A History of Muhlenberg County (Kentucky)

Otto A. Rothert

HERITAGE BOOKS
2007

HERITAGE BOOKS
AN IMPRINT OF HERITAGE BOOKS, INC.

Books, CDs, and more—Worldwide

For our listing of thousands of titles see our website
at
www.HeritageBooks.com

Published 2007 by
HERITAGE BOOKS, INC.
Publishing Division
65 East Main Street
Westminster, Maryland 21157-5026

Copyright © 1913 Otto A. Rothert

All rights reserved. No part of this book may be reproduced or transmitted in any form or by any means, electronic or mechanical, including photocopying, recording or by any information storage and retrieval system without written permission from the author, except for the inclusion of brief quotations in a review.

International Standard Book Number: 978-0-7884-0454-2

TO THE MEMORY OF

THE PIONEERS OF MUHLENBERG

who by their resolute deeds and heroic lives made possible the achievements of a later day, this History of Our Own Times and of theirs is

DEDICATED

CHAPTERS AND ILLUSTRATIONS

	PAGE
PREFACE	xi-xiii
INTRODUCTION	xv-xvii

1. GENERAL MUHLENBERG 1-7
    Statue of General Muhlenberg, Philadelphia.
    Muhlenberg Delivering his Farewell Sermon.

2. SOME OF THE FIRST-COMERS. 8-28
    A Survivor of "the Forest Primeval."
    The Site of Pond Station.
    Old Caney Station Graveyard.
    Mrs. Samuel Russell, 1845.
    Robert S. Russell, 1870.
    The "Cave Hut Cliff."
    The Jesse McPherson House.
    The Jonathan Hunt House.
    Zillman Wood, 1850.
    Graves of Judge and Mrs. Wm. Worthington.
    Kincheloe's Bluff.
    Pioneer Moses Wickliffe, 1817.
    Mr. and Mrs. William J. Dean, 1850.
    Mr. and Mrs. John Noffsinger, 1865.
    Mr. and Mrs. Peter Shaver, 1865.

3. HENRY RHOADS 29-35
    The Henry Rhoads House.
    Grave of the "Godfather of Muhlenberg County."
    Henry Rhoads (grandson of pioneer), Wife and Daughter, 1854.
    McHenry Rhoads, 1912.

4. BEGINNING AND BOUNDS OF THE COUNTY 36-40
    Map of the original Logan County.
    Map of Muhlenberg County, 1798-1854.
    Map of Muhlenberg County, 1912.

5. COURTS AND COURTHOUSES 41-55
    Facsimile of Commission of County's First Justices, 1798.
    The Second Courthouse (erected 1836) and Clerk's Office.
    The Second Jail (erected 1864-65) and Jailer's Residence.
    John Edmunds Reno, 1895.
    William H. Yost, 1912.
    The Present Courthouse, erected 1907.
    Jail and Jailer's Residence, erected 1912.

6. THE WEIRS 56-62
    Pioneer James Weir, about 1840.
    Mrs. Anna C. R. Weir, about 1825.
    Edward R. Weir, Sr., 1875.
    Mrs. Harriet R. Weir, 1900.
    E. R. Weir (Colonel), 1865.
    Max Weir, 1900.

CHAPTERS AND ILLUSTRATIONS

7. MUHLENBERG MEN IN THE WAR OF 1812 63-75
    Larkin N. Akers, 1865.
    Mosley Collins Drake, about 1870.
    Ephraim M. Brank, about 1850.
    The Ephraim M. Brank House.
    Alney McLean, about 1820.
    The Isaac Davis House.
    Mr. and Mrs. Joseph C. Reynolds, 1867.

8. CHARLES FOX WING 76-80
    Charles Fox Wing, 1850.
    Mrs. Charles Fox Wing, about 1850.
    The Charles Fox Wing House, 1891.

9. EDWARD RUMSEY 81-83
    Edward Rumsey, about 1845.

10. THE POND RIVER COUNTRY........................... 84-103
    The Michael Lovell Old Place, 1900.
    Michael Lovell, about 1865.
    The John Adair Allison Old Place, 1900.
    John Adair Allison, 1874.
    The Hutson Martin Old Place, 1900.
    Strother Jones, about 1845.
    Clark's Ferry Bridge.
    Harpe's "House," on Harpe's Hill.
    Mrs. Elizabeth Earle Oates, 1870.
    Mrs. Clara G. Stanley, 1855.
    The Hugh W. McNary House.
    Hugh W. McNary, 1871.
    The So-called Daniel Boone Rock.
    The "David Short Old Brick."
    Murphy's Lake.
    Pond River.

11. OLD LIBERTY CHURCH............................. 104-109
    A Sweep and Well and an Old Oaken Bucket.
    Old Liberty, 1900.
    Ruins of Old Liberty, 1912.
    Old Liberty Burying-ground, 1912.

12. LIFE IN THE OLDEN DAYS.......................... 110-132
    A White Oak and a Yellow Poplar.
    Ground-sled or "Landslide."
    "Wolf Sculp" Certificate.
    Passenger or Wild Pigeons.
    "The Weir Corner."
    Some Old Chimneys.
    A Hog Harvest.
    Cooksey's Mill.
    Hazel Creek Church.
    Newman Graveyard.

13. THE STORY OF "LONZ POWERS"..................... 133-149
    James Weir, author, 1850.
    Residence of Pioneer James Weir.
    The Lonz Pennington House, 1912.
    Graves of Lonz Pennington and Wife, 1912.

14. GREENVILLE AS DESCRIBED IN "LONZ POWERS"........ 150-164
    Mrs. William H. Yost, Sr. (Mrs. Jonathan Short), 1864.
    Old Presbyterian Church, Greenville, erected about 1825.
    Charles Metzker, 1849.
    The Metzker House, 1895.
    The William A. Wickliffe Residence.
    The William G. Duncan Residence.
    Main Street, Greenville, 1912.

CHAPTERS AND ILLUSTRATIONS vii

15. THE OLD MILITIA MUSTER..................................165-175
 Facsimile of William Bradford's Commission as Captain, 1799.
 Ruins of the O. C. Vanlandingham, Sr., Residence.
 Ruins of the "Jim Taggart Old Place."
 The Mosley Collins Drake House.

16. THE STORY OF THE STACK..................................176-190
 The Stack in 1905.
 Ruins of the Buckner Milk-house.
 Andirons made at The Stack in 1840.
 "The Stack House."
 Friendship Baptist Church.
 Aylette H. Buckner, 1824.
 Simon Bolivar Buckner, 1846, 1906.
 John Jenkins, 1857.
 The Buckner Cradle.
 Alfred Johnson, 1864.
 Alvin L. Taylor, 1912.

17. MUHLENBERG MEN IN THE MEXICAN WAR......................191-193
 Arthur N. Davis, 1870.

18. ISAAC BARD 194-207
 Isaac Bard, 1850.
 A White Oak Shade Tree.
 Mount Zion Presbyterian Church.
 Dr. Alfred M. Jackson, 1864.

19. POST-PRIMARY EDUCATION IN MUHLENBERG...................208-219
 Teacher and Pupils, McClelland School, 1905.
 The Shaver or Philadelphia Schoolhouse.
 Residence of Henry C. Lewis (Presbyterial Academy Building), 1912.
 William L. Green, 1900.
 James K. Patterson, 1909.
 Greenville College, 1881.
 Edwin W. Hall, 1888.
 South Carrollton Public School Building.
 Central City Public School Building.
 Greenville Public School Building.
 Bremen Public School Building.
 Drakesboro Public School Building.

20. PARADISE COUNTRY AND OLD AIRDRIE.......................220-241
 Paradise and the Highway Thereto.
 O. C. Vanlandingham, Sr., about 1850.
 George W. Haden, 1895.
 The Airdrie Furnace, 1912.
 The Stone House, Airdrie.
 The Stone Steps, Airdrie.
 Alexander Hendrie, 1852.
 Mill Chimneys at Airdrie, 1900.
 Some of the Abandoned Houses, Airdrie, 1895.
 Ruins at Airdrie, 1900.
 The Old Hotel Building, Airdrie, 1895.
 Entrance to "McLean Old Bank," Airdrie.
 McLean Old Spring, Airdrie, 1900.
 General Don Carlos Buell, 1866.
 Buell's Private Park, Residence, and Boathouse, Airdrie, 1900.
 Buell's Residence, Airdrie, 1900.
 Ruins of Buell's Residence, Airdrie, 1912.

CHAPTERS AND ILLUSTRATIONS

21. CHARLES EAVES 242-249
    Charles Eaves, 1884.
    Beech Tree, a "Philosopher of the Forest."
    The H. L. Kirkpatrick Residence, Greenville (former Eaves residence).

22. MUHLENBERG IN THE CIVIL WAR..........................250-284
    Benjamin J. Shaver, 1890.
    Myers' Chapel and Grangers' Hall.
    John K. Wickliffe, 1860.
    Garst's Pond.
    Greenville and Rumsey Road.
    Breastworks, South Carrollton (1862), in 1912.
    Residence of John L. Taylor, South Carrollton.
    "Our House" or "Lovelace Tavern," South Carrollton.
    Bethlehem Baptist Church.
    "Alvin's Avenue."
    The Edward R. Weir, Sr., Residence, Greenville.
    Sullivan's Barn.
    Some Civil War Veterans, 1912.

23. R. T. MARTIN'S "RECOLLECTIONS OF THE CIVIL WAR"..........285-317
    Richard T. Martin, 1912.
    Mount Pisgah Church.
    The Old Prowse Bridge, 1911.
    Where the "Bogus Cavalry" was organized.
    The Thomas C. Summers Residence.
    S. D. Chatham, 1870.
    Public Road near Old Liberty.
    The Greenville Hotel Building, 1912.
    Reno House, Greenville, 1897.

24. ROBERT M. MARTIN......................................318-325
    Robert M. Martin, 1866.
    The Muhlenberg County Poor Farm.

25. SOME OF MUHLENBERG'S CIVIL WAR SOLDIERS................326-337
    John Coombs, Wife and Son, 1874.
    Japha N. Durall, 1861.
    Francis M. Finley, 1869.
    Thomas M. Finley, 1869.
    J. K. Freeman, 1864.
    S. P. Love, 1895.
    R. T. Vincent, about 1863.
    J. L. Wilkins, about 1863.
    William S. Grundy, about 1863.
    Henry C. McCracken, 1861.
    Isaac Miller, 1861.
    Joseph Mitchell, 1861.
    Joseph F. Richardson, 1861.
    J. L. Roark, 1863.
    M. J. Roark, 1863.
    W. C. Shannon, 1864.
    E. E. C. Shull, 1862.
    William H. Smith, 1862.
    John L. G. Thompson, 1861.
    R. W. Wallace, 1865.
    Joseph D. Yonts, 1864.

CHAPTERS AND ILLUSTRATIONS ix

26. SLAVERY DAYS 338-344
        "Uncle" John Oates, 1912.
        Slave Cabins.

27. LOCAL WRITERS AND THE LOCAL PRESS......................345-352
        Ruric N. Roark, 1906.
        Clarence B. Hayes, 1905.
        Muhlenberg's First Newspaper.
        Facsimile of Editorial Title.

28. IN 1870 353-367
        Dr. Alexander McCown, 1870.
        House occupied in 1870 by M. C. Hay & Co.
        Old Cumberland Presbyterian Church, Greenville, about 1870.
        Old Brick Bank Building, 1890.
        Wiley S. Hay, about 1850.
        Finis McLean Allison, 1870.
        A Load of Saw-logs, 1894.
        The Jonathan Short Residence.
        Y. M. C. A. Building, Greenville.
        The Hugh Martin House.

29. THE RAILROAD BONDS 368-379
        Illinois Central Bridge over Green River, Rockport.
        Twin Tunnel, between Bellton and Penrod.
        Big Cut, near Midland.
        Facsimile of one of the original Railroad Bonds, 1869.
        Ben and Bob Wickliffe, about 1890.
        T. J. Sparks, 1912.
        Illinois Central Depot, Greenville.

30. TOBACCO 380-386
        Dabney A. Martin, 1855.
        C. Y. Martin & Co.'s Tobacco Rehandling House, Greenville.
        Thomas L. Martin, 1856.
        A Cropper's Log Cabin, 1912.
        Old-time Log Tobacco Barn, 1912.
        A Tobacco Field.

31. COAL MINES AND IRON ORE................................387-403
        Mud River, near Mud River Mine.
        The Dr. Roberts House.
        Tipple and Power House, Central Mine, Central City.
        Power House and Double Tipple, Graham-Skibo Mine, Graham.
        Tipple and Power House, Black Diamond Mine, Drakesboro.
        Power House and Steel Tipple, Kentucky-Midland Mine, Midland.
        William G. Duncan, 1912.
        James W. Lam, 1912.
        William A. Wickliffe, 1912.

x   CHAPTERS AND ILLUSTRATIONS

32. COLLINS ON MUHLENBERG, QUOTED AND EXTENDED............404-431
    Road from Boat Landing to South Carrollton.
    Dr. J. T. Woodburn, 1912.
    Methodist Episcopal Church, Central City.
    St. Joseph's Roman Catholic Church, Central City.
    Central City's First Post-office.
    Broad Street, Central City, 1912.
    H. D. Rothrock, 1870.
    Black Lake and Cypress Trees.
    Main Street, Drakesboro, 1912.
    Dr. A. D. James, 1905.
    A Collection of Indian Relics.
    A Prehistoric Mound.
    Site of a Prehistoric Mound.
    R. Y. Thomas, 1912.

APPENDIX.

A. JUDGE HALL'S STORY OF THE HARPES........................435-441

B. JOURNAL BY JAMES WEIR, 1803.............................443-448

C. TWO LOCAL STORIES BY EDWARD R. WEIR, SR.................449-453

D. DUVALL'S DISCOVERY OF "SILVER ORE," BY R. T. MARTIN.....455-459

E. "RIDING THE CIRCUIT," BY LUCIUS P. LITTLE...............461-465

   INDEX 467-496

PREFACE

THE gathering and compiling of the traditions and history of Muhlenberg County has occupied much of my time for some years. These pages have been written solely because of the pleasure and interest I have taken in the work, and are here presented in book form that they may be read not only by those who are now interested in the subject, but that they may be preserved also for future generations. I found Muhlenberg's history a very fascinating subject. All Muhlenbergers, with few exceptions, are interested in the history and traditions of the county, but I dare say the subject appealed to me, a newcomer, more than it would to most of the men and women who were born and reared in the county. To them it had become somewhat familiar and commonplace, while to me it is new and filled with the picturesque. I am, in a sense, a stranger in Muhlenberg. My first trip to the county was made in the fall of 1902, for the purpose of looking after some land my father had bought there a few years before. During that first trip I saw comparatively nothing of Greenville, but passed my time in the country, occupying my leisure hours with hunting, and listening at night to the traditions and reminiscences of old residents. Out of these began to develop a strong desire to call up the stories that would begin with "I've often heard my grandfather say that when he was a boy," etc. I was in the presence, it seemed to me, of pioneers themselves, once or twice removed. Their very words were coming to me through the lips of those that had picked them up from now-silent voices, and who had cherished them through the long years.

One night in the fall of 1905 a number of us were sitting near the old Stack of the long-abandoned Buckner Furnace—in the upper Pond Creek country, in the neighborhood to which my annual visits up to that time had been confined—when the vague traditions of that old landmark again became the subject of discussion. All agreed it was unfortunate that the Story of The Stack had never been written. Alvin L. Taylor, my host, suggested that since the object of my hunting was apparently drifting from "digging out foxes to digging up facts," I spend the remaining half of my visit in gathering the traditions of The Stack. The novelty of the suggestion appealed to me at once. The next day I began a systematic investigation of the subject. In the course of two weeks I spent a day or more with every "oldest citizen" in the neighborhood, and from them and some of their children and grandchildren I gathered the materials from which was written the first version of "The Story of The Stack." This was published in the Greenville Record in the spring of 1906.

In the fall of 1906, shortly after returning to Muhlenberg, I found that there still lingered a longing to hear the horn of the hunter and the trailing of the hounds, for one night the "call of the wild" led me three miles from the Buckner Stack to the Russell Old Field. There, while listening to the musical bark of the running dogs, I began an investigation of the traditions of the Russell Race Track and Muster Field. A few weeks later the results were published in the Greenville Record. And so, fall after fall, I drifted into new fields in the southern part of the county, and submitted various sketches to the local press. In 1910 the pleasure had become a preoccupation of deep interest, and I decided to compile a history of the county and publish it in book form. That fall and the two following I laid aside gun and lantern, took camera and note-book, and spent a total of about six months making pilgrimages, through rain and shine, to every place in the county where there might be gathered facts worth preserving in a printed history. On returning to Louisville I began arranging my notes, and took up the laborious but absorbing task of searching through books for any Muhlenberg history they might contain. The results of these years of earnest effort to produce a volume that would be worthy the memory of the valiant and resolute men and women who settled and established Muhlenberg County are contained in this completed book. While it is submitted with proper diffidence as to my ability to do the subject full justice, it is nevertheless presented as an honest effort in which no difficulty has been evaded or shunned.

This volume pertains principally to the history of the county from its beginning down to 1875, but is extended more or less briefly in some practical aspects from 1875 to the present day. Much remains for a later historian to write about the wonderful advancements Muhlenberg has made during the past twenty years. The events of general interest during the past quarter of a century are not only fresh in the memory of many of the men and women of to-day, but are likely to be remembered or handed down until a history is written covering that period, whereas much of the material I am here trying to preserve would otherwise, in all probability, soon pass away with the many other local traditions and unrecorded facts that have already disappeared and are forgotten.

The records of the county and circuit courts from the beginning have been preserved in the courthouse at Greenville, and in all probability will always be preserved. I have, therefore, made no attempt to write a history based principally on these ever-available records, but have confined my work as much as possible to collecting the now vanishing traditions and to presenting the less available material. Much of this heretofore unpublished as well as published material is woven into this volume. I found in printed books comparatively little that bore on Muhlenberg's past. Practically all I found in print I quote, and thus give the reader an opportunity to read the statements in the language in which they were originally recorded, preferring this to expressing the facts in my own words.

Of the more than two hundred illustrations here presented, comparatively few are of modern buildings or of active men and women of to-day. Most of the pictures are of some of the old citizens, the old houses, and the old landmarks. More than one fourth are copies of pictures made between 1817 and 1872. All except those taken in 1911 and 1912, which comprise about one half, are dated. It is a well-known fact that the portraits and biographies that appear in many county histories are published in consideration of a stipulated price, and it may therefore not be amiss to state that this absolutely has not been done in this book.

I have, either in the text or in some of the foot-notes, given the names of the children of a number of pioneers, and have thus laid a foundation for those of their descendants who may desire to compile a family tree. I made no attempt, except in a few cases, to procure the names occurring in the third and succeeding generations. I feel that the lists of names for the second generation are in most instances complete, for only such of the many lists as I have been able to verify, to a greater or less extent, are printed in this volume. Very few of these lists were copied from written records; most of them were compiled for me within the past few years by men and women who depended on their memory, family traditions, and tombstones upon the graves of their ancestors for their data. Any one who has given his family tree even comparatively little thought will realize the difficulty of preparing an accurate list from such sources, if he but attempt to recall and record the names of the brothers and sisters of any of his four grandparents, and he will also realize that omissions and other errors are likely to occur in any first-published list.

Many of the local traditions woven into the various chapters of this history are seldom heard beyond the immediate neighborhood to which they belong, while some of the other local stories and incidents are familiar to practically every Muhlenberger. A few of the traditions have almost as many versions as they are years old. Where various versions are in circulation I have accepted the one that, in my opinion, seemed the most authentic.

I here express my thanks to Mr. Richard T. Martin, of Greenville, and to the many other Muhlenbergers whose aid and encouragement in gathering data have made the writing of this history of Muhlenberg County not only a possibility but a pleasant occupation; also to Mr. George E. Cross, of Louisville, for copying old oil paintings, daguerreotypes, ambrotypes, tintypes, and photographs, and for preparing many photographic views for reproduction; to Mrs. Jennie C. Morton, of Frankfort; to Judge Lucius P. Little, of Owensboro, and Doctor Samuel A. Braun, of Louisville, for material bearing on the subject; to Colonel Reuben T. Durrett, of Louisville, for many suggestions and for the use of his large library on Kentucky history; and last, but by no means least, to Mr. Young E. Allison, of Louisville, for suggestions growing out of his experience as an editor in preparing matter for the press.

OTTO A. ROTHERT.

Louisville, Kentucky, March 15, 1913.

INTRODUCTION

BEFORE taking up the history and traditions of Muhlenberg County it may be well to recall a few dates pertaining to the beginning of the nation, and also to review some of Kentucky's history to the time of the organization of Muhlenberg County in 1798.
The Declaration of Independence was adopted in Philadelphia on July 4, 1776. The first battle in the American Revolution was fought at Lexington, Massachusetts, on April 19, 1775, and the surrender of Cornwallis took place at Yorktown, Virginia, on October 19, 1781. Washington was President of the United States from April 30, 1789, to March 4, 1797, and John Adams from 1797 to March 4, 1801.

Doctor Thomas Walker, in 1750, passed through Cumberland Gap, and was probably the first white man to wander within the present borders of Kentucky. In 1751 Colonel Christopher Gist traveled over the eastern part of the State. In 1769 Daniel Boone made his first trip to the Dark and Bloody Ground. The "Long Hunters" started on their expedition in 1770. Simon Kenton began his explorations in 1771. In 1775 the Transylvania Company appeared on the scene with Daniel Boone as their chief guide and pathfinder, and opened up land offices and attempted to form a proprietary colony or government in the territory lying between the Kentucky and Tennessee rivers, which territory they had purchased from the Cherokee Indians, who claimed to have the right to dispose of it.

At Harrodstown, afterward Harrodsburg, the first permanent white settlement was begun in 1774. The first fort was built at Boonesboro in 1775 and a town started. Louisville, although partly laid out on paper by Captain Thomas Bullitt as early as 1773, was not settled until 1778, when George Rogers Clark and other pioneers built a few houses on Corn Island, opposite the site of the present city—an island in the rushing waters of the Ohio which has long since disappeared. As time rolled by many other settlements were made.

In 1778 George Rogers Clark traveled down the Ohio, landed at Fort Massac, opposite the mouth of the Cumberland, and thence began his celebrated and eventful march to Kaskaskia and Vincennes. In 1780 he went down the same river, built Fort Jefferson at Iron Banks, on the present Kentucky shore of the Mississippi, five miles below the mouth of the Ohio, within the Chickasaw country. After Clark had erected this fort he proceeded with two men on foot to Harrodsburg. They crossed the Tennessee River, met a few hunters and trappers (Butler's History of Kentucky, page 115), and then continued their tramp through the territory which later became the original Logan County. (Smith's History of Kentucky, page 174.) The hunters they then met were probably some of the "Long Hunters" who entered Western Kentucky about 1771, or other pioneers who followed a few years later. The account of Clark's trip is probably the earliest authentic record regarding the first white people who saw that section of the State of which Muhlenberg now forms part.

In 1783 Transylvania Seminary, the first school for higher education in the West, was founded in Danville, and six years later was removed to Lexington; in 1798 it received the name of Transylvania University.

In 1784 John Filson wrote the first history of Kentucky. On his "Map of Kentucke" Filson gives the names and general course of all the rivers and many of the creeks in the District, and shows about twenty roads, a number of springs and licks, and locates about fifty of the settlements and mills and the eight towns then in existence. In his history Filson says, on page 11: "There are at present eight towns laid off, and building; and more are proposed. Louisville, at the Falls of Ohio, and Beardstown, are in Jefferson county; Harrodsburg, Danville and Boons-burrow, in Lincoln county; Lexington, Lees-town, and Greenville, in Fayette county; the two last being on Kentucke river." The Greenville and Leestown here referred to were located a short distance below where Frankfort now stands. This Greenville passed out of existence before the close of the Eighteenth Century, before the beginning of Greenville in Muhlenberg County; Leestown was abandoned during the early part of the Nineteenth Century.

After ten years of debating and delaying Kentucky was finally admitted into the Union on June 1, 1792, and became the fifteenth State of the new confederation. Vermont was the fourteenth, and Tennessee, in 1796, became the sixteenth. The administration of Isaac Shelby, the first Governor of Kentucky, extended from June 4, 1792, to January 1, 1796, and the two terms of Governor James Garrard from 1796 to 1804. During the closing years of the Eighteenth Century the political doctrine of Nullification, as embodied in the Kentucky Resolutions of 1798 and 1799, was warmly debated throughout the Union.

Up to about the year 1800 many of the pioneers experienced much trouble with the hostile Indians, but after that date no massacres or battles of any great consequence took place in the State, for by that time most of the Indians had been killed or driven out of the Dark and Bloody Ground. The homeseekers from the old colonies emigrated into Kentucky in larger numbers during the last fifteen years of the Eighteenth Century and began many permanent settlements. Local traditions and records show that among these newcomers were some German-Virginians who, as early as 1784 or before, located in the country a part of which later became the northern section of Muhlenberg County. These German-Virginians were soon followed by other Virginians, some of whom, after building temporary homes at Caney Station about the year 1795, started the town of Greenville in the spring of 1799. Many of the earliest settlers in the southern part of the county came from North Carolina during the last years of the Eighteenth and the first quarter of the Nineteenth Century.

The great increase in population throughout Kentucky resulted in the creating of many new counties out of parts of the older ones. Kentucky was originally a part of Fincastle County, Virginia. In 1776 Fincastle was divided and the County of Kentucky was established. The new county embraced all that is now included in the State. In 1780 the County of Ken-

tucky was divided into Jefferson, Fayette, and Lincoln counties. Jefferson included the country between Kentucky and Green rivers; Fayette the land north of Kentucky River, and Lincoln the remaining territory. In 1784 all of Jefferson County south of Salt River became Nelson County. In 1785 Bourbon County was formed from part of Fayette, and during the same year Mercer and Madison counties sprang from parts of Lincoln. In 1788 Mason County was formed from part of Bourbon and Woodford County from part of Fayette, making up to that date a total of nine counties in the District of Kentucky.

In 1792, the year Kentucky was admitted into the Union, seven new counties were established, among them being Logan, which was formed from part of Lincoln. Logan was the thirteenth county organized in the State. It was then the most westerly county, and embraced practically all that part of Kentucky lying west of Green and Barren rivers. During the next two years three more counties were laid off in various parts of the State. In 1796 six new ones were started, including Christian, which was formed from part of Logan. In 1798 thirteen more sprang into existence, among them being Muhlenberg, the thirty-fourth, which was formed from parts of Christian and Logan. In the course of years many others were formed from Logan County or its former territory. By 1860 the original Logan County was divided into twenty-nine counties. The State of Kentucky now contains one hundred and twenty counties.

The seven counties bordering on Muhlenberg were organized as follows: Logan in 1792; Christian in 1796; Ohio in 1798; Hopkins in 1806; Butler in 1810; Todd in 1819; McLean in 1854. Of these, Christian, Hopkins, and Butler counties were named after officers of the Revolutionary army; Muhlenberg was also so named, in honor of General John Peter Gabriel Muhlenberg, one of Washington's brigadier-generals.

A HISTORY

OF

MUHLENBERG COUNTY

I

GENERAL MUHLENBERG

MUHLENBERG COUNTY was so called in honor of General John Peter Gabriel Muhlenberg, an officer of high distinction and patriotism in the American Revolution.[1]

General Muhlenberg made two trips to Kentucky in 1784, but did not see any part of that section which fourteen years later was formed into a county and named after him. It is more than probable that he did not visit any section of the Green River country. His life, however, is part of the history of Muhlenberg County, not only because the county is a namesake of his but also because many of its pioneers fought under him in the Revolution. General Muhlenberg's career is woven into the history of the Revolution and into the history of the nation during the first quarter of a century following that struggle. A volume entitled "The Life of Major-General Peter Muhlenberg, of the Revolutionary Army," was published in 1849 by Henry A. Muhlenberg, a nephew of the distinguished soldier. From this work I gather the following facts.

Reverend Henry Melchoir Muhlenberg, the father of General Muhlenberg, emigrated to Pennsylvania from Hanover, Germany, in 1742. He founded the Lutheran Church in America, and died at Trappe, near Philadelphia, on October 1, 1787. His son, J. Peter G. Muhlenberg, was born at Trappe, Pennsylvania, on October 1, 1746. At the age of sixteen Peter was sent to Halle, Germany, to be educated. While in Europe he incidentally gained a little knowledge of military drills that was, in later life, of great advantage to him. In 1767 he returned to America and became a minister in the Lutheran Church, serving as a pastor to various congregations.

Previous to the Revolution there was a union of Church and State in Virginia, where the Church of England was established by law; "and in

---

[1] The pronunciation of the name of the county doubtless gave rise to the difference among early historians as to the correct spelling. Lewis Collins (1847) followed the pronunciation, and spells the name uniformly Muhlenburg; Richard H. Collins (1874) corrects the error when referring to the man but not when referring to the county, and this error has been repeated in his various editions. The name is also occasionally misspelled in some of the early maps and county records, but never in those of a later day. The proper spelling of the name is as here given.

order that the rector could enforce the payment of tithes, it was necessary that he should have been ordained by a Bishop of the English Church, in which case he came under the provision of the law, although not a member of the established church." To meet these difficulties Muhlenberg decided to be ordained in the official church. In 1772 he went to England, where he was "ordained by a Bishop of the English Church," and then returned to Virginia and preached at Woodstock until the Revolutionary War broke out. In the early part of 1776 he organized a regiment of soldiers, the Eighth Virginia, known as the "German Regiment." He participated in the fights at Charleston and Sullivan's Island. On February 21, 1777, he was made brigadier-general and took charge of the Virginia line under Washington, and was in chief command in Virginia in 1781 until the arrival of Baron Von Steuben. He was in the battles of Brandywine, Germantown, and Monmouth, and was also at the capture of Stony Point. He was second in command to LaFayette in resisting the invasion of the State by Cornwallis. He took part in the siege of Yorktown, and was present when Cornwallis surrendered on October 19, 1781. On September 30, 1783, he was promoted to the rank of major-general. A few months later the army was formally disbanded, and he returned to his family in Woodstock. In November he moved to Trappe and shortly afterward made Philadelphia his home.

In 1784 he made two trips to the Falls of the Ohio, to superintend the distribution of lands in Kentucky granted to himself and other officers and soldiers of the Virginia army. His diary kept on these trips shows that he did not go down the Ohio below Louisville. In the fall of 1785 General Muhlenberg was elected Vice-President of Pennsylvania, Benjamin Franklin being at the same time chosen President. He was reëlected to that office every year until 1788, when he was chosen one of the members of the First Congress, to serve from March 4, 1789, to March 4, 1791. He also served in the Third Congress and in the Fourth Congress. His brother, Frederick Augustus, served as Speaker of the First Congress assembled under the Constitution. In February, 1801, General Muhlenberg was elected United States Senator from Pennsylvania. On the 30th of June, 1801, having been appointed Supervisor of Internal Revenue for Pennsylvania, he resigned his seat in the Senate. In July, 1802, he was appointed Collector of the Port of Philadelphia, which office he held up to the time of his death, October 1, 1807. He is buried at Trappe, Pennsylvania, where rest also the remains of his father.

His biographer, commenting on the career of General Muhlenberg, says:

He was one of those characters which in a revolution always find their level. He was by nature a soldier. . . . He entered the church, doubtless, with as sincere and honest purposes as any of her ministry, but the agony of his country called him from the altar with a voice that touched every chord of his soul. The time for fighting had come—the time to try men's souls. His whole heart was with his country; rebellion against tyrants was obedience to God, and so feeling and so thinking, he went forth from the temple to the field. He was brave and generous to a fault, a proper brigadier to Greene, *who loved him*. Cool in danger, sound in judgment, indifferent to fame, zealous in duty: these were his distinguishing traits as a soldier. His virtues in private and political life were all cognate to these.

Such, in brief, was the career of General Muhlenberg. Many interesting incidents occurred during his life, the details of a number of which are re-

STATUE OF GENERAL MUHLENBERG, PHILADELPHIA, ERECTED IN 1910
Copyright, 1911, by J. Otto Schweizer

corded in his biography. Among them is the dramatic event that took place at Woodstock, Virginia, in the early days of "'76." Times, as Muhlenberg was wont to remark, had been "troublesome," and the colonies were preparing to declare and fight for their independence. Muhlenberg was appointed colonel of the Eighth Regiment, which was then far from fully organized. His acceptance of this office necessitated his resignation as pastor of his churches. The scene that took place when this "fighting parson" delivered his farewell sermon is thus described by his biographer:

Upon his arrival at Woodstock, his different congregations, widely scattered along the frontier, were notified that upon the following Sabbath their beloved pastor would deliver his farewell sermon. Of this event numerous traditionary accounts are still preserved in the vicinity in which it took place, all coinciding with the written evidence. The fact itself merits a prominent place in this sketch, for in addition to the light it sheds upon the feelings which actuated the American people in the commencement of the Revolutionary struggle, it also shows with what deep earnestness of purpose Mr. Muhlenberg entered upon his new career.

The appointed day came. The rude country church was filled to overflowing with the hardy mountaineers of the frontier counties, among whom were collected one or more of the independent companies to which the forethought of the Convention had given birth. So great was the assemblage, that the quiet burial-place was filled with crowds of stern, excited men, who had gathered together, believing that something, they knew not what, would be done in behalf of their suffering country. We may well imagine that the feelings which actuated the assembly were of no ordinary kind. The disturbances of the country, the gatherings of armed men, the universal feeling that liberty or slavery for themselves and their children hung upon the decision the colonies then made, and the decided step taken by their pastor, all aroused the patriotic enthusiasm of the vast multitude, and rendered it a magazine of fiery passion, which needed but a spark to burst into an all-consuming flame.

In this spirit the people awaited the arrival of him whom they were now to hear for the last time. He came, and ascended the pulpit, his tall form arrayed in full uniform, over which his gown, the symbol of his holy calling, was thrown. He was a plain, straightforward speaker, whose native eloquence was well suited to the people among whom he laboured. At all times capable of commanding the deepest attention, we may well conceive that upon this great occasion, when high, stern thoughts were burning for utterance, the people who heard him hung upon his fiery words with all the intensity of their souls. Of the matter of the sermon various accounts remain. All concur, however, in attributing to it great potency in arousing the military ardour of the people, and unite in describing its conclusion. After recapitulating, in words that aroused the coldest, the story of their sufferings and their wrongs, and telling them of the sacred character of the struggle in which he had unsheathed his sword, and for which he had left the altar he had vowed to serve, he said "that, in the language of Holy Writ, there was a time for all things, a time to preach and a time to pray, but these times had passed away"; and in a voice that reëchoed through the church like a trumpet-blast, "that there was a time to fight, and that time had now come!"

The sermon finished, he pronounced the benediction. A breathless stillness brooded over the congregation. Deliberately putting off the gown, which had thus far covered his martial figure, he stood before them a girded warrior; and descending from the pulpit, ordered the drums at the church-door to beat for recruits. Then followed a scene to which even the American Revolution, rich as it is in bright examples of the patriotic devotion of the people, affords no parallel. His audience, excited in the highest degree by the impassioned words which had fallen from his lips, flocked around him, eager to be ranked among his followers. Old men were seen bringing forward their children, wives their husbands, and widowed mothers their sons, sending them under his paternal care to fight the battles of their country. It must have been a noble sight, and the cause thus supported could not fail.

Nearly three hundred men of the frontier churches that day enlisted under his banner; and the gown then thrown off was worn for the last time. Henceforth his footsteps were destined for a new career.

RELIEF ON THE PEDESTAL OF GENERAL MUHLENBERG'S STATUE, PHILADELPHIA
Representing Muhlenberg in the act of delivering his farewell sermon,
Woodstock, Virginia, in January, 1776

Copyright, 1911, by J. Otto Schweizer

This event occurred about the middle of January, 1776; and from that time until March, Colonel Muhlenberg seems to have been busily engaged in recruiting. After the great impulse already received, it is natural to suppose that his success was rapid, and such accordingly we find to be the fact. It was probably the first of the Virginia regiments ready for service, its ranks being full early in March. By the middle of that month he had already reported this fact to the Governor, and received orders to proceed with his command to Suffolk. On the 21st the regiment commenced its march for that place.

A little less than a half century after the death of General Muhlenberg, and about five years after his biography was written, a poem, based on the incident that took place at the church in Woodstock, was published by Thomas Buchanan Read. This poem, "The Rising," is printed in McGuffey's old Fifth Reader, where most of us have read it, and from which I quote a few lines:[2]

> Out of the North the wild news came . . .
> And swelled the discord of the hour. . . .
>
> The pastor rose; the prayer was strong;
> The psalm was warrior David's song;
> The text, a few short words of might—
> "The Lord of hosts shall arm the right!" . . .
>
> When suddenly his mantle wide
> His hands impatient flung aside,
> And lo! he met their wondering eyes
> Complete in all a warrior's guise. . . .
>
> The enlisting trumpet's sudden roar
> Rang through the chapel, o'er and o'er, . . .
> And there the startling drum and fife
> Fired the living with fiercer life. . . .
>
> "Who dares"—this was the patriot's cry,
> As striding from the desk he came—
> "Come out with me, in Freedom's name,
> For her to live, for her to die?"
> A hundred hands flung up reply,
> A hundred voices answered "I!"

General Muhlenberg was less than forty years of age when he left Virginia and returned to Pennsylvania, where he spent the last twenty-two years of his life in the upbuilding of his native State and the new nation. Pennsylvania has expressed her appreciation of his great work by placing a statue of him in Statuary Hall, Washington, D. C. His memorial stands in the southeast corner of the Hall, and although a graceful piece of work, the sculptor, Blanche Nevin, evidently was not familiar with the stature and physiognomy of her subject. Muhlenberg's biographer and other writers

---

[2] This and other incidents in the life of General Muhlenberg are the subjects of a number of poems written in German by German-Americans. Among them are the following, which are published in the records of the German Society of Pennsylvania, and for copies of which I am indebted to Mr. C. F. Huch, of Philadelphia, the custodian of the archives of that organization: "Peter Muhlenberg" and "General Peter," by Joseph Zentmayer; "Muhlenberg," by F. Moras; "Peter Muhlenberg," by Philip Haimbach, and "The Farewell Sermon," by William Miller. Mr. Huch also informs me that General Muhlenberg is the subject of two dramas that were written in German and are occasionally produced by German dramatic companies: "Peter Muhlenberg, or Bible and Sword," in five acts, by Frederich H. Ernst, of New York, and "Cowl and Sword, or General Muhlenberg," by Victor Precht.

describe him as "tall in person," which statement is verified not only by paintings now extant but also by tradition. Nevertheless the sculptor represents Muhlenberg's height as not much more than five feet. His face, in this marble statue, looks more like that of a poet or musician, and not like that of a preacher and still less like that of a soldier. On the base of the statue is carved the name MUHLENBERG; the pedestal is marked PENNSYLVANIA.

In October, 1910, the German Society of Pennsylvania erected a statue to General Muhlenberg in Philadelphia on the City Hall Plaza. It is a good likeness and a masterly piece of work by J. Otto Schweizer, of Philadelphia, one of the foremost sculptors in America. A portrait of this statue is here reproduced. Every detail of this fine work of art is true to its subject and is based on paintings and descriptions still preserved.

The relief on the face of the pedestal of this statue is by the same artist, and is probably the best work of that character in the country. The elevations are so delicately balanced that the depth of the church with all pews and people comes within a thickness or height of only an inch and a half. The scene represents Muhlenberg in the act of finishing his farewell sermon. The church depicted is the old one in Trappe, near Philadelphia, which has been preserved unchanged since the middle of the Eighteenth Century, and is the same in which General Muhlenberg and his father often preached.

In the Pennsylvania Capitol a large painting was recently finished by Edwin A. Abbey, symbolizing the "Apotheosis of Pennsylvania." Among the celebrities who appear in this large picture is General Muhlenberg.

Such, as I here give it, is a glimpse of the life of the man after whom Muhlenberg County is named, and also a glimpse of the esteem in which he was and still is held. As already stated, General Muhlenberg probably never visited any part of the county that now helps perpetuate his name, nor even saw any part of the Green River country. Nevertheless, pioneer Henry Rhoads, in 1798, very fittingly procured for the entitlement of the county the name of the man who was a friend, pastor, and general to many of its earliest settlers.

II

SOME OF THE FIRST-COMERS

STATISTICS show that from the close of the Revolution to 1786 about 2,500 newcomers settled in Kentucky every year. After 1786 the army of emigrants gradually grew larger until 1795, when the in-flow increased to about 25,000 annually and continued at that rate for a number of years. In 1790 the population of Kentucky was 73,677. By 1800 it sprang to 222,955. It was during this big inflow of the last years of the Eighteenth Century that many of the homeseekers drifted into the Green River country and became its first permanent settlers.

Under the heads of the various counties bordering on Muhlenberg I gather, from Collins' History of Kentucky, the data here given relative to their first settlements. About a half-dozen stations were established between 1780 and 1784 in what is now Logan County. Among them was one that, later, became Russellville. In Ohio County the first settlements were Hartford and Barnett's Station, both of which were settled "before 1790." As early as 1794 a trading-post had been established at Berry's Lick, in Butler County. "Hopkinsville was laid out in 1799." The beginning of Madisonville, Morgantown, and Elkton dates back to the first years of the Nineteenth Century. Under the head of McLean County, Collins says: "The first fort or station was built, where Calhoon now stands, in 1788, by Solomon Rhoads, and called Vienna. In 1790 James Inman built Pond station, a few miles southeast of Calhoon." That Caney Station was what might be regarded as the first settlement in what is now Muhlenberg County is only parenthetically stated by Collins, and without the date of its beginning, which tradition says was about 1795: "One mile north of Greenville, near old Caney Station—which was the first settlement in the county—are several mounds."

From the foregoing statements it will be seen that a few settlements were made in this part of the State as early as 1780, and that most of the places which became permanent settlements were begun during the last few years of the Eighteenth or the first of the Nineteenth Century.

Tradition does not say who were the first white people to come into what is now Muhlenberg County. It is, however, probable that the first men who made this locality their home were Revolutionary soldiers who wandered westward immediately after that war. Tradition goes no further back than about 1784, to which time a few of the families in the county can trace the arrival of their ancestors.

After Pond Station had been started and after Henry Rhoads began inducing more German-Americans to locate near that station and in other sections of the country, and while Caney Station was being built by Virginians, the inflow of newcomers began to increase rapidly. A number of pioneers from North Carolina and Virginia settled along Pond River. John Dennis and a few other North Carolinians, some of whom probably came as early as 1785, settled in the Pond Creek country. Kincheloe's Bluff or Lewisburg, on Green River, was settled and made a "port of entry" before the close of the Eighteenth Century. It was there that Thomas Irvin and his party of stone-cutters landed about 1797 and helped open up the Nelson Creek country. Stum's Landing, now Paradise, was also a well-known river point as early as 1798. It was during this period of the country's his-

A SURVIVOR OF "THE FOREST PRIMEVAL"
Upper Pond Creek Country

tory that the outlaw, Big Harpe, was killed near what has ever since been known as Harpe's Hill.

Jesse McPherson was one of the earliest settlers in the Clifty Creek country. John Hunt and James Wood were among the influential first-comers in the Mud River country. Among the first to settle in the Long Creek country were the Drake, Duke, Welborn, and Wells families.

A number of the pioneers, as already stated, were Revolutionary soldiers, but more of them were sons of such veterans. The names of the Revolutionary soldiers living in the United States in 1840 were compiled for the census of that year. Collins gives the seven reported from Muhlenberg County: John Bone, Joshua Elkins, Sihez Garriz, Andrew Glenn, William

Hopkins, Benjamin Neal, and Britain Willis. The average age of these seven in 1840 was eighty years. They must therefore have been about twenty-one years old at the close of the war. Life insurance statistics show that about 18 per cent of men who reach the age of forty are likely to reach the age of eighty. At this rate, if seven Revolutionary soldiers aged eighty were still alive in 1840, they represent what were thirty-eight men, aged forty, in 1800. We may thus assume that there were thirty-eight Revolutionary soldiers in Muhlenberg in 1800, who at the close of that war were twenty-one years of age.

On the supposition that the number of older soldiers who came here after the Revolution and who died before 1800 is equal to the number of younger soldiers who were still alive in 1800 and represented by thirty-eight men, we may infer that about seventy-six Revolutionary soldiers were among the first settlers of Muhlenberg. If we assume that each soldier was the father of five children, then there were 380 sons and daughters of Revolutionary soldiers in the county in 1800. These children (380) with their parents (twice 76) make a total of 532. According to Collins, the population of Muhlenberg in 1800 was 1,443. That being the fact, we may infer that about 5 per cent of the pioneers who settled in Muhlenberg in the Eighteenth Century saw service in the Revolutionary War, and furthermore, that about one fourth of the pioneers were children of such soldiers.

Although these figures, based partially on statistics, may be wrong, and these conclusions be far from representing the actual but unrecorded facts, these estimates nevertheless are more likely to be nearer correct than any based on mere supposition or a groundless guess.

The first of the early settlers of whom we have any tradition or history were Henry Rhoads and his brothers, who settled Rhoadsville, which later became Calhoun. Of the original party who began this station only a few remained permanently in the immediate neighborhood. Henry Rhoads was probably the first to leave it. After living a few years near what later became Hartford, Ohio County, he settled in the neighborhood of what is now Browder, Muhlenberg County. In 1790 James Inman left Rhoadsville and moved five miles south, where he built Pond Station in the territory which, in 1798, became a part of Muhlenberg County, and in 1854, when McLean County was organized, became in turn a part of that county.

W. G. Stroud, of Semiway, McLean County, in a letter written to me in 1912, says: "There is a tradition to the effect that at one time a party of Indians came to the fort at Pond Station when it was occupied by only one man and several women. The other men were out either hunting or at work. The Indians made an attack on the fort, but were successfully repulsed by the occupants. About the year 1850, when I was a boy of ten, Thomas Worthington told my father that his grandfather was an inmate of the fort and that he (Tom) when a small boy visited him there and saw fine corn growing on the site of the old pond. The pond from which the Station took its name was made by beavers closing a gap in a ridge with a dam, causing the water to cover about twenty-five acres of ground. Local tradition gives no dates, and I am not able to give you, even approximately, the time when Pond Station was discontinued as a fort or station."

Pond Station was located on the east side of the Greenville and Rumsey Road, on the lands now owned and occupied by J. W. West and R. D. H. Beasley. In 1840 the Baptists in that neighborhood organized a congregation and called their church Old Station Church, in honor of Pond Station. Many years later a new structure was erected by that organization on a site about a mile from the original, and since known as Station Church.

About the year 1795—that is, about five years after Pond Station had been started and about two years after Henry Rhoads settled in Muhlenberg County—Caney Station was started, near the present site of Greenville. This forerunner of Greenville was established by Colonel and Mrs.

SITE OF POND STATION, McLEAN COUNTY

William Campbell, who with William Bradford and a few others, together with a number of slaves, came from Lexington for the purpose of opening a settlement on General William Russell's and Colonel Campbell's military grants. John C. Russell and Samuel Russell, it seems, did not appear upon the scene until after Caney Station had been begun by their brother-in-law and sister.

Caney Station was located on a stretch of elevated and rolling ground, semicircled by Caney Creek. It was about a mile and a half northwest of where Greenville is now, and near what later became the Earles and Lower Madisonville Road. A few log houses were erected. According to one version of this tradition, a stockade was also built. However, this spot was not decided on for a permanent home or future town. So, when the place for the courthouse had been selected (June, 1799), the people of Caney Station were all more or less prepared to move to the new town site.

A few years after Greenville was started Caney Station was entirely abandoned. In the course of time the few log houses began to tumble down, and finally all traces of the old buildings disappeared. The only thing left to mark this historic spot is an abandoned graveyard, which was used by a few of the pioneer families for over half a century. Its dozen or more fallen tombstones are almost hidden by briars and myrtle, running rampant under a few walnut trees and old cedars.

The square selected for the courthouse and the lots facing it were presented to the county by Colonel William Campbell. John Dennis, it is said, offered to donate the same amount of ground if any of his survey (about three miles southeast of Caney Station) were chosen for the county seat.

OLD CANEY STATION GRAVEYARD, NEAR GREENVILLE
The shaft on the right marks the grave of Edward Rumsey, the stone on its right the grave of Charles Fox Wing. These stones have long since fallen, but were temporarily raised to mark the graves for this picture.

The pioneers objected to Caney Station as a town site because the locality was then considered as lying too low for such a purpose. The place selected for the county seat was chosen because it was high and therefore more healthful, and because near it were two good springs, and furthermore because two old trails intersected upon it or not far from it.

There is a vague tradition to the effect that an old trail ran from Hartford, crossed Green River at Benton's Ferry (or Rockport), and running about two miles south of what later became Central City, continued through or near Caney Station or Greenville and crossed Pond River above Harpe's Hill, at what is now called Free Henry Ford. At some point west of Greenville another trail branched off the main route and extended through the Murphy's Lake country to the southwest, and like the main trail connected with the trail that became the Highland Lick Road. Another old trail started from Owensboro, or Yellow Banks, went through Rhoadsville (Calhoun) and Pond Station to Caney Station or Greenville, and passing the John Dennis house, continued to Russellville. It is probable that these two main trails intersected near the spot where the courthouse was built, and that they were old trails used by the Indians up to the time they stopped passing through this section of the country.[1]

General William Russell, to whom was granted the land on which Caney Station and Greenville were built, was an officer in the Revolution. His regiment formed part of General Muhlenberg's brigade, which at times was in General Greene's division. General Russell participated in the Brandywine, Monmouth, and other battles, and was present at the surrender of Yorktown. He also fought in the French and Indian War, and led several expeditions against the Indians. General Russell was born in 1735 and died in 1793. His first wife was Tabitha Adams; his second wife was Mrs. Elizabeth Henry Campbell, widow of General William Campbell and sister of Patrick Henry. General Russell was the father of sixteen children, many of whom came to Central Kentucky shortly after the Revolution. His second son was Colonel William Russell, after whom Russell County is named. Three of General Russell's children by his first wife, after a short stay in Fayette County, located, as already stated, in Muhlenberg: John C. and Samuel Russell and their sister Mrs. Tabitha A. R. Campbell.

Tabitha Adams Russell Campbell was the wife of Colonel William Campbell, who was a son of Patrick Campbell and a cousin of General William Campbell. General William Campbell was the hero of King's Mountain, where he defeated the British on October 7, 1780, and fought what proved to be "the turning in the tide of success that terminated the Revolution." In the autumn of 1800, shortly after Greenville's first courthouse was completed and the new town started, Colonel William Campbell broke his leg and was obliged to ride in a saddle to Lexington for medical treatment. There, in the home of his friend, Colonel Robert Patterson, he died

---

[1] I am informed by Julian W. Allen, of Ennis, that about two and a half miles above the mouth of Rocky Creek are evidences of an old buffalo trail, three or four feet wide, and that where it crossed the creek it is now worn down to a depth of about six feet. This trail apparently led from the barrens in Christian County through the Mud River country of Muhlenberg, crossed Mud River about eight miles below Mud River Mine, into Butler County to Conley's Lake, which, before the dam was built at Rochester, was a salt lick. This salt lick, in the olden days, covered the ground (about twenty acres) where the lake now is. It is said this worn-down area was formed by buffaloes and other animals trampling and wallowing on the ground while there for the purpose of licking salt. From a point on the Muhlenberg side, near the Mud River crossing, the main trail followed the general course of Mud River down toward its mouth. An old road that led from Bowling Green to Owensboro followed this trail through the Mud River bottoms from the lick, over the old Mud River crossing into Muhlenberg, and then continued over the hills toward the north. Evidences of this old buffalo trail can also be seen in some of the woodlands between Dunmor and Penrod. There are indications that below the Mud River country a trail led off from the main buffalo trail toward Greenville, through what is now the Pallas Dwyer farm. Since some of the old surveys refer to this main trail as the Old Buffalo Trail, it is more than likely that traces of it were far more apparent in the days of the first-comers than they are now. Evidences indicate that another old trail ran from Berry's Lick, Butler County, crossed Mud River about a mile below Mud River Mine, intersected the Old Buffalo Trail south of Rocky Creek, and then continued over the Muhlenberg hills toward Christian County.

November 19, 1800, aged forty-one years. Distance and transportation facilities were such that the body could not be brought from Fayette County, and for that reason the Father of Greenville is not buried in Muhlenberg.

After Colonel Campbell's death his family continued to live in Greenville. His widow, being a woman of education and means, was in a position to give their five children many advantages. She died in Greenville, July 26, 1806. Their only son, Samuel Campbell, married Cynthia Campbell, but had no children. Their daughter, Elizabeth, became the first wife of Elder Barton W. Stone, and up to the time of her death in 1810 traveled with her husband, who was then beginning his great evangelizing work in Western Kentucky. The other three daughters became the wives of some of Muhlenberg's most prominent men: Tabitha married Judge Alney McLean, Anna S. married Charles Fox Wing, and Mary married Ephraim M. Brank.

MRS. SAMUEL RUSSELL, 1845

John C. and Samuel Russell were identified with the upbuilding of Greenville and Muhlenberg County. John C. Russell, who married Anna Clay, died November 17, 1822; Samuel Russell, who married Lucy Roberts, died October 23, 1835.[2] These two men were not represented in the county as long, nor as numerously, as the descendants of Colonel William Campbell. The name of John C. Russell, who in 1805 located three miles southeast of Greenville, in what is now the Pleasant Hill neighborhood, is still perpetuated in the traditions of the Russell Old Field. Samuel Russell, in connection with other business, conducted the Russell House, which after his death was continued by his widow, who was succeeded by their son, Robert S. Russell. This well-known tavern was run until 1861, a period of sixty-two years. It was a two-story log house, built in 1799, on Main Street, due west of the Public Square. Samuel Russell's eldest son, Robert S. Russell, was the last of the Russells to leave the county. He moved to Paris, Tennessee, in 1865.[3]

---

[2] After the death of Mrs. Tabitha A. R. Campbell in 1806, Mrs. Lucy Roberts Russell, wife of Samuel Russell, became "The Mother of Greenville." She died in the famous Russell House in 1851. A number of years later Mrs. Lucy Wing Short Yost became known as "The Grand Old Lady of Greenville."

[3] Robert S. Russell was born in Greenville November 13, 1810. In 1839 he married Celia McLean, daughter of Doctor Robert D. McLean. They were the parents of Lucy R., Rebecca W., Samuel, and Edward M. Russell. In 1850 he was a member of the State Senate. He represented Muhlenberg's southern sympathizers in the Confederate Legislature at Russellville in November, 1861. He died in Paris,

William Bradford, as already stated, accompanied Colonel William Campbell to the unsettled country that later became Muhlenberg County, and helped to build Caney Station. When Greenville was laid out, one of the streets was named after Bradford. He was one of the first captains in the local militia, and held various county offices in the early days, representing Muhlenberg in the Legislature in 1801, 1803, 1810, and 1811. It is more than probable that William Bradford was one of the most influential of the first-comers in the county. His name, like the names of many of the other pioneers, appears here and there on the pages of the old court records, and like the names of a number of his contemporaries is now seldom heard. As far as I am aware, he is forgotten by all the repeaters of local traditions except two—William A. Armstrong and Judge William H. Yost.

William A. Armstrong told me that about the year 1855 Charles Fox Wing, speaking of local men who had died years before, referred to William Bradford as a man who had

ROBERT S. RUSSELL, 1870

spent the last years of his life trying to better the laws of the State and improve the environment of the people of Muhlenberg. Captain Wing also told him a story to the effect that Bradford showed heroism in battle on one occasion. A bombshell had been thrown into a fort, and Bradford, while the fuse was still burning, picked the shell up and threw it on the enemy outside the fortification before it exploded, and thus saved the day for the Americans. Armstrong's recollection as to where Captain Wing stated that this took place was very vague. He, however, was of the opinion that it occurred during the second war with England, if not during the Revolution or during General Anthony Wayne's campaign in Ohio in 1794. I failed to find William Bradford's name on the roster of officers and privates who enlisted in Kentucky during the War of 1812. However, since that list is far from complete, he may nevertheless have served as a soldier from this State.

Judge William H. Yost, in a letter sent to me recently, writes: "Some time between the years 1870 and 1875, while the clerk's office in Greenville was undergoing some repairs, Judge Charles Eaves and myself found in one of the old record books two copies of a printed circular, written by Wil-

Tennessee, October 4, 1873. Edward M. Russell, of Paris, Tennessee, in a letter to me, writes: "Except for the eyes, the enclosed photograph of my father, made in 1870, is a very good likeness. He had large gray eyes, but during the last few years of his life they were very much weakened by disease. . . . I have often heard my father speak of the howling of the wolves in Greenville at night, so wild and unsettled was the country when he was a young man."

liam Bradford and addressed to the voters of Muhlenberg County. It was headed 'In Prison Bounds.' It announced his candidacy for the Lower House of the General Assembly at the ensuing election. Judge Eaves told me Bradford was elected and his election took him out of 'Prison Bounds.' Judge Eaves also told me that the judgment fixed Bradford's 'Prison Bounds' to the limits of the Courthouse Square. I remember how, in his circular, he mercilessly flayed his creditors for confining him to 'Prison Bounds.' I was told that their action resulted in his election, and that during the rest of his life he did much toward repealing the old laws inflicting imprisonment for debt."

The old laws according to which men were sentenced to the State prison or confined to local "prison bounds" for debt were modified during the years that Bradford was a member of the Legislature. All of these laws, with the exception of a few, were repealed by 1821, which in all probability was after his death.

No one knows the place and time of William Bradford's birth or death. I find no trace of any descendants and therefore infer that he was a bachelor or a childless man. In his day he undoubtedly worked faithfully for the betterment of the life and laws of his fellow-men, and having done what he regarded as his duty, he probably was indifferent whether or not he would be remembered by posterity. Nevertheless, like many others who have gone to their reward, if he were to return to his earthly haunts he could but say, "How soon we are forgotten!"

THE "CAVE HUT CLIFF"
Near Dunmor

Jesse McPherson was probably the first of the first-comers who settled in the southeastern part of the county. According to one tradition he arrived upon the scene before either Pond or Caney stations were started. It is said that during 1790, or before, he left his wife and two or three children in Virginia and came to Kentucky, and while looking for a place to settle selected a tract of land three miles from what later became the town of Cisney or Rosewood. He spent the winter and spring clearing two fields, one near the foot of a cliff facing a valley leading to Clifty Creek, and another on the top of the same cliff. In the meantime he lived in his "cave hut" near his bottom field. This improvised house was made by erecting two short walls of logs in front of a small cove at the foot of the cliff, and placed in such a way that the top of the concave opening in the cliff served as a roof and the rock wall of the cliff and the two log walls served as walls to the "cave hut." The following summer, after having set out a crop of corn in each of his fields, he returned to Virginia for his family. He brought them to Kentucky and they lived in the "cave hut" until a log cabin on the bluff was finished. A few years later, or about 1800, he began building the spacious house known as the Jesse McPherson house, now occupied by William H. Pearson and his wife, the latter a great-granddaughter of Jesse McPherson. The logs used in the construction of the "cave hut" have long ago disappeared, but the rock-roofed cove in "Cave Hut Cliff" has for more than a century been used as a hay bin.

Jesse McPherson was one of Muhlenberg's best-known pioneers. When the county was organized he was appointed one of the justices of the peace.

THE JESSE McPHERSON HOUSE, NEAR DUNMOR

He ran a tanyard, horse mill, and distillery for many years. Tradition says that he feared nothing. On one occasion his neighbor Billings was attacked by a bear whose cub he had taken. McPherson, hearing the cry for help, rushed to the rescue and killed the animal with a hickory club. A few years later McPherson took a trip to Arkansas, and upon his return showed Billings some hickory nuts he had brought from that State. Billings suggested that they plant one of the nuts where McPherson had saved his life from the ferocious bear. This was done, and to-day a large hickory tree, standing near the "Cave Hut Cliff," marks the spot where, as one of the local oracles puts it, "Billings came near getting the stuffings squeezed out of him by a big bear."[4]

---

[4] Jesse McPherson was born in Virginia February 15, 1765, and died May 14, 1849. His wife was born February 16, 1772, and died August 25, 1822. Both are

Among other pioneers in the southeastern part of the county were John Hunt and James Wood. Hunt, a Revolutionary soldier, came to Muhlenberg from North Carolina about the year 1806 and settled in that part of the Mud River country known ever since as the Hunt Settlement. The house erected in 1825 near Gus by his son, Jonathan Hunt, was later occupied by the latter's son, Jefferson Hunt, and he in turn was succeeded by his son Amos L. Hunt, who now lives in this well-preserved landmark.

About the year 1816 James Wood, also of North Carolina, settled a few miles above the Hunt Settlement, north of what is now Dunmor. Many of the descendants of John Hunt and James Wood still live in the Hunt Set-

THE JONATHAN HUNT HOUSE, NEAR GUS

tlement and other parts of the Mud River country, where they are highly respected farmers.

Among the children of James Wood was Zillman Wood, who was born in 1814 and died in 1859, and who in his day was one of the most influential men in the Mud River country. One of the sons of Zillman Wood is James Willis Wood, a Federal soldier, who was born in 1841 and who all his life did much for the good of the county. Among the sons of J. W. Wood is Ed S. Wood, who was county clerk from 1898 to 1906.[5]

---

buried near their old home near Rosewood. They were the parents of seven children, all of whom lived in the southeastern part of Muhlenberg County, where they were well-known citizens: Lewis, John, Alexander, Amos, Alney, and Jesse McPherson, and Mrs. Nancy (Samuel) Davenport.

[5] Pioneer John Hunt and his wife, Charity Hunt, were the parents of Jonathan, John, Elijah, Owen, Daniel, and Gasham Hunt, Mrs. Charity Davis, and Mrs. Joan Whitaker.

Pioneer James Wood and his wife, Susan Wood, were the parents of Mrs. Sally (Enoch, son of Jonathan) Hunt, Zillman, John, Mrs. Mary (Daniel, son of Elijah) Hunt, and Mrs. Elizabeth (J. S.) Hughes.

Richard C. Dellium and James Forgy were among the pioneers of the Mud River country, in Butler County. Forgy's Mill on Mud River was among the first mills built along that stream. Dellium owned much land in Muhlenberg, and about 1815 built a large log house which, although no longer used as a residence, is still standing, one mile west of Gus. Collins, in his "History of Kentucky," under the head of Butler County, says: "Richard C. Dellium carried on a trading station at Berry's Lick, and James Forgy settled near there, about 1794. They had to go to Nashville to mill along a footpath through a solid canebrake."

ZILLMAN WOOD, 1850

Judge William Worthington was one of the most influential first-comers in that part of Muhlenberg which later became a part of McLean County. He owned a large tract of land on what, for more than a century, has been known as the "Island"—a territory of about eight square miles, surrounded during high water by back water from Green River, the Thoroughfare, Black Lake, and Cypress Creek. His home was about a half mile north of what is now the town of Island. The post-office for that section of the country was at his residence for many years, and bore the name of Worthington up to about 1860, when it was transferred to Point Pleasant on Green River. When the Owensboro & Russellville Railroad was built, a station was erected near the old Worthington place and a new post-office established. This was appropriately called Island Station, and formed the nucleus of the town now known as Island, which in 1910 had a population of 547. A more appropriate name, however, would have been the former name of Worthington, for no pioneer in Muhlenberg was more worthy of having his name perpetuated in that manner. Worthington's Chapel, three miles west of Island, called so in honor of his son Thomas, who gave the land on which this church is built, is now the only place that bears the name of this pioneer family.

William Worthington came to Muhlenberg about fourteen years before the county was organized. He took part in many of the early county court meetings and often presided over the court of quarter sessions and a number of the circuit court meetings. He was a member of the State Senate from 1814 to 1826. About the year 1830 his residence burned, and practically everything in it was destroyed. Among the few things saved was the cane presented to him a few years before by his fellow-members of the State Senate. This walking-stick is now owned by T. M. Worthington, of Dallas, Texas.

About the year 1845 Judge Worthington moved to Point Worthington, a plantation in Mississippi owned by one of his sons, and a few years later died there. His body was packed in salt and shipped by boat to his old home in Kentucky, where he had spent more than sixty years of his life, and was there buried by the side of his wife. Two stone-walled graves, each covered with a marble slab, mark the last resting-place of the old judge and his wife. On one is carved, "Wm. Worthington, Died June 5, 1848, aged 87 years."—on the other, "Mary Worthington, Died August 25, 1827, aged 66 years."

GRAVES OF JUDGE AND MRS. WILLIAM WORTHINGTON
Near Island, McLean County

Judge and Mrs. Worthington were the parents of a number of children. Two of them lived and died in Muhlenberg or McLean counties, near Worthington's Chapel—Mrs. Elizabeth Kincheloe and Thomas Worthington. One daughter, Mrs. Polly Wickliffe, lived in the South.[6]

---

[6] Elizabeth Worthington married Reverend William Kincheloe. They lived on a farm about two miles southeast of Judge Worthington's home. William Kincheloe was for many years one of the few preachers in that neighborhood. After his children became large enough to go to school he employed a teacher for them and extended an invitation to the boys and girls of his neighbors to attend this school at his expense. He ran a store for many years, and in that connection made a number of trips by boat to New Orleans and return. R. M. Kincheloe, of Sacramento, who represented McLean County in the Legislature in 1891 and 1892, is a grandson.

Thomas Worthington, son of Judge Worthington, was born May 27, 1786, in Fort Vienna, now Calhoun. There is a tradition to the effect that his parents,

The Kincheloes, like the Worthingtons, were among the most influential and highly educated first-comers in the Green River country. Local tradition, however, is very vague regarding the history and genealogy of this family, although the name of Kincheloe, like that of Worthington, is very familiar to those who are versed in local traditions. It is quite probable that Lewis Kincheloe, who lived at Kincheloe's Bluff for many years and who took part in the battle of the Thames, was a brother of Reverend William Kincheloe, who married a daughter of Judge William Worthington, and that he was also a brother of Thomas Kincheloe, whose son Jesse W., of Breckinridge County, was elected circuit judge in 1851 in the district then embracing Muhlenberg County. One of the pioneer

KINCHELOE'S BLUFF, GREEN RIVER

Kincheloes, who lived in Muhlenberg, died, it is said, on his way to Tippecanoe in 1811. He was probably a brother of Lewis, Reverend William, and Thomas. One tradition has it that all the pioneer Kincheloes were soldiers in the War of 1812 and were sons of Lieutenant William Kincheloe, who fought in the Revolution and died in Western Kentucky about 1798.

with their two small daughters, had a few weeks before gone to the Fort for protection from the Indians. In 1808 he married Elinore Barnes, of Ohio County, and shortly after settled near Cypress Creek on a farm that had been presented to him by his father. He, like his brother-in-law William Kincheloe, was a preacher, and also maintained a school in his neighborhood at his own expense. He died near Worthington's Chapel in 1853. Shortly after his death his wife and all their children, except three daughters, moved to Mississippi. These three were Mrs. Matilda (W. B.) Lawton, the mother of Alexander Lawton, of Rumsey, Mrs. Caroline (James) Henry, the mother of Joseph G. Henry, of McLean County; Mrs. Emily (Joseph L.) Gregory, who is the mother of Reverend Thomas Gregory, now of Marshall County.

Polly Worthington, the second daughter of Judge Worthington, married Aaron Wickliffe. They moved to Greenville, Mississippi, and there he became one of the wealthiest planters in the South. They had no children, and left their estate to one of Judge Worthington's grandsons, whom they had adopted.

Among the many other first-comers were Arington and Robert Wickliffe and their nephews, Colonel Moses Wickliffe and J. W. I. Godman. Arington and Robert Wickliffe were sons of John Wickliffe, of Prince William County, Virginia. They settled in northeastern Muhlenberg about 1800, where Robert died in February, 1820. Both were influential pioneers.

Arington Wickliffe was born in Virginia in 1750. He was an officer in the Revolutionary army, and took part in many of the battles. Shortly after the Revolution he married Catherine Davis, daughter of Captain Jesse Davis, of Virginia. In the winter of 1819-20 he rode from Muhlenberg to his old home in Virginia on horseback and returned a few weeks later; he died, as a result of the exposure, in March, 1820. He was the father of ten children, one of whom was William B. Wickliffe, who was born near South Carrollton February 15, 1808, and died in Greenville, July 12, 1892. William B. Wickliffe was at one time a large landowner and slave-holder. He was the father of William A. Wickliffe, of Greenville.

Colonel Moses Wickliffe was born in Virginia in 1779 and settled in Muhlenberg about 1795. A few years later he made a trip to Virginia to report to some of his kinsmen and friends the condition and prospects of the Green River country. In 1799 or 1800 he came back to Muhlenberg accompanied by his two uncles, Arington and Robert, and their families. They brought with them J. W. I. Godman, then a child about a year old. Colonel Wickliffe did much toward encouraging not only some of his kinsmen, but many others, to settle in Muhlenberg. His integrity and his interest in the development of the community soon placed him among the best-known men in the county. Tradition says that during the War of 1812 and again during the Mexican War he organized a company of soldiers, but in each case, just as he was ready to leave with his men for the scene of action, he received news that peace had been declared. He often served as magistrate. He represented the county in the Legislature from 1816 to 1819 inclusive. He was always ready to lend a helping hand, and never hesitated to express his opinion when he thought that by so doing he could benefit any one. It is related of him that, although not a member of the Nelson Creek Baptist Church, he often presided over the business meetings held by that congregation. On one occasion he rebuked the members present, saying, "Unless you work in peace and harmony the devil will never let loose his hold on this church. I tell you the

PIONEER MOSES WICKLIFFE
From Pen-and-ink Sketch made in 1817

devil himself is in this church now, and right here in your own pulpit this very moment!" One of the members called the attention of the audience to the fact that Colonel Wickliffe himself was at that moment occupying the pulpit. The Colonel, nevertheless, finished his argument, and soon restored peace and harmony in the congregation.

In 1814 Colonel Wickliffe married Nancy Young, of Muhlenberg. They were the parents of ten children, all of whom were well-known citizens of the county. He died in 1854 at his home near what is now known as Bevier.[7]

J. W. I. Godman was not only a kinsman but a protege of Colonel Moses Wickliffe. Although an infant when brought from the old settlements by the Wickliffes, the Godman baby was nevertheless one of Muhlenberg's first-comers. This baby boy was carried in the arms of one of the women of the party who, in 1799 or 1800, rode horseback from Virginia to Muhlenberg. It is an interesting fact that about fifty years later this infant first-comer became Muhlenberg's first elected county judge.

Judge John Wickliffe Israel Godman was born in Virginia, December 8, 1798. He was the only child of John Allen Godman and his wife Susan (Wickliffe) Godman, both of whom died shortly after he was born. He was named for his two grandfathers, John Wickliffe and Israel Godman. When his mother's family moved to Muhlenberg he was reared by his grandparents and his cousin, Colonel Moses Wickliffe. Young Godman's early education was limited to such learning as the schools of his neighborhood then offered. This, however, he supplemented with extensive reading, and became one of the best read and most practical men in the county. He was universally regarded as a superior man. Among other things, he read law and medicine. At one time he intended to take up law as a profession. In the absence of lawyers and physicians he practiced, gratuitously, both professions among his neighbors. After his marriage he settled on a large tract of land in the northeastern part of the county, near Green River, where he spent most of his time farming and merchandising. Through these he accumulated a good estate. He made trips to Louisville to buy goods, and also to New Orleans to sell produce. Henry Clay, some time between 1825 and 1830, visited him in Muhlenberg, and engaged him to look after the Blackburn lands lying near the Godman farm and belonging to a ward of Clay's. In this way the two men became the best of friends and carried on an extensive correspondence. The letters received from Clay, although preserved by the family for many years, can not now be found.

Godman was for long a justice of the peace, and being skilled in the writing of legal documents he was for many years the only man in his section on whom the people relied for the preparation of their most impor-

---

[7] Colonel and Mrs. Moses Wickliffe were the parents of (1) Aaron, (2) William Y., (3) Mrs. Susan Jane (William Y.) Cundiff, whose husband was a son of pioneer Bryant Cundiff, (4 and 5) Benjamin Singleton and Robert McLean, twins, the two well-known bachelors, (6) Moses, a bachelor, who resigned as sheriff of the county to join the Confederate army and who later often served as a magistrate, (7) Mrs. Agnes Elizabeth (John F.) Davis, (8) Charles Bryant, who served as sheriff and who represented the county in the Legislature in 1889-'91, (9) John Kincheloe, a Confederate soldier killed during the war, and (10) Miss Mary Frances Wickliffe.

tant papers. At the first general election held under the Constitution of 1850, which took place on the second Monday in May, 1851, he was elected county judge, and thus became the first man elected to that office in Muhlenberg. He was devoted to his family, and when attending court at Greenville, discharging his official duties, he made it a rule to ride home every night, a distance of fifteen miles. In this way, through exposure to inclement weather, he contracted a severe cold, from the effects of which he died December 23, 1852. He was buried in the private burying-ground near his home, where a large marble slab marks his grave. That Judge Godman was "the right man in the right place" is a statement made by those who are familiar with the lives of the county's most influential men, and is verified by his record as a citizen and judge. He left no portrait. He had one made a few years before he died, but permitted it to be erased in order that the plate might be used to make a portrait of one of his children.

MR. AND MRS. WILLIAM J. DEAN, IN 1850

Judge Godman married Elizabeth Nicholls, who was born in Muhlenberg December 2, 1801, and died February 6, 1891. She was a daughter of pioneer James Nicholls and his wife Margaret Randolph, a daughter of Captain John Randolph, who was a cousin of the celebrated John Randolph of Roanoke. Captain John Randolph was also the father of pioneers Robert[8] and John Randolph, jr., and Mrs. John Reno. Judge and Mrs. Godman were the parents of three children: Sarah Jane, who married Edmund M. Blacklock[9]; Mary Eliza, who married William Johnson Dean[10]; and John Allen, who died in 1854.

---

[8] Pioneer Robert Randolph died in 1817. He was the father of (1) Ashford D., who married Geraldine Oates, daughter of William Oates and among whose children are John R. and E. M. Randolph, (2) Elizabeth, who married Bayless Oates, son of William Oates, (3) Robert, jr., who married Harriet Oates, daughter of Jesse Oates.

[9] Mr. and Mrs. Edmund M. Blacklock were the parents of seven children, all of whom spent the greater part of their lives in Muhlenberg: (1) Mrs. Elizabeth (Benjamin E.) Young, whose second husband was Judge Q. B. Coleman, (2) Mrs. Mary C. (Allison) Kincheloe, (3) Mrs. Sue M. (William) Leiter, (4) John A., (5) Mrs. Lena (Jacob) Kittenger, (6) Miss Jennie, and (7) Edmund Blacklock.

[10] Although William Johnson Dean was born in Breckinridge County (January 17, 1827), where he spent his entire life and where he died (October 10, 1901), he

Andrew and Peter Shaver were among the prime movers in what was for many years called the "Dutch Settlement," now known as the Bremen country. These two pioneers did not appear upon the scene until about twenty years after the county had been organized. A number of German-Americans and other Virginians had already settled in the northern part of Muhlenberg. Among the pioneers who appeared during or before the coming of Andrew and Peter Shaver were Benjamin Coffman, Reverend Samuel Danner, Jacob Garst, the seven Gish brothers, John Gossett, Rudolph Kittinger, Jacob, Daniel, and Doctor John Noffsinger, Lot Stroud, the three Vincent brothers, and Jacob Whitmer.[11]

MR. AND MRS. JOHN NOFFSINGER, ABOUT 1865
From a damaged tintype.

Andrew and Peter Shaver were sons of Andrew Shaver, sr. (originally spelled Schaber), who was born in Bremen, Germany, came to America shortly after the Revolution, and died in Virginia from wounds received during the War of 1812, in which war he had fought, together with his son Peter. John, Jonathan, and David Shaver, sons of Andrew Shaver, sr., settled in Muhlenberg some time between 1820 and 1825, but left the county before 1840. Parthenia, who married John Kittinger, and Mary Magdalene, or Polly, who married Jacob

---

was nevertheless identified with Muhlenberg County. He had an uncle (Charles F. Robertson) living in Muhlenberg, and often visited the county both before and after his marriage. He cultivated the acquaintance of the prominent men of the county, and always took much interest in its affairs. He supervised the farming and other business operations of Judge Godman's widow, and spent much time in the county. His wife was born (August 12, 1829) near what is now Moorman, and lived there until her marriage, November 14, 1849. Mr. and Mrs. W. J. Dean were the parents of nine children, all of whom lived to be grown: (1) Godman S., of Greenville, the father of Harry M. Dean, (2) John Allen, the well-known lawyer of Owensboro, (3) Summers, (4) William Johnson, jr., (5) Mrs. Mary Elizabeth (David C.) Herndon, (6) Miss Amanda R., (7) Mrs. Jennie L. (Charles M.) Reid, (8) Mrs. Margaret W. (Charles L.) Cornwell, and (9) Charles Wickliffe Dean. Of these, two sons, Godman S. and Summers, have lived in Muhlenberg for many years, and are among the best-known men in the county.

[11] Benjamin Coffman came to Muhlenberg in 1803, where he died in 1847. He was the father of John L., Isaac, Benjamin F., Jacob, Joseph, Mrs. Katherine (Daniel) Plain, Mrs. Betsy (Peter) Johnson, Mrs. Nancy Stoghill, Mrs. Hannah (James) Nall, and Mrs. Sarah (Jefferson) Rust.

Reverend Samuel Danner, a Dunkard preacher, was born April 1, 1784, came to Muhlenberg about the year 1800, and died near Bremen July 7, 1857. Reverend and Mrs. Danner were the parents of nine children: John and Samuel Danner, Mrs. Susan (John M.) Gish, Mrs. Nancy (Jacob) Hill, Mrs. Elizabeth (William H.) Kittinger, Mrs. Sallie (George) Branson, Mrs. Francis (David) Gish, Mrs. Mary (Jacob L.) Groves, and Mrs. Harriett (John) Hendricks.

Jacob Garst was born in 1795 and died in 1865. His wife, Mary Magdalene (Polly) Shaver, was born in 1796 and died in 1871. They were the parents of eight

Garst, were daughters of Andrew Shaver, sr., and like their brothers Andrew and Peter Shaver are to-day represented by many descendants in Muhlenberg. Mrs. Andrew Shaver, sr., died in Muhlenberg about 1840, and is buried near Shaver's Chapel.

Andrew Shaver, jr., married Susan M. Bower in Virginia, and came to Muhlenberg about the year 1820. He was a successful farmer and did much toward encouraging others to settle in the "Dutch Settlement." His career, unfortunately, was a short one. One day two strangers, passing through the country, came to the Andrew Shaver home and asked for supper and lodging. They were admitted, for in the olden days strangers were welcomed in the homes of the pioneers, if for no other reason than for the news they might bring from the outside world. Although the wanderers com-

children: Alfred, John, Philip P., Andrew, Jacob, jr., Mrs. Sarah (Samuel) Short, Mrs. Mary Jane (David J.) Fleming, and Mrs. Margaret (Rudolph) Kittinger.

Christian Gish, during the year 1800 or earlier, while on his way to Muhlenberg from Virginia, was killed in the Cumberland Mountains by a team of horses. His widow, Elizabeth Stintz Gish, and her seven sons took the corpse with them and upon their arrival at their destination, near Bremen, buried the body. These seven sons were George, who was married to Betsy Peters; John, to Betsy Noffsinger; David, to Lydia Wiley; Samuel, to Elizabeth Wiley; Abraham, to Mrs. Francis Hill; Joseph, to Sarah Landies, and Christian, to Susan Knave.

John Gossett, who was born in 1776 and died in 1854, married Mary Noffsinger in Virginia and came to Muhlenberg about 1812. They were the parents of ten children: Samuel, John, Isaac, Jacob, Daniel, Mrs. Betsy (Robert) Wright, Mrs. Rachael (John) Danner, Mrs. Polly (James) Miller, Mrs. Susan (Esquire John) Whitmer, jr., and Miss Kate Gossett.

The Kittingers (six of the children of Jacob Kittinger, who was a native of Switzerland) came to Muhlenberg about 1820. They were Rudolph, Joseph, Martin, Jonathan, Mrs. Lucinda (Jacob) Miller, and Mrs. Bethena (Martin) Miller. Jacob and Martin Miller, who married Lucinda and Bethena Kittinger, were sons of pioneer Martin Miller, sr., who was a brother of Henry Miller, the great-grandfather of F. Marion Miller, of Bremen.

Jacob Noffsinger married Susan H. Stoner, who was born in 1764 and died in 1836. They came to Muhlenberg about the year 1800. The following is a list of their children and to whom they were married: Nancy, to Mr. Cook, then to J. Thomas Hill; Mary, to John Gossett; Samuel, to Sallie Rhoads; Betsy, to John Gish; Jacob, to Mary Noffsinger; Catherine, to Reverend Samuel Danner; Hannah, to Samuel Reid; Susan, to Bradford Rhoads, jr.; Rebecca, to John Noffsinger; Sally, to George Humphry; Joseph, to Betsy Bowman; Miss Rachael Noffsinger, and John Noffsinger. John Noffsinger was born in 1803, farmed east of Bremen, married Harriet Reno, and died in 1872. Mrs. Harriet R. Noffsinger was born in 1807 and died in 1897. A picture of Mr. and Mrs. John Noffsinger appears among the illustrations in this chapter.

Daniel and Doctor John Noffsinger were brothers of Jacob Noffsinger. Daniel Noffsinger's only child married Wilson Turner. Doctor John Noffsinger died about the year 1835, at the age of eighty. He was the father of a number of daughters, but only one son, John H. Noffsinger.

Lot Stroud, who was born February 8, 1778, came to Muhlenberg about the year 1800, and died November 22, 1824. He settled in what was for many years called Stroud, and is now known as Brucken. There he died November 22, 1824. He was the father of six children: Mrs. Fanny (Richard) Morton, Reuben, Jesse, Asher, Mrs. Edna M. (Samuel M.) Ross, and Isaac Stroud.

Three Vincent brothers came to Muhlenberg about the year 1800. They were John, Charles, and Thomas Vincent.

John Whitmer was born June 24, 1752, came to Muhlenberg about 1795, and died December 10, 1828. He was the father of eight children: Jacob, John, Michael, Valentine, or "Felty"; Mrs. Eve (John) Phillips, Mrs. Susan (Martin) Miller, Mrs. Sally (Anthony) Donahue, and Mrs. Dossett.

plained of being ill, they nevertheless gladly told the news they had heard along the road. The next morning it was discovered, to the surprise of all, that one of the men had smallpox. His companion nursed him through the siege, and although every precaution was taken to prevent the disease from spreading, Andrew Shaver contracted smallpox and died. He was born November 5, 1793, and died June 13, 1837. His wife, Susan Shaver, was born February 14, 1791, and died May 8, 1874.[12]

MR. AND MRS. PETER SHAVER, 1865

Peter Shaver was born in Virginia January 18, 1790, and died November 17, 1866. His wife, Nancy Peters, daughter of pioneer Christian Peters, was born December 25, 1798, and died September 21, 1879. Peter Shaver came to Muhlenberg about 1815, and was regarded as one of the best educated men in the "Dutch Settlement." He did much toward the moral, educational, and industrial development of the northern part of the county. It was he who, in honor of his father's birthplace, had the post-office called Bremen, a name it still bears. He was a progressive farmer, and wielded the axe, the hammer, and the pen with equal grace. A letter written to his son, Benjamin J. Shaver, in 1861, is quoted elsewhere in this volume. The day he and his wife celebrated their golden wedding they had their portraits made. On the same day he recorded the following in their family Bible: "November 30, 1865: Peter Shaver was married to Nancy Peters November 30, 1815. We, the above-named Peter and Nancy Shaver, have, through the blessing of God, lived fifty years in the state of matrimony and

---

[12] Mr. and Mrs. Andrew Shaver, jr., were the parents of eight children: Peter, who was married to I. McIntire; Jacob B., to Ann McIntire, then to Harriett McIntire, then to Margaret Wilkins; Barbara Ann, to Michael Whitmer; Elizabeth Jane, to Bradford Noffsinger; Mary, to Felix Naul, then to Absalom Whitmer; Susan, to Joseph Hendricks; Caroline, to Wesley Hunt; and Nancy, to Martin Kirtley.

are this day in good health and able to take care of ourselves. God be praised for his mercy and goodness."[13]

Such, as I have given it, is a glimpse at some of the first-comers. But there were many other prominent pioneers. The Muhlenberg men who fought in the War of 1812, the first settlers in the Pond River country, the Paradise country, and the Rhoads and the Weirs, were among the other first-comers. The part taken by these pioneers in the settling and upbuilding of the new county is recorded in some of the other chapters in this history. They, like the men and women referred to in this chapter, helped to make Muhlenberg what it is to-day.

---

[13] Mr. and Mrs. Peter Shaver were the parents of five children: Andrew, who was married to Theodosia A. Timmens; Benjamin J., to Susan Jagoe, and then to Ann Morehead; David, to Mildred Taylor; Polly, to Thompson Miller, and John M., to Catherine Welsh.

III

HENRY RHOADS
"THE GODFATHER OF MUHLENBERG"

AMONG the pioneers who first settled that section of the Green River country which is included in what is now the northern part of Muhlenberg County were some who had fought in the Revolution under General John Peter Gabriel Muhlenberg. Most of the first settlers in the central and southern sections of the county were Virginians and Carolinians, mainly of English, Scotch, and Irish extraction.

Representatives of General Muhlenberg's army drifted to this part of the Green River country from Southern Pennsylvania and Northern Virginia. Most of General Muhlenberg's soldiers were born in America, but their fathers came from Germany and Holland long before the Revolution. Among these was Henry Rhoads, "the Godfather of Muhlenberg County," who not only procured the name of his general for the county but was also a prominent pioneer in Western Kentucky and identified with the early development of Muhlenberg and the entire western section of the Green River country.

In Perrin's "History of Kentucky," page 997, a brief sketch of the life of Rhoads is incidentally introduced in a biography of Professor McHenry Rhoads, the well-known educator, who is a son of Absalom J. Rhoads, a grandson of Solomon Rhoads, and a great-grandson of Henry Rhoads.[1] From this sketch I quote:

Henry Rhoads was born in Germany in 1739 and died in Logan county in 1814. [He died in Muhlenberg County.] He and two of his brothers came to America about 1757 and settled in Bedford county, Pennsylvania. In 1760 he married Elizabeth Stoner of Maryland. He fought for his adopted country through the great struggle for Independence, under the leadership of General Muhlenberg. After the war for Liberty, having lost heavily in the cause, he, with his two brothers and their families, came to Kentucky. They stopped first at Bardstown where they left their wives and children, and then went out in the wilderness to find a site to build a town. The place selected was at the falls of Green river where they started a settlement and called it Rhoadsville. After three years of peaceable possession an action was entered in the Ohio circuit court, styled "John Hanley vs. Henry Rhoads and others," for the possession of the land on which the new town stood. The suit was gained by the plaintiff. Henry Rhoads and a few of his friends then removed to Barnett's Station, on Rough Creek, where he lived five years, during which time the present town of Hartford was laid out and a few houses built. He next moved to Logan county and settled . . . where he owned 7,000 acres of military land. He represented

---
[1] The name Rhoads is occasionally spelled Rhoades and Rhodes, but pioneers Henry and Solomon Rhoads and their descendants never so wrote it.

the county [Logan and what became Muhlenberg] in the legislature of Kentucky in 1798, [and] on its formation [in December, 1798] as a county, named it in honor of General Muhlenberg.

Collins, in his "History of Kentucky," under the head of McLean County, says that the first fort or station in McLean County was built where Calhoun now stands, in 1788, by Solomon Rhoads, and called Vienna, and that in 1790 James Inman built Pond Station, a few miles southeast of Calhoun.

Other authorities and most traditions say that Henry Rhoads established a station some time between 1784 and 1788 where Calhoun now stands, and

THE HENRY RHOADS HOUSE, NEAR BROWDER

that he was assisted in this work by his brother Solomon Rhoads and another brother whose name is usually given as David. At any rate, a few years after Henry Rhoads established or helped to establish Rhoadsville or Fort Vienna, he lost the title to all his land in that vicinity, and after living for a while near Hartford he moved into what is now the Browder Mine neighborhood, in Muhlenberg County, which at that time was part of Logan County.

From a letter written to me by Judge Lucius P. Little, of Owensboro, the highest authority on the history of the Green River country, I quote:

"When Henry Rhoads came to this part of the Green River country he stopped at Barnett's Fort, on Rough River, above Hartford. He first located his claim for land at the site of the present town of Calhoun, and laid out a town in 1784 and called it Rhoadsville. When Rhoads was defeated by Captain John Hanley, agent for the Dorseys, of Maryland, the name of the town was changed to Vienna. Rhoads then went back to Barnett's Fort for a short time and soon after located in the bounds of the present county of Muhlenberg, five miles from Paradise on Green River and a mile from the present town of Browder on the Louisville & Nashville Railroad.

"Simultaneously with the departure of the Germans to the south side of the river, they erected a fortification about five miles south from Rumsey for refuge in case of Indian attack. This was called 'Pond Station.' This was in Muhlenberg until the territory embracing it was made a part of McLean County. About the same time such of the residents of Fort Vienna as owned slaves quit the fort and opened up farms north of the river, where some of their descendants are still to be found.

"As late as 1840 the settlement south of Cypress Creek and extending far enough south to embrace Sacramento and Bremen was commonly called 'The Dutch Settlement.' While these people were thrifty, yet few of them owned slaves."

In 1798, a few years after settling in Logan County, Henry Rhoads became a member of the State Legislature and on December 14, 1798, an act was passed creating a new county out of parts of Christian and Logan. It was Henry Rhoads who proposed and secured the name of Muhlenberg for the new county. Ed Porter Thompson, in his "School History of Kentucky," page 162, says:

General Muhlenberg was at no time a resident of Kentucky. His name and his deeds, however, are of interest to us because some of the gallant members of his church who followed him when he left his pulpit to fight for independence, had grants of land for military service, which they located on and below Green River, soon after the close of the Revolution, and made their homes in what are now Muhlenberg, McLean and Ohio counties. One of them, the Hon. Henry Rhoads, was a member of the legislature in 1798 when Muhlenberg county was established, and procured it to be named in honor of his pastor and general. . . . Through the influence of one to whom General Muhlenberg had been a pastor in peace and a valiant captain in the fight for freedom, his ever enduring monument (a county's name) was erected, not in his own land, but in the wilderness of Kentucky.

While faithfully and successfully serving the public, Henry Rhoads had, for a number of years, more or less trouble in establishing his claim to the land to which he was entitled and on which he lived after he moved into what later became a part of Muhlenberg. This land, of which he finally gained possession, lay in what was up to 1798 a part of Logan County. It was part of a grant of almost 7,000 acres which he had surveyed in 1793 for General Alexander McClanahan, with the understanding that he was to receive part of it. It is possible that 1793 was the year Henry Rhoads first settled in what is now Muhlenberg. In 1797 the State of Kentucky issued to McClanahan and Rhoads a patent for this survey. In October, 1801, a commission of six men was appointed to divide this tract between the two and issue a deed to each for his share. Order Book No. 1, page 1, gives the names of these commissioners, all of whom were prominent pioneers—John Dennis, Henry Keith, Matthew Adams, William Bell, Benjamin Tolbert, and Solomon Rhoads Deed Book No. 1, page 66, shows that they granted Henry Rhoads two thousand acres of the survey, for which he received a deed October 26, 1801. Thus, after a long and patient struggle, he held a title to land against which no priority of claim was ever brought. In 1798 he bought an adjoining survey of five hundred acres that had been granted to General George Matthews.

GRAVE OF THE "GODFATHER OF MUHLENBERG COUNTY"

It was on this 2,500-acre tract that he built his home, shortly after his arrival from Hartford. The original dwelling has undergone many changes, but is still standing, near the Greenville and Rochester Road about nine miles from Greenville. The farm on which this house stands has passed from father to son for more than a century, and is now owned by Professor McHenry Rhoads. Near this historic house is the old family graveyard. In it, among five generations of Rhoads buried there, is the grave of the "Godfather of Muhlenberg County," on which was placed, almost a century ago, a sandstone about two feet high and marked: "H. R., B. J. 5, 1739, D. M. 6, 1814."

Henry Rhoads died on the 6th of March or May, 1814, aged seventy-five. His "last will and testament" was written April 15, 1812, witnessed by "J. W. McConnell and Wm. Sumner." It was recorded in 1813 and probated in August, 1814, as attested by "C. F. Wing, Clerk," in Will Book No. 1, page 194:

In the name of God, Amen. I, Henry Rhoads, of the county of Muhlenberg and State of Kentucky, being weak in body but of perfect mind and memory, do make and ordain this my last will and testament.

First, I recommend my soul to the Almighty God, and as touching my worldly effects wherewith He has helped me, I give and dispose of them in the following manner.

First, I give and bequeath to my beloved wife Barbay Rhoads all the property she brought with her after we were married, agreeable to contract, and one cow, a large heifer and one iron pot and the corner cupboard and chest and my large Bible, and the low posted bedstead, one large and one small wheel including all the furniture we have got since we were married. I also give and bequeath to my beloved wife Barbay all that is allowed to her agreeable to the courts of a bond on my son David Rhoads bearing date August 23, 1810.

Secondly, I give and bequeath all my debts, dues and demands and all the property I own in this world except what is expressly mentioned in this my last will to my children, namely my sons, Jacob Rhoads, Daniel Rhoads, Henry Rhoads, Solomon Rhoads, David Rhoads, Susanah Nighmyoir and Caty Jackson, Elizabeth VanMeter and Hannah Jackson, all my daughters, to be equally divided among them, at the discretion of my executors at my decease.

Lastly, I do hereby nominate and appoint my brother Daniel Rhoads and Solomon Rhoads and David Rhoads as executors of my last will and testament, hereby ratifying and confirming this and no other to be my last will and testament, hereby revoking all other wills by me made as witness and seal this 15th day of April in the year of our Lord 1812 and the presence of viz: Henry Rhoads. (Seal)[2]

HENRY RHOADS (GRANDSON OF PIONEER HENRY RHOADS), HIS WIFE AND DAUGHTER, IN 1854

When Henry Rhoads settled on his tract of land Muhlenberg was practically an unbroken wilderness. Many wild animals, large and small, held sway. A number of stories are told about the game that roamed over these hills in olden times. I here repeat two of these stories, because they are characteristic of life in the wilderness and because they are incidents from the life of Muhlenberg's first great pioneer, handed down by local tradition.

When Henry Rhoads was building his log house his neighbors were few and far between, but all came with a helping hand and a happy heart to take part in his "house-raising." These old-time house-raisings were attended as much for the sake of their social features as for the purpose of building a house.

One afternoon, while the crowd was busily engaged on the roof of this building, a large bear leisurely wandered into sight. When the men saw the

---

[2] The descendants of Solomon Rhoads, son of Henry Rhoads, are represented more extensively in Muhlenberg County and other parts of the Green River country than any other of Henry Rhoads' children. Solomon Rhoads was born June 7, 1774, and died near Browder November 19, 1849. (This Solomon Rhoads was a nephew of the Solomon Rhoads who, with Henry Rhoads and another brother, started the station which later became Calhoun.)

Among the children of Solomon Rhoads was Henry Rhoads, whose picture, taken with his wife and daughter, is here reproduced. This Henry Rhoads was born in Muhlenberg in 1806, where he died in 1864. His wife, Elizabeth Morton Rhoads, was born in Muhlenberg in 1808 and died near Greenville in 1907. They were the parents of Morton and Doctor Solomon Rhoads and Cynthia Ann, who in 1863 became the wife of Robert W. Browning.

Luther Bard Rhoads, of Drakesboro, is a son of Isaac W., grandson of Barnabas and a great-grandson of David Rhoads, who was a son of Henry Rhoads.

animal they stopped work and immediately started on a bear chase. Some ran after him with axes and others with guns. The women of the wilderness always lent a helping hand. In this instance one woman followed in the bear chase with a pitchfork. After an exciting time old Bruin was finally killed. That night a large bearskin was stretched on the new log wall and barbecued bearmeat was served in abundance at all the other meals prepared for the house-raising party.

But the noise made by the bear-chasers evidently did not scare all the wild animals out of the neighborhood. About a year after that event Henry Rhoads, while walking in his wood, which is still standing a short distance north of the old house, espied a large drove of wild turkeys. He slowly raised his flint-lock rifle for the purpose of shooting a fine gobbler strutting under a white oak within close range. When he was about ready to pull the trigger he heard a rustling in the dry leaves behind him. Rhoads looked around, and to his great surprise saw a huge panther preparing to spring upon him. Without stopping to take sure aim he fired at the threatening beast. Luckily, the bullet hit the animal between the eyes and killed it instantly. A half-hour later Rhoads walked back home with the panther skin on his arm and his trusty flint-lock on his shoulder.

These old flint-locks were, as a rule, fine-sighted and unerring. They were slow but sure, although they did not kill every panther they were aimed at. Compared with modern rifles they were slow in all the operations that preceded and resulted in the discharge of the bullet.

Most of the local traditions are subject to a variety of versions. The old panther story, as I have related it, has probably changed very little from the original since Henry Rhoads' day. However, another version of this incident has also crept into circulation, and shows to what extent some traditions are changed. This new version has it that when Henry Rhoads saw the wild turkey in the woods he took steady aim and then pulled the trigger of his flint-lock. He had no more than pulled the trigger when he heard the panther back of him. Rhoads turned, immediately swung his gun around and aimed at the panther, then in the very act of making a long leap from a limb down upon the hunter. But the old pioneer was quicker than the discharging powder or the charging panther, for he had the gun pointed at the animal before the bullet left the barrel, and thus killed the panther with the load that, a few seconds before, had been started toward the turkey! This same version continues with the statement that the animal did not drop to the ground after it was shot, but fell across the shoulder of the hunter, who then leisurely walked home and did not throw the panther down on the ground until he reached the front of his house. I do not adopt this version, but merely record it for its vivacity and novelty.

Henry Rhoads, as already stated, was a member of the State Legislature from Logan County when, in 1798, Muhlenberg was formed, and he was the first man to represent the new county in the House of Representatives. He was sixty years of age when the county was organized. Although he declined various county offices offered to him, he nevertheless continued to work for the good of the community, and probably did as much for the county, if not more, than any of the other early pioneers. He helped draw the plans for the first courthouse and also did much toward promoting the interests of Greenville, the new county seat. He was bondsman and adviser to a number of the younger men whom he successfully recommended for office. Tradition says that many, and probably all, of the German-American pioneers in Muhlenberg came to the county through his direct or indirect influence.

During his last years Henry Rhoads spent much of his time looking after his farm, tanyard, and other personal affairs, but nevertheless lost no opportunity to bring in new settlers and perform such acts as he thought would a d v a n c e Muhlenberg County and its people. To-day a small sandstone is all that marks the spot where rest the bones of this influential pioneer. Some day his labors will be more fully recognized and appreciated and an appropriate memorial will then, I dare say, be erected over the grave of the Godfather of Muhlenberg County.[3]

McHENRY RHOADS, 1912

---

[3] Professor McHenry Rhoads, a great-grandson of Henry Rhoads, was born in Muhlenberg County on July 27, 1858, and entered West Kentucky College, South Carrollton, in 1876, from which institution he was graduated in 1880. He held the chair of natural science in this college until 1885, when he was elected vice-president of the Hartford College and Business Institute, where he taught science and literature until 1891, when he was elected Superintendent of City Schools at Frankfort, which position he held for nine years. In 1900 he was elected to the superintendency of the city schools of Owensboro, which position he held for eleven years. In the fall of 1910 he was appointed State Supervisor of High Schools under the General Education Board and elected to the professorship of secondary education in the State University, which position he now holds. He has been a member of the National Educational Association since 1891, and has served in the capacity of director, vice-president, and treasurer. His work as State Supervisor of High Schools arises out of a dual position, he being connected with the State University and the Department of Education at Frankfort.

IV

BEGINNING AND BOUNDS OF THE COUNTY

A FEW DAYS after the State Legislature began its regular session, November 5, 1798, the subject of forming a number of new counties was brought before the House. Henry Rhoads was then representing Logan County. Through his efforts the act establishing a new county out of parts of Christian and Logan was passed. It was he who proposed and procured the name of Muhlenberg for the new county. This act, passed at the first session of the Seventh General Assembly, creating Muhlenberg, reads as follows:

An act for the erection of a new County, out of the Counties of Logan and Christian. Approved, December 14th, 1798.

§ 1. *Be it enacted by the General Assembly,* that from and after the fifteenth day of May next, all that part of the counties of Logan and Christian included in the following bounds, to wit: Beginning at the mouth of Mud river, running up said river with its meanders within three miles of the mouth of Wolf Lick fork on a straight line; from thence with a straight line to the Christian county line, six miles below Benjamin Hardin's; from thence on a straight line so as to strike Pond river, two miles below Joel Downing's; from thence down Pond river with the meanders to the mouth; from thence up Green river to the beginning, shall be one distinct county, and called and known by the name of MUHLENBERG. But the said county of Muhlenberg shall not be entitled to a separate representation until the number of free male inhabitants therein contained above the age of twenty-one years, shall entitle them to one representative, agreeable to the ratio that shall hereafter be established by law. After said division shall take place, the courts of the said county shall be held on the fourth Tuesday in every month, except those in which the courts of quarter sessions are hereby directed to be held. And the court of quarter sessions shall be held in the months of March, May, July and October, in such manner as is provided by law in respect to other counties in this state.

§ 2. The justices named in the commission of the peace for said county of Muhlenberg, shall meet at the house of John Dennis, in the said county, on the first court day after the division shall take place, and having taken the oaths prescribed by law, and a sheriff being legally qualified to act, the court shall proceed to appoint and qualify their clerk, and fix on a place for the seat of justice for the said county, and proceed to erect the public buildings at such place. *Provided always,* that the permanent seat of justice shall not be fixed, nor a clerk be appointed (except pro tempore), unless a majority of the justices of the court concur therein, but shall be postponed until such majority can be had.

§ 3. It shall be lawful for the sheriffs of the counties of Logan and Christian to make distress for any public dues or officers' fees unpaid by the inhabitants thereof at the time such division shall take place, and they shall be accountable in like manner as if this act had not passed.

The courts of the counties of Logan and Christian shall have jurisdiction in all actions and suits depending therein at the time of said division, and they shall try and determine the same, issue process, and award execution thereon.

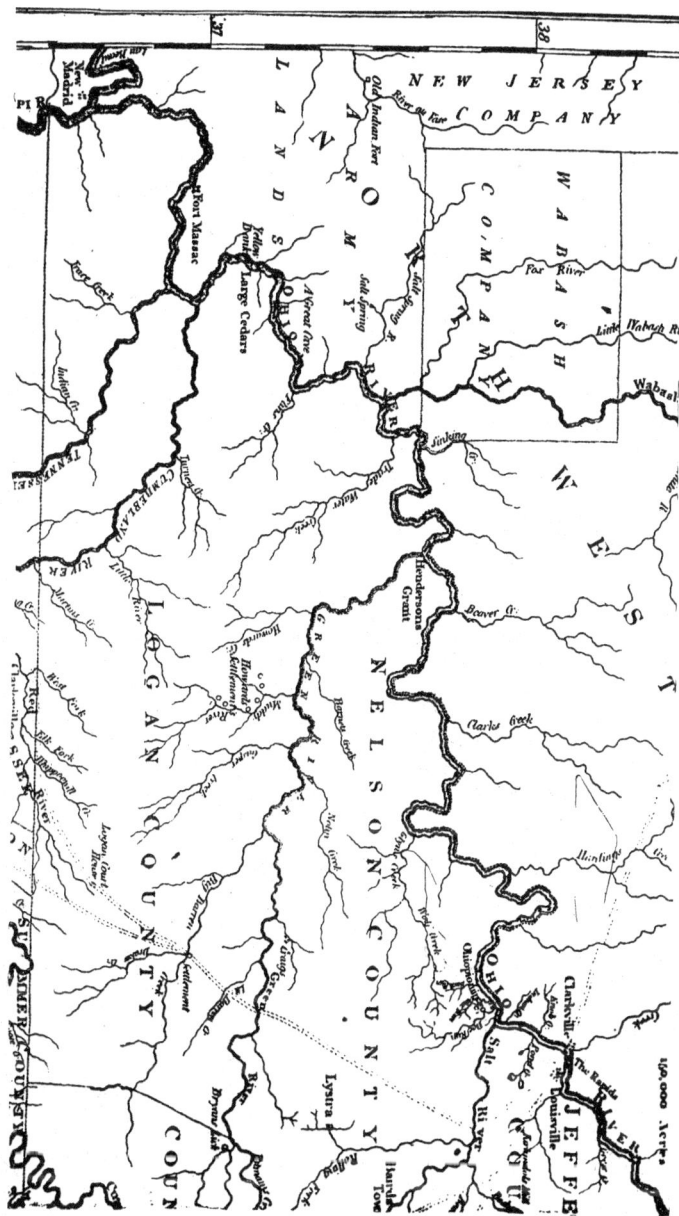

Section of J. Russell's "Map of the State of Kentucky with Adjoining Territories," published in 1794, showing extent of the original Logan County from 1792 to 1796. Among the errors on this old map is the location of "Howards Settlements," which were on Gasper River and not on Mud (or Muddy) River as here indicated.

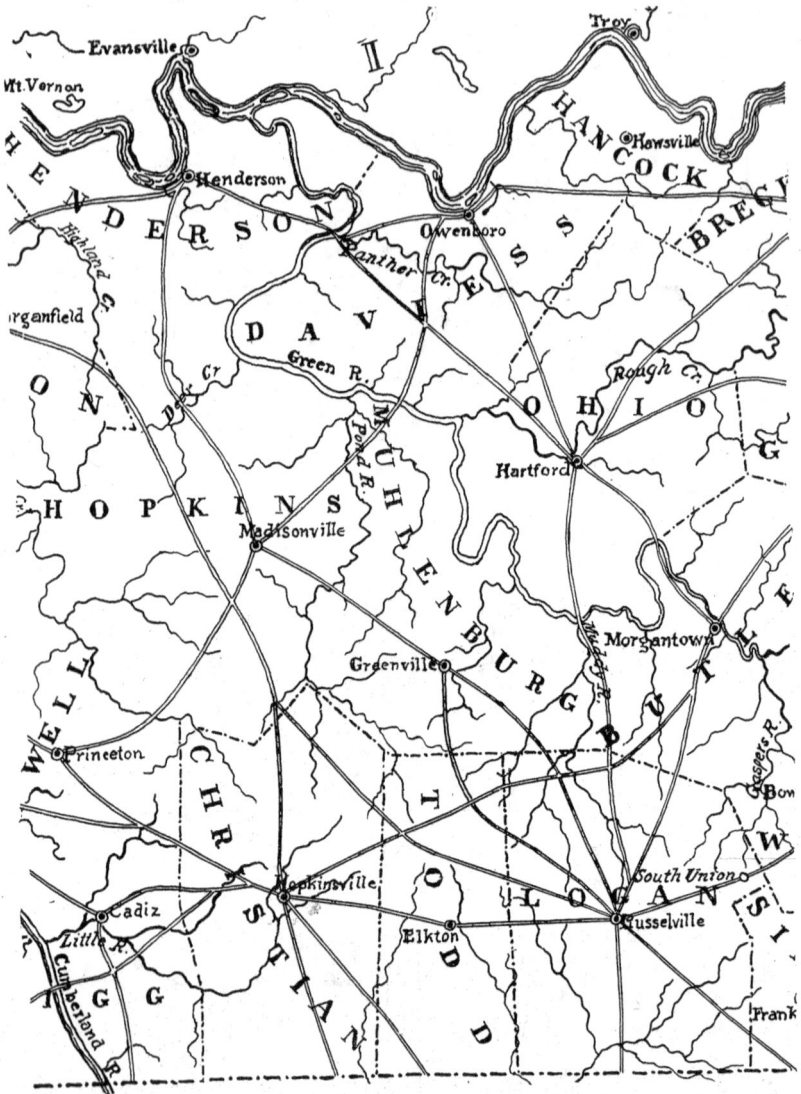

Section of Munsell's Map of Kentucky, published in 1835, showing outline of Muhlenberg and adjoining counties up to 1854, when McLean County was formed

BEGINNING AND BOUNDS OF THE COUNTY

The line that, before the formation of Muhlenberg, separated Logan from Christian and lay within the bounds of what became Muhlenberg, is described in the act creating Christian County as follows: "Beginning on Green river, eight miles below the mouth of Muddy river[1]; thence a straight line to one mile west of Benjamin Hardin's." In other words, this former dividing line ran in a southwesterly direction from a point on Green River

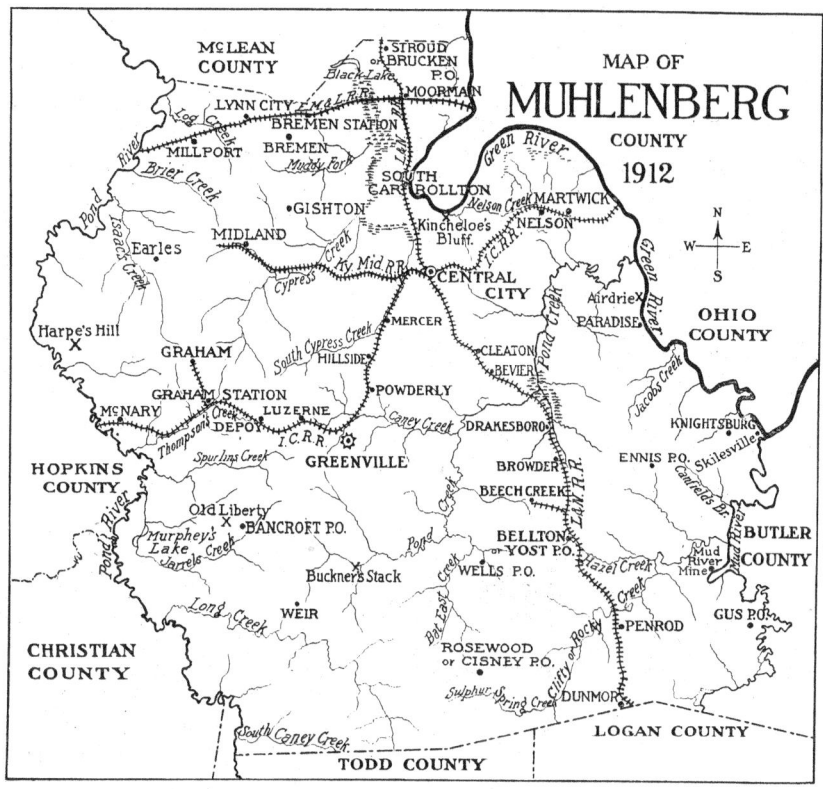

Map of Muhlenberg County compiled from six atlas sheets issued by the United States Geological Survey (1907-1912)

eight miles below the mouth of Mud River to a point in the neighborhood of what later became the northwest corner of Todd County. That being the fact, about three fourths of the original area of Muhlenberg County, or about two thirds of the present area, was taken from Christian, and the remainder—the southeastern part of Muhlenberg—was taken from Logan County.

---

[1] Mud River, up to about 1860, was more frequently referred to as Muddy River than Mud River. Pond River, on Elihu Barker's map of Kentucky published in 1795, is marked "Muddy or Pond River." Neither Pond River nor Mud River is correctly named or placed on Russell's map, published in 1794.

I judge that after the southern line had been surveyed it was discovered that certain lands originally intended to fall within the bounds of Muhlenberg were, according to the "calls for running the county line," not included in the new county. At any rate, on December 4, 1800, the Legislature passed "An act to amend and explain an act, entitled 'an act for the division of Christian county,'" which I here quote in full:

WHEREAS, it is represented to the present General Assembly that the act passed in December, 1798, for the division of Christian county is imperfect, and wants amending:

Be it therefore enacted by the General Assembly, that so much of the act as calls for running the county line from six miles below Benjamin Hardin's, to strike Pond river two miles below Joel Downing's, be and the same is hereby repealed; and the line shall run from said six mile tree to Job Downing's on Pond river, so as to include said Downing's dwelling house in Muhlenberg. This act shall commence and be in force from and after its passage.

An act to establish the county of McLean was approved by the Legislature on January 28, 1854, and set "the second Monday in May, 1854," as the time for the beginning of the new county. Muhlenberg, Ohio, and Daviess counties furnished the territory. Muhlenberg's part (about thirty-five square miles) was all the land that lay between Green and Pond rivers north of the line described thus in the acts of 1854: ". . . the mouth of the Thoroughfare branch; thence up the Thoroughfare branch to the mouth of Big creek; thence up Big creek to a point where the road from Rumsey to Greenville crosses the same; thence a straight line to the head of the island on Pond river, at the Horseshoe bend."[2]

In 1890 a change was made in a part of the southeastern boundary of the county. An act passed April 30, 1888, provided for the appointment of commissioners "for the purpose of establishing the lines between Muhlenberg and Butler counties." An act approved May 22, 1890, briefly states: "That Mud river be, and the same is, made the line between Butler and Muhlenberg counties." This act added to Muhlenberg a triangular strip of land covering a few square miles touching on Mud River below the mouth of Wolf Lick Fork. It incidentally ended the occasionally disputed question as to which county the land really lay in, and therefore also settled the discussion as to which county governed it in the sale of liquor. It is said that this strip was, up to 1890, invariably "wet," regardless of whether Muhlenberg or Butler were "dry."

---

[2] The county line between Todd and Muhlenberg was "run and re-marked" in February, 1853 (Deed Book No. 17, page 336), and the line between McLean and Muhlenberg in August, 1872 (Deed Book No. 25, page 452).

V

COURTS AND COURTHOUSES

ALTHOUGH Greenville is Muhlenberg County's first and only county seat, the first six county courts and first three meetings of the court of quarter sessions were held elsewhere, before the town was begun. These initial meetings took place at the home of pioneer John Dennis, about two miles southeast of Greenville on the Greenville and Russellville Road. The original Dennis house was a large three-room log house put up about 1790 by John Dennis, who in 1810 built a two-story brick of four rooms adjoining it. Both houses were torn down in 1902 by W. I. Gragston, who erected a frame residence on the site of the old landmark.

Back of the original log and brick residence were scattered a few slave cabins, a smoke-house and an ice-house; across the road stood a large log barn, a blacksmith shop, a horsepower corn mill, and several sheds, all of which gave the Dennis farm the appearance of a small town. But all these barns and other accessory buildings erected by John Dennis were torn down many years before the log and brick residence disappeared.

The old Dennis house was one of the earliest "stopping-places" in the county, and in its day one of the most noted. Among the other early places of entertainment for man and beast were the Tyler Tavern at Kincheloe's Bluff and the Russell House in Greenville. The Dennis tavern was situated on a comparatively much-traveled public road leading from Nashville and Russellville to Owensboro and other towns. Stage coaches, loaded with passengers and their deerskin trunks and carpetbags, halted at this tavern in the olden days. All travelers over this route, whether in public conveyance, horseback, or afoot, or in their own sulkies, buckboards, wagons, or landslides, lingered here. Those who were on long trips made it a point to spend the night with the genial John and the members of his household. Circuit riders occasionally appeared on the scene and held services in the house or under an arbor near by.

Before Greenville was started, the Dennis place was the principal headquarters for the pioneers who lived in the southern part of the county. On the stile-blocks and around the large open fire-places the local happenings were related by the pioneers, who came not only to discuss such affairs but also to trade in the store and to hear the latest news brought by the traveling public. But after Greenville became the county seat one patron after another changed his trading and meeting place to the new town, and long before 1822, when John Dennis died, the Dennis place had been relegated to the past. In the meantime, one after another, the pioneers died, and many of the stories of their adventures that had often been told by them were no longer heard, and so in the course of time most of the long-past events gradually ceased to be topics of conversation, slowly faded out of memory, and were finally lost forever. Only a few of these once-familiar facts were handed down for a generation or two, and are now but dimly remembered as traditions.[1]

Written official records are required by law, and these, from the beginning down to the present, are still preserved and are now on file in the courthouse at Greenville. The first of the county court records I quote in full:

May 28th, 1799. At the house of John Dennis, in the county of Muhlenberg, on Tuesday the 28th day of May 1799.

Agreeably to an Act of Assembly entitled an Act for Forming a New County out of the Counties of Logan and Christian, a commission of the peace from his Excellency, James Garrard, Esquire, was produced, directed to James Craig, John Dennis, William Bell, Isaac Davis, John Russell, Robert Cisna, Richard Morton, John Adams and Jesse McPherson, appointing them justices of the peace in and for the county aforesaid, which being read, thereupon John Dennis, Esquire, administered the oath to support the Constitution of the United States, the oath of fidelity to this Commonwealth, and also the oath of a justice of the peace to James Craig, Isaac Davis and William Bell, whereupon the said James Craig administered the said several oaths to John Dennis, Esquire.

And thereupon a court was held for said county. Present: James Craig, John Dennis, Isaac Davis, William Bell, Esquires.

John Bradley, Esquire, produced a commission from his Excellency the Governor appointing him Sheriff in and for said county which being read, he, the said John, thereupon took the oath to support the Constitution of the United States, the oath of fidelity to this Commonwealth and also the oath of office of Sheriff, and together with Isaac Davis and William Worthington, his securities, entered into and acknowledged their bond in the penalty of Three Thousand Dollars conditioned as the law directs.

The court appointed Charles Fox Wing their clerk pro tempore who thereupon took the oath to support the Constitution of the United States, the oath of fidelity to this Commonwealth and also the oath of office, and together with Henry Rhoads, Sen., and William Campbell, his security, entered into bond in the penalty and conditioned as the law directs.

Alney McLean, Esquire, produced a commission from his Excellency the Governor, appointing him surveyor in and for the county of Muhlenberg,

---

[1] The Dennis house was occupied by a number of well-known persons after it had been vacated by the Dennis family. Among those who in later years lived in this house was the Reverend William Leftwich Cornett, who came to Muhlenberg in 1874 and continued to live in this historic brick residence until 1884. He died April 15, 1892, aged eighty. He was preacher, farmer, blacksmith, and saddler. One of his old church members says: "Brother Cornett was the Saint Paul of the Pond Creek country. He plowed and preached, worked and worshiped, on and on, for the now and the hereafter." Reverend Cornett and his wife, Harriet Ward Cornett, were the parents of thirteen children, among whom are Ulysses C., Edward E., and Andrew Jackson (who is an old bachelor, and is known throughout Muhlenberg as "Uncle Jack").

whereupon he took the oath to support the Constitution of the United States, the oath of fidelity to this Commonwealth and also the oath of office, and together with Robert Ewing and Ephraim McLean, Sen., his securities, entered into and acknowledged their bond in the penalty of six hundred pounds conditioned as the law directs.

On the recommendation of Alney McLean, Esquire, surveyor of the county, William Bradford, George Tennell and James Weir, Esquire, were

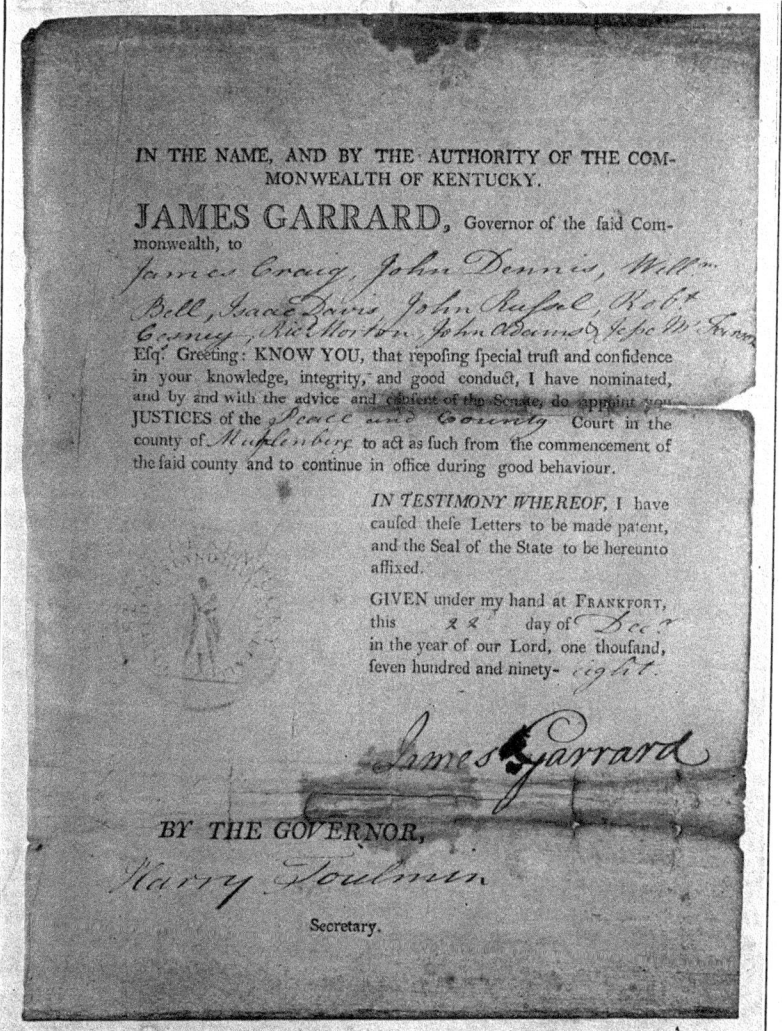

REDUCED FACSIMILE OF COMMISSION
Showing appointment of Muhlenberg County's first justices, December 22, 1798

admitted as his deputies, who thereupon took the oath to support the Constitution of the United States and the oath of fidelity to this Commonwealth and also the oath of office as deputy surveyors.

Peter Lyons' stockmark: two smooth crops and a nick under each ear. On his motion ordered to be recorded.

Henry Davis' stockmark: a hole in each ear. On his motion is ordered to be recorded.

The court appointed John Anderson constable for the county of Muhlenberg, who thereupon took the oath to support the Constitution of the United States, the oath of fidelity to this Commonwealth and also the oath of constable, and together with Richard Tyler, his security, entered into and acknowledged their bond in the penalty and conditioned as the law directs.

On the motion of Richard Tyler leave is granted him to keep a tavern at his house in Lewisburg whereupon with Lewis Kincheloe, his security executed bond in the penalty and conditioned as the law directs.

Ordered that the next court he held at John Dennises.

Ordered that the court be adjourned until court in course.

The minutes of these proceedings were signed by

JAMES CRAIG.

The second meeting of the county court took place in the John Dennis house on Tuesday, June 25, 1799. The record covers about three times as many pages as the first, and is signed by John Dennis. Charles Fox Wing was appointed county clerk "during good behavior." Evidently his behavior was considered good and his books well kept, for he held the office more than half a century.

James Weir was appointed to compile a list of the taxable property in the county. The following oaths were administered: Robert Cisna and Richard Morton, justices of the peace; William Bradford, deputy sheriff; John Culbertson, coroner; Peter Boggess and Thomas Morton, constables.

Sixteen men had their stock-marks recorded. Six roads were considered, and for each a committee was appointed to "view and mark the most convenient way." A number of "bargains and sales" were recorded. Ferries were established at Smith's Landing and Lewisburg, on Green River. John Dennis was granted license to keep a tavern at his house. Tavern rates and ferry charges were fixed. Among such items are:

> Dinner ....1 shilling 6 pence.
> Breakfast or supper ....1 shilling.
> Whisky, per half pint ....9 pence.
> Peach brandy, per half pint......1 shilling.
> Corn, per gallon ....6 pence.
> Stableage, 24 hours ....4 pence.
> Ferry for a horse, single..............4½ pence.
> Ferry for a man, single ....4½ pence.

The following is quoted from page 15 of the records of the same meeting of June 25, 1799:

The court proceeded to vote for a place for the permanent seat of justice for the county of Muhlenberg. A majority of all the justices concurring, it is ordered that Colonel William Campbell's[2] headright on Caney adjoining the lands of the heirs of William Russell, deceased, be and is hereby fixed upon as the place for the permanent seat of justice for said county, and that the public buildings be erected at said place.

Henry Rhoads, Charles Lewis, and William Bell were appointed commissioners to prepare plans for a courthouse.

The third county court took place on Tuesday, August 27, 1799, in the house of John Dennis. The minutes were signed by James Craig. The proceedings are similar to the earlier meetings, with the additional feature of the filing of several applications to establish grist mills. On page 28 the record reads:

The persons appointed for the purpose of exhibiting into court a plan for building the public building, which being examined and approved of is ordered to be recorded: "A memorandum of the dimensions of the court house of Muhlenberg county, to be built of hewn logs seven inches thick, nine inches on the face or more, 26 feet by 18, seventeen feet high, a joint shingle roof put on with pegs, except the outside rows with nails, a joint plank floor and loft with a good staircase, the lower story twelve feet high with one door and three windows, a partition upstairs, a window in each room and shutters to each window, and a door, a judge's bench barred around, an attorney's bench barred around, also a sheriff's box, a clerk's table and seat. The cracks of the house to have shaved boards pegged in on the inside and daubed in on the outside, and a sufficient number of jury benches.

Another paragraph informs us that "The court appointed Isaac Davis Esquire to build a stray pen on the public square two and thirty feet square, five feet high, to be finished by the fourth Tuesday in September, next."

An entry written at this meeting concludes with the statement: "Satisfactory proof being made to the court that the said Benjamin lost a part of his left ear by a bite from the accused Mathew in a fight, which is ordered to be recorded."

The fourth meeting is dated Tuesday, September 24, 1799. The fifth meeting was the last held at the Dennis house and took place on November 26 and 27, 1799. The following is quoted from the proceedings of November 26, 1799, page 49 (here the word Greenville makes its first appearance on the court records):

On the motion of William Campbell, and it appearing to the court that it will be advantageous to the public and it also appearing that legal notice

---

[2] Three other men named William Campbell were identified with the early history of the county.

The first of these was the William Campbell who came to Muhlenberg about 1805, lived on the northwest corner of Main and Main Cross streets, and moved to Nashville about 1820. His daughter, Cynthia Campbell, married Samuel Campbell, son of Colonel William Campbell. They had no children.

The second was the William Campbell who, with his brothers David and Charles, located west of Greenville about 1805. He moved to Illinois about 1835.

The third William Campbell was a son of the above-mentioned David Campbell. He married a daughter of Benjamin Hancock, and about 1860 moved to California. Another of the sons of David Campbell was John Campbell, who was a tanner in Greenville for many years.

having been given agreeably to law, it is ordered that a town be established on his land at the seat of justice in this county on Caney, including thirty acres of land to be called and known by the name of Greenville, whereupon the said William Campbell together with John Bradley and Charles Fox Wing, his securities, entered into and acknowledged their bond in the penalty of five hundred pounds, conditioned as the law directs. It is further ordered that the said town be vested in Samuel Russell, Alney McLean, Henry Rhoads, Charles Fox Wing, William Bradford and John Dennis, who are hereby nominated and appointed trustees of the said town of Greenville, agreeably to law.

The fifth meeting ends with the statement that it is "Ordered that the next court be held at the town of Greenville, the Seat of Justice of this county."[3]

The sixth begins as follows: "At a county court held for Muhlenberg county at the house of Samuel Russell in the town of Greenville on Tuesday the 24th day of December, 1799." Among its many items is one showing that Samuel Russell was granted license to keep a tavern at his house in Greenville.

The seventh, dated Tuesday, January 28, 1800, also took place in the Russell house. One of the items, which is the first of its kind, reads: "On the motion of the Reverend William Nexon, who produced credentials of his ordination and of his being in regular communion with the German Baptist Church who thereupon took the oath prescribed by law and together with John Culbertson, his security, entered into and acknowledged their bond as the law directs, license is thereupon granted him to solemnize the rites of marriage."

The eighth meeting was the first to be held in the new log temple of justice. Its record is headed: "At a county court held for Muhlenberg county at the court house on Tuesday the 25th day of February 1800." The new building, although occupied, had evidently not been completed, for the record of April 22, 1800, shows that "On the petition of the commissioners who were appointed to let the building of the court house of this county, ordered that leave be given the undertakers until the first day of August next to complete the same."

At the meeting held on June 24, 1800, an entry was made relative to a jail: "Ordered that the sheriff pay Jacob Severs two hundred dollars for building the county jail, being a part of the price of said jail." On August 26, 1800, is recorded: "The court this day received the jail as built by Jacob Severs which is received and considered as the jail of the county. On the nomination of John Bradley, esquire, sheriff Samuell Russell was appointed jailor of this county."

---

[3] John Dennis, in whose house the first five county courts were held, was the father of a number of children. Among those who made Muhlenberg County their home was Abraham Dennis, who was born in 1784 and died near Greenville in 1875. Abraham Dennis and his wife Tabitha (Rice) Dennis were the parents of eight girls and three boys, among whom was Alney McLean Dennis, who was born in 1822 and died in 1900. Alney McLean Dennis was the father of four children, one of whom is Robert A. Dennis, who is the father of William Rufus Dennis of Greenville, who in turn is the father of Master William McDavid Dennis, a great-great-great-grandson of pioneer John Dennis.

The twelfth meeting is dated Tuesday, September 23, 1800. "The court received the court house of the undertakers as being done agreeably to their bond and it is ordered that the bond entered into by the said undertakers be destroyed."

On the same date "A plan of the town of Greenville was exhibited into court and ordered to be recorded." The plan is recorded on page 75 of Transcribed Deed Book No. 1. The surveying was done by Alney McLean. He divided Colonel William Campbell's donation of thirty acres into fifty-

MUHLENBERG COUNTY'S SECOND COURTHOUSE
Erected in 1836; the clerk's office (one-story brick house) was built in 1865. Both were demolished in 1906. The old stone jail is shown in the background, between the two brick buildings

six lots, all of which lay in the vicinity of the two-acre public square. The proceeds from the sale of these lots was used to help defray the expense of building the new courthouse. The map shows the public square at the southeast corner of streets designated as Main Street and Main Cross Street. Running parallel with and east of Main Street are McLean and Water alleys, and parallel with and west of Main Street are Wing and Bradford alleys. Parallel with and south of Main Cross Street are Campbell and Wood alleys, and parallel with and north of Main Cross Street are Thompkins and Russell alleys. Adjoining the thirty-acre plot is another map, designating ten lots of five acres each. From one of these lots two acres are cut off for a graveyard, and five of the ten are granted to Alney McLean, the surveyor.[4]

---

[4] James Craig, William Bell, and Peter Boggess, referred to in these early court meetings, were, like many of the others who participated in those meetings, among the well-known pioneers.

Captain James Craig was a Revolutionary soldier, born in 1734, who came to Muhlenberg at an early date and died March 5, 1816. Among his children were:

The second courthouse was built in 1834; so, leaving the intervening county court records untouched, I quote from Record Book No. 4, page 135, under date of January 27, 1834:

The persons appointed for that purpose report the situation of the court house of this county, at this court, upon the examination thereof, deem it inexpedient to make any repairs on the present building; that it would be greatly to the public's good to build a new house instead of repairing the old one, and a majority of all the justices in commission of the place being present and concurring therein, it is ordered that Edward Rumsey, Strother Jones, Charles Fox Wing, James Taggart and Wm. Hancock be and they are hereby appointed commissioners to draft a plan of a building for a new court house for the county and that they make a report thereof to the next county court.

On page 139, under the date of March 31, 1834, the subject is continued as follows:

The commissioners appointed for that purpose reported that they had drafted a plan for a new court house for this county, which being examined and accepted of by the court, it is therefore ordered that Ephraim M. Brank, Wm. Martin, Coroner R. D. McLean and Charles Fox Wing or any three of them be and they are hereby appointed commissioners to let to the lowest bidder the building or erecting of said house upon the ground whereon the present building stands, after giving due notice by advertising the same, which building is to be completed on or before the first day of August, 1835, to be paid for by installments, that is to say, $500 to be paid as soon as the building shall be covered in, and the balance to be paid in two annual installments, payable out of the county levy, in such money as the said levy may be collected in, taking bond with approved security for the faithful performance of the work on said house with the said plan annexed.

I did not find the plans annexed to this document. However, I will state that according to my memory the old brick courthouse was about thirty-two feet square and two stories high. The court room took up the entire lower floor, while the second was divided into three small rooms, reached by steps erected on the outside of the building against the south wall.

The contractor, after having almost finished a certain part of his work, was obliged to tear it down and rebuild it in order to comply with his agreement. This delayed matters, and the house was not finished "on or before

---

Garland D., Mrs. Susan S. (James H.) Wright, Mrs. Peggy (Reverend James) Tolbert, and Mrs. Elizabeth (Thomas) Robinson.

William Bell and his brothers Josiah, Robert, and Thomas Bell came to Muhlenberg County about the year 1797. All of them became well-known men. Although the name of Bell is now extinct in the county, they are still represented by many descendants through their daughters. William Bell was born in 1768 and died in 1826.

Peter Boggess was a bachelor, a son of pioneer Richard Boggess, who came to Muhlenberg from Virginia about 1797 and settled near Pond Creek, above the Russellville Road, where he died about 1805. Richard Boggess was the father of Richard, jr., J. Warren, Joel, Peter, Robert, William, Lemuel, and Eli Boggess.

the first day of August, 1835." An entry on page 239 notes that a commission was appointed "to examine the court house just finished by Wm. W. Hancock and receive the same if finished according to contract, and report to the next court."

On November 28, 1836, it is recorded that the house was accepted. It may be well to add that the old log temple of justice stood a short distance north of the brick house, and was not torn down until after the second courthouse was occupied. The third or present structure stands on the site of the second.

MUHLENBERG COUNTY'S SECOND JAIL
Built in 1864-65, and jailer's brick residence adjoining—abandoned and demolished in 1912

In Record Book No. 8, page 13, June 24, 1865, is a record to the effect that Alfred Johnson had completed the stone work on the jail satisfactorily and it was ordered to be paid for. This building was used until December, 1912. In this same volume, on page 78, is an entry showing that Finis M. Allison and Jesse H. Reno were awarded the contract for building a clerk's office on the site of the old one. This brick building was completed a few months later. The clerk's office was one story high and contained two rooms, each about eighteen feet square, with a hall six feet wide between them.

The old brick courthouse and the clerk's office were torn down in 1906, and in their place now stands, not only a new courthouse, but one of the best and finest in the State. The first county court in the new building was held on "the last Monday" in September, 1907. Two metal tablets were placed in the front wall of the courthouse. One reads: "Erected A. D. 1907.

R. O. Pace, County Judge. W. O. Belcher, County Attorney. Magistrates: R. T. Johns, J. W. Stuart, C. W. Cisney, Bryant Williams, O. T. Kittinger. Bailey & Koerner, Contractors." The other reads: "Erected A. D. 1907. Building Committee: T. J. Sparks, Chairman, T. B. Pannell, W. G. Duncan, J. W. Lam, W. A. Wickliffe. Architects, Kenneth McDonald and W. J. Dodd." A bench mark erected in 1911 by Charles W. Goodlove, of the United States Geological Survey, shows that the courthouse yard is 568 feet above sea level.

5 JOHN EDMUNDS RENO, 1895

As stated in the beginning of this chapter, the first three meetings of the court of quarter sessions were held at the residence of John Dennis. The first justices of this court were William Campbell, Henry Rhoads, and William Worthington, appointed by Governor James Garrard December 22, 1798. Charles Fox Wing was chosen clerk. The first meeting took place on May 28, 1799, and the third on October 22, 1799. The fourth and following meetings took place in the courthouse, William Worthington, John Dennis, and Charles Morgan usually presiding. The last session was held in the spring of 1803, and coincides with the establishing of the circuit court in the county.

The first grand jury impaneled for the court of quarter sessions met on July 23, 1799, and was composed of: Isaac Davis, foreman; Henry Davis, William Cisna, Daniel Rhoads, jr., John Culbertson, Charles Lewis, Gilbert Vaught, Henry Keath, William Luce, George Brown, Benjamin Garris, Richard Nelson Alcock, William Hynes, John Cornwell, William McCommon, Thomas Bell, and Thomas Ward. They presented three indictments.

---

5 John Edmunds Reno was a son of pioneer Lewis Reno, jr., and a grandson of pioneer Lewis Reno, sr., who settled at Kincheloe's Bluff about the year 1800. Another son of Lewis Reno, sr., was John Reno, the father of Lawson R. Reno, who for many years conducted the Reno House in Greenville. Lewis Reno, jr., married Sallie Kincheloe, a daughter of pioneer William Kincheloe. Lewis Reno, jr., was the father of five children, among whom were Jesse H. Reno and John Edmunds Reno. Jesse H. Reno was born in 1817 and died in 1895. He was a prominent man, held a number of offices, and was for many years in the mercantile business.

John Edmunds Reno was born May 20, 1820. During his earlier business career he conducted a store and tobacco rehandling house in South Carrollton, and later ran a store in Greenville. He held various county offices. In 1852-53 he helped fill the unexpired term of Judge Godman. In 1874 and 1878 he was elected county clerk. His first wife, the mother of his three children, was Ademine Downer. To them were born: (1) Lewis Reno, banker, born June 25, 1847, died April 25, 1906, and who in 1870 married Mary Short, daughter of Jonathan Short; (2) Lizzie Reno, who married Judge William H. Yost, son of Doctor W. H. Yost; (3) Sue Reno, who married C. W. Short, son of Jonathan Short.

The first petit jury of the court of quarter sessions was impaneled on March 25, 1800, and was composed of: Charles Lewis, David Rhoads, Dempsey Westbrook, David Robertson, John Cornwall, Isaac Rust, John Keath, John Culbertson, Jesse Littlepage, Matthew McLean, William Boggess, and Daniel Rhoads. Their first case was that of "Commonwealth against Andrew Hays." The judgment shows that Hays was charged with assaulting Richard Nelson Alcock, and was fined "twelve dollars besides cost."

From the first day's record of the first meeting of the circuit court I quote:

March Term, 1803: At the courthouse of Muhlenberg county on Monday the 21st day of March 1803.

Pursuant to an Act of the Assembly passed the 20th day of December 1802 entitled an "Act to establish Circuit Courts," and an Act to amend an Act entitled an "Act to establish Circuit Courts passed the 24th day of December 1802." A commission was produced from his Excellency the Governor directed to William Worthington and William Bell, Esquires, appointing them Assistant Judges in and for the Muhlenberg Circuit. And they also produced a certificate of their having taken the oath of office, they having heretofore taken the oath to support the Constitution of the United States and also the oath of fidelity to the Commonwealth, which certificate reads as follows, to wit:

[6] WILLIAM H. YOST, 1912

"Muhlenberg County, Sct: I do hereby certify that William Worthington and William Bell this day came before me, one of the Justices of the peace for said County, and took the oath of Assistant Judges for the Muhlenberg Circuit, they having heretofore taken the oath to the United States and the oath of fidelity to the Commonwealth, March the 21st 1803.

WILLIAM GARRARD."

---

[6] Judge William H. Yost was born in Greenville April 17, 1849. He is a son of Doctor William H. Yost and Mary Jane Brank, who was a daughter of Ephraim M. Brank and a granddaughter of Colonel William Campbell, the founder of Greenville. Judge Yost, after attending school in Greenville, finished his education at Kentucky University, Lexington. In 1870 he began the practice of law in Greenville, where he was associated with Joseph Ricketts. He was county attorney from 1870 to 1875. From 1890 to 1895 he served as judge of the Superior Court of Kentucky. In 1903 he moved to Madisonville, where he now lives. He is a member of the law firm of Yost & Laffoon, who have offices in Madisonville and Greenville. No lawyer in Western Kentucky is better known; none is more highly esteemed or more closely identified with Muhlenberg's courts and courthouses than Judge Yost.

And thereupon a court was held for said Circuit.
Present: The Honorable William Worthington and William Bell.
The Court appointed Charles Fox Wing clerk pro tem to the Muhlenberg Circuit Court who thereupon took the Oath of Office, he having heretofore taken the oath to the United States and also the oath of fidelity to the

MUHLENBERG COUNTY'S THIRD COURTHOUSE
Erected 1907

Commonwealth and together with Sam'l Caldwell and Jesse Reno, his securities, executed bond in the penalty of One thousand pounds, conditioned as the law directs.

The Court appointed Christopher Tompkins, Esquire, attorney for the Commonwealth in the Muhlenberg Circuit.

Sam'l Caldwell, Sam'l Work, Henry Davidge, Robert Coleman, Matthew Lodge, Christopher Tompkins, Reason Davidge, John Davis, James H. McLaughlen and John A. Cape, Gentlemen, were on their motion admitted to practice as attorneys at law in this Court who produced a License as required by Law and thereupon they severally took the oath of office, they having heretofore taken the oath to support the Constitution of the United States and also the Oath of Fidelity to the Commonwealth.

William Hynes, foreman, Charles Crouch, Jacob Studebaker, Thomas Dennis, Solomon Rhoads, Rob't Robertson, William Roark, William Baugus, Jacob Taylor, John Keath, John Cain, Sam'l Weir, John Cargle, Thomas Littlepage, Dempsey Westbrook, Jacob Severs, John Stom, Jesse Jackson and Edmund Owens were sworn a Grand Jury for the body of this Circuit, who after having received their charge retired from the bar to consult, &c., and after some time returned into Court & having nothing to present were discharged. . . .

ORDERED that Court be adjourned until tomorrow morning 10 of the Clock.
WM. WORTHINGTON.

The first petit jury impaneled for the circuit court served at the March term, 1803, and was composed of: Samuel Handley, John Dennis, David Casebier, David Robertson, Thomas Bell, Thomas Littlepage, Thomas Randolph, Henry Unsell, George Nott, Henry Davis, Jacob Anthony, and Philip Stom. The first case tried was that of "The Commonwealth against Peter Acre, sometimes called Acrefield." Peter Acrefield was charged with assault, and was fined "one penny besides costs."

William Worthington or William Bell, with Christopher Greenup or Ninian Edwards, presided over the three sessions of the circuit court that followed. Judge Henry P. Broadnax, of Logan County, was next appointed circuit judge, and served from June, 1804, to March, 1819. Up to 1815 two associate judges in each county sat with the presiding judge, and William Worthington and William Bell usually acted in that capacity. Judge Broadnax was succeeded by Judge Benjamin Shackelford, who served from March, 1819, to September, 1821. He was succeeded by Judge Alney McLean, of Greenville, who served from 1821 to 1841, the time of his death. Judge John Calhoun served from 1842 until the new Constitution displaced him in 1851.[7]

---

[7] Of the five men who were appointed and served as circuit judges previous to the adoption of the Constitution of 1850, one, Judge Alney McLean, was a citizen of Muhlenberg. The other four here named were, like Judge McLean, among the best-known men in Western Kentucky:

Ninian Edwards was a son of Hayden Edwards, of Prince William County, Virginia, who afterward moved to Kentucky. In 1796 and 1797 Ninian Edwards represented Nelson County in the State Legislature. In 1798 he moved to Logan County. In 1806, at the age of thirty-one, he became Chief Justice of Kentucky. In 1809 he was appointed Governor of Illinois Territory, and held that office until 1818, when Illinois became a State. He was United States Senator from 1818 to 1824, and in 1826 was elected Governor of Illinois for four years. He died in 1833. His son, Ninian W. Edwards of Springfield, Illinois, married the sister of Abraham Lincoln's wife, became one of his most intimate friends, and supplied Lincoln's biographers with much data regarding him.

Judge Henry P. Broadnax was a native of Virginia, and came to Kentucky in his youth. He lived in Logan County, where he died in 1857, aged about ninety. He was an accomplished man and an able judge. Mrs. Chapman Coleman, in her "Life of John J. Crittenden" says: "Judge Broadnax was a stately, high-toned Virginia gentleman, who dressed in shorts, silk stockings, and top boots. He had an exalted sense of the dignity of the court, and a great contempt for meanness, rascality, and all low rowdyism."

Judge Benjamin Shackelford was a son of Benjamin Shackelford, and was born in Virginia, April 24, 1780. In 1802 he located in Lexington, where he practiced law

Prior to 1850 the circuit judges were appointed by the Governor. Since that time the following elected circuit judges have served: Judge Jesse W. Kincheloe, of Hardinsburg, 1851-1856; Judge George B. Cook, of Henderson, 1856; Judge Thomas C. Dabney, of Cadiz, 1857-1862; Judge R. T. Petree, of Hopkinsville, 1862-1868; Judge George C. Rogers, of Bowling

MUHLENBERG COUNTY'S JAIL AND JAILER'S RESIDENCE
Erected 1912

Green, 1868-1870; Judge Robert C. Bowling, of Russellville, 1870-1880; Judge John R. Grace, of Cadiz, 1880-1892; Judge Willis L. Reeves, of Elkton, 1893-1897; Judge I. Herschel Goodnight, of Franklin, 1898-1901; Judge Samuel R. Crewdson, of Russellville, 1901-1903; Judge William P. Sandidge, of Russellville, from 1904.

---

until 1807, when he moved to Christian County. In 1815 he was appointed circuit judge in the judicial district which embraced Christian County (which for a few years included Muhlenberg), and served in that capacity uninterruptedly until the adoption of the Constitution of 1850—a period of thirty-six years. Few men in Kentucky occupied the circuit bench longer than he. It is said that during that time fewer of his decisions were reversed by the higher courts than any other judge's in the State. He died in Hopkinsville, April 29, 1858. His two sons were Richard and Doctor Charles Shackelford. General James M. Shackelford, of the Federal army, who spent the early part of his life in Hopkins County, was a member of another branch of the Shackelford family.

Judge John Calhoun was born in Henry County in 1797, and shortly after came to the Green River country with his father. In 1820 and 1821 he represented Ohio County in the Legislature. About 1825 he moved to Breckinridge County and represented that county in the Legislature a number of times. He was a member of Congress from 1835 to 1839. In 1841 he was appointed circuit judge by Governor Letcher. He was a good orator and an accomplished lawyer. Calhoun, the county seat of McLean, was named in his honor.

COURTS AND COURTHOUSES 55

The following have served as circuit clerks: Charles Fox Wing, 1851-1856; Jesse H. Reno, 1856-1868; Nat J. Harris, 1868-1880; Doctor George W. Townes, 1880-1892; Thomas E. Sumner, 1893-1903; Clayton S. Curd, from 1904.

Prior to the adoption of the Third Constitution all county officers were appointed. Up to that time none of the officers of the State, with the exception of the Governor, Lieutenant-Governor, members of the Legislature, electors for President and Vice-President of the United States, and members of Congress were voted for by the people. The manner of filling offices in cities and towns was regulated by their charters. Trustees of towns were either appointed by the county courts or elected by the people. The Legislature controlled the subject, and the regulation of the subject was by no means uniform. The reader curious on this subject is referred to the State Constitution of 1799. From 1850 to 1890 the general elections for county and State officers were held on the first Monday in August. Since 1890 such elections have taken place on the first Tuesday after the first Monday in November. The following county judges, county attorneys, county clerks, jailers, and sheriffs have served Muhlenberg since 1850:

COUNTY JUDGES, ATTORNEYS, CLERKS, AND JAILERS.

	JUDGES	COUNTY ATTORNEYS	CLERKS	JAILERS
1851-54	J. W. I. Godman[7]	Joseph Ricketts	Wm. H. C. Wing	Sam H. Dempsey.
1854-58	Wm. G. Jones	B. E. Pittman	Jesse H. Reno	" "
1858-62	" "	" "	" "	James Simpson.
1862-66	Ben J. Shaver	" "	T. J. Jones	John L. Williams.
1866-70	S. P. Love	" "	Thomas Bruce	W. D. Shelton.
1870-74	" "	Wm. H. Yost	" "	John M. Williams.
1874-78	J. C. Thompson	Eugene Eaves	J. Ed Reno	John S. Miller.
1878-82	" "	W. Briggs McCown	" "	" "
1882-86	John H. Morton	W. A. Wickliffe	W. T. Stiles	John Coombs.
1886-90	Q. B. Coleman	W. Briggs McCown[8]	" "	" "
1890-94	D. J. Fleming	M. J. Roark	Joe G. Ellison	R. H. Lyon.
1895-97	" "	" "	" "	" "
1898-01	T. J. Sparks	J. L. Rogers	Ed S. Wood	Wm. T. Miller.
1902-05	" "	" "	" "	" "
1906-09	R. O. Pace	W. O. Belcher	F. L. Lewis	Geo. M. York.
1910	Jas. J. Rice	T. O. Jones	H. L. Kirkpatrick	" "

COUNTY SHERIFFS.

1851-52	Wm. Harbin.	1879-82	Geo. O. Prowse.
1853-58	Ben J. Shaver.	1883-86	Alex Tinsley.
1859-60	H. D. Rothrock.	1887-90	T. B. Pannell.
1861-62	Moses Wickliffe.[9]	1891-93	M. L. Prowse.
1863-66	J. P. McIntire.	1894-97	D. T. Hill.
1867-68	Wm. Irvin.	1898-01	W. H. Welsh.
1869-70	Tom M. Morgan.	1902-05	W. D. Blackwell.
1871-74	C. B. Wickliffe.	1006-09	J. A. Shaver.
1875-78	W. A. Mohorn.	1910	T. L. Roll.

[7] Judge Godman died December, 1852, and his unexpired term was filled by John Edmunds Reno and Joseph Ricketts.
[8] W. Briggs McCown died in 1889 and his unexpired term was filled by John Allison.
[9] Moses Wickliffe resigned in 1861 and his unexpired term was filled by S. D. Chatham and John Jenkins.

VI

THE WEIRS

NO NAME is better known in Muhlenberg than that of Weir. James Weir, sr., was a pioneer merchant and the founder of a family whose history is closely interwoven with all the history of the county. James Weir, sr., was a son of William Weir, a Revolutionary soldier of Scotch-Irish descent. He was a surveyor by profession, and in 1798, at the age of twenty-one, came to Muhlenberg on horseback from his home at Fishing Creek, South Carolina. This trip was the first of his many long horseback journeys, and extended over a period of eight months.

While on this expedition in search of a place to begin his career he spent some of his time writing sketches and poems bearing directly or indirectly on the places he visited. His account of this trip to Muhlenberg he himself styles "James Weir's Journal: Some of James Weir's travels and other things that might be of interest."

The old journal is still preserved, and although it throws very little light on the history of Muhlenberg, his observations, made in the Green River country and elsewhere, show the character of a young man who, immediately after his arrival in the county, became one of its most influential citizens. He evidently idled away no time on this trip, and the same may also be said of his entire journey through life. His first entry in the journal begins: "March 3, 1798, I set out from South Carolina, the land of my nativity, with the intention to explore the western climes." He gives a graphic description of the country through which he passed on his way to Eastern Tennessee. Writing of his short stay in Knoxville, he says: "In the infant town of Knox the houses are irregular and interspersed. It was County day when I came, the town was confused with a promiscuous throng of every denomination. Some talked, some sang and mostly all did profanely swear. I stood aghast, my soul shrunk back to hear the horrid oaths and dreadful indignities offered to the Supreme Governor of the Universe, who, with one frown is able to shake them into non-existence. There was what I never did see before, viz., on Sunday dancing, singing and playing of cards, etc. . . . It was said by a gentleman of the neighborhood that 'the Devil is grown so old that it renders him incapable of traveling, and that he has taken up in Knoxville and there hopes to spend the remaining part of his days in tranquillity, as he believes he is among his friends,' but as it is not a good principle to criticise the conduct of others, I shall decline it with this general reflection, that there are some men of good principles in all places, but often more bad ones to counterbalance them."

These few lines show that although Mr. Weir thought the "infant town of Knox" was a very wicked place he, nevertheless, did not wholly condemn it. From Knoxville he rode to Nashville, where he remained a few months and where he "kept school at the house of Colonel Thomas Ingles, a gentleman of distinguished civility." Before leaving Tennessee he wrote:

Thinks I, is this that promised land? Is this that noble Tennessee whose great fame has filled the mouths and fired the breaths of many through the different states? If so, I do not doubt your fame is more than you are in reality, which is commonly the case of new countries. . . . I have now traveled six months in the state of Tennessee and have set out for Kentucky. . . .

On the 8th day of October, 1799, I crossed the Clinch River and there took to the Wilderness, which is 95 miles without a house or inhabitant. I met two gentlemen who proved very good company through this lonely wilderness. This wilderness land belongeth to the Indians, who will not suffer anybody to settle on it. The land is for the most part barren and mountainous. After three days' travel we arrived into Cumberland, a Country whose fertility of soil and pleasant situation I could not pass over, without particular attention. This country is well settled with people.

PIONEER JAMES WEIR, ABOUT 1840

Having tarried there a few days in a friend's house, I passed over into the state of Kentucky and travelled through some of the lower parts, viz., on Green River and Red River. This country is for the most part newly settled, their buildings and farms but small. Some live by hunting only, which explore the solitary retreats of the wild bear and buffalo. Others, being more industrious, cultivate the soil, though not as properly as they might for want of implements. The land yields exceedingly well, corn, wheat, cotton and all other grains and plants common to the southern states. The latitude is nearly the same as that of North Carolina.

The range for cattle is good in the summer and for hogs I suppose it is equal to any in the world. There are low flats and marshes which overflow at certain seasons which after the water is departed make excellent range for hogs. I saw a gentleman here who from four of a stock raised 200 head in three years. These flats lie along on Green River and up some of the creeks that empty into it. They would produce rice or grass, I think, very well, and in some places corn, as she does not overflow in the summer season. It is thought that near to these flats it will be sickly on account of vapours and thick fogs which exhale from them and which also breed numbers of mosquitoes which infect the inhabitants even unto their houses. It is thought when the country is settled they will be done away.

Green River is navigable all seasons of the year for large boats, which may pass to and from Illinois and from thence to the Atlantic Ocean. It is thought that it will be a place of great trade in time to come.

Here I made a stop again, and kept school six months in Muhlenberg county on this River, in a Dutch settlement. Some of them are of distinguished kindness. Their profession is Dunkards and Baptists. They appear to be very sincere, God only knows their hearts.

MRS. ANNA C. R. WEIR
First Wife of Pioneer James Weir, about 1825

The journal ends with this brief statement relative to his first six months in Muhlenberg. He evidently found the place that pleased him and therefore settled in Muhlenberg and closed his story of the trip he made in search of the promised land.

Pioneer James Weir arrived in Muhlenberg County about the time the county was formed. He took an active part in the first county court meetings and also helped Alney McLean lay out the town of Greenville and did much toward the moral and commercial development of the community. He was instrumental in getting a number of people to settle in the county. His sister, Jane Weir, and her husband, pioneer Joseph Poag,[1] and his brother, Samuel Weir,[2] who lived and died near Paradise, were, like him, influential persons.

---

[1] Pioneer and Mrs. Joseph Poag were the parents of six children, all of whom were well known in the county: Miss Parthenia; Mrs. Jane (Isaac) Clifford; Mrs. Elizabeth (Christian) Vaught; Mrs. Anna (James) Rothrock; Mrs. Margaret (Joseph) McIntire, and James W. Poag, who married Angeline E. Solomon.

[2] Pioneer Samuel Weir was born in South Carolina in 1769 and died near Paradise in 1830. His farm was one of the best-managed places in the county. It was at his home that his mother, Mrs. Susan Weir, died. On the marble slab marking her grave are no dates; the well-carved inscription reads simply, "Susan Weir, the Best of Mothers." Samuel Weir married Elizabeth Vanlandingham, sister of

He was the first merchant and banker in Greenville. His business increased very rapidly in the new town, and he soon established another store at Lewisburg or Kincheloe's Bluff. In the course of time he conducted mercantile houses in Henderson, Hopkinsville, Morganfield, Madisonville, and Russellville. He also had a store in Shawneetown, Illinois. But Greenville, from the time of its beginning, was his home and headquarters.

James Weir bought practically all his merchandise in Philadelphia, to which place he made more than a dozen trips on horseback, accompanied by no one except his faithful body-servant Titus. Most of his goods were transported in wagons to Pittsburgh and thence by boat down the Ohio on their way to his various stores. The boxes intended for Muhlenberg County were sent up Green River, unloaded at Lewisburg, and then hauled on wagons to Greenville. These wagons were always at the river landing when the freight arrived, but the teamsters were often obliged to wait many days for the expected boats. Mr. and Mrs. Weir made a number of trips together to the Eastern market. On one occasion they bought some of the best furniture for sale in Philadelphia. They transported it to Pittsburgh and there unpacked it, furnished their own stateroom, and used it while traveling down the Ohio and up Green River to Lewisburg and then sent it to their home in Greenville.

EDWARD R. WEIR, SR., 1875

He made many trips down the Mississippi to New Orleans, from which place he returned to Greenville either via land or via ocean boat to Philadelphia, where after making his purchases he continued his journey by land and river. He wrote an account of a trip taken in 1803, giving his experience while traveling down the Mississippi, then via ocean and up the Delaware to Philadelphia. It is an interesting story and is quoted in full in an appendix to this history. One of the ledgers kept in his Greenville store about 1814 is still preserved and is described in the chapter on "Life in the Olden Days."

James Weir was born in South Carolina in 1777 and died in Greenville on August 9, 1845. His first wife, Anna Cowman Rumsey, mother of his

pioneer Oliver C. Vanlandingham. They were the parents of seven children: Elizabeth, who was married to Isaac Roll; Susan, to T. J. Rice; Nancy, to Elijah Smith; Margaret, to O. C. Vanlandingham, jr.; Esther, to Josiah Maddox, and Samuel M., to Elizabeth B. Vanlandingham. Samuel M. Weir was born in 1826 and died near Paradise in 1908.

children, was born in 1792 and died in 1838. She was a daughter of Doctor Edward Rumsey (of Christian County), who was a brother of James Rumsey, the inventor. Doctor Edward Rumsey was the father of eight children, four of whom are identified with Muhlenberg history: the Honorable Edward Rumsey; Anna C. Rumsey, who married James Weir, sr.; Harriet Rumsey, who married Samuel Miller, and whose only child, Harriet R. Miller, married Edward R. Weir, sr.; and Emily Rumsey, who married Richard Elliott, of Hartford, Kentucky.

James Weir was the father of five children:

MRS. HARRIET R. WEIR, 1900

(1) Edward Rumsey Weir, sr., who, as just stated, married Harriet R. Miller. Mr. and Mrs. Edward R. Weir and their children are referred to in this and other chapters.

(2) James Weir, jr., of Owensboro, who married Susan C. Green. He was a banker, lawyer, and well-known writer. Among his books is "Lonz Powers." A review of this work is given in another chapter, where also appears a biography of the author.

(3) Sallie Ann Weir, who married Edward R. Elliott, a son of pioneer Richard Elliott. Mr. and Mrs. Edward R. Elliott moved to Jacksonville, Illinois, in 1851. They were the parents of Edward, Richard, Frank, J. Weir, and Henry Elliott, and Mrs. Anna R. (William S.) Devine.

(4) Susan M. Weir, who married Professor William L. Green. Professor Green, as stated in the chapter on "Post-Primary Education," was one of the first promoters of higher education in Muhlenberg.

(5) Emily Weir, who married Samuel M. Wing, son of Charles Fox Wing. The names of their children are given in the chapter on "Charles Fox Wing."

Of the elder James Weir's five children only one, Edward R. Weir, sr., lived in Greenville all his life. Edward R. Weir, sr., was born in Greenville on November 29, 1816, and died February 5, 1891. He was an influential merchant, lawyer, and politician, a slave-holder, an abolitionist, and a strong Union man. He was wealthy and charitable; always active in church work and in the elevation of his fellow-men. Nearly every act of his life was directed toward the moral and commercial good of Muhlenberg County. He represented the county in the State Legislature in 1841, 1842, and in 1863-65. In 1848 he built, on Caney Creek, a mile north of Greenville, the first steam saw and grist mill in the county.

The large brick residence erected by Edward R. Weir, sr., about the year 1840, on South Main Street near the foot of Hopkinsville Street, was in its day one of the best-built homes in the county. It not only afforded him and his family every possible comfort, but stood as an example of what enterprise can do. He dug what is probably the most symmetrical stone-lined well ever made in Kentucky. The brick cabins built for his slaves, and the greenhouses and icehouse, have been torn down, but the solid old residence and hexagon-shaped office near it still show that what Edward R. Weir, sr., did he did well.

He was also an author. Among the articles written by him are "A Visit to the Faith Doctor," published in the Western Magazine, of Cincinnati, in November, 1836, and "A Random Sketch by a Kentuckian, E. R. W." describing a deer hunt, which appeared in the March, 1839, issue of the Knickerbocker Magazine, and are here reviewed in one of the appendices. These sketches pertain to some of his experiences in Muhlenberg County. Some time during the '40s of the last century he wrote a short history of the Harpes, which it is said was published in the Saturday Evening Post of Philadelphia. Although I have tried to obtain a copy of this article, I have failed to do so. If printed, it probably appeared under some assumed name and under a heading other than "The Harpes."

E. R. WEIR (COLONEL), IN 1865

Harriet Rumsey (Miller) Weir, wife of Edward R. Weir, sr., was born in Christian County March 16, 1822. Mrs. Weir came to Greenville in early youth and lived there for three quarters of a century, when, after the death of her son Max Weir, she moved to Jacksonville, Illinois. Few Muhlenberg women were better known in their day than Mrs. Weir. She took an active interest in her husband's affairs, and always helped him in his business and in his various efforts to do good. During the last fifty years of her life she was generally referred to as Lady Weir, for all who knew her realized that she was a noble woman in every sense of the word. She died at the home of her son Miller Weir on February 16, 1913, and is buried at Greenville. The day after her funeral the Greenville Record said: "Her long life was an active one, spent in simpleness and goodness. She was a brilliant woman; in manner, ever kind and attentive. She was one of the most loved women in the whole county. Her religious activities were varied and effective, doing much in that line without show or ostentation."

Five of the children born to Mr. and Mrs. Edward R. Weir, sr., reached maturity:

(1) Edward Rumsey Weir, jr. (better known as Colonel E. R. Weir), was born August 13, 1839, and died March 30, 1906. After the close of the Civil War, Colonel Weir became a merchant in Greenville and later a leading lawyer. Eliza T. Johnson, daughter of Doctor John M. Johnson, was his first wife and the mother of his children, who were: Frank Weir, who was killed September 19, 1890, in Eastern Kentucky while in the revenue service; Jerome Weir, of the U. S. Army; Harry Weir, of Greenville, who married Ruth Grundy; Louise B. Weir, who married W. D. Reeves, and Anna C. Weir, who married Max Layne. Colonel Weir's second wife was Alice Culbertson, of the State of New York, to whom he was married in 1898.

MAX WEIR, IN 1900

(2) Anna C. Weir, who married David W. Eaves, a son of Sanders Eaves. Their children are: Elliott, Lucian, Lucile, Harriet, Ruth, and Belle Eaves.

(3) Miller Weir, who early in life settled in Jacksonville, Illinois. He is a banker and is identified with the politics of Illinois. He married Fannie Bancroft. Their only child, Fanita, married Edward P. Brockhouse, a banker and lawyer of Jacksonville.

(4) Virginia Weir, who died at the age of sixteen.

(5) Max Weir, who was born December 23, 1863, and died May 18, 1904. He was a bachelor, a popular merchant in Greenville, a devout Christian, and a local and State Y. M. C. A. worker. In 1899 he wrote "From the Father's Country," a pamphlet of a religious character, which was published shortly after his death.

VII

MUHLENBERG MEN IN THE WAR OF 1812

WHEN on June 18, 1812, war against Great Britain was declared by the United States, no State responded to the call for volunteers more readily than did Kentucky. The second war with England lasted over two and a half years, during which time three companies that presented themselves for service were organized in Muhlenberg. Most of the men in these three organizations were citizens of the county. From the "Roster of Volunteer Officers and Soldiers from Kentucky in the War of 1812-15," compiled in 1891 by Samuel E. Hill, Adjutant-General of Kentucky, I copy the following list of officers and privates of these three companies and also the dates as there recorded. These names are here given as printed in the roster, although many of them are evidently misspelled. The only additions I have made to this record are the notes stating that Captain Kincheloe's company took part in the battle of the Thames, and that Captain McLean's company fought in the battle of New Orleans.

ROLL OF CAPTAIN ALNEY MCLEAN'S COMPANY.

In First Regiment Kentucky Mounted Militia, commanded by Lieutenant-Colonel Samuel Caldwell.
Enlisted September 18, 1812. Engaged to October 30, 1812.

Alney McLean, Captain.
Charles Campbell, Lieutenant.
Jere S. Cravens, Ensign.
William Oates, Sergeant.
Parmenas Redman, Sergeant.
Thomas Glenn, Sergeant.

James Martin, Sergeant.
John Ferguson, Corporal.
John January, Corporal.
Moses F. Glenn, Corporal.
John C. Milligan, Corporal.
John Earle, Trumpeter.

PRIVATES.

Ash, James	Dennis, Abraham	Houser, Christopher
Anthony, Jacob	Dudley, Robert	Harrison, Isaac
Bond, Cornelius	Everton, Thomas	Hunsinger, George
Bennett, John	Edmonds, George	Hill, William
Bower, Jacob	Everton, James	Jarvis, Simon
Campbell, William, sr.	Evans, John	Langley, John W.
Campbell, William, jr.	Foster, Thomas	Luce, David
Cummings, Moses	Good, John	Lynn, George
Conditt, Moses P.	Gillingham, Jno. B. C.	Morton, William
Carter, William	Hewlett, Alfred	McFerson, John
Cochran, Bryant	Hemman, George	Maxwell, Robert
Davis, William	Hines, Isaac	Martin, Samuel

Nunn, John
Robertson, Robert
Rice, Samuel
Salsbury, Thomas
Sanders, George

Stroud, John
Skillman, James
Stanley, Mark
Tyler, Charles
Thompson, Philip

Todd, William
Vaught, Abraham
Winlock, Joseph
Wilkins, Bryant
Young, Benjamin

ROLL OF CAPTAIN LEWIS KINCHELOE'S COMPANY.

In Kentucky Mounted Volunteer Militia, commanded by Colonel William Williams.
Enlisted at Newport, Kentucky, September 11, 1813.
(This company took part in the battle of the Thames, October 5, 1813.)

Lewis Kincheloe, Captain.
Charles F. Wing, Lieutenant.

John Dobyns, Ensign.
John W. Langley, Corporal.

PRIVATES.

Baldwin, Herbert W.
Brown, Frederick
Butler, Samuel
Culbertson, Robert W.
Davis, Randolph
Davis, William
Drake, Mosly
Graves, John C.
Ham, David
Harris, Richard
Haws, John
Hill, Asa

Hill, John
Hill, William
McFerson, John
Miller, George
Murphy, Samuel
Neff, Henry
O'Neal, Spencer
Pace, Daniel
Pace, Joel
Penrod, George
Row, Henry

Redman, Parmenas
Roark, William
Raco, Henry
Segler, Jacob
Shelton, John
Smith, Hugh
Uzzell, Thomas
Wilcox, Thomas
Worthington, Isaac
Jones, Fielding
Langley, James

ROLL OF CAPTAIN ALNEY McLEAN'S COMPANY.

In Kentucky Detached Militia, commanded by Lieutenant-Colonel William Mitchusson.
Enlisted November 20, 1814. Engaged to May 20, 1815.
(This company took part in the battle of New Orleans, January 8, 1815.)

Alney McLean, Captain.
Ephraim M. Brank, Lieutenant.
William Alexander, Lieutenant.
Isaac Davis, Ensign.
John Stull, Sergeant.
Henry Nusell, Sergeant.
Enoch Metcalf, Sergeant.

Jordon O'Brien, Sergeant.
James Langley, Corporal.
Moses Matthews, Corporal.
Edward H. Tarrants, Corporal.
George Hill, Corporal.
Abner B. C. Dillingham, Fifer.

PRIVATES.

Apling, Henry
Anderson, John
Anderson, John, jr.
Allen, Linsey
Allison, McLean
Bishop, James
Barker, Samuel

Bone, Cornelius
Bonds, Lott
Carter, James
Craig, John
Combs, Jesse
Cob, Elijah
Craig, Robert

Crouch, Isaac
Claxton, Jeremiah
Dewitt, William
Donnald, James
Evans, James
Ferguson, John K.
Foley, Mason

Fox, Nathan
Fowler, Jeremiah
Gany, Matthew
Gant, Thomas
Gamblin, John
Grayham, William
Hewlett, Thomas
Hubbard, Liner
Hines, John
Howard, Isaac
Hensley, Leftridge
Hewlett, Lemuel
Janis, Edward
Kern, George
Kennedy, George F.

Lott, James
Lynn, Gasham
Lynn, Henry
Leece, Samuel
McGill, James
Moore, Thomas
Matthews, Jacob
McFerson, James
Martin, John
Macons, Peter
Nanny, Spencer
Norris, Thomas
Nixon, James
Penrod, George
Ripple, Michael

Row, Adam
Ripple, Jacob
Rhodes, Bradford
Sever, Michael
Sumner, Thomas
Sumner, William
Sunn, John F.
Sanders, George
Voris, John
Wilcox, Elias
Williams, Noah
Wade, Hendley
Wilson, John
Williams, William
Yaunce, Lawrence

A century has passed since the War of 1812 began. It is said that for many years after this war accounts of daring deeds performed by Muhlenberg men were told by the soldiers who participated in some of the battles. With the exception of a few, all of these old stories, although handed down for a generation or two, are now forgotten. Most of the men who saw service in the second war with England passed away before the close of the Civil War. George Penrod, who died January 22, 1892, at the age of about one hundred, was the last of the Muhlenberg veterans of 1812.[1]

Practically all that is now told in local traditions of this war forms part of the story of the life of eight well-known local men: Larkin N. Akers, who ran the gantlet after the battle of the River Raisin; Charles Fox Wing and Mosley Collins Drake, who took part in the battle of the Thames; Ephraim M. Brank, Alney McLean, Isaac Davis, Joseph C. Reynolds, and Michael Severs, who took part in the battle of New Orleans.

Larkin Nicholls Akers came to Greenville about twenty-five years after his miraculous escape at River

LARKIN N. AKERS, IN 1865

Raisin. He was a private in a company organized in Central Kentucky, where he lived at the time he enlisted. The famous massacre of River Raisin took place in Michigan on January 23, 1813, and was one of the most cruel and bloody acts recorded in all our history. The American forces, mainly

---

[1] George Penrod was a son of Tobias Penrod, who about 1800 settled near what has since been called Penrod. George Penrod was the father of Lot, David, Samuel, William, Leander, Thomas, and Martin Penrod and Mrs. Nancy (David) Russell.

Kentuckians, after fighting a fierce battle against a superior number of British soldiers and their Indian allies, surrendered under promise of protection from the Indians. But the British made no attempt to carry out their promise. On the contrary, they encouraged the bloodthirsty Indians by offering them pay for all the scalps they would bring in. The unprotected and defenseless American prisoners, who were crowded into a few cold houses and pens, were soon in the hands of the merciless savages. Some of them were killed outright or cruelly burned to death; a number were scalped alive. Many were tortured in various ways, some by being compelled to run the gantlet. In the confusion not many made their escape. But of those few who ran the gantlet and came out alive, Larkin N. Akers was one.

Akers often told the sad story of his River Raisin experience to his family and friends while sitting around the fireside or while working in his tailor shop in Greenville. The treatment he received during that massacre was almost beyond human endurance. His body was virtually covered with scars. Up to the time of his death, which occurred in July, 1865, he frequently suffered intense pain from a fractured skull and other wounds inflicted by the Indians.[2]

MOSLEY COLLINS DRAKE, ABOUT 1870

Mosley Collins Drake was among the Muhlenberg men who took part in the battle of the Thames. This battle took place on October 15, 1813, in Southern Ontario, near the Thames River, and was the victory gained by American forces under General William Henry Harrison over the British under General Proctor and their Indian allies, led by Tecumseh.

Like some of the other Muhlenberg men who belonged to Captain Lewis Kincheloe's company and who took part in the battle of the Thames, Drake claimed that he saw Tecumseh after the great Indian chief was killed, and often remarked that if any of the soldiers skinned Tecumseh and "made razor strops out of his hide" they must have done so after he saw the dead body.

Mosley Collins Drake was born in North Carolina in 1795, came to Muhlenberg in 1806 with his father, and farmed in the lower Long Creek

---

[2] Larkin N. Akers married Sally Harrison, who was related to General William Henry Harrison. Mr. and Mrs. L. N. Akers were the parents of five children: (1) Anna Akers, who married John A. Stembridge; (2) Jane Akers, who married William Lindsey; (3) Matilda Akers, who after the death of her first husband, David Donevan, married Joseph Randall, both of whom lived in Hopkinsville; (4) Thomas Akers, who married Lera Boswell, of Princeton; (5) Sarah Catherine Akers, who married Charles W. Lovell, of Muhlenberg.

country the greater part of his life. He died in 1885. His wife was Louraney Wells, daughter of pioneer Micajah Wells.[3]

Ephraim McLean Brank's heroic act on the breastworks in the battle of New Orleans, January 8, 1815, is one of the most thrilling incidents recorded of any Muhlenberg man, as it is a fine one in national history. To his family and friends he seldom described the part he played in this battle. However, his friends and comrades, John Shelton, Mike Severs, and others, frequently told the story, and although their version was never written, it was in nearly every detail the same as the one here re-quoted from McElroy's "Kentucky in the Nation's History."

McElroy, by way of introduction, says: "The effect produced upon the British army by the daring coolness of a single Kentucky rifleman is thus graphically described by one of the British officers who took part in the historic engagement." He then quotes:

"We marched in solid column in a direct line, upon the American defenses. I belonged to the staff; and as we advanced we watched through our glasses the position of the enemy, with that intensity an officer only feels when marching into the jaws of death. It was a strange sight, that breastwork, with a crowd of beings behind, their heads only visible above the line of defense. We could distinctly see their long rifles lying on the works, and the batteries in our front, with their great mouths gaping toward us. We could also see the position of General Jackson, with his staff around him. But what attracted our attention most, was the figure of a tall man standing on the breastworks, dressed in linsey-woolsey, with buckskin leggings, and a broad-brimmed felt hat that fell round the face, almost concealing the features. He was standing in one of those picturesque, graceful attitudes peculiar to those natural men dwelling in forests. The body rested on the left leg, and swayed with a curved line upward. The right arm was extended, the hand grasping the rifle near the muzzle, the butt of which rested near the toe of his right foot. With the left hand he raised the rim of the hat from his eyes, and seemed gazing intently on our advancing column. The cannon of the enemy had opened on us, and tore

---

[3] Mosley Collins Drake was a son of pioneer Albritton Drake. Albritton Drake and James Drake, his father, were Revolutionary soldiers. It is said they were descendants of Sir Francis Drake. When Albritton Drake joined the Revolutionary forces he called on his sweetheart, Ruth Collins, to bid her goodbye. The story is told that when the two parted they chanced to be standing under an apple tree on which a few dried "second growth" apples were hanging. The girl plucked one of them and gave it to Albritton, saying, "Keep this in your pocket as a reminder of me." He carried it in his pocket, not only during the Revolution, but up to the day he and Ruth Collins were married. That same apple—much shriveled and very hard—was preserved by Mosley Collins Drake for many years, and is now owned by John R. Drake, son of William Drake.

Albritton Drake was one of the best-known pioneers in the lower Long Creek country, where he died in 1834. His wife died in 1847. They were the parents of Reverend Silas, Mosley Collins, Reverend Benjamin, J. Perry, Edmund, and William Drake.

Mr. and Mrs. Mosley Collins Drake were the parents of eleven children: (1) Ruth Ann, the second wife of Moses M. Rice; (2) Albritton M., married to Elizabeth Hancock; (3) Sarah Amandaville, to Moses M. Rice; (4) John Perry, a bachelor; (5) Edmund L., to Ruth Drake; (6) James Marion, to Mary E. Saddler; (7) William M., a bachelor; (8) Susan P., to John Wells, then to John Jenkins; (9) Jackey L., to Thomas S. Saddler; (10) Sophia V., to James P. Drake; (11) Mosley Collins, jr., to Amanda Saddler.

through our works with dreadful slaughter; but we continued to advance, unwavering and cool, as if nothing threatened our progress.

"The roar of cannon had no effect upon the figure before us; he seemed fixed and motionless as a statue. At last he moved, threw back his hat rim over the crown with his left hand, raised the rifle to the shoulder, and took aim at our group.

"Our eyes were riveted upon him; at whom had he leveled his piece? But the distance was so great, that we looked at each other and smiled. We saw the rifle flash and very rightly conjectured that his aim was in the direction of our party. My right hand companion, as noble a fellow as ever rode at the head of a regiment, fell from his saddle.

"The hunter paused a few moments without moving his gun from his shoulder. Then he reloaded and assumed his former attitude.[4] Throwing the hat rim over his eyes and again holding it up with the left hand, he fixed his piercing gaze upon us as if hunting out another victim. Once more the hat rim was thrown back, and the gun raised to his shoulder. This time we did not smile, but cast glances at each other, to see which of us must die.

EPHRAIM M. BRANK, ABOUT 1850

"When again the rifle flashed, another one of our party dropped to the earth. There was something most awful in this marching on to certain death. The cannon and thousands of musket balls playing upon our ranks, we cared not for, for there was a chance of escaping them. Most of us had walked as coolly upon batteries more destructive without quailing, but to know that every time that rifle was leveled toward us, and its bullet sprang from the barrel, one of us must surely fall; to see it rest motionless as if poised on a rack, and know, when the hammer came down, that the messenger of death drove unerringly to its goal, to know this, and still march on, was awful. I could see nothing but the tall figure stand-

---

[4] Tradition says E. M. Brank did not load the guns he shot from the breastworks. He used flintlocks, and fired them as rapidly as Mike Severs and Robert Craig reloaded and handed them up to him.

ing on the breastworks; he seemed to grow, phantom-like, higher and higher, assuming, through the smoke, the supernatural appearance of some great spirit of death. Again did he reload and discharge, and reload and discharge his rifle, with the same unfailing aim and the same unfailing result; and it was with indescribable pleasure that I beheld, as we neared the American lines, the sulphurous cloud gathering around us, and shutting that spectral hunter from our gaze.

"We lost the battle; and to my mind, the Kentucky rifleman contributed more to our defeat than anything else; for while he remained in our sight our attention was drawn from our duties; and when, at last, he became enshrouded in the smoke, the work was complete; we were in utter confusion, and unable, in the extremity, to restore order sufficient to make any successful attack—the battle was lost."

McElroy's footnote, page 365, following this quotation, reads: "This manuscript is marked 'Kentucky Rifleman in battle of New Orleans,' Durrett Collection. The hero here described was E. M. Brank, of Greenville, Kentucky." The manuscript referred to is not signed, but gives the name of E. M. Brank as the hero of the sketch. The late Z. F. Smith informed me that this description was first printed about the year 1820 in one of George Robert Gleig's books on the campaigns of the British at Washington and New Orleans. I have not had access to any of these works by Gleig and am unable, therefore, to refer the reader to the quotation in the original. At any rate, this interesting description was quoted as early as 1832 by Walter Walcott in "The Republican" of Boston, and later republished, but slightly changed, by various Kentucky papers, clippings of which are still preserved by Rockwell S. Brank and other descendants of E. M. Brank.

Ephraim McLean Brank was born in North Carolina August 1, 1791, and died in Greenville August 5, 1875. He was a son of Robert Brank and Margaret (McLean) Brank, who was a sister of Judge Alney McLean and Doctor Robert D. McLean, sr. His first wife, the mother of his children, was Mary (Campbell) Brank, daughter of Colonel William Campbell. She was born March 27, 1791, and died in Greenville December

THE E. M. BRANK HOUSE, GREENVILLE

4, 1850. His second wife was Ruth B. Weir, the third wife and widow of pioneer James Weir.

E. M. Brank came to Muhlenberg about 1808. He was a lawyer by profession, but devoted most of his time to surveying. He lived in Greenville on Main Street, half a mile north of the courthouse. Although his later years were spent in farming, he nevertheless continued to take a great interest in the progress of the town. Captain Brank was a man of stately proportions and wonderful physical constitution. He was a "crack shot" and an enthusiastic hunter; a well-read and a resolute and systematic man, and very kind to all those with whom he came in contact.[5]

Of all the citizens of Muhlenberg County who took part in the second war with England probably none worked with more zeal or did more for his country than Alney McLean. Immediately after the news reached Western Kentucky that war had been declared he organized a company of volunteers, and was always ready to leave with them at any time they might be called. The official records show that his first company was "enlisted September 18, 1812," and was "engaged to October 30, 1812." Whether or not this company saw any service other than to march from Greenville to Frankfort or Newport, and after remaining in camp awhile, returning home, I can not state with any certainty. However, one tradition says that after this company had been accepted it was discovered that the supply of volunteers was far greater than the number of arms and other necessary war material at their disposal, and that it fell to the lot of McLean's company to turn over their self-supplied equipment to such men as had none but were members of companies that had been chosen for immediate service.

After Alney McLean helped organize Lewis Kincheloe's company in the fall of 1813 he formed another of his own, drilled his men often and had them prepare, like the minute-men, to report on a moment's notice. At the head of his second company he took an active part in the battle of New Orleans. Judge Little, in his "Life of Ben Hardin," says:

After the battle he was assigned to very arduous fatigue duty, of which he complained to General Jackson. He received an insulting rebuff, for which he never forgave his old commander.[6] . . .

By change of districts Judge McLean, of Greenville, in 1822, succeeded Judge Broadnax in the Breckinridge district. He was always an active politician. His accession to the bench and twenty years service there did not diminish his interest in public affairs. He had served as a captain at New Orleans, and while not with the Kentucky troops, who, in the language of General Jackson, "ingloriously fled," yet he resented this stigma cast upon his State. He was ever an opponent of "Old Hickory." Naturally enough

---

[5] Mr. and Mrs. E. M. Brank were the parents of five children: (1) Louisa, who married James M. Taylor (no children); (2) Tabitha A., who became the second wife of Doctor William H. Yost (no children); (3) Samuel C., who died in childhood; (4) Reverend Robert G. Brank, who married Ruth A. Smith. He was born November 3, 1824, and died in St. Louis August 21, 1895. Among their four children is Reverend Rockwell Smith Brank. (5) Mary Jane, who became the first wife of Doctor William H. Yost. Through his skill, liberality, and long service "Old Doctor Yost," as he was called, became one of the best-known physicians in Muhlenberg and adjoining counties. Doctor Yost was born July 5, 1820, and died in Greenville November 1, 1894. Doctor and Mrs. Yost were the parents of three children: (1) Mary W. Yost, the first wife of Doctor T. J. Slaton. Their two children are Doctors Henry Y. and Brank Slaton. (2) Judge William H. Yost, who married Lizzie Reno. Their two children, who reached maturity, are Doctor E. R. Yost and Mrs. Mary B. (Reverend W. H.) Fulton. (3) Doctor E. B. Yost, who married Bertha Grimes (no children).

[6] John F. Coffman, who during the campaign around New Orleans served as one of General Jackson's bodyguard, was, it is said, the only man in Muhlenberg to vote for Jackson in the presidential election of 1825.

he was a friend of Henry Clay. He was, while judge, chosen a Clay elector in 1824 and again in 1832. His taste for and activity in politics shocked those of his constituents specially sensitive as to the proprieties of the bench.

Under the head of McLean County, Collins, in his "History of Kentucky," publishes a brief biographical sketch of Judge McLean:

Judge Alney McLean, in honor of whom McLean county was named, was a native of Burke county, North Carolina. He emigrated to Kentucky and began the practice of law at Greenville, Muhlenburg county, about 1805, but had little to do with politics before 1808. He was a representative from that county in the legislature, 1812-'13; a captain in the war of 1812, a representative in Congress for four years, 1815-'17 and 1819-'21; one of the electors for president in 1825, casting his vote and that of the state for Henry Clay; again in 1833 an elector for the state at large, when the vote of the state was cast a second time for the same distinguished citizen. He was appointed a circuit judge, and for many years adorned the bench. One of the oldest and ablest of Kentucky ex-judges, in a letter to the author, speaks of Judge McLean as "a model gentleman of the old school, of great courtesy and kindness to the junior members of the bar," an honored citizen and a just judge.

ALNEY McLEAN, ABOUT 1820

The following is copied from the record entered by the clerk of the Muhlenberg Circuit Court in Record Book No. 8, at the March term in 1842. It verifies not only some of the statements given above but adds other facts, and also shows the high esteem in which Judge McLean was held by his contemporaries:

Thereupon, on motion of John H. McHenry, the Court suspended all further proceedings for the purpose of attending the following meeting.

And thereupon Edward Rumsey, Esq., offered the following preamble and resolved statement, to wit: At a meeting of the members of the Muhlenberg Circuit Court, on Monday, the 21st day of March 1842, the Hon. John Calhoun was called to the chair, and the following statement and resolution being presented, were unanimously adopted:

"The Honorable Alney McLean, late presiding judge of this Court, was born in the state of North Carolina, in May 1779. In June 1799 he removed to this county, and commenced the practice of law, which he successfully pursued, through a long series of years, securing by his integrity, ability and courtesy the confidence of the bench, the friendship of the bar, and the esteem of the public. In 1812 & 1813 he represented his county with fidelity and distinction in the General Assembly.

"In 1813 and 1815 he aided in repelling the invaders of his country in the memorable battle of New Orleans, at the head of his company, acted the part of a gallant officer and devoted patriot. With honor and reputation he represented his district in the 16th and 18th Congresses. In 1821 he received the commission of Judge of the 14th District in which he presided with eminent impartiality, dignity, and ability, for more than twenty years. The 31st day of December, 1841 his active and useful life was suddenly terminated by a severe attack of bilious pneumonia. Regret and grief for his death, though great and general, may well be somewhat alleviated by the reflection that he lived not in vain, that he died after a long career of public and private usefulness—full of honor, high in the affection of his friends and the esteem of his countrymen, leaving a bright fame, a beloved memory behind."

Alney McLean was the first county surveyor of Muhlenberg, and laid out the town of Greenville in 1799. He took an active interest in all movements that might help develop the county. His popularity is also shown by the great number of children named in his honor by their parents. Doctor Robert D. McLean, sr., of Greenville (born 1783, died 1875), in his day one of the best-known surgeons in Western Kentucky, was his brother.

Judge McLean was a son of Ephraim McLean and Eliza (Davidson) McLean. His father, in 1820, at the age of ninety, removed from North Carolina to Greenville, and there died three years later. Judge McLean married Tabitha R. Campbell, daughter of Colonel William Campbell. She was born in Virginia January 25, 1785, and died in Greenville February 17, 1850. No one among the pioneers is more frequently and more creditably mentioned in local traditions than Judge McLean. In his day he was esteemed one of the greatest men in the Green River country, and as such his name will always be recorded in its history, much to the credit of Muhlenberg County.[7]

Isaac Davis was an officer in Alney McLean's company, and was among the Muhlenberg men who took part in the battle of New Orleans. Tradition says he frequently referred to his military experience as "a tramp around with the boys." While camping at New Orleans, so runs the story, he, like

---

[7] Judge and Mrs. Alney McLean were the parents of ten children, all of whom were born in Muhlenberg County. Six of them were married and lived the greater part of their life in Mississippi, where they died: William D., Reverend Thornton, Judge Robert D., Samuel, Mrs. Eliza A. D. McBride, and Mrs. Transylvania McBride. None of the four children who made Muhlenberg their home were ever married: Tabitha was born May 25, 1815, and died September 10, 1898; Alney was born October 27, 1819, and died May 29, 1905; Charles W. was born October 27, 1819, and died October 13, 1893; Rowena was born October 22, 1827, and died September 10, 1861.

Judge William C. McLean, of Grenada, Mississippi, who during 1910-11 was an Associate Justice of the Supreme Court of Mississippi, is a son of Judge Robert D. McLean.

the others, suffered many hardships. He was accustomed to fresh butter and sweet milk, and these he missed far more than any of the other things of which he was deprived. Before leaving New Orleans he vowed that upon his return to Muhlenberg he would not only build a comfortable house, but also dig a large cellar and keep it well supplied with butter and milk. Practically all the well-to-do pioneers used cellars, but none, according to this tradition, was better equipped and supplied than was the one dug by Isaac Davis. The old Isaac Davis house still stands—near Green River, east of Martwick—and although its cellar is no longer noted for its abundance of butter and milk, it is still pointed out as the "Isaac Davis milk cellar."

THE ISAAC DAVIS HOUSE, NEAR MARTWICK

Davis lived on a farm that in early days was regarded one of the best-managed places in the county. He owned many slaves and much stock, and raised large quantities of corn and wheat. He did not plant tobacco, for he considered tobacco injurious to the soil. It is said that he protected his ground so well and cultivated his corn so carefully that he never had a crop failure, and that even during the dryest years his ridge land never produced less than fifty bushels to the acre. His corn-cribs were always well filled. When his neighbors' crops failed he sold them corn for their immediate need at any price they cared to pay, even though that price was less than half the prevailing market price. If they were in poor circumstances and could pay nothing, he gave them the corn.

In his earlier years he frequently taught school, for which he invariably declined pay. He instructed the rising generation "for the good of the community," as he expressed it, although in the meantime he had "more than enough to do at home."

Isaac Davis was born in Virginia October 9, 1782, came to the Nelson Creek country while a boy, and died in Muhlenberg June 6, 1858. His wife, Mary, was a sister of pioneer Moses Wickliffe. She was born April 22, 1785, and died September 14, 1870.[8]

Another of the well-known veterans of the War of 1812 was Joseph C. Reynolds, who was born in North Carolina May 17, 1793, and who while still a boy came to Muhlenberg, where he died January 13, 1868. While visiting in Tennessee he enlisted in a company organized in that State. He showed great bravery at the battle of New Orleans, where he experienced a number of narrow escapes. Tradition has it that General Andrew Jackson complimented him on his courage in battle.

---

[8] Mr. and Mrs. Isaac Davis were the parents of seven children: Mrs. Eliza Jane (Richard H.) Jones; Mrs. Mary K. (William Mc.) Sharp; Mrs. Julian Ann (George) King; Mrs. Ellen (Elias Wickliffe) Davis; Aaron W., William, and Edward Davis.

Joseph C. Reynolds was for fifty years one of the best-known men in the county. He was a successful farmer, and up to the time of the emancipation of the slaves was one of the largest slave-owners in Muhlenberg. He was a liberal man, and never hesitated to volunteer to help a neighbor or friend when he felt his help was needed. In January, 1820, he married Mary Fortney Reynolds, a daughter of pioneer Richard D. Reynolds, sr., a Revolutionary soldier. They were the parents of six children, all of whom were influential citizens. Mrs. Reynolds, like her husband, always had the good of Muhlenberg at heart and did much toward the moral advancement of the county. She came to Muhlenberg in her youth, and died near Greenville August 31, 1868.[9]

MR. AND MRS. JOSEPH C. REYNOLDS, 1867

In addition to Akers, Drake, Wing, Brank, McLean, Davis, and Reynolds, there were many other Muhlenberg men in the War of 1812. Traditions regarding most of them are very vague. Even Michael Severs, who helped load the guns that Ephraim M. Brank shot while standing on the breastworks at New Orleans, and who in his day was one of the most picturesque characters in the county, is now almost forgotten.

Severs lived in the Bevier neighborhood, where he died about the year 1850. He came to Muhlenberg some time before 1800. He was then, and ever after, a typical backwoodsman and a true representative of the pioneer days. Although manners and customs changed as he advanced in years, he nevertheless continued to wear the hunting-shirt and to use a flintlock rifle. During all his life he wore moccasins in winter and went barefooted in summer.

He was a member of Alney McLean's company and, as already stated, took part in the battle of New Orleans. One story is to the effect that after the victory all the men in McLean's company rode back to Kentucky except Mike, and that although he walked he reached Greenville a few days before any of the others. One of the local traditions has it that he killed General Pakenham in the battle of New Orleans. Whether he is entitled to this distinction can probably never be determined. At any rate he was highly esteemed, especially by the local men who took part in the War of 1812. Every time he came to Greenville such men as Alney McLean and Charles Fox Wing prevailed on him to be their guest while in town. Although clad

---

[9] Mr. and Mrs. Joseph C. Reynolds were the parents of Richard D., Thomas H., John T., sr., Benjamin F., Mrs. Nancy Y. (C. C.) Martin, and Mrs. Susan E. (J. A.) Stokes.

in buckskin breeches and hunting-shirt, and often without shoes, he was always placed at the head of the table and given the best room in the house, regardless of other guests.

The progress of the world and the making of money had no attractions for him. He was always interested in his immediate surroundings, and whatever he undertook he did with great enthusiasm. After the death of his second wife, which occurred many years before his own, he lived in a log cabin, but spent most of his days tramping around and hunting. When night overtook him, or when he cared to stop, he went to the most convenient house, walked in without knocking, presented his game, made himself at home, and remained until he was ready to start on another hunt. He was gladly received by every one who knew him. Every man considered it an honor to have Mike Severs enter his smoke-house or corn-crib and help himself. This he often did, for he realized that he was more than welcome to anything he wished to take. He made quantities of maple sugar every year, and distributed his entire "bilin' " among those who cared for "tree sugar."

Severs was evidently a most interesting and unusual character. Very little regarding the story of his life is now remembered by those who heard of him in their youth. The bones of this old hunter rest in the Duke and Whitehouse burying-ground near Bevier, and his contented soul, in all probability, is now wandering around in the happy hunting-grounds of another world.

Many years after his death some of the people in the Bevier neighborhood purposed to erect a shaft over his grave, but unfortunately their plans were never carried out. Severs Hill, overlooking lower Pond Creek, and the nearby Severs Ford, crossing the same stream, now perpetuate the name of Mike Severs, the old soldier and old-time backwoodsman.[10]

---
[10] Michael Severs was the father of nine children, among whom were Michael, William, and Gabriel Severs, Mrs. Nancy Jones, Mrs. Lucinda Underwood, and Mrs. Archa M. Bibb.

VIII

CHARLES FOX WING

NO MAN in Muhlenberg ever came in closer touch with a larger number of the citizens of the county than Charles Fox Wing. No man living in the county was more highly esteemed by his contemporaries. From 1798, when he first came to Muhlenberg, to 1861, when he died in Greenville, he had the respect and confidence of every man with whom he came in contact.

He was the youngest son of Barnabas Wing, who was for many years one of the wealthiest and most prominent men in New Bedford, Massachusetts, where he was extensively engaged in shipbuilding and various other enterprises. During the Revolution Barnabas Wing loaned money to the colony of Massachusetts Bay with which to carry on the War of Independence. During this struggle his home and all his other property was confiscated by the English, and at the close of the war he was a penniless man. It was during these trying times that Charles Fox Wing was born. About the year 1790 Barnabas Wing moved to Central Kentucky, and there, at the age of about fifty-seven, he began life anew. He and his wife had no desire to try to regain their lost fortune, but worked as best they could for the education of their younger children. They undoubtedly impressed upon their youngest son the sacredness and the cost of independence, for no man venerated the flag and its makers more than did Charles Fox Wing during all of his long life. Barnabas Wing moved to Greenville about 1809, and died there at the home of his son, October 4, 1815.

Charles Fox Wing was born in Massachusetts, according to one record, on January 25, 1779, and according to another, on January 15, 1780. In either case he was less than twenty-one years of age when, on May 28, 1799, he was appointed county clerk. He had previous to this time served in the office of Thomas Allen, of Mercer County, and Thomas Todd, Clerk of the House of Representatives. The experience gained under these two men undoubtedly made him far more competent to fill the position of county clerk than many men who had reached the age required by law. He served as clerk of the court of quarter sessions, and in March, 1803, when the circuit court was established, he became its clerk. He continued as clerk of the circuit and county courts until the adoption of the Third Constitution in 1850. He was then more than seventy years of age, and had devoted more than a half century to the writing and preserving of official records. When the Constitution of 1850 was adopted the office of circuit clerk and all county offices became elective. Captain Wing, at the urgent solicitation of the citizens of the county, became the candidate for clerk of the circuit court, and was elected without opposition; his son, William H. C. Wing, who had assisted his father for many years, was elected county clerk.

When, in 1812, war was declared against England, no Muhlenberg man responded to the call to arms with greater enthusiasm or with more patriotic

CHARLES FOX WING, 1850

feeling than did Charles Fox Wing. He and Captain Lewis Kincheloe organized a company and awaited orders from the Governor. In the early part of September, 1813, their company marched to Newport, and on October 5th of the same year took part in the battle of the Thames. Wing was the lieutenant of this company, but on Captain Kincheloe's death, which occurred before the battle, he was placed in command.

The details of Captain Wing's action in this short but decisive battle are, unfortunately, among the many other things that have passed away with the men and women who were familiar with them. The story of his connection with this battle has dwindled down to the statement that he was "a hero at Thames, and saw Tecumseh after he was slain." This brief statement is probably founded on some act of heroism, for tradition says that all the veterans of 1812 not only referred to him as "a hero at Thames" but always gave him the seat of honor at their soldiers' reunions. Those who knew him best declare that his recollections of the part he took in the second war with England were among the many things that, in old age, gave him the satisfaction of feeling that he at least had tried to do his duty toward his county and his country. No man in the county or State was more devoted to the American flag or regarded it with more sacred feeling. Every year, on the Fourth of July, from 1799 to 1861, he hoisted Old Glory on a pole in front of the courthouse and also in front of his own home. This fact is referred to by James Weir in his recollections of Greenville as published in "Lonz Powers" and quoted in this volume. The Louisville Daily Journal, shortly after Captain Wing's death, commenting on his devotion to the flag, says:

MRS. CHARLES FOX WING, ABOUT 1850

His love for the American flag has been a marked feature of his whole life. His devotion to the Star-spangled Banner was proverbial in all this region. It amounted to a passion. It was the one form in which, throughout his declining years, the rich and intense loyalty of his nature sought full expression. Every Fourth of July for the last quarter of a century and upwards, as regularly as the glorious anniversary dawned, he had raised the Stars and Stripes in his humble dooryard, and had kept them flying proudly until the close of day. The sight of the starry banner of the Republic, though rendered dim by the cloud of age, was to him a solace and an inspiration, bringing tears of mingled pride and joy to his failing eyes and smiles of hope to his sunken lips and his withered cheeks. He had been born under the American flag; he had lived under it and fought under it; and, now that he was dying under it, he asked, as his last request on earth, that ere he should be consigned to the grave he might be wrapped in the folds of that worshipped banner—that it might be his shroud in death as it had been his canopy through life. He died with this prayer on his lips.

This request was granted. His body was not only wrapped in the American flag, but in the very flag he had hoisted in front of the courthouse during the last ten or fifteen years of his life, and thus lowered into the grave. General Buckner and his army passed through Greenville September 26, 1861, the day after Captain Wing died. The General viewed the remains of his old and fatherly friend, commented on the befitting manner in which his body was wrapped in the Stars and Stripes, and then returned to the troops under his command. Such are the facts regarding this incident. I have verified this version by many men and women, among them General Buckner himself, who in August, 1912, fifty-one years after the incident occurred, still remembered all the circumstances connected with his call at the Wing home.

One of the other versions has it that General Buckner offered to bury Captain Wing with military honors, his offer being declined; another has it that General Buckner, finding the body of Captain Wing wrapped in the Stars and Stripes, insisted on removing the Federal flag and burying the old patriot in the Confederate flag. A variety of other groundless statements can be traced to these two often heard but false stories.[1]

On October 18, 1861, the Louisville Daily Journal published a brief sketch of Captain Wing, signed "T." From this I quote:

It was his rare merit to be all that he seemed to be, a distinction seldom attained by those who have figured on the public stage of life or have received its highest honors. He was the chief supporter of the little Presbyterian Church of his preference, and with unfailing constancy his venerable form was seen and his earnest voice heard whenever two or three were convened to worship God. For thirty years, with untiring patience, he presided over and sustained the Sunday-school. His departure makes a great void. Who can fill it? A life of great beauty and excellence was closed by a most triumphant faith in the joys beyond the grave.

In 1806 Charles Fox Wing married Anna S., or "Nancy," Campbell, daughter of Colonel William Campbell and Tabitha A. (Russell) Campbell. Mrs. Wing was born March 13, 1788, came to Muhlenberg about eight years later, and died January 17, 1863. She was buried in Caney Station buryingground by the side of her husband. Captain Wing died in Greenville September 25, 1861, aged about eighty-one. The inscription on his tombstone, "Died September 15, 1861," is incorrect, and has been so recognized since the stone was erected in 1862.[2]

---

[1] Charles Fox Wing, in all probability, was named in honor of Charles James Fox, the great English orator, who entered Parliament in 1768 at the age of nineteen and at once took rank as the most brilliant speaker and statesman after Pitt. He was a friend of the American colonies. Some of his great speeches were in opposition to George the Third's war on the colonies. Fox thought the Americans ought to have home rule or independence. By the time Charles Fox Wing was born the fame of Fox had become worldwide, and was at its height when he (Fox) died in 1806, aged fifty-seven.

The name "Charles Fox" indicates the patriotism of the parents of Charles Fox Wing. It is more than probable that both father and mother often told their son Charles of the sufferings and losses endured during the Revolution, and thus impressed upon him the cost of American liberty and the meaning of the American flag.

[2] Mr. and Mrs. Charles Fox Wing were the parents of eight children: (1) William H. C. Wing, a bachelor. (?) Jane M., who married Edward Rumsey. (3) Lucy, who married Jonathan Short, to whom were born: Mrs. Mary (Lewis) Reno, Charles W. Short, Mrs. Lucy (Samuel) Landes, Mrs. Minnie (J. J.) Kahn, and Miss Anna Short. After the death of her first husband, Jonathan Short (who was born May 24, 1822, and died August 27, 1882), Mrs. Lucy Wing Short, in 1888, became the third wife of Doctor William H. Yost. She was born in Greenville June 16, 1822, and is now the oldest living citizen in the town. (4) Lucilia, who married Professor James K. Patterson, to whom was born an only child, William A. Pat-

The log residence built by Captain Wing shortly after he was married stood on the southeast corner of Main Cross and Cherry streets, Greenville. The building was later enlarged and covered with weatherboards. The Wing house was, for more than fifty years, Muhlenberg's center of hospitality and refinement. This famous old landmark was torn down in 1905 and a few years later a modern residence was erected on the site by J. L. Rogers.

THE CHARLES FOX WING HOUSE, GREENVILLE, IN 1891
Taken thirty years after the death of Captain Wing and about fifteen years before the building was torn down

Captain Wing's long service as clerk of county and circuit courts, his unselfish interest in the community and his usefulness as a citizen, are referred to in other chapters. He was in every respect an upright, intelligent, useful, and charitable man. He was worthy of the great respect he commanded, and his name is well deserving of the great esteem in which it is now held.

terson. (5) Samuel M. Wing, who married Emily Weir, to whom were born seven children: E. Rumsey, Theodore W., Samuel C., Mrs. Emma (W.) Yerkes, William, Charles F., and Albert. (6) Caroline, (7) Anna, and (8) Matilda Wing; the last three never married.

E. Rumsey Wing, son of Samuel M. Wing, was appointed Minister Resident of the United States to Ecuador, November 16, 1869, and died at his post October 6, 1874. His widow, about twenty-five years later, became the third wife of Colonel W. C. P. Breckinridge.

IX

EDWARD RUMSEY

FOUR Muhlenberg men while citizens of the county became members of Congress—Alney McLean, Edward Rumsey, Doctor A. D. James, and R. Y. Thomas. Edward Rumsey, the second to attain this distinction, came to Muhlenberg in his youth, shortly after the close of the second war with England, and made Greenville his home during the rest of his life—a period of fifty years. Citizens now living who knew Edward Rumsey in their younger days usually begin and end their talks regarding him, whether short or long, with a sentiment that is best expressed in a paraphrase of the familiar quotation:

"None knew him but to love him,
Nor named him but to praise."

He was very modest and unassuming and usually a man of few words, but when addressing the public his speech became eloquent.

Some have it that the town of Rumsey, in McLean County, was named after him. Others assert that the place was so called after his uncle, "James Rumsey, who built the first steamboat." However, the version generally accepted is that when, in 1839, the people proposed naming the new town after Edward Rumsey, he modestly declined the honor, and his friends then compromised with him and called the place Rumsey in memory of his uncle. Thus, although the town may have been named after James Rumsey, it was really so called after Edward Rumsey.

The death of his two children, aged three and six, in the spring of 1838, was soon followed by the loss of all ambition on his part to climb the ladder of fame. His friends vainly urged him not to cast aside his many bright prospects of a public career. Although his interest in public affairs practically ceased when he was forty, no man in Muhlenberg was better known and more admired during his entire life than Edward Rumsey. He was a gentleman of the "old school." During the Civil War the Southern sympathizers looked upon him as their adviser. He married Jane M. Wing, daughter of Charles Fox Wing. She died October 15, 1868.

Much could be written about Edward Rumsey based on the verbal reports of to-day, but such a chapter would probably be more of a eulogy than a biographical sketch. Ten years after his death an article on his life and character was printed in "The Biographical Encyclopedia of Kentuckians of the Nineteenth Century," which I here quote in full:

Hon. Edward Rumsey, lawyer, was born in Botetourt county, Virginia, in 1800, and removed with his father, Dr. Edward Rumsey, to Christian county, Kentucky, when quite a boy.

His uncle, James Rumsey, is claimed to be the first who applied steam to navigation in America, if not in England. It was also claimed that the evidence submitted before the National House of Representatives, in 1839, is conclusive as to his priority over John Fitch. A letter written by George Washington, in 1787, mentions that James Rumsey had communicated his steamboat invention to him in 1784, and that subsequently John Fitch had laid his claim to the invention before him, asking his assistance, he declining to give it, stating that James Rumsey had previously introduced the same idea to him.

EDWARD RUMSEY, ABOUT 1845

It is certain that James Rumsey propelled a steamboat on the Potomac River, against the stream, at the rate of four miles an hour in 1784. He afterward went to England and procured patents for steam navigation from the British Government in 1788; constructed a boat of one hundred tons burden, with improved applications, covered by his patents, which were in advance of those of James Watt. He was on the eve of complete success when his sudden death from apoplexy, while discussing the principles of his invention before the Royal Society, terminated his career. His boat and machinery went to satisfy his creditors; and Robert Fulton, then in London, profited by his intimacy with the inventor.

Edward Rumsey was educated in Hopkinsville by Daniel Barry, one of the famous classicists of Kentucky. He studied law with John J. Crittenden, who became his lifelong friend. He settled in Greenville and practiced in Muhlenberg and adjoining counties. His reputation for candor and thorough honesty, coupled with his clear sense of justice and wonderful faculty of expression, soon placed him at the head of the bar. With all his natural qualifications to shine in public life he was remarkably timid and modest, his diffidence at times becoming almost morbid. Owing to this fact, no doubt to a great extent, may be attributed the loss from public affairs of one of the most refined and brilliant men of the times.

At the urgent solicitation of his county, he consented, in 1822, to represent its interests in the Legislature, where he immediately took rank as a leader, making a great impression by his earnestness, modesty and uncommon ability. In 1837 he was nominated for Congress, and was elected by an almost unanimous vote of his district. While in Congress he made the famous speech on the resolution recognizing his uncle's claim to the invention of the steamboat and bestowing on that uncle's blind and only surviving son a gold medal as a mark of such recognition.[1]

While serving in Congress his two children died of scarlet fever. After that no argument of his friends or constituents could ever induce him again to enter public life. He strove to drown his sorrow in mental and physical toil; living in the future and the past. He never entirely recovered his elasticity and soon became prematurely old.

The outbreak of the Civil War brought with it new calamities. He loved his country next to his children. He believed that the General Government had no right to coerce a State. Although he survived the war, grief and apprehension aided greatly to break the thread of life. He died in Greenville, April 6, 1868.

On February 9, 1839, Edward Rumsey delivered his famous speech before the House of Representatives of the United States. In this speech he reviewed the history of the invention of the devices for propelling boats by steam, showed that his uncle, James Rumsey, was entitled to the distinction of being the first inventor, and asked that Congress present to James Rumsey, jr., the only surviving child of James Rumsey, a suitable gold medal, commemorative of his father's services in giving to the world his discovery of using steam for the propulsion of boats and watercraft. The resolution awarding such a medal passed the House by a unanimous vote, but for no reason given was rejected by the Senate. It is probable that the Senate recognized Fulton as the first man to put steam to practical use in connection with navigation, and therefore ignored the fact that Rumsey was the real inventor. At any rate, there was no gold medal nor reward for the Rumseys, notwithstanding reports to the contrary.

The Rumsey claim had its advocates many years before Edward Rumsey delivered this speech. It has them now, more and more every year, and will in all probability continue to have them in increasing numbers until Rumsey is universally recognized as the original inventor. No man in recent years gathered more evidence in defense of James Rumsey's claim than did John Moray, of Berkeley Springs, West Virginia, whose manuscript on the subject was almost finished when he died, January 15, 1912.

No stone marks the grave of James Rumsey; no monument has been erected to his memory. He was buried in London, in that part of St. Margaret's churchyard which has since been converted into a thoroughfare. The fact that James Rumsey was the real inventor of the application of steam for the propulsion of boats will in all probability be some day recognized by the world. Edward Rumsey's speech will then be more fully appreciated, and Muhlenbergers will refer with even greater pride to the fact that he was a citizen of Greenville.

---

[1] James Rumsey's only son, James (who was deaf and dumb as well as blind), and his brother, Doctor Edward Rumsey (the father of Honorable Edward Rumsey), lived and died in Christian County.

X

THE POND RIVER COUNTRY

THE Pond River country of Muhlenberg is a section of the county that offers the archæologist, geologist, botanist, and local historian a very interesting field of research. Murphy's Lake and all the other so-called lakes of the Pond River country are now, as in days gone by, frequented by many fishermen. Few localities are better known to local Nimrods than the Pond River bottoms and the Pond River hills. In olden times deer and turkeys were more numerous in this part of the county than in any other. The last deer was shot about the year 1890.[1] No wild turkeys have been seen during the past few years. None of the old pigeon-roosts have been visited by wild pigeons since about the year 1860. The 'coon, 'possum, and fox hunters or those looking for squirrels or birds still find this a good field for game. It is also a good field for those who are interested in local traditions. Some of the county's most prominent pioneers settled near Murphy's Lake and in other parts of the Pond River country, and many of them are still represented there by descendants.

Murphy's Lake is twelve miles southwest of Greenville. There are many interesting places between the courthouse and the lake. The first of these along the road from Greenville is Fair View Farm, where, beginning in 1885 and continuing for about eight years, the Muhlenberg County Fair was held. A few miles farther on is Sharon Baptist Church, and near it, under a concave bluff of sandstone, is the well-known Rock Spring. Where the Murphy's Lake road turns off from the Lower Hopkinsville road is Mount Pisgah Church, built in 1851 and abandoned a few years ago. Less than a half mile from Mount Pisgah are the ruins of Old Liberty, and beyond this famous landmark—in what, years ago, was sometimes called "The Hoe-Cake Country"—are Olive Branch and Green's chapels. Of these five churches Old Liberty is by far the oldest and most historic.

Old Liberty is now a ruin—four tottering log walls, each about twenty-five feet long, enclosing a sunken floor and a caved-in roof, mingled with broken benches and a weatherbeaten pulpit. The hewed logs, partly shaded by a large white oak, show that they at one time were well chinked with wood and pointed with sand and lime. Its four window- and two door-

---

[1] Up to the year 1867 deer were plentiful in the Pond River country. The high water of that year forced them to the hills, where a great number were slaughtered. In 1884 they were again driven to the hills by high water and practically all of them were shot.

frames will soon collapse; with them will fall the walls, and so, bye-and-bye, no part of this old landmark will be left to mark the site of the once famous church. Near the ruins is the Old Liberty burying-ground. In it are the myrtle-covered and stone-marked graves of many a Martin, Lovell, Eades, Shelton, Allison, Brothers, Luckett, and Jameson, all of whom were among the old families of this community.

More people have ancestors buried at Old Liberty than in any other country graveyard in the county. Tradition says the original church was built about 1816, and was then called New Liberty. In the course of time

MICHAEL LOVELL'S OLD PLACE, NEAR OLD LIBERTY, IN 1900
A few years after it had been abandoned by the Lovells and much of the original building had been removed

the first log house was replaced by a second, which was abandoned about 1851. Some years later the third or last house was erected, and was used until about 1890.[2]

Among the well-known first-comers who lived in the Old Liberty neighborhood and the Murphy's Lake country were: Samuel Allison and his son, John Adair; John S. Atkison, sr., John Bone, Divinity Grace, N. Green, William and Jacob Imbler, pioneer Jarroll or Joiles (perhaps Jerrold), Jesse Kirby, Michael Lovell, the Martins, Jesse Murphy, Jacob Oglesby, John and Edmund Owen, George O. Prowse, Miles Putnam, Joseph C. and Richard D. Reynolds, William Rice, John Richardson, Newton B. Riddick, Richard Thompson, and Reverend Samuel M. Wilkins. One of the earliest

---

[2] A chapter on "Old Liberty Church," by R. T. Martin, appears elsewhere in this volume.

of these settlers was Michael Lovell, who in his time was, and to this day still is, referred to as "the Man from Maryland."[3]

Most of the other pioneers of the Old Liberty neighborhood were Carolinians and Virginians. Among the North Carolinians were pioneer Samuel Allison and his wife Margaret Dickson, both of whom were born in the province of Ulster, Ireland. They came to Logan County about 1796, and a few years later settled in what became known as the Friendship neighborhood. Samuel Allison was famous for his wit and as being the best rifle-shot in his end of the county. He was born about 1767 and died January 20, 1827. His wife was born about 1773 and died December 24, 1834. Both are buried near Friendship Church. Mr. and Mrs. Allison were well educated, and so were their children. Their daughter, Nancy R., married Samuel Jackson. Their sons were Charles McLean, William Dickson, Young Ewing, John Adair, and Samuel Henley.

Charles McLean Allison, who was among the first to enlist in Alney McLean's company, died in camp at New Orleans of swamp fever, three weeks after the battle was fought in 1815.

MICHAEL LOVELL, ABOUT 1865

John Adair Allison was the only one of the five sons who lived and died in Muhlenberg. He was born February 3, 1803, and during his day was one

---

[3] John Bone was a Revolutionary soldier, one of the early settlers near what is now the Webster McCown farm (south of Bancroft), and who died there about 1841. He was the father of Mark, Thomas, John, Mrs. Louisa (Peter) Duvall, Mrs. James Green, Mrs. Wyatt Collins, and Mrs. George Barnett.

Nathaniel Green came to Muhlenberg in 1816, where he died about 1850. He was the only son of Joseph Green and his wife, who was a Miss Eaves. He was born in Virginia, where he married Lucy Richardson, daughter of Thomas Richardson, and in 1815 came to Kentucky. They were the parents of James, William Joseph, Thomas M., Samuel, Miss Polly, and Mrs. Martha (Doctor) Lowe, all of whom, like their parents, were well-known Pond River people.

Michael Lovell's first wife was Mary Ingram. To them were born Joseph, John, Sarah Ann, and Mrs. Mary E. (William K.) Morgan. His second wife was Rachel Eades. To them were born Charles W., Sam B., Lewis H., Miss Frankie, Leander W., Michael, jr., and Thomas J. His third wife was a daughter of John Reno. To them was born one child, James Lovell. Michael Lovell died near Old Liberty on February 26, 1874, aged about one hundred years.

William Rice, a Revolutionary soldier and army blacksmith, settled in Muhlenberg about 1800 and died near Bancroft March 16, 1824. Among his fourteen sons and four daughters were William, jr., Jesse, Larkin, Matthew, Claborn, T. Jefferson, James Benjamin, and Ezekiel Rice. Ezekiel Rice was born in 1774, married Ann Watkins, daughter of pioneer James Watkins, and died in 1847. Among Ezekiel Rice's children was Moses M. Rice (born 1817, died 1894), who married Sarah Amandaville Drake, and among whose children is Judge James J. Rice.

of the most prominent citizens in the Pond River country. He died near Old Liberty, April 2, 1875. He and his wife, Frances Watkins, were the parents of five children, among whom was Finis McLean Allison, who, as stated in the chapter entitled "In 1870," was a State Senator and one of the best-known men in the county.[4]

The other three sons of Samuel Allison removed to Henderson County in early manhood. William Dickson Allison was deputy clerk of Muhlenberg under Charles Fox Wing. He went to Henderson in 1822 to become deputy clerk there. In 1824 Judge Alney McLean appointed him clerk, and he held

JOHN ADAIR ALLISON OLD PLACE, WEST OF GREENVILLE, IN 1900

that office without interruption until his death in 1860. Young Ewing Allison went to Henderson in 1824 to become his brother's deputy, became presiding justice and afterward county judge, succeeded his brother as clerk, and was in office fifty years. Samuel Henley Allison was sheriff of Henderson County for one term—the three brothers holding office at the same time.

As Charles Fox Wing in Muhlenberg trained and equipped young men for public service, so the Allisons did in Henderson, and a large number of successful men of affairs were started from the Henderson courthouse under them. The Allisons were all men of strong personality, and their wit and humorous exploits were quoted widely. In James Weir's "Lonz Powers"

---

[4] John Adair Allison was the father of James Watkins, Finis McLean, Samuel Henley, and William Young Allison, and Mrs. Ann Luro (W. Britton) Davis.

Samuel Allison and three of his sons are sketched under the disguise of "Allston and the Allston boys." But they were also men of great usefulness and influence.

Among those who during the first years of the Eighteenth Century settled in the neighborhood of Old Liberty was Mrs. Susannah Walker Martin, widow of Thomas Martin of Virginia, who was a Revolutionary soldier. She moved to Muhlenberg in 1805. Her three daughters, Betsy, Mary, and Nancy, remained only a short time. Her son, Dabney Amos, who had located in Georgia in 1800, later moved to Alabama, where he died in 1850. Of her six children two settled in the county—William Martin and Hutson Martin. These two are the forefathers of all the Martins in Muhlenberg except the few who are descendants of Jefferson Martin and another William Martin, who were brothers of Hugh Martin. William Martin, son of Thomas, was the pioneer of the plug-tobacco manufacturing business in Muhlenberg. Hutson Martin was a successful farmer near Old Liberty, and one of the foremost men in the county. His wife, Anna Lockridge Martin, treated many of the sick in the neighborhood with her own preparations, made of native herbs, and up to the time of her death, which occurred in her eighty-second year, was known as "Mother Martin."[5]

JOHN ADAIR ALLISON, 1874

---

[5] William Martin was born in Virginia December 23, 1776, and died in Muhlenberg County November 5, 1851. His wife, Jane (Campbell) Martin, was born in Virginia October 22, 1776, and died near Old Liberty in August, 1851. Mr. and Mrs. Martin were the parents of eight children: (1) Thomas Lawrence, among whose eight children (as stated in the chapter on Tobacco) is Richard T. Martin; (2) William Campbell, who married America Niblack, their two sons being Hugh Niblack and Thomas Hutson Martin; (3) Mrs. Eliza Ann (Reverend Samuel M.) Wilkins; (4) Mrs. Susannah W. (James) Hancock; (5) Dabney A., who married Lizzie Britt, their only child, Jennie, marrying Hanson Browder, of Clinton, Kentucky; (6) Charles C., who married Nancy Y. Reynolds; (7) David; (8) Ellington Walker, who married Emily Elliott, daughter of Richard Elliott.

Hutson Martin was born in Virginia May 27, 1781, and died in Muhlenberg July 7, 1838. His wife died January 29, 1869, aged eighty-one years. Mr. and Mrs. Hutson Martin were the parents of twelve children: (1) Andrew L., who married Fannie Rice; (2) Mrs. Mary (George) Ingram; (3) Mrs. Jane (Jackson) Rice; (4) Lucrecia; (5) William W., who married Mary Ann Lovelace; (6) Mrs. Susan (James) Rice; (7) John; (8) Mrs. Ellen (John) Grigsby; (9) James, who married Elizabeth Bell; (10) Felix J., who married Caroline Eaves; (11) Mrs. Laura Ann (James W.) Allison, who is the mother of Mrs. Anna Allison Holmes and Professor B. Frank Allison and who, after the death of her first husband, married Azel M. Terry; (12) Miss Luro Martin.

Among the well-known first-comers who settled in the Pond River country above Old Liberty and Murphy's Lake was Micajah Wells, who came from North Carolina before the county was organized, settling in the lower Long Creek country, where he and his three brothers did much toward opening up that section. He became a candidate for the Legislature in 1810, and remained one for sixteen successive years, when, in 1826, he was finally chosen. Although he wanted the office "just once for the fun of it," as he expressed it, he nevertheless did much, tradition says, "for the good of the county his whole life long." He served as a justice of the peace for many years, and also filled various other county offices.[6]

HUTSON MARTIN OLD PLACE
Near Old Liberty, in 1900

One of Micajah Well's neighbors was Strother Jones, who lived near Long Creek, in the southern part of what is known as the Lead Hill country. Strother Jones was in his day one of the most polished citizens in the southwestern part of the county. He was born September 20, 1781, came to Muhlenberg in 1822, and died on his farm February 17, 1859. His eldest son and only child by his first wife was Judge William G. Jones, who served as county judge from 1854 to 1862. Judge Jones was born June 4, 1813, and died August 6, 1891. Strother Jones' second wife was Elizabeth Ann Hancock. Three children were born of this second marriage: Thomas J. Jones, who was county clerk during the Civil War, and who at the time of his death (February 22, 1904) was

STROTHER JONES, ABOUT 1845

---

[6] Micajah Wells was born January 1, 1772, and died October 19, 1851. He and his brothers John, Frank, and Wyatt Wells were among the pioneers in the upper Pond River and Long Creek country. Micajah Wells was the father of six children: (1) Mosley P.; (2) Mrs. Lourana S. (Mosley Collins) Drake; (3) Mrs. Sally Grissom; (4) Mrs. Patsy (Reverend Silas) Drake; (5) Mrs. Anna (Edmond) Drake; (6) Joseph J., who was drowned in Pond River February 12, 1832. His sons-in-law Mosley Collins, Reverend Silas, and Edmond Drake, jr., were sons of pioneer Albritton Drake.

running a store he had established in Greenville about fifty years before; John M. Jones, a Confederate soldier, and James M. Jones. The two last were "Forty-niners."

A story Strother Jones heard relative to a small band of Indians which, a number of years before his arrival in the county, had passed through the neighborhood in which he settled, is still told by a few of his descendants, and runs as follows:

One day at noon a man named Walker returned to his cabin from his work in the field. He sent one of his children, a girl nine years of age, to a spring some two hundred yards away to get some fresh water. While the girl was at the spring she heard screaming at the house, and a moment later saw some Indians set the place on fire. Being frightened, she concealed herself in some bushes. After the house had burned almost to the ground, there being nothing to indicate that the Indians were still about, she walked to the ruins and discovered that her parents and the five other children had been murdered and their bodies thrown in a pile near the burning house. She immediately notified the nearest neighbor. A pursuing party was at once organized. They trailed the Indians to the Pond River bottoms, but there all trace of the murderers was lost. Upon their return the pursuers buried the Walkers near the ruins of the cabin, which stood within two hundred yards of the spot where Strother Jones' house was later erected.

The Clarks, who were among the pioneers living below Murphy's Lake, are no longer represented in the county, but their name is perpetuated in the name of Clark's Ferry Bridge, built across Pond River where, for many years, the Clarks ran a ferry and grist mill. For a while the place was called Pond River Mills. The first bridge built here was a wooden bridge placed on stone abutments, erected by Alfred Johnson about 1858. In December, 1861, this bridge was burned by Confederates under Forrest. In 1862 the ferry was reëstablished and operated until 1890, when the New Clark's Ferry Bridge was erected on the old but solid stone abutments. In this same neighborhood stood the well-known David Clark sugar camp.

CLARK'S FERRY BRIDGE, POND RIVER

About the year 1880 Fobel & Krauth, of Louisville, attempted to establish a small colony of Germans and German-Americans on the site that had been abandoned by the Clarks and their associates. Although the few German-Americans who moved there remained but a short time, since then this region has been known as the "Dutch Farm."

A mile below Clark's Ferry Bridge is Harpe's Hill, overlooking the Pond River bottoms and also overlooking an "arm" or "bay" of "second bottom," which extends far beyond the river bottoms and is semicircled by Harpe's Hill and other high and picturesque hills. Crops never fail in this fertile area of well-drained farms. In biblical days people used to go down into Egypt to buy corn. Harpe's Hill valley is, therefore, frequently referred to as "Egypt." When their own crops fall short many of the farmers of Muhlenberg and Hopkins counties go to this never-failing region, where they can be supplied with corn and other agricultural products that are not only as good as the best, but usually "a little bit better." Near the foot of one of the hills overlooking the level and slightly rolling floor of this gigantic amphitheater is the home of William A. Armstrong, a mathematician and student of the classics, who before his retirement was one of the best-known surveyors in the county.

Major Jesse Oates was the first of the prominent pioneers who settled in the Harpe's Hill country. He was a Revolutionary soldier, having fought under Francis Marion in South Carolina. He came to Muhlenberg about 1795 or shortly thereafter. He opened up what was for many years considered one of the best farms in the Pond River country. He owned thirty or more slaves, all of whom were employed on his plantation. Although he never held any of the high county offices, few men of his time did more to promote public interests than Major Oates. He died August 10, 1831, at the age of seventy-five years.

THE SO-CALLED HARPE'S "HOUSE"
On Harpe's Hill, near Pond River

Major Jesse Oates was born in North Carolina about the year 1756. He was a son of Jesse Oates, sr., who although not a soldier in the Revolution did much toward promoting the war. Jesse Oates, jr., however, much to the satisfaction of his father, took an active part in the struggle. After the Revolution Jesse Oates, sr., gave his son Jesse practically all his estate, to the exclusion of his son-in-law Coghill, who it is said was either not in sympathy with the American colonies or was an outright Tory. Having received none of the expected fortune, Coghill's feeling toward his brother-in-law was anything but friendly.

In those days every man was obliged to attend the militia musters, which took place once a month. Coghill and Oates were members of the same company, and on nearly every drilling day a fight would take place between the two. Coghill was large and strong, Oates was small; the consequence was that Oates got the worst of the fight every time. Matters went on in this way for several years, when one day Oates notified his brother-in-law that if he attacked him at the next muster he would kill him. The day arrived and Coghill, according to his custom, gave Oates his usual whipping. Oates had his flintlock with him and threatened to shoot, and would have done so had Coghill not begged him to give him a chance for his life. Oates agreed to let Coghill go home—a distance of two miles—to get the gun he said he preferred to use in this duel instead of the one he had with him. The two men and some of their friends then mounted their horses and started for Coghill's farm. When the crowd arrived at the end of the short lane leading up to the house, Coghill put spurs to his horse and told Oates to shoot. Coghill evidently felt confident that Oates would miss him, and that his gun being loaded he could kill Oates before Oates could reload. Oates fired and killed Coghill instantly.

Oates rode home, procured some money and a pocket compass, bade his family good-bye, mounted his horse, and with his flintlock lying across his saddle started west. He rode through Tennessee into Mississippi. While at Natchez, stopping at a tavern, he picked up a newspaper and there read an advertisement giving a full description of him and also offering a reward for his capture. That same day he started for Kentucky and shortly afterward landed in the Pond River country, procured some land, notified his family of his whereabouts, and had his oldest son, William Oates—who was then a young man—move the family, slaves, and personal property to the new home he had provided for them. His friends in North Carolina advised him not to return, for although he would not be prosecuted he would in all probability be killed by some of Coghill's friends. During the course of a number of years advice was frequently sent him to be on his guard, for some of the friends of Coghill were coming to kill him. Although he for a while feared he would be shot from ambush, no attempt to kill or arrest him was ever made.

Major Jesse Oates and his family lived happily and prospered in their new home. After the death of his first wife, who was the mother of his five oldest children, he married again and became the father of twelve more. All of his children except one, Mrs. Campbell, settled in Muhlenberg, where most of them are now represented by many descendants.[7] His oldest son, William, married Elizabeth Earle, who was a daughter of pioneer Bayless Earle, a Revolutionary soldier. Her husband was a soldier in the War of 1812. Her brother, Richard Bayless Earle, was a Mexican War soldier. She was the grandmother of four Federal soldiers, William Oates Randolph, Lieutenant Ed M. Randolph, George Oates, and Wallace W. Oates, and of one Confederate soldier (who fought on the side with which she sympathized), Charles R. Oates. Her eldest son, Bayless Earle Oates, was the father of J. Wallace Oates, who was one of the most progressive farmers and stock-men in the county. Mrs. Elizabeth Earle Oates was one of the

---

[7] The first wife of Major Jesse Oates was, according to a vague family tradition, a Miss Caraway, sister of a Captain John Caraway. His second wife was Zilpah Mason, to whom he was married April 13, 1798, and who died October 1, 1849. Major Jesse Oates was the father of (1) William; (2) Jethro; (3) Mrs. Nancy (Charles) Campbell; (4) David; (5) Bryant; (6) John Mason; (7) Mrs. Betsy (V. L.) Dillingham; (8) Jesse; (9) Richard M.; (10) Rachael (Mrs. Lemuel Boggess, later Mrs. Wickliffe); (11) Mariah; (12) Mrs. Zilpah (Edmond) Dunn; (13) Matthew Mason; (14) Harriet (Mrs. Gough, Mrs. Robert Wickliffe, jr., Mrs. Williams); (15) Oliver Hayes (bachelor); (16) Wyatt; (17) Charles Campbell Oates.

best-known and most highly esteemed women of the Pond River country. She was born in 1790 and died in 1884.[8]

Another well-known woman in the Harpe's Hill country was Mrs. Clara Garris Stanley. She was probably the last of the pioneers to pass away who had seen the headless body of Big Harpe lying near Harpe's Hill.[9]

John S. Eaves, in 1805, settled in the valley near the foot of Harpe's Hill, not far from the Jesse Oates plantation. He became one of the most influential men in Muhlenberg, representing the county in the Legislature in 1834. He died in Greenville in 1867. He was the father of seven children, all of whom were well-known people. No man ever born in Muhlenberg County was more highly esteemed than his youngest son, Charles Eaves, who long before 1857, when at the age of thirty-two he was elected to the Legislature, had won the love of his fellow-citizens. John S. Eaves' fourth son, John S. Eaves, jr., was for many years a merchant and farmer near Clark's Ferry. John S., jr., was in turn succeeded in his business by his son George W. Eaves, jr., who until his removal to Greenville was identified with the development of the Harpe's Hill country.

MRS. ELIZABETH EARLE OATES, 1870

Members of the Legislature are, as a rule, among the best-known citizens in their counties, and because of this their lives are discussed by a greater number of people and for a longer time than are those of other citizens, who are seldom heard of in tradition outside their own neighborhood, regardless of the good they may have done in their vicinity. The lives of the members of the Legislature who lived in the Pond River country are therefore, as a rule, more widely discussed in the oral history of the earlier days than are the lives of some of its other one-time prominent men.

---

[8] William Oates and his wife Elizabeth Earl Oates were the parents of nine children: Bayless Earle, Mrs. Geraldine M. (Ashford D.) Randolph, Thomas, Charles, Jethro, William W., Martha, Jesse, and James Wilson Oates.

[9] Mrs. Clara Garris Stanley, wife of James Stanley, was in her day one of the most accomplished women in Western Muhlenberg. It is said she was one of the best-informed women on the early history of the Pond River country. She lived near Harpe's Hill when Big Harpe was killed, and continued to make that locality her home until shortly before her death in 1864. She had read Judge Hall's story of the Harpes and also T. Marshall Smith's version, and often remarked that both were in the main correct. Mr. and Mrs. James Stanley were the parents of Russell, Alfred, Wickliffe, David, and Gilbert Stanley and Mrs. Elizabeth (William) Dillinder and Mrs. Matilda (Henry) Thomas.

The first man living in the Pond River country to represent Muhlenberg County in the Legislature was John Morgan. Micajah Wells, as already stated, was a member of the Legislature in 1826. In 1828, and during the eight years following, Muhlenberg was represented in the Legislature by men who lived in the lower Pond River country. Most of the members who served from 1838 to 1853 came from the Pond River country, and many of those who were elected during a later period were born and reared in that same section of the county. Among the well-known first-comers who settled in the Pond River country below Harpe's Hill were the McNarys, Shorts, and Morgans.

The McNarys lived about six miles below Harpe's Hill near the edge of Pond River bottom, on the lower Greenville and Madisonville Road. William McNary was the forefather of this well-known family. He was born in Scotland, and shortly after his arrival in America settled near Lexington, where he lived for more than twenty years, doing much toward promoting the interests of the Presbyterian church. In 1812 he settled on what has ever since been called the McNary place, or Ellwood. McNary Station, although some distance from the old home, was so called in honor of his son, Hugh W. William McNary was the father of three sons, Hugh W., William C., and Doctor Thomas L.; the latter lived and died near Princeton.

MRS. CLARA G. STANLEY, 1855

William C. lived near the place first settled by his father, where he died in 1871 at the age of seventy-four. He represented the county in the Legislature five times between the years 1830 and 1853. He was a member of the State Senate from 1846 to 1850. None of his four children made Muhlenberg their home.

Hugh W. McNary was born in Fayette County, Kentucky, November 25, 1790, and came to Muhlenberg at the age of twenty-two. In 1816 he went to South Carolina, where for ten years he dealt in groceries and speculated in cotton. In 1822 he married Miss Sarah A. Scott, one of the most highly accomplished young ladies of Columbia, South Carolina. In 1826 he returned to Muhlenberg with his wife, reinvested the money he had made in the South, and soon accumulated a fortune. He was at one time one of the wealthiest men in Muhlenberg County. He owned a number of slaves, ran a large farm, bought and sold livestock, operated a large still, and found a market not only for his own products but for those of most of the people living in the lower Pond River country. None of his local contemporaries were more generous, better read, or more refined than he. In 1850 he erected a frame residence which, up to 1879 (when the McNary family moved to Greenville), was considered one of the best built and most artistically furnished homes in the county. The mantels and many of the door- and window-frames were hand carved. The front porch was torn away a few years ago, and owing to its removal and to a lack of paint and repairs the building has lost much of its former beauty; nevertheless, the most casual observer can not fail to see that it must have been an exceptionally beautiful residence in its day. It was in this house that Hugh W. McNary died, October 7, 1872, at the age of eighty-two.[10]

David Short came to Muhlenberg County from Virginia some time during the first ten years of the Eighteenth Century and settled on a tract of

HUGH W. McNARY HOUSE, LOWER POND RIVER COUNTRY

land bordering on Pond River, about a mile above what is now the McLean County line. The house he erected—"The David Short Old Brick," as it is called—was when it was first built, and is now, one of the largest and most substantial brick residences in Muhlenberg. An inscription painted in the arch of the door-frame reads, "D. 1821 S." This, although it has evidently been repainted since first recorded there, undoubtedly indicates the year the house was built. David Short devoted most of his time to the cultivation of his large farms and to the promotion of better laws. His well-built house proclaims the fact that he was a man of means. He was a member of the

---

[10] Hugh W. McNary and his wife Sarah A. McNary (who was born December 16, 1806, and died October 15, 1868) were the parents of six children: W. Scott, Samuel F., John A., Miss Anna, Mrs. Sally (George W., jr.) Eaves, and Miss Mattie McNary, who is and long has been one of the most highly esteemed women in the county.

Legislature in 1828, 1829, and 1832. His son William T. Short filled the same office in 1847, and his son George W. Short filled it in 1849. David Short was born January 19, 1779, and died December 30, 1845. He was the father of ten children, all of whom were influential citizens.

Among others who settled in Muhlenberg about the same time as David Short were Jacob Short and Jacob Jagoe, whose wife, Susan (Short) Jagoe, was a sister of David Short. Samuel Short, another brother, after living in this neighborhood awhile moved to Illinois and later returned to Sacramento, where he died. The family name, it is said, was originally spelled Schartz. One tradition has it that the Shorts were born in Germany and came to Virginia in their youth, while according to another they were born in Virginia.[11]

John Morgan, who represented the county in the State Legislature in 1806, was one of the early settlers in the Pond River country. None of the pioneers took more interest in saddle-horses or owned better ones than he. Every winter, for more than fifty years, he wore a cap made from the fur of white foxes he occasionally caught in the hills near his home. He and his brothers Willis and Charles Morgan, who were also well-known early settlers, ran a grist mill at old Millport for many years. John Morgan was a dignified and scholarly man, a wealthy farmer and an extensive slave-owner, and was also one of the most liberal men of his day. He was born in Virginia March 17, 1779, and died at his

HUGH W. McNARY, 1871

---

[11] David Short and his wife Jane Scott Short, of Virginia, were the parents of: (1) Mrs. Sarah (David) Evans, who later married A. M. Spurlin; (2) George Washington Short; (3) Joseph Poague Short; (4) David T. Short, who first married Martha Henry, next Elizabeth Arnold; (5) Mrs. Jane P. (Sanders) Eaves; (6) William T., who married Elizabeth Greu; (7) Miss Elizabeth; (8) Jacob L., who married Emma Mitchell and who later moved to Texas; (9) Jonathan Short, who married Lucy Wing; (10) Mrs. Susan Ann (William) Harbin.

Jacob Short was born August 20, 1772, and died October 26, 1858. His wife, Isabelle Scott Short, was born August 18, 1787, and died October 19, 1860. They were the parents of: (1) Mrs. Mary (or Polly) (Samuel) Whitmer; (2) Mrs. Eva (Louis) Phillips; (3) Jacob (bachelor); (4) Samuel, who married Sarah Garst; (5) William, who married Nancy Miller, daughter of Captain Isaac Miller. Jacob Short's children lived in the lower part of Muhlenberg and in southern McLean County, where all of them were well-known people.

Jacob Jagoe was the father of three sons, Abraham G., Benjamin, and William Jagoe. These three brothers in their day were among the best-known farmers in the lower Pond River country.

home north of Earles September 25, 1858. His wife, Jane Morgan, was born in 1783 and died in 1844.[12]

A few years ago David W. Whitmer, while cutting down a beech tree on his farm on the edge of Pond River bottoms, near old Millport, unearthed a slab of sandstone on which was carved "Daniel Boone, May 22, 1772." This rock was covered with a few inches of soil, and one end of it was partly overgrown by a large root. Conditions indicated that it had lain there about fifty years. The fact that Daniel Boone's name and an old date appear on it caused many to declare that the carving was done by no other than Daniel Boone. Although Boone made his first trip to Kentucky in 1769, and may have been in the State in 1772, he evidently did not cut his name on this rock. The lettering is like that found on many of the old grave-stones in the southern part of the county, and it is therefore quite likely that this slab was taken to Millport many years ago by some experienced stone-cutter to serve as a sample of his work.

THE SO-CALLED DANIEL BOONE ROCK

The fact that pioneer John Morgan had a son named Daniel Boone Morgan, who lived in this locality for many years and was a well-known physician, may have influenced the stone-cutter to select the name of the great scout on which to show his skill. This stone weighs eighteen pounds, is three inches thick, and its face measures about nine by twelve inches.

Murphy's Lake,[13] as stated in the beginning of this chapter, is in the Pond River country, about twelve miles southwest of Greenville. This so-called lake is about three miles long, but its width is by no means in proportion to its length, for it is only from forty to fifty feet wide. It is part of the old Pond River bed and meanders for some three miles in Pond River bottom, at a distance of about half a mile from the river itself. The lake proper consists of two long, deep bends of the old river, connected by a number of smaller and shallower crooks. In places above and below these two lagoons the old bed is nothing more than a filled-up or marshy slough. The upper of these two bodies of water is known as Fisherman's Bend or Big

---

[12] John Morgan and his wife Jane Irvin Morgan were the parents of eight children, Charles, John, Doctor Daniel Boone, Doctor James Robert, William K., Mrs. Susan Lovin, Mrs. Margaret Lovin, and Mrs. Jane (William) Eades.

William K. Morgan and his wife, Mary E. Lovell Morgan, were among the best-known people in the Pond River country, where they lived on a farm and where they reared eight sons and four daughters, most of whom live in the county and are among Muhlenberg's most progressive citizens.

[13] Murphy's Lake was so called after Jesse Murphy, who was born in 1781, settled near the banks of the lake about the year 1805, and who lived there until his death in 1846. Jesse Murphy was the father of Thomas Murphy, who was born in 1825 and died in 1862. Thomas Murphy was the father of James R., W. Jesse, and Samuel W. Murphy and Mrs. Mary (Julian) Wicks.

Bend, and the lower is called Green's Bend. The Murphy's Lake bridge crosses one of the shallow links that help unite the two bends. During the dry season practically all the water disappears from these shallow intervening crooks, and at such times they show that they are nothing more than a chain of brush-grown sloughs, more or less filled with logs and snags. These various sloughs are by no means picturesque. However, Murphy's Lake proper offers many attractive views. Varieties of aquatic plants flourish in the lake and on its banks. Among such vegetation are great clusters of a species of lily known as Bonnets or Spatterdock. In many places the two large bends are gracefully lined down to the very water's edge with small willows and other shrublike growths. On the shore stand majestic old oaks, beech and gum, shading here and there a growth of short cane. Some of these trees, draped with wild grapevine, bend over the banks of the lake and in many places form unbroken arches with those leaning from the other side.

The territory lying between the present bed of Pond River and Murphy's Lake, with its inlet, sloughs, outlet, and "scatters," comprises some three thousand acres, all of which with the exception of about two hundred acres is rich bottom land. In fact, the richest soil in the county is found in the Pond River bottoms. Most of it, however, is subject to floods, and therefore comparatively little of it is as yet under cultivation. Much of it probably never will be redeemed until certain parts of the river's channel are straightened out and the many sloughs properly drained.

Isaac Bard recognized the superior quality of this soil, and in 1853 made an attempt to give the three thousand acres around Murphy's Lake better drainage. He dug a straight ditch from the head of the "scatters" of Murphy's Lake to Martin's Creek. He abandoned the ditch, however—not because his work was ridiculed by many of the people, but because his time was taken up with other affairs. No attempt has since been made to restore Bard's Ditch, and the land in that vicinity is still awaiting better drainage.

Lakes of this character, originating from disappearing streams, are found in a number of places in the Pond River bottoms. Above Murphy's Lake is Atkinson's Little Lake, or as it is frequently called, "The Little Lake at Fish Pond Hill." This lake is about three hundred yards long. Old Lake, a quarter of a mile below Clark's Ferry Bridge, is a crescent-shaped lagoon with its two points coming up to Pond River. Boat Yard Creek or White Ash Pond, near Harpe's Hill, is another lake of this character, but receives most of its water from the small streams that drain the valley near it. All these lakes, including Murphy's Lake, have an inlet and an outlet, which are as a rule simply long, narrow, winding swags. In these places, where the outlets are very shallow, occur the so-called "scatters," which during an overflow permit the water to run in any and every direction until it finds its way to the main channel of the river.

The lagoon known as Boat Yard Creek is so called from the fact that in the early days, and down to as late as 1860, flat-boats were built on its banks. Richard Aycock was one of the best-known boat-builders at this place. Some of the flat-boats made here were loaded with hoop-poles cut in the Pond River country and shipped to New Orleans, while others were sent down to Green River and there sold to men who used them for various purposes. John S. Eaves sent tobacco, pork, and lard from this neighborhood to New Orleans as early as 1818. William Oates built a number of flat-boats here and shipped many loads of hides and produce to the South.[14]

The west bank of Big Bend, or Fisherman's Bend, of Murphy's Lake has for almost a century been a favorite camping-place for fishing parties.

THE "DAVID SHORT OLD BRICK"
Near Pond River and the McLean County Line

One of these is well remembered locally because it terminated in the drowning of J. Lindsey Spurlin and Ellington Eades. This tragedy occurred on the 5th of July, 1866. J. Lindsey Spurlin was a man of about forty-four years and Ellington Eades was a boy of nineteen, a son of R. W. Eades and a grandson of pioneer Barnett Eades. Besides the two who were drowned the

---

[14] Bridge Lake, near the mouth of Mud River, may at one time have been a channel of Green River or Mud River. It is now more of a bayou or back-water slough than a lagoon of the character of those in the Pond River bottoms. During high water Bridge Lake becomes a channel and flows into Green River below the mouth of Mud River. Abram, Campfield, Horseshoe, and other small lakes above it on the Muhlenberg side are probably old channels of Mud River.

Black Lake, located in the extreme northern part of the county, is a long, narrow lagoon, the origin and nature of which is a matter of speculation. An arm of Green River may have run, ages ago, from the mouth of Thoroughfare branch to the region of Black Lake and then continued down Cypress Creek, or down some other course, back into Green River.

Near Pond Creek occur a few small, narrow ponds known as "old sloughs." Above the old Jack Ford, near the Greenville and Elkton Road, is one which, previous to about 1860, formed part of the Pond Creek main channel.

party consisted of Theodore Spurlin (son of J. Lindsey Spurlin), K. L. Terry, John Luckett, and Alfred Luckett. Their nets having become entangled, Ellington Eades waded into the water to straighten them out. While thus engaged a cramp caused him to lose all control of himself. J. Lindsey Spurlin jumped into the lake to help his sinking friend, but in his attempt both sank to the bottom.[15]

About twenty years before J. Lindsey Spurlin was drowned he had participated in a hunt that took place in this same part of the Pond River country. Wild turkeys and squirrels were in such abundance in the olden times that corn was more or less subject to destruction by these "pests" from the time it was planted to the day it was gathered. In 1845 the people living near Old Liberty and Murphy's Lake declared war on the wild turkeys and squirrels, for during that year they had become unusually troublesome. Thomas Murphy and Joseph C. Reynolds were selected as captains to fight a prolonged battle against these foes of the farmer. Each leader chose an equal number of men and boys for his company. It was agreed that after sixty days of bombardment the two captains and their hunters were to return to a designated camp between Murphy's Lake and Old Liberty. The company bringing the smaller number of scalps (that is, tails) was to prepare a barbecue for the entire neighborhood. When the fight began, those who could procure no shotguns or rifles marched along depending on sticks and stones for their ammunition. For two months the old muzzle-loaders scattered lead in every direction, and everything small that could be picked up and thrown was "fired" at the corn-field enemy. Reports differ as to how many squirrels and turkeys were slaughtered in this great battle. One enthusiastic fisherman, whose grandfather was then a mere boy, declares that "Grandpa kept a horse and landslide busy every day and most every night for two months carrying tails to Murphy's headquarters, and the Lord only knows how many others were kept busy on the same job." Facts usually undergo some changes in the hands of tradition, and it has therefore been supposed by some that the *tails* referred to by this grandson were in reality *tales*, or daily reports carried to Tom Murphy's camp to keep that captain informed in regard to the movements of his own and his rival's progress. At any rate, all versions agree that "there was a terrible sight of fur and feather tails" displayed at the barbecue, and that Tom Murphy and his crowd, having brought in the larger number of "scalps," were that day crowned the kings of the killing. The next year, so the story runs, and for many years after, every farmer in the neighborhood raised more corn than Carter had oats—"except when the crows were bad."

Tradition takes us further back than the "Tale of the Tails," for in the legend of Lew Allen Hill we are carried to the days of the roving Indians.

---

[15] J. Lindsey Spurlin was a son of John Spurlin, an Englishman who settled in Christian County about 1800, where he married Rebecca N. Utley. The Reverend James Utley Spurlin, who died in 1909 aged eighty-two and who for more than fifty years preached in Muhlenberg and some of the adjoining counties, was also a son of John Spurlin. J. Lindsey Spurlin came to Muhlenberg about 1845. When he drowned he left a widow with eight small children, all of whom have since become well-known citizens: Theodore, Miss Rebecca, Mrs. Mary (Jacob) Colley, Mrs. Elizabeth F. (Hiram W.) Lee, Mrs. Prince (Douglass) Laswell, Miss Luro, James T., and J. Lindsey Spurlin, jr.

The much-talked-of Lew Allen (or Lewellyn) Hill is located in Pond River bottom, about two miles south of Murphy's Lake. The size of this hill is not at all in proportion to its fame. It is an elevation of only about twenty feet, and has the general form of a broad low cone with a more or less oval-shaped base. It is surrounded in every direction by the level bottom land of Pond River for a distance of half a mile or more. Its area, including its sloping sides, is about one acre. It is covered with beech and sugar trees of

MURPHY'S LAKE

various sizes. On the top, near the center, is the stump of a recently cut black oak tree three and one half feet in diameter.

The legend of Lew Allen Hill is an old and likewise vague tale. In fact, there are two versions of it. One is to the effect that shortly after the Revolution a Captain Knight and his associates settled somewhere on Pond River between what later became the site of the Jesse H. Reno mill (which was built in the early '50s and stood near Prowse's Bridge) and Grace's Fish Trap Ford, farther down the river and opposite the picturesque Grace's Bluff. There, it is said, these pioneers built a strong block cabin and fort. Captain Knight was a trapper and Indian fighter and seemingly the Daniel Boone of the upper Pond River country. Tradition does not tell how many men were connected with his little station. The probabilities, however, are that there were only a few. Among the Captain's companions was one Lew Allen, or Lewellyn, who—so the story runs—while out looking after some bear traps wandered from the camp to this little hill, a distance of about two miles. He was standing on the moundlike elevation, trying to locate a favorable spot for another trap, when suddenly he was attacked and killed by a number of Indians. Knowing that his friends would be likely to search the woods for him, the red men dug a hole on top of the hill, threw the corpse in, and then made an effort to conceal the hiding-place. The following morning, after a diligent hunt, Captain Knight's men discovered Lew Allen's body, and reburied it in its original Indian-made grave. The few small pieces of sand rock now scattered over this knoll are said to have served at one time as the murdered man's tombstone.

POND RIVER

According to the other version, Lew Allen and another prospector came to this neighborhood from what is now Hartford, in Ohio County, which was then one of the few settlements in Western Kentucky. These two men, having been caught in a heavy rain near Pond River, built a fire and put up a wigwam of brush on the top of the hillock, for this purpose more suitable than the wet bottom land surrounding it. They removed all their drenched clothes except their buckskin hunting-shirts. While engaged in drying their wearing apparel and preparing a meal they found themselves, without a moment's warning, attacked by three or four Indians. Some say the Indians rushed upon the two white men simply for the fun of scaring them. At any rate, a few shots were exchanged and Lew Allen was killed. His frightened companion, however, made his escape through the woods and found his way back to Hartford, where he arrived clad in nothing but his badly tattered hunting-shirt.

The hunting-shirt of the early pioneer, it might be well to add, was a long buckskin garment that served the double purpose of a coat and a shirt. It encircled the body down to about eight inches above the knees, and could be worn either with the lower part hanging loose over the breeches or stuffed in them, as desired. In pattern it somewhat resembled the modern woolen military coat-shirt.

Such are the two versions of the legend of Lew Allen Hill. Each has its enthusiastic upholders and its equally enthusiastic deniers. The same may also be said concerning the two theories regarding the origin of the hill. On one hand are those who have come to the conclusion that it is nothing more or less than a natural hill like many of the other hills, large and small, scattered over Pond River bottom; on the other hand are those who believe that it is artificial, the work of the Mound Builders, evidence of whose former existence can still be found in the Pond River country and other parts of Muhlenberg. [16]

Mounds and other signs of the prehistoric men of the Pond River country are rapidly disappearing, and the same may also be said of the few remaining landmarks erected by its pioneers. The primeval forests have long since given way to new farms, and many of the long-abandoned fields are now being redeemed. Modern buildings are taking the places of old-time houses. After better roads shall have been built, Pond River straightened out, and the bottoms properly drained, the Pond River country will rank—as it did in the olden days—second to none in Muhlenberg.

---

[16] A superficial investigation with a pick and shovel strengthened my opinion that Lew Allen Hill is not the work of man. To me it looked like an accumulation deposited by some of the sediment-laden currents in the big floods that prevailed during some of the great overflows in prehistoric times, when the hills of this section were formed by the intervening valleys being washed out. If Lew Allen Hill showed a formation consisting of stratified rocks, such as occur in the hills bordering upon Pond River bottom, then we could conclude that it is the remains of one of the many hills that once existed here, but which were eroded and removed when Pond River was making its wide bottom.

I presume the isolation of Lew Allen Hill and its shape, combined with the fact that a number of prehistoric mounds exist throughout this and other parts of the upper Pond River country, suggested the possibility of its being an artificial mound. The fact that a number of arrow-heads and stone axes have been found not only on this small elevation but also on the nearby Reynold's Turkey Hill and Owen's Island, is considered by some as further evidence that Lew Allen Hill is an artificial mound. Such relics indicate nothing more than the presence at some time of prehistoric men.

XI

OLD LIBERTY CHURCH[1]

SOME time ago I visited the ruins of Old Liberty, six and a half miles west of Greenville. It stands on a spot where the pioneers built a church that flourished for many years. My companion and I sat down by the old forsaken and forgotten log house and then wandered around in the graveyard. Old Liberty, as we saw it, probably presented to my companion a scene showing nothing more than the ravages of time and neglect. I saw not only the view that lay before us, but I also could see in my mind's eye the many changes that had taken place, year after year, since the days when I was a boy.

Liberty was built by the pioneers in the early history of the county—in 1816. A short time after Liberty was built Reverend James Johnston organized a Cumberland Presbyterian congregation there, it being one of the first Cumberland Presbyterian congregations organized in the county. The Presbyterians held their regular meetings of worship at Liberty until 1851, when they erected a new church house on the lower Hopkinsville Road and called it Mount Pisgah. Liberty Church was built as a union church house, free to all denominations. The Methodists used Liberty as a place of worship until about 1880, when they abandoned it.

Liberty Church had a noted record of religious worship and revivals. When this church was built, houses of worship were scarce in the western as well as in the other parts of Muhlenberg. No other place in the county was more noted for religious revivals than Liberty. During the summer and fall of every year protracted meetings were held, and people and preachers of all denominations gathered and remained for weeks. Large arbors were made for outdoor service. Basket meetings were frequent, and cooking was sometimes done on the church ground. No such revival services take place now-a-days. The earnest appeals of the preachers, the zealous songs, long prayers, and loud shouts of joy that were heard and realized at Liberty long ago are seldom heard in the worship of to-day. I can remember the old pioneers as they would shake hands with each other with smiles of hope and joy.

Liberty was called "the mother of preachers." Many of the young men of this and adjoining neighborhoods became ministers of the Gospel under the influence of the revivals that took place at Liberty. Among them were Thomas and Mark Bone, sons of John Bone; George and Thomas Reynolds, sons of Richard D. Reynolds, who was the grandfather of John T. Rey-

---

[1] This entire chapter is by Mr. Richard T. Martin. It is a delightful mingling of history and personal reminiscences, by one who knows his subject well. The sketch was originally printed in the Greenville Record, April 25, 1912.

nolds, sr.; Charles and Kincheon Hay, sons of Kinnard Hay, a schoolteacher, and brothers of Wiley S. Hay, who represented the county in the Legislature in 1845 and 1846, and who later became a State Senator; Henry and Felix Black, sons of Henry Black and brothers of Judge Nathan Black, who later became a noted lawyer in Western Kentucky; Duran Alcock, Stephen Goodnight, Charles Campbell, Adlai Boyd, and Samuel Wilkins, through the influence of Old Liberty, also became preachers. None of these men spent much time in Muhlenberg after they became preachers except Adlai Boyd and Samuel Wilkins.

Liberty was sometimes used as a place for political gatherings and barbecues. It was also used as a schoolhouse until 1855, when a school was built a mile east of the church. W. A. Armstrong taught the last district school at Liberty, in the fall of 1855. In the early times the county was not divided into school districts, and the children of about fifteen families came from a radius of two miles to attend school at Liberty. The first school that I attended was at Liberty. It was then (in 1846) taught for two sessions by James F. Messic, a young Presbyterian preacher. He was born in 1819 and died at Dixon, Webster County, in 1885. His students ranged from five to twenty in years and from thirty to forty in number. Liberty was then standing in the midst of a beautiful forest surrounded by clustered oaks proudly waving their long arms of green foliage to the summer winds and forming a delightful shade. A beautiful and ample playground extended all around the house.

A Sweep and Well and an Old Oaken Bucket, near Old Liberty

In my memory I can plainly see, as if it were but a few years ago, the children that attended the school taught by Messic coming up to Liberty along the different roads and paths in the early morning hours with their baskets, buckets, and books. They were neatly dressed in homespun apparel and came with merry hearts and rosy cheeks, greeting each other with a smile. It was an ambition among the boys and girls to be first at school and to get there before "book time," which gave them a chance for play. The old blue-backed spelling-book was used, and it took two copies to last some pupils through the school. The old-time readers were also used. We all admired the poem about the sailor boy whose name was Patrick Green, who said, "Would you know my story? I have been across the ocean blue and seen it in its glory." Most of the boys and girls used thumb-papers to protect their books. In the early schools the children were allowed to read and spell out and sometimes the schoolhouse would appear like a beehive with a general hum of variegated voices. We tried to see which could spell and read the loudest. W. H. Rice, who died forty years ago, was the champion in loud spelling.

Messic was king, and waved the scepter o'er Liberty's domain. What he said was law and gospel. He would read his rules every Monday morning, commencing first, second, and so on to the tenth rule. He backed up his rules with two keen switches, a large and a small one, which he placed in a rack over the door.

OLD LIBERTY CHURCH, IN 1900

The greatest attraction at school was recess and playtime. At twelve o'clock Messic would say, "Put by books for dinner." Then a general hustling commenced and continued until "books" was again called. After dinner was over, play commenced. The games were "Bull-pen," "Prisoner's Base," "Catball," "Andy Over," and marbles. The recess would last an hour. James F. Shelton, now in his seventy-seventh year, was the "fox" of the school. A number of boys would act as "hounds," and many a time they chased Shelton around through the woods, but never caught him.

Messic had a sweetheart, who lived about a half mile from Liberty, and sometimes after dinner he would make a call, and then our playtime would be extended. We were all glad to see Messic step off down the road, for we felt that we could do as we pleased during his absence.

How well I remember the old well that stood west of the house and near the road! It was nicely curbed up with stone. We used a pole and a sweep to draw water from its depths. There we often stood to drink of the fresh water from "the old oaken bucket, the iron-bound bucket, the moss-covered bucket that hung in the well." But now neither vestige nor sign of this old well can be seen.

On one occasion a man named Loving came to the Messic school. I remember him as well as if it had been yesterday. He was a middle-aged man with light hair and blue eyes; his face was considerably marked with smallpox. Messic called the school to order and Loving took out his watch and

RUINS OF OLD LIBERTY CHURCH, IN 1912

commenced his examination with the smallest pupil. He asked this small boy, "If you had this watch and should break it, to whom would you take it to get it fixed?" This he asked of some others. Most of them said that they did not know. Some answered that they would take it to the blacksmith; others said to the gunsmith or to the carpenter. Finally Loving came to a boy who had been listening and watching very earnestly. He asked the boy, "Son, if you had this watch and should break it, where would you take it to get it fixed?" The boy looked wise and smacked his mouth and said, "Well, sir, I would take it to God." "Oh, no," replied Loving, "you could not do that." This lad was the well-known C. Y. Shelton, who in 1864 moved to Arizona and who died at Pittsburgh, Pennsylvania, in 1887, and was buried at Old Liberty.

On another occasion during Messic's school, John Campbell, a mathematical genius of the country, came to Liberty, as we supposed, to test Messic's mathematical ability. Campbell stated several problems and asked

Messic to solve them. One of them was: "How large is that piece of land or section of country which, if fenced, the number of acres enclosed would be equal to the number of rails around it, the rails being ten feet long and laid ten rails high, and so placed that every two lengths of rails formed a pole of the boundary?" Messic said he did not think the problem could be solved. Campbell then figured it out and showed in what size tract it was that, under the specified conditions, the number of acres and the number of rails was just the same. Messic and all of us then saw that it could be done, and I, for one, have not forgotten it.

A novel event during Messic's time was the geography singing-school. A man named Burr came into the Liberty neighborhood and made up a class of about twenty scholars. It was a singing-school of geographical names. Burr had these names so classified and arranged that by giving them the proper accent and singing them to some familiar tune they would make interesting music as well as impress geographical names on the memory. Burr had a large chart which he used, and the pupils all had maps. In those days maps and geographies were printed in separate books. During the process of singing some of the mischievous girls, in calling out the names of some of the lakes, would substitute the name of Messic. For instance, instead of Lake Michigan they would sing "Lake Mr. Messic." This singing-school was taught Saturdays and Sundays. Messic was not a member of the singing class, but would attend as a spectator.

The young men of the neighborhood occasionally met to discuss different questions. However, Liberty was more frequently used as a meeting-place for singing classes. Such singing classes met during the summer season and sang according to the old four-note system called the fa, sol, la, me. These classes were kept up for many years. The songs were called "Montgomery," "Mt. Zion," "Edom," "Ocean," "Huntington," "Delight," and "Easter Anthem," and they were fine music. James W. Rice was the leader for many years. The books used were called the "Missouri" and "Southern Harmony." Sometimes the singers would bring their dinners and spend the day at Liberty. Uncle John Allison (who would rather sing bass than eat) was one of our best singers. Allison, Morton, and Buchannon gave us music equal to a brass band.

Many of the boys and girls with whom I went to school at Liberty have passed away. Some of them are scattered in other States; only a few are now living in the county, and they have reached their threescore years and ten. Soon after Liberty was built a graveyard was started near the church. This burying-ground has slowly increased, and now a number of the people of the neighborhood, including some of those who attended Liberty school and church during, before, or after my youth sleep within its confines.

My companion and I walked around in this graveyard and read the inscriptions on the tombstones. As we passed along I pointed out the unmarked grave of the Reverend Adlai Boyd, once a noted pioneer Cumberland Presbyterian preacher. He was born in the first years of the Nineteenth Century and spent fifty-odd years of his life in earnest devotion to the cause of the Christian religion. Boyd was an eloquent and impressive speaker and one of the ablest preachers that ever lived in the county. He was pastor of Liberty Church for some years. Many a time his clear and distinct voice rang out within and about Liberty Church, interesting and instructing many of those that are now slumbering with him in the dust of death. He lived northeast of Greenville, and was a man of some means. He owned a good farm of five hundred acres of land, underlaid with coal, which is now included in the Hillside coal holdings. He owned a house and lot in Greenville. His first wife was Joanna Cesna. They raised a good-sized

OLD LIBERTY BURYING-GROUND, 1912

family, consisting of four boys and three girls. His first wife died about 1864 and was buried in Liberty graveyard. Some years afterward Mr. Boyd married again and removed to Henderson. In the spring of 1882 he came to Greenville on a visit, took sick and died, and was buried at Liberty by the side of his first wife. He devoted his life to the betterment of his race, in persuading men and women to become allied to the Christian religion.

In 1902, when the Cumberland Presbyterians of Greenville tore down the old building that had been erected in 1848, they placed in their new building four memorial windows, one of which is "Sacred to the Memory of Adlai Boyd, First Pastor. Matthew 28:19." Few who now read his name in that window know that he was one of the most influential preachers of his day and that he is buried at Old Liberty.[2]

---

[2] The four memorial windows in the Cumberland Presbyterian Church of Greenville are in memory of—Adlai Boyd, first pastor; Mrs. Anna Allison Holmes, first organist; J. C. Howard, for twenty-one years superintendent of the Sabbath-school, and A. J. Martin, ruling elder.

XII

LIFE IN THE OLDEN DAYS

WHEN the first settlers came to look for homes in that portion of the State which is now Muhlenberg County they found the hills and valleys covered with one continuous forest. Gigantic oak, poplar, hickory, walnut, beech and many other species of hardwood trees flourished in great numbers, especially in the bottoms and valleys and on the north hillsides; tall pines stood on the cliffs overlooking Clifty Creek, and large cypresses shaded the banks of Black Lake. Little or no underbrush grew in this virgin forest. Men and women experienced no trouble in riding or walking under the trees. Wagons encountered few obstacles other than deep streams or steep hills.

The pioneers believed that the best land on which to settle was where good springs and running streams existed and where good timber for houses, fences, and fuel was plentiful. Wood and water they found here to their satisfaction, and in a territory they judged sufficiently large to provide them and their successors with "new ground" for many centuries. The supply of standing timber then seemed as inexhaustible as the water in the everlasting springs and ever-running streams. They did not imagine that the conservation of forests and the redeeming of the so-called "worn-out land" would, in less than a century, be among the problems of the day. Nor did they realize that they were treading on ground under which lay great deposits of coal, and that this coal would some day be developed and rank as the county's greatest natural resource.

The Indians had, for more than a century, given up this section of the State as a place of residence, but had not abandoned it as a hunting-ground until a short time before the first white men began making their settlements. The few red men who were seen by Muhlenberg's pioneers were in all probability rovers, belonging to no tribe at all. In the olden days deer, bear, turkeys, and other game were plentiful; wolves were numerous, and panthers, although comparatively few, were likely to be encountered at any time.

Such, in brief, was the wilderness into which the first-comers penetrated to open up a new country and to establish homes and fortunes for themselves and for their children. In this vast forest the pioneers made their clearings, erected their houses, raised their crops, cut their roads, built their churches, put up their courthouse, reared their families, and blazed the way for posterity.

The providing of food and shelter occupied the greater part of the time of the first-comers. Self-reliance became of necessity a strong characteristic.

Every family was thrown absolutely on its own resources, except in cases where two or more families came in a body and settled in the same place for mutual protection and assistance. Help of any and every kind was cheerfully given to neighbors; but neighbors were as a rule few, and in most cases the nearest lived several miles away. The men cultivated the crops, shot game for meat, and attended to what marketing there was of their scanty products. In the meantime the women not only performed the regular household duties, but also spun the yarn and flax and wove the cloth for most of the clothes then worn.

WHITE OAK　　　　　　　　　　YELLOW POPLAR

Trees like these two (oak six feet, poplar four feet in diameter) were numerous in the olden days. They are among the few giants still standing in the Upper Pond Creek country

As the number of newcomers increased, the exchange of labor and products became more frequent and more practical, and pleasure as well as profit brought about a more frequent commingling of the people. Business and social, religious, and educational intercourse not only led to an exchange of views but also to the broadening of ideas. Nearly every farm became not only a place for work but also a social center. Those who lacked an interest in social, religious, or educational affairs and avoided these gatherings soon deteriorated, no matter how great their accomplishments or how high their social standing might have been.

Neighbors intermarried, and as every neighborhood was in social touch with those surrounding it, all neighborhoods, in time, were linked together. The German-Americans in the northern and eastern part of the county, the Virginians in the middle section, extending from Green River to Pond River, and the Carolinians in the southern part, soon became more or less united into one settlement, with Greenville as its center. More than half of the citizens now living in Muhlenberg, who trace their ancestry to the pioneers of the county, are related, although in many cases this kinship has been lost sight of or is expressed in the vague term, "some sort of a cousin from way back."

The early settlers in the county were of various extraction. Most of them were German, English, Scotch, or Irish descent. But since environment plays a more important part in the development of a people than the nationality of their ancestors, and since in the early days all were under the influence of the same surroundings, conditions, and laws, the pioneers soon drifted more or less into the same way of living and into the use of the same language and the same local forms of expression. A few of the pioneers were Germans, and a number were German-Pennsylvanians and German-Virginians; but all traces of the old Vaterland customs and speech disappeared from Muhlenberg three or four generations ago. This change extended even to the spelling of the German names, most of them having been long since Americanized.

The Virginians and Carolinians of English, Scotch, and Irish extraction were more numerous than any other class of settlers, and their life, language, and laws prevailed to such an extent that their characteristics soon influenced the manners and customs of the entire population of the county. As time rolled on and new conditions presented themselves new customs slowly developed, and as the customs of colonial Virginia and the Carolinas that had long prevailed in Muhlenberg passed into the days gone by, there gradually developed another American people—Muhlenbergers—who were not only among the earliest of typical Kentuckians, but whose descendants, changing with the times, are typical Kentuckians of to-day.

A large portion of Virginia's military grants lay in Kentucky south of Green River. A number of the first-comers and other pioneers, consequently, were people who came to take possession of the military lands granted to them or to their fathers. Others traveled into this wilderness to buy offered tracts or to claim tracts they had bought. Some wandered here to settle on unclaimed public lands, or to "squat" on wild lands with a view of later obtaining a patent for their newly acquired farms. Some, stirred by the "call of the wild," came to hunt and fish. Others, drifting on the tide of adventure, indifferent about land or game, had—as a local expression puts it—"come to be a-coming."

Many who had land warrants located them, irrespective of any other claim, on any ground that seemed desirable, for the country had not been surveyed and "sectioned" by the government. As early as 1775 Richard Henderson proposed that the lines run on the territory claimed by the Transylvania Company be made "by the four cardinal points, except where rivers or mountains so intervene as to render it too inconvenient." The neglect of Virginia to provide for the general survey of Kentucky, and the failure of the pioneers to adopt Henderson's idea, resulted in complications all over the State, many of which are still unsettled.

Many of the settlers employed professional surveyors, but more often had the tracts they intended to occupy laid out according to their own notions, independent of their neighbors' lines. However, most of the pioneers did their own surveying. Some, it is said, "ran their lines with grapevines, using a portable knot-hole for a transit, the sun for a compass, and a dogwood saplin' for a flag-pole." In modern parlance, it was "the Eye-See Way." They, like the professional surveyors, also established courses by planting stones and pegs or by marking "a hickory on a hill," "a beech near a branch," or by blazing any convenient trees along a line or near a corner, or by following the meanderings of a stream. The old maps represent most of the military lines (lines bounding military grants) "as straight as an arrow," but many of such old lines are in reality, as one man expressed it, "as crooked as a dog's hind leg." The fact that many of these old calls can not be traced as originally run out has given rise to the report that the description of a certain line in the county reads, "from a ben' in a creek, thence a kinder south-like forty poles, more or less, to a nigger in a fiel'."

Mr. R. T. Martin, speaking of the pioneers, said:

"The first settlers of Muhlenberg County were people of nerve, enterprise, and industry. They braved the hardships and obstacles of a wild and unbroken forest. They came, stayed, and conquered, and laid the foundation for future greatness. We have many advantages over our forefathers; they had only about two over us. They had a wonderful range for stock. Pea-vines were knee-high all over the county, fast canebrakes stood in many places, and there was always an abundance of mast. On all these the horses, cattle, and hogs fared exceedingly well. The other advantage was in the abundance of game, which supplied them with much of their meat and leather.

"Most of the pioneers had apple and peach orchards. Many of the apple trees planted by them produced fruit for thirty years, and some as long as fifty years. Dried apples and dried peaches were a commodity with the old settlers. Their cider and vinegar have never been equaled. Their whisky, apple jack, and peach brandy, made at the various still-houses in the county, were according to all reports very fine.

"Their method of preparing meals was very different from that of today. Cooking was done in pots, skillets, and ovens around a large open wood fireplace. They beat and chopped their meat into sausage with cleaver and hammer made in the blacksmith shop.

"One of their great burdens was in their disadvantage as to transportation facilities. Most of the traveling was done afoot, on horseback, or in a public stage-coach. There were no two-horse wagons in those days. Ox-carts and ground-sleds were used for farm purposes. In nearly every neighborhood there were one or two six-horse wagons run by regular wagoners, who in the earliest times hauled much of the produce to shipping points on the Ohio River, but about the beginning of the Nineteenth Century, when Kincheloe's Bluff was made a landing-place, all produce for the outside world was sent there, and later, after South Carrollton was settled, all the hauling was to and from that point."

In the early days, and even until comparatively recent times, some of the farmers used a ground-sled or a "landslide" for short hauls. It was built on the principle of a sled, and so used during all seasons. The so-called "truck wagon" was also frequently seen in the olden days. Its wheels were discs sawed from a solid black gum log, and were about two and a half feet high. It was usually drawn by a yoke of oxen. The owner lubricated the axles with homemade soap before starting from his farm, but after driving two or three miles and allowing the wagon to stand in the sun for a few hours the lubricant would waste away. On his return home the screeching of the old wagon could be heard for more than half a mile.

Many of the pioneer families not only "killed" or raised their own leather but also made their own shoes and harness. They went to the tanyards to have the hides tanned. The process of tanning required almost a year, and although the tanner often had hundreds of hides in his tan-pits at one time, he could "tell any man's hide" in his tanyard. No matter how much the "unhairing" and other processes may have changed the original skin, he would return to each customer the identical hide that had been brought months before. In payment for his work the tanner usually received one third of the leather.

GROUND-SLED OR "LANDSLIDE"

Practically all the pioneers wore clothes that were made from homespun cloth. Flax was more or less extensively cultivated in the county until about 1850, but since 1870 this crop has not been raised. Flaxseed was usually sown on Good Friday. The plant cultivated in Muhlenberg was from two to three feet high, branching only near the top, and stood about as thick as wheat stalks. The harvesting began by pulling the plant out by the roots. It went through a number of processes before the fibre was finally separated from the "bone." The women, after spinning this fibre into thread, wove it into linen. Their linsey or linsey-woolsey was a homespun cloth made of home-grown linen and home-grown wool.

A few of the pioneers, some of their children, and even some of their grandchildren, experimented with the raising of cotton in Muhlenberg. The local cotton crop was usually a very small one, although it is said that on one or two occasions it was greater than the local demand.[1]

Speaking to me of the old days, Judge David J. Fleming said:

"I have often heard my father, Samuel C. Fleming, tell of an incident that took place about the year 1815, or shortly after my grandparents set-

---

[1] Up to 1900 Mrs. Cynthia B. (J. K.) Gary raised all the cotton she used in her quilts, and ginned it with a device that resembled and worked on the principle of a clothes-wringer. In 1847 John Staples built a small public cotton gin near Friendship. A few years later he sold it to Thos. Terry, who moved it three miles west of Greenville; although a number of people tried to raise cotton during the Civil War, not enough was produced to justify the running of the gin. In 1870 W. H. James moved the gin to near Pleasant Hill Church (Russell Old Field), and after three years' trial sold it to E. V. Tate, who transferred the rollers, sweep, and other parts back to the Friendship neighborhood, where they were used for various purposes.

tled in the Mud River country. Ammunition was scarce in those days, but game was plentiful and easily caught. My grandfather, David L. Fleming, had cleared a small field, in which he built a turkey-pen for the purpose of trapping wild turkeys. One day at dinner my grandfather told my father, then a boy of about ten, to go over to the turkey-pen after dinner and see whether any turkeys were in it. Shortly before supper father walked over to the pen, but found no turkeys nor any signs. On his return he followed a path through a strip of dense woods. Soon after entering the woods he heard a noise like a crying child. He glanced around, and seeing nothing rushed home and told his father, who was then in the blacksmith's shop at

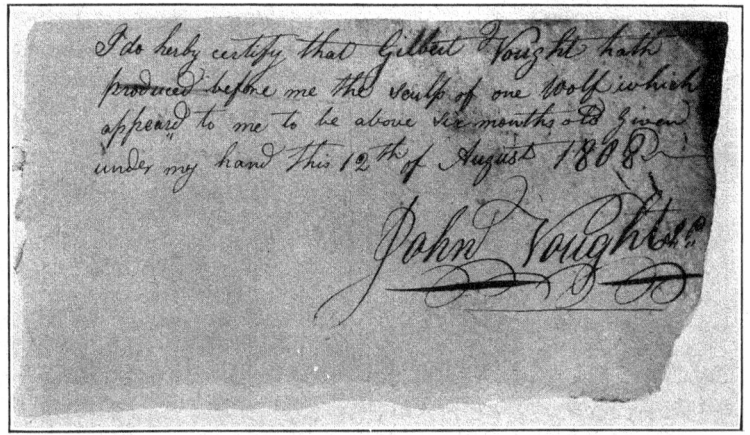

REDUCED FACSIMILE OF A "WOLF SCULP" CERTIFICATE

work. The old gentleman remarked that he had often heard a 'child' crying in the woods at night, but never before so early in the evening. Grandfather picked up his gun and followed the path leading to the turkey-pen. He entered the woods, looked and listened, and after hearing the expected cry hid himself behind a tree and from there mimicked the slowly approaching beast. When it came within safe shooting distance he blazed away and killed one of the largest 'Tom' panthers ever seen in Muhlenberg County. The animal measured eleven feet from the end of his nose to the tip of his tail. Although I was not born until about eighteen years later, I remember using this old panther skin for a pallet.''

No panthers have been seen in Muhlenberg since about the close of the Civil War, notwithstanding that even to this day reports are occasionally circulated that one had been seen, or rather heard, in the Clifty Creek country. Wolves, too, have long ago disappeared. The desire to exterminate wolves, and incidentally to receive the bounty paid for their scalps, resulted in a war on wolves that lasted as long as there were any to be killed. Any one producing the head of a wolf before a justice of the peace, stating under oath when and where he killed the animal, was granted a certificate to that effect. These certificates, upon presentation to the sheriff, were paid for at the rate of two dollars and a half for wolves over six months of age and one dollar for those under that age. A reduced facsimile of one of these certificates is here reproduced.²

Great flocks of wild pigeons or passenger pigeons frequented Muhlenberg in the olden days. Up to about 1850 they were, on occasions, seen in great numbers passing over the country while moving from place to place or at some of the pigeon-roosts in various parts of the county. Since about 1860 none have been seen at all. That "they came by the millions and were killed with clubs by the thousands," and that while flying over the country "they hid the sun even more than the blackest cloud" and "turned day into night" is verified by many local traditions. Amos M. Jenkins, now eighty years of age, declares that wild pigeon meat was better than the best quail. One tradition is to the effect that in the olden times some of the farmers near Paradise fattened their hogs on them. A few places in the Pond River country and along Green River are still pointed out as old pigeon-roosts. However, all evidences of the presence of pigeons have long ago disappeared.³

PASSENGER OR WILD PIGEONS
1. Male. 2. Female.
(From a drawing by Audubon)

---

² In a bundle of old documents marked "Medley of papers" in the courthouse I found many "wolf-sculp" certificates. Four, selected at random, read:

"March 4th, 1800. This day came Jacob Wiley before me, one of the Justices of the Peace of Muhlenberg County and brought a wolf's head which appears over the age two years and took the oath prescribed by law. Given under my hand. Isaac Davis."

"I hereby do Certify that Sharp Garness Brought before me a Justice of thee peace for Muhlenberg County four Groan Wolf Sculps and proved them as the Law directs. Given under My hand thee 27 day of August 1800. W. Bradford, J. P."

"October the 7th 1805. Jacob Groves produced one grown woolfe skulp to me and proved it as the law directs. Charles Lewis, J. P."

"Muhlenberge Countey. This day about 2 o'clock I killed a large wolf and Jacob Short witness. November 23, 1805. Joseph Arnold, Sener."

³ Audubon, in his work on "Birds of America," publishes a sketch on The Passenger Pigeon (Vol. V, pp. 25-36). In this he relates that on one occasion in the autumn of 1813 he saw "immense legions" of wild pigeons passing over the country near the mouth of Salt River, and that they continued "passing in undiminished numbers . . . for three days in succession." "The air was literally filled with pigeons; the light of noonday was obscured as by an eclipse."

In this same sketch he says that he repeatedly visited one of the roosting-places "on the banks of Green River in Kentucky." This particular roosting place was probably near the mouth of Green River, for there "two farmers from the

Probably the first store opened in the county was the one started by pioneers James Weir and James Craig in Greenville in 1799. After a time they dissolved partnership and James Weir and Oliver C. Vanlandingham conducted the store. In the course of a few years they dissolved partnership. Weir continued the business in Greenville, and Vanlandingham returned to his large farm near Paradise. Much of the merchandise brought from the East by old James Weir was exchanged for wild pork, rawhides, produce, and tobacco. These he shipped to New Orleans on flatboats, where he sold them for cash, with which he bought more goods in Philadelphia.

Harry Weir has in his possession an old ledger kept from 1813 to 1815 by James Weir, his great-grandfather, whose store at that time had already been moved from the log house on the west side of Main Street to the brick building on the opposite side and a little farther north, on what is now and has been for a century known as the Weir corner. South of the brick store and facing Main Street he erected, about the year 1816, a brick residence. Both houses are still standing, and are among the county's most interesting landmarks.

This ledger of long ago gives us some facts and figures pertaining to the olden times. It is a book about sixteen inches long, six inches wide, and more than two inches thick. Although its leather covers and its five hundred pages show their age, both are remarkably well preserved. The penmanship is good, and evidently by one Jacob Zimmerman. It contains the accounts of three hundred and twenty people, all of whom probably lived in Muhlenberg at the time the transactions took place. The first entry is dated August 5, 1813, and the last was made in August, 1815. All prices and

vicinity of Russellville, distant more than a hundred miles, had driven upwards of three hundred hogs to be fattened on the pigeons, which were to be slaughtered . . . The pigeons, arriving by the thousands [shortly after sunset], alighted everywhere, one above another until solid masses were formed on the branches all around. Here and there the perches gave way under the weight with a crash, and, falling on the ground, destroyed hundreds of the birds beneath, forcing down the dense groups with which every stick was loaded. . . . Thousands were knocked down by the polemen. . . . The pigeons were constantly coming, and it was past midnight before I perceived a decrease in the number of those that arrived. . . . No one dared venture within the line of devastation. The hogs had been pent up in due time. . . . The dead, the dying, and the mangled . . . pigeons were picked up and piled in heaps [the next morning] until each had as many as he could possibly dispose of, when the hogs were let loose to feed on the remainder."
In his minute description of the adult male, Audubon says: "Length 16¼ inches, extent of wings 25 inches. . . . Bill black. Iris bright red. Feet carmine purple, claws blackish. Head above and on the sides light blue. Throat, fore-neck, breast, and sides, light brownish red, the rest of the under parts white. Lower part of the neck behind and along the sides, changing to gold, emerald-green, and rich crimson. The general color of the upper parts is grayish-blue, some of the wing-coverts marked with a black spot. Quills and larger wing-coverts blackish, the primary quills bluish on the outer web, the larger coverts whitish at the tip. The two middle feathers of the tail black, the rest pale blue at the base, becoming white towards the end."
The adult female: "Length 15 inches; extent of wings 23 inches. . . . The colors of the female are much duller than those of the male, although their distribution is the same. The breast is light greyish-brown, the upper parts pale reddish-brown, tinged with blue."

totals are in English pounds, shillings, and pence, except the few connected with Eastern houses, the post-office, and one pertaining to the sale of a slave, which are in dollars and cents. English money as a medium of valuation passed out of use in Muhlenberg shortly after 1815, and the dollar, which had been more or less extensively adopted as a standard since the days of the first settlers, became the sole standard in all financial transactions. The slave referred to was "one negro woman, Leah," bought on December 5,

"THE WEIR CORNER," GREENVILLE, ERECTED 1812, AS IT APPEARS TO-DAY

1814, for $350, by Jesse Murphy, who paid about half in cash and the balance in "pork and lard." To-day the value of a pound sterling is a little less than five dollars, a shilling twenty-five cents, and an English penny two cents. However, the calculations in this ledger indicate that at the time of these accounts the value of a pound was about three dollars, which made the shilling fifteen cents and the penny a little more than one cent. The entries here given are copied verbatim and show the prices charged for goods. The first column represents the number of pounds, the second shillings, and the third pence. The items are taken at random and are confined to single purchases, for when more than one article was bought the entry was transferred from the day book and the total recorded in the ledger as either "merchentdise" or "sundries." Among the hundreds of single items are the following:

LIFE IN THE OLDEN DAYS

	Pounds	Shillings	Pence
4 lbs. sugar	0	6	0
1 lb. coffee	0	3	0
½ lb. Imperial tea	0	10	6
1 peck salt	0	4	1
7 bu. corn	0	10	6
1 qt. wine	0	9	0
½ gal. whisky	0	3	0
1 qt. rum	0	6	0
½ lb. alum	0	1	1
1 dose calomel	0	1	1
1 bx. Antibillious Pills	0	1	6
1 bx. Itch Ointment	0	2	0
4 lbs. logwood	0	6	0
1 fine shawl	1	4	0
5 yds. calico	1	13	9
5 yds. muslin	0	11	13
1 wool hat	0	7	6
1 fine hat	1	10	0
1 fine hat to S. W.	2	14	0
3 yds. country linen	0	9	0
1 yd. crape	0	18	0
2 yds. flannel	0	18	0
1 paper pins	0	3	0
1 fine pair socks	0	6	0
1 handkerchief	0	3	0
1 pr. cotton cards	0	15	0
1 pr. wool cards	0	7	6
1 ax	0	16	0
1 carving knife	0	6	0
1 pen knife	0	3	9
1 mill saw	2	14	0
1 cythe blade	0	15	0
2 hoes	0	15	0
1 door lock	1	1	0
1 lb. nails	0	1	6
1 bridle bit	0	3	9
1 pr. saddle bags	1	6	3
1 fine woman's saddle	5	8	0
1 fine man saddle	4	4	0
1 pr. shoes	0	9	0
1 pr. boots	3	12	0
1 thimble	0	0	9
1 pr. specks	0	6	0
1 gun lock	1	13	0
1 dozen flints	0	2	3
1 skillit	0	12	0
1 spelling book	0	1	6
1 hymn book	0	6	0
1 Esop's Fables	0	2	3
2 vols. British Poets	0	11	3
1 Bible	1	1	0
1 quire paper	0	2	3

Tobacco was the principal crop raised for the market, and was in many es the source of most of the farmer's "cash." According to the Weir ger the price paid for tobacco in 1813 and 1814 varied from twelve to fifa shillings per hundred pounds. The account kept with George Davis ws that he bought merchandise and also received cash at various times, all of which he received credit as follows:

"August 27, 1813. By 3687 lbs. tobacco at 12 s. £22 2 s. 6 d.
March 19, 1814. " 1949 " " " " £11 19 s. 10 d."

Benjamin Coffman is credited with "Four hogs, tobacco weighing 4954 15 s.=£37, s. 1½ d."

Samuel Dukes is credited with "3734 lbs. tobacco at 12 s.=£22, 8 s. d."

Four others sold their tobacco to Weir—Thomas Hesper, Edmond Hopas, Benjamin Johnson, and Christian Peters.

Comparatively few men settled their bills by paying the actual cash. A umber of pioneers bought large quantities of goods and in many cases paid r them with some of their home products. From among the various credit ems I gather the following:

David Campbell is credited with among other things: "By 121½ gallons whisky, £22, 15 s. 7 d." and "By Four barrels to hold it, £1, 4 s."

James Corder: "By a spinning wheel, £1, 4 s."

Abraham Dennis: "By 550 lbs. pork, £4, 2 s. 6 d."

Leroy Jackson, on December 23, 1814: "By 6¼ lbs. butter, 4 s. 9 d."

John January is credited: "By one buro, £5, 8 s."; "By letter box, 6 s. d."; "By hinges, 1 s. 6 d."; "By Framing two pictures, Perry and Lawence, 9 s."; " By Mending wagon, 12 s."; "By one dressed deer skin, 6 s."

Alney McLean's account has among its credit items: "By cash and pork, 22, 2 s. 10 d.'"; "By Fees up to this date, £14, 5 s."; "By cash, £39, s. 9 d."

Presley Pritchett is frequently credited, "By 12 wool hats, £4, 1 s."; 'By working over my hat, 4 s. 6 d."

Thomas Pollard: "By one dose calomel, 1 s."

Ezekiel Rice: "By black smith bill, £2, 18 s. 9 d."

John E. H. Rogers: "By ½ doz. razor strops, 10 s. 6 d."

Mathias Zimmerman: "By one boat, £30"; and "By one 40 foot boat, £24."

Henry Phillips and Thomas Glenn are each credited: "By Orleans voyage, £3."

Jeremiah Langley is credited for trips to Lewisburg and Hopkinsville and trips from Shawneetown and Henderson. William McCommons evidently made a number of trips between Greenville and Shawneetown. David Robison made a number of trips to and from Lewisburg.

In the older days many of the people exchanged their products for various things in the store, just as butter, eggs, poultry, etc., are now exchanged by some farmers for articles sold by the merchants.

Abraham Dennis exchanged "chickens" for "one oz. barks, 3 s."

Michael Lovell exchanged "11 yards linnen" for "one fine dressed bonnet, £1, 3 s."

James McCown exchanged "12 lbs. sugar" for "one wool hat, 12 s."
George Miller exchanged "feathers" for "Ballance spoon, 4 s. 6 d."
Matthew Rice's account is debited: "Sundries, per his mother," and credited "By midwife fees, 13 s. 4½ d."
Charles Vincent exchanged "Five yards linnen, full," for "Sundries, 10 s."

SOME OLD CHIMNEYS
1. Chimney in David Whitmer house, near Bremen, built 1832.
2. Rough rock chimney in John Wright house, near Carter's Creek Church, built 1810. Erected against a rib-roofed wall.
3. Stick and dirt chimney in Starling Duke house, near Weir, built 1865.
4. One of Alfred Johnson's dressed rock chimneys, in "The Stack House." Most of the old chimneys are of this type.
5. Brick chimney in old James Weir house, Greenville, built 1816.

These items give a wonderfully intimate glimpse into the everyday life of these people and let us see, as it were, in actuality how they lived.

A grist mill was regarded by some of the pioneers as a greater necessity than a store, a courthouse, or a professional physician. Corn was the first crop raised by the pioneers, and has been one of the principal products ever since. Cornmeal was the pioneer's most essential food. Going to mill to have the corn ground was always looked forward to with great expectancy, for the mill was, in olden days and even until recent times, the best place to hear the latest news. Every farmer had occasion to go or send to the mill many times during the course of a year, for he usually took no more than a bushel or two of corn or wheat at a time. As a rule the bag into which the grain had been placed was thrown across the horse's back and used by the rider as a saddle.

All the mills in the olden days were run by water-power or horse-power. When wheat was ground it was bolted by hand-power. Grinding was a slow process, and men were obliged to remain around the mill until their "turn" was ground. This time was usually spent in hearing and telling the news. Every man waited and got his cornmeal or flour from the grain he took to mill. Now he can get his "turn" without delay by taking some of the "grinding" that is carried in stock by the miller.

Reverend G. W. Ford, writing to me about the old Staples Mill in the Friendship neighborhood, says:

"My grandfather, J. B. Staples, ran a horse-power mill in which wheat and corn were ground. Across the road he ran his turning lathe and cotton gin. It would take from an hour to an hour and a half to grind a bushel of corn. I remember hearing him tell of a little incident that occurred at his mill one day. A tall, bony young man, always hungry, rode to the mill and being a little late quite a number of turns were ahead of him, so he had to wait until his time came. It was late in the afternoon when his corn was poured into the hopper. While it was being ground he stood at the meal spout and caught the fresh meal in his hand and ate it as it came slowly from the burrs. Grandfather watched the young fellow for quite a while and then asked him, 'How long could you eat that meal?' and he answered, 'Until I starved to death!' "[4]

Preparing corn for the mill was a comparatively simple affair. After it had been gathered and sufficiently well dried it was shucked and then taken to the mill, either on the cob or off. Wheat, however, in the olden days required a more complicated process. The wheat was cut in the field with the old-fashioned scything cradle and then either bunched or swathed on the ground. This was done by one man. Another man followed, binding the wheat into bundles as fast as it was cut. Two good hands could cut and shock about seventy-five shocks a day. These shocks stood in the field until

---

[4] Laborn Ford, the father of Reverend G. W. Ford, was born in North Carolina in 1811, settled in Muhlenberg in 1839, and died near Friendship in 1897.

In 1840 Laborn Ford married Lucy Ann Staples, daughter of John Burton Staples, who was born in Virginia in 1785, came to Muhlenberg in 1835, and died near Friendship in 1867. The Staples Mill, near Friendship, disappeared many years ago, but the farm on which it stood is still known as the Old Mill Place.

Mr. and Mrs. Laborn Ford were the parents of Mrs. Virginia Ann (David M.) Durham, Mrs. Arritta (J. B.) Browning, John Laborn, Samuel Henry, Reverend George William, James Riley, Napoleon Monroe, and Laborn ("Sonny") Ford.

Reverend G. W. Ford was born in 1853 and married Susan Eliza Allen, daughter of William Booker Allen, who came to Muhlenberg in 1845, raised eighteen children, and died near Friendship in 1900, aged eighty-six.

they were thoroughly dry. They were then hauled and stacked near a plot of level ground. When the time came to separate the wheat from the straw and chaff, the farmer would decide on one of two processes.

Following one method, he built a rail pen, some three feet high and near to his wheat stack. He covered the top of this enclosure with other rails laid side by side, and then placed some of the wheat from the stack on this platform of rails, laying the heads close together and all in one way or direction. Then he proceeded to flail out the grain on the pen with a hickory pole about eight feet long and the thickness of an average man's wrist. The farmer had previously prepared this pole by beating a wide band around it about two feet from the end, which was done with an ax or hammer, to make the stick bend easily without breaking. With this limber-ended pole

A HOG HARVEST ON THE ALVIN L. TAYLOR FARM, 1910

he flailed out his wheat by striking heavily on the bundles. This knocked out the grain, which then fell to the ground through the cracks between the rails.

In following the other method the farmer took a hoe and scraped off the top of a level piece of ground and formed a circular space some twenty or twenty-five feet in diameter. He made the ground inside the circle perfectly level and smooth and tamped it down as solidly as possible. The dirt scraped off was banked up in the shape of a circus ring around the prepared yard. Then the farmer took enough of the sheaves from the stack to make a batch. The bundles were laid down as closely as possible, with the heads pointing toward the center of the ring and the butt-ends against the ridge. When this outer row was laid, another was made by turning the butts toward the center of the circle and lapping the heads just over the heads of the first layer. This left a space of from eight to ten feet in the center of the yard, which was reserved for the purpose of piling the grain. The farmer now brought two horses into the ring, put a boy on one, and let him lead the other. The horses walked around and around until they had "tramped" out the grain. They were then led out, the straw was raked away and thrown on the outside of the circular ridge, and the grain and chaff were piled in the center of the yard. This process was repeated until all the wheat had been "tramped out."

After the farmer separated the grain by either of these two processes he ran it through a wheat fan. This fan was something like the one now used for cleaning wheat preparatory to sowing it, except that it was much larger and more heavily built. The wheat and chaff were thrown into the hopper of the machine, which was run by a crank turned by one man. This work was kept up until all the wheat was fanned out, sacked, and stored away. The grain was still mixed with more or less chaff, but this was then the only way they had to clean it.

Some of the old-style mills were run for many years; others were in operation only a short time. Some were well known, others were not. Among the comparatively few that are still occasionally recalled in local traditions are Tom Wagoner's Mill, at Findley's Ford on Long Creek; Hancock's Mill, on lower Long Creek; Thompson's or Green's Mill, near the mouth of Long Creek; McKinney's Mill and Reno's Mill, on upper Pond River; Clark's Mill, above Harpe's Hill; Morgan's Mill, near the mouth of Isaac's Creek; Tiding's Mill or Needham's Mill, on Pond River near Millport; Turner's Mill, on Log Creek; Calvert's Mill, near Black Lake; Morehead's Horse Mill, near what is now Central City; Weir's Mill, on Caney Creek; Leonard Stum's Mill, above Paradise; Henry Stum's Mill, in Paradise, later known as Kirtley's Mill; the Ely Smith Mill, on Pond Creek near Paradise, which was established in 1796 and a few years later became the Elias Smith Mill, and in 1850 the Smith Brothers Mill, by which name it was known until 1896, when it quit running; Haden's Mill, in Paradise; Brewer's Mill at the mouth of Mud River; Forgy's Mill and Barr's Mill, on Mud River; Taggart's Mill, near Hazel Creek Church; Staples Mill, near Friendship; Martin's Mill, on Jarrell's Creek, and Cooksey's Mill, on Clifty Creek.

Other water and horse mills were erected in various parts of the county, but all, with the exception of Cooksey's Mill, have either been abandoned or have been replaced by small steam saw mills, most of which are now prepared to grind corn on Saturdays. However, the greater part of the flour and cornmeal now consumed in the county is ground at the few steam mills, that run every day and confine their work to the grinding of wheat and corn.

In 1848 Edward R. Weir, sr., set up the first steam mill. It was a saw and grist mill, built on the banks of Caney Creek about a mile and a half north of Greenville, on what is now called the Central City Road. A number of other steam mills were established shortly after.

Cooksey's Mill, the only survivor of the old-time grist mills, was started about the year 1810 by Alexander McPherson and some of his neighbors, who built an overshot wheel and ran a mill on the site that has ever since been used for "grinding." They were succeeded by Henry Myers, who converted the wheel into an undershot. Shortly after the Civil War the original building was torn down and a new house erected with a turbine waterwheel. Cooksey's Mill still grinds at least once a week. Now, as in years gone by, "turns" are carried there and are paid for in "toll." Cooksey's

Mill and other grist mills of old, like "the mills of God," though they grind slowly, "yet they grind exceeding small"—and exceeding well. The old-fashioned stone burrs still work in the old-fashioned way, grinding out the old-fashioned cornmeal by slowly crushing the grain, without heating and robbing the meal of its natural flavor.

In the olden days, as now, Greenville was the center of the county from a business and social standpoint as well as from a geographical standpoint.

COOKSEY'S MILL, ON CLIFTY CREEK, OLDEST IN THE COUNTY

From its beginning it was the county seat. The courthouse and Russell's Tavern, both of which were of logs, formed the nucleus of the new town of Greenville. The town was slow of growth. It is probable that not only the small population of the county but the lack of good roads limited the early development of the county seat. Then, as now, all roads in the county led directly or indirectly to Greenville, but then, more than now, the roads were wellnigh impassable at some seasons of the year, and it was no easy matter to get into or out of the county seat. Except in the Long Creek country and south of it there is no stone suitable for road building, and the problem of good wagon-roads was therefore a serious one for the pioneers, and is still for the citizens of to-day. The streets of Greenville were unpaved mud roads.

In 1800, according to the census report, Greenville's population was 26; in 1810 it was 75, and in 1830 it had grown to 217. In 1830 there were probably fewer than forty residences, business houses, and mechanic's shops in the town. The location of some of these was, according to tradition, as follows:

The John January house was near the southwest corner of Main and Hopkinsville streets. The homes of Ezias Earl and John Walker were on the south side of Hopkinsville Street. Edward Rumsey then lived on the west side of Main Street near Hopkinsville Street. James Weir's store and his residence stood where they are still standing, on Main Street south of the courthouse. On the west side of Main Street, opposite Weir's store, stood his tobacco and storage house. On the northwest corner of the public square, not far from the log courthouse, stood the "old brick bank" building.

Among the houses on Main Street opposite the courthouse, facing its main entrance, were Russell's Tavern and a few stores. Isaac Bard lived on the northwest corner of Main and Main Cross streets. Doctor Robert D. McLean's office was on Main Street a little north of Bard's. Opposite Doctor McLean lived Doctor Thomas Pollard. North of Pollard's house was a wool-carding factory. On Main Cross Street, near where the Y. M. C. A. now stands, lived Alney McLean. A short distance north of McLean's house, near a good spring, was a tanyard. The Charles Fox Wing home was on the southeast corner of Main Cross and Cherry streets. Across the street and west of Captain Wing's home was the home of his brother, John Wing. On the east side of Cherry Street, a few hundred feet north of Main Cross Street, stood the Greenville Seminary, and near it a small graveyard. About two hundred yards east of Weir's store stood the Presbyterian Church. E. M. Brank lived about a half mile from town on the west side of the Rumsey road, and about a half mile farther down this road was Weir's Mill on Caney Creek.

Although the county's leading lawyers, physicians, and merchants lived in Greenville and were extensively identified with the growth of the county seat and the development of the county, they were by no means the only prominent men in Muhlenberg in the olden days. In the Pond River country, the "Dutch Settlement," the Green River and the Long Creek countries, as well as in and around Greenville, there lived many men who were in their day among the county's most intelligent and influential citizens.

Samuel Russell was Greenville's first postmaster. He was appointed April 1, 1801, and served until October 1, 1809, when he was succeeded by Parmenas Redman. Later James Weir became postmaster at Greenville. It was at Weir's store that for many years the pioneers received and sent their mail. Weir's store was for more than half a century the principal headquarters for Muhlenberg men and women who had things to buy, sell, or exchange. Among their many customers were old Revolutionary soldiers and men who had fought in the War of 1812.

Such business as must be transacted in the courthouse made it necessary for many people living in and out of the county to frequent the log "Temple of Justice." Of those who were compelled to remain in town many were the guests of friends; others stopped at the Russell Tavern. All, no matter whose guests they might be while in town, congregated during a few hours each day at the Russell Tavern or "The Hog Eye" tippling house. There they not only heard the news from other sections of the county and the outside world, but also had many opportunities to quench their thirst.

Practically every man and woman living "out in the county" had occasion, or at least a desire, "to go to town" one or more times during the year. Some went for business, some for pleasure, some for "business and pleasure combined." Many arranged to make their trips to town on county court days. In the olden times county court days were "big days" in Greenville, and are such even to this day. Then as now, of the number of people who went to Greenville on county court day only a few had court business to attend to. Some went to trade, some to meet friends and discuss business or social matters with them, some to "swap" horses, and some "to see what was going on."

Other meetings, besides those that took place in Greenville, around the mills and in the stores, offered the pioneers an opportunity to intermingle. Public speakings, militia musters, picnics on the Fourth of July, and, after the battle of New Orleans (January 8, 1815), the celebrations on the eighth of January, brought together many people from all parts of the county. House-raisings, log-rollings, hog-killings, quiltings, wedding celebrations, harvesting, hunting, fishing, shooting-matches, frolics, dances, fiddlers' contests, and racing, also, served as a blender of the early settlers. However, churches and baptizings, camp-meetings and buryings, brought them in closer and more intimate touch with each other than any other form of gathering.

Many of the first-comers were more interested in religion than in any other one subject. Their fathers and many of the pioneers themselves were Revolutionary soldiers, and had fought for political and religious liberty. Liberty stood foremost among their thoughts and deeds. Thus the church established by the pioneers near Murphy's Lake was called by them New Liberty—now known as Old Liberty. They were willing to continue to devote their time and fortunes, and even to sacrifice life itself, for the liberty that had been won not many years before. A spirit of altruism prevailed in those days. The patriotic pioneer did not dream of the probability of an age of dollars—an age characterized by its selfish men who with little thought of honor or justice accumulate or try to accumulate a fortune, and look on the making of money as the only victory in life. When in 1812, and again fifty years later, volunteers were called for, men responded with a patriotic spirit and unselfish motive.

To the pioneer the Bible was as symbolic of political and religious liberty as was the Flag.[5] Those who could read were sure to read the Bible often. In the beginning, when as a rule farms were far apart and church

---

[5] Mrs. James Duvall, of Greenville, a great-granddaughter of pioneer Samuel Allison, has in her possession a Bible published in 1815 by M. Carey, Philadelphia. It is a large, well-printed volume, bound in calf. It was published by subscription, and in it are given the names of the subscribers (about six hundred and fifty) then living in Kentucky, Ohio, Illinois, and other sections of the West. The fact that these men subscribed for a Bible of this character indicates that they were men who appreciated good books and could afford to buy expensive volumes. Eighteen Muhlenberg men appear among the names of the subscribers to this Bible: "Samuel Allison, John Bone, William Campbell, Hugh Carter, B. Coffman, W. Campbell, Abraham Dennis, Samuel Drake, John January, I. Langlis, Job Matthews, Solomon Rhodes, D. H. Stephens, Thomas Salisbury, James Wier, Charles F. Wing, Lewis Webb, J. Zimmerman."

houses, in most locations, were impracticable, religious exercises were held in turn in the homes of the pioneers. These services were conducted in English. In some homes there were no Bibles other than German—copies that had been brought by the German-American pioneers—nevertheless the services were conducted in English. Henry Rhoads, it is said, frequently addressed audiences and read chapter after chapter from a German Bible, translating them into English with more grace and rapidity than some of his contemporaries who on other occasions read a Bible printed in English.

Hazel Creek Baptist Church was organized December 3, 1798, and was the first church organized in the county. This is not only the first but also the oldest church organization in Muhlenberg. Furthermore, it is the only church in the county of which a history has been published. In 1898 Professor William J. Johnson, who then lived near Wells, printed a seventy-page pamphlet entitled "History of Hazel Creek Baptist Church." This church, like many of the other early churches, became the mother of other organizations. Relative to the twelve churches originating from Hazel Creek, Professor Johnson says:

"In 1799, twelve members were authorized 'to continue an arm at George Clark's, on the west side of Pond Creek,' which doubtless led to the formation of Nelson Creek church, June 10, 1803. June 1, 1805, eighteen members were dismissed from Hazel Creek church to form Midway church, now Monticello. August 2, 1806, eighteen members were dismissed to form what is now Cave Spring, near Pond river, on the road from Greenville to Hopkinsville. Cypress church, McLean county, was formed from this church in 1808. Antioch, Todd county, was formed from this church, and also Whippoorwill church in the year 1819. May 6, 1820, the arm known as Hebron (now Mt. Vernon) was made a constituted body. In 1840, thirteen members from this church formed new Hebron church (Muhlenberg). Ebenezer was organized with twenty-six members from this church, January 3, 1851. Macedonia was formed from this church on November 22, 1856. New Hope church (Muhlenberg) was formed of material mostly from this church, in 1858; but is now extinct. Sugar Grove was constituted with twenty-five members, mostly from this church, in January, 1873."

It may be well to add that the Hazel Creek congregation built its first house in 1800, its second in 1807, and its third in 1857, all of which were of logs. Its fourth (the present) building was erected in 1906.

Mount Olivet (three miles northeast of Central City) is probably the oldest Methodist church in Muhlenberg. Mount Zion (one mile east of Central City) is among the oldest Presbyterian organizations. Although Mount Zion was organized as early as about 1802, the congregation, it is said, did not erect its first house until about twenty years later. As a rule, the church houses built by the pioneers were union churches—that is, buildings erected jointly by two or more denominations, who conducted their services independently of one another. In Greenville, up to about 1825, the academy building served the purposes of a school and a union church. As far as I have been able to ascertain, the Presbyterians of Greenville were the first in that town to erect a building of their own. I tried to procure data relative to the early history of all the old churches in the county, but an investigation showed that in only a few cases had the old church records been preserved.

In religion, as well as in politics and business, the pioneers of Muhlenberg were always conservative. The "Great Revival" of the first part of the last century, that spasmodically stirred what was then called the West, did not throw many of the people of Muhlenberg into "jerks" and other mysterious "exercises." In Kentucky its effect was felt more in the southern and central sections of the State.

HAZEL CREEK BAPTIST CHURCH, ERECTED 1906

This "Great Revival" began in Logan County in 1799, under the ministry of John McGee, of the Methodist church, and his brother William McGee, of the Presbyterian, and soon spread over the State. Tradition says that the local men and women who had gone to Logan and Christian counties to attend these great camp-meetings were the only ones affected by the "exercises."

Reverend Barton W. Stone (who married Elizabeth Campbell, daughter of Colonel William Campbell) in his "Autobiography," published in 1844, says that while at Greenville in July, 1801, he heard of the wonderful things taking place at some of the revivals in other sections of Kentucky. He and his wife "hurried from Muhlenberg" immediately after they were married, and went to Cane Ridge, Bourbon County, to see and study the extraordinary phenomena. His description of the "bodily agitations" is the best that has been written. Had any of these "exercises" taken place in Muhlenberg he in all probability would have stated the fact in his book.

Peter Cartwright in his "Autobiography," published in 1856, also gives an interesting account of these revivals, but refers to Muhlenberg only once. Commenting on the widespread effect of one of his great camp-meetings held some time during the year 1812, while he was riding the "Christian circuit," so named after Christian County, he says (page 122): "From this meeting a revival spread almost through the entire country round, and great additions were made to the Methodist church. This circuit was large, embracing parts of Logan, Muhlenberg, Butler, Christian and Caldwell counties in Kentucky and parts of Montgomery, Dixon and Stewart counties in Tennessee."

It is more than probable that Peter Cartwright conducted a number of meetings in Muhlenberg. Tradition, however, tells of only one place where he did so—the Old Camp Ground, located north of Cleaton and near the Greenville and Seralvo Road. Tradition has it that he preached there not only once but often, and that all his meetings were well attended. One of Peter Cartwright's personal friends and disciples in Muhlenberg was Reverend Silas Drake, one of the best-known local Methodist preachers and circuit riders, and of whom the following characteristic incident is related:

Preacher Drake was opposed to the wearing of things that were more ornamental than useful, declaring that such apparel was indicative of pride, and that "ear bobs are the devil's stirrups." One day, while addressing a crowd at an arbor meeting, he observed a woman with large bows of ribbon on her bonnet. He called her by name, reproved her, and told her that such bows were of absolutely no use. She, without hesitating, retaliated by saying, "Neither are the buttons on your coat sleeves or on the back of your coat!" He immediately pulled off his coat, cut off the buttons referred to, and never afterward wore a coat with buttons sewed on the sleeves or back.[6]

No matter whether affected permanently, temporarily, or not at all by the "Great Revival" or any other revivals, all of the early settlers exercised more or less influence over their contemporaries and descendants. However, it is an indisputable fact that many, if not most, of the good influences exerted by the early settlers were due directly or indirectly to the work of the women of the community. Written records as well as local traditions fail to give the women who lived in the olden days the credit they deserve for their moral and religious influence. They always showed courage on trying occasions. They were the doctors of the times, and in some instances the sole preservers of hard-earned homes or farms.

---

[6] Reverend Silas Drake was a son of pioneer Albritton Drake, a Revolutionary soldier who settled in southern Muhlenberg in 1806, where he died in 1834. Albritton Drake married Ruth Collins. They, as already stated, were the parents of Reverend Silas, Mosley Collins, Reverend Benjamin, J. Perry, Edmond, and William. Reverend Silas, Mosley Collins, and Edmund Drake married daughters of pioneer Micajah Wells. Reverend Silas Drake was born in 1790 and married Patsy Wells; he preached for a half century, and in the meantime farmed in the Long Creek country, where he died in 1858. J. Perry Drake married Priscilla Buell, who was a sister of General Don Carlos Buell's father. The parents of General Buell died while he was still a child, and the rearing and educating of young Buell was assumed by his uncle and aunt, Mr. and Mrs. J. Perry Drake, who were then living in Indianapolis. J. Perry Drake was a Mexican War soldier and a well-known Indiana lawyer. One of his daughters, Elmira Drake, became the wife of General W. T. H. Brooks of the Federal army.

In the olden days, as now, the foundation of the career of every man and woman depended largely on the training received in youth from his or her mother. The control of many mothers was confined to their own family fireside, where while also attending to their domestic duties they were not only mothers to their children but often assumed the duties of schoolteacher. In many cases the mother, a grandmother, or an aunt was the only guide through the "three R's" the child of an early settler ever knew. The

SECTION OF THE NEWMAN GRAVEYARD, FOUR MILES EAST OF GREENVILLE
The three stone box-grave covers in the foreground are "coffin-shaped"; the other two are "box-shaped"

influence of some mothers was felt far beyond their own home and neighborhood. Local public schools were few and far between. Post-primary schools were not established until the middle of the last century.

Among the best known and one of the noblest of the pioneer women of Muhlenberg was Mrs. Tabitha A. R. Campbell, "the Mother of Greenville." Local tradition still tells many interesting things regarding Mrs. Campbell's great work in the moral and religious unbuilding of the new county and her deep interest in social and educational affairs. Her path through life was followed by her four daughters and her son. The same can be truly said of many others of the pioneer mothers of Muhlenberg, who although now perhaps forgotten, yet who in their day smoothed the rough paths over part of which many of their sons and daughters of the present generation are still treading. They were of that strong and generous type of pioneer women, great in virtue and sacrifice and deserving to have their names inscribed on a monument erected to the Mothers of Muhlenberg.

On most of the old farms in Muhlenberg one can find small groups of old-time graves, where rest those who lived during the days of the early settlers. Public cemeteries were rare and frequently inaccessible. Few congregations had established a common graveyard adjoining their church lot before 1870. Many of the old graves in these private burying-grounds are marked with crude and unlettered rocks. Most of them, however, are identified by slabs of lettered sandstone; a few are of white marble. In some sections, especially in the southern part of the county, a large number of the old graves are marked with stone box-covers placed over them many years ago. These covers were made of slabs of dressed sandstone erected either in the form of a long, narrow box, or in the shape of a stone coffin. They were placed over the graves as markers, and not—as is now sometimes stated—to prevent animals from digging down to the buried body. The custom of constructing these vault-like grave-covers was introduced by the pioneers and prevailed to a great extent during the first quarter of the Nineteenth Century. Very few graves were marked in this solemn and picturesque manner after the year 1850.

The olden days were the heroic age. What Judge Little has said in summing up the men of Kentucky and their life in the early days is particularly applicable to the men and women of Muhlenberg: "Existing conditions produced a type of men surpassed by no other time or country. . . . Without contrasting them or measuring them by a common standard, it is conceded that the type of the pioneer differs from his descendant of the third and fourth and subsequent generations. The latter, with less daring, is more intelligent, with less vigor lives longer, with less fortitude is more patient, with less activity accomplishes more. To the pioneer belongs the warrior's laurel—to his descendant the moral and intellectual achievements of peace.

" 'Peace hath her victories no less renowned than war.' "

XIII

THE STORY OF "LONZ POWERS"

AN EPITAPH we frequently find carved on old tombstones is "Gone but not forgotten." These words could also very appropriately be applied to "Lonz Powers, or The Regulators," a novel published by James Weir in 1850 and now obsolete.

"Lonz Powers" is a historical story based on the actual operations of a number of outlaws, and of a class of citizens known as Regulators. These bands of Regulators, in the early history of many sections, felt themselves called on to enforce the law which was being violated by the outlaws, who had no regard for law, human or divine. Organizations like the Regulators, which took the law into their own hands, are not only found in the early history of many communities but also exist, to some extent and in one form or another, even to the present day. The Ku-Klux Klan had its rise and fall. Up to a few years ago White Cap raids, that took place in some sections of this and other States, were frequently reported. Unorganized bodies such as mobs and lynchers still occasionally take the law into their own hands.

What might be called the reign of the Regulators did not begin in Muhlenberg until about a quarter of a century after the county was organized. Regulators here were, as a rule, composed of members of some of the best families. Most of them were sons of pioneers, and like their fathers were men of good standing. For a period of about ten years, beginning about 1820, there came into southern Muhlenberg and northern Todd and Christian counties some settlers who, through their dishonesty, became undesirable citizens. The fact that they either escaped the officials of the then slow-acting law, or were ignored by them, resulted in the organization of the Regulators, whose reign lasted until about 1850.

The outlaws or "Roughs," whose misdeeds form a part of Muhlenberg's traditions, were the Andersons, the Shepherds, and the Penningtons.

Tom Anderson was a horse and slave thief, and lived on Long Creek near Lead Hill Church. The Regulators burned his home about 1837 and drove him and his gang out of Muhlenberg County. Jack Shepherd was a horse-thief, and lived in Todd County near New Harmony Church, where he was killed by William Welborn, who with others attempted to arrest him together with two of his brothers and Isom Sheffield. Alonzo, or "Lonz" as he was called, and Morton Pennington lived in Christian County. It is the career of these two Penningtons, and the movements of the Regulators who finally brought one of them to justice and ran the other out of the State, that form the plot of "Lonz Powers, or The Regulators." The situation is one frequently found in the early history of new and sparsely settled countries. Only a few of the scenes are laid in Muhlenberg County. The book is here reviewed more as a literary work by a Muhlenberg man than as a story bearing on Muhlenberg's local history. Before attempting to sketch a brief history and outline of "Lonz Powers," and before commenting on the theme of the book, I will give a few facts from the author's life.

James Weir was born in Greenville, Kentucky, on June 16, 1821, and died in Owensboro January 31, 1906. He was the son of James Weir, sr., and Anna Cowman (Rumsey) Weir, daughter of Doctor Edward Rumsey, who was a brother of James Rumsey the inventor. James Weir was graduated from Centre College, Danville, in 1840, and the following year completed a course in the Lexington Law School. In 1842 he left Greenville and settled in Owensboro, where he began the practice of law and where for more than forty years (up to his retirement from the profession) he was a leading member of the local bar. He not only had the reputation of being a lawyer of the highest rank but was likewise well known as a scholarly author, a banker of ability, a man with a kind, generous heart, and always worthy of the distinction that "among his fellow-citizens he stood preëminently as

JAMES WEIR, THE AUTHOR, IN 1850

the first citizen of Owensboro."[1] Many words of praise could be quoted regarding the life and career of James Weir, but since it is one of his literary works we are about to review I shall confine myself to a few paragraphs from "Kentucky Biographies" on the subject. In this we read that in 1850 he wrote "Lonz Powers, or The Regulators," and in 1852-53 "Simon Kenton, or The Scout's Revenge," and "Winter Lodge, or Vow Fulfilled," which novels were published by Lippincott of Philadelphia. From "Kentucky Biographies" I quote:

These three novels gave promise of a brilliant future, but since that time Mr. Weir has been too much engrossed in his profession and other business matters to devote much time to literature, and his work in that direction has

---

[1] James Weir married Susan C. Green. They were the parents of ten children, eight of whom reached maturity: Mrs. Ann Belle (Clinton) Griffith, John G., Arthur W., Doctor James, Mrs. Susan Green (James Lee) Maxwell, Mrs. Norah (R. S.) Triplett, William L., and Paul Weir. Paul Weir is an attorney and banker in Owensboro. Doctor James Weir wrote two books, "Religion and Lust" and "The Dawn of Reason," of a scientific nature, and numerous magazine articles of the same character.

been limited to an occasional sketch for the newspapers and magazines. The stories referred to were written in Owensboro before Mr. Weir was thirty years of age.

The first of these was "Lonz Powers, or The Regulators," a romance of Kentucky, based on actual scenes and incidents of the early days of the "Dark and Bloody Ground." The second, "Simon Kenton," was designed to give a sketch of the habits and striking characteristics of the people of western North Carolina, immediately following the Revolutionary times, and to introduce Simon Kenton, the scout and Indian fighter, and also his opponent and enemy, Simon Girty, the Tory renegade. In this volume the character which Kenton represented came off victorious. "Winter Lodge" is a sequel to "Simon Kenton," in which the author introduces many of the most striking characters who were prominent in the early history of Kentucky, with descriptions of scenery, Mammoth Cave, the battles in which Kenton and Girty were engaged, and the habits and marked characteristics of the pioneers. The name "Winter Lodge" is derived from a cabin erected by Kenton, for the hero and heroine, which was ornamented with carpets and buffalo hides and lined with furs. Mr. Weir intended in his younger days to write a third volume of this series, coming down to the war of 1812 and the death of Kenton and Girty, but his increasing business prevented him from accomplishing this, and his literary work of late years has been undertaken as a pastime and recreation rather than a matter of business.

Immediately after its publication "Lonz Powers" became the most popular and enthusiastically discussed book in Western Kentucky, and in fact it attracted attention in literary circles throughout the whole country. The edition was soon exhausted, and as the writer refused to permit the issuing of a second edition until he could find time to revise the book, it was soon out of print. Later, when time for revision might have offered itself, the inclination on his part seemed lacking.

It is probable that after the publication of "Lonz Powers" Weir, realizing that since his romance would be likely to help perpetuate the name and deeds of his hero, decided to let its circulation spread no further. He was undoubtedly aware that frequently a character's fame depends more upon the power of his historian than upon the hero's actual acts. Furthermore, through "Lonz Powers" the writer gives his opinion on a thousand and one subjects, and it is quite possible a few of these expressions being in advance of his day and time were then somewhat harshly criticised, while these same ideas, with one or two exceptions, are to-day accepted. This slight opposition, and the desire not to perpetuate the name of Lonz Pennington, or "Lonz Powers," probably influenced James Weir to refuse the issuing of a second edition of this book.[2]

Whatever the reason, the work was not republished, and the few volumes printed of the first and only edition were soon sold or loaned to neigh-

---

[2] There is a story, affirmed by some and denied by others, to the effect that James Weir did not issue a second edition of "Lonz Powers" because a number of the outlaws, having recognized themselves as the originals of characters portrayed therein, sent the author an anonymous note in which they requested him to suppress the further circulation of the book and threatened to kill him if he issued another edition.

bors and friends and to kith and kin, far and near, until now, sixty years after, it is almost an utter impossibility to obtain a copy. But in spite of this fact, "Lonz Powers" is still discussed not only by the old citizens of Western Kentucky—many of whom read it when it first appeared—but is also talked about by those generations which have come upon the scene since the Civil War, among whom, however, there are but few who have even seen a single page of it. Thus, as I have said, "Gone but not forgotten" is the book's most appropriate epitaph.

And now, "lest we forget," I shall attempt to perpetuate this old story in at least its outlines. Practically all the men and women who were old enough to appreciate and remember "Lonz Powers" when it first appeared have passed into the Great Beyond. Very few of their successors have had an opportunity to read it. Some have permitted their imaginations to mislead them concerning the nature of the book. Thus it is that we frequently hear it compared to "The Life of Jesse James," "The Texas Rangers," or "Tracy, the Bandit." No comparison could be more erroneous or absurd. To suggest that this story more closely resembles that of "Robin Hood" better approaches the mark, especially in the cave life of the bandits.

The book is divided into two volumes, making a total of about seven hundred pages. On the title page is printed:

LONZ POWERS
or
THE REGULATORS
A Romance of Kentucky
founded on facts
by
James Weir, Esq.
Published by Lippincott, Grambo
& Co.
Successors to Grigg, Elliot & Co.
Philadelphia
1850

Most of the scenes in the story are laid in and around Christian County. It would be impossible to quote all pertaining to Muhlenberg and other counties of Western Kentucky without reproducing the greater part of the text. I shall, however, in the course of this chapter, copy many paragraphs word for word.

Turning page after page we soon recognize the literary merits of this work, note the accuracy with which Mr. Weir records local history and the vividness with which he portrays the early days. We are affected by the pathetic little sketches scattered throughout the book. We thrill at his tragedies and laugh at his ever-recurring humor, wit, and fun.

It is the story, the author tells us, of a people living "away from the busy haunts of commerce and from the brick, mortar and marble of the city; away from the hacks and pavements; away from baronial castles, brave knights and fair ladies." In the preface he says he confidently believes "few works, claiming the title of romance, have ever comprised so many real characters and actual incidents. Throughout the particular localities of the story hundreds of persons may be found who will detect, in the career of the hero, a transcript of the life and adventures of one Edward Alonzo Pennington; and although the author, in the exercise of one of the privileges of the craft, has brought many of the minor characters and incidents of the book into a new juxtaposition, yet many of these will also be recognized, with equal facility, as real and true.''

As to the identity of some of the other characters represented, or to what extent they are true portrayals of the originals, no one seems now to

RESIDENCE OF PIONEER JAMES WEIR, GREENVILLE
Built about 1816. In this house the author of ''Lonz Powers'' was born

be able to state with any certainty. Tradition has it that Francis P. Pennington is the name of the father of Alonzo and Morton, and that Alonzo's wife was a Miss Oates, a granddaughter of pioneer Jesse Oates. The "O'Rourke" of the book was Simon Davis, a stone mason. "Old Sisk" is very likely drawn from a certain Frank Cessna, or Cisney, and also a Sheffield. According to tradition—which differs in some instances greatly from the written romance—Alonzo Pennington was pursued and arrested by Doctor Reece Bourland, living near Hopkinsville, who captured the outlaw while he was playing a "breakdown" on his fiddle at a cowboy dance in Northeastern Texas. But, according to the author, Lonz was captured in the Lone Star State by "Charles Burton," a leading but fictitious character whose romantic career adds much to the interest of the book. The court records show that John McLarning was the prosecuting attorney for Christian county when Alonzo Pennington was tried and condemned in April, 1846, and Colonel James F. Buckner, then of Hopkinsville, was employed by the defense, a duty that was considered dangerous, yet discharged with courage by young Buckner.

The plot of "Lonz Powers" is a very thrilling one. It holds the reader's interest from the beginning to the end. Now and then the author leads up to a melodramatic climax. But after all it is not, in my opinion, the exciting plot that gives the book its value. It is the author's literary style, his portrayal of the Regulators and their times and his frequent digressions, in which he expresses himself on various subjects, that give the work its value. I shall attempt to give a brief outline of the plot, incidentally accompanying that outline with quotations from the book, and add a few remarks based on tradition.

The story begins at a time when Southern Kentucky was yet almost a wilderness. The Powers farm, "Forest Home," "presented as beautiful and inviting a scene as the most impassioned lover of Nature could desire." Its two hundred acres "lay imbedded in a deep and almost impenetrable forest." Its well-kept barns sheltered blooded stock, and evidences were many that the inmates of the comfortable home lived in a style befitting country gentry of the time and place. The sons of the house, Lonz and Morton, were young men of widely different dispositions—Lonz even then a stern fatalist, and Morton gay, brilliant, changeable, and led at all times by his elder brother.

To pay a gambling debt, Lonz Powers stole several blooded mares from his father's farm. The fact that Lonz was guilty of this theft was known only to four persons—to himself, his brother Morton, to a character we shall later know as "the Colonel," and to Charles Burton. Burton and his wife, Laura, had a few years previous removed to this neighborhood from Virginia. It was by mere chance that Burton discovered Lonz taking the horses.

In this same neighborhood lived a man called, from his prematurely gray hair, "Old Sisk." Previous to his settlement in Kentucky he had committed crimes, knowledge of which had followed him, and though he had lived uprightly in the midst of a little colony of which he was head by reason of his superior intelligence and education, his past record being against him he was arrested and placed in jail for Lonz Powers' crime—namely, that of horse-stealing.

On the day preceding the trial of Old Sisk, Lonz pleaded with Burton to divulge none of the proceedings he had accidentally witnessed. But silence on the part of Burton would have meant the imprisonment of Old Sisk for a theft committed by Lonz. So Burton told Lonz he would "tell the truth, the whole truth, and nothing but the truth," no matter whom it helped or hurt.

That night, just before retiring, Charles Burton, "leaving his chair by the fire, walked to the open door and there leaning against the rustic pillar of the porch, while gazing at the moon, just rising over the dark veil of the forest, was shot" from ambush by Lonz Powers, who had shrewdly taken every precaution to cover his tracks and divert suspicion.

During the few years preceding this murder various persons had been robbed along the highways and byways and many horses had been stolen, but no guilty parties had ever been located by officials or other citizens. The murder of Charles Burton now shook the whole community, which, as it gathered around the dead man's home and there beheld his young widow and their son, Charles, about eight years old, declared it had now fallen on the citizens to avenge this daring and bloody deed.

Every man present seemed enthusiastically in favor of such action—none more than Lonz Powers himself, whose own father was made chairman of the assembly. A few of the wiser and cooler heads were for lawful proceedings, but the majority were moved by the insinuations of Lonz (whose purpose is clear to the reader) that Old Sisk, though in jail awaiting trial, was the instigator of this foul deed. Morton (who was ignorant of the fact that his brother was the murderer) made a speech to the crowd, during the course of which he said:

But they say we have no proof of the guilt of Old Sisk or the guilt of his gang in this murder. If they are innocent then who can be guilty? . . . Old Sisk knew that Burton was a witness for the Commonwealth . . . and that such a witness as Burton was more than enough to cause his conviction and death. . . . The citizens of a neighboring county were long infected by just such another band. Tom Anderson and his fierce crew of outlaws, for years and years, committed crime after crime, and the law made futile and fruitless efforts to convict and punish them. At last the people, having borne and suffered as long as to bear and suffer was wise and honorable, arose in their power and majesty, and casting aside for the moment laws—in that case vain and useless—swept in the hour of their anger this entire band from the county, and drove them homeless and houseless to another land. Shall we now follow their example, and treat in the same manner this cursed gang? Or shall we weakly submit and retire to our homes, leaving this atrocious and cowardly assassination of a friend and neighbor unpunished and unavenged?

The crowd, fired by his daring speech, soon left the Sisk home a pile of smoldering ashes, and made his wife and children fugitives. Thus took place the organization of this band of Regulators, according to the author of "Lonz Powers." Old Sisk, an unfortunate victim of prejudice and popular excitement, was convicted of the crime of horse-stealing, of which he was innocent, and sent to prison for fifteen years. There was, of course, no evidence to convict him of Burton's murder.

Fifteen years have joined the endless train of eternity since the scenes described in our foregoing chapters. Fifteen years of sunshine and storm, of winter and summer, of springtime and harvest, have come and gone. Treading on with quiet, but regular and ever-moving steps, old Time has gingerly tripped along, like some light-hearted maiden over the dewy grass, scarcely leaving a trace of his passage. For fifteen full, long years have the flowers bloomed only to wither, and man has been born only to die. For fifteen years Time, like interest, has never slept, but has stolen by with noiseless tread while we were sleeping; thus hurrying on, careless, reckless, and ignorant, still nearer to the grave. . . .

But you must not suppose, gentle reader, that because fifteen years have gone, and we have seen proper to pass them over in silence, that they have fled like a day, without producing many changes. During that period, wars and revolutions have convulsed the world; kingdoms have sunk into ruin and risen again; men, religion, politics, the sciences and arts, have all been remodeled, and have thrown off their ancient garbs and appeared in holiday dress, to suit the march of intellect or change in taste. Like flowers transplanted, the change has bettered some and injured others.

During these fifteen years many strange inventions have startled the eye of man. The iron horse has trampled his way through forest and over mountains, dragging after him long trains of wealth, and driving away, with his wild whistle and hoarse snort, the old rumbling conveyances of our fathers, and speeding along with all the force and power of steam, reckless alike of toil or distance. The bright forerunner of the thunderbolt has been snatched from the whirling clouds, and made the post-boy of this intelligent and progressive age. Steam has dashed aside the dark bosom of the ocean, and careless alike of wind or wave, brought the old and new worlds in a few days' travel of each other. . . .

During that period many changes have occurred in the scenes and characters of our present story. The country, then almost a wilderness, is now teeming with life; the activity and energy of our moving and restless race has filled the old forests; and broad farms, golden with grain, and made glad by all the comforts and necessaries, and even luxuries of life, have taken the place of wild wood and tangled briar. The little village of Hopkinsville now aspires to the dignity of a city; the sluggish waters of Pond River have now, by the wisdom of our Legislature, been declared (what God never intended) navigable—whether for steamboats, broadhorns or dugouts, our wise lawmakers did not see proper to mention. . . .

Fifteen years have fled! Long, weary and solitary to Old Sisk, for they had been spent in the gloomy, silent cells of a prison, and had been made even longer and more dreary than they really were by the fierce raging of never-sleeping passion, coupled with an insane and almost hopeless longing for freedom. . . . In person he was almost gigantic—a perfect specimen of thews and sinews; and as he wielded his hammer in the forge of the penitentiary, with his stern face illuminated by the blazing metal, and dark with passion and malice, he would have made a glorious picture for the God of the Infernals. He loved that work, for every stroke he gave the fusing iron, he fancied it a death-blow to an enemy and oppressor. . . . He loved to hear the ringing sound of his blows, and see the firm iron crush beneath his stroke; for he knew then that the power and force of his arm was not yet destroyed, and that he was still able to execute the vengeful schemes of his dark and unforgiving heart. . . .

Old Sisk is now, after fifteen years' absence, approaching with slow and wearied but steady and firm tread the location of his once comfortable, and to him, perhaps, happy home. No wife or child or kindred are there to greet and welcome that old man; to soothe him in his hour of darkness, and rejoice over his return. . . . He slept that night stretched on the green sod where once stood his pleasant home, and there will he dream either of happier days or of bloody vengeance.

Thus is freed the instrument of fate.

This intermission of fifteen years brings the story of "Lonz Powers" down to about 1844. Charles Burton, jr., who after the death of his father had been sent to his grandfather in Virginia, had grown to young manhood and had just returned to Kentucky, the scene of his early life. Old Sisk, having served out his prison term, had come back, as already shown, an embittered, revengeful man. Lonz Powers had married Mary Warren, and was living on a farm near his old home. He and his brother had a bad reputation in the neighborhood, but no one could point to any real lawbreaking on their part. Their old father, still living at "Forest Home," almost a ruin, sat dreaming over his wrecked fortune and the almost ruined reputations of his once darling sons.

During these fifteen years the hypocrites among the Regulators withdrew from the association, declining, as they put it, to ally themselves with such an organization, but secretly associated themselves with a band of outlaws by whom many former crimes had been committed.

The writer says: "For a space of two years previous to the present period of this narrative the entire southern portion of Kentucky, from the Ohio River, or from the counties around Fort Massac in the State of Illinois, across to the Tennessee line, running along up through the counties of Hickman, Caldwell, Hopkins, Christian and so on to Nashville, and through Tennessee to the States of Mississippi, Alabama and Georgia, had been infested and preyed upon by a daring gang of robbers, horse-thieves and counterfeiters, who had, as yet, escaped all discovery or punishment."

The representatives of that fraternity of outlaws who plied between the Green and Tennessee rivers established their headquarters in a cave, described in this story as being located near Pilot Rock in Christian County. Of this organization Lonz Powers was the leader. Among themselves this retreat was known as "The Hermitage." Besides Lonz, to whom they referred as Captain, there were about five other leaders and a greater number of subordinates or "strikers."

Morton Powers was usually second in command. The Monk, Pilot, or Dick Murdock, as he was variously called, was an old flatboat man and river pilot, and frequently entertained his brothers with a raft full of fun. Old Sisk was another of the leaders, for he had joined this band after his release from prison as a means of being more easily revenged on his enemies, the Regulators. Then, too, there was a character known as the Parson, who, in the capacity of circuit rider, held camp-meetings while his brothers in crime preyed upon the praying mourners by appropriating their horses. Last, but not least in wickedness by any means, was the Colonel, the gambler who had first led Lonz Powers into crime and who was the sharer of his first guilty secret.

In the course of the narrative each man tells the story of his life to his assembled companions while idly sitting around in the cave. Some of these are daring, some pathetic, some humorous. Each would make an interesting story in itself. The Colonel, a card sharp, was not sparing of humor, and among other things, while speaking of his past, is made to remark: "In those days I scattered my money about like a prince. No one, you know, had a better right than myself to ape the luxury and expense of royalty, for all my funds had been given me by kings and queens."

Returning to the plot, it develops that a young Irishman named O'Rourke is making preparations to visit his native isle, and it is therefore supposed he will have money on his person. Lonz hears that O'Rourke intends to come to the muster which is to take place at Pleasant Hill, a drilling ground in the northwestern part of Christian County.[3] For Lonz to hear was to plan, so he at once made up his mind that not only the Irishman's money but his rich farm should soon become his own. Thus, working on the revengeful mind of Old Sisk by telling him that O'Rourke had been among the destroyers of his home, he plots to kill O'Rourke on his way from the muster.

Lonz and the Irishman meet after the muster and proceed toward their homes, and according to Lonz's prearranged orders they are soon overtaken by Old Sisk, who is to deal the death blow when Lonz pronounces the words, "And this is the end?" O'Rourke tells the story of his life, his early struggles, his final success; of his love and his loss, and of his mother and sister who eagerly await him at his old home in Ireland, where they are happy in the hope of returning to America with him. By this time "they had traveled four miles from the training ground and were in the midst of a broken and rugged chain of hills." Thus they reached Cave Hill, near what is now Haley's Mill, in Christian County. When O'Rourke had finished his story, Lonz, unaffected by the pathetic recital, gave the signal, "And is this the end?"—in response to which Old Sisk struck the fatal blow, but it was not without much struggling that their wicked work was finished and their victim robbed and his body thrown into a nearby pit, since known as Davis Cave.

Lonz's versatile talents were next to be applied to accomplishing a robbery on a larger scale than any he had yet attempted. It was rumored that the safe in the Bank of Kentucky in Hopkinsville contained "six hundred thousand dollars" (more or less). Lonz decided to enrich himself with at least a part of that amount. As usual, he played upon Old Sisk's desire for retaliation by putting him under the false impression that the cashier had been present at the burning of his home, fifteen years before.

On the night set for the robbery Lonz stationed a number of his men at various places around the bank to act as guards, while he and Old Sisk were to do the actual work. They concealed themselves in some shrubbery in the yard near the rear door of the building, prepared to make a charge on the cashier, whom they judged was alone at the time, for the front door had been locked several hours before. But it suddenly developed that another man was with the cashier. The robbers did not know that young Charles Burton had returned to Kentucky.

At this moment Burton, walking to the open door of the bank, folded his arms across his bosom, and leaning against the post, gazed thoughtfully out over the garden. Lonz sank upon the ground as if a bullet had passed through his brain, while his heart beat quick and fast, and he gasped and struggled for breath, like a man when laboring under a horrible nightmare. Covering his blanched face with his hands, as if he would shut out some terrible sight, he murmured: "'Tis his ghost! And standing in the same position and attitude as when I last saw him fifteen years ago!"

---

[3] James Weir's description of the old militia muster is quoted in full in the chapter on "The Old Militia Muster."

Young Burton having heard this outburst of surprise and horror, quietly, but much bewildered, stepped back into the bank. In the meantime the robbers, suspecting they were detected, returned homeward and gave up the attempt. In the course of a few hours, however, the enraged Lonz learned that the "ghost" he had seen standing in the open door was not that of Charles Burton, the man he had killed fifteen years before, but the living son of the murdered father, to whom the son bore a striking resemblance.

The next morning young Burton left Hopkinsville on his return to the home of Major Thompson, whom he was visiting and whose daughter Julia was receiving much of his attention. Young Burton had not seen Lonz Powers since his early childhood. By a strange and unfortunate coincidence he was overtaken by Lonz, who introduced himself as Jack Randolph. In the course of their conversation Burton, wishing to show a friendly feeling toward his new acquaintance, who claimed to be an old friend of his father, kindly suggested to Randolph, "If you ever need the services of a strong arm or the aid of a long purse, never be backward in calling on the son of your old friend." These overtures were declined with thanks by his new acquaintance, who pretended to be much insulted by such an offer. Burton then begged his pardon, after which Randolph remarked, "No man was ever seriously insulted by the offer of money, for that is an insult very seldom given and when once given very soon forgotten."

That "a man may smile and smile and be a villain still" certainly is applicable to Lonz, for a few moments after their pleasant conversation he deliberately shot Burton, robbed him, and left him lying apparently dead on the highway, where he was soon afterward discovered by some friends and taken to Major Thompson's home, where he received the best attention from his prospective mother-in-law, his ladylove, and fox-hunter Thompson, and soon recovered.

At some time in the life of almost every daring man we find he overreaches himself. This was to be Lonz's fate, and he was about to engineer a robbery, small in itself, but upon which depended his final undoing. Some of his band descended upon the then quiet village of Greenville, and robbing a store there, were followed by the fully awakened townsmen; one of the thieves was captured. This reference to Greenville, the town of Mr. Weir's birth and youth, arouses a reminiscent spirit, resulting in a description of which the author of "Sleepy Hollow" himself might well have felt proud.[4]

Now we shift the scene to Pilot Rock, in Christian County, where a small party of young lovers are picnicking, among whom are, of course, our hero Charles Burton and his heroine Julia Thompson. This famous rock and resort is, according to "Lonz Powers," located in the immediate vicinity of the cave of the robbers, and being so frequently visited by picnic parties the outlaws decided to make the place less popular in the future by capturing the girls of this jolly party and holding them prisoners in their hidden and undiscovered retreat. This they did, and left the struggling young men bound to trees. After the young men had liberated themselves, failing to

---

[4] James Weir's description of Greenville is quoted in the chapter entitled "Greenville as described in 'Lonz Powers.'"

locate the whereabouts of the stolen girls, they rushed home to their families and friends, spreading the alarm of this daring abduction.

By noon of the following day more than five hundred men were gathered upon and about the rock. Every stone and crevice in the neighborhood had been examined for some traces of the girls or robbers, but as yet without success.

In the meantime Old Sisk and his companions and their captives were securely concealed in the cave. One robber, as said, had been captured near Greenville a few days before. He was brought to the scene by some of the Regulators. Having refused to make a confession, he was stripped and bound to a tree and then whipped, and after much pounding and persuading and a promise of liberty he revealed the names of the outlaws.

"He was ignorant of the seizure of the girls and the names of their abductors, but had no doubt they were some of the band to which he belonged. He declared that Lonz and Morton Powers were the leaders of the daring gang which had so long infested the country, and gave the names of many of the citizens of the country and surrounding counties who were secret members of the numerous and widespread association." Every name mentioned created a surprise. Even Lonz and Morton Powers were heretofore unsuspected.

A consultation followed, after which about fifty Regulators marched to the home of Morton, and marching away again left it in flames. They next visited the home of Lonz, determined to burn it down also and give him a good lashing. Through his wife's heroic intercession he was spared on condition that he leave Kentucky at once. Then the Regulators turned toward "Forest Home," having resolved to send the father of these two outlaws out of the State, but the pleadings of the innocent old man were so pathetic that the Regulators changed their resolution and permitted him to remain.

In the meantime the girls were still captives in the undiscovered cave. Five dark and weary days and nights they spent anxiously waiting to be rescued. However, all this while they were gallantly protected from Old Sisk and the other villains by the Pilot and the Parson, who although outlaws like their companions in iniquity had still some traits of decent character. Five long and diligent days and nights were spent around Pilot Rock by the searching party. At last their efforts were rewarded, for Burton discovered the entrance to the secret cave.

Lonz and Morton being absent during the abduction, the besieged, quarrelling among themselves in the cave, could hold out no longer. An exciting conflict followed between the robbers and the rescuers. One of the outlaws dashed out the brains of the Colonel. Two or three of the other bandits were killed, among whom unfortunately was the Parson, who had so courageously aided the Pilot in defending the fair prisoners. The girls were liberated, safe and unharmed but nervous and exhausted, and, of course, "Julia, half crazed with delight, sprang forward to meet Burton and fell fainting upon the bosom of her lover and deliverer."

The lash was applied freely to all the captured outlaws except the Pilot, who having helped protect the girls was now left unwhipped, and who was later pardoned by the Governor on Burton's petition. The revengeful Old

Sisk willingly made a confession, for he had long entertained a secret determination to betray Lonz and Morton, whose connection with his false conviction and imprisonment for horse-stealing he had learned from bits of their overheard conversation and hints from the Colonel, who knew the real criminals. Old Sisk gave a brief history of the maneuvers of the outlaws, saying, among other things, that "Lonz was the thief of his father's horses, for which crime I suffered fifteen years imprisonment; he was the mur-

THE LONZ PENNINGTON HOUSE, CHRISTIAN COUNTY, AS IT APPEARED IN 1912

derer of Burton's father, who was witness of his guilt; he was the instigator of the Regulators who drove away my family and burnt my home. Since that time he has been a gambler, a robber, counterfeiter and kidnapper. A few weeks ago he murdered the young Irishman, O'Rourke, and threw his body into the pit. It was Lonz Powers who planned to rob the bank in Hopkinsville, but failed because when he saw Burton standing in the back door he believed him to be his father's ghost, and the next day, under the false name of Jack Randolph, he came very near murdering young Burton."

This certainly was a very interesting confession to the Regulators. However, Old Sisk failed to relate his own connection with the murder of O'Rourke. About this time Morton Powers suddenly disappeared, and according to the story was seen only once after this exposure.

Lonz having learned from some of his secret associates that the cave had been discovered and that he had been betrayed by Old Sisk, "fled as fast as horse and terror and money could take him, for flight was now his only hope of safety," until finally he arrived at "one of the most remote settlements in Texas, then the great valley of refuge for felons." There he associated with a crowd of strangers, who like himself were fugitives from justice.

Burton, now knowing his father's murderer, determined to avenge the terrible deed. He pursued Lonz, and with the aid of the Pilot arrested him in Texas, where he was taking part in a cowboy dance.

While Burton and the Pilot were pursuing Lonz in Texas the Regulators were still at work in Kentucky. Old Sisk was confined in the jail at Hopkinsville, where he had remained until the present moment. The community, hoping that Lonz Powers might be taken, and trusting with the evidence of Old Sisk to be able to convict him of the murder of O'Rourke and bring him to punishment, had quietly permitted the old convict to remain in jail. But when week after week rolled by and nothing was heard of the fugitive, secret whisperings and threats against the prisoner were bandied about among the Regulators, or rather those who had the strongest reason to fear the bloody vengeance of the fierce old man; and as the time for the convening of the circuit court was drawing rapidly near and he would soon be taken under the power and control of the law, and as they feared, on account of want of testimony, would either escape or be sentenced to only a few years of imprisonment, they determined to take vengeance into their own hands and thus rid themselves of all future fear.

In order to carry out these plans Old Sisk and his fellow-prisoners were secretly supplied with a small file and a highly tempered saw, accompanied by a note signed by "friends from without," saying "at 12 o'clock to-night we intend to undermine the northwest corner of your jail and set you at liberty." The prisoners filed away all day and at midnight crawled, to their great surprise, into the arms of the Regulators. They were taken to the spot where O'Rourke had been murdered by Lonz Powers aided by Old Sisk. Old Sisk admitted he had aided in the murder of the young Irishman on his return from the muster, but explained that it was all done at the instigation of Lonz. Old Sisk pleaded for his life, and begged to be permitted to live until he could kill Lonz, swearing by all things living and dead that after he had seen Lonz die and thus satisfied his aching for revenge he would return and submit to any punishment they cared to inflict.

But his prayers were all in vain. "Directly in front of Old Sisk stood twenty men grasping their long rifles, and silently awaiting the command of their leader. They had been chosen by lot before the coming of the victim, and only ten of the rifles were loaded with ball, and so prepared that the executioners might be ignorant who were the real destroyers." A quick, ringing volley followed the signal of their leader; Old Sisk fell, and disappeared into the mouth of the same cavern into which he and Lonz had thrown the body of O'Rourke a few weeks before. The other outlaws who had been taken from the jail along with Old Sisk were each given a hundred lashes and then driven out of the county.

In due time Lonz was brought from Texas and safely lodged in the Hopkinsville jail. The authorities, learning from experience, did not lock him in the cell recently vacated by Old Sisk, but placed him under heavy guard to prevent his escape or rescue. During his imprisonment his true and faithful wife called on him frequently, consoled him, and even to the last believed him innocent.

Lonz was tried for the murder of O'Rourke, found guilty, and hanged. On the day of the execution, which took place Friday, May 1, 1846, people came from far and near to witness the hanging. Very likely Charles Burton and his bride Julia were in the great crowd, for their gay and festive wedding celebration had taken place shortly after Burton returned from the West with his prisoner, Lonz Powers. Morton Powers, too, according to the story, was among the spectators of the hanging, but in disguise. Tradition says that some years after Lonz's death Morton appeared at the home of his brother's widow, where as an unwelcome guest he lingered for a few weeks. Fearing that his shiftless life would have a bad influence on her children, Mary Powers called in her neighbors to run him away. At her request he was given an application of "hickory oil," after which he fled the county without delay.

Lonz met death bravely and without any unusual demonstrations. Thus ended the life of a brilliant but misguided and misguiding man, who if his abilities had been applied in a legitimate course might have had as great an influence for good as he had for evil. As it is, he has the distinction of being one of the greatest outlaws in Western Kentucky, and also the distinction of being the first man legally hanged in Christian County.

There is a tradition to the effect that when Lonz stood on the scaffold with the hangman's rope around his neck he asked for his old violin, which was handed to him and he played a musical composition of his own, entitled "Pennington's Farewell." Nothing is said about such a scene by the author of "Lonz Powers," and it is therefore likely that this sometimes confirmed but usually denied incident is groundless.

Another tradition says that in the first attempt made to hang Lonz the rope broke, and he then cried out, "See, gentlemen, this is proof of my innocence!" The sheriff, however, proceeded with the work, and thus ended Lonz's earthly career. A denial of his guilt, and not a tune on his fiddle, was "Pennington's Farewell."[5]

In justice to the Penningtons, it must be said that Lonz's heartbroken father was an honest and upright man. Lonz's wife (who remained a widow and died in 1892) and their five children all lived to old age, and each during his or her entire life proved a credit to their county. So, too, his many grandchildren, now living in various parts of Kentucky, are all, without a single exception, good and highly respected citizens.

As to the Regulators and their methods, the author brings up many arguments for discussion. He admits that lynch law as a general custom may be injurious and in some cases unjust. In this instance he asks the reader to bear in mind the fact that at the time and in the country described the inhabitants were few and lived far from any seat of government; that they were constantly suffering from the bold and unpunished work of outlaws, and that most of them practically depended upon themselves and their own efforts for obtaining their necessities. They raised their own bread, shot their own meat, spun their own cloth, and also enforced their own laws.

---

[5] One version has it that the day Pennington was hanged he not only played "Pennington's Farewell" on his violin, but also recited what has ever since been referred to as "Pennington's Lament":
"Oh, dreadful, dark and dismal day,
How have my joys all passed away!
My sun's gone down, my days are done,
My race on earth has now been run."

Commenting on this subject, Mr. Weir says: "Had not the Regulators pursued the course described in the present case, they never would have discovered the nest of villains, and they might have gone on step by step, until it would have become dangerous for an honest man to move from his door, unless armed and guarded as if in the country of an enemy. It is true, lynching may at times result in the punishment of innocent men. Rascals may ever and anon take advantage of the custom to revenge themselves upon their enemies. The law itself may, in a manner, be brought into con-

Two rocks on the graves of Lonz Pennington and his wife, buried in Christian County, and A. Webster McCown and Richard T. Martin, who after a long and careful search located them

tempt by a reckless indifference of appealing to it for punishment or protection. But, upon the whole, taking everything into consideration, time, place and circumstances, we think regulating or lynching, although an evil, was then sometimes a necessary one."

"A multitude of furious, reckless and unmanageable men," continues Mr. Weir, "assembled together in some city, bent upon the destruction of property or punishment of obnoxious persons, is called a mob. A company of men assembled with the same purpose or design, but meeting in the woods instead of the city, are dubbed with the title of Regulators. A community uniting together with the intent of resisting the laws of the land and overthrowing the regularly constituted government, if unsuccessful, receives the odious name of rebels; but if their attempt be crowned with victory, then, instead of rebellion, it is dignified with the more exalted and glorious title of revolution."

After referring to Ireland's wrongs, to "Louis Philippe with a recollection of a former revolution in France," to the troubles of Germany and Italy, and to how "Emperor and Pope have alike been compelled to submit to the expanding will of the people," the author adds (failing, however, to refer to anarchy and its troubles): "Our Regulators, who were nothing more nor less than a country mob, had their evils to remedy, and, as they met with entire and complete success in all their undertakings, the only question that now remains is whether they, like the victorious French, shall be applauded, or like the unsuccessful Irish, meet with condemnation." Since the work of the Regulators and the execution of Lonz Pennington resulted in a general suppression of lawlessness and a general reformation of the country, Mr. Weir is, of course, inclined to say "they shall be applauded."

One is indeed tempted to refer to many other arguments and incidents introduced by the author and to quote from them. But the selection is so large and varied that one scarce knows which to choose. Besides, lack of space limits this chapter to a short biographical sketch of the author, to a rough outline of the plot of "Lonz Powers," and to a few remarks on the subject of the Regulators. These three subjects I have briefly reviewed. However, this review would be far from complete if I did not refer to the fact that during the course of the story the author discusses, at length and in a very entertaining manner, the many subjects that are incidentally introduced.

These communings, meditations, descriptions, and moralizations are interesting and unusually humorous. Among "the themes which skirt the roadside of the narrative" are Mr. Weir's description of the old military muster, Pilot Rock and The Barrens, a dog supper, a steeplechase, and the improbable style of conversation as given in fiction; hereditary vices and virtues; the tree of life; influence of victuals on verse; prospects of war in the indissoluble Union; modes of deer-hunting in Kentucky; botanizing as an art in courtship; knitting and its effects upon lovers and the price of socks; hypocrisy among the so-called admirers of Milton's Paradise Lost; the road-working age of old men and young boys; grammar from a theoretical and practical standpoint; the bliss of a brandy cocktail, and a score or two of other themes.

I have tried to present a general idea of "Lonz Powers, or The Regulators," the author's versatility, literary style, his complete conception of the subject, and his thorough knowledge of the old-time Regulators. I found it an extremely interesting book from a historical and literary as well as from a local standpoint.

XIV

GREENVILLE AS DESCRIBED IN "LONZ POWERS"

AS already stated, "Lonz Powers" was published in 1850. The author devotes his twenty-ninth chapter to the town of his birth—Greenville. This entire chapter, with the exception of about one page of irrelevant dialogue, is here reproduced.

In the early part of his reminiscences Mr. Weir gives a picture of Greenville as it was when he was a schoolboy in the early thirties of the last century. The "Village Tavern" referred to was the old Russell Tavern, which was among the first houses built in Greenville and was conducted by the Russells for more than half a century. The "sweet little church" was the old Presbyterian church east of the courthouse. The "old soldier of the second war" of whom he writes is Charles Fox Wing. The "auger-hole" incident, according to the story of "Lonz Powers," took place in 1844. The "Dutchman's" store, tradition says, was run by two brothers, Isaac and Simon Oberdorfer, who after living in Greenville for a few years returned to their native town in another part of the State.

It may be well to remind the reader that in the preface to "Lonz Powers" Mr. Weir remarks that his story is "founded on fact," but that as an author he sometimes indulges in "the privileges of the craft." To what extent he has here, at times, indulged in an author's license can be more readily seen than told. In the whole sketch we may read the good-humored satire of the young Greenvillian who had removed to a larger and more bustling community. Nevertheless it contains much that is tender recollection. The sketch follows:

The little town of Greenville located on, if not seven hills,—like the immortal city of the Cæsars,—at least half that number, was, a few days after the events described in our last chapter [his chapter XXVIII], the theatre of great excitement, and not a little wonder and astonishment. You must understand, dear reader, that year after year, for at least one generation preceding the incidents we are now about relating, the good citizens of this primitive town had lived, or rather vegetated, in one great, grand calm, unruffled by a single storm.

From time immemorial (or at least so far back as my memory runneth, for this quiet spot was my birthplace) the bell on the village tavern had rung out its alarm-notes for breakfast long before the peep of day; dinner followed at eleven, supper at four, and by seven, or eight at the outside, all the sober and respectable portion of the villagers were in bed. Yet I have known—although it was by no means a frequent thing—some wild, dissipated young blades (as they were then called), greatly to the horror and grief of the elder inhabitants, set upon a spree, eating eggs and hickory-nuts, at least an hour later than the prescribed time.

The customs of this retired village were as ancient as the village itself, and never changed nor varied in the least, for the good villagers not once dreamed of wandering a hair's breadth from the old beaten path of their fathers. Week after week, month after month, and year after year, quietly stole by, but the people, the town, and the fashions continued one and the same, unchanged, and, in their estimation, unchangeable.

The citizens sat at the same corners, and under the same shade-trees, and nearly, if not altogether. the same men and boys, father and son, day by day, as they had done for a quarter of a century. A s t r a n g e r might have ridden through that quiet and peaceful little town, at the period of which we are speaking, continued his journey through Europe, Asia, and Africa, consuming half a lifetime, and then returning, would have found exactly the same company, sitting in the same place, engaged in the same business, and talking pretty much about the same things. The houses, gardens, yards, shops, stores, and taverns never changed owners, occupiers, or signs, and, what was still more singular, never grew any better or worse. They remained always looking just the same as though death had swept away the entire community, and time, with its ravages and decay, so far as they were concerned, had ceased to be.

[1] Mrs. William H. Yost, sr. (Mrs. Jonathan Short), in 1864

The old seminary (a sacred and holy place in our memory) perched upon one hill—the sweet little church upon another—and the courthouse and jail (as if typical of justice guarded by religion and education) immediately between, have remained just in that position, never improving nor growing worse, until the memory of man knoweth not to the contrary. We have many pleasant memories of that old seminary, and of the ancient pedagogues who figured and flourished there in the happy days of our boyhood. Like the village itself, our old schoolmasters were an odd, unaccountable set, with queer notions of their own, for those fashioners and formers of the mind, those polishers and beautifiers of the most glorious gift of God to man, those workers not in gold and jewels, but in a far more precious and priceless commodity, who figured upon the stage in my day, were a species

---

[1] Lucy Wing, daughter of Charles Fox Wing, in 1846 married Jonathan Short, who died in 1882. In 1888 she became the third wife of Doctor William H. Yost. She was born in Greenville, June 16, 1822, and has lived there all her life—more than ninety years. She is known as the "Grand Old Lady of Greenville." During the time referred to by James Weir in his recollections of Greenville she was a girl of about ten. (See footnote 2, page 79.)

strange and unique, and bearing very little, if any, resemblance to the genus pedagogue of this steam-engine age.

I well remember one of these ancient trainers of the young mind, who, for want of a better, was for a time made grand Czar of the old seminary, and I can never, even now, think of his little school, and the rare scenes enacted under his reign and superintendence, without a burst of laughter.

OLD PRESBYTERIAN CHURCH, GREENVILLE
Erected about 1825 on a lot presented by pioneer James Weir; abandoned as a place of worship about 1867; now used as a warehouse

He was an odd, disjointed little fellow,—a reverend, by the by,—without much knowledge of books and with still less of politeness or etiquette, yet on every Friday evening would he make his entire school go through a thorough drill in "curtseys," "bowing," "leaving and entering the room," and in "formal introductions one to the other," done up, as he imagined, in the best Chesterfield (Count D'Orsay was not then in vogue) style, and, as I know myself, much to the gratification and amusement of his red-headed, bare-footed, and ragged disciples.

I have been a little awkward and stiff in my bowing ever since those polishing Fridays of my younger days, and believe in my soul I never will forget the ungraceful, formal bows drubbed into me by this schoolmaster of the "ancien regime."

This same little fellow had also a great, and I might say, superlative idea of female loveliness, and conceived it to be not only his duty to polish the minds and manners of his scholars, but to add, if possible, new charms to their natural beauty. He was in the habit of saying, at each one of these drill days, and sometimes even during the week, "that the most lovely and attractive feature of the female face was the serene smile." Hence regularly, on these stated evenings, would he form all the girls of his school in a long line, and then go through the exercise of putting on the "serene smile." Jupiter and Bacchus, what a sight! Cruikshank should have seen that review! A good sketch would have made his everlasting fortune, and caused the death or life of every sour anti-laugher in the Union.

There we sat—the boys dirty, barefooted, and grinning with delight— while first the little, ungainly, cross-eyed (for he had a horrible squint) teacher would draw up his mouth to a proper focus, and, with a smirk and heavenly roll of the eye, give a sample of the "smile serene," and then girl after girl, along down the line, would follow with grim contortion and grimace his most beautiful and charming example; and thus we had the "serene smile" with all the variations. Some of the larger and more intelligent girls, struck with the ridiculousness of this "serene review," would merely smile in derision and contempt; and to these he invariably gave the badge of excellence in this particular branch of his exercises. To this day the young ladies of this little village, remembering the "serene exercises" of their ancient beautifier, often catch themselves unconsciously going through the "serene smile"; and his scholars generally may now be pointed out and known by the great serenity of their countenances. Peace be to the old pedagogue! If he is still alive, may he die with a "serene smile" upon his lips; and if he is dead, may his scholars remember the lesson he taught them, and "smile serenely" to his memory.

I remember still another famous teacher, who flourished for many years as superior of this academy when we were a wild boy; and his name must and shall not go down to the grave unhonoured and unsung, as long as we have a goose-quill and ink to dot down his peculiarities. When inflicting punishment, he never used the rod, but vented his ire by pulling the nose, ears, and hair of the offender. To such length did he carry his nose and ear-ology that the trustees of the school were compelled by public opinion, and the elephantine growth of the junior villagers' proboscies, to call a special meeting and pass a law forever forbidding any further elongation of these necessary members of the face divine. Once set by the ears, and fully alive to the importance of the occasion, the trustees not only put a stop to the squeezing of smellers, but forever put an end to "ear-pulling." This special statute was all that saved us; for even as it was, these features had got such a start, that they are now much larger and longer than there is any particular necessity for. But, as the commercial papers would say, after this decline of ear and nose punishments, there was a visible and rapid increase in the demand for hair.

Our good teacher being deprived, by one stroke of the trustees' pen, of his two greatest gratifications, took to wool-gathering in the most serious and most extensive manner. There is no telling how many of us would now be patronizing the wig-makers (for, as it is, we are generally coolly covered about the cranium) had not a young friend and myself hit upon a glorious plan of putting a stop, and forever, to this last pleasure of our old master.

On a certain morning, without any cause or provocation (as you may all well know), this hair-plucking teacher of ours, who wore a wig himself, and therefore held all hair in utter abomination, took it into his head to give my young friend, who was blessed with white locks, and myself, who had just the opposite, a long pull, a strong pull, and a pull all together, and such a pull that made our heads tingle, and which we (or at least I can speak for myself) have not yet forgotten. Like a second-rate power when insulted by a superior, we smothered our ire for the time; but the hour of vengeance was at hand, for we had hit upon a plan of operations and only awaited a fit season to put it in execution. So, when the school was dismissed for dinner, revenge took the place of hunger, and we spent the entire vacation in picking up and gathering together every stray hair we could find in the school-room. No lover ever thought more of, or treated with greater respect and tenderness, the flowing ringlets of his mistress, than we did each straggling white, red, or black hair, gathered on that day from the dust and dirt of that little room.

To these, when wearied with searching, we added a bunch pulled from the white locks of my friend, by *particular request*; and folding them all neatly together, making quite a respectable collection, he bore them triumphantly, as a memento of our teacher's cruelty and barbarity, to his father. The old man, although a pleasant and kind-hearted gentleman enough, was very apt to use his knotty cane, and that, too, without much delay or examination, whenever he was excited by anything mean or outrageous, and we counted upon this trait in his character for vengeance. Our teacher, however, by some means unknown to the author, escaped the drubbing he so well deserved, and which we so confidently anticipated, but was forever after very chary how he pulled hair.

The citizens of this little place have lived so long together, having the same habits and customs, enjoying the same sunshine and shade, taught by the same teachers, and worshipping in the same church, that they all bear a faint resemblance to each other, and look for all the world like a great family of relations. The old men never grow any older, and the young men remain in "statu quo"; only they all have a premature appearance of middle age. Smoking, until a few years back, was a thing unknown, or known only to be universally condemned. Railroads, steamboats, and telegraphs, and all such things, would do to talk about, but were believed to be rather sinful inventions, made for the purpose of desecrating the Sabbath, and therefore not very favourably received. The fashions were never changed; for these retired people cared not a fig for Paris, or the latest style. The same old tailors who did the cutting and modelling when I was a boy still remain, and form and fashion the Sunday finery of the modern dandy. During the week, or working days, the clothes of the community were about the same in fashion, material, and appearance. The lawyer, divine, merchant, clerk, mechanic, and labourer all alike wore shocking bad hats, ragged coats, patched pants, and unblacked shoes, and were equally indifferent as to dress. They have not yet entirely forgotten their ancient habits, and a little patching and blacking would not be at all injurious or unbecoming. If they kill the poor brute for his hide, we think it nothing but fair and right and proper that they should keep his skin always in mourning. Humanity requires this much at their hands.

But when Sunday came, it was quite another thing. This was a day for ransacking old trunks and bandboxes; and you wouldn't begin to know your acquaintances of the week, without a fresh introduction. The villagers mounted their best, and now was the time to tell who was who; for the swinging black, laid away during the week, made its seventh-day appearance, glittering in the sunshine; and blankets, casinets, and jeans coats,— very respectable on common occasions,—were nowhere in comparison with

[2] CHARLES METZKER, 1849

---

[2] Charles Metzker was the last of the German-American pioneers to settle in Muhlenberg. He came to Greenville from Virginia in 1836, and for twenty years ran a large and well-known blacksmith and wagon shop, in which he made and repaired many of the farming implements and wagons used in the county. He was born October 21, 1810, and died in Greenville October 8, 1857. Among his eight children was William H. Metzker, who married Susan E. Paxton, a daughter of Joseph Paxton. Joseph Paxton died August 15, 1884, at the age of eighty-five.

the wool-dyed, short-napped, imported broadcloth. This custom of all going alike during the week, and in the same careless, ragged manner, was and is not done on account of meanness or parsimony; not at all,—for the citizens of Greenville have always been noted for liberality and generosity,—but merely because they are all known to each other, very seldom see any strangers, and can not understand or conceive any particular use or necessity in troubling themselves about their apparel. On Sunday it is another thing altogether; for their fathers before them set the custom of shaving and dressing up on this particular occasion, and they but follow in their footsteps. It is a mark of respect to the sacred day and answers the purpose of a kind of almanac to let them know how time is passing. They have strange notions of the world in this little town, for they look upon every foreigner as an enemy, and watch his movements with a rather suspicious and jealous eye. They have heard from their merchants, who travel East once a year (and are therefore considered most daring and wonderful voyagers), of robbers, pickpockets, and other such fellows, and have, from the horrible accounts given by these travelers, come pretty much to the conclusion that all the remainder of the world outside of their boundaries are engaged in one or the other of these laudable occupations, and are to be at any rate considered dishonest until they prove themselves the contrary.

As to whiskers or other hirsute ornaments, they are not only esteemed prima facie evidence, but proof positive of rascality and villany of the darkest grade. No such a thing has ever been tolerated, but have always been held in the strictest abomination; and a person visiting this village with one of these hairy appendages would run a great risk of being mobbed, or at least thrown into prison on suspicion of horse-stealing. One or two men in my remembrance have been convicted and sent to the penitentiary on no other evidence; and one fellow, who had only escaped the same fate by a hung jury, was at the next term acquitted by acclamation, he having followed his lawyer's advice and freed himself from this suspicious encumbrance. The good citizens have always laid it down as an axiom (and with some degree of reason) that no honest man would thus attempt to conceal his countenance. The lawyers who practice at this court are the most *barefaced* in the circuit; and those sporting whiskers generally spend the better part of the Sunday previous in getting up a clean face—I won't add heart, for they are not generally supposed to be troubled with any such commodity.

One poor devil of a half-military attorney was so green, or ignorant of the customs of this Rip Van Winkle village, as to make his appearance during term-time ornamented not only with whiskers, but a moustache. He only escaped the penitentiary, prison or mob, by a slight mistake as to his genus, being taken by most of the citizens for a stray baboon from a travelling menagerie. As such he was looked upon, admired, wondered at, and followed around by the boys and negroes, and last, through humanity for a poor dumb brute, allowed to escape. It was only their ignorance, that such a thing as a moustache was ever worn, that saved the poor fellow. As it was, he made a most narrow escape; and, upon learning the dangers and perils through which he had passed, became so alarmed that he fled the country immediately, and has never been heard of to this day.

The amusements of this quiet town were as simple and harmless as might be expected with such primitive, unsophisticated people. At the period of which I am speaking, the old and middle-aged sat in the shade talking politics, or dreaming away their days in listless indolence, only varying their monotonous life by going to church regularly on Sunday. The young gentlemen, being a little more full of life and spirit than their fathers, played marbles, and, when tired of this manly amusement, did the same as the old men, only they gave tone to their sittings by vigorous whittling on boxes and benches, now and then adding variety to their innocent sport by slyly gallanting the girls to church, whenever they could catch an opportunity of doing so, without being observed by their friends or mammas. Card-playing, wine-bibbing, balls, horse-racing, dancing, and other such pleasures were things unknown, or if known, never happened during my day and

³ THE METZKER HOUSE, GREENVILLE, IN 1895
(Side view)

generation; for they were all esteemed and considered most heinous and wicked contrivances of the devil to destroy men's souls.

Christmas, the 8th of January, and 22d of February, our three great national holidays, were either forgotten—considered no better than their other three hundred and sixty-two fellows—or passed by unnoticed, merely from indifference or their total repugnance to all noise and confusion. The glorious Fourth of July—that most celebrated and memorable of all our days—would have shared the same silent fate, had it not been for an old soldier of the second war. Regularly did this old patriot, from my earliest recollection (and it was a great and bright epoch in my boyish days), rear his liberty pole and cap of freedom on every coming Fourth. On the third, let it be sunshine or storm, he would repair to the woods, and there felling the loftiest pole he could find, always eschewing hickory,—for he

---

³ What was for many years known as the Metzker House, Greenville, was begun in 1824 by Reverend Ezias Earle. The place was purchased in 1847 by Charles Metzker, who erected the two-story addition in front of the original house. Later the entire log structure was weatherboarded. It was occupied by the Metzker family for many years. This landmark was torn down in 1911, and on the site the William A. Wickliffe residence was built.

was a most inveterate Whig,—he would remove it to the public square, and on the morning of the Fourth, bright and early, before the rising of the sun, would he bring out his old banner, with its stripes and stars, and proudly send it up into the heavens. For three days would he let his eagle, his stars, and his stripes flutter gaily in the winds, in honour of the day and to the memory of his gallant ancestors; but on the fourth he would again take down his worn and sometimes tattered banner, and folding it up, sacredly lay it away, to do the same honour to the coming year. It was a simple and touching act of devotion, and well worthy of the old soldier's heart. Our

THE WILLIAM A. WICKLIFFE RESIDENCE, GREENVILLE
Erected in 1911 on the site of the Metzker House

country's proud flag is dear to all of us, but still more so to him who has fought and suffered under its protecting folds. The old man's gray hairs, and his glad shout, and his deep emotion when his banner would sweep out from the flagstaff, and his old eagle unfold her broad wings and flap them joyfully in the wind, will never be forgotten by us.

The rearing of that cap of liberty and flag was the most memorable event of my childhood days. I waited for it, and dreamed of it, and sprang up with the coming light to see the first and last of it, and danced and sang around it, and shouted with joy as the old man cheered its upward flight. May that gallant old soldier and honourer of the Fourth live to unfold his star-decked banner through many a coming year; for, when he dies, then will this old flag be forgotten, this proud act of devotion lie buried with his throbless heart, and this ancient village, the home of my infancy, be left without an honoured day.

Those were bright days—the days of our early youth, when every passing event brought happiness; when every thought was the genuine outpouring of unsophisticated nature, and when all our hopes and dreams were of a golden hue. They are gone now—and no longer do we wake to cheer the old flag in her upward flight; no more will we wander by the little branch, and lave our limbs in its bright waters; and never again will we sit in that old seminary, or carve the name of our boy-love upon the widespreading beech. We wished then for manhood, and prayed then for the time when we would mingle with the world. We have got our wish, and would like right well if we were a boy again. The world is not what we expected; for the glorious garden of our young anticipations has its thorns as well as its flowers. Glory has proven a bauble; and love, patriotism, and friendship are too intimately combined with selfishness, hypocrisy, and deceit to afford much pleasure. We would gladly exchange our manhood, with all its proud privileges and cares, for "the days when we went gipsying a long time ago," through the hills and valleys around that retired little village. We had far more heartfelt pleasure in fishing in that little branch and stringing our minnows, than we have ever had, or ever will have, in fishing for "gudgeons or whales" in this great world-sea of ours.

No wonder the good citizens are wedded to that quiet place, and think no home so lovely and enchanting as that forest-embowered home of theirs. The neat little church, the silent, sunny dells, the quiet, retired graveyard, the old oak covered with the wild vine, the gay, sweet-scented rose, springing up over fence and hedge, the tumbling brook, and the still, dreamy quietude of the place, give such an air of rural beauty and patriarchal innocence to that retired and peaceful spot that no one could but love that fairy scene.

Death but seldom left the footprints of his sad tread within the boundaries of that quiet town. He walks abroad in the crowded city and swarming thoroughfare, leaving behind him a gloomy path of sorrow, marching to the wail of the living and the last sigh of the dead; but to this retired place he but rarely takes his way, only mowing down those who are ripe for the sickle, and leaving the young vines green and flourishing, until time shall wither their soft young tendrils and fit them for the reaper and the grave. Yet that shady little graveyard, where a man would almost be willing to lie down and sleep forever, with its short, myrtle-covered mounds and little head and foot-stones, tells of fair young flowers, crushed in their first bloom of infantile beauty, untimely withered; of prattling tongues hushed in their sunny glee; of earthly treasures swept away; and that "Thou hast all seasons for thine own, O Death!"

Many a sad tale of heavy affliction is brought again to our memory by looking upon those monuments of love in that still and silent resting-place of the dead, and many a simple but sorrowful story could be told of those who people that village graveyard. For, although sickness and death but rarely visited that retired spot, yet long years had brought many to that last home.

That grave, far away by itself, alone and without companionship, unmarked by head or foot-stone, desolate and solitary, and almost smooth with the common turf, is as vivid now in my imagination as when, shuddering, I crept stealthily by it many years ago. It is the last resting-place of the suicide. His was a sad fate, and one of the strangest and most horrible events that ever disturbed the quiet monotony of the village. He came there a stranger, upon an errand of love, and no doubt with a heart alive to gladness and gay with brilliant anticipations of the coming future. His business was to obtain the necessary papers to consummate his marriage with the fair young girl he had wooed and won. He was successful, and when upon his return to the home of his intended bride, while yet upon his way, little dreaming of evil, he was met by an enemy and cruelly insulted. Resenting the injury, he in his rage threatened further punishment to his foe, and that foe, too cowardly to meet him, as a brave man, hand to hand, took a coward's revenge by having him arrested and taken before a magistrate. He was there, upon the oath of his craven antagonist, bound over to keep the peace, and as he was a stranger, and no one appeared to go his security, was committed (as the law directs) to prison for the want of bail. The same sun that beheld him joyous and light-hearted, leaving the little village and hurrying with sparkling eye to the presence of her he loved, beheld him again, and ere it had sunk to rest in the distant west, with bondaged arm, desponding heart, and gloomy brow, placed within the cheerless walls of the village prison. This may be a necessary law, but it often works great injury and injustice, and we have known it too frequently made the engine of a coward's vengeance. It has been said that

"The wildest ills that darken life
Are raptures to the bosom-strife;
The tempest in its blackest form
Is beauty to the bosom's storm."

The poor prisoner must have undergone this fierce bosom-strife, or sunk in utter despondency under this heavy blow, at one stroke crushing all his fond hopes and joyous imaginings; for on the following morning, when visited by the jailer, he was found suspended by the neck—dead! a horrible and terrible object, with his purple swollen face and starting eyes! In the hour of solitude and madness, he had become the victim of his own hand, and died in prison. Instead of embracing his bride, he clasped death to his bosom, and now his soul was in eternity, and his disfigured corpse left to the wonder of the gaping villagers.

Well do we remember that ghastly and terrible scene, and the cold, chilly sensations that stole through our heart as we looked upon that shuddering sight, and beheld his now useless license, and that plain gold ring glittering with pale, unearthly light upon his swollen finger. No one thought of moving that ring from his stiff, clammy hand! It was the last fond gift of a doting mother, a gentle sister, or, may be, one even dearer than these. But there it was—he prized it when alive, and it rests with him now in his dishonoured grave. His body was taken by the jailer and his assistants and carried to his last long home—that lonely grave; and there, without a friend, without a mourner, without a sigh, a tear, or a prayer, was buried the stranger suicide. There, upon the top of the hill, rest the whites; a little farther down, placed below those who were their masters before death made them all equal, sleep the blacks; and there, still farther down, below them all, without a stone or a monument, without even a head-stone or a line to tell his name and fate, slumbers, quiet and still enough, the victim of suicide. Solitary and alone, separate and apart, and away from his fellows, as if there were not enough solitude in the grave, rests the mouldering remains of that unfortunate man. We shunned that humble grave when we were a boy, for there was something startling and terrible to our young heart when we thought of his mournful death; but in after years we often stood by that lonely mound, and mused long and sorrowfully over his sad, sad fate.

But our story is not of the past nor of the dead,—and we must leave this beautiful and sacred spot, with all its sad memories, and mingle again with the living.

We know, gentle reader, you will pardon this wandering of ours; for who can think of his childhood, and the merry days of youth—when all was sunshine and song—without paying a passing tribute to the good old days of yore, and to the memory of his ancient home. This was indeed a strange little town, with its queer old habits and customs, and its simple-hearted, contented inhabitants. But, notwithstanding they thought not as the world thinks, and had little to do with the novelties, amusements, and fashions of the day, yet within that quiet, unpretending village, as novel as it may appear, there were men of the highest talent and genius; and as a general thing, the citizens were as intelligent and well educated as in any place, of the same population, in Kentucky or the world. Then we must not forget the ladies. Unlike the males, who cared so little for dress or fashion, they have ever followed the customs of the changing age, if not as strictly as some, at least close enough never to be odd, or to attract attention by the antiquity of their apparel. Inheriting all the beauty of mother Eve, blessed with rare intelligence, gifted with much natural grace, and remarkable for their modesty and gentleness of heart, they are well fitted in every respect to grace the drawing-rooms of the proudest and loveliest of all our land, and cannot be excelled in anything becoming or lovely in the character of a woman.

Taking all things together, this quiet little village was as pleasant a home as could be found in many days' journey, a kind of modern Arcadia, with its peaceful calmness,—"a happy valley" (something like that from which Rasselas escaped), where a man could live and dream away life, unruffled by a single storm.

But, as we have already remarked, a long time ago, in the commencement of this chapter, the great, grand Dead Sea calm which had fallen upon this waveless and billowless village was now broken and rent asunder. The quiet and peace which had rested over that ancient town for so many years was now destroyed, and destroyed forever! Never again will our old home be what it once was, when we were a boy, and when the good old teacher went through his "serene review," giving forth his riband of honour to the successful "smiler." All the male inhabitants of the village, from the oldest to the youngest, were now gathered together in awful wonderment, crowding with staring eyes (and for them, frightful commotion) around, not the mouth of the raging Vesuvius, or a great opening in the earth, such as Curtius closed,—patriotically closed,—but around nothing more nor less than an "auger-hole." Yes, gentle reader, it was not another sack of Rome, neither was it another rape of the Sabines, but it was a genuine, bona fide "auger-hole," and, in the language of Free Tom, "it wasn't nothing else." But this unusual and unlooked-for sight (found where it was) was quite sufficient to stir up all the latent energies of that hitherto sleeping community.

Old Rip, once awake, has never again been caught napping, and, from the morning of this commotion, there has been a rapid and wonderful change going on in the habits and notions of the people, and in the appearance of that little village. The lethargy and apathy which had so long borne heavily upon them, crushing their motive power, and laying a distinctive mark between them and the balance of the world, once broken, never again resumed their sway. From that day you may date the first inroad of cigars and whiskers. From that hour, old houses have become new—old coats have been trimmed, and docked, and remodelled—bell-crown hats have given away to sharp tops—round-toed to square-toed shoes—and the peace of that hitherto silent town is now nightly broken by the braying of a "brass band" and the puff of a steam-engine, and, what is still more strange, all these changes and improvements are mainly ascribable to that "auger-hole."

You must not suppose that these quiet villagers were ignorant of mechanics or mechanical instruments, and had never before seen an "auger-hole"; for it was not so, since for many years they had been well acquainted with the science of "boring." Do not think, for a moment, that we use the

THE WILLIAM G. DUNCAN RESIDENCE, GREENVILLE. ERECTED 1912

word "boring" in its fashionable sense, for we have no such intention, and, if we did, it would not be true, for the good citizens, among their other strange peculiarities, were not in the habit of talking much, but, on the contrary, were rather reserved and much given (if such a thing can be) to silence. This particular "auger-hole," which was then creating so much excitement and which has since been the cause of such wonderful changes, was discovered in the window-blind of the Dutchman's store, one of their principal stores, a very unusual place, not at all necessary, either for light, safety, or beauty. No wonder they were surprised and suspicious; for that little hole, although then harmless, and not large enough for a fairy to slip through without greasing, still augured, not only the presence of an auger (they could have forgiven that), but of a robber and burglar!

Like the footsteps discovered by Crusoe upon the sandy beach of his little island, it told of danger, and that they were no longer safe, unless secured by lock and bar. The good citizens wondered much, studied long, looked intently, and shook their heads; pointed at the ominous hole, and talked in low whispers; suspected every man with whiskers that they could bring to memory, and yet they hesitated, and were in doubt what to do or where to turn for safety. But, while still deep in their mazy cogitations, they were suddenly aroused by loud cries of distress, and the little Dutchman, wringing his hands and swearing, burst in upon the amazed crowd, crying out that he had been robbed. . . .

The crowd had now a faint inkling of the cause of his wailing, and, like politicians deserting a fallen star, left, without a sigh or backward look, the hitherto fearful and wonderful and mysterious "auger-hole," and rushed pellmell to the Dutchman's store.

And there, sure enough, were all the marks and evidences of the midnight robbery, for the burglars had left broad traces of their recent presence. The money-desk had been broken open, and all the poor Dutchman's hard-earned spoils, with the exception of a handful of coppers and a few German pieces, not considered pure coin (and which the thieves had scorned to take), carried away. His goods, too, had not been treated with that gentleness and care with which a well-trained salesman would have handled such articles, but were thrown about in wild confusion over counter and floor, and all that were of any great value had been removed, by the very choice and select robbers, to some other market.

While the excited crowd were still gazing with speechless dismay and horror upon these unmistakable evidences of a daring robbery, committed in their very midst, a countryman rode up, and, being informed of the cause of this unprecedented tumult, declared that he had seen, only a few hours previous, a band of bearded men, travelling with great rapidity along a certain solitary road, and that they had many bundles and packs, so many that he had taken them for movers or a company of hunters.

"You are certain they wore whiskers?" shouted one of the bystanders.

"Yes," replied the countryman.

"Then they are the robbers!" exclaimed the same voice.

"Ay, they are the robbers!" shouted the whole assembly, without a dissenting voice, now that they had certain proof as to the whiskers,—for they would have convicted any man on such evidence as that.

A few moments later, a company of well-armed and well-mounted men, led by the countryman as guide, dashed from the village in hot pursuit of the daring invaders. Nor was it many hours before they discovered, in a lonely wood, Lonz Powers and a band of his desperadoes, for they were the robbers and burglars who had thus rudely disturbed the security of that unguarded town. The villagers were bold men, excited with the hope of making a terrible example of those daring villains who had so rashly destroyed the peace of their quiet realm, and did not hesitate how to act when once in view of their retreating foe. So soon as within shooting distance, they poured in a volley from pistol, shotgun, and rifle, and with a loud shout charged gallantly upon the enemy. The robbers were well mounted, for they had the pick of the country in their horses, and, not choosing to meet their enraged pursuers, dropped their spoils, dashing off helter-skelter through the woods, every man for himself, as fast as their steeds, urged by whip, and spur, and voice, could carry them. With but one exception, they all escaped; and he, his horse being disabled by the first fire, fell into the hands of the villagers, and was afterwards induced by some very *striking* reasons given him (by the Regulators, into whose tender hands he was in a few days committed), to make very valuable discoveries, which eventually put an end to the career of Lonz Powers and his companions.

Proudly the exulting conquerors returned to the village, loaded with the recovered goods of the Dutchman, and bearing in their midst, bound hand

and foot, a fierce, dark-visaged, black-whiskered bandit. The prisoner was a sullen, devilish-looking cut-throat as one would care about meeting; returning stare for stare with the gaping villagers, and refusing to answer any questions, or doing so only in a dogged, sullen tone, defying them to do their worst, and threatening every imaginable vengeance.

Many a rusty, long-disused fowling-piece or pistol was dragged from its hiding-place on that memorable night. Many a door, that never knew a lock before, was made intimately acquainted with that civilized guard; and many an anxious citizen had a weary, broken sleep of it, dreaming of huge

MAIN STREET, GREENVILLE, IN 1912
Looking north from opposite the main entrance of the Courthouse

whiskers as big as the court-house cupola, flourishing away upon the faces of terrible and hideous robbers; starting at every slam of a crazy window-shutter, and imagining the gnawing of the hungry rat the file of the desperate burglar. It was a dreadful, uneasy night to the nervous villagers—that first night after the robbery—and it will not be soon forgotten, for, since that time, they date all events from that memorable epoch; and it has become just as much a habit with them to say, "from the year of the great robbery," as it used to be, "from the year of the shakes."

Alas! sweet little village! thy quiet and spirit-like stillness so dreamy and fairy-like, is now gone; and, I fear me much, gone never to return. Thy citizens have tasted excitement, and for one entire day the usual places of resort have been deserted, and the ordinary amusements swallowed up in wild astonishment, first, at the "auger-hole," then, at the actual scene of robbery, and, last of all, in gazing upon the fierce whiskers of an actual live robber.

From that ever-to-be-remembered day—that day of horror and tumult—the good citizens have never been able to fall back into their old habits and customs and peculiarities. It is true, the young men still play marbles, and the old men still talk politics and go regularly to church; but then they have other sources of pleasure, and take delight in far different amusements from what they did in our day.

The march of improvement, an impetus having been given by this robbery, is now onward. New merchants, new tailors, new lawyers, and new divines are now moving in, and the old settlers, forced by necessity, are compelled either to change their musty habits or be driven by public opinion, in disgrace, from their ancient hunting-grounds. The bell at the old tavern, with its famous and well-known landlady, still sticks out for the ancient customs, ringing as it did of yore the summons to meals, at daylight, eleven, and four o'clock; but many of the citizens, smitten with the lazy fashions of modern improvers, disregarding its shrill call, sleep long after that little bell has pealed out its alarum; and many of them have even gone so far as to dine at twelve and sup at dark, and sit up as late as nine, although the majority, I am happy to say, still fall to sleep at the good old hour of seven.

As for the public, or high-days and holidays, the good people of **Greenville**, wishing, no doubt, to make up for past neglect, now celebrate not only Christmas, the 8th of January, 22d of February, and 4th of July, but throw in some three or more for good count, upon which day-offering they have braying from the brass band and puffing from temperance orators. Had the robbers never bored that "auger-hole," or robbed the Dutchman, they might have continued their thriving to this day; and that little village would have remained enjoying its ancient nap, and never awakened to the fuss, turmoil, and improvements of this changing age. They might have robbed almost any other town, and the robbery would have created no disturbance; but unfortunately, in an evil hour for them, they fell upon this quiet, out-of-the-way place, where the mere boring of an auger-hole shook the entire community to its very foundations, and led, not only to their future overthrow and ruin, but to the happiness (that is, in the estimation of the age), prosperity, and final greatness and glory of this hitherto slumbering, but now thoroughly awakened village.

Alas! my ancient home, you have changed, but I will not say for the better. I remember only thy quiet old days, when the hum of the singing insect, and the buzz of the floating bee, was the only and loudest music heard within thy silent borders. I will not think of thee as thou art now, noisy with the clattering hammer and shaken by the hoarse belching of steam, but will continue my slumber, forever dreaming that thou art now what thou used to be, my own, still, quiet, peaceful home!

XV

THE OLD MILITIA MUSTER

UP to the year 1850 every man in Kentucky considered himself a soldier, and was so considered in the eyes of the law. Until the Third Constitution was adopted, every male citizen from the age of twenty to forty-five, with a few exceptions, was on the enrolled militia and reported at a mustering place on specified dates and there took part in military drills. Such was the law old Virginia inherited from England, and it was also the law when Kentucky became a State, and, as before stated, remained a law until 1850. To-day every able-bodied man from eighteen to forty-five years of age is enrolled as a soldier of the United States under compulsion to respond if called upon in time of war. If he does not belong to the regular army or navy, or is not a member of the national guard, he then belongs to the reserve militia.

Previous to about the year 1820 the militia muster was a gathering of citizen-soldiers who met for the purpose of drilling, and all devoted their time while on the muster grounds to military exercises conducted according to military tactics. However, about five years after the second war with England, interest in the military features of these gatherings began to decline, and during the second quarter of the century all of the musters were more or less a farce.

The law required all able-bodied men, with a few exceptions, to report for duty at the musters, and imposed a fine for non-attendance. The company musters usually took place in April, June, August, and September; the battalion usually in May, and the regimental in October. In the early days a company consisted of from fifty to one hundred men, including officers; two to four companies constituted a battalion, and two to four battalions formed a regiment. The number of men in these various organizations was governed principally by the extent of the population in the locality.

Among the many places in the county on which companies met to drill were: The courthouse yard, the Russell Old Field, the Andy Craig place, Kincheloe's Bluff, Morehead's Field (now Central City), the George Clark place, Thomas Sumner's farm, the Solomon Rhoads farm, the Hunt Old Field, William Bell's, the Vanlandingham Old Place, the Jim Taggart farm, Wyatt Wells', the Mosley Collins Drake farm, Old Liberty, Mike Lovell's, Old Millport, and the Gish Old Field. Up to about 1820 most of the battalion and regimental drills took place in Greenville. After that time the place of rendezvous for the men in the southern part of the county was changed to the Russell Old Field, southeast of Greenville, near what is now Pleasant Hill Church. In the meantime regimental musters also took place on the Gish Old Field, south of Bremen, and other fields in the northern part of the county. These two regiments, it is said, on several occasions drilled together on the Russell Old Field.

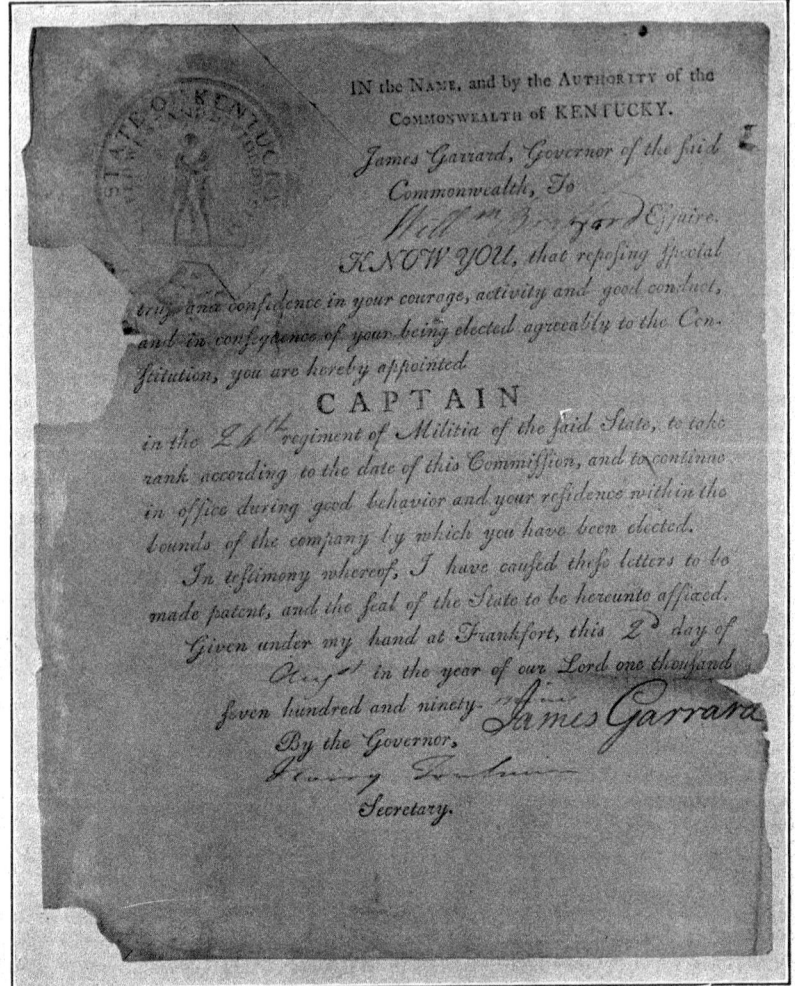

Reduced facsimile of commission showing appointment of William Bradford as Captain of Militia, August 2, 1799

Very little documentary data bearing on the early history of the militia in Muhlenberg is now extant, and as far as I am aware none exists pertaining to its later history in the county. An old commission, still preserved, shows that William Bradford was among the first local men to serve as a captain. Others may have been appointed at the same time, but none preceded him. He probably later filled other positions in the militia. A photograph of the Bradford commission is here reproduced. On the back of the original is written: "Muhlenberg County, Sct. This day came William Bradford before me, a justice of the peace for said county, and made oath as Captain of the Militia company. Given under my hand this 20th day of February, 1800. Wm. Bell."

From a few of the other commissions still preserved I gather the following facts: Charles Fox Wing was "appointed Lieutenant in the Twenty-fourth regiment of Militia, on August 2, 1799"; Alney McLean was appointed Ensign in the same regiment on the same date; Lewis Kincheloe on September 30, 1800, was "appointed Lieutenant-Colonel commandant of the Fortieth regiment of Militia to fill the vacancy occasioned by the resignation of William Campbell, Esquire." William Bell, on February 9, 1801, was "commissioned Paymaster, with the rank of Lieutenant in the Fortieth regiment." Lewis Reno, on May 24, 1802, was "commissioned Ensign in the Fortieth regiment." Thomas Randolph, on March 22, 1803, was "commissioned Captain in the Fortieth regiment."

A certificate of exemption, written on letter paper, reads: "Kentucky. At a court-martial held for the Fortieth Regiment of Militia in the County of Muhlenberg on the 24th day of May, 1802: Ordered, that George Lovelace be and he is hereby exempt from military duty in future for and on account of his having his arm broke. A Copy Test. Charles Fox Wing, Judge Advocate."

An official notice, written on a small piece of paper and addressed to Captain Samuel Weir, reads:

Battalion Order, March 12, 1811.

Sir: You will have your Company parade at Solomon Rhoads's on the 17th day of May next by ten o'clock in order to hold a Battalion Muster. You will also have your Company parade in like manner at William Bell's on the second day of October next in order to hold a Regimental Muster. The Drill Muster will be held on the last Wednesday and Thursday in September next at William Bell's. The Court of Assessment of fines will be held also at William Bell's on the last Monday in November.

THOMAS BELL, Majr. Comdt.
1st Battalion of the 32nd Regt. K. M.

As already stated, from about the year 1825 until the law obliging all men to drill was abolished, the musters were more or less a farce. The laws regulating the militia of the Commonwealth were amended and changed so often that, as a consequence, they became more complicated than the maneuvers were unmilitary. Humphrey Marshall, in 1824 ("History of Kentucky," Vol. 2, page 14), wrote: "It is in vain to suggest that neither officer nor soldier will ever trouble himself to know the law, when it may, and probably will, be changed before he has an opportunity of reducing his knowledge to practice." Musters became gatherings in which everybody participated, regardless of age or social position. The men who attended were not so much prompted by a desire to drill, and thus live up to that article of the Constitution, as they were to take advantage of the chance to mingle with the crowd of men, women, and children, renew old friendships, make new ones, hear the news, see the races, trade horses, partake of a good dinner, and incidentally have a good time at "the big to-do."

The military features of these affairs grew insignificant as compared with those of their social, political, and business nature. The ordinary picnic basket was too small for these gatherings. Trunks and boxes packed with fried chicken, boiled ham, roasted pork, pies and other edibles, with coffee-pots and whisky-jugs, were brought to the place of rendezvous in wagons, and everybody was welcome to their contents. Gunsmiths were in abundance. Since the greater number of people came in wagons or on horseback, there was necessarily a large aggregation of horses, from colts and two-year-olds down to worn-out plow-horses, and from carefully groomed quarter-nags to neglected horses whose tails and manes were filled with burrs. This led to the appearance of blacksmiths, who repaired wagons and shod horses. It also resulted in much "horse swapping," which in turn gave occasion for betting and horse-racing. The combination led to drinking, and drinking frequently brought on "fist and skull fights" and other disturbances.

In those days, as in the earlier days, every man furnished his own gun—muzzle-loaders of any sort, flintlock rifles, muskets, shotguns, or horse-pistols. Those who had no firearms to bring, or who had forgotten them, would enter the drills with a trimmed sapling or a cornstalk—consequently the name, the Cornstalk Militia.

When the captain was ready to order his company into ranks he usually mounted a convenient stump, rail fence, or empty barrel and called out: "Oh, yes! Oh, yes! Oh, yes! All you who belong to Captain So-and-so's company (giving his name) fall into ranks and parade!" The "Oh, yes," it might be well to add, is derived from the old French "oyez"—"hear ye." Hence the Court of Oyer and Terminer—to hear and to finish. If the captain's first order failed to move his men he would again appeal to them—"Everybody in my company, off the fence there and fall into line! Now come on, men, come on, everybody, and let's get started with our *revolutions!*" After all, or nearly all, of his company had responded to his call, he ordered "'Tention, the whole!" after which most men gave him more or less attention. Right or left dress was usually lengthened into the command to "Look to the left and dress!" or right, as the case might be. "Stop!" or "Hold!" was the command for halt. It is also said that although keeping step was a matter of indifference or beyond the control of some of the privates, they were nevertheless permitted to remain in ranks and follow as best they could or would through the drills.

Company, battalion, and regimental drills were conducted on the Russell Old Field from May to October, making a total of at least six different musters on that tract every year. It became a great gathering-place, especially when a Big Muster (a battalion or regimental drill) was scheduled. Horse-races on such occasions were then by far the most prominent feature on the program, and they soon became more frauds than the drills were farces. In fact, the Russell Old Field is even to-day more frequently referred to as the Old Russell Race Track than the Old Russell Muster Field, although no races have taken place there since the days of the militia muster.

The Russell Race Track and muster grounds, like every other historic place in the county, is the subject of many absurd tales. One of these pertains to the threshing of wheat. In the early times one of the methods the farmer employed to get his wheat out of the chaff was to "tramp" it out. He located a stretch of ground that would pack solid. On this he built a ring fifty to one hundred feet in diameter. After scattering his wheat on

RUINS OF THE O. C. VANLANDINGHAM, SR., RESIDENCE, PARADISE COUNTRY
Standing near a number of fields used as drilling-grounds

the inner edge of this circle he walked his horse over it and thus trod out the grain. On some farms this was done on the wooden floor of the barn. At any rate, the story is told that after the Russell Race Track was finished a certain farmer brought his wheat, stock and all, to the track on a race day and scattered it over the course, and that while running the races the horses trod all the grain out of the chaff, thus relieving the raiser of that wheat of any further work except to "rake up the golden grain."

All the traditions regarding this old Muster Field teem with romance and comedy except one—the killing of Isom Sheffield by Bob Jenkins. This tragedy took place in the fall of 1842 and during the time the Regulators were hunting down the outlaws. It is said Jenkins was in sympathy with the Regulators and that Sheffield disapproved of some of their work. These two men had argued this question on several occasions, and their disagreement soon developed into enmity. Both came to the Big Muster. Jenkins was sitting on a log when Sheffield, who was approaching from the rear, either by accident or intention hit Jenkins with a sumac stick. A few short words had passed between them an hour before, and now the provocation for a fight presented itself. After a short but fierce struggle Sheffield ran away from Jenkins, some say because he feared the many friends of Jenkins who had gathered around, while others declare he ran to get a weapon concealed in his wagon. Jenkins, highly infuriated, followed him with an open knife in his hand. When Jenkins had gotten within a few feet of his antagonist and was ready to make a stab, Sheffield tripped on a root and fell. Jenkins immediately thrust his knife into Sheffield's back, killing him instantly. Jenkins surrendered to the authorities, gave bond, and the following year was acquitted on the plea of self-defense, but some years later was shot from ambush.

After this fatal event the preachers and church people began a campaign against the meetings on the Russell Muster Field. For a year or two the races were discontinued, but soon large and reckless crowds gathered again and things went from bad to worse until 1850, when the militia musters were discontinued throughout the State.[1]

James Weir, in his boyhood days, saw the decline of the old militia muster, and in 1850, shortly after he wrote "Lonz Powers," saw its final fall. He frequently attended the drills on the Russell Race Track. Observations made there and at Old White Plains in Christian County suggested, it is said, much of what appears in his chapter on the old military muster. Historians generally either refer simply to the old-time military musters, or in the course of a few words vaguely suggest what they were. The following satirical description, taken from "Lonz Powers," is probably the only thing of its kind ever written, and deserves to rank among Kentucky classics:

Every nation has a memorable day—a day of songs and rejoicings. With us the fourth of July, twenty-second of February, and Christmas, are all holidays, or days of joy and pleasure. But of all the grand days in this martial old Commonwealth of ours, those set apart for militia training are (at least in the estimation of militia captains) the grandest and most exciting. If you should happen within ten miles of a militia muster on one of these eventful days, every step you took, and every object that met your gaze, would remind you of war, with its glorious and thrilling panoply, its noise and wild tumult. Boys, negroes, and men, on foot and on horseback, in cart, wagon, and carriage, single, double, and treble, are crowding from every direction and hurrying with anxious speed toward the scene where mimic battles are to be fought and won. Old shotguns, rusty rifles, long-untried fowling-pieces, cornstalks, and hickory sticks are in great demand, while the Sunday fineries, drawn from their secret hiding-places, adorn the martial forms of their proud-treading owners. Cider-wagons, ginger-cakes, apples, whisky, and all the other et ceteras of the camp, are rushing pellmell into the place of rendezvous. Arriving at the parade field,

---

[1] The Russell tract was first settled by John C. Russell, who moved on it about the year 1805 and remained there until 1820. After he moved to Todd County his level fields and abandoned houses were used for mustering purposes for many years. John C. Russell represented the county in the Legislature from 1807 to 1809. He was a liberal and kind-hearted man. His farm, in its day, was one of the best equipped in the county. No traces of his large log residence can now be seen. Even the ruins of the old stone milk-house have almost disappeared.

your ears are greeted with every imaginable noise—the squealing of pigs, neighing of chargers, barking of dogs, braying of asses, laughing of happy negroes, and hoarse commands of military chieftains being mingled together in the most harmonious concord of discord. Jingling spurs, rusty sabers, black cockades, and the fierce little red plume, everywhere meet your wandering eye and fill up the interstices of this moving, animated scene.

Such an exhibition of warlike enthusiasm might have been seen, if you had only been present, dear reader, at Pleasant Grove, on the morning after

RUINS OF THE "JIM TAGGART OLD PLACE"
Standing on the Russellville Road near Hazel Creek Church. Built about 1810, abandoned 1900. Many militia musters were held here

the night described in our last chapter. Noise and wild confusion were the order of the day. The thrilling fife and a cracked drum were pealing forth their stirring notes, and calling loudly upon the brave sons of old Kentucky to shoulder their arms and sustain the glory of their ancestors. Generals, colonels, majors, captains (we have no lack of titled gentry in Kentucky), and privates were mingled together in a confused mass, talking, laughing, shouting, swearing, drinking, and every now and then taking a pleasant knock-down, merely to vary the bill of entertainment, keep up the excitement, and cultivate a proper military ardour. Candidates were there, too (like all other aspirants for office), shaking hands, treating, speaking, and making known to the warlike assembly the past, present, and future (they were no prophets, merely reasoning from cause to effect) glory and renown of Kentucky and her gallant sons. Horse-racing, cock-fighting, rifle-shooting, wrestling, and boxing, upon this occasion, all had their votaries, and all were busily engaged in their respective amusements. Babel, in her palm-lest day, was a mere "tempest in a teapot" compared with a militia muster in the backwoods of Kentucky. The Carnival at Rome or the ancient Saturnalia of the Romans, in the very height of their revelling, would be tame and insipid when placed in juxtaposition with such an occasion. We know of nothing that can be compared, for noise and wild confusion, with a regiment of boisterous, merry, reckless militia, along with their chivalrous leaders, adorned with flowing red sash, bullet-button coats, tin-foil epaulets, and stiff, ragged, red plumes, just preceding or succeeding "the training."

But suddenly a great change comes over the moving, tossing mass gathered on the battlefield at Pleasant Grove. Some order (a devilish little, by-the-by, if it can be called order at all) takes the place of the late disorder, and a comparative calm—in a figurative sense—settles down upon this raging storm. The commanding officer of the day, stripping his saddle of its red girth, belts on his trusty, trenchant blade, dons his swallow-tailed blue, adorned with bullet-buttons and red tape, borrows the best charger he can find, scrambles on his back with the assistance of a stump or a kind hand, and, when once safely moored, waves his plumed beaver around his warlike head, and shouts his orders to parade. Now comes a busy, stirring, wild, and moving panorama. Men, before ignoble and unknown from the common herd, draw from their bosoms, pockets, and hats the red plume and sash (that is, if they are so lucky as to have any), and soon become the leaders and chieftains of the day. A fierce struggle now commences who shall get their companies first formed into a line, or who shall first gain a preëmption right to the shade of a tree, under which to marshal and form. Although each company has, or rather has had at some former time, a captain and inferior officers (for they often assemble on parade-ground without any), in reality every man in the corps, being fully competent to command, takes the responsibility of giving orders.

It may be thought an easy matter by the inexperienced to form a company of men into a straight line; but if it is so, our militia captains have never discovered that fact. They commence at one end of the winding line, and with threats, entreaties, and much trouble get a tolerably fair and straight row, especially if there be any corn-ridges in the immediate neighborhood, but, unfortunately, before they reach the other extreme, their soldiers having a predisposition for Mahometanism, are generally in a crescent, and then they are compelled to begin afresh. And thus we have seen them go on for hours and hours, and at last end their labours, not being in much better array or condition than at the beginning of their arduous and impossible undertaking. Tall, low, long, short, thin, and fat, old and young, men and boys, clothed with fur and wool hats, caps, and no hats at all; cloth coats and jeans, calico and linsey, and no coats at all; boots, shoes, and moccasins, and no shoes at all; new and old pants, white, black, and striped, and no pants at all; shirts ruffled and unruffled, white, black, green, and gray, cotton, linen, and calico, and no shirts at all—are all mingled together in the most beautiful and checkered confusion, giving a motley and ludicrous appearance to the ununiformed, straggling, and crooked corps.

The officers are generally the most silly and ignorant men of the community, for none but such will seek a command in so farcical a concern as a militia company; and most frequently elected, as the saying is, unanimously, for they are considered most "unanimous fools," and no one will vote either for or against them. As for a knowledge of military tactics, they never dream of any such a thing. They are unable (with a few exceptions, of course) to form even a straight line, unless they have the assistance of a ditch or a corn-row, and as for giving any other orders save "About face!" (to which they add "right!") "March!" it is a thing not only unknown but unheard of. Those who can read are accustomed to carry "Scott's Tactics" in their pockets, from which they read out the different commands or manœuvres, but as for knowing what is then to be done, after spelling through the various movements, they don't think of such a thing, for it is none of their business. They are placed there to give the orders, and it is the duty of the company to obey; and if they fail to do so, then it

THE MOSLEY COLLINS DRAKE HOUSE, LONG CREEK COUNTRY
Built in 1816, abandoned in 1912. Many company drills took place in a field near by

is their own fault, for their skilful captains have read out all the necessary instructions *as plain as Scott* himself could give them.

We know of but one real, genuine, whole-souled, praiseworthy militia captain, and he has now left the country and moved to Arkansas. He was a glorious, jolly fellow, that old captain of ours, and if ever a military leader deserved a monument of brass, he was that one; and we will give a ten at any time we are called on towards bestowing that honour to his memory. He was, during his soldiering life, the most popular chieftain of the age—always excepting Old Hickory and his sons, the young Hickories— and we will venture to say his company was the most numerous and well-attended of the regiment, so long as he was permitted to drill under his own laws and in his own *spirited* way.

His mode of operating (and we make it known for the benefit of martial spirits) was to form his corps as near into a straight line as possible; but he only attempted this difficult manœuvre once a day, and that very early in the morning, for after that, not even with the assistance of a fence or ditch could he keep them either perpendicular or rectilinear. Then marching at the head of his brave companions, he opened with a vigorous pursuit of the enemy, and at a suitable and convenient spot, made known to him by his spy (for he always threw out an advance guard), he generally discovered the foe, disguised and changed by the fairies into a half dozen blue or red (most frequently red) pails, and well filled with mint julep, a ladle in each (a trick of the enemy to induce a charge) and commanded by that old bruiser and man-overthrower John Barleycorn, always ready and willing (like Wellington at Waterloo) to be attacked. There is no shrinking or giving back in John, and, like Old Zack, the word retreat is unknown in his tactics, let the enemy be ever so fierce and numerous.

Our gallant captain was one of the same sort, a real Murat for daring charges; and, forming his men into platoons of six—for he scorned to take advantage of his superior number—led them manfully to the contest, full upon the battery of the foe, although ready to *pour* out destruction upon himself and followers. "Make ready!" was his hoarse command, and down went the dippers; "Take aim!" and up they came on a level with the mouth; "Fire!" and away goes the liquid stream, not of fire, but of fire-water, down the thirsty throats of his soldiers. "Next platoon, march!" (there was no pricking of bayonets to urge them on); "Make ready, take aim, fire!" and thus each individual of the band had an opportunity to display his nerve and steadiness under a point-blank shot from the stubborn foe. Nor was our noble captain content with battling this little squad of the enemy, for, like a true hero that he was, he allowed the foe to send after fresh ammunition, and bring up the reserve, squad after squad, and still continue the fight, showing no quarter and asking none, until he alone of all that gallant corps is left *standing* to face the "red coats." "I see them on their winding way," was the favourite air of this fighting band of heroes, and many a battle have they fought with the "Britishers," as the red pails were called, when spirited on by this good old tune.

The followers of the captain, unlike other militia, were far more steady when going into the fray than when coming out. We remember you well, most jovial son of Mars, and wherever you may now be, and whatever may be your fate, we will never cease to give you honor, although you were a militia captain. We have fought and have been defeated under your banner, but never disgraced, for, like conquerors, we always slept upon the field of battle and close around the battery of the enemy.

The martial farce is now over; the red plumes have vanished; the bullet-buttons are numbered among the things "that were," and bright sabers no longer glitter in the sunbeams. They who but a moment since lorded it over their fellow-men, dubbed as generals, colonels, majors, and captains, and as grandly and gloriously as Napoleon and his marshals, or the Grand Turk and his pachas, are now but common citizens, without command, and no longer in authority; and (what is still worse for them) liable at any moment to be soundly thrashed by any of the sovereigns they may have been so unfortunate as to insult during the drill!—a privilege not unfrequently enforced, very much to the discomfort of the gallant commanders.

The soul-inspiring drum and fife have ceased, and the old forest no longer echoes back the martial roll. Boys, negroes and stragglers, wanting the excitement of military music, and glutted with warlike pageantry, are now making hasty preparations for departure. Cider-barrels and cake-baskets are empty; and their happy owners and venders, shaking their swelling purses, go on their way rejoicing. All are now gone, or preparing to leave, save those brave spirits who intend to sleep upon the field and upon their arms, for the very simple reason that they have fallen victims to Bacchus and are unable to leave.

And such is a militia muster—a great, grand, sometimes laughable but always silly farce, and not only tolerated, but legalized and even commanded by our laws. Yet do we suffer, and, like good citizens, obey—three times annually leaving our labour and business to undergo this most absurd of all absurdities, a "militia training."

XVI

THE STORY OF THE STACK

THE ruins of the old Buckner Furnace, known as "The Stack," form one of the most desolate, yet interesting landmarks in the county. As far as I am aware, nothing, save one paragraph in the First Kentucky Geological Survey, has ever been written on the history of this once flourishing place. The deed books in the county clerk's office record the dates of land transfers, but reveal none of the romances and tragedies that make up the Story of The Stack. Members of the younger generation—many, at least, of those with whom I have come in contact—simply know the remains of the Buckner Furnace as "The Stack," the "Old Furnace," or the "Pennsylvania Furnace," and that General Simon Bolivar Buckner had been in some way connected with the old iron works. Collins in his 1847 edition refers to it as the "Henry Clay Iron Works." So the old people were the only ones from whom I could gather any information, and they frequently disagreed on very important points. The Stack, I find, was erected in 1837 and was operated only a few years. The few men and women now living who saw the place when it was running were all too young to remember their visits; some of them, nevertheless, are well versed in the traditions of the old Furnace.

One young man, who might have learned something of the history of The Stack from his grandparents, unaware of his ignorance regarding local and national history, "informed" me that The Stack was built by General Buckner during the Mexican War, and a few years later, when the American Revolution broke out, General Buckner furnished Washington and Andrew Jackson with guns and swords with which to whip the French and British; that if General Buckner had not been prepared to supply the iron from The Stack for the making of American cannon, and if saltpeter had not been discovered in Mammoth Cave about this time, England would have won the fight and helped Jeff Davis defeat the North! All of which, if not history, is at least interesting.

The land on which The Stack stands was for a long time owned by a company of capitalists, and is therefore frequently referred to as "the Company land." However, the same young man insists that this title originated from the fact that many of the people living on this tract of land in olden times had "a heap of company."

Another rural philologist, pointing out a piece of pig iron made at The Stack three quarters of a century ago, "informed" me that his grandfather said that this pig iron is so called because on "hog-killing" days General Buckner heated these chunks of iron and then threw them into barrels of water in order to bring the water to a temperature sufficient to scald the skin of the hogs, preparatory to scraping off the hair. This process of heating water for cleaning hogs is as old as the hills, the only difference being that ordinary rocks are almost invariably used instead of pig iron.

THE STACK AS IT APPEARED IN 1905

It seems that about the year 1833 one William Miller, of Massachusetts, claimed to have received a revelation (written on some hen eggs he found in a hollow stump) to the effect that the destruction of the world would take place in 1843. He preached this doctrine throughout the United States, and had a few followers in Muhlenberg County. When, in 1842, the Furnace was abandoned, Miller's converts declared Buckner closed down his iron works because he did not want to be running a hot furnace on Judgment Day. Those who did not know why operations were discontinued immediately drew the conclusion that Buckner had become a Millerite. The absurd story thus started is still heard in a few of the local traditions.

Such confusion of the details of national history of which there is a written record, and the telling of such ridiculous tales as these I have just cited, are to be expected, and they serve to show that many statements regarding old places, like many reports regarding current events, are not only false but often absurd, and that "investigation brings out the truth."

At any rate, the discovery of the extensive deposits of surface iron ore in southern Muhlenberg County prompted Aylette H. Buckner (the father of General Buckner) and Cadwalader Churchill to organize a company for the purpose of working this ore. In 1837 they erected a furnace near the junction of Pond Creek and Salt Lick Creek, five miles south of Greenville, and before the close of the following year the iron works were put in operation. The Stack was built at the foot of a hill, and a level gangway was placed from the top of the hill to the top of the furnace, where there was a charging platform over the opening through which the ore was fed. The Stack was a double wall of local sandstone, hooped with six iron bands, the whole forming one massive tower about eighty feet high, forty feet wide at the base, and twenty-five feet across at the top.[1]

Alfred Johnson, Garland Craig, and Thomas Welborn, Muhlenberg's best stone-masons, with the help of others, did the stone work. They must have been masters of their craft, for in spite of the fact that some of the iron bands were removed about the year 1875 and that twenty years later two vandals dynamited it for the purpose of taking the heavy iron bars used to support the four arches, the walls stood for seventy years. It was the irreparable damage done by the two old-iron gatherers that, on January 14, 1907, caused the final collapse of the old landmark, which is now nothing more than a heap of dressed rock.

The Stack and its wooden gangway were by no means the only structures erected by Buckner and Churchill. They also put up a substantial two-story log house of ten rooms, used as a residence, office, and store by the Buckners. It is said that three yoke of oxen were required to transfer Buckner's private library from Hart County to this place. The Buckner house was the largest structure of its kind in the county. It was about one hundred and fifty feet long, constructed of hewed logs, had good glass windows, and floors of sawed lumber. There were three large chimneys and a dozen open fire-places. The building contained a spacious dining room, used by some of the white employes. In an adjoining room, known as "the

---

[1] The first iron furnace in Kentucky was the Bourbon Furnace, built in Bath County in 1791. Iron ore was not discovered in Western Kentucky until about a quarter of a century later. A few years previous to 1837 iron ore had been found in Trigg, Lyon, Hart, and Livingston counties and near Mud River, and was being worked at a number of furnaces when Buckner and Churchill began The Stack. It was at Eddyville, Lyon County, that William Kelly, in 1851, discovered the so-called Bessemer process, which entirely revolutionized the steel industry.

store," goods were kept for the convenience of the people connected with the Furnace and for the purpose of exchanging merchandise with farmers for produce. Opposite the south end of the log house, and built in the hillside, was the stone milk-house, through which there constantly ran a stream of spring water.

Not far from The Stack stood a grist mill, to which corn was brought by the farmers, who gave one sixth of their meal for the grinding. This mill, used later as a tobacco barn by Ben Mitchell and others, was burned to the

RUINS OF THE BUCKNER MILK-HOUSE

ground about 1870, with a large crop of Yellow Pryor in it. Many of the white miners and wood-choppers and the forty slaves occupied log cabins north of The Stack, but all traces of their quarters have now disappeared. In fact the large pile of rock that now marks the site of the Furnace, a few pieces of slag, the ruins of the milk-house, two half-buried corn burrs, two half-filled wells, and a few small mounds where chimneys once stood—all more or less hidden in a jungle of bushes or second-growth timber—are the only evidences of the great work that flourished around The Stack a few years before and after 1840.

As already stated, the discovery of iron ore in Muhlenberg County prompted Buckner and Churchill to organize a company to develop this mineral. Investigation revealed the fact that there was not only sufficient surface ore to justify the building of a furnace, but that there also existed enough good ore below the surface to supply them for a century or more. The furnace they built was in operation about four years, during which time various processes were experimented with. Besides making a great quantity of pig iron they also manufactured a number of iron utensils, among them kettles without legs or "ears," ovens, shovels, tongs, and andirons or dog-irons, some of which can still be found in the county.

The pair of dog-irons of which a picture is here given were made at the Buckner Furnace about the year 1840. Notwithstanding the fact that they

ANDIRONS MADE AT THE STACK IN 1840

were used during cold weather for seventy years, they are for all practical purposes as good now as the day they were cast. The part which supports the log of wood is in one solid piece, about fifteen inches long by four inches high and an half-inch thick. The base is kept in an upright position by a winglike pedestal which spreads out in front. The upright, which keeps the forestick from rolling off on the hearth, is twelve inches high and is a representation of the head of some animal of uncertain identity. It resembles somewhat the head of a camel on the neck of a goose.

Many pairs of dog-irons of this type were made at The Stack, but tradition does not tell who designed them. The designer, if we apply the F. C. Morse theory, evidently was not a "Campbellite"; for Morse, in a book on "Furniture of the Olden Times," says that immediately after the Revolution andirons known as "Hessians," in which the upright was the figure of a Hessian soldier, were very popular, and that "the figures of the hated allies of the British thus received the treatment with flame and ashes that Americans considered the originals to merit, to say nothing of worse indignities cast upon them by the circle of tobacco-using patriots.''

The dwellers in the Buckner colony lived on the best the country then afforded. They not only used the produce and meal furnished by the neighboring farmers, but also supplied themselves with game, fish, and forest fruits. In those days fish were plentiful in Pond Creek.[2] Deer were so numerous and so destructive to crops that many farmers were obliged

"THE STACK HOUSE," NEAR THE STACK

to guard their cornfields to keep the deer from trampling down the growing plants. Raising beans was almost an impossibility, for the deer loved sprouting beans better than some of us like venison. Turkeys were in abundance, and wild pigeons were more plentiful than sparrows are now. 'Coon and 'possum hunting was on the program nearly every night in the fall.

A story is told of a certain Scotchman who, shortly after arriving from his native land, procured a position at the Furnace and one day shot some turkey buzzards while wandering around in Pond Creek bottom, mistaking them for a bird he had eaten in Scotland. With these he prepared a surprise dinner for his friends. All enjoyed the meal very much until the

---

[2] Pond Creek is the longest creek within the bounds of Muhlenberg County. It rises in the Friendship Neighborhood, near the church, and flows into Green River near Paradise.

"Scotch fowl" was indulged in. Many commented on the peculiar flavor of the meat, but, fearing they might offend their host by declining to eat abundantly of his much-prized dish, they partook freely. They begged to know more about this peculiar "Scotch fowl." After some persuasion he proudly told them where and how he had captured this most palatable of birds. The guests threw up their hands in horror. They not only refused to continue the meal, but even declined to keep what they had already accepted!

Much of the salt used by the Furnace people was procured from Deer Lick or Salt Wells, or Salt Lick Creek, about one mile above The Stack, where common salt was made by the evaporating process from the waters of a small spring. It was a well-known lick even before the days of the Buckners, and for many years supplied the immediate neighborhood with this essential. About the year 1855, so runs the story, some men, thinking a stronger solution of salt could be found here, dug three wells near the lick. But the water from the wells proved to be no stronger than that coming from the spring. This was a disappointment to the investigators. Salt water was then boiled and evaporated for a number of days, and the salt thus obtained thrown back into the wells; a Greenville capitalist was then invited to inspect the new "gold mine." He made a hasty inspection and analysis of the water, bought the farm, and some time later learned that there is such a thing as "salting" a salt well.

The Furnace folks spent some of their leisure time on the hill west of The Stack, on the old Indian burying-grounds. Some of the picnic parties that spend a day around or near the ruins of The Stack climb this hill and view what is now left of the seven mounds that once stood there. It is a joke among some of the neighborhood boys to tell the newcomer that if he wishes to know why these Indians were killed he need but stand on any of the mounds and solemnly cry out, "Lo, poor Indian, for what did the white man kill you?" Not hearing a response, the newcomer is urged to ask the question again. He finally discovers that "Nothing" is the answer.

Louis Greenway was one of the many interesting characters around the Furnace. He made a wager he could lead a certain blind horse over the trestle to the top of The Stack and then safely back him off again, "with ten drinks in him." Tradition does not say whether "in him" had reference to the man or to the horse. At any rate, it was successfully done.

Shoemaker was the name of the official shoemaker. He exchanged shoes for untanned cowhides. His dealings with his patrons were anything but satisfactory to them, so one day they all joined in and gave him a "cowhide." He has not been heard from since. It was rumored that he joined Lonz Pennington, the outlaw, who was maneuvering in this part of the State at that time. The only thing Shoemaker left behind was a large trough, made from the trunk of an oak tree, and prepared by himself to be used as his coffin. After his departure his intended coffin was used as a feeding trough in a pig-pen.

Many of the men and women connected with The Stack attended church very regularly. Some went to Greenville, while others worshiped with the members of the then newly organized Friendship congregation. Friendship Baptist Church, two miles northwest of The Stack, was then and still is located in what is very appropriately called the Friendship Neighborhood. This congregation was organized in the old Hickory Withe Schoolhouse a few years before The Stack was built. In 1837 its members put up a log house on land donated by Charles Metzker. The third (the present) building was erected in 1893. The burying-ground adjoining was started in 1883, and is now one of the best-kept country graveyards in the county. In it are buried a number of men and women who in their youth saw the Buckner Furnace in operation. One of Friendship's best-known preachers was the Reverend William Dodd Pannell, who was born in Todd County in 1824, came to Friendship about 1855, and died on his farm, near the church, in 1877. He was the father of James P., Thomas B., and Frank B. Pannell.

FRIENDSHIP BAPTIST CHURCH
Upper Pond Creek country

There is a variety of stories told regarding the negro Isaac, who was hanged Friday, July 6, 1838, for attempting to kill Buckner. Some say Buckner had treated him shamefully by starving him and refusing to let him wear shoes, but such statements can not possibly be founded on facts, for Buckner was a tall and portly man, with the reputation of having a heart as kind as he was large. At any rate it was rumored among the slaves that Churchill was willing to abandon the Furnace, and would have done so had Buckner agreed to it. Isaac belonged to the Churchills, who then lived in Elizabethtown, and being dissatisfied with his surroundings came to the conclusion that if he killed Buckner then Churchill would desert the Furnace and he would be allowed to return to his master's home. Supported by this simple logic, the negro proceeded to carry out his plan. He approached Buckner with an ax, and without a word of warning began striking him in the face. Buckner was rescued by some men who happened on the scene, but not until he had fallen unconscious to the ground with two long gashes in his face, the scars of which never disappeared. In the confusion that followed the negro made his escape, and had fled to a point on the Russellville road, a little north of what is now Dunmor, when he was discovered by the Grabel boys, who found the exhausted slave sleeping alongside a log. Not knowing of his bloody deed they were about to release him, when Robert Jackson appeared and recognized him as the negro who had tried to assassinate Buckner. He was sent to Greenville, tried by the court, and sentenced to death. While confined in jail he was frequently visited by Mrs. Churchill, who read religious books to him and also helped him in his prayers.

On the morning of the hanging Isaac was taken from his cell, put on a wagon, where his coffin served as a seat, and was thus driven to the edge of the woods, about half a mile south of Greenville. He was hanged between two poplar trees, and the same wagon and coffin on which he rode to his execution were used as the platform and trap of his gallows. He stood erect on his coffin with a suspended rope around his neck. The horses pulled the wagon forward, Isaac fell, and a few minutes later was prepared for burial.

AYLETTE HARTSWELL BUCKNER, IN 1824

Upon presentation of a certificate of death, signed by the sheriff, Churchill received the sum of one thousand dollars from the State as compensation for his executed slave.[3]

According to some tellers of the story, the negro was not killed by the hanging, but showed signs of life after he was placed in his coffin; whereupon his head was chopped off with the same ax he had used on Buckner, and placed on the end of a hickory pole at the side of the Russellville road, where it remained exposed to the public for a number of days. This statement is not true. However, a circumstance of that nature took place some years later, when a negro by the name of Gray was lynched in Greenville in 1870.

Shortly following his trouble with Isaac, Buckner had another narrow escape. A well was being dug north of The Stack. After reaching a depth of about twenty-five feet one of the charges of powder placed in the bottom did not explode, although a reasonable time was allowed for that purpose. Suspecting carelessness on the part of the man who did the work, Buckner directed one of the negroes to let him down in the box attached to the windlass. He had descended only a short distance when the fuse began to sizz. Buckner immediately commanded the slave to pull him up, but the negro became excited, lost his grip on the winch, and ran away. By the time Buckner had dropped half-way down the well the explosion took place, throwing him and the box up through the opening, landing him some ten feet from the rim.

The negro, having been punished for deserting his post, planned revenge. One of his duties was to dump the iron ore from the platform down

---

[3] This was the first of the legal hangings that have taken place in the county, and is referred to in the chapter on "Slavery Days." The second, as there stated, took place in 1850, and the third in 1853. The fourth and last was the hanging of Alexander Harrison on August 9, 1906. All were negroes, and all but Isaac were convicted of criminal assault.

into the furnace. One day while Buckner was inspecting that part of the works the negro sprang upon him, intending to throw him into the burning oven. Suspecting the slave, Buckner was on his guard. After a short struggle the negro discovered stronger resistance than he had anticipated. Having nothing but death and revenge on his mind, he decided to jump into the furnace, pull Buckner down with him, and thus cause both to perish together. He clutched at his master's arm, but instead caught hold of a loose shirt-sleeve. As he made the fatal leap Buckner's sleeve was torn, and the negro, with his hands clutching a bit of rag, fell into the fiery furnace alone. One version of this incident goes on to say that immediately after the negro fell into the furnace a long white flame gushed out of the top and the

1906   1846
SIMON BOLIVAR BUCKNER

sky above was filled with black smoke, and that next day a black heart-shaped cinder was found in the ashes.

The local trade on dog-irons and other domestic utensils made at the Furnace was far more extensive than was anticipated, but in the meantime the operating expenses grew greater, month after month, while the net receipts from the sale of pig iron increased comparatively little. However, Buckner and Churchill did not give up hope of success. In 1840 they mortgaged the works and their forty-five hundred acres of land to the Bank of Kentucky and various individuals. It is a well-known fact that about this time Eastern mines became better equipped, and being located in more accessible sections were able to place their material on the market at a lower figure than Buckner and Churchill could. The Stack's long road to Green River led to its financial grave. The hauling of the pig iron to Kincheloe's Bluff or South Carrollton, a distance of eighteen miles, over new and rough roads, involved an enormous expense that could in no way be reduced. So the Furnace was abandoned in 1842. Many families connected with it returned to their native towns, while others bought farms and remained in the county. No man in southern Muhlenberg did more to assist Buckner and

Churchill while they were in the county, and none did more to encourage those who remained, than Esquire John Jenkins.[4]

From page 139 of the First Kentucky Geological Survey, compiled by David Dale Owen and published in 1855, I quote:

> The discontinuance of the operations of the Buckner furnace was not due to any deficiency or defect in the ores, but for want of capital, and from the bad condition of the stack, which was entirely too large a diameter for the blast. . . . The gray limestone used as a flux was obtained one mile south of the furnace. . . . Both the analysis of the ore, the thickness of the ore beds, and proximity of all the necessary materials, with an ample supply of forest timber, all indicate a favorable position for iron works; especially if by the construction of a railroad through Muhlenberg County to the Ohio River a more direct line of communication to a market were established.

JOHN JENKINS, 1857

Simon Bolivar Buckner was a young man in those days. He was born in Hart County April 1, 1823. In the spring of 1839, after finishing a course of studies at a private school in Hopkinsville, he was given a position as clerk at his father's furnace. Here he worked for about two years, during which time he made many trips to Greenville, then a town of about three hundred people. It was in this way that he met Charles Fox Wing, who took a fatherly interest in him. In fact the two kept up a correspondence for twenty years, until the time of Captain Wing's death, which, as stated in the chapter on the Civil War, took place the day before General Buckner passed through Greenville with his army.

In June, 1840, Charles McLean, son of Judge Alney McLean, returned from West Point because of his dislike for military discipline and his longing to be at home with his brother Alney, jr. These twin brothers were bachelors and inseparable companions all their life long. Charles died in Greenville in May, 1895, at the age of seventy-six, and was followed ten years later by Alney, jr. Upon Charles McLean's return from West Point, Simon Bolivar Buckner, then employed at The Stack, was appointed a

---

[4] Squire John Jenkins was one of twelve children of pioneer Amos Jenkins, who is now represented in the county by many descendants. Pioneer Amos Jenkins was born in 1784 and came to Muhlenberg in 1810, where he died in 1839. His wife, Grace Dearing, was born in 1788 and died near Olive Grove Church in 1883. They were the parents of (1) Mrs. Elizabeth (Henry) Bivins, (2) John, (3) Henry, (4) Robert, (5) Mrs. Parky (Joseph) Gates, (6) Mrs. Sally (Henry) Gates,

cadet to succeed him at the military school. He was graduated from the Academy on July 1, 1844, and, as is well known, was immediately assigned to the army. A daguerreotype, made in 1846, represents him as brevet captain, aged twenty-three; another picture, also here reproduced, is a copy of a portrait made sixty years later.

Although General Buckner lived in the county only two years, Muhlenberg has since that time regarded him more or less as a son, and the General looks upon Muhlenberg as the place where his destiny was shaped. This feeling he not only expressed in public when, in 1861, he marched through the county with his army, but again showed in 1887, when he visited Greenville as a candidate for Governor, to which office he was elected; and again in 1896, when as a candidate for Vice-President on the National Democratic Gold Standard ticket he stopped in town for a short time.

Colonel Aylette Hartswell Buckner, the father of General Buckner, was a son of Philips Buckner. He was born in Albemarle County, Virginia, in 1792, and came to Kentucky in 1803 with his parents, who settled in Hart County. A. H. Buckner was in his twenty-first year when, in 1813, he enlisted in Colonel James Simrall's regiment. He was present during the siege of Fort Meigs and also took part in the battle of the Thames. Like his friend Charles Fox Wing, he was always greatly interested in the soldiers of the War of 1812. In his day he was one of the best-known men in the State. About the year 1832 he built the Henry Clay furnace in Hart County, and about five years later left Hart County for Muhlenberg, where he erected the Buckner Furnace, or The Stack. As early as 1832 he prophesied that within a hundred years every county in the State would be reached by lines of railroad and that people then would travel in iron cars and sleep in beds at night while traveling, and that iron would in many things take the place of wood. During his four years' stay in Muhlenberg he did much toward the advancement of the county's interests. In 1842, when The Stack was abandoned, he moved to his plantation at B e e c h l a n d , near Camden, Arkansas, where he died in 1852.

THE BUCKNER CRADLE

When the Buckners came to Muhlenberg they brought with them the cradle in which their son Simon Bolivar and their older children had been rocked as babies. When they left the county Mrs. Buckner presented the old cradle to her friend Mrs. John Adair Allison, who handed it down to her daughter, Mrs. W. Britton Davis, in whose family it has since remained. It is thirty-nine inches long, sixteen inches wide and

---

(7) Lemuel Harvey, (8) Mrs. Julia (Jonathan) Shutt, (9) Mrs. Jane (Frank) Gray, (10) Thomas, (11) Alney McLean, and (12) Miss Mahala Jenkins.

John Jenkins, better known as Squire Jenkins, was born July 7, 1807, and died May 11, 1885. He was one of the best-known and most progressive men in the southern part of the county, where he owned large tracts of land. He was frequently called the Lord of the Long Creek Country. Among his ten children is Amos M. Jenkins, who was born December 22, 1832.

about fifteen inches deep. It seems to be of yellow poplar, put together with wrought iron or "shop" nails, and is typical of the cradles of the olden days. The rockers are off, and a stool that went with it has been lost.

A few years after the Buckner Furnace had been abandoned and the Buckners had vacated the large house, it was occupied by Alexander Hendrie, known as "Scotch Henry," who was then looking after the interests of R. S. C. A. Alexander. On a piece of land he cleared north of The Stack, about 1853, and on which he raised several crops of corn, the original ridges can still be easily traced in spite of the heavy second growth of timber now scattered over them. For a short time "Scotch Henry" was associated with J. Jack Robertson in the milling business. Their grist and saw mill was located on Pond Creek, on what is known to-day as the Welborn farm or the Jack Robertson old place. The well-known "Jack Ford" in this immediate neighborhood, now used by Carter's Creek Church as a baptizing place, derives its name from the fact that in olden times the farmers forded the creek there on their way to Jack's Mill. This mill was in operation until 1864, although Alexander Hendrie had withdrawn about ten years before.[5]

ALFRED JOHNSON, 1864

The Buckner house was next occupied by Joseph Turner. He was followed by Alfred Johnson, the famed stone-mason and chimney builder. At the age of eighty "Uncle Alf," or "Old Honesty" as he was called, was baptized in "Jack Ford." In his later days, although he had grown old in

---

[5] James Jackson Robertson was born in South Carolina in 1802 and died at his home on Pond Creek July 31, 1871. About the year 1810 he came to Muhlenberg with his father, pioneer Robert Robertson, who died near Carter's Creek Church in 1843. Robert Robertson was the father of (1) John, who married Charlotte Wright; (2) Thomas, who married Elizabeth Craig; (3) James Jackson, who married Susanna W. Campbell; (4) Mrs. Rachael (T. P.) Morton; and (5) Mrs. Jane (Eli) Jackson. James Jackson Robertson was the father of seven children, among whom are Thomas C. Robertson, Mrs. Nancy A. (Thomas M.) Finley, and Mary Lura Robertson, whose first husband was W. G. Claggett.

John Robertson's wife, Charlotte, was a daughter of pioneers John and Elizabeth Grigsby Wright, who came to Muhlenberg about 1808, where they died in 1864. Although John Wright left no son to perpetuate his name, he nevertheless is a forefather of more people in southern Muhlenberg than any other pioneer. All of his six daughters, except Lucy, became mothers of large families. (1) Charlotte, as just stated, married John Robertson; (2) Winnie married Alfred Johnson; (3) Lourana married John Jenkins; (4) Elizabeth married Isaac Bodine; (5) Jane, whose first husband was Moses Smith and her second Peter Smith; (6) Lucy married Lewis McCown.

years he remained young in spirit. A peculiar thing about him was that up to the time of his death (1896, aged eighty-five) his mustache remained black, although the hair on his head had been white for a quarter of a century.[6]

Among those who occupied the famous old Buckner house after Alfred Johnson were James P. Drake, Isaac, Joe, and Ben Mitchell, James Dune, Eli Skipworth, Ferney and Hutson Driskell, Plunket Parnham, William Warren, and J. F. Driskell. Stanford Lee was the last man to make this noted house his home. He left about 1875, after which the deserted place soon began to collapse. The last of the old logs and chimney rocks were removed in 1890, and since that time nothing but a few broken stones have marked this historic spot. In 1880 Tom B. Johnson built a substantial log house on the Furnace land near The Stack, for the erection of which he procured much material from the abandoned Buckner house. There it stands to-day. "The Stack House," as it is called, is by no means as large as the original or of the same design. Although put up many years after the days of the early settler, it is a good type of the log house built in olden times.

The ground on which The Stack was built was part of a six-hundred-acre s u r v e y patented by James Weir, sr., and sold to Buckner and Churchill,

ALVIN L. TAYLOR, 1912

who at the same time purchased all the land in the neighborhood, making a total of forty-five hundred acres. After they disposed of this tract it passed through several hands and in 1851 was bought by R. S. C. A. Alexander, who shortly after procured about twelve thousand acres on Green River

---

[6] Alfred Johnson was one of the six sons of pioneer Jacob Johnson, who is the forefather of nearly all the Johnsons in southern Muhlenberg, some of whom spell the name Johnston. Pioneer Jacob Johnson came to Muhlenberg with his father Josiah Johnson about the year 1810, and died in 1845. Jacob and his wife Elizabeth (Wells) Johnson were the parents of (1) Alfred, (2) John, (3) Jacob, jr., or "Proctor"; (4) Burt H., (5) Hines, and (6) James.

Alfred Johnson, or "Old Honesty," was born in 1811 and died October 25, 1896. During his life he was one of the best-known farmers and stone-masons in the county. Although he was never a soldier, other than a member of the old militia, his interest in military affairs was such that during the Civil War some of his friends persuaded him to have his picture taken while wearing a Federal officer's uniform, which they borrowed for that purpose. This picture is here reproduced.

near Paradise. In 1854, as is told in another chapter, Alexander opened up the Airdrie mines. In 1865 General Buell leased the mineral rights to all the Alexander lands for forty years, including the Buckner Furnace tract. However, the mineral on the Buckner land was not developed, for General Buell devoted his time to the Airdrie mines and furnace on Green River, which had been abandoned ten years before. In 1890 all the Alexander lands in Muhlenberg County were deeded to Alexander's sister, Mrs. Lucy A. Waller, who in 1893 sold the Buckner Furnace tract, then about three thousand acres, to Koerner Brothers, of Indiana, who cut staves off it for a few years. It was while connected with this company that Alvin L. Taylor and a number of others came from Indiana and settled in the county.[7] The land has since changed owners a number of times, and is now the property of the Rothert family, of which I am a member. Although the place is reduced somewhat in size, the original six-hundred-acre survey on a portion of which the ruins of The Stack stand is still a part of what for three quarters of a century has been known as the Buckner tract or Furnace land, this history of which it has given me pleasure to write.

---

[7] Alvin L. Taylor was born near Adeyville, Indiana, August 25, 1862, and moved to Muhlenberg in 1893, since which time he has been regarded as one of the most influential citizens in the southern part of the county. After spending a few years in the stave and saw-mill business he opened up some ground near The Stack, where he has since lived and maintained a good farm. Mr. Taylor introduced many of the up-to-date farming methods and much of the newer agricultural machinery now used in the county.

XVII

MUHLENBERG MEN IN THE MEXICAN WAR

MEXICO had never acknowledged the independence of Texas, which had been declared by the people of that State in 1836; so when, in 1845, the new republic was annexed to the United States, war with Mexico followed. Kentucky was called on for twenty-four hundred men. Volunteers were promptly organized everywhere in the State. Ten thousand offered their services, but less than half were accepted. The others were not needed. History also says that by far the greater number of Kentuckians who fought in the Mexican War came from the central sections of the State, and that comparatively few lived in the western part. Muhlenberg's representation, as far as I can learn, was very small; no smaller, in proportion to its population, however, than the other counties of the section.

The story of Muhlenberg's connection with the Mexican War is a brief one. Tradition does not say whether a company was organized in the county during the beginning of the war, but in the latter part of 1847 Colonel Moses Wickliffe formed a company and was prepared to leave, but his commission was delayed and not delivered to him until after the news that peace had been declared reached Greenville. It is probable that the few men who enlisted and saw service, while citizens of Muhlenberg, became members of companies in the Fourth Regiment Kentucky Foot Volunteers, organized at Owensboro, Princeton, and Smithland.

As far as I am aware General S. B. Buckner is the only soldier of the war who lived in the county before hostilities but not after. More than half the veterans of the Mexican War who made Muhlenberg their home became citizens of the county after the conflict; most prominent among these were Colonel S. P. Love, who moved into the county in 1849, and General Don Carlos Buell, who came in 1866. Veterans of the Mexican War residing in Muhlenberg and some of the adjoining counties held several reunions under the leadership of Colonel Love. No record of these meetings was kept, at least none is now to be found. I compiled the following list of fifteen names of Muhlenberg men who were in the Mexican War and who were citizens of the county when the war began or became citizens later. This list, notwithstanding the fact that I devoted much time to it, is probably far from complete: Richard Aycock, Don Carlos Buell, Perry Clemmons, Harrison Clifford, Granville Corley, Arthur N. Davis, Mosley Collins Drake, jr., Richard Bayless Earle, Henry Greenwood, S. P. Love, James Nunan, Raisin Pool, Levi Pruitt, Isaac R. Sketo, and Jonas Walker.

I have no memoranda on the lives of Aycock, Clemmons, Clifford, Drake, Earle, and Walker, beyond the fact that they were Mexican War soldiers. Arthur N. Davis, Raisin Pool, Levi Pruitt, and Isaac R. Sketo fought in both the Mexican War and the Civil War. Granville Corley, S. P. Love, and Don Carlos Buell were also veterans of the two wars. Elsewhere in this book are given the biographies of S. P. Love and of General Don Carlos Buell.

Captain A. N. Davis was born in Tennessee in 1826. He joined the army for Mexico in Tennessee, Colonel David Allison's regiment. He came to Muhlenberg in 1847, and in 1861 helped organize Company D, Third Kentucky Cavalry, and became the company's first captain. He took part in a number of battles in both wars, and about 1872 was killed on his farm, three miles south of Greenville, by the falling of the bough of a tree under which he and his family chanced to be driving. Raisin Pool, it is said, was captured by the Mexicans, and was also among the soldiers liberated from Libby Prison at the close of the Civil War. Levi Pruitt, although seriously wounded in the Mexican War, was among the first to enlist in the Federal army after volunteers were called for. Captain Sketo fought through the greater part of the Mexican War and was killed at Shiloh on April 7, 1862.

ARTHUR N. DAVIS, 1870

Henry Greenwood, while still living in North Carolina, enlisted as a soldier in the Mexican War. He came to Muhlenberg about 1855, and lived in the Cisney neighborhood, where he died July 15, 1907. James Nunan, while a boy in his early teens, became a member of a company organized in Louisville which shortly after saw service in the Mexican War. He was born in Dublin, Ireland, in 1832, and nine years later came to this country with his parents. His father, James Nunan, sr., was a well-known educator in the Bluegrass region. James Nunan moved to South Carrollton about the year 1873, while engaged on the construction of the Owensboro & Russellville Railroad, and continued to live there until his death, May 12, 1909. One who knew him well says: "James Nunan was one of the foremost civil engineers and railroad contractors in the State. He built and at one time owned the Owensboro & Russellville Railroad. He was noted for his extensive travels and superior mental attainments. During his eventful career he made and lost several fortunes."

The county's veterans of the Mexican War have now all passed away. The last to answer the call was Granville Corley, who died on Tuesday,

October 24, 1911. At the time of his death the Greenville Record published the following:

Muhlenberg lost one of its eldest and most widely known citizens Tuesday morning, when Mr. Granville Corley died at the home of his grandson, Mr. Thaddeus E. Corley, about two miles west of Earles, on the Madisonville Road. Mr. Corley was born July 9, 1822. The afflictions of age, coupled with an accident in which he fell and broke his leg a year ago, caused his death. His death removed the last of the veterans of the county who saw service in the Mexican War; he was also a veteran of the Civil War, a distinguished member of Company K, Eleventh Kentucky Infantry. He has lived to see many of his comrades fall before that unconquerable enemy, the Death Angel, after having endured the rigors of war. Mr. Corley was one of the county's pioneers, and a gentleman of the old school. His wife had been dead more than a score of years. They had only one child, Mr. James Corley, who died August 9, 1909. Interment was in the family graveyard near Graham, and was largely attended by people from all over the county. The funeral was conducted by the Masons of the John T. Crandall Lodge, of Earles, of which he was one of the charter members. Several old soldiers were also in attendance, and a silk flag was placed at the head of the grave after the mound had been covered with flowers. The ceremony was a very impressive and affecting one.

XVIII

ISAAC BARD

THE Reverend Isaac Bard came to Muhlenberg in 1823, then in his twenty-sixth year, and from that time for almost a half century led a very active life in the community. No local preacher was better known in his day than "Preacher Bard." It is quite probable that during his more active ministerial career he was heard by every citizen then residing in the county. Those who listened to his sermons evidently remembered that fact, for although he died thirty-five years ago all the older native-born citizens now living, and to whom I have mentioned the name of Isaac Bard, invariably remarked that they had heard him preach.

He devoted about half his time to ministerial work; much of the remainder he gave to his farm on Bard's Hill, south of Depoy. He owned extensive tracts of timber lands in the Pond River country, on which he ranged his stock. It is said he was often heard calling his hogs with a fox-horn. He was a tall, muscular man, kind and generous to every person with whom he came in contact, and extremely gentle to all animals. One who knew him well says: "Preacher Bard was a scholar and a gentleman of the old school. He was one of the most sober looking and at the same time most pleasant men I ever met. I remember he always had cold feet and usually kept them wrapped up in heavy cloth, and frequently complained of the discomfort."

Isaac Bard was a son of William and Mary (Kincaid) Bard, and was born in Nelson County, Kentucky, near Bardstown, January 13, 1797. He died at his home, seven miles west of Greenville, June 29, 1878. After spending a few years in Transylvania University, Lexington, he began, in 1817, a course in Princeton Theological Seminary, New Jersey, and on April 27, 1820, was licensed to preach. During the same year he entered in the Senior class of Union College, Schenectady, New York, from which school he was graduated in 1821, and shortly after returned to Kentucky.

On July 26, 1823, he was ordained in Greenville by the Muhlenberg Presbytery and immediately took charge of the Presbyterian Church at Greenville and the congregation at Mt. Zion, near Green River. In autumn of the same year he organized Mt. Pleasant Church, near Pond River. These three congregations remained in his charge until about 1833. During this period he built a brick church in Greenville on a lot presented by pioneer James Weir. The old brick house was long ago abandoned as a place of worship, and is now used as a warehouse.

After the year 1833 no congregation was solely under his supervision, for from that time, and continuing for many years, he extended his ministerial work among many of the Presbyterian churches in Muhlenberg and all the adjoining counties. In 1862, when the division of the Presbyterian church took place, Mr. Bard adhered to the Southern General Assembly.

On March 15, 1827, he was married to Matilda Miranda Moore, daughter of pioneer Maurice Moore. They were the parents of five children: Henry Clay Bard, Luther Bard, Mrs. Verona Mary (Carrol) Larkins, Mrs. Martha Amaryllis (R. P.) Howell, and Doctor LaFayette Bard, all of whom made Muhlenberg their home.

ISAAC BARD, 1850

When, in 1823, Isaac Bard first came to Muhlenberg, many of the Revolutionary soldiers and other pioneers were still alive. He was a college man, who from childhood had been in touch with the progress made in various cities and centers of culture and refinement. His constant association with the pioneers and their children undoubtedly had an influence in modernizing their habits and practices; and on the other hand, living among these people, many of their characteristic manners and customs became his own.

Farms, in those days, were few and far between. The county was still regarded as a new country. Most of the sermons then heard by the local people were delivered by men who, although deeply interested in religious work and well versed in the Bible, had a limited knowledge of theology and of logic. When Mr. Bard appeared on the scene he found a good field for the exercise of his college education and religious training. The uneducated as well as the educated recognized his ability as a "sermonizer."

He kept pace with the times at home and abroad, and in some respects was ahead of his day. He lived during that period of the country's history when "freedom and liberty" were known to be permanently established, and fighting for them was therefore no longer one of the principal objects in life. Local political questions, although discussed from the time the county was organized, were rapidly becoming more and more the leading topics of the day. Among some of the citizens the acquiring of land and wealth was gradually becoming the sole object in life. Isaac Bard was swayed by these times. He not only performed the duties of a preacher and a doctor and looked after his farm, but also took an active interest in national and local politics, and in the meantime, like some of the other citizens, invested in land. He was the first man to advocate the draining of the Pond River bottoms, and about the year 1850 made an attempt to redeem some of the rich soil he owned below Murphy's Lake; but owing to the abundance of other good land, not subject to overflow, and owing to the scarcity of labor, he abandoned the work. When, a few years after the Civil War, the building of a railroad was proposed, Mr. Bard was enthusiastically in favor of a bond issue, for he realized that such means of transportation was necessary for the upbuilding and advancement of the county.

As already stated, he was always in touch with his times. The following letter quoted from "The Private Correspondence of Henry Clay," compiled and published in 1856 by Calvin Cotton, Cincinnati, shows that Mr. Bard was an admirer of good and influential men, and that if he so desired he could write in a style that showed he was a man of literary ability:

Greenville, Kentucky,
March 27, 1828.

Mr. Henry Clay,
    Ashland,
        Lexington,
            Kentucky.
Dear Sir:—

I know you will not think it strange if an unknown friend should address a letter to you. Have you not given yourself to your beloved country, devoted yourself to her cause, and may not the citizen claim you as his property and inheritance? If so, why should an humble citizen be shy and stand aloof from him whom he has long loved and admired?

Will you be so kind as to indulge me in some desultory remarks? When I was pursuing my education in Lexington, I first heard you deliver an oration at the laying of the corner-stone of the Hospital. As a student and boy I was much pleased. Once on Poplar Row, on the pavement, I met you and there were none else on the whole street, and you spoke to me so politely and friendly, it, though a little thing, made no small impression. The next time I saw you was when I was at College and the Divinity School, you passed through Princeton, sitting by the driver on an outside seat of the stage, spoke to Mr. William Warfield, who was with me coming up street. To say the least, the way you spoke to him (an acquaintance) impressed me that you, in no ordinary degree, were a man of friendly feeling, of openness and urbanity of manner.

But it is not merely the pleasing qualifications and attractions of private character, your eloquence and ratiocination, the boon of God, but your political course, and those important national principles of internal improvement, smiling on rising republics, that enhance you in the approbation and give you such a scope in the affections of your fellow-citizens. You have already established an imperishable reputation. A wreath of evergreens encircles your brow, and will entwine around your name while time shall last. Your reputation the storms of persecution have tried to carry away; but it is built on a basis that wondering ages can not waste. Ethiopia will remember your colonization efforts. South America and Greece will couple your name with liberty and independence. Your Tariff speech of 1824 has opened the eyes of the American people and they will not forget you. Roads and canals and manufactures, in fine, the American system, will hail you as their founder and father. Sir, if I understand flattery, it is stating what is false, but I believe I am telling the truth. Truth that is already written in American history—written in the hearts and affections of the American people, more indelible than letters engraven on adamant.

For many years I have read with pleasure your speeches and observed your public course. I have witnessed with heartburning and disgust the vituperation and slander of ambitious, wicked men. In private conversation I have often pleaded your cause and that of the President, and of your policy. I approve heartily of your course. When my friend told me that Mr. Adams was President and you had voted for him, a sudden exultation of joy flashed through my bosom.

We (of Greenville) had a large number of your defenses printed at Russellville, and I have spread them from my store far and wide (for I am a merchant and Presbyterian preacher). Be assured they are operating powerfully. It is the best antidote against lying and slander that has ever been used. Many of the Jackson men of this county (Muhlenberg) have turned completely around. We are decidedly Administration here, by a very large majority. I hope you and Mr. Adams will not be discouraged, but keep up good spirits.

In writing you this letter I mean no more than an expression of my friendship for you, my country, the prosperity of the nation and the welfare of civil and religious liberty. I am in the habit of praying for you in secret and in public. If I have an interest at the court of Heaven, I have tried to make it for you. Think; they didn't say, at Hopkinsville, they knew I was an Administration man from my prayer, as I prayed for the President, etc. But it is not a cause I am ashamed or afraid of; for if even "Old Hickory" should be elected, we will not give up you. You must come next. You are consecrated to your country and you are ours.

Permit me to say, I have named my first-born son Henry Clay Bard. I did it for two reasons: 1. As a mark of affection and friendship for you; 2. That your character might stimulate him to worthy deeds.

Will you be so good as to give my respects to Mrs. Clay? Will you be so good as to give my respects to the President, Mr. Adams? Tell him I pray for him and his cabinet. May God bless Mr. Clay. May God bless the President. May God guide and direct him and his counsellors. May you all fear God, pray to him, keep his "commandments that it may be well with you."

ISAAC BARD.

Mr. Bard was always interested in good books, and in the course of years accumulated a large library. He was very systematic and kept a written record of many of his transactions. His residence burned in 1876, two years before he died, and all his books and papers were destroyed except two of his own documents. One of these is a diary and the other contains some notes on local history. Isaac Bard probably never expected that these records would some day form a contribution to a printed history of Muhlenberg County.

The first of these personal documents is Bard's Diary. This is a leather-bound book of two hundred pages, written with a quill pen. Although many pages are faded, the records are still legible. The greater part of this journal is devoted to the years 1848 to 1851; but it extends, with occasional entries, down to 1855, after which date about a dozen more records are added, bringing it to May, 1872. The diary evidently was written for his own gratification and convenience, and was not intended for publication. I have gone over it carefully, and here give verbatim all that bears on the history of those communities referred to in Muhlenberg County and also all such other items as, in my opinion, will interest the reader. The extracts quoted comprise about one tenth of the whole:

EXTRACTS FROM BARD'S DIARY.

July, Thursday, 13, 1848. My commission [as colporteur and missionary minister, probably], dated January 1, 1848, now begins, and I started to-day. Rode to South Carrollton and thence to John Baxter's. Staid all night, thence rode to McCrearysville, Mouth of Muddy River, and preached at Ellzy Hamilton's to an attentive audience. Then rode to Caneyfork Church, Butler County, and preached Saturday, Sabbath, and Monday, three days and four sermons to large and attentive audiences, visited seven families. Then rode and preached at Salem, Thursday, Friday, Saturday, and Sabbath to large and attentive audiences. Preached six sermons, visited seven families, then came home. Gone twelve days and rode 126 miles. . . .

Friday, Saturday, Sabbath, and Monday, including first Sabbath of September, 1848, at Mt. Zion and South Carrollton. Preached three sermons and I shoveled the first dirt so that John Morgan and John Clark laid the corner-stone of the Presbyterian Church of South Carrollton. I made a short address and prayed standing on the corner-stone, which was the northwest corner for the building, . . . on September 4th, 1848. . . .

Tuesday, November 7th, 1848: Rode to Rumsey and voted for Gen. Taylor to be president. May the Lord deliver our country from despotism and monarchy under the false name and disguise of Democracy. O Lord, have mercy on us as a nation, give us the grace of repentance that we may see our wickedness, turn from our national sins and seek forgiveness of Thee through the blood of atonement. O Lord, choose our rulers, preside in our destinies and make us a great people, distinguished for righteousness, love for pure civil and religious liberty and that we may grow in grace and in the knowledge of our Lord and Savior Jesus Christ.

1848, November 22. The news has come by Lightning, by the Telegraph Lines, that Gen. Taylor is elected. If this be so what a change for the good of our country! O Lord, Thou knowest, to Thy name be the glory. . . ,

Soon after November 7, 1848, preached at Wm. Keith's on Cypress in Muhlenberg at a night meeting, also at Mr. Arnold's a few days after and also a night meeting. Both liberal Baptists, and had good and attentive audiences. I was surveying some land on Cypress and Green river. The people were very kind and attentive to me. . . .

March, Saturday, 24, 1849. Rode to Rumsey. Preached March 25 in Rumsey. . . .

March, Tuesday, 27th, rode to Livingstone (Luther Bard was with me) one mile of Owensboro. Wednesday, March 28th, got on board General Worth Steam Boat. Went over the Falls of Ohio River while asleep and got to Louisville before light Friday morning. Much talk of cholera. It exists below on the coast of Mississippi River. . . . Went to Bardstown, . . . returned by stage to Louisville, and thence by General Worth home. Preached two sermons, visited eighteen families and traveled 400 miles.

April, Saturday, 14th, preached at South Carrollton. . . .

Preached and lectured at South Carrollton on the 3rd Sabbath of June. Went and staid at the Bluff with Col. Wilson (old school) Baptist. They treated me kindly, had worship night and morning. We debated Emancipation. My great surprise is how any true Whig or true Democrat should oppose it. I have heard men oppose it which said nothing for their Republicanism or piety. Yet the Colonel is an exception to the above remark. Yes, there are men who oppose Emancipation who are influenced by low, sordid and selfish notions, whose public spirit reaches no higher than the length of their arm or lower than their belly. . . . They say if Kentucky should emancipate her slaves we would be ruined. Bob Wickliffe said: "The Darkies are the best shade I have ever seen." Perhaps some think they will be ruined if they can not sit in the shade quite so much. Indeed, I think some more sunshine would be better for health and as a cure for empty corn-cribs and barns as well as a good cure to ignorant, idle and dissipated youth. . . . And if our daughters were more trained in the science of cooking, washing, and the wheel and the loom, they would have better health and constitutions, less liable to vanity and extravagance. . . .

1st Sabbath of July, 1849. I preached to-day on Passover and Lord's Supper, Ex. 12-8-11. A good attention was paid. Some young men staid out in the church yard and talked. I had to reproach and talk plainly of such bad conduct. Brother Baxter talked of cutting the tree down they sat under; that if they were so ill mannered and reckless to stay out they must go further. It is far worse than heathen to do so to the House of God, to stay out during Divine Service and interrupt a worshipping congregation. It is in keeping with the worst conduct or vice. . . .

August, Monday, 7, 1849. Mr. Donaldson and I went up to Greenville. I voted for Edward R. Weir, the Emancipation candidate. While here I met with Col. Wm. McNary and we got into an argument on Emancipation. At last we got on the Scriptures on this subject and he said he would go and get a Bible and read it and show I was in error. He got the Bible and read it and I answered him by reading several verses, Ex. 21 ch. and Leve. 25 ch. on jubilee and extended my remarks on the scope of the Old and New Testaments. Some private questions, not manly, were asked me by G. C. and J. E., and also H. R. made an unbecoming remark of private nature. The Rev. John Donaldson was present and heard what passed, which took place under a locust tree in the court yard. Before I left the Rev. Jones and —— came up. The former opened his Bible and the latter drew out a written paper. Both were about to answer me and some person remonstrated and got them to go away. Mr. Donaldson, standing on the outer edge of the crowd, said he heard several say, "They had better let Bard alone." When I saw Jones and —— come up and ready to speak, I got on a bench and remarked publicly: "I wish it understood I do not seek controversy, but I do not care how many come and speak, I will answer them." Maj. McNary said: "Well, I do not think that that remark is called for." So terminated this little debate. Several told me afterwards: "They made nothing off of you. You outdone them and you are able to do it." Donaldson said some of them said: "When they go to the Scriptures they have no business with Mr. Bard." O Lord, bless my speech and may much good and no evil come of it. Help us to love our neighbor as ourself.

11th August, Tuesday, 21. . . . Mrs. Dickson, whose husband's funeral I preached by request, and I rode forty miles to do so, made me a present of $10. I thanked her and also feel thankful to the Lord, for my expenses, though we live frugal and economical, have increased my debt for several years. When a man's expenses at the end of a year are not paid by his income, and expenses and income prudently managed, it proves that his income is less than his expenses. It is often so with us preachers, and our preaching often brings us in debt to men. God, our surety, may relieve us, but no other.

February 20, 1850. Rode last Friday to Greenville and assisted Rev. A. Housley in a sacramental meeting. Delivered two lectures and two sermons. There was solemn attention both times. Delivered an address and administered sacrament. I took subscriptions for a Presbyterial Academy to near $3,000 in two days. Attended the burial of my old and dear friend, Mrs. Tabitha McLean, who was buried at old Caney Station Grave Yard, with a large concourse of citizens. Delivered two addresses at the burying and a prayer. Sister McLean was an extraordinary woman, distinguished for talents, orthodoxy and genuine piety. "Precious in the eyes of the Lord are the death of his saints."

Saturday, March 2 (1850). Left home early and rode to Mt. Zion . . . lectured on a chapter and then preached on Education and urged the importance and utility of a Presbyterial Academy and some prospects of having it in Greenville. . . .

Friday, 15th March, 1850. . . . In my tour to Elkton as Agent Committee of the Muhlenberg Presbytery and also missionary, I was gone six days, visited four families and rode about seventy miles. I wrote a subscription and got three names to it for $200; but it put down payable so far in the future and partly in trade that I gave it back and declined it at present.

Attended Presbytery April 11, 1850, and Presbytery adjourned Saturday evening (April 13). . . . I delivered about a dozen speeches on the Presbyterial Academy. I preferred and besought other ministers to advocate and make speeches for the Academy, but none except Mr. Housley at the end of the debate made a little speech for it. Mr. McCullough, elder of

Henderson, made several speeches against its location at Greenville, to whom I had to reply and also to make speeches in favor of having such an institution. Such are facts, and I am sorry I have to speak myself in reference to them. Again, I have spent much time in getting subscriptions and arguing and pleading with individuals for the Academy, when in that time I could have preached several sermons; besides I had to take some time to prepare the people; to get them to think about it before subscribing. . . . Also delivered one address. After an interesting address of Brother McCullough.

WHITE OAK SHADE-TREE WEST OF BREMEN

on Sabbath afternoon at 3 o'clock before the members of our Presbytery and the congregation in the Presbyterian Church at Greenville. At this meeting we made Mr. Charles F. Wing Life Member of the America Sunday-School. On this occasion I gave one dollar and fifty cents to Prof. James Grayham because he gave fifty cents. I said we ought to raise it and give it to him because he gave it for Mr. Wing. "A cup of cold water" will not lose its reward.

Saturday, May 11, 1850. As trustee I visited Unity Church, opened the meeting with singing, delivered a short lecture on 2 Sam. 7-1-2. . . . Unity Church is a frame house about 25 by 36, and half finished, no stove, no glass, no ceiling, and the question was to finish it. After much debate and settling other questions, we, the four sects to whom Maurice Moore deeded the land (Baptists, Presbyterians, Methodists and Cumberland Presbyterians), agreed to try and finish the house and get a stove. Brother Stephen Harris and I drew a subscription each and I got $34.50, subscribed on May 12, 1850. . . . O Lord, bless my poor labors and take all the glory to Thyself. . . .

July 29, 1850. Vernal Grove, my home, in Muhlenberg County, six miles from Greenville, Ky. Having bought a buggy, a one-horse carriage, at $40, and received two boxes of the books of the Board of Publication from Hopkinsville, I took the books of the smaller box and put them in a trunk and new box in my buggy, and started on my tour, the upper end of Muhlenberg Presbytery. According to a list of appointments published in the Presbyterian Herald at Louisville, I went first to Unity Meeting House three miles. One-fourth of said house belongs to the Presbyterian Church. Here I lectured on the First Psalm and sold two books of the Board of Publication and received the first money, fifty cents, from Mr. E. R. Dillingham. Distributed some Tracts. . . .

July 31, 1850. Wednesday I went to the Brick Church, preached to an attentive audience, sold a few books, and got only $2.50 subscribed to the Presbyterial Academy. This afternoon went up to Greenville and put up with Br. Wing.

1850, August, 4th Sabbath, 25. Rode three miles in my buggy from Br. Andrew Cochran's to Salem Church, lectured and preached. Had some fever when I got there. Caught cold by sleeping on straw bed, thin covering and windows up. Then went and dined with James Sawyer; ate too hearty, too much milk. Then went to Bro. Ben Sawyer's; James went with me. Fever was now very high, very, very sick. Got better and better until Wednesday morning. Took Cook's pills every night . . . but now, August 30, I am much better and hope, by the Lord's blessing, to set out for home on to-morrow. Blessed be God for his mercies, and I thank him it is no worse.

MOUNT ZION PRESBYTERIAN CHURCH
East of Central City

September 1, 1850. The places I have preached during the last four months are as follows: Mt. Zion, Brick Church, Greenville, Unity, Rumsey, Edward Combs, Rochester, Caneyfolk, Cochran's and Salem[1]; delivered thirty-four lectures, twenty-four sermons, visited fifty-nine families, traveled 369 miles, collected $9.70 for the Board of Missions.

January 21, 1851. . . . Luther Bard began to board at John Cochran's January 19, 1851, and to go to school to Rev. J. Donaldson. Board

---

[1] Unity Church, near McNary Station, is now a Missionary Baptist church. The Brick Church, referred to by Isaac Bard, was located a mile southwest of Earles; it was torn down about the year 1897. Mount Pleasant Church, now known as Pleasant Hill Church, is also in the Pond River country below Harpe's Hill. Mt. Zion is east of Central City. This congregation had a nominal existence as early as 1804, but was not organized until 1823, when Mr. Bard appeared on the scene. The building now occupied by the Mt. Zion congregation was erected in 1900. It stands on the site of the old church, and near one of the oldest church burying-grounds in Muhlenberg.

seventy-five cents per week, including washing, cut his own wood, find his own candles, and Cochran to find him a room and bed.

1851, April 1. Went to Greenville and took my daughters, Verona and Mary Bard and Martha Amaryllis Bard, to Mr. Green's Female Academy. Then engaged in selling and distributing books.

May 16, 1851. The Rev. A. C. DeWitt, a Methodist minister of Muhlenberg County, and the Rev. James Bennett, a Baptist minister of Ohio County, held a debate on Baptism in Greenville on Tuesday, Wednesday, Thursday and Friday, the 13, 14, 15 and 16th of May. Hon. Robert S. Russell, Isaac Bard and Rev. Kinchen Hay were moderators. There was a good deal of shrewdness, talent and reading manifested by the debate. . . . Baptism is not settled and must be more fully studied by Pedo-Baptists so as to keep the Baptists from most dangerous delusion.

June, 1851, Thursday, 19th, at 4 o'clock. I, chairman of the Building Committee, laid (the other members assisting) the corner-stone of the Presbyterial Academy. I stood on the corner-stone and made a short speech and a prayer, asked the blessing of the great Jehovah on the enterprise. O Lord, cause this house to be built and make it a great blessing to the church and State.

July 1, 1851. I have just reported to the Rev. W. W. Hill, from March 1 to July 1, 1851—four months. The places I have preached at are as follows: Mt. Pleasant, Antioch, Jefferson, Martin's, Mrs. Rebecca Summers', West Salem, Rumsey, Greenville, Unity and Myers' Chapel. Visited sixty-nine families, rode 462 miles, preached thirty-three sermons and lectures and delivered fourteen addresses. Labored ten months on this Mission and resigned in order to act for the Academy. O Lord, bless my labors, Isaac Bard. . . . On Saturday, July 5th, got to Judge Broadnax's of Russellville.

Tuesday, July 15. Brother J. Williamson went with me down to Allensville, 8 miles southeast of Elkton. Here we organized the Allensville Church of nine members, ordained two elders, Messrs. James Bibb and John W. Glass. Lectured and preached on two occasions in the Baptist Church in Allensville and on one occasion at the school house near there. Sold books one day as colporteur. . . .

This day, July 20, 1851, attended the Campbellite Church near Allensville, Todd County, because I never before had attended a meeting of that order. . . .

1851, November 1st. . . . Lost my saddle-bags from my buggy on my way to Rumsey. Had some cholera medicine in them and some reported and insinuated that it was brandy, etc., etc. I explained and denounced publicly at Mt. Pleasant and Antioch the error and slander.

1853, April, Thursday, 28th. Left home to-day to visit the upper part of the State to collect funds for our Presbyterial Academy. Staid all night in Greenville with E. M. Brank.

29th, started to Russellville and on way staid all night with Rev. A. C. DeWitt. 30th, arrived in Russellville. . . . Stopped at Shakertown . . . and then put for Bowling Green. . . . Also when at Bowling Green I visited the tomb of the Rev. Joseph B. Lassley. His tomb of white limestone is on the ground where the pulpit of the old church formerly stood. When he stood there and I stood there and preached, little did he think, or yet I, that that was to be the place of his tomb!

From mishap I visited the Mammoth Cave. It cannot be described. It is grand and awful, beautiful and picturesque. I often was brought to think of the unconverted and converted state of the sinner; but hell with its horrors was more associated in my mind. Gorin's Dome, Fat Man's Misery, Bottomless Pit, River Styx, Cyclop's Tomb and the Star Chamber were grand and interesting objects.

Went to Glasgow. . . . Munfordsville . . . Red Mills Church on Nolin Creek. . . . June 4, 1853, I went to Elizabethtown. . . . June 7th. Left Hodgensville, the county seat of LaRue County . . . and went out to the Glasgow Turnpike Road, passed the high and terrible Muldrow Hill and arrived at my niece's, Mrs. Jonathan Rogers, in Bardstown, my native town. . . . The road on Muldrow Hill is a magnificent work and does credit to Kentucky. May God bless the spirit of improvement in our country so that railroads may pass through our country between all important points, so as to facilitate, equip and promote civilization and the Gospel. . . . Returned home.

July 15, 1855. The Democratic Party are fraternizing or forming a league with two other great parties, the Abolitionists of the North and the Foreigners, so as to make a great and strong Party to carry the election, and if the American Party, who discards Abolitionism and Foreignism, does not prevail, what will become of our Union?

July 30, 1855. . . . The next day I went to Henderson, dined with Robert Beverly and there met at dinner Gov. Powell. We had a debate about Popery. His arguments were the subterfuges of Papists; nothing solid, but declamation.

January, 1st Sabbath and 6th day, 1856. Rode to the Brick Church. Preached to an attentive audience on Ps. 103-2, "Bless the Lord, O my soul, and forget not all his benefits." In afternoon dined with Col. Wm. McNary and rode to Madisonville with a view to preach, but was too late; dark when I got there and extremely cold. Monday, 7th, it snowed. I staid all day there. In the meantime got my buggy mended. January 13, 1856. Rode to Rumsey, crossed Pond River at the mouth on the ice. . . .

Total of whole service from May 1, 1855, to May 1, 1856: Preached 187 sermons and lectures, visited 270 families and received ten persons, and traveled 1997 miles, Amen.

June 1, 1864. It seems that from July 21, 1861, to June 1, 1864, near three years, I had no commission from the Board of Missions, owing to the War and our Presbytery not meeting. Indeed, we can not now, or since the War, travel thirty miles without serious damage. . . .

May 1, 1865. I have labored three months since December 1, 1864 (excepting January and February). The bad weather, high water and guerrillas prevented my preaching. I have labored in said churches since above report. There has been increased attention and large audiences.

(1865) . . . I preached a funeral sermon of a distinguished man, Dr. A. M. Jackson, at which there was the largest and most solemn audience I have ever seen in Muhlenberg County.[2] . . . I have concluded to spend

---

[2] Doctor Alfred Metcalf Jackson was born in Shelby County, January, 1816. After finishing a course in the Louisville Medical College he moved, about the year 1842, to South Carrollton and there followed his profession. He soon became one of the best-known practitioners in Muhlenberg, Ohio, and McLean counties. In 1849 he represented the county in the State Constitutional Convention. He died February 16, 1865. In 1845 he married Martha S. Fentress, daughter of John Fentress. Their children now living are Mrs. Carrie A. (Charles A.) Robertson and Ursulas Jackson, of Muhlenberg, John M. Jackson, of Logan County, and Honorable Alfred M. Jackson, of Winfield, Kansas.

more time at Mt. Zion and Mt. Pleasant and other vacancies. . . . I hope to do much work this winter—the Lord willing.

The next to the last entry is dated December 1, 1865. The last entry was made six and a half years later, when Mr. Bard had reached the age of seventy-five, and from it I quote:

As well as I recollect, I resigned the care of Mt. Zion, Brick Church or Mt. Pleasant and South Carrollton churches early in 1868. . . . Sometimes I visited them. . . . My health has been so delicate I could not go abroad. . . . Recently I attended Presbytery at Paradise and delivered three sermons (being six ministers and six elders). We had a pleasant time. 1872, May 17.

ISAAC BARD.

DOCTOR ALFRED M. JACKSON, 1864

The second of Isaac Bard's documents that has been preserved is what he designates a "Lecture on Muhlenberg County." This is a sketch that seems to have been prepared for a lecture delivered some time after 1870. He digresses into national history so frequently that "Our County and Our Country" would have been a more appropriate title for his lecture. Much of what he records was obtained by me from other sources and woven into various parts of my manuscript before I learned of the existence of his interesting paper. Nevertheless I quote all that he gives bearing on local history, omitting only such statements as do not pertain directly to Muhlenberg County:

BARD'S LECTURE ON MUHLENBERG COUNTY.

Greenville is the name of the county seat of Muhlenberg County, Kentucky. Greenville was named after Gen. Greene of the Revolutionary War, and Muhlenberg County was named after General Muhlenberg, another officer of the Revolution. The gentlemen and fathers who gave the names to our town and county indicated their patriotic sentiments by perpetuating the names of Greene and Muhlenberg to time and posterity. . . .

John Bone and Hugh Martin, elders of the Greenville Church, and Andrew Glenn, elder of Mt. Zion Presbyterian Church, were Revolutionary soldiers. They lived and died in Muhlenberg County.

In order to get at the history of Muhlenberg County we must say a few words about the first families who settled in this county, the churches and preachers of the different sects, the lawyers and doctors, the part our citizens took in the English-Indian War, the Mexican War and our late Civil

War, the steam navigation of Green River, our steam mills and our railroad clear through the county with its terrible tax of $400,000.

When I came here in 1823 I became acquainted with certain respectable families who had been, I suppose, in the county long before, namely, Judge Alney McLean, James Weir, Charles F. Wing, Hon. Edward Rumsey, Hon. Edmund Watkins, Samuel Russell, John January, John Bryant, John Rothrock and John Campbell. These included nearly all the men of Greenville There were also some leading families in the country, namely, James McCaleb, Maurice Moore, Maj. Jesse Oates, Jesse Murphy, Hugh Martin, Col. Wm. McNary, Hugh McNary, Charles Summers, Stephen Harris, Capt. John Smith, Robert Branscome, Andrew Glenn, John Culbertson, Thomas Irvin, David Rhoads, Solomon Rhoads, Wm. Martin, John Bone, Hutson Martin, Samuel Allison and Richard D. Reynolds.

The Presbyterian Church was organized in Greenville at an early date. The Reverends Nelson, Wm. Gray and James McCready were her first preachers. They acted as stated supplies and missionaries. More late were Reverends Isaac Bard, McAfee, Templeton, Housley, and Morton, who acted as pastors and supplies. The Presbyterian Church was first built, with Isaac Bard its pastor. After the Methodist, Cumberland Presbyterian and Baptist churches were built. The Presbyterial Male Academy and Female Collegiate School were built by Presbyterians, old school.

The first Baptist churches in Muhlenberg were Hazel Creek, Bethel and Unity; Reverends Benjamin Tolbert, Daring Allcock and John Bowling were their first preachers. They were pious, liberal, good men; evangelical and eloquent, the most so of any I ever heard to have so little education. It was remarkable what good language they used. . . . But all the helps of their native genius and piety did not supersede Education, for if they had had it they would have shone out still brighter and as stars of the first magnitude.

The first circuit court judges of our county were Judge Broadnax and Judge McLean. They were both eminent men, able in the law and stood high as jurists. Charles F. Wing and Jesse H. Reno were our first county clerks; the former acted in that capacity some fifty years. Both stood high in office and preserved an untarnished reputation. Dr. Robert McLean and Dr. Thomas Pollard were our first doctors. After them came Dr. W. H. Yost. All of them were very respectable; so much so that I cannot add laurels to their fame. . . .

. . . These were the causes of the last British War . . . and this was why Judge McLean, Ephraim Brank, Edward Jarvis, Mike Severs, Joseph McCown, John Shelton, Isaiah Hancock and others of Muhlenberg fought the British. It is said that Ephraim Brank and Edward Jarvis mounted the breastworks and there fired into the British army, as they marched up, as fast as their friends could load the rifles for them. I see it stated lately in a highly respectable paper that Mr. Brank brought down several British officers in their march up to our breastworks at the battle below New Orleans.

During our Civil War or war of four years, when brother was arrayed against brother, North against South, in bloody conflict, the citizens of Muhlenberg County were honestly divided and took sides, and now we stand as parties Radicals and Democrats. . . . The old question is a bygone thing and the constitution is the umpire. . . .

The main staples or commodities of Muhlenberg County are corn, wheat, tobacco and pork. In proportion to our soil and climate I do not know that any of our neighbors do excel us. We are certainly capable of making hay, another important staple, as we have the best bottom lands to suit the purpose; and as our hills get more worn and washed off, for want of grass, our farmers will have to betake themselves to the bottom lands to feed their stock and save half their corn. But what does all our coal lands and staples amount to when we have been beguiled and are about to be forced to pay $400,000.00 and interest?

Whisky was once a staple of this county. Thousands of bushels of corn and thousands of bushels of apples and peaches have been used to make whisky and brandy. . . . But, I forbear. I have said more about bust-head whisky as a "filthy lucre" than I intended. I am talking to-day on the history and the future of Muhlenberg County.

I would hereby call your attention to two very important cardinal laws that ought to be amended. They now form part of our history. I mean, fellow-citizens, the District School Laws and the Law of Suffrage. . . .

When parents are so ignorant, stupid and criminal that they will not or do not send their children to school when the teacher or tuition is paid by the State, we positively advise as a remedy that the history of Muhlenberg may be disgraced no longer, that such parents and guardians be fined an amount equal to what their tuition would have been by the State.

The Law of Suffrage in these United States ought certainly be so amended that no man ought to be allowed to vote who cannot read and write the English language. . . .

The day will come in the Millennium, not far away, when the Jews and all the Gentile nations of all the earth will be so many republics. When that bright day comes the pillars of those republics will not be built on Ignorance and Vice. No, those republics will be built, so to speak, figuratively, on the Granite Rocks of Virtue, Intelligence, the Bible and Christianity. . . .

ISAAC BARD.

XIX

POST-PRIMARY EDUCATION IN MUHLENBERG

SOME of the pioneers of Muhlenberg were men and women of education and refinement; some were not; others occupied an intermediate position. All, however, with very few exceptions, were respectable people. The sons and daughters of educated and well-bred parents, of course, had an advantage over those children whose parents, owing to a lack of education or to a lack of hereditary instincts of refinement, were not qualified to teach their offspring better manners than they themselves possessed. Many of those who were members of such families acquired some polish through their association with those whose education and home training were of a higher order. On the other hand, those who continued to associate with their moral and intellectual inferiors drifted to a lower level. Those who, during their leisure time, sought the companionship of good books and mingled with honest and progressive people rapidly became citizens for whom the community had the greatest respect. Then, as now, a man was judged by the company he kept.

Representatives of some of the better pioneer families, owing to a lack of education, deteriorated in the course of a generation or two, but comparatively few such sons or daughters ever lost all traces of their better blood. One citizen, now past seventy-five, informs me that he did not learn to read or write until after he was married. He is the son of a religious man, whose education was limited, but the grandson of a pioneer whose education, judging from all reports and from documentary evidence, was of a superior order. Each of the children of this old man spent about six years in a country school, and his grandchildren attended school until they reached the age of about eighteen. Thus, in the course of five generations, this family went down the hill of education for a half century, and in about an equal length of time—from 1850 to 1900—climbed back to the starting point. Religion held a firm and constant grip on each generation, but not until education again took hold did the family return to its original plane. Commenting on the essentials of a happy life, this grandson of a pioneer said to me:

"I have noticed, again and again, that from 'shirt sleeves to shirt sleeves' is often a matter of only three generations, and that from silk stockings back to silk stockings is usually a matter of at least five generations. In my opinion there are three essentials to a happy life. From the days of my youth and down to the present, I have heard the preachers preach on the Father, Son, and Holy Ghost, and I have always believed in the Trinity.

But I must say my father and my grandfather failed to realize that there is a trinity in the right way of living, and that unless each part is practiced in about equal proportions, life is bound to be a failure. This is the trinity of Learning, Labor, and Love of the Lord. My labor has given me a comfortable home on earth, and my religion, I feel, has prepared me for the next world, but my life has been a failure for want of education. From as far back as I can remember, and down to the day of her death, my mother sang a song I shall never forget. It went like this:

TEACHER AND PUPILS, McCLELLAND SCHOOL
Upper Pond Creek country, in 1905

'Tis religion that can give
Sweetest pleasures while we live;
'Tis religion must supply
Solid comfort when we die.

After death its joys will be
Lasting as eternity!
Be the living God our friend,
Then our bliss shall never end.

"It is a beautiful hymn, but if I could write I would weave into this old song education and work along with religion, and make this trinity the source of the 'sweetest pleasures while we live.'"

It is not my purpose to argue the question as to whether "Learning, Labor, and Love of the Lord" are the three essentials of a happy life. However, it is an indisputable fact that where any one or any two of these essentials existed without the others—that is, where the "trinity" was incomplete—life to the citizen of Muhlenberg in the Nineteenth Century was seemingly a failure. When all three were missing, life was a deplorable failure. Such men as "didn't have no larnin'," "done a heap of nothin'," and went to church "just to devil the preacher," were, fortunately, few.

It was the lack of better education and not the lack of sincere religion and honest occupation that began to tell on a number of the citizens who were born in the county during the first half of the last century. During that same period some of the families living in various sections sent their children to Lexington, Danville, and other cities to be educated. Among such pioneer families as the Allisons, Bells, Campbells, Eaves, McLeans, McNarys, Randolphs, Renos, Russells, Shorts, Weirs, Wickliffes, and Worthingtons were found some of the best educated people in the county. Their training indirectly helped to educate many of the local people with whom they came in contact but who were not in position to attend any but local schools.

The Shaver or Philadelphia Schoolhouse
On Greenville and Rumsey Road—one of the few log schoolhouses now in the county

In the meantime, the schoolhouses throughout the county were open only a few months each year. A short time after Greenville was founded the pioneers built a one-story, two-roomed brick schoolhouse on the east side of Cherry Street north of Main Cross Street. This house was used many years, both as a schoolhouse and as a place of worship. It was usually known as the Greenville Academy, but is sometimes referred to as the Greenville Seminary. It was established by an act of the Legislature approved January 18, 1810. For many years it was used as a district school and later also as a county school, it being a higher graded school than any other in the county. It served as a district schoolhouse until about 1890, when it was torn down and another building secured elsewhere for that purpose. M. J. Roark taught school in the old house for a number of years, including the early sixties.

None of the schools in Muhlenberg County went beyond primary work until about 1850, when post-primary classes were first taught by Professor William Lewis Green, who is regarded as the first teacher of higher education in the county. During the course of the second half of the last century five colleges were organized, all of which have since passed out of existence. Professor Green's school, the Greenville Female Academy, although started in the fall of 1850, was not established by an act of the Legislature until

February 11, 1854. The Presbyterial Academy of Greenville was established by an act approved January 7, 1852. The Greenville College, which was practically the successor of the Female Academy, was started in 1880 by Professor E. W. Hall, who for a few years during the sixties had taught a private school in Greenville. The South Carrollton Male and Female Institute, which in 1886 became known as the West Kentucky Classical and Normal College, was established by an act approved February 23, 1874. The Bremen College and Perryman Male and Female Academy was incorporated April 3, 1890.

RESIDENCE OF HENRY C. LEWIS, GREENVILLE
Formerly Presbyterial Academy Building

R. T. Martin, writing about the early history of higher education in Greenville, says:

"During the year 1850, one William L. Green began the establishment of what was called the Greenville Female Academy. He built houses upon a site perhaps not excelled anywhere in the State for beauty and attractiveness. South of the brick study hall, which faced College Street, he erected a large frame dormitory and east of it a brick cottage, all shaded by large forest trees. Professor Green married Susan M. Weir, daughter of pioneer James Weir. He was a man of high intellectual attainments, a Presbyterian preacher and a fine sermonizer. The whole tenor of his life seemed based and centered upon education. He spent a fortune of $50,000 for the betterment of education in Greenville and Muhlenberg County. He not only erected the buildings now owned by the Greenville School District, but he also assisted greatly in building other schoolhouses in different parts of the county.

"Professor Green organized the Greenville Female Academy under the very best discipline and regulations and supplied it with competent teachers, some of whom came from the East. He offered all the necessary comforts required of a good school. He soon had a large attendance of young lady students from different parts of the State, and his Academy rapidly gained a widespread reputation. But after a few years his means failed him, and he was unable to further conduct the school successfully. So, after having spent his time and money in procuring educational advantages for his town and county, he disposed of his school property to the Cumberland Presbyterian Church, left the State a poor man, and never returned. He spent a long, eventful, and useful life in other States.[1]

WILLIAM L. GREEN, 1900

"When, about 1858, the Cumberland Presbyterian Church came into possession of Professor Green's Academy, they continued the school under the same discipline and regulations and employed many of the teachers who had served under him. For the first few years this institution was placed under the care of Miss Susan M. Anthony and Miss Abbott, both experienced educators. It was next placed under the superintendency of William C. McNary, who in turn was succeeded by Reverend J. C. Bowden, William C. McNary, Reverend W. L. Casky, Reverend James Morton, and Reverend Azel Freeman, shortly after which, or about 1878, the property was purchased by Reverend W. L. Casky, who conducted the college a few years and in 1880 sold the property to Professor E. W. Hall, of the Methodist Episcopal Church. Thus ended the life of the Greenville Female Academy, sometimes called the Greenville Female Collegiate Institute or Greenville Female College, and thus also began a new school conducted by Professor and Mrs. Hall.

---

[1] Professor William Lewis Green was born near Danville, Kentucky, in 1825. After being graduated from Centre College he continued his education in the East and in 1850 came to Greenville, where during his stay of more than six years he devoted his time and all his money to higher education in Muhlenberg. He was the first man in the county to establish a post-primary school. After leaving Greenville he and his wife resumed educational work in Wisconsin. He was a widely known Presbyterian minister, an orator and an exceedingly well-informed man. After preaching in Illinois and Kansas for a few years, he returned to Wisconsin in 1882 and established a Presbyterian school at Poyenette, of which institution he had charge up to about the time of his death, July 28, 1903.

"About the time Professor Green established the Greenville Female Academy he, together with others, urged the importance of establishing a male school. So, in the early fifties, the Presbyterians, with outside help, erected a two-story brick building on the north end of Cherry Street, near a fine spring. This was called the Presbyterial Academy of Greenville. It was first placed under the charge of Professor John Donaldson, who conducted it until 1856, when Professor James K. Patterson became president and was assisted in his work by his brother, William Patterson. The Pattersons were young men of fine education and were gifted educators. They soon established a school of considerable reputation. Young men, not only from Muhlenberg and adjoining counties but from many other parts of the State, came to Greenville to attend the Patterson school. The Academy grew rapidly until the Civil War broke out, when many of its students joined the army and the school closed. Professor James K. Patterson married Lucilia Wing, daughter of Charles Fox Wing. After the Presbyterial Academy closed the Pattersons continued their educational careers elsewhere, and Professor James K. became one of the most celebrated educators in Kentucky."[2]

JAMES K. PATTERSON, 1909

In 1864 Professor and Mrs. E. W. Hall, of New York State, were employed by some of the citizens of Greenville to teach a school in the old Presbyterial Academy building. They taught there until 1866. During the two years following they conducted a school in a building on Main Street known as Temperance Hall. Mr. and Mrs. Hall were succeeded in the old Presbyterial Academy building by Professors Crow, Hageman, O'Flaherty, and Helm, after which, about 1873, the school was discontinued and the place became the property of Doctor T. J. Slaton, who in 1885 sold

---

[2] Professor James K. Patterson was born in Glasgow, Scotland, March 26, 1833. He came to America in 1842 and in 1856 was graduated from Hanover College, Indiana. From 1856 to 1859 he was at the head of the Greenville Presbyterial Academy, in which school he was succeeded as principal by his brothers William K. and Andrew M. Patterson. He taught in Stewart College, Clarksville, Tennessee, from 1859 to 1861, and from 1861 to 1865 was principal of Transylvania High School, Lexington. He was Professor of History and Latin in the Agricultural and Mechanical College, Lexington, from 1865 to 1869, and President of the State University from 1869 to 1910. In 1910 he retired from the educational world, after an active career of more than half a century devoted to higher education.

it to R. T. Martin and D. E. Rhoads, by whom the building was used as a tobacco manufacturing establishment for two years. In 1887 it was sold to the Greenville School District and used for school purposes a number of years. It was next purchased by a few citizens who lived in the immediate neighborhood. In 1904 it was bought by H. C. Lewis, who remodeled the building and now occupies it as a residence.

In 1880 Professor and Mrs. Hall returned to Greenville and, as stated above by Mr. Martin, bought the Greenville Academy property. They es-

GREENVILLE COLLEGE
From a wood-cut made in 1881

tablished the Greenville Ladies' College and the Greenville College for Young Men, two separate schools under one administration.

The Halls were assisted by a good faculty, among their teachers being Professor W. S. Hall, a brother of Professor E. W. Hall. Their college opened in September, 1880, and soon gained a wide reputation for the efficiency of its management and the thoroughness of its courses. In February, 1889, after a very brief illness, Professor Hall died of pneumonia. His widow, Mrs. Sarah T. Hall, continued the schools, acting as President for eight years. She was assisted by her son, Professor Elmer T. Hall, and a competent faculty. In 1897 Mrs. Hall retired from school work and sold her college property to the Greenville School District, since which time it has been used for public school purposes. The outside walls of the old frame dormitory were stuccoed and the entire building remodeled and equipped in modern style.[3]

---

[3] The Reverend Edwin Walter Hall was born in Jefferson County, New York, March 4, 1838, and died in Greenville February 27, 1889. He was graduated from Genesee College (now Syracuse University) in 1863, and shortly after received the degree of A. M. from his alma mater and also from Wesleyan University, Middletown, Connecticut. In August, 1863, he married Miss Sarah D. Trowbridge, of

About six years before Professor and Mrs. Hall returned to Greenville, Professor Wayland Alexander established a college in South Carrollton, which was conducted for about twenty years. One of the frame buildings erected by Professor Alexander is now used as the South Carrollton public school. When the South Carrollton Male and Female Institute was chartered in 1874, the citizens of South Carrollton were enthusiastic about their new venture. It brought many young men and women to the town, and the place seemed destined to become the Athens of the Green River country. Its course of studies was of a high order. Graduates were given license to teach in any of the public schools in Kentucky without passing an examination before the State board or the superintendent of public schools of the county in which they had been chosen to teach. When the Institute was incorporated in 1874, many unlimited scholarships were sold at the rate of three hundred dollars each, good for an indefinite period and transferable. A number of men invested in these scholarships and sold them to students at the rate of about forty-five dollars a year, thus realizing fifteen per cent on the investment.

EDWIN W. HALL, 1888

The students who attended this school during its early career received the benefit of all the capital derived from the paid-up scholarships, but in the course of a few years all the money derived from the sale of these scholarships was used to pay teachers' salaries, and the scholarships that had been sold became the source of obligations involving expense which the Institute had made no provision to meet. Financial aid was occasionally given, and the school was thus temporarily revived. This state of its finan-

---

Lima, New York, who was also educated at Genesee College. They taught together in the Watertown High School, New York, until 1864, when they went to Greenville to teach. In 1869 they removed to Missouri, where Professor Hall had accepted the position of President of Macon College. A few years later he became President of Craddock College, Quincy, Illinois. In 1878 he was placed at the head of Cazenovia Seminary, one of the oldest schools in Central New York. In 1880, at the solicitation of many old friends and former students, he returned to Greenville, where he established a college for young ladies and one for young men, and continued as their President up to the time of his death. Though his special work was that of an educator, he was nevertheless considered one of the best preachers in the Louisville Conference of the Methodist Episcopal Church, South, of which body he was an honorary member. One of his old pupils said of him: "Professor Hall did much toward the intellectual improvement of Greenville and the surrounding county. He did as much, if not more, for the morality of Greenville than any other man."

cial affairs, coupled with increasing competition, resulted in the closing of the college.

By an act of the Legislature approved April 7, 1886, the name of the Institute was changed to the West Kentucky Classical and Normal College. However, it was usually called the West Kentucky College. With the exception of a few years, the place was constantly under the charge of Professor Alexander. Notwithstanding its financial and other difficulties, the enrollment often reached two hundred. Its popularity was due greatly to the

SOUTH CARROLLTON PUBLIC SCHOOL
Formerly one of the West Kentucky College Buildings

reputation of Professor Alexander, whose scholarly attainments and ability as an instructor were well known, and to the fact that he always employed well-trained college men and women for instructors.[4]

The Bremen College and Perryman Male and Female Academy was opened September 9, 1889, with Milton T. Brown as President. The first trustees were Joseph A. Shaver, John J. Humphrey, Peter Shaver, Reverend John B. Perryman, and Joseph Whitmer. The object of the school was to offer a preparatory course to those intending to enter the ministry of the Methodist Episcopal Church, and also to give a general education to any others who wished to take advantage of the scholarships.

Reverend John B. Perryman, an Eastern man, was the original promoter of the school. He devised a scheme whereby scholarships were sold to such persons as wished to buy them without using them and thus con-

---

[4] Professor Wayland Alexander was born in Jefferson County, Kentucky, June 26, 1839. He taught his first school at Sacramento, McLean County, in 1858, and fifteen years later became identified with educational work in Muhlenberg. He also taught in Hartford and Owensboro. During his many active years he was one of the best-known educators in Western Kentucky. He died in Hartford, Ohio County, August 28, 1911.

PUBLIC SCHOOL BUILDING, CENTRAL CITY, ERECTED 1909

PUBLIC SCHOOL BUILDING, GREENVILLE
Formerly the College Dormitory

tribute a specified amount toward the cause, and to such prospective students as might desire to procure scholarships with the expectation of attending school during part or all of the time specified in the contract.

Perpetual scholarships were sold for one hundred dollars each, eight-year scholarships for seventy-five dollars each, and four-year scholarships for fifty dollars each. Warranty deeds were issued for the paid scholarships which expired four or eight years from date, or never, as the case might be. In this way three thousand dollars was raised the first year, but

PUBLIC SCHOOL, BREMEN
Formerly the College Building.

this amount was not sufficient to meet the teachers' salaries and to pay Joseph A. Shaver for erecting the new building. Although the time and price of scholarships was changed, and although Mrs. Fannie Speed, of Louisville, and a number of local citizens, contributed much toward the support of the institution, the trustees, for lack of funds, were obliged to discontinue the school in the spring of 1900, since which time the college building has been used for a public school. Among the teachers were: Professor J. C. M. Ellenberger of Pennsylvania, Professor Peter G. Shaver of Bremen, and Professors Brown, Gordon, and Carhart. From fifty to one hundred students attended the school every year, over half of whom lived in Muhlenberg County.

Thus, from 1850 to 1900, five colleges were opened and closed in Muhlenberg. At the time these institutions were in progress, the best public schools in the county were not much above what is now a common graded school. These five colleges not only included many of the post-primary studies in their courses, but also a number of primary studies that are to-day confined to primary schools.

Many of the country schools are now better supplied with desks, charts, and libraries than were some of the town schools during the time of the colleges. There are at present one hundred and two school buildings in Muhlenberg, in which one hundred and twenty-six teachers are employed to teach the nine thousand children in the county, of whom about sixty-eight hundred are enrolled. Six towns have graded schools: Central City, Greenville, Drakesboro, South Carrollton, Dunmor, and Bremen. There are high schools at Central City, Greenville, Drakesboro, and South Carrollton, with

PUBLIC SCHOOL BUILDING, DRAKESBORO

a total attendance of one hundred and sixty-eight pupils. Any one who now is graduated from any Muhlenberg County high school receives an education equal to any that was given by the minor colleges of fifty or even twenty-five years ago.

The schools in the county are progressing with the times. Modern methods have been introduced, and in most instances new and well-equipped houses are used. Even the five or six old log schoolhouses still occupied are equipped with comparatively modern furniture. That the children themselves are becoming more and more interested in their schools and school work was manifested on November 15, 1912, when Muhlenberg held its first School Fair and Corn Show. Six thousand people, of whom two thousand were school children, came to Greenville that day to see the exhibit of drawings, paintings, needlework, carvings, inventions, etc., made by the school children who were attending the common, the graded, and the high schools in the county.

XX

PARADISE COUNTRY AND OLD AIRDRIE

AIRDRIE and its furnace were built in 1855 by R. S. C. A. Alexander, and since that time it has been one of the most interesting spots along Green River. General Don Carlos Buell made it his home in 1866, and continued to live there until his death in 1898. In the course of years Airdrie's twenty-five or more frame houses have all been abandoned. The Deserted Village became a demolished village, and to-day little is left to mark the site of this once-flourishing town. No trace of the buildings that stood on Airdrie Hill can now be found. Some of the houses were carried off in the shape of lumber, others tumbled down years ago and rotted away. The Buell residence, erected by William McLean many years before Airdrie was started, was not only the largest and oldest residence in the place but was also the last to pass away. It burned in 1907. This historic mansion stood in a beautiful park near the top of Airdrie Hill, on which the town was built. The landscape viewed from this spot, up and down Green River and across the stream and overlooking the farms and forests in Ohio County, is an unusually beautiful one. This riverside park, so well kept by General Buell during his lifetime, is now almost a jungle. The winding paths are rampant with ivy and honeysuckle, the foot-bridges are tottering, and what was once a shaded lawn is now overgrown with wild weeds and run-wild shrubbery.

On the narrow strip of land between the water's edge and the top of the hill, and running parallel with the river, are now found the only evidences of the old iron works and old mines. Among the cedars and sycamores are the ruins of a large brick chimney, and near it lie two rusty boilers. Here and there, protruding from the ground, can be seen traces of old stone walls that remind one more of the work of prehistoric mound-builders than of a foundation laid by mill-builders. Two of the old shafts look like long-abandoned wells, and another like a mere hole in the ground. The opening on the hillside leading into the abandoned drift mine, known as the "McLean Old Bank," looks like the entrance to a cave that has never been explored.

The stack of the furnace still stands, a majestic old pile, fifty-five feet or more in height. But the days of this picturesque landmark are evidently numbered. Near the stack is the Stone House, whose massive walls seem able to defy storm and sunshine for many years to come. This house, used in former times for machinery, is a sandstone structure three stories high, fifty by twenty feet. The wooden floors and window frames have long ago fallen away. This fortlike building was at one time covered with a slate roof, which was ruined by visitors throwing rocks on it from the top of the bluff at the foot of which the house stands. The shingle roof placed on it by General Buell has since met with the same fate. About half-way up the wall of the Stone House, between two windows, the thoughtful architect placed a large stone bearing the inscription, "AIRDRIE, 1855."

The hillside stone steps leading from a point just beyond the Stone House to the top of Airdrie Hill, where the town stood, are most picturesque. Virginia creeper has found its way up the solid stone foundation, and the drooping branches of the nearby trees shade the beds of heavy moss and

PARADISE AND THE HIGHWAY THERETO

clusters of clinging ferns. The sixty stone steps, although without railing, can still be climbed in safety.

The stack of the old furnace, together with the Stone House and the stone steps, as they stand to-day (about fifty yards from the river), suggest a bygone time with which one's imagination could associate any long-past age in the world's history, if the "1855" chiseled deep into its ancient walls did not keep the mind from wandering back further.

Such, as I have tried to describe it, is the Airdrie of to-day. Although Airdrie's history does not begin until 1855, the traditions of that neighborhood go back to the end of the Eighteenth Century. Airdrie Hill is about one mile below Paradise. Paradise is one of the oldest places in the county, and is built on land first settled by pioneer Leonard Stum (or Stom), who opened up a farm and with his sons Jacob and Henry conducted the first store where the town now stands. Their boat landing was for many years known as Stum's Landing, and it is very probable that before their death, along in the '40s, the name of the settlement was changed to Paradise.

Jacob Stum, it is said, was "long, lean and lank," weighed only seventy pounds, and measured about six feet in height. He was never known to be ill but once. On that occasion, while confined to his room with "the slow fever," a new doctor, who was unacquainted in the neighborhood, was summoned to his bedside. The physician had never seen his patient "stand on his pegs," so tradition says, nor had he ever heard of his feathery weight. When, therefore, he stepped into Jacob's room he asked to be shown the sick man. At the sight of the "skin and bones" the frightened doctor rushed from the house, saying Jacob was even less mortal than a living skeleton. He informed the family that the patient, although "able to sit up and eat a snack," must have died some months ago, but owing to the absence of flesh the worms made no attack on him, and that the voice they heard was the voice of Jacob's spirit "talking through his hide." Nevertheless, the sick man recovered from the attack of typhoid fever and, says tradition, continued to "play hookey from the graveyard" for many years.

His brother Henry, on the other hand, was a man of normal proportions, but never enjoyed the best of health. Both were upright and highly respected men and lived to a ripe old age, and are now represented in the county by many descendants. Pioneer Leonard Stum was the father of Henry, Jacob, and George Stum, Mrs. Judith (Aaron) Smith, and Mrs. Frank Kirtley.

Matthew or Mattheis Hamm was among the early settlers who lived near Pond Creek, in the Paradise country. He came to Muhlenberg from North Carolina in 1797, accompanied by his wife and what was then their only child, and also by his mother, Barbara Hamm, who died three years later. He was a well-to-do farmer and at times served his community as a preacher. The German Bible he brought with him is now the property of J. Luther Hamm, son of Reverend Jacob Hamm. Unfortunately, the title page of this old and heavily bound volume is among the few leaves that have disappeared, and the time and place of its publication are unknown.

In 1802, when pioneer Peter Shull (or Scholl) came to Paradise from Pennsylvania, he found no one living in the immediate vicinity but the Stum families. Peter's father served seven years in the Revolutionary War; Peter himself served two years in the War of 1812, and Peter's son, E. E. C. Shull, the well-known hotel-keeper at Paradise, served four years as a Federal soldier in the Civil War, making a total of thirteen years of active military service in three generations of Shulls.

Among other first-comers in this neighborhood were three of the sons of Peter Smith, of North Carolina—Aaron, James, and Elias Smith, who have many descendants in Ohio and Muhlenberg counties. William H. Smith, the old Federal soldier, is a grandson of Aaron and Judith (Stum) Smith. Isaac Hunsacker and Joseph Heck were early settlers there.

Five members of the Yonts (or Yontz) family came to the Paradise country from North Carolina about 1812 and became well known in Muhlenberg County. They were Philip, Rudolph, and Lawrence Yonts, Elizabeth, who married William Heltsley, and Susan, who married Michael Heltsley. All of them settled near the home of Eli Smith, who was a kinsman of the Elias Smith just referred to.

Abraham Roll, although not one of the earliest settlers in the Paradise country, was one of the most influential men in that section. He was born in Virginia May 27, 1798, came to Muhlenberg from Hardin County in 1826, and died on his farm, near Paradise, January 30, 1838. He was the father of Mrs. Elizabeth (Philip) Heltsley, David B., Michael F., and Thos. J. Roll, Mrs. Sally Ann (A. L.) Depoyster, and Mrs. Tiney (Henry) Moore.

None of the first-comers in the Paradise country were better known than Oliver Cromwell Vanlandingham, sr., who in his day was one of the most polished and liberal self-made men of the county. He was born in Northumberland County, Virginia, in 1784. While still a small boy he, with his parents and his sister Elizabeth, left Virginia for Muhlenberg. The father died on the way. After burying her husband Mrs. Vanlandingham and the other members of the party resumed their trip and finally arrived near P a r a d i s e, where she procured some land. There she and her two children worked hard and soon placed themselves in comfortable circumstances. She was a well-educated woman, and up to about the time her children were married devoted practically all her evenings to their education. Her daughter Elizabeth married Samuel Weir, a prominent farmer, brother of pioneer James Weir. Her son, O. C. Vanlandingham, sr., was for a few years associated in the mercantile business with pioneer James Weir. After he and Weir dissolved partnership he made a number of trips to New Orleans, where he sold the hides and produce he bought in the eastern part of the county. In 1823 he married Mary A. Drake, of Louisiana, and shortly after removed to Shawneetown, Illinois. In the meantime he retained the property he owned in Muhlenberg, including the place on which he had erected a large log dwelling. His wife, during one of their many visits to Muhlenberg, died on their farm near Paradise, December 22, 1844. In 1845 he and his five children, including O. C. Vanlandingham, jr., moved to Baton Rouge, where he had bought a large plantation. There he married Amelia Blount, of Louisiana. He died on this plantation October 2, 1856, aged seventy-two. His remains were brought to Kentucky and buried by the side of his first wife, near what he always called his "old Muhlenberg home."

O. C. VANLANDINGHAM, SR.
About 1850

In 1847 his eldest son, O. C. Vanlandingham, jr., returned to Muhlenberg and married Margaret J. Weir, daughter of Samuel M. Weir. He remained in the county for ten years, looking after his father's property. In 1857, after the death of his father, he moved to Louisiana to take charge of the Vanlandingham plantation. At the breaking out of the Civil War he became a member of a Confederate cavalry regiment and served during the greater part of the war. During the war practically everything on the Louisiana plantation was burned or ruined and the hundred or more slaves owned by the Vanlandinghams were set free, leaving nothing of the great estate but the ground. About the year 1868 he and his family returned to their farm near Paradise, where he died in 1905. He owned a large library, and was regarded as one of the best-read men in the county. O. C. Vanlandingham, jr., and his wife were the parents of two daughters and six sons, all of whom live in the Paradise country, among them being Samuel P. and Oliver C. Vanlandingham, the two well-known farmers.

Among the influential men who began an active career in the Paradise country during the second quarter of the last century was George W. Haden, who was born in Maryland December 6, 1813. He was a son of Joseph Haden, a pioneer of Kentucky, who at the time of the birth of his son was temporarily located in Hagerstown, Maryland. His parents made the return trip west over the mountains and through Kentucky on horseback, carrying their little son George with them. George W. Haden's mill was the first saw mill erected in the vicinity of Paradise. After running a horse-power "upright saw" or "sash saw" for a number of years he put in a circular saw run by steam, the second of its kind in the county. His mill business was well established when Alexander began building Airdrie. He sawed all the lumber used in the erection of its houses. He also built the first flat-boats used by the various coal operators who mined at Airdrie before the arrival of Alexander. Mr. Haden lived on his large farm east of Drakesboro, and for almost a half century was connected with various saw mills in Muhlenberg. He was a Southern sympathizer, and made many sacrifices for the Lost Cause. Mr. and Mrs. Haden were the parents of Joseph C. Haden, Mrs. Amanad (Doctor J. G.) Bohannon, and Roy Haden. Mr. Haden died in Greenville November 10, 1904.

GEORGE W. HADEN, 1895

The land on which the town of Airdrie was later built was for a short time the property of Judge Alney McLean. His son, William McLean, in the latter part of the '30s, began, near the building once occupied by his father, the house afterward known as the Alexander house and which later became the Buell house. William McLean was the eldest son of Judge Alney McLean, and was the first, so it is said, to work the coal around Airdrie. After the death of his father in 1841 he moved his mother and her children from Greenville to his new residence. While the McLean family was living here William McLean married. A few years later he and his wife moved South, but frequently returned to visit their old home. In the meantime the coal mine opened by him was worked by William Duncan, of Bedford, Indiana, and J. W. Newlan, who were succeeded by Thomas Carson, of Bowling Green, who was probably the last to work the McLean coal bank before the arrival of Alexander.

In those days steamboats plied on Green River between Bowling Green and Louisville. None ever passed the McLean house without a salute. It was from the McLean landing that many Greenville and other Muhlenberg people took passage. What was, in 1846, the newest and finest boat on Green River was named "Lucy Wing," in honor of the daughter of Charles Fox Wing. Captain Culiver was always in charge of this boat. It is said he was a great admirer of "Poems by Amelia," and that he presented many of his passengers with copies of that work. This was a book published in 1845 by Amelia Welby, a popular Ohio poetess of that time, whose writings were exploited by George D. Prentice.

Airdrie derives its name from a small city of the same name in Scotland, situated between Edinburg and Glasgow. It is the old home of the titled Alexanders. Robert Sproul Crawford Aitcheson Alexander, the founder of Airdrie in Muhlenberg, was born in Frankfort, Kentucky, in 1819. He was a son of Honorable Robert Alexander and a grandson of Sir William Alexander and his wife, who was a Miss Aitcheson, of the House of Airdrie, Scotland. The Honorable Robert's eldest brother was a bachelor and was named, like their father, William; he succeeded to the title. This Sir William, the bachelor, promised his brother Robert, then living in the Bluegrass region of Kentucky, to educate his oldest son Robert and let him succeed to the title and estate if he would send him over to Scotland for that purpose. This was done, and after Sir William's death young Robert fell heir to the estate. Some years after the death of his uncle he decided to return to America in order to be near his brother and sisters (Alex-

THE AIRDRIE FURNACE

ander John Alexander, Mrs. J. B. Waller, and Mrs. H. C. Deeds). Besides, his supply of Black Band iron ore in Scotland was about exhausted. He made a search for similar ore in America through his geologists, Charles Hendrie, sr., and his son Alexander Hendrie, who discovered the existence of a desirable ore, in 1851, first near the abandoned Buckner Furnace and then near Paradise. Alexander bought about seventeen thousand acres of land in Muhlenberg, all of which with the exception of the Buckner Furnace lay along Green River.

Alexander believed the Scotch were the most competent iron-workers in the world, and so, during the latter part of 1854, he brought many of his former employes and their families to his new Airdrie. A special ship, it is said, was chartered for the trip. It required six weeks for their sailing-vessel to cross the ocean. Tradition has it that their boat had a collision with a waterlogged boat, which resulted in changing their course to such an extent that they landed at New York instead of Philadelphia. From Pittsburgh they came down the Ohio, and after some delay in Louisville started up Green River. Upon arriving at Airdrie, their "New Scotland," they immediately set to work finishing the houses begun in the new town by Alexander Hendrie and a number of local masons and carpenters, among whom were Alfred Johnson and his son Lonz Johnson, and Thomas Sumner and his son Alney McLean Sumner.

THE STONE HOUSE, AIRDRIE

Alexander spared no expense in his work. The capital at his disposal for this undertaking was practically unlimited. It is said he invested over $350,000. He enlarged the McLean house, in which he retained a few rooms for his personal use. Besides the furnace, Stone House, and mill he erected a two-story frame hotel, a few two-story frame dwellings, and about twenty frame cottages of three rooms each. These houses were lathed and plastered and supplied with massive chimneys and large open fire-places. Everybody around the works, regardless of position, was comfortably housed.

After considerable drilling, digging, and delaying, the furnace was finally started. Alexander, as said before, believed the Scotch were the most competent iron-workers in the world, and he therefore gave them full sway. While his men may have been thoroughly familiar with the handling of the Black Band iron ore of Scotland, they evidently did not realize that the ore here required a different treatment. Three or four unsuccessful attempts were made to run the furnace. The trouble lay not in the ore, but in its management. Had they changed some of their methods, the probabilities are that the undertaking would have been a grand success.

Alexander's patience soon gave out. He cared very little about the money involved, for it was only a small part of his fortune. He set a date for the discontinuing of the work, and although the drillers discovered more iron ore on the preannounced last day, Alexander nevertheless clung to his firm resolution and abandoned the work. This was in the fall of 1857. He retired to his stock farm near Lexington, where he did probably more than any other one man toward the improvement of blooded stock in this State. At the time of his death, on his farm December 1, 1867, he was reputed to be the richest man in Kentucky.

Sir Robert S. C. Aitcheson Alexander was a bachelor. After the death of his uncle he became known as Lord Alexander. He was a quiet, modest,

THE STONE STEPS, AIRDRIE

unassuming man. His employes called him "the lord." On one occasion a backwoodsman named Williams paid a visit to Airdrie, and upon his arrival immediately asked for "that there Lord." Alexander was pointed out to him. Williams "sashayed around him and sized him up from head to foot," and then expressed his astonishment by saying, "So you are the Lord, are you? By gum, you are nothin' but a human bein' after all, and a plain, ordinary, say-little sort of a feller at that. They said you was a Big Bug, but five foot six will reach you any day in the week, by Washington!" This amused Alexander, for he realized how unconsciously but truthfully the speaker had described him. He gave Williams a hearty handshake, and a few weeks later the backwoodsman presented "Lord Ellick" with "enough venison for all Scotland."

Notwithstanding the fact that the furnace was a failure from a commercial standpoint, life in the colony was happy. Although the men spent most of their time at work connected with the mines and furnace and the women were occupied with their household affairs, amusements of many sorts were frequent. The women attended afternoon gatherings of various sorts, and did much toward introducing new customs among the native families with whom they came in contact. The men were good fishermen and splendid swimmers. Archie Pollock, one of the jolliest of the Scotlanders, was the "champion fist-fighter." In fact, friendly fist-fights were on the program more than any other sport. Dances were frequently given. Some of the old Scotch airs introduced by them can still be heard at "old fiddlers' contests" occasionally held in the county.

Although the town of Airdrie was short-lived, its establishment resulted in the introduction of many new and desirable families into Muhlenberg. After the withdrawal of Alexander practically all the men and women who came from Scotland remained in the county, and are to-day represented by many descendants.

Andrew Duncan and his brothers Robert and David Duncan left Scotland for America in the early part of 1855, and a few months later Alexander sent for them to come to Airdrie. They were practical miners, and Alexander gave them a contract to sink a shaft. One of the brothers managed the day shift and the other the night crew. William G. Duncan, now the best-known mine operator in Kentucky, is a son of Andrew Duncan, and David John Duncan, the well-known insurance man of Greenville, is a son of David Duncan.

James Gilmour and his brother Matthew Gilmour were among Alexander's trusted employes. James spent most of his life in the Paradise country, and died there in 1895. James G. Gilmour, of Paradise, is his son. Matthew returned to Scotland and there managed a large coal mine.

Robert Kipling, the patternmaker, was an Englishman and came to Airdrie with Frank Toll. After the works were abandoned he located on a farm near Paradise, where he died March 10, 1902. Among his children now living in the county are Miss M. Bettie, Miss Rhoda A., George S., and R. Henry Kipling. Kipling, like every other man in Airdrie, was an admirer of J. Jack Robertson, of the upper Pond Creek country. Kipling designed and cast a number of door-props called "Old Jack Robertson." They were iron figures about ten inches long and five inches high, representing "Old Jack" sitting on the floor with his legs stretched out, a goose between them, and he in the act of carving it. A few of these iron door-weights can still be found in the county.

Alexander Hendrie was Alexander's geologist. His father, Charles Hendrie, sr., was manager of the estates belonging to the House of Airdrie. Alexander Hendrie, or "Scotch Henry," was born in Airdrie, Scotland, June 24, 1820. In 1848 he came to the United States in search of iron ore for Alexander. In 1850 he located in Paducah, where by prearrangement he met his father, with whom he made an exploration of the deposits of iron ore in Western Kentucky. In the course of a few months they began an investigation of the Buckner Furnace tract and there found the ore that they considered was what they were looking for. Their recommendation of the iron ore found on this tract resulted in Alexander's buying the place in 1851.

Hendrie, wishing to be near his work, moved into the abandoned Buckner house, which he had restored for that purpose. While living near The Stack he occupied some of his leisure time farming. In the meantime he explored various parts of the county, and among other places discovered iron ore near Paradise. Alexander visited Hendrie on the Buckner place and discussed with him the questions of quality, quantity, and location of the iron ores on the various tracts that had been bought. Hendrie advised Alexander not to repair The Stack, where transportation facilities were an obstacle, but to build a new furnace on Green River. In 1853 they selected a site below Paradise and named it Airdrie. Hendrie, assisted by Matthew Gilmour, immediately began the new town. Alexander Hendrie's brother, John Hendrie, while still in Scotland, drew the plans for the new furnace and Stone House.

About 1853 Alexander Hendrie moved to Airdrie. In the meantime he superintended the farming on the Buckner place. He continued to look after that tract until he resigned as manager of the Airdrie furnace. He

ALEXANDER HENDRIE, 1852

made many trips between the two places on his celebrated mare "Susie." This animal was burned to death while hitched in one of the Buckner stables; however, shortly after, George W. Haden presented him with a mare, "Dolly," that for many years was considered one of the most beautiful and intelligent animals in the county. Alexander Hendrie had a good education, and notwithstanding one report to the contrary, was a sober and industrious man. Tradition says his only fault lay in the fact that he was "too good for his own good." After his resignation as manager of Airdrie he continued his visits to Lexington, where he was invariably the guest of his friend Alexander. Shortly after he left Airdrie he became connected with the Riverside mine, where he remained until about 1864, when he moved to his farm in Ohio County, where he died in May, 1874. One of his sons is Charles Hendrie, the well-known mining engineer of Central City.

John Macdougal, the father of William Macdougal, was also among those who held responsible positions at Airdrie. Gilbert Muir, the father-in-law of James Gilmour, was the "driver" or engineer, and retained charge of the machinery long after the furnace was abandoned. Robert Patterson was the bookkeeper and also one of the civil engineers. It was he who surveyed a line from Airdrie, while the furnace was in operation, to the old Buckner Furnace, from which place Alexander was planning to get ore. Henry Southerland was a shoemaker in Scotland, and continued in that line of work at Airdrie and Paradise.

William Torrence was the engine-builder, in which capacity he had also worked in Scotland. Shortly before the works were abandoned he became one of the overseers. After the place was shut down he farmed across Green River from Airdrie. At the breaking out of the war Torrence became a member of Company I, Eleventh Kentucky Infantry, and later settled in Rockport, where he died. Frank Toll held various positions at the furnace.

MILL CHIMNEYS, AIRDRIE, 1900

Much has been written about Airdrie. As far as I am aware, the sketches that have been published are all, with one exception, nothing more than absurd murder and ghost stories, that evidently originated in the minds of those who wrote them. The exception I refer to is "A Report upon the Airdrie Furnace and Property," republished by the Kentucky State Geological Survey from an original record made in 1874 by P. N. Moore to Professor N. S. Shaler, then in charge of the Survey. It is a report of twenty-eight pages on the character of the coal and iron resources on the Airdrie property. One page is devoted to a description of the furnace and about three pages to its history. These I quote:

The furnace was built in 1855-56. It has an iron shell stack, resting upon a masonry base, twenty-six and a half feet square by twenty-one feet high. The outside diameter of the shell is twenty-three feet. The internal dimensions of the furnace are as follows: height fifty feet, diameter of bosh seventeen feet, height to bosh twenty-four feet (bosh cylindrical for six feet), diameter of throat eleven feet. The hearth is four feet high (elliptical in shape), seven feet four inches by (about) five feet.

The furnace is entirely open-topped, having no facilities for saving the gases, and requiring separate firing for both boilers and hot-blast.

There are two hot-blast ovens of the old-fashioned pistol-pipe pattern, with thirty-four pipes in each oven, ten curved pipes on each side, with seven straight at each end. The pipes are eight feet long, elliptical in cross-section, nine by eighteen inches, with diaphragm through the center of each.

There are four boilers, each forty inches in diameter by twenty-eight feet in length, each boiler having two flues. The engine is vertical, with direct connection between the steam and blast cylinders, and also connected with a heavy walking-beam and fly-wheel, the walking-beam working with a counterpoise at one end.

The steam cylinder is twenty inches in diameter and nine feet stroke; the blast cylinder six feet ten inches in diameter, stroke same as steam cylinder.

The engine-house is a splendid stone structure, built of a fine freestone, which occurs at the furnace. Everything about the furnace is constructed in the most thorough and durable manner.

The top of the furnace is about the level of the No. 11 Coal, to be hereafter described, and the ore and coal from the No. 12 seam were brought to the furnace mouth through a tunnel cut in the No. 11 Coal. The engine is in good order and well preserved.

The furnace proper stands perfectly sound (1874) and could, in a very brief time, be put in condition to go into blast; but among the buildings attached thereto the lapse of many years since they were in use has not been without its effect, so that repairs to both buildings and hot-blast apparatus will need to be made before they can be used again.

The Airdrie Furnace property consists of about 17,000 acres of land in Muhlenberg County, Kentucky. This land is not all in one body, but lies in various sized lots, ranging from 500 to 5,000 acres. The greater portion of the estate lies within a short distance of the furnace; but one tract of about 5,000 acres—the old Buckner Furnace property—is about five miles from Greenville, the county seat of Muhlenberg County, and fifteen miles from Airdrie. . . .

Having thus considered in detail the resources of this property, and seen the remarkable advantages it possesses for obtaining fuel and cheap and varied supplies of ores, the question naturally presents itself: why, then, with all these advantages, was the furnace no more successful on its former trial? This is a serious and important question, for the reproach of failure laid against an enterprise of this kind outweighs many advantages.

Into the answer a number of reasons enter, and to render them properly understood it will be necessary to go into the history of the former campaign of the furnace in some detail, and to refer to the management of the enterprise in language which is unmistakable, although it may seriously reflect upon the business sagacity of some persons once connected with it who are no longer living. It should be premised that the information upon which the following account is based was obtained partly from the books of the furnace and partly from men who were on the ground, connected with the furnace in various capacities.

The enterprise seems to have been conceived by its proprietor in a spirit in which benevolence, national pride, and the desire for a profitable investment were strangely mingled. Being a Scotchman, and having some knowledge of iron manufacture as practiced in Scotland, he not unnaturally believed men of that nationality to be the most competent and desirable persons to conduct establishments for iron-making.

He, therefore, committed from the beginning the serious mistake of employing almost exclusively newly arrived foreigners, men who, however competent at home, were without any knowledge of American prices and metallurgical practice, or experience with American ores and fuel.

Having found what was firmly believed to be the equivalent of the celebrated Scotch Black Band iron ore, and an associate coal which it was thought could be used raw in the furnace, he proceeded to erect a furnace modeled after the Scotch pattern. He brought over large numbers of Scotch miners and furnace men, and employed them almost exclusively; giving them to understand, it is reported, that it was to improve their condition, rather than in hopes of great returns, that he had made the investment. He employed as superintendent and manager an uneducated, dissipated Scotchman, a man wholly unfit to fill so important and responsible a position, and to him he gave almost entire charge of the whole enterprise, often not visiting the property for months at a time.

Under such conditions, it is no wonder that there was mismanagement, and that ill-advised expenditures were made.

For three years, while the slow process of development was going on, the furnace and machinery erected, entries driven, and the great shaft, five and a half by eighteen feet, sunk to a depth of four hundred and thirty feet in search of a mythical ore (known to exist fifteen miles distant and nowhere

SOME OF THE ABANDONED HOUSES AT AIRDRIE
As they appeared in 1895

between), the proprietor continued uncomplainingly to increase his investment.

At last the furnace was started. It ran a few days very unsuccessfully, producing iron of a poor quality and in small amount, when an accident to the boiler compelled it to be blown out.

Repairs were made in due time and the furnace again started. The working was no better than before, and the iron not improved in quality or quantity. In twenty-two days from the time of starting the saddle-plate of the walking-beam broke, disabling the engine and compelling the furnace to be shoveled out. Again it started and again, after a short run, no more successful than the last, an accident happened to the engine, the cast-iron shaft of the fly-wheel broke, and once more the furnace was shoveled out.

In all three of these unfortunate campaigns the furnace was not in blast altogether more than six weeks or two months.

After the last blast the manager concluded that the coal did not work well raw, and so made a large amount of coke from it to be tried at the next blast, but the next blast never came; the proprietor's patience was exhausted; he stopped operations entirely, discharged his men, and shut up the mines and furnace.

Since that time (November, 1857) the furnace has never been in operation. The No. 11 Coal has been worked largely for shipment to the Southern market, but beyond that the property has been lying idle and unproductive.

The closing of the furnace at that time was a mistake no less serious than some committed in starting it. The manager was beginning to learn, by the only method by which a so-called practical, uneducated man can learn—his own dear-bought experience—that American ores and fuel are not exactly like the Scotch, and that different practice is required for their treatment. Had he been allowed to go on, using coke for fuel, it is not unlikely that his next campaign would have proved much more successful.

It can be truly said that the furnace has never been subjected to a fair trial. A total campaign of six weeks or two months, divided into three short blasts, affords no fair basis for judgment as to the merits of furnace, fuel or ore.

After the withdrawal of Alexander his lands in Muhlenberg County were placed in charge of Colonel S. P. Love. He was succeeded by Thomas Bruce, a merchant and one-time county clerk, who looked after Alexander's interests a short time. Along in these years Doctor Shelby A. Jackson was in some way connected with Airdrie. Doctor Jackson was one of the most widely known men of his day. David B. Roll followed Thomas Bruce as agent of the land. "Squire" Roll, as he was familiarly called, was a magistrate for ten years in succession, a well-to-do farmer and stock-raiser, and the owner of considerable property. The overseeing of the Alexander tracts was in "Squire" Roll's hands when General Don Carlos Buell appeared on the scene.[1]

Immediately after the close of the war General Buell began a search for an oil field. He came to Airdrie from Marietta, Ohio, in 1866, for the sole purpose of working the oil on the Alexander lands. He took a forty-year mineral and oil lease on Alexander's seventeen thousand acres. Alexander was to receive, among other things, one tenth of all "the petroleum or other oil or oily substance obtained from the land." This company, of which General Buell was president, was known as the Airdrie Petroleum Co.

Buell drilled extensively on the Alexander property along Green River and also on the Buckner Furnace tract. Airdrie being on Green River, and having the best transportation facilities, he decided to establish himself

---

[1] Don Carlos Buell was born at Lowell, Ohio, March 23, 1818; moved to Indianapolis, Indiana, in his youth, and entered West Point in 1837, from which military academy he was graduated July 1, 1841. He fought in the Mexican War, and from 1848 to 1861 served as chief of various departments. In July, 1861, he was made Brigadier-General of Volunteers, and in March, 1862, Major-General. The timely arrival at Shiloh of the Army of the Ohio, under his command, resulted in the saving of Grant's army from defeat; his rapid and successful march to reach Louisville in time to prevent the city from being occupied by Bragg, and his driving of the Confederate army from Kentucky after the battle of Perryville, are among the military achievements of General Buell that are matters of national history. On October 30, 1862, through the influence of some of his enemies in the Federal army, he was superseded by General Rosecrans. Among other things with which he was then charged were failure to capture Bragg's army and to confiscate certain property held by non-combatants. A military commission was appointed, before which he was summoned, and after an investigation covering a period of many months there resulted some criticism upon some of his movements, but nothing affecting his honor or military standing. In May, 1864, at his own request, he was honorably mustered out of service. Thus ended the military career of a soldier who, while a soldier and later while a civilian, received little of the great credit due him for the military services he had rendered. His military career is not properly a subject for this book, but is for others to write.

there. Furthermore, after the death of Alexander, the Alexander heirs, wishing to dispose of some of the property which they had inherited, entered into an agreement with Buell whereby the latter received a deed to the Airdrie furnace and about a thousand acres around it for having released the forty-year lease that he then held. He thereafter confined his work to his own property near Airdrie. However, the coal Buell discovered while looking for oil was in such abundance that he changed his plans and directed most of his attention to coal development.

RUINS AT AIRDRIE IN 1900
Shortly before the last of the frame houses disappeared

In the meantime (1868) The Green and Barren Rivers Navigation Company leased Green River, which stream up to that time had been directly controlled by the State of Kentucky. The increased freight rate demanded by the new corporation was so much that Buell could not meet the prices of his competitors, to whom a lower freight rate was given. He fought the corporation through the Legislature for some fifteen years. His long, hard, and time-sacrificing work resulted in the Federal government purchasing the unexpired lease of the Navigation Company in 1888. The river was then put in good order and the old locks were improved and new ones added. For this work alone he deserves a monument.

After Buell had won his transportation rate fight he felt too far advanced in years to again begin his work of developing the mines. In the meantime much of the machinery had gone to wreck and ruin, and some of it had been sold. On one occasion, it is said, an old-iron peddler agreed to buy all the old pig iron and scrap iron lying around the furnace. The peddler loaded his barge, however, not only with scrap, but with all the machinery on the place except the two boilers standing there to-day. Under the circumstances, and in spite of the available mineral, it is not at all surprising that nothing further was undertaken by General Buell.[2]

Of all the extravagant stories told about Airdrie, few are more absurd than those relative to the Stone House, sometimes—but erroneously—called the Old Prison. Some declare Alexander worked prisoners in his mines; others say Buell used them in connection with his work. One young man's idea was that Buell here held the prisoners he had captured in the

THE OLD HOTEL BUILDING AT AIRDRIE IN 1895

Civil War. A number of people are under the impression that the Stone House was built by and for some of the State convicts. In fact, one can hear anything and everything in regard to the "prisoners" except that they were free workmen brought over from Scotland by Alexander.

The truth of the matter, however, is this: About 1884, when Eddyville prison was being enlarged, arrangements were made with General Buell to quarry stone on his place, to be used in the new penitentiary. About fifteen prisoners were sent by the State for the purpose of getting out the rock, who while at Airdrie were quartered in the Stone House. They remained only a few weeks, for in the meantime other stone had been discovered by General Lyon near Eddyville, and the State then transferred the prisoners to the new quarry.

---

[2] Although coal has been mined at Airdrie for many years and by various men, this rich field is practically untouched.

Many ghost stories are connected with the old hotel building at Airdrie. It was the largest frame house erected by Alexander. It remained unoccupied after Alexander abandoned the furnace, and its weatherbeaten walls, broken windows, and generally dilapidated condition gave rise to a report that the place was haunted. Although all traces of the hotel have disappeared, the ghost stories have continued to increase in number and variety. Many of them begin with a murder scene and end with the maneuvers of a headless ghost. No one was ever killed in or near the building, all reports to the contrary notwithstanding.

Entrance to the "McLean Old Bank," Airdrie

The stories about the haunted hotel and of "prisoners" being worked by the owners of Airdrie are as groundless as those circulated over the country regarding the kinship or friendship that is said to have existed between General Buell and General Bragg. These two soldiers were not related by blood or marriage, and did not "sleep in the same bed the night before the battle of Perryville." General Buell on November 19, 1851, married the widow of General Richard Barnes Mason, who was a grandson of General George Mason of Revolutionary fame. General Bragg's wife was Miss Ellis, of Louisiana. General Buell's wife before her second marriage was Mrs. Margaret (Turner) Mason, the mother of Miss Nannie Mason. Mrs. Buell died in Airdrie on August 10, 1881. After her death Mrs. Course, the General's sister, made the place her home until 1885, when she died. General Buell died at Airdrie on November 19, 1898, and his body was sent to Belfontaine Cemetery, St. Louis. His estate was willed to Miss Nannie Mason, who a few years after his death made Louisville her home and died there November 19, 1912. In 1908 she sold the Airdrie lands to the Five J. Coal Company, of which Shelby J. Gish, of Central City, is general manager.

McLEAN OLD SPRING, AIRDRIE, 1900

After the General's death William Shackelton occupied the house for about two years. He was succeeded by Lorenzo D. Griggs. John Hendrie, the then aged architect of the old stone structures at Airdrie, occupied the house from September, 1904, to November, 1906. David Rhoads came next,

DON CARLOS BUELL, 1866

and was living in the historic mansion when, on the night of October 26, 1907, it was destroyed by fire.

During its seventy-five years of existence many of Muhlenberg's pioneers loitered under its roof. Alexander entertained a number of renowned

American and foreign visitors while living there. Charles Eaves was General Buell's most intimate friend in the county and likewise his most frequent visitor. During Buell's residence in Airdrie many men prominent in military and social circles were his guests. None, however, no matter how distinguished, was received with more open arms than his neighbors and friends of the Green River country.

GENERAL BUELL'S PRIVATE PARK, RESIDENCE, AND BOATHOUSE, AIRDRIE, 1900

General Buell lived in this house thirty-two years, including the four years (1885-1889) he made Louisville his headquarters while Pension Agent for Kentucky. In 1880 and during a number of years following he was one of the Commissioners of the State Agricultural College. He was one of the early members of the Kentucky State Historical Society, and was also identified with many conventions that have aided in the development of the resources of the State. In 1890, when the Shiloh Military Park Commission was organized, he was appointed one of its members, and served on that board up to the time of his death. Although never an applicant for office, General Buell's name has been mentioned in connection with many high offices, among them being the presidency of the United States.

When, owing principally to his efforts, the Federal government assumed charge of Green River, General Buell had reached the age of seventy. In his declining years he spent most of his time on his two hobbies—working in his little carpenter shop, and looking after the trees and shrubbery in his park, which he kept always in good condition. He had a mechanical

GENERAL BUELL'S RESIDENCE, AIRDRIE, IN 1900
Seven years before its destruction by fire

turn, and among other things constructed in his carpenter shop a model of a large dish-washing machine, such as are used in hotels, whereby one man can do the work of four. He never patented it.

General Buell never engaged in farming, but rented out a small portion of his land to others, from whom he received enough hay and corn for rent to supply his own needs. He was always an admirer of native trees, wild birds, and good saddle-horses. From the time he first came to Muhlenberg until shortly before his death he could be seen almost every day riding in the country near Airdrie with his wife or daughter. When, about 1880, his favorite horse "Shiloh" (presented to him during the war) died, he buried him on Airdrie Hill, putting a small rock at the head of the grave. He treated every animal on his place with the gentleness that a loving father would a small child. In his old age he continued to walk and ride with a military air. Everything he did was done in a most systematic manner. He was well informed on current events and subjects generally, and all who knew him personally speak of him as a most interesting conversationalist.

He was an optimist and never found fault with anything. One of his most intimate friends in Muhlenberg says: "Not once did he as much as intimate to me that the Government had given him little or no reward for the services he had rendered in peace and in war."

General Buell, while living at Airdrie, wrote on various subjects. Among his writings are three articles pertaining to the Civil War—"Shiloh Reviewed," "Operations in North Carolina," and "East Tennessee and the Campaign of Perryville," all of which were published in 1887

RUINS OF GENERAL BUELL'S RESIDENCE, AIRDRIE, 1912.

by The Century Company in "Battles and Leaders of the Civil War." General Buell, shortly after the death of his wife, wrote the following poem, heretofore unpublished, for a copy of which I am indebted to his stepdaughter, Miss Nannie Mason:

THOU AND I.

Strange, strange for thee and me,
    Sadly afar,
Thou safe, beyond, above,
    I 'neath the star;
Thou, where flowers deathless spring,
    I, where they fade,
Thou, in God's holy light,
    I, in the shade.

Thou, where each gale brings balm,
    I, tempest tossed,
Thou, where true joy is found,
    I, where 'tis lost;

Thou, counting ages thine,
    I, not the morrow,
Thou, learning more of bliss,
    I, more of sorrow.

Thou, in eternal peace,
    I, where 'tis strife,
Thou, where care hath no name,
    I, where 'tis life;
Thou, without need of hope,
    I, where 'tis rain,
Thou, with wings dropping light,
    I, with Time's chain.

Strange, strange, for thee and me,
    Loved, loving ever,
Thou, by life's deathless fount,
    I, near Death's river;
Thou, winning wisdom's love,
    I, strength to trust,
Thou, with the seraphim,
    I, in the dust.

XXI

CHARLES EAVES

AMONG Muhlenberg's men of the last half of the Eighteenth Century none was more universally loved than the late Judge Charles Eaves.

His father, John S. Eaves, was born near Roanoke River, Virginia, in 1783, and after a short stay in Nashville and Russellville settled in Muhlenberg in 1805 and became one of the county's most influential pioneers. He located on Pond River, near Harpe's Hill. He was an intelligent man and a thrifty farmer, served as justice of the peace and sheriff, and in 1834 represented the county in the State Legislature. He died in Greenville in 1867. John S. Eaves married Lurena Ingram. She was a talented woman and like her husband very much interested in the development of the county. They were the parents of seven children, of whom Charles Eaves was the youngest son.[1]

From early youth and through all the years of his life Charles Eaves was a student not only of law, history, and literature, but also of the natural sciences. During his boyhood and early manhood he devoted most of his winter evenings to the reading of good literature, and in the warmer season spent much of his spare time wandering through the Pond River forests studying Nature or sitting under an old sycamore on the banks of Eaves Creek, near his old home, perusing good books. To him the monarchs of the forest were philosophers and friends. His poetical idea of the interpretation of the trees is beautifully expressed by his personal friend, James Lane Allen, in "Aftermath."[2] Judge Eaves recognized the great educational value of travel. At the age of twenty-two he made a trip on horseback to Dakota and other Western sections, and later in life visited some of the Eastern cities and the Southwestern States.

[1] Mr. and Mrs. John S. Eaves were the parents of: (1) Sanders, who married Jane Short; (2) William, married Sarah Walker; (3) George W., sr., married Mary Peters; (4) John S., jr., married Miss Turbiville; (5) Charles, married Martha G. Beach; (6) Mrs. Mary (Reverend Isaac) Malone; (7) Mrs. Caroline (Felix J.) Martin.

[2] "How sweet that smoke is! And how much we are wasting when we change this old oak back into his elements—smoke and light, heat and ashes. What a magnificent work he was on natural history, requiring hundreds of years for his preparation and completion, written in a language so learned that not the wisest can read him wisely, and enduringly bound in the finest of tree calf! It is a dishonor to speak of him as a work. He was a Doctor of Philosophy! He should have been a college professor! Think how he could have used his own feet for a series of lectures on the laws of equilibrium, capillary attraction, or soils and moisture! Was there ever a head that knew so much as his about the action of

A brief biography of Judge Eaves was published in J. H. Battle's "Kentucky, a History of the State," twenty years before his death. From this I quote:

Charles Eaves was born January 20, 1825, nine miles west of Greenville. He was educated chiefly at home. In early boyhood he became a voracious reader. He gathered books and spun his own web of knowledge. On his father's farm his habit was to read half the night, after working on the farm all day. At the age of eighteen he took up the study of law on the farm, reading Blackstone, Story, Chitty, Stevens, Starkie, Greenleaf, and numerous other textbooks, and after three years' reading obtained license to practice law. He was admitted to the Greenville bar in September, 1846. Since then he has devoted his life to the study and practice of law and to the study of literature.

He is now a ripe, thorough lawyer, ranking high in his profession. His knowledge is encyclopedic. As a pleader he is skillful, accurate, thorough; as a speaker, never rhetorical, but plain, direct, compact and clear; always fair and honorable in the conduct of a case, and generally successful. If eloquence he has,

CHARLES EAVES, 1884

it is the eloquence of conviction and clearness. He wins his cases by careful preparation, clearness of statement and fairness of argument. He served Muhlenberg County one year as county attorney, one year as school commissioner, and one term (1857-59) as representative in the Legislature.

In 1865 he removed to Henderson, Kentucky, and after a residence there of twelve years returned to Greenville, where he now resides in his quiet, tree-embowered suburban home. At Henderson he was city attorney for three years. The office was unsought, and he held it till he resigned it.

---

light? Did any human being ever more grandly bear the burdens of life or better face the tempests of the world? What did he not know about birds? He had carried them in his arms and nurtured them in his bosom for a thousand years. Even his old coat, with all its rents and patches—what roll of papyrus was ever so crowded with secrets of knowledge? The august antiquarian! The old king! Can you imagine a funeral urn too noble for his ashes? But to what base uses! He will not keep the wind away any longer; we shall change him into a kettle of lye with which to whiten our floors."—From James Lane Allen's "Aftermath."

From having frequently presided as special judge in the circuit courts he is generally known as Judge Eaves.

Not old at sixty; six feet high, and though not obese, weighing two hundred pounds, healthy and strong, with a memory like a chronicle, with a love of books unabated, reading a new law book with as much zest as a novel, drinking in its meaning as a sponge absorbs water, Judge Eaves is likely to survive the present century as an active member of his profession, honored and respected by bench and bar as well as by the people, and after his death his ghost may possibly be seen by his old associates about the courthouse with a law book or bundle of papers under his arm.

In 1852 Charles Eaves married Martha G. Beach, of Greenville, formerly of Rochester, New York. They became the parents of five children. Their first two children, Rufus and Frances, died before reaching maturity. Their sons, Charles and Ridley, left Muhlenberg in early manhood. Their fifth child, Miriam, was a beautiful but unfortunate woman, highly accomplished and an excellent musician. She made Greenville her home during the greater part of her life. She was murdered in Louisville on November 12, 1892. This dreadful tragedy and the circumstances leading to it was the great sorrow of Judge Eaves' life, the shock of which left a deep and lasting impress on him.

No citizen was better versed in local traditions, and no man could tell the stories of bygone days more interestingly and more accurately, than Judge Eaves. He always showed a great and sympathetic interest in any legend he might be reciting. He was a brilliant conversationalist. Few men in telling old traditions, discussing literature, or explaining law could go so deeply into minute details and yet hold their listener's uninterrupted attention as he did. Unfortunately, he wrote nothing on local history and very little on any other subject. A poem said to have been written by him, and one of his letters, are quoted elsewhere in this chapter. On his death many oral traditions lost their last narrator and much of Muhlenberg's unwritten history faded into the mass of things forgotten.

Judge Eaves loved Muhlenberg and everything associated with it. No hills and valleys appealed to him more, and no county's future seemed to him brighter, than Muhlenberg's. He often, and in all sincerity, told his friends that his soul could not pass away peaceably in any other community, and that his bones would not rest quietly in any other place than in this land where he had spent a life of so many joys and sorrows. He was past eighty when the final summons came. He died in Greenville on August 17, 1905, and was buried by the side of his wife, who had preceded him to the Great Beyond on January 17, 1902.

On September 23, 1905, these resolutions on the death of Judge Eaves were passed by the members of the local bar and inscribed in the records of the Muhlenberg Circuit Court:

Resolved: That in the death of Judge Eaves we have lost not only the senior of our bar and a revered and respected friend, but also the last member of a distinguished number of lawyers who began the practice of law under that system known as the Common Law Practice, which was in force in Kentucky prior to our Code Practice.

Resolved: That we revere his memory and cherish with grateful recollections many favors bestowed by him, as well as many pleasant associations with him.

Judge Eaves was a student all his life long. A volume could be written relative to his instructive and entertaining conversations on the books he had read. Judge Jeptha Crawford Jonson, one of the best-known attorneys in the Green River country, who moved from McLean County to Greenville in 1892, where he died April 10, 1912, aged seventy-nine, speaking to me of Judge Eaves, said: "During the thirty-five years intervening between 1868 and the date of his death Judge Eaves and I were intimately associated, and I esteemed him greatly. He was an omnivorous reader and could describe vividly the characters in any story he had read, discuss in detail any essay he had perused, and repeat many and long extracts from the better-known poets. His memory was excellent. His assimilation and digestion of what he had read was perfect. He was thoroughly familiar with the Bible and with many of the Greek and Latin authors, with Shakespeare, Milton, and the Brownings; with Cowper, Scott, Bulwer, and Dickens; with Irving, Cooper, and Hawthorne, and with a number of the French authors."

Shortly after 1866, when General Buell made Muhlenberg his home, Judge Eaves and the General formed a friendship that continued until the death of Buell in 1898. Judge Eaves and his family frequently visited General and Mrs. Buell and their daughter, Miss Nannie Mason, at Airdrie, for many years. After the death of the General, Judge Eaves continued his visits to "dear old Airdrie." During all these years, upon his return home, the Judge invariably wrote his host a letter of appreciation. All his letters were destroyed when the Buell residence burned in 1907 except one which is addressed to Miss Nannie Mason, who after the death of the General continued to live at Airdrie for a few years. Although the Judge here expresses himself in the form of a letter, it is a good sample of the style of conversation into which he often drifted. It is dated Greenville, June 26, 1902:

I loved Airdrie from the first of my knowledge of it as the home of General Buell and his family—admired it for its beauty—loved it greatly for its dwellers—love it now for its old associations and its present owner.

It was and is out of sight of roads and of people. A place where you may spread yourself—your whole self—without disturbance; where you escape the dust and smoke and folk; where you dwell in the presence of the beautiful river, which is ever on its tranquil pilgrimage, bearing messages from the woods to the sea; where you know every tree, every plant, every walk, every footpath, every bird, every note of every bird; where, indeed, the birds have plenty of hiding-places, and they must need tell of it to others, until it becomes their summer garden as well as yours. You did not wait until Sunday to go to church; but every morning in the week you and the birds had your orisons at four o'clock and your evening benedictions at sunset. One who has never heard the birds from four o'clock until six, of a summer morning, as I have done at Airdrie, has never rightly heard God praised. You had your friends there. Some shaded you, some fed you; the catbird chatted with you; the hens took food from your hands; the roses never talked politics, but simply went on, clothing themselves with more beauty and evolving sweeter fragrance for your sake. Often you got down to the soul of things; for everything has a soul. Surely the bees and the butterflies have soul-life—made up of taste, affection, fancy, will, and hereditary instincts. The General's horse might have been immortal, without injustice to other animals. Was there ever a genuine Anglo-Saxon cow there—a great, rich, red-hided Durham? Such a cow would have become the place, and would doubtless have had a clean, sweet yard, where the apple trees leaned across the fence to shade her, and the moon looked in of nights to see her chew her cud. Such a cow would have spoken to you in modulated tones and looked at you with affection

But the home, the dear old home, perched on the hillside, overlooking the beautiful river, the house enriched by its tender and precious associations, is by far the most interesting inanimate object at Airdrie, if, indeed, it be inanimate. In this house a truly great man, of noble nature, lived and died; a beautiful and lovely woman lived and died, and a no less beautiful and lovely woman lived and loved to live and would again love to live. Of the walls of this house where these beautiful lives have been lived, where so many precious experiences have been passed through, might not one say exactly what Joshua said about the stone that he set up in Shechem (Joshua xxiv, 27): "They have heard all the words of the Lord which He spake unto you?" And

BEECH TREE
One of Judge Eaves' "Philosophers of the Forest"

indeed the parallel goes farther. The words which your household walls have heard from God, and which they are still uttering, are the same words which He had spoken in the presence of the old stone at Shechem, and of which that stone was a perpetual witness to the people. Think of this house which has become monumental. Its walls have other and far deeper values than were paid the architect and the carpenter for designing and building them. These walls are steeped in truth, and each room speaks it in its own peculiar voice—the old truth of Covenant between man and God—the necessity and blessing of obedience. It is not put in the hard old Jewish way as it speaks to you out of the walls of your Christian home. It is richened and deepened. But it is the same old truth. The wondrousness of life, the blessedness of life, and the tie between all life and God, who is the everlasting and all-creating one; that man's life belongs to God, and that there is no true life in man except in God.

In these rooms you faced the awful mystery of death; you watched that slow, sure, gentle, irresistible untwisting of the golden cord, and saw mortality fade into immortality before your very eyes. Can these rooms ever be silent to you again? God gave you there at once the keenest pain and the sublimest triumph over pain that the human heart can know. There He taught you at once the necessity and blessedness of submission.

It was here that some of your most precious friendships grew and ripened. It was here I first met you, your mother and the General, and learned to love you and yours. It was here you met and loved my wife and my granddaughters, Mabel and Bessie Reno. It was here in this auditorium of

THE H. L. KIRKPATRICK RESIDENCE, GREENVILLE
For many years the Charles Eaves Residence

heaven, amid all these sacred and inspiring associations, that you "heard the voice of the Lord which He spake unto you," bearing "witness unto you lest you deny Him." He bore ever "fresh and present witness" of Himself in your heart. Every morning His voice was new. Every evening His voice pursued you to your rest. Besides this direct continual presence He filled your world of association with utterances of Himself. The world will become to you more and more full of monumental pictures of human nobleness, patience, self-sacrifice, courage, meekness, so that you shall be more and more sure that goodness and heroism are possible for man. Not that you are lacking in any of these, but they will grow and ripen.

The transforming power of association is wonderful. It is the greatest enrichment of the world by man. Herod builds a temple at Jerusalem. With vast labor he levels the rough places and hews the great stone blocks into shape. When it is done, his temple shines like a jewel on its hill. But who cherishes the memory of its builder? Jesus comes right across the little valley to the Mount of Olives. He changes nothing outward. He sticks no spade into its surface. He leaves each bush and olive tree as he finds it. But there He ofttimes resorts with his disciples. There he lies prostrate in the struggle of Gethsemane. There at last His feet touch the earth as He ascends to Heaven, and ever since those days Mount Olivet burns in the dearest and most sacred memory of man.

Judge Eaves' life was filled with profound sorrows that would have crushed a less philosophic nature than his. Keen and bitter disappointments in his life followed one after another, leaving him a desolate and lonely man. What these disappointments were are still fresh in the minds of his surviving contemporaries and do not come within the scope of this sketch or of this volume. He met sorrow uncomplainingly and without any appeal for sympathy. Sympathy was universally felt, but nobody could invade the sanctity of the burden of grief that the disappointed old man carried to his grave without murmuring. His nature, which rose above resentment, and his philosophy, which contemplated with stoical endurance all the varying fortunes of life, were shown by his voluntary appeal, in simple and direct words, to a jury about to decide the fate of the murderer of his daughter. A plea of guilty had been entered. The deed was without legal extenuation, and without hearing evidence the court was about to submit the case to the jury. At that moment the prosecuting attorney asked permission for Judge Eaves to make a statement. This, although an unusual proceeding, was granted by the court. Judge Eaves, rising and advancing toward the jury, and speaking slowly with solemnity and feeling, said:

"By permission of the court I wish to state that I am the father of Miriam Wing. I wish also to state that it will be satisfactory to me if the jury will sentence Bert Wing to penal servitude for life. I have reasons for this. I, who am sixty-eight years of age, can not afford to act against any man from mere resentment. I can not help but feel some pity for a man with whom drinking was such a disease. Gentlemen, it will suit me, if it will suit you, to say in your verdict that his punishment shall be confinement in the penitentiary for life."[3]

After the death of Judge Eaves the following poem was found among his personal papers. The words were in his own handwriting and not in quotations. This fact, coupled with the subject of the poem, makes it appear that he may have been the author. He was a man of poetic temperament, but no one knows of his having written or published any other poem. On the other hand, it may be one of those stray waifs of impressive and solemn inspiration that sometimes find anonymous publication and which he had found in print somewhere, adopted in his heart, and copied in his own hand. It so faithfully portrays the sorrow that fell upon his old age that it would naturally appeal to him as a full summary of human fate under sorrow. Nevertheless, many of his friends think that he wrote these lines out of the fullness of his own heart:

---

[3] This case was tried in Louisville on February 17, 1893. The jury, after considering the matter an hour and twenty minutes, agreed to a sentence of life imprisonment. The Courier-Journal of the following day, in an account of the trial, reported:

"That the verdict of death did not follow Wing's admission of guilt was due to the plea made in his behalf by Judge Eaves. After the jury had rendered its verdict, Judge Eaves said: 'Whatever blame attaches to this tempering of justice with mercy, let it fall on me. I am responsible. I had intended to say this to the jury.'"

GOD'S PLOW OF SORROW.

God's plow of sorrow! Sterile is
  The field that is not turned thereby;
And but a scanty harvest his
  Whom the great Plowman passeth by.
God's plow of sorrow! All in vain
  His richest seed bestrews the sod;
And spent for naught the sun and rain
  On glebes that are not plowed of God.
He ploweth well, he ploweth deep,
  And where he ploweth angels reap.

God's plow of sorrow! Gentle child,
  I do not ask that he may spare
Thy tender soul, the undefiled,
  Nor turn it with his iron share.
Be thine his after-rain of love,
  And where his heavy plow hath passed,
May mellow furrows bear above
  A holier harvest at the last!
He ploweth well, he ploweth deep,
  And where he ploweth angels reap.

God's plow of sorrow! Furrowed brow,
  I know that God hath passed thy way;
And in thy soul his heavy plow
  Hath left its token day by day.
Yet from the torn and broken soil,
  Yea, from thy loss and from thy pain,
He hath due recompense of toil,
  Be sure he has not plowed in vain.
He ploweth well, he ploweth deep,
  And where he ploweth angels reap.

God's plow of sorrow! Do not think,
  Oh careless soul, that thou shalt lack.
God is afield, he will not shrink—
  God is afield, he turns not back.
Deep driven shall the iron be sent
  Through all thy fallow fields, until
The stubborn elements relent
  And lo, the Plowman hath his will!
He ploweth well, he ploweth deep,
  And where he ploweth angels reap.

XXII

MUHLENBERG IN THE CIVIL WAR

THE Civil War began on the 12th of April, 1861, when General Beauregard ordered the batteries in front of Charleston, South Carolina, to fire on Fort Sumter, and it ended on the 9th of April, 1865, when General Lee surrendered his army to General Grant at Appomattox Court House, Virginia.

For at least ten years before the actual outbreak of the Civil War the probability of war was discussed by every Muhlenberg man and woman. This topic was also the subject of much of the correspondence that passed between relatives and friends. A letter written by Peter Shaver a few weeks before the breaking out of the Civil War, sent to his son Benjamin J. Shaver, who at that time was at Frankfort representing Muhlenberg County in the Legislature, is here quoted. It is dated at Bremen, February 6, 1861:

> I find the people in this part of the county and McLean firm for the Union, but all that we can hear appears to be gloomy and doubtful. I still hope that a settlement of the difficulties will be reached.
> It seems to me that the Southern aristocratic Democrats have neither reason nor judgment. I cannot see what they expect to gain. But when a people are doomed they are blind and will work out their own destruction. I think that when they feel the heavy taxes that will fall on them, they will revolt and return to the Union. I am proud Virginia has taken such a noble stand. She always was brave and patriotic. She has great influence and I hope that her plan will be successful and that peace and harmony may be restored.
> I am astonished that there are so many disunionists in our State. I perceive that a goodly number are in the Legislature. If the Union must be dissolved, will we not be in a worse condition than Mexico? If this Union is divided Kentucky will go with the Southern division. [1]
> Times are hard now, but they are nothing whatever to what they will be if this rupture takes place.
> There is no class of citizens that have contributed more to cause this distracted state than the clergy of the North. Their influence is great. They have "gendered" envy, hate, strife and bitterness in society, whereas their Master, whom they pretend to serve, taught nothing but peace and good will to all people. As a nation we have been the most happy and prosperous in the world. Perhaps we have grown too rich, too proud and corrupt, and that we need some chastisement to bring us to our senses; then we will do what is right again.

---

[1] South Carolina seceded on December 20, 1860; Mississippi, Florida, Alabama, Georgia, and Louisiana followed in January, 1861; Texas in February, Virginia in April, Arkansas and North Carolina in May, and Tennessee in June. The citizens of Kentucky and of Missouri were divided in sentiment on the question of secession.

Dear son, you complain of the great responsibility that rests upon you. All that I can advise you, is to have confidence in your own judgment, and be swayed by no man's opinion without mature consideration.

I hope the people of Kentucky will pause and consider what they will do before it is too late. Just think of seeing garrisons from the mouth of the Sandy to the mouth of the Ohio, and all our effective men stationed there! Then every small farmer that is not able to have a negro will be compelled to sell his farm to a slave-holder and be a servant. I greatly fear that while some are contending to free the negro they will enslave the white man, and we will be the most unhappy people on earth, with no one to blame but ourselves.

A reform is certainly wanting in the Federal government;—too many officers, an empty treasury and a large debt have accumulated in time of peace. I hope all the States will return to the Union, and if South Carolina will not, she will be no loss to the government; she has never done any good; a perverse member she always was.

Now all that I can say, fall on what side we may, let us be loyal citizens so that we may lead peaceful and quiet lives. As for myself, I have nothing to lose or gain; it is for posterity that I feel interested. My prayer is for peace and prosperity and the Union forever.

Your most affectionate Father.

P. SHAVER.

Postscript: I hope you will be home soon. I can not see what good the Legislature can do now. Perhaps they have done too much already. I kindly tender you my thanks for the Commonwealth until you are better paid.

P. S.

[2] BENJAMIN J. SHAVER, 1890

---

[2] Benjamin Johnson Shaver, son of Peter Shaver, was born near Bremen, September 11, 1818, and died on his farm near Greenville October 17, 1894. He served as constable for eight years in the Bremen district. In 1850 he moved east of Greenville, and in 1851 was elected constable for the Boggess district. He next served as deputy sheriff for a few years, and then two terms as sheriff. In 1859 he made the race for the Legislature on the Union ticket, defeating Charles Eaves, Democrat, by six votes. In 1862 he was elected county judge without opposition. In 1875 he was elected to the Legislature on the Democratic ticket. On the expiration of his term in the Legislature he retired from public life and spent the remainder of his years on his farm. He served the county well. He always merited and received the confidence and esteem of the people. His first wife was Susan Jagoe. After her death he married Ann Morehead. Two of his children—Robert A. Shaver and Mrs. Nannie E. (first wife of George W.) Morgan—made Muhlenberg their home. His other children—George, Horace, William, Benjamin, and Joseph Shaver—settled in the West.

Collins is the only historian who has recorded any account in a history of Kentucky relative to Muhlenberg during the Civil War, and his is a very brief reference. Under the head of Muhlenberg County he writes:

"During the War of the Rebellion, Greenville was, for some time, an outpost of both armies, or rather neutral ground between them. It was taken by General Buckner in February, 1862, and some time after by John Morgan, and was once or twice partially sacked by guerillas. Muhlenburg County sent 836 men to the Federal army."

Collins' statement that Greenville "was taken by General Buckner in February, 1862," is erroneous both as to the date and the act. General Simon Bolivar Buckner passed through Greenville on September 26, 1861, but did not take possession of the town nor did he attempt to do so. General Buckner was in the neighborhood of the Cumberland and Tennessee rivers, near the Tennessee State line, during the first half of February, 1862, and on February 16th, when he surrendered Fort Donelson, he was transported to Indianapolis, whence he was sent a military prisoner to Massachusetts.

The statement made by Collins that Greenville "was once or twice partially sacked by guerillas" does not apply to the maneuvers of Generals S. B. Buckner, N. B. Forrest, or John H. Morgan, for their movements were more in the nature of a ride through the county than a raid on it. However, of the sections visited by such men as Dave Cain, Morris Moore, Jake Porter, Quantrill and others it may, in many instances, be said that they were "partially sacked by guerillas."

The marches made by Generals Buckner, Forrest, and Morgan were among the stirring events that transpired in Muhlenberg during the war, and will always rank among the most interesting incidents in the county's history. Although the coming and going of these troops may have frightened many people, such frights were insignificant compared to the experiences the citizens lived through while subject to the guerrilla raids and highway robberies that took place in Muhlenberg during the war. Many of these predatory invasions are woven into R. T. Martin's "Recollections of the Civil War," published elsewhere in this history, and to avoid repetition are eliminated from this chapter on the Civil War. The military career of Colonel Robert M. Martin in Muhlenberg and other parts of the country is also given in another chapter.

Edward R. Weir, sr., of Greenville, was looked upon as the leader of the Union men in the county. In September, 1861, he organized Company B, Eleventh Kentucky Infantry, and partially equipped it. His daughter, Anna Weir, presented to each of the officers and privates a pin-cushion or "housewife"—a small baglike cushion supplied with needles, thread, and buttons. James H. Brown, of Central City, carried his through the war, and still preserves it as one of his most precious war mementos. Edward R. Weir, jr., was chosen captain of Company B. He later resigned his captaincy and in 1863 helped raise the Thirty-fifth Kentucky Mounted Infantry, of which he became colonel. [2]

---

[2] Throughout the war E. R. Weir, jr., was always accompanied by his "waiting boy," Jesse Weir, who continued to serve his master faithfully for many years after slaves were emancipated. Jesse Weir died in Greenville in 1900, a highly respected negro.

Muhlenberg was more numerously represented in the Eleventh Kentucky Infantry than in any other Federal regiment. Most of the local men joined companies B, H, I, or K. At the resignation of Colonel Pierce B. Hawkins the Eleventh was commanded by Colonel S. P. Love, then of South Carrollton. The names of all the officers and privates in this and the other Union regiments organized in the State appear under a brief history of each regiment in "The Union Regiments of Kentucky," a book published by the Courier-Journal Job Printing Company in 1897. After the resignation of Captain Edward R. Weir, of Company B, William F. Ward became captain. Captain Isaac R. Sketo was killed at Shiloh, and Jesse K. Freeman was then elected captain of Company H. Joseph D. Yonts was first lieutenant of the same company. Joseph Fox and James R. Wise, of the Paradise country, served as captains of Company I. After Captain M. J. Roark, of Company K, was wounded at Shiloh he was succeeded by Captain Columbus H. Martin and Captain W. C. Shannon. James L. Roark was first lieutenant of this company.

The county was also well represented in the Third Kentucky Cavalry, organized by Colonel James S. Jackson, of Hopkinsville, who in July, 1862, was made brigadier-general and was succeeded as colonel by Major Eli H. Murray. Arthur N. Davis was captain of Company D until he was captured at Sacramento, when he was succeeded by Captain Thomas J. Lovelace. Captain Isaac Miller, of Company F, was succeeded by Captain Elisha Baker. A number of local men were attached to the Seventeenth Kentucky Infantry, raised by Colonel John H. McHenry, of Owensboro, and a few enlisted in the Twenty-sixth Kentucky Infantry and the Forty-eighth Kentucky Mounted Infantry.

It is probable that less than one hundred and fifty Muhlenberg citizens were in the Confederate army. No company of Confederates was organized in the county. Some men joined Buckner's command when he passed through in September, 1861, and a few became attached to companies that were recruited in Hopkins and Christian counties. Muhlenberg's largest representation in the Southern army was in Company C, Ninth Kentucky Infantry. This was recruited at Hartford by Doctor John Ed Pendleton, who served as its captain until its arrival in Russellville, when he was appointed chief surgeon of the regiment and later advanced to higher positions on the medical staff of the brigade.

From Ed Porter Thompson's "History of the Orphan Brigade" I copy the following names of the Muhlenberg men who were members of Company C. All here given were Muhlenberg men, although many of them are not so designated by Thompson: Moses Wickliffe, first lieutenant; Hume H. Harris, second lieutenant (seriously wounded at Baton Rouge); James H. Faughender, second lieutenant; C. C. Ambrose, second corporal (wounded at Stone River); James W. Yonts, second corporal (wounded at Chickamauga). Privates: John L. F. Ambrose (died at Atlanta); W. D. Burney (died at Griffin, Georgia); Joel Craig (died on retreat from Corinth); Richard Green (captured at Stone River); Joseph Hall; Harry Hendricks (killed at Shiloh); M. C. Hay (wounded and captured at Shiloh); John F. Jernigan; Benjamin G. Jernigan (wounded at Shiloh);

C. K. Jones (died of wounds received at Jackson, Mississippi); J. Ed Jones (killed at Shiloh); R. Wickliffe Jones; A. H. Kincheloe; A. J. Kirtley (wounded); Elisha B. Kirtley; W. C. Lander; N. R. Letner; John J. Mahan; William C. Pendleton; James H. Roll (killed at Shiloh); George Raney (wounded at Shiloh); Charles W. Rothrock; Elias G. Smith (killed at Shiloh); David Saulsburg (died of wounds received at Columbus, Mississippi); Gus Thompson (died of disease at Russellville); Henry L. Vickers (wounded at Shiloh); James W. Weeks (wounded at Chickamauga); M. L. Weeks; John K. Wickliffe (killed at Resaca); R. W. Wallace.

The names of John L. Taylor, of South Carrollton, and Jesse H. Wallace, of Paradise, are omitted by mistake from the list published by Thompson. Among other Muhlenberg men who joined the Confederate army in the South was Noah D. Rothrock, Benjamin L. Rhoads, James Drake, John M. Jones, and David Hay.

All the men who became members of Doctor Pendleton's company did not enlist at Hartford. This company left Hartford on Sunday, September 22, 1861, crossed Green River at South Carrollton and marched to Greenville, where they were joined by about twenty men under Moses Wickliffe, who had resigned as sheriff of the county to take up the cause of the South. After remaining in Greenville an hour this company resumed its march, and on the evening of the 23d arrived at Myers' Old Chapel, where after they had prepared to camp for the night they received a report that they were being pursued by a regiment of Federals. They immediately started for Logan County, but soon discovered that the report was false. The next morning they arrived in Russellville, and their company became part of what was later known as the Orphan Brigade.

In the meantime, that is, on the "fourth Sunday in September, 1861," Elisha B. Kirtley, of Paradise, made preparations to join the Southern army. While shaving he told those who were in his room that he would not shave again until the Confederate government was established beyond all doubt. He walked to Bowling Green and there enlisted in the Confederate cavalry, but later joined Company C of the Ninth Kentucky Infantry. At any rate, although he had many "close shaves" at Shiloh, Chickamauga, and Missionary Ridge, he never shaved his face after the "fourth Sunday in September, 1861," but wore a long beard during the remainder of his life, more than fifty years. Resolutions of similar nature were often made by Federal as well as Confederate soldiers, and many

MYERS' CHAPEL AND GRANGERS' HALL
Russellville Road, near Clifty Creek; built 1880, abandoned 1895; as it appears to-day

of them were carried out. These men stood on the brink of eternity every day, and naturally many of them had presentiments of death. A number of these forebodings came to pass. The following relative to a citizen of South Carrollton is quoted from a faded newspaper clipping which was probably published shortly after the battle of Stone River, December 31, 1862:

"In the celebrated detour of General Wharton to the rear of the enemy on Tuesday, December 30th, he was completely successful in his daring undertaking, but several gallant spirits fell never to rise again. Among these we may mention Noah D. Rothrock, of Muhlenberg County, Kentucky, and adjutant in Colonel Howard's Alabama Cavalry. He was shot just at the moment of victory, and such was the severity of his wound that he had to be left in the rear. Lieutenant Waller Overton remained with him and saw his body decently interred with an appropriate gravestone placed over it. The Abolitionists took Lieutenant Overton prisoner and paroled him. The body of Adjutant Rothrock they merely robbed of his cap and spurs. Noah Rothrock was one of nature's noblemen—a kind, generous and accomplished gentleman. He entered the service at the inception of the war and served with great faithfulness until the hour of his death. The day previous to receiving the fatal wound he remarked to his immediate companion that he had a presentiment of disaster to himself and told him that he would fall and the ball would pass through the picture of his sweetheart, Lilian, then in his pocket, and requested him to tell her of this presentiment and its coming true. Sure enough, the messenger of death first defaced the consecrated and enshrined picture and then laid low in death the gallant Rothrock."

In this connection it may be well to refer to John K. Wickliffe, another of the Muhlenberg soldiers who lost his life fighting for the South. John K. Wickliffe was a son of Colonel Moses Wickliffe, and one of the most popular men in the county. He was born in 1834 near Bevier, enlisted in Company C, Ninth Kentucky Infantry, fought at Shiloh, Vicksburg, Baton Rouge, Hartsville, Stone River, Jackson, Chickamauga, Mission Ridge, and Rocky Face Gap, and was killed at Resaca, Georgia, May 14, 1864. No soldier's death was more keenly deplored in the county, by both Northern and Southern sympathizers, than that of John K. Wickliffe, who had won his way into the hearts of all with whom he had come in contact. Lycurgus T. Reid, of Rockport, Ohio County, writing to me in July, 1912, relative to the death of this brave man, says:

"Although I may have forgotten some of my war experiences, I remember the time John K. Wickliffe was killed. I had my hand on his back when the fatal ball struck him. This incident, in all its detail, is as clear in my mind to-day as it was the day he was shot. I need but close my eyes to see the whole scene reënacted. It will be impossible for me to picture to you all the details of the event. However, I will attempt to give an outline of the facts.

"We were at Resaca. We had dug out shallow trenches and on top of the low embankment we had placed an old log, leaving a space between the top of the embankment and the lower side of the log, through which to shoot at the Yankees should they attack us. We had left our arms back of the breastworks while we were working on this embankment. Suddenly the rally to arms was sounded and every mother's son of us made for our guns. I, being a small man, was posted on the left of Company C (the color company of the Ninth Regiment), near the flag and John K. Wickliffe, who was our second sergeant and left company guide. Something, at times, makes me think he was color sergeant that day, but if he was he held on to his gun and accoutrements. We fell into the slight works and began to arrange ourselves for a good, square fight. The Yankees were in sight and coming fast. Wickliffe lay down on his stomach and, finding his cartridge box under him, asked me to push it up on his back. While I was attempting to do so a minie ball from the Yankee column struck the lower edge of the log, just above our heads, and glanced down, striking Wickliffe in the forehead, a little to the right of the center, passing through his head. He suddenly rose to his feet and fell backward, outside of the works, a dead man. He scarcely moved a muscle after he fell. I fired a number of shots over his prostrate body at the approaching enemy. During the course of the fight that followed I was obliged to change my position, but before doing so I took another look at my old friend and then covered his face with a blanket. That was the last I saw of John K. Wickliffe."

JOHN K. WICKLIFFE, 1860

Soon after war was declared no less than a dozen Muhlenberg families were represented in both armies. Many families and friends were divided in their sympathies. Arguments followed, and as a result the dividing line was usually more distinctly drawn. While those on the same side agreed on most questions, they occasionally held opposite views regarding certain points. Among those whose sympathies were the same but who disagreed in their opinion as to the final outcome of the war were William and Henry Young, of the Nelson Creek country. One day in the fall of 1861 these two brothers were sitting by the stove in Samuel Henry's shoeshop in South Carrollton, again arguing the question as to which side would win in the Civil War, when Henry remarked to his brother that if General Thomas L. Crittenden moved his troops from Calhoun into Muhlenberg County some of the local people "would make it as hot as blazes for his soldiers." Just then a Federal soldier stepped into the shop, and having heard none but the last few words, demanded that the remark be repeated. Henry hesitated, and William answered: "He was just saying that if General Crittenden had stoves like this in his tents he could make them as hot as blazes for his soldiers."

That evening, on their return home, each tried again to convince the other of his view as to which side would win. Henry held that the South was bound to come out victorious: William declared that the North would conquer. They agreed that since they could not "argue it out" they would "fight it out," and that the result of the war would be settled by them "once for all" in a "fist-and-skull fight." A friendly battle followed, and ever after both felt convinced that the North would subdue the South.

Shortly after Doctor Pendleton's company left Hartford, General Simon Bolivar Buckner passed through Muhlenberg at the head of about fifteen hundred men. General Buckner marched from Bowling Green to Rochester, where some of his recruits attempted to destroy the lock and dam below the mouth of Mud River. His men continued over the Greenville, Rochester, and Mud River Road to Greenville, and on the evening of the 26th of September, 1861, camped at the Ellison Spring, about two miles southwest of town. Charles Fox Wing, whom General Buckner had known intimately for twenty years, had died in Greenville the day before. Buckner, hearing of this, called at the Wing home at Cherry and Main Cross streets and there viewed the remains of his old friend.

When Buckner's men passed through Greenville they carried the Confederate flag at half-mast. On that occasion a few Southern banners were waving from some of the house-tops, most conspicuous among which was the one at the home of Robert S. Russell. Edward Rumsey, during the entire war, although a Southern sympathizer and looked upon as an adviser of those who espoused the Southern cause, never hung out any other flag than a white one—the flag of peace. Many Union flags were unfurled on this memorable 26th of September, and although greater in number they were not displayed with any greater enthusiasm than the Confederate colors. At the breaking out of the war the Federal flag was raised on the lawn in front of the residence of Edward R. Weir, sr., and remained there day and night, year after year, until peace had been declared. When General Buckner and his soldiers arrived in Greenville they saw the large flag waving in front of the Weir house. One of the Confederates attempted to pull it down, and probably would have done so had not the General immediately stationed some of his men near the flag to guard it. "Every man has a right to express himself," said the General, and then gave orders to his men not to molest this or any of the other flags they might see displayed along their line of march.

During this short but memorable stay in Greenville General Buckner chanced to see a horse ridden by George W. Haden, who happened to be in town that day. The General expressed his admiration of the animal and offered to buy it. But this sorrel being the pride of the whole family, the owner did not feel at liberty to give or sell him to any one. Upon his return home, near Drakesboro, Mr. Haden informed his wife of the General's desire to own this horse, "Reindeer." Mrs. Haden immediately sent the horse back to Greenville and presented him to General Buckner with her compliments. One version has it that this same animal was shot from under General Buckner five months later, at Fort Donelson, February 15, 1862. General Buckner informed me, however, that while he was attending the conference of officers which arranged for the surrender of Fort Donelson this horse was stolen and taken across the river, and that about a year later, while at Knoxville, the animal was returned to him by order of General Floyd, and that it died a natural death before the close of the war.

On the morning of the 27th of September Buckner's command left the Ellison place and resumed its march. They crossed Pond River at Reno's Bridge, now Prowse's Bridge, and on the 29th entered Hopkinsville, where they left a few troops. When the Union men of Greenville learned of Buckner's departure for Hopkinsville they immediately sent this information to the Federals in that town. John Breathitt, of Christian County, carried the news. The moment he received the message he sprang upon a horse belonging to Colonel James S. Jackson, disappeared up the high road in a cloud of dust, and in three and a half hours had raced over the thirty-two hills between Greenville and Hopkinsville.

Buckner's men arrived in Bowling Green on October 3, 1861, after a march of about one hundred miles. The object of this detour was to arouse an interest in the Southern army and thus gain recruits, for the enlisting of volunteers at Owensboro and Henderson was rapidly drawing men into the Federal army. However, as a result of this march General Buckner did not increase his force by much more than a dozen citizens from Muhlenberg, for most of the local men who had decided to fight for the South had already enlisted in Doctor Pendleton's company.

Colonel Nathan B. Forrest and about three hundred of his men were the next to appear on the scene in Muhlenberg. They passed through Greenville on Friday morning, December 27, 1861. They had a few days before left Hopkinsville, which at that time and until the first part of February, 1862, was an outpost of the Confederate force stationed at Bowling Green. Colonel Forrest and his men were then on a scouting expedition in the territory south of Calhoun, where about a month before General Thomas L. Crittenden had established his headquarters. Many of Forrest's squadron stopped for a late breakfast at the Weir farm north of Greenville, which at that time was managed by an overseer who was evidently a Southern sympathizer, for he not only treated them to milk and honey but also filled many of their knapsacks from the best in his smokehouse. Shortly before crossing the Muhlenberg County line into McLean they encountered about one hundred and seventy Federal soldiers under Major Eli H. Murray and Colonel S. P. Love, who were skirmishing in that neighborhood. In the battle that followed about eight men were killed, a dozen or more wounded, and a number taken prisoner. This fight took place on December 28, 1861, near Sacramento, in that section of McLean County which a few years before was part of Muhlenberg. R. T. Martin's account of this encounter is printed in this volume in his "Recollections of the Civil War." Descriptions of this fight are also published in "The Life of General Nathan Bedford Forrest," by J. A. Wyeth, and in "Confederate Operations in Canada and New York," by John W. Headley. From "The Partisan Rangers," by General Adam R. Johnson, I quote:

In a short time we [Adam R. Johnson and Robert M. Martin, scouts for Colonel Forrest] were on the road [from Hopkinsville] to Greenville. Martin's parents living in the vicinity, he determined to visit his home, and wanted me to accompany him. But I preferred to remain to meet Colonel Forrest if he came up. It was late in the afternoon, and I passed the remainder of the day in ascertaining where supplies for cavalry could be obtained, leaving the impression that they were for the Federal cavalry under Jackson. Next morning early Bob Martin rejoined me and we started back, meeting Forrest in the road a few miles out. When informed that provisions and forage were to be had, and the country was clear of the enemy, Forrest determined to go into the town with his little force.

Some Federal soldiers, while watering their horses at Garst's Pond, one half mile south of Sacramento, McLean County, after a skirmish in Northern Muhlenberg, were surprised and routed by Colonel Forrest's squadron and driven through Sacramento to Calhoun, December 28, 1861

A long march over the rough, muddy roads required a short rest for the men and horses, but Martin and I were ordered to move down the road to Rumsey, ascertain the movements of the Federals, and report the results of our observations. Pushing forward, when we reached Rumsey we ascertained that the enemy had built a pontoon bridge and were crossing their cavalry. Thereupon I returned to report to Colonel Forrest, while Martin remained in the vicinity to observe the movements of the enemy.

I met Forrest on the road beyond the little town of Sacramento, and the Colonel hurried forward his regiment to attack them. The news that the Federals were not far away, and that a combat was imminent, seemed to send a thrill of pleasure through the entire command, for these young warriors already felt in anticipation "the rapture of the fight." When the order "gallop" was given, the men who rode the fleetest steeds impetuously crowded to the front. As I looked back at this confused body of riders, each rushing to meet the foe first, a fearful sickening dread came over me which I well recall to this day, and I almost presumed to call Forrest's attention to this disorderly mass of men galloping pellmell at breakneck speed, when suddenly there came into view a young woman on a bareback horse, wildly dashing up, frantically waving her hat, while her long hair was flying in the wind like a pennant, and her cheeks were afire with excitement as she exclaimed: "There the Yankees are! right over there!" pointing back over the hill whence she had just galloped.

Forrest, not checking his horse in the least, shouted: "Johnson, go and see right where they are!"

Letting my eager animal have the reins, I was soon up with the two advanced videttes of Forrest's regiment. They were fortunately riding good horses, and at my word increased their speed. Observing a high point on one side of the road not far in advance, I rode up to its summit and spied just over the crest of the hill a large body of cavalry drawn up in a V-shape and a small platoon stationed in the road in advance of the main force.

I rode back rapidly to Colonel Forrest with this information; he was trying to persuade the brave girl, who was riding by his side, to retire.

I, of course, expected him to halt his disorderly men and order a proper formation to make battle. But this fiery leader, without checking his charger, galloped on until he had reached the videttes, whom I had left on the hilltop to watch the enemy, now quite close to them. Jerking his gun out of the hands of one of them, and without a moment's hesitation, he fired at the Federals. The Confederates in his rear gave "the wild Rebel yell," and the Yankee advance guard fled back to their command. From his post of observation Forrest could plainly see the great odds which he was so eager to attack, but, undisturbed, he halted his men right in face of the enemy and ordered his captains to reform their companies. Under less serious circumstances this would have seemed altogether ludicrous; as the captains rode to right and left commanding their men to form around them, not one of them succeeded in collecting more than a dozen or two men out of the confused mass, every fellow seemingly "on his own hook." Just at this juncture Captain Gould, of the Texas company, coming up and hearing the order to form, dashed to the summit of the hill immediately in the front of the astonished Federals, and shouted in his deep, sonorous voice: "All you Texas boys rally round your leader!"

Gould had more men to the front because his company had the best horses, and as they rushed ahead to "rally round their leader" the Federals likely could see their peculiar saddles and so perhaps concluded that not only Forrest's regiment was in their front, but the entire regiment of the Texas Rangers. At any rate, they began to fall back in disorder, and Forrest throwing out flankers, both right and left, adopting thus in his very first fight those tactics which he afterwards made so formidable, swept down like an avalanche upon the Federals, now in almost as much disorder as his men had lately been.

The Southerners, led by this impetuous chieftain, swooped down upon their foes with such terrific yells and sturdy blows as might have made them believe a whole army was on them, and turning tail, they fled in the wildest terror, a panic-stricken mass of men and horses, Forrest's men mixed up with them, cutting and shooting right and left, and Forrest himself in his fury ignoring all command and always in the thickest of the melee. Never in any battle did leader play a fiercer individual part than did Forrest on this day. With his long arm and long sword, once during the fight and chase he was some distance ahead of his men, making a pathway as he cut and slashed on this side and that, and the demoralized Yankees, looking back and seeing a man whom their excited imaginations doubtless magnified into a veritable giant coming down upon them, pressed to either side, thus widening his path into a lane. Finally he came up with a man who had been a blacksmith, as large as himself, muscular and powerful. While engaged in combat with this man, another Federal was in the very act of running his sword into Forrest's back, when a timely shot from Lieutenant Lane felled this second antagonist. Forrest hewed the big man to the ground by a mighty stroke.

Near the large tree on the right, on the Greenville and Rumsey Road north of Sacramento, McLean County, Captain Albert G. Bacon, of the Third Kentucky Cavalry, was killed in the retreat of the Federals from Garst's Pond to Calhoun. Station Church is shown in the background

Wildly onward rushed the fleeing and pursuing masses, all in the most disorderly manner, until again Forrest was engaged in an unequal contest with two Federal officers and a private, the latter shooting a ball through his collar, and Forrest quieting him with a pistol-shot just as the two officers made an attack upon him with their swords, which he eluded by bending his supple body forward, their weapons only gashing his shoulder. The impetus of his horse carrying him a few paces forward, he checked and drew him a little to one side and shot one of his antagonists as his horse galloped up, and thrust his saber into the other. Severely wounded, both of these officers fell from their steeds, which now uncontrolled, sharply collided with each other at full speed, falling together over the bottom of an abrupt hillock. Forrest, eager in the pursuit, inadvertently rode his horse over these two prostrate animals, causing him to fall and his rider to dart ten feet over his head. Seeing Forrest down, and fearing he had been shot, I leaped my horse over the fallen horses just in time to see him spring to his feet and call out: "Johnson, catch me a horse!" His own horse was badly crippled. Catching one that came plunging down the road, I handed him the bridle, but the saddle did not suit him, and while he was getting his own saddle his men gradually withdrew from the pursuit.

After the defeat of this cavalry force I was ordered forward to reconnoiter, and gathering up a few men on the way, I pushed forward to the top of the ridge, where I could observe the road for some distance; finding it clear, I left the men there as a guard and rode back to Colonel Forrest. There I found Bob Martin in high glee over the rôle he had played in the late tragedy. He was leading a horse and had his belt full of pistols.

"Hello, Bob; what have you been doing?" I asked him as I rode up.

"I've been trying to get even with a fellow that stole my horse—old Beauregard," he replied laughingly, meaning the high-headed, slender-limbed gray horse he had lost.

"What success?"

"Well, here is his horse, this is his pistol, and this is his gun," he said as he smiled.

"What became of the Yank?" I inquired.

"I left him over yonder in that strip of woods you see to the left of that road," he replied.

Collecting the guns which the Federals had thrown away, Forrest returned to Hopkinsville.

Forrest's squadron passed through Greenville late Saturday afternoon, December 28, 1861, and that night camped at Mount Pisgah Church, near Pond River. In the meantime the routed Federals returned to their camp at Calhoun, and although General Crittenden sent out five hundred soldiers that same night to capture Forrest and his men, they failed to locate him.

General Thomas L. Crittenden, who had taken command of the Federal forces at Owensboro on October 9, 1861, moved his headquarters to Calhoun during the latter part of November. As already stated, it was while stationed at Calhoun that some of his men encountered Colonel Forrest near Sacramento. On January 16th Crittenden's division moved to South Carrollton, where it remained until January 28, 1862. On the two hills south and southwest of South Carrollton, General Crittenden threw up breastworks, remains of which can still be seen. In a number of places at the foot of these hills and in the valley between them he felled wide rows of trees and thus constructed an abatis for the defense of his position. What is now the residence of John L. Taylor stood near the camp of the Eleventh Kentucky Infantry, and was used by that regiment as a hospital during their stay at South Carrollton. General Crittenden's headquarters were in the hotel long known as "Our House" or "Lovelace Tavern."

The history of Crittenden's stay in Muhlenberg is told in five of the official communications that passed between him and General Buell, whose headquarters were then in Louisville. These letters are here quoted from the "Official Records of the War of the Rebellion," Series I, Volume 7:

HEADQUARTERS DEPARTMENT OF THE OHIO,
Louisville, January 10, 1862.

Brigadier-General T. L. CRITTENDEN,
Commanding Fifth Division, Calhoun, Ky.:

Sir: The general commanding directs that you move your division without delay to South Carrollton or near there. Take a strong position on the north side of the river which can be held by a small force.

BREASTWORKS NEAR SOUTH CARROLLTON, THROWN UP JANUARY, 1862
From photograph made fifty years later

Take your bridge with you or provide other means of crossing rapidly. Leave a regiment at Calhoun to guard the lock.

I am, sir, very respectfully, your obedient servant,

JAMES B. FRY,
Assistant Adjutant-General, Chief of Staff.

HEADQUARTERS FIFTH DIVISION,
Calhoun, January 18, 1862.

J. B. FRY, Assistant Adjutant-General:

Captain: My entire command is now here. The Fourteenth Brigade, under Colonel Jones, and Jackson's cavalry reached here yesterday evening.

On the 16th instant we crossed the river at Calhoun and marched to Sacramento, with all our wagons, bringing nothing but a little forage. The roads of course are bad, but we got there without accident or damage. Colonel Cruft's command was so conducted as to occupy the town before the inhabitants were aware of the approach of troops.

The order to march, though dated the 10th, did not reach me until the 14th. This made me, of course, more anxious to be rapid in my movement. To do this I was forced to cross at Calhoun and march to South Carrollton, on the south side of the river. I considered this movement imprudent unless South Carrollton was first occupied. For this reason Cruft's command was sent by the steamboat and barges, as the only expeditious way of occupying the town. I confess to great anxiety of mind when I saw over 2,000 troops crowded on the boats, and determined that, except in a great emergency, I would not start such another expedition. In the present condition of the road it would have taken me five or six days to reach this place, marching by the north side of the river.

RESIDENCE OF JOHN L. TAYLOR, SOUTH CARROLLTON

My command is now in South Carrollton, on the south side of the river. This is, I am aware, in violation of General Buell's order, at least the spirit of it. It is impossible to execute the order, there being no strong position on the north side of the river in the vicinity of South Carrollton.

Unless I occupied this place, 1,000 men could have stopped me from crossing at any point where there is a road by which I could march. This is a position of great strength and my command ought to hold it against 15,000 good troops.

If I must move to the north side of the river, I will be compelled to go at least 2 miles back to find ground high enough to camp on, and it would take me two days to cross the river here if ordered to advance. I consider my command safe here. I assure you I have endeavored to obey orders, and have done so as far as practicable—obeying what I considered most important where all could not be obeyed. I could not have secured a passage across the river at or near this place by occupying any position in the vicinity of South Carrollton, on the north side of the river.

For miles around this place, on the north side of the river, the land is flat, and so low as to overflow when the river is up. If I move over and cross this flat, as I should be compelled to do, and the river should rise, I could not cross at all.

South Carrollton is situated on a hill, rising abruptly from the river, 150 feet high. There are only two ways of approaching the place from the south—one by the road which I came, through a swamp, and which could be defended by a small force; the other through a wooded country and up hill.

"OUR HOUSE" OR "LOVELACE TAVERN," SOUTH CARROLLTON

Captain Edwards, of the U. S. Army, doubtless known to you as an educated and accomplished soldier, fully concurs in my views as to the strength of the place. With another battery of artillery it seems to me I could hold the place until starved out, and as it is can hold it against any force the enemy can send.

Respectfully, your obedient servant,
T. L. CRITTENDEN,
Brigadier-General, Commanding.

HEADQUARTERS FIFTH DIVISION.
South Carrollton, January 27, 1862.

Captain J. B. FRY,
Assistant Adjutant-General.

CAPTAIN: I have heard that a large force from Bowling Green had come under Buckner to Russellville, with a view to intercept me if I advance or come here and attack me if I remain for any length of time where I am.

I am strongly posted, and am making my position stronger by erecting earthworks on the heights for the protection of the men.

I should have no apprehension for the result if attacked by 15,000 men, the reported force of the enemy with which we are threatened, but shall, of course, use every exertion to become still stronger.

If I am to remain here any time a few guns in position would aid me immensely.

Most respectfully, your obedient servant,

T. L. CRITTENDEN,
Brigadier-General, Commanding.

HEADQUARTERS DEPARTMENT OF THE OHIO.
Louisville, January 28, 1862.

Brigadier-General T. L. CRITTENDEN,
    Commanding Fifth Division, South Carrollton:

Sir: It is presumed that you have before this received the general's dispatch of the 24th (26th) instant, directing the return of your division to Calhoun, and the general trusts that you have complied with it.

Your position at South Carrollton (being on the south side of Green River, which is impassable at this time) is a very unsafe one, and you will lose no time in moving your command to Calhoun and placing yourself on the north side of Green River.

If you should be attacked or too seriously threatened to undertake this move with time to accomplish it, you must, of course, defend yourself to the last extremity in the strongest position you can take, and see that the enemy does not cut your line of communication at or near Calhoun. It is hoped, however, that you will move to Calhoun promptly and without interference.

I am, sir, very respectfully, your obedient servant,

JAMES B. FRY,
Assistant Adjutant-General, Chief of Staff.

HEADQUARTERS FIFTH DIVISION.
South Carrollton, January 28, 1862.

General BUELL,
    Commanding Department of the Ohio:

GENERAL: Your dispatch of the 26th instant was received before daylight this morning, and the barges and steamboats are now being loaded with commissary stores and forage. I shall get the supplies which I have of these things to Calhoun before night, I hope, and the boat back during the night. I hear of no advance of the enemy, and unless I do, will march back, as soon as I can rid myself of every incumbrance, by the road I came. It is a very bad road, but the best and much the shortest. It would be almost impossible for me to cross the river here, because of the steep and muddy banks and the high water. I shall endeavor to have every possible arrangement made to cross the wagons and troops with despatch as soon as they arrive opposite to Calhoun.

Owing to the terrible condition of the roads between here and Calhoun I shall send my camp equipage by the boats, so as to have my wagons light as possible. I shall send down at least a regiment in the same way, with instructions to construct a bridge of the boats by the time I arrive with the troops and train, and if the current of the river is too swift for the bridge, to make the best possible arrangements for ferrying.

This evening or to-morrow morning I will send Colonel Jackson with 500 cavalry, to Greenville, to remain there until I leave here with the column, and then march to Sacramento by the road leading from Greenville to that place.

This, I think, will certainly conceal my movements until I have actually started, and protect me on the only quarter from which I could be surprised and harassed by cavalry. I anticipate, however, no difficulty except from the roads and river, though I will prepare as well as I can for every kind of difficulty.

Respectfully, your obedient servant,

T. L. CRITTENDEN,
Brigadier-General, Commanding.

N. B.—I cannot send you a telegram, because I cannot spare a boat, and the high water has obstructed the right road to Evansville. I hope this letter will reach Owensboro to-night, and, if so, it will be the quickest way in which I can communicate with you.

Respectfully,

T. L. C.

There were five Kentucky and four Indiana regiments at Calhoun under General Crittenden until the early part of January, when the Seventeenth and Twenty-fifth Kentucky Infantry and the Thirty-first and Forty-fourth Indiana Infantry were ordered to join General Grant, who was then directing his movements against Forts Henry and Donelson. His division at South Carrollton consisted of the Eleventh and Twenty-sixth Kentucky Infantry, Third Kentucky Cavalry, the Forty-second and Forty-third Indiana Infantry, and Behr's battery of artillery, making a total of a little less than five thousand soldiers, not including the men who were left at Calhoun to guard the locks.

BETHLEHEM BAPTIST CHURCH, NEAR BREMEN

On February 16, 1862, a little more than two weeks after General Crittenden returned to Calhoun from South Carrollton, his men were ordered to Tennessee. Some of the infantry marched to Owensboro and proceeded by steamers to Nashville, while others were taken down Green and Ohio rivers and up the Cumberland to the same place. The Third Kentucky Cavalry marched from Calhoun through Muhlenberg County to Nashville. They spent the first night in and around Bethlehem Baptist Church, near Bremen, and the next day resumed their trip up the Rumsey Road to Greenville, where they halted a few hours. The second night they camped on McClelland's Hill, including what is now the Alvin L. Taylor farm, on which was planted, in 1907, what has since been known as "Alvin's

Avenue." From McClelland's Hill the cavalry continued their march south. General Crittenden's men were reunited in Nashville and later proceeded to Pittsburg Landing, where as part of General Buell's army they came to the relief of General Grant and helped save the day for the Federals at Shiloh.

Many letters were undoubtedly written to their families and friends by Muhlenberg men while in the army, and a number of them, I hope, are still preserved. However, only a few have been submitted to me. One of these was written by E. R. Weir, jr., then captain of Company B, Eleventh

"ALVIN'S AVENUE," SIX MILES SOUTH OF GREENVILLE.

Kentucky Infantry, and addressed to Jesse H. Reno, who was quartermaster of that regiment until about the middle of May, 1862, when on account of ill health he resigned and returned to his home in Greenville. This letter is dated "Field of Shiloah, April 24, 1862," which was seventeen days after the fight. Before quoting this letter it may be well to explain why the writer was still on the field so long after the battle.

The battle of Shiloh, or Pittsburg Landing, was fought on Sunday and Monday, April 6 and 7, 1862. Immediately after this bloody fight Generals Buell and Grant began making preparations to attack the somewhat shattered army of Confederates who were retreating to Corinth, in Northern Mississippi, about twenty miles from Shiloh. The Federals were about ready to pursue when, on April 12th, General Halleck arrived on the scene, and being superior in rank took chief command of the troops. The army loitered on the battlefield awaiting the arrival of more forces ordered by General Halleck. The march of the augmented army against General Beauregard at Corinth did not begin until April 27th. It was during this delay on the field of Shiloh that E. R. Weir, jr., wrote to his friend Jesse H. Reno. It is printed as written, as a battlefield souvenir.

Field of Shiloah, April 24, 1862.

Dear Reno:—On the morning of the first day of battle we were within 9 miles of Savannah. About 7 o'clock A. M. Sunday we heard the fire of cannon in the distance. Orders were given to forward in quick time. Of course our boys pushed forward with speed. We arrived within one mile of Savannah at 1 o'clock P. M. Our General then received orders that we were not wanted, so we began to pitch tents.

About sundown we were ordered forward to Savannah. We then took transportation to Pittsburg Landing, arriving at Pittsburg Landing at about 11 o'clock P. M. We remained under arms until daylight when we were ordered out to the field about 2 miles from the Landing, toward Corinth.

Our Brigade was composed of the 13th Ohio, 26th & 11th Ky. and the 14th Wisconsin. The 13th Ohio was drawn up on the left, the 26th next & the 14th Wis. next. We were ordered to the support of Mendenhall's Battery. We were drawn up in its rear & were ordered to lie down so as to protect ourselves from the bombs. But we were not suffered to remain long in this position, for the 14th commenced giving way & we were ordered to take its place. General Crittenden gave the order to charge bayonets.

The Eleventh, with shouts of Kentucky & Crittenden rushed forward about 300 yards beyond our lines. Capt. Isaac R. Sketo here fell by my side; also John B. Morgan who was in our advance. Capt. Jeff. Roark was also wounded. Having broken our ranks & being exposed to the direct & cross fire of their Batteries we were compelled to fall back and form. At the 2nd charge we advanced about 800 yards beyond our line of battle. In the charge we took four guns & six cannon from the enemy, bayonetting the cannoneers at their post. Having completely routed them in front we were about to be flanked; so we fell back to our line of battle. Having reformed we advanced slowly on our second charge, reinforced by Bartlett's Battery & the 13th Ky. under Col. Grider on our left. We took possession of the Battery; the enemy were put to flight on our right & left. They fled in a great rout, leaving behind everything of value. Guns, casons, muskets, rifles & knapsacks were scattered in every direction. Our cavalry followed them for 5 or 6 miles until night overtook them.

I can form no estimate of the amount of dead Rebels. In front of where we fought were 300 or 400. We had the advantage of them; their shot would fall short of us by 20 or 30 feet nearly always. During the day we fought against Gen. Withers of Mississippi under Gen. Beauregard. At one time we were fighting against the 5th Ky. Rebels.

Some of our boys said that they recognized one as Charles W. Rothrock; Charles McBride was almost confident that it was he. I did not know him well enough to say. Ben Jernigan, from near Greenville, was pointed out to me by Louis Dwyer. M. C. Hay was wounded & taken prisoner by our forces.

After the battle I went over the battle field, at least over about one fourth of it. No pen can tell of its horrors; thousands lay dead. At some places 200 or 300 were upon one acre of ground. On Tuesday a detail of about 5000 men began the burying of the dead. Our men were, of course, buried first. The work steadily progressed until Friday when all in the immediate neighborhood of our camps were interred. The number on Thursday evening was upward of 7800.

Not long ago we were ordered out on picket duty about 3 miles from our camp. The road all the way was strewed with knapsacks, guns, cannon, etc. During the day I went beyond our lines about three fourths of a mile. I found, I believe it was, nineteen dead Rebels in one pile that had been left behind by them in their flight. A little below we found about 2000 knapsacks. Our scouts bring in the report that the road out of Corinth is blockaded for miles with wagons and caissons. These are plain facts about the battle.

If the Rebels say in Muhlenberg that they won the battle, it is a fabrication. You can tell them there is a day of retribution coming yet. The boys of Muhlenberg and the men that chased them down last winter when they were on furloughs, can never live together again; one or the other of us will have to leave the country forever. When we return home we will have no military law to restrain us and we will clean out the County of our enemies. All of us have strong hands and willing hearts for a work of this kind. We can never live together; they shall drive us or we them.

Yours,

WEIR.

I do not know, positively, to what incident Weir refers in the last paragraph of his letter. It may be he had in mind what has since become known as "Old Ed's Rush to Rumsey," the story of which is as follows:

One day in February, 1862, a band of about ten desperate-looking young men entered Greenville. Some of them, it is said, were citizens of the county, among whom were a few Confederate soldiers then on furlough. It appears that these young men came to the conclusion that if they captured Edward R. Weir, sr., they could hold him for a large ransom, for he was one of the most ardent workers for the Federal army in the county.

Anna Weir, his daughter, was at home sitting near a window, and when she saw the crowd coming in the yard she started toward the front door, where she met them with a pistol in her hand. The leader asked her whether "Old Man Ed" was in the house. Although she knew that her father was in his room taking a nap, she did not answer the question, but asked them to tell her the nature of their call. They shouted that they had come "to get Old Ed's scalp and meant to have it." Her serving-woman, Elvira, hearing this threat, quietly entered the house, woke Mr. Weir, and informed him of what was taking place downstairs, and added: "I jes' know Miss Anna aims to hol' 'em till you can haste away."

In the meantime Anna Weir was detaining the band, for she felt confident that neither her father nor any other man would trust his life in the hands of such characters, and that he, if he had a chance to escape from them, would do so.

While she was talking to the mob and thus gaining time for her father, one of the men attempted to pull down the flag that hung from a pole near the front of the house. Perceiving his intention, she raised her pistol and aimed it at him, saying, "If you touch that flag I'll kill you and as many others of your gang as I can. It's my father's flag and mine too and I'll die by it. I tell you father's not on the place, but I'm here and I'm ready to die by that flag now or at any other time!"

After Mr. Weir heard Elvira's warning he took a peep at the noisy crowd, and after telling her he would leave sent the woman back to her mistress. He crawled out of a back window, ran down to the stable, and ordered his negro, Lewis, to saddle his swift horse "Jack Monkey." He mounted the animal and was soon on his way toward Rumsey, where a number of Federal soldiers were guarding the lock and dam. Anna Weir refused to let the crowd search the house, and although they did not enter they nevertheless soon left convinced that "Old Man Ed" was not at home.

THE EDWARD R. WEIR, SR., RESIDENCE, GREENVILLE
Built in 1839, occupied by the Weirs for seventy years, now the home of L. Z. Kirkpatrick.

A little less than seven months after the battle of Shiloh, and about ten months after General Forrest had had his encounter with the Federals near Sacramento, General John H. Morgan passed through Muhlenberg County. Immediately after the battle of Perryville, October 7, 1862, General Bragg's army withdrew from Kentucky. During this withdrawal General Morgan, at the head of a command of about eighteen hundred men, took an independent westerly course and on November 4th arrived at Gallatin, Tennessee. General Morgan entered Muhlenberg County at Skilesville. All local traditions bearing on this subject give the time of his arrival as Friday night, October 24, 1862. General Basil W. Duke, in his "History of Morgan's Cavalry" places the date two days earlier. General Morgan was then on his ten days' march from Gum Springs to Hopkinsville. He traveled via Elizabethtown, crossed Green River at Morgantown and Mud River at Rochester, and from there proceeded to Greenville, and on Sunday, October 26th, started for Christian County.

General Duke, in his history, devotes only a few lines to Morgan's march through Muhlenberg County, all of which I here quote. After stating that he left Morgantown on the morning of October 23, 1862, General Duke says (page 204):

"We crossed Mud River that night at Rochester, on a bridge constructed of three flat-boats, laid endwise, tightly bound together, and propped, where the water was deep, by beams passing under the bottoms of each one and resting on the end of the next; each receiving this sort of support they mutually braced each other. A planking, some five feet wide, was then laid, and the horses, wagons and artillery were crossed without trouble. The bridge was built in about two hours. On the 24th we reached Greenville; that night a tremendous snow fell—tremendous, at least, for the latitude and season. After crossing Mud River there was no longer cause for apprehension, and we marched leisurely."

Morgan's cavalry passed through Greenville during the afternoon of October 25, 1862. Morgan spent the greater part of that evening in Greenville, and in the meantime his men camped near the Joe C. Reynolds place, about three miles southwest of town. It was an exceedingly cold day for that season. That night his tired soldiers, as usual, slept under their blankets in long rows. They were unmindful of the snow which fell softly above them, hiding alike the sod and the sleepers and forming what appeared to be a snow-covered graveyard, for each soldier's snow-heaped body made a distinct mound in this camp-ground of Morgan's Immortals. When the bugler sounded his bugle for rising, he beheld a scene which well might make one think of that last day when Gabriel shall blow another trumpet, for each snow-covered grave opened and gave up, not its dead, but its living.

From the beginning of the Civil War until its close many good and bad reports and true and false alarms were constantly being put into circulation. John R. Randolph, in his "A Muhlenberger's Recollections of 1862," published in the Muhlenberg Sentinel, May 5, 1911, gives an account of two incidents which, in their general character, are representative of the experiences many people in the county were subjected to throughout the war:

When the Civil War broke out, Clark's Mill, on Pond River, near Harp's Hill, was in full operation. Clark ran the mill and Eaves conducted a dry-goods and grocery store. Clark and Eaves each owned 30 or 40 slaves. This mill was one of the largest and best known mills along Pond River. Besides his many slaves, Clark employed a number of families who lived in the immediate vicinity of the mill. In fact, the place looked more like a small town than a mere store and mill. Clark and Eaves were both clever men and well liked by all who had any dealings with them.

Nearly all the people in that vicinity in Hopkins County, and nearly all those who lived in Muhlenberg near Clark's Mill and Harp's Hill, were Southern sympathizers. The mill soon became a great gathering-place for those who had war measures to propose or war news to tell.

It was well known that my father, Ashford D. Randolph, was not only a strong Union sympathizer but also did all he could for the Union men. He was very outspoken, and his remarks frequently incurred the ill-will of those who differed with him on the situation. Many who were his best friends during his free-trade days became his bitterest enemies.

In the summer of 1862, after both Northern and Southern armies had gone South, a number of prowling guerillas began to form themselves into little squads. One day a band of guerillas came to Clark's Mill, and in the course of a few hours a number of their sympathizers appeared on the scene. Two of these sympathizers told the captain of this band that my father was making himself conspicuous in the Union cause and that they wanted him disposed of. In this band was one of my father's nephews, who was acquainted with his uncle's habits. This kinsman knew that if at any time the chickens on his place squalled he would get out of bed at once to investigate the nature of the disturbance in his hen-house. This nephew, therefore, assured the band that they could get my father by simply making a chicken squall; and he further suggested that when my father stepped out of the door on his way to the chicken-house, any one could easily "blaze away at him." After a little discussion of the matter it was decided that some of the band should march over and kill my father that night.

There was a school going on at Clark's Mill that summer. One of the scholars was standing in the crowd of men and overheard all their plans. That evening, as soon as school was dismissed, he sent word to our home. It was getting dark when the message reached us. My father and those of our family who were at home talked the matter over and agreed that father should take his gun, leave the house and stay out in the woods until the band left. So, he started out at about 10 o'clock.

Shortly after he had gone we heard the chicken squall. My brother's wife looked out of the window and saw four men, one holding a chicken and the other three standing behind some low shrubbery and ready to shoot. Seeing no men come to the windows or door, the band after a while evidently concluded that no men folks were at home, and therefore left the place.

My father saw the guerillas as they walked away and could easily have shot one or two of them, but decided that, under the circumstances, he had better let them escape, rather than suffer any outrages the survivors and their associates might commit on the place. Suspicious-looking men prowled around our home for about a week, and my father did not stay at home at night until he felt confident they had left the country.

One night in the winter of 1862, after Capt. Netter, of the 26th Kentucky Infantry, had attempted to destroy the L. & N. bridge across Whippoor-will Creek, my father was hailed by some one at the gate. He opened the door and learned that the man who had called was George Driskill, piloting Netter's men. Driskill had heard that my father was always ready and willing to help a Federal, so he came to our house for assistance. He had six or seven men with him, all of whom were wounded. One soldier, by the name of John Mayhan, was so sick he could not move any farther. He was left at our house, while my father piloted the others toward Sacramento.

The next day was mill day and I was sent to Clark's Mill. This mill stood on the bank of Pond River, but the store was on a rise overlooking the bottoms on the Hopkins County side. From the store we had a clear view, for almost a mile, of the road leading in the direction of Hopkinsville.

While I was standing on the platform in front of the store I looked across the river and saw about a dozen mounted men, each carrying a gun. I asked the merchant, who was weighing something on the scales, who these mounted men were. He looked up the road and then said, "By George!

It is the cavalry!" I knew they couldn't be Union soldiers, for they were coming from the wrong direction, and besides the appearance of their uniforms, even from that distance, indicated that they were not Federals. My first thought was of the sick and crippled John Mayhan. It struck me that this squad was on its way to our house after him or any other of Netter's men. I also thought of the many bad things this squad might do to our home and farm should they find Mayhan quartered there. I took another good look at the approaching cavalry. They were now about a half mile from the store. I ran down to the mill, got my horse, and asked the miller to bring out my turn. He did so, and threw the bag of meal over the horse's back. This miller was generally very careless about balancing a sack for a boy, but this time he happened to strike even halves. I don't think there was an ounce difference in the ends. I poked out my foot to the miller and he hoisted me on the horse, for I was then only twelve years old, and after adjusting the bag I started off in a gallop. I knew every hog-path and short cut between the mill and our home. Over the most direct of these I hurried as fast as I could, up hill and down hill and through the woods, until I came to the fence at the back of my father's farm; I got off my horse, laid down a few rails, climbed back on the animal and went tearing through the fields. When I came within hearing distance of the house I yelled, "Get Mayhan out to the weeds, for the Rebel cavalry is coming after him!"

There happened to be several men at our house when I got there, and my father said to them that Mayhan must be saved at all hazards. He and the men rushed upstairs to where the sick man lay and told him the Rebel cavalry were coming after him. When my father picked up Mayhan to carry him down the steps Mayhan begged the men to let him jump down to the lower floor, saying that if it killed him he would be better off. But my father said, "No, I'll take care of you at the risk of my own life."

While my father was carrying him down he shouted to some of the other men to bring the feather bed and some quilts. They carried Mayhan out into the woods, laid him on the feather bed, spread the quilts over him, then covered him with leaves, and returned to the house. In the meantime my mother performed her part. She rearranged the vacated bed and made it look like it had not been occupied.

We waited and waited, but the Rebel cavalry never came. Finally my father sent out one of the men to spy around. He returned with the information that the cavalry had gone to old man George W. Eaves' farm on Pond River to get some hogs for the Rebel soldiers located at Hopkinsville.

When the men learned this, they realized that the alarm I had given was a false alarm, so they brought Mayhan back into the house. A few days later my father disguised his patient, put him in a buggy, and sent him to Calhoun, where a regiment of Federal soldiers was still encamped.

The spring of 1863 marked the beginning of the third year of the Civil War. Of the many letters that were sent by Muhlenberg men while serving in the army only a few, as previously stated, have fallen into my hands. The one written by E. R. Weir while at Shiloh has already been quoted. Among the others is a letter of different character, but it serves as a sample of its kind. The writer, by taking his "pen in hand," succeeds in telling, in his own way, something about his life with the soldiers in Warren County:

Bowlingreen, Ky.
April 23th, 1863.

Mr. R. C. J. I with pleasure take my pen in hand once more to drop you a few lines and I am happy to say thes lins leaves me in good helth and I hope when this coms to hand it will find you and famly injoying good helth. I have nuthing interestin to writ this time, only the boys is all in good helth and as lively as ever. I am agoin to send you the history of this Regiment to you and I want you to get a fram and put it in if you pleas. I wood be glad if I could com home once more but thar is no chance. I wood be glad to see you all, but you must writ, it gives me much plasure to Read your leters, tell Jeff that pal he is well and ed is not hear, he is in scotts ville, but when he left he was well but wee ar looking for them back every day.

My Respecs to sarah Jane and I hope you ar well, I have had my picture taken and I tell you it is nice, it looks very much like me I think, but I was mad when it was taken. and I will tell you weir mounted but I gess you have heard it before now, and we will make the grillars get up and cluck when wee will get after them on our old broak down horses, and when the boys chases one anuther tha want to no what tha hav dun that tha ar ridin a rail. so no more of my foolshines. So I must clos, you must writ soon, so nuthin more only far you well.

B. G. W.

Two letters written during the latter part of 1863 by D. C. Humphreys, of Spring Station, Woodford County, to Gilbert Vaught Rhoads, contain much that pertains to this period of Muhlenberg's history. D. C. Humphreys for many years owned a tract of timber land lying near the Louisville & Nashville Railroad, between Browder and Bellton. Shortly before the Civil War broke out Alexander Todd came to Muhlenberg to look after this land for his uncle, and with a view of making this his permanent home. He opened a small farm and built a cabin, in which he lived for a few years. D. C. Humphreys' sister, Elizabeth Humphreys, was the second wife of Robert S. Todd, who by his first wife was the father of six children (among whom was Mrs. Abraham Lincoln) and by his second wife was the father of seven children, among whom was Alexander Todd and Mrs. Ben Hardin Helm. Alexander Todd, having received a special invitation from Abraham Lincoln, went from Muhlenberg County to Washington City to witness the inauguration of his brother-in-law, March 4, 1861. Shortly after his return he joined the Southern army, became ordnance sergeant in the First Kentucky Cavalry, was made aide-de-camp on the staff of General Ben Hardin Helm, and on August 5, 1862, was killed at Baton Rouge. "Aleck" Todd was a bright young man, and during his stay of a few years in the county was a great favorite among the old people as well as among those of his own age. Although he had a well-furnished cabin of his own, he spent much of his time in the homes of two of his neighbors, David and Absalom J. Rhoads. Alexander Todd, after his death, was succeeded as overseer of the Humphrey tract by his friend Gilbert V. Rhoads:

Spring Station, Kentucky.
13th November, 1863.

Gilbert V. Rhoads, Esq.—My dear friend:—Your very acceptable letter of 30th September I received a short time since. It arrived while I was absent in Illinois which will account for your not receiving an answer sooner. I am happy to learn you have recovered from the dangerous attack of sickness you had in June last, and that you bid fair to be in the enjoyment of your usual health again. What a blessing it is to enjoy health and how thankful we all are to Him in whom we live and move and have our being for it.

I have been anxious for two years to pay you a visit, and had made my arrangements to send some hands down to open a large tobacco farm, but this cruel and unnatural war has broken up all my arrangements, and now I don't think it worth while to count upon the work or value of my negro labour. If the war lasts much longer all our young and valuable negroe men will be pressed into the service to make railroads, cut wood, drive wagons, make fortifications or perhaps enlisted as soldiers. I think the abolitionists are determined to give a finishing blow to slavery in America. Should they succeed I pity the poor negroes. I hope God will overrule and govern all things for our present and eternal good, the good of his church and his glory.

I have been speaking to a man who has lived with me several years about going to Muhlenberg and living on my land. He has not yet made up his mind on the subject. I don't wish you to rent my place to any one until you hear from me. My rent corn dispose of as soon as you can for the best price you can get, and retain the money in your hands until further instructions. Write to me and let me know the amount you receive for it. Corn here is in good demand at $3.00 per barrel in the field and will be higher. The crop of corn in Indiana and Illinois is very poor; the drought and the early frost have cut it down to almost nothing in places. Last year in Illinois I got only 12½ cents per bushel for my rent corn; this year I am offered 40 cents.

I am glad to learn that my old friend Mrs. Rachael Rhoads is still enjoying good health. Remember me kindly to her and all the family. Give my kindest regards to my old friend Isaac Woods who I sincerely hope is prepared to live or prepared to die whenever God in his providence shall see fit to call him. When you see Mr. Baker remember me to him and his wife whose kindness and hospitality I can never forget.

My family are all well except my grandson David who has been confined for seven weeks with a swelled knee. I fear it is white swelling. He is much better and I hope will recover without a stiff knee.

Write me soon and believe me sincerely Your friend,
D. C. HUMPHREYS.

Spring Station, Kentucky.
9th December, 1863.

Mr. G. V. Rhoads,—Dear Sir:—I am just in receipt of your kind letter of 21st November which by some mistake was missent. I am glad to learn you are enjoying peace and quietness and sincerely hope you may long be exempt from the horrors of war. It is bad enough at a distance, but when it comes into our own houses it is dreadful.

I notice your remarks about Chancy. My sister Mrs. Todd is now in Alabama where she got permission from President Lincoln to go for her daughter (who was married to General Helm who was killed at the battle of Chickamauga.) She gave me no special directions about Chancy, but I am satisfied she wishes her and her son and daughter hired out and would consult Chancy's wish in a considerable measure as to whom she would like to live with. Certainly from my knowledge of Mr. Taggart my sister will have no objection to his having Chancy, and if he is willing to give a fair price for Chancy and she is anxious to live with him, let him have her.

You said nothing in your letter about my rent corn for the year 1863. Write to me about it on receipt.

I would like to pay a short visit to Muhlenberg this winter if I thought the Guerillas would not overhaul me. I hope the country will soon be free of them.

Remember me to Mrs. Rachael Rhoads and all the family and accept for yourself and family my best wishes for your health, happiness and prosperity. Yours truly,

D. C. HUMPHREYS.

These two letters, it might be well to add, were found in the attic of an old two-story weatherboarded log house standing on a hill overlooking Browder. A few years ago a number of old papers, regarded as rubbish by the man who had rented the house, were burned after they had been removed from between two of the logs in the wall of this building. Evidently these two had slipped down behind the lower log when the other letters were removed. At any rate, they were there discovered by Miss Amy M. Longest, who recognized their value as documents bearing on local history.

On or about May 10, 1864, there took place what is known as the Fight at Sullivan's Barn. Captain Henry L. Vickers, a recruiting officer for the Southern army, whose home was near Paradise and who while a member of Company C, Ninth Kentucky Infantry, was wounded at Shiloh, was scouting in Ohio and McLean counties and had with him sixteen Confederates, most of whom were recruits. In their march through Ohio County this squad appropriated a horse belonging to Ashby Woodward. When Woodward discovered that his animal had been taken he declared he "would get his horse back or die in the attempt." He reported the robbery to his brother, Captain Steven Woodward, of the Twenty-sixth Kentucky Infantry, who was an officer of the Home Guards of McLean and Ohio counties, and who immediately organized a pursuing party of about thirty-two men.

In the meantime Captain Vickers and his squad rode toward Green River, crossed that stream at Point Pleasant, four miles below South Carrollton, and at about four o'clock in the evening arrived on the Raleigh Sullivan farm in Northern Muhlenberg, three miles west of Green River. Knowing that he had come to the home of a Southern sympathizer, Captain Vickers asked Sullivan for food for his men and forage for his horses, which request was readily complied with.

After feeding their animals in the barn all the men walked to the house, a distance of about one hundred yards, to eat the meal that had been prepared for them. They, however, failed to put out any sentries.

This was either through an oversight or because Captain Vickers felt confident that such a precaution was unnecessary. At any rate, he evidently anticipated no trouble or attack, and least of all did he suspect that the owner of the stolen horse had traced the theft to them and that a pursuing party was near at hand.

While Captain Vickers and his men were enjoying their meal, Robert N. Sullivan, the son of their host, heard two gunshots fired somewhere on the north or far side of the barn. The boy rushed into the house and gave the alarm. These two shots had been fired by Captain Woodward's pur-

SULLIVAN'S BARN, NEAR MOORMAN

suing Federals, who, believing that they were close upon the Confederates, wished to learn whether or not Vickers' men were concealed in the barn, and also desired to draw their fire in order to approximate the size of the squad.

As soon as Captain Vickers learned that the Federals were upon him he rose from the table, and grasping a revolver in either hand and calling to his men to follow him, ran toward the barn. Most of Captain Woodward's soldiers were in the barn, and Captain Vickers was therefore unable to form any idea as to the size of the party he was attacking. There being only a few Federals in sight, he told his comrades they "would soon chase the Yanks away," and ordered them to rush forward and to fire as they advanced. When they had covered about half the distance to the barn, crossing the little ravine that separates the two elevations upon which the house and barn stand, one of the Confederates, Mitchell, a boy about sixteen years of age, was shot through the bowels and fatally wounded. The Confederates continued their advance, and in the meantime the Federals fell back on the north side of the barn.

This retreat gave Captain Vickers' men temporary possession of the building. While attempting to hold a position near the entry until his men could get their horses, Captain Vickers sought to shield himself behind a narrow post. This post probably saved his life, for while he was standing behind it a Federal soldier fired at him with a gun loaded with buckshot, two of which lodged in Captain Vickers' neck, inflicting painful though not serious wounds. The shooting continued for about five minutes, when the Confederates, having regained their horses, hastily retreated under fire. They ran down the road and around a hill, and soon got beyond the reach of bullets.

As a result of this fight the young Confederate, Mitchell, who had been shot, died in the Sullivan home a few hours later. His body was interred in the New Hope Church burying-ground near by and remained there for a number of years, when it was exhumed by relatives and taken to Daviess County. Captain Vickers was captured and sent to Camp Chase, Ohio, where he was imprisoned until the close of the war. A young unwounded Tennessean was captured near the barn. The Federals lost one man, Ashby Woodward, who was shot through the heart. His corpse was taken to his home near Livermore. Only one of Captain Woodward's squad was wounded—a man named King, who was shot in the leg. A horse owned by the Federals, another belonging to the Confederates, and five of Sullivan's sheep that were penned up in the barn preparatory to shearing, were killed in the fight.

That night Captain Woodward quartered his troops in the Sullivan house, which he kept well protected during his stay by posting sentries in the immediate neighborhood. The next morning he returned to Ohio County with his two prisoners; not with the stolen horse, but with the corpse of Ashby Woodward, who the day before had declared that he "would get his horse back or die in the attempt."

One day toward the end of December, 1864, the people living in and near Greenville were very much aroused by what might be called "a false alarm." It was reported that General Hylan B. Lyon had burned the courthouse at Madisonville and was on his way to Greenville and Hartford to burn the courthouses there. When this report reached Greenville the citizens became alarmed and immediately prepared to defend the place. All the people, whether sympathizing with the North or the South, seem to have ignored their antagonistic principles and stood united in their desire to save the courthouse. They made ready to resist by improvising what might serve the purpose of defense works. Alfred Johnson and Henry Jenkins were then building the stone jail. These two men pushed out a few stones from its unfinished walls and thus constructed some portholes. The brick building on the northwest corner of Court Square was converted into a fort. The windows on the second floor of the Weir store were opened and arranged as places to shoot from, and in one of the brick walls which had no windows two holes were cut.

While all these preparations were being made, some of the people became very excited and others grew very impatient. Sebastian C. Vick, or "Captain Bass Vick," as he was called, was in town at the head of a company of citizen-soldiers. After the supposed time of General Lyon's arrival had passed, Bass Vick and his men mounted their horses and rode up the Lower Hopkinsville Road, hoping to locate the expected enemy. However, they saw nothing of him. When they reached Mount Pisgah Church they concluded that General Lyon must have heard of Greenville's preparations for defense and therefore had marched on and left the place in the hands of its five hundred plucky and patriotic citizens. Vick and his men then returned to town and informed the people that General Lyon had gone elsewhere and that all danger was past and the courthouse saved.

One version of this incident ends by saying that when Bass Vick reëntered Greenville with his men he was hailed as the hero who had saved the town, and that if he had killed every man in General Lyon's command he could not have had a more rousing reception.

It is probable that on this raid General Lyon did not come within the bounds of Muhlenberg County. He and his squadron left Tennessee during the early part of December, 1864, and after going to Hopkinsville, Princeton, Eddyville, and Madisonville they crossed Green River at Ashbyburg, in Hopkins County, and then continued to Hartford, Leitchfield, and various other places and arrived in Hopkinsville January 15, 1865. In Hartford and some of the other county seats they burned the courthouses. [3]

Possibly all the men who had joined either army were anxious to return home long before they were mustered out of service; nevertheless they were willing to "stick to the end" in spite of the many hardships they had experienced. This feeling is shown in the following letter written near Atlanta [4] by James W. Wood, of the Mud River country, who enlisted in Company B, Eleventh Kentucky Infantry, in September, 1861, and remained in that company until his regiment was mustered out in December, 1864. The letter is addressed to John H. Wood, Laurel Bluff, Muhlenberg County.

---

[3] In this connection Colonel James Q. Chenoweth, in his chapter in Adam R. Johnson's "The Partisan Rangers," says, on pages 190 and 191:

"We entered the town of Hartford, garrisoned by a battalion of Federal troops who, on our approach, took shelter in the courthouse. They were speedily surrounded, captured and paroled and the courthouse burned. Just here I beg to remark that all the courthouses burned by General Lyon on this raid through Kentucky were in every case used as Federal garrisons or prison-houses for our Southern friends. . . . It was considered by General Lyon 'a military necessity' to destroy these courthouses. These courthouses were no longer needed by the citizens of Kentucky as houses of law and temples of justice, but as military barracks and stockades for Federal soldiers and prison-houses for unoffending Kentuckians who dared to entertain any sympathy for the Southern cause."

[4] Mr. L. D. Griggs, who since 1885 has made Muhlenberg County his home, was a member of Company D, Twenty-fifth Indiana Volunteer Infantry, which saw hard service in front of Atlanta in July, 1864. During this siege he found time to compose a prayer that has been widely published and commented on: "Our Father Abraham, who art in Washington, honored be thy name. Thine administration come. Thy will be done in the South, as it is done by the Republicans in the North. Give us this day our daily ration of hard tack, beans and bacon. And forgive us our foraging, as we forgive those who forage upon us. And lead us not into the field of battle, but deliver us from the land of the enemy: for thine is the administration, and the power, so long as thou art in office. Eight men."

Camp near Atlanta, Georgia. August 16th, 1864.

Dear Brother John H.:—I received your kind and welcome letter the other day, dated July 22nd. I am always glad to hear from you, Mother and the children. I wrote Mother yesterday. . . .

We have had a hard time during this campaign; but we have no right to grumble, for our regiment hasn't suffered hardly any compared to what some of the others have. Our regiment hasn't been in any general fight lately, though our company had several men wounded and two killed in a skirmish on the 6th of this month. I have written all about it to John. The wounded were sent back and the last we heard of them they were doing very well.

I am sorry to hear that the boys have to work so hard on the farm. I hope I will be at home to help them next year. I know I could enjoy hard labor at home better than soldiering, for soldiering is hard on both mind and body. I do hope and trust that this wicked war will soon be over, but I fear it will be a long time before it is ended. I believe if the head leaders on each side had to come out and lay on the skirmish line and fight and undergo the hardships that we do there would be peace soon.

I don't know what they will do here but there is one thing, we all hope this campaign will soon be over so that we can go home and live in peace with our friends as we have in bygone days. I think it has been on hand long enough, but no matter how much longer it lasts I'll stick to the end.

It is now almost a year since I was at home and the time appears that long to me too. But there is one good consolation: if we live, it will not be long till we see each other again. If we are not permitted to see each other again in this world I feel that we will all meet beyond this vale of sorrow and tears where all our war troubles and earthly toils will be over.

You said in your letter that you had been to the preaching. I am glad to know you all have the privilege of going to church. It is more than I have. I was on picket last Sunday night. There was preaching in some regiment; I could hear them singing but I could not leave my post to go. I always look forward to the day when I can go to church of a Sunday in place of going on picket. I have heard but two sermons preached since we left Kentucky.

Harvey received a letter last night from cousin Allen, dated August the 5th. He said there were no guerilas in that neighborhood now. I was glad to hear it, for I expect the people back there will have a hard time anyhow, without having their property taken by the rogues.

I would like very much to see you and the folks, but it is hard to tell just when that will be. We are getting along pretty well, considering the hardships we have to undergo. We have a pretty hard time, but the boys take it cheerfully. We are getting plenty to eat now and the boys are generally well and in fine spirits.

H. Y. and J. L. Wood and C. W. McBride are well and send their respects to you all. Give my love and respects to all enquiring friends, the girls in particular, and keep a good portion for yourself. If our friends knew how highly we appreciate their letters down here they would write oftener.

Write soon and give me all the news, let me know how you are getting along and how the crops look. Your affectionate brother until death

JAMES W. WOOD.

The following letter was written by the same writer about a month before his regiment was mustered out at Bowling Green, December 16, 1864:

Louisville, Kentucky, November 11, 1864

Dear Mother:—We are in old Kentucky once more, and I'm glad of it. We will be mustered out before long. The prospects of peace and of us getting home again has put every single one of us in a very lively mood. We are seeing a fine time here. I am glad I'll be with you soon. . . .

H. Y. Wood is not with us. He was left at Chattanooga guarding some government beef cattle, but we are looking for him on every train. The balance of the boys are well and in fine spirits. John McBride is here with us and is well and hearty.

We saw a hard time after we left Decatur, Georgia. We left there on the 4th day of October and had to march nearly every day for over a month. We took the cars at Dalton, Georgia, last Sunday and passed through Bowling Green Wednesday. They had our old battle flag on the depot and you ought to have heard the old Eleventh cheer when they saw it. We had a fine time. I was glad to be so near home.

The cars were so crowded some of us had to ride on the roof. It rained every day and that made it bad for those who were on top.

This is the first letter I have had a chance to write since we left Decatur, and it has also been some time since I heard from you or had a chance to.

Give my love to grandfather and the children. . . . Your affectionate son

JAMES W. WOOD.

James R. Gross, of Bremen, carried a pocket memorandum book with him during the war and in it made brief entries of his movements. With the exception of a few memoranda relative to short visits home after his regiment left Kentucky, all his records pertaining to his career in or near Muhlenberg are written on the first and last pages. These I quote:

October 4th, 1861. Joined the Eleventh Regiment Kentucky Volunteers at Calhoun. P. B. Hawkins, Colonel; S. P. Love, Lieutenant-Colonel.

24th, Thursday, marched to Sacramento, McLean County, and camped.

25th, Marched to South Carrollton and returned.

26th, To Bethlehem, Muhlenberg County.

27th, Went home.

28th. Back to Camp Calhoun.

December 28th. Went to Spottsville, Henderson County, on the L. W. Eaves, staid there two hours and returned to Camp Calhoun.

January 16th, 1862. Struck tent, marched to South Carrollton, and camped.

February 1st. Left South Carrollton, returned to Camp Mottley on the L. W. Eaves.

February 16th. Marched to Owensboro.

17th, Monday. Got on board the N. W. Thomas and went down the Ohio River.

18th. Landed at Smithland, mouth of Cumberland River. Distance 170 miles.

19th. Returned to the mouth of Green River.

20th. Back to Smithland.

21st. To Paducah. Staid there a while.
22nd. Went up Cumberland River.
February 24th. Landed at Fort Donelson.
25th. P. M. Landed at Nashville.
December 14th, 1864. Wednesday, at Bowling Green, Kentucky, turned over arms and accoutrements and was mustered out of service.

Returned home in Muhlenberg County, Kentucky, the 16th and 17th days of December, 1864. Distance 65 miles.

Traveled from time of enlistment until mustered out of U. S. service and returned home, 6212 miles.

SOME CIVIL WAR VETERANS, 1912

These fifteen veterans attended the soldiers' reunion held on May 4, 1912, at the home of William H. Smith, near Paradise. All had fought in the Federal army except Lycurgus T. Reid, who was a Confederate soldier.

Back row, left to right: W. H. Smith, Samuel Robertson, Ed Williams, G. W. Allen, R. J. Dobbs. Front Row: H. C. McCracken, W. M. Lewis, R. W. Casebier, John Coombs, J. N. Durall, Lycurgus T. Reid, Mitchell Mason, L. D. Griggs, E. E. C. Shull, John L. G. Thompson.

Shortly after the close of the war the Grand Army of the Republic was organized. The first post in Muhlenberg was the Columbus H. Martin Post No. 7, Greenville, organized in October, 1883, with Doctor J. W. Church as commander. On March 25, 1908, this post was reorganized and its name was changed to the J. N. Paxton Post No. 17, Greenville. H. C. McCracken became commander of the new organization, and has held that office ever since. The post at Central City is the James N. Durall Post No. 64, organized July 4, 1889.

Many reunions of Civil War soldiers have taken place in Muhlenberg County during the past forty years, and they are still taking place. As years roll by the veterans are rapidly decreasing in numbers; nevertheless it is more than likely that the holding of reunions will continue until the last of the comrades are laid in their graves. All those in this county have been held under the auspices of Federal soldiers. Confederate veterans were always and are still invited to these gatherings. The reunions that have taken place under the auspices of organizations consisting of old Southern soldiers, to which the men of Muhlenberg have belonged, have been held in Logan, Christian, and Hopkins counties, where the fighters for the Lost Cause are more numerous than in Muhlenberg.

Many of the soldiers' reunions in Muhlenberg have been conducted by the G. A. R. posts. In recent years most of these gatherings have taken place at the homes of old soldiers, where all veterans, neighbors, and others were the guests of the man who had invited the assemblage. Thus "on the first Saturday in May, 1912," William H. Smith, near Paradise, gave a semi-annual reunion at which there were present one Confederate and fourteen Federal soldiers, a brass band, and seventy other guests, all of whom ate dinner and supper at the Smith house and took part in an all-day picnic. Now, as in the past, the "boys who wore the gray" are as welcome at these gatherings as the "boys who wore the blue."

XXIII

R. T. MARTIN'S "RECOLLECTIONS OF THE CIVIL WAR"

NO CITIZEN in Muhlenberg is better versed in the traditions of the county than Richard Thompson Martin. His ancestors came to Muhlenberg more than a century ago. He has lived in the county all his life, and has from early youth been interested in local traditions and current events. During the past few years Mr. Martin has published a number of sketches of local history in the Greenville Record and in the Muhlenberg Sentinel. Much that he has written of past men and events does not find a place in formal history. It has, however, a value and interest all its own, being in the nature of personal recollections that vividly recall and repeople old times in an atmosphere of singular charm, of appreciative sentiment and personal interest. Mr. Martin will always deserve a high place in the estimation of those who love native reminiscence. His published recollections will increase in value with the years, and should be preserved in some permanent form for the benefit of later generations.

Mr. Martin is the third son of Thomas L. and Mahala (Bell) Martin. He was born on a farm near Old Liberty on February 27, 1841, and went to the county schools in that vicinity. He later attended the school taught in Greenville by Professor E. W. Hall, and completed his English education during the Civil War. For several years he taught school in Ohio, Muhlenberg, and Christian counties, and then engaged in farming. In 1879 he married Viva Atherton, of McLean County, a daughter of A. J. and Susan C. Ranney Atherton. In 1882 he left the farm and took up his residence in Greenville, where he engaged in manufacturing tobacco until 1902, when he retired, leaving the business to his only son, Buren Martin, who is one of the influential young men of the county.

Richard T. Martin is a member of the Cumberland Presbyterian church. He has always been a Republican in politics. No man in Muhlenberg is better known. He was about twenty years of age when the Civil War broke out. His sketch, "Recollections of the Civil War," was originally written in January, 1911, and published in the Muhlenberg Sentinel. It was later rewritten for this history.

RECOLLECTIONS OF THE CIVIL WAR

The statements that I here make concerning some of the incidents that took place in Muhlenberg County during the Civil War may not be correct in every detail, for nearly a half century has passed since they occurred. We have no written record of these local happenings, so what I say is according to my recollections, some of which have been verified by the recollections of a few other men who lived in Muhlenberg during war times. I find that a number of these events have been almost forgotten, and that a few are recalled somewhat differently by different people. However, most of these incidents, as recalled by those who are still living, are about the same as I here give them.

Before the war, citizens of Muhlenberg County occupied a different status from what they do now. The people were then under the persuasion of the old-time religion and the regulations of the old Constitution; their manner of procedure and their customs of living were different from what they are to-day.

On November 6, 1860, Abraham Lincoln was elected President of the United States, greatly to the surprise of all the Southern States and to Kentucky and Muhlenberg County. Nevertheless, the election of Lincoln occurred in the course of human events and undoubtedly proved a blessing to the entire country, although it drenched the nation with the blood and tears of the sons of liberty.

The people of Muhlenberg, in the election of 1860, were divided on John Bell, Stephen A. Douglas, and John C. Breckinridge. I have always understood that Abraham Lincoln received only two votes in the county: that of Leonard Lewis and Andrew McClelland. In the spring of 1861, after Lincoln had taken his seat, agitation became alarming; secession commenced in the South; war-clouds began to gather on the horizon, and a revolution seemed inevitable.

Before entering into general details, I shall tell of an occurrence that took place the latter part of August, 1861, which will show the feeling then existing among some of the Muhlenberg people at the beginning of the war.

A protracted meeting was in progress at Pisgah Church, about six miles west of Greenville. One William Harrison, who was born and reared in Christian County, a son of Harvey Harrison, came over to attend the meeting, and during his stay put up with a cousin. Harrison wore, all buttoned up, a full suit of Southern soldier's uniform, of which he seemed very proud. He attracted a good deal of attention in his war apparel. The people were considerably worked up about the rebellion of the South. Harrison was an incessant talker and braggart. He claimed to have been at the battle of Bull Run, which was fought on July 21, 1861. He did much bragging and boasting about this, telling the people how the Southern soldiers made the Yankees run and how they mowed the Federals down and cut them to pieces with corn-knives and scattered the retreaters like sheep. He also asserted that the Yankees were all cowards, and that the South would whip them before long. Harrison was not advised of the sentiment of the people in the Pisgah neighborhood, who were then largely in favor of the Union. Although they had remained neutral up to that time in regard to the war, they had no inclination to worship a rebel hero, especially during a protracted meeting. Harrison attended the meeting only at night. His continued abuse of the Yankees and the Federal government began to create considerable excitement, and the Union boys discussed the question of whipping Harrison and making him leave. Although he seemed to have found out something of the intended whipping,

RICHARD T. MARTIN, 1912

he nevertheless hung around. He would go to Greenville during the day, where he was associated with some young men who expected to join the Southern army. Harrison brought them out to the church with him the next night after the whipping was first talked about, to serve as a kind of bodyguard. They all wore caps and improvised Southern uniforms. There was no whipping done that night, for it was then believed, and afterward found out, that Harrison and his company were all armed. The next night all of them came riding up again while the church people were assembling. But no fighting or whipping took place.

That night an old gentleman informed the elders of the church that he had discovered some guns behind a log in the edge of the woods not far away. So the elders thought best, under the exciting conditions, to adjourn the meeting. When the people had about all assembled, and while most of the men were still standing around outside, one of the leading elders went to the front door and announced that the meeting had closed and that the people could all go home. He did not give a reason, but simply said that it was thought best to close the meeting. The young men around Pisgah were greatly incensed because the services had to be closed on account of Harrison's capers. That same night three young men rode over the neighborhood and notified a number of persons in whom they had confidence to meet at Old Liberty Church the next morning at sunrise.

MOUNT PISGAH CHURCH, NEAR BANCROFT

At the appointed time about twenty met, among whom were five old men who had also heard of the arranged meeting. The object of coming together was to consider the propriety of hanging Harrison. Most of the young men favored the hanging. The old men dissented; they reasoned with the young men. One old man got up on a log and made a little talk to them, saying: "Boys, we seem to have a fearful future before us. Our county and State are apparently in great danger of being made a bloody field of battle. Armies are being raised in bordering States, north and south. A big war, I believe, is inevitable, and we do not know into whose hands we shall fall. Our homes may be in the midst of battle, and we should be very careful how we act and what we say and do. To hang Harrison would not profit any one, but such an act might be the means of great harm to ourselves." The old man, in closing his argument, said: "Boys, take an old man's advice for once. While you are doing well, let well alone." After the old men had talked with the young men, they proposed that one of the crowd go and notify Harrison to leave the county at once. This was done, and Harrison's cousin immediately conveyed him back to Christian County. That was the last seen of Harrison around Pisgah. He died afterward, in Hopkinsville.

Most of the citizens of Kentucky sought neutrality, and wished to take no part in the disturbance. The majority of the people of Muhlenberg County were opposed to war, but were for a peaceable settlement of the difficulty if possible. While some few were for secession, a large majority were for the protection and perpetuation of the Union on peaceable terms. The step taken by Kentucky and her counties was armed neutrality; the State Guard was organized and went into camp service at once, and in the various counties the Home Guards were formed and held in reserve. Three

Home Guard companies were made up in Muhlenberg—one commanded by Edward R. Weir, sr., of Greenville, one by Doctor Shelby A. Jackson, of Paradise, and a third was formed in the southern part of the county. The company of Edward R. Weir, sr., was the largest in the county and was drilled regularly at Greenville. These companies were organized in the spring of 1861, and were at that time composed entirely of Union men, who were opposed to the dissolution of the Union. All of the Secession element looked upon the Home Guard procedure with suspicion.

In the spring of 1861 the veterans of 1812 and of the Mexican War held a reunion the day the Home Guards gathered to drill. Many of the old soldiers were present, some of whom took part in the exercises. But the maneuvers were according to a later manual, and the old men appeared a little awkward in the new commands. Of the War of 1812 soldiers I saw that day I now recall Joseph C. Reynolds, John Shelton, M. Collins Drake, Joseph McCown, Ephraim M. Brank, George Penrod, Charles Fox Wing, Larkin N. Akers, and Thomas Terry.

Thomas Terry, the father of Azel M. Terry, took the new company through some of the evolutions used during the War of 1812, and gave the crowd a good idea of the old-time drill. Thomas Terry was a soldier in the second war with England, and his son, Azel M. Terry, was a Federal soldier in the Civil War.

At this gathering Edward Rumsey addressed the old soldiers, complimenting them on their great service in the defense of their country. Rumsey seemed a little trammeled on this occasion. In his early life he was an advocate of the principle of the abolition of slavery, but now his sympathies had turned. A short time afterward he issued a printed circular stating that his sentiments were with the South. He was the owner of some negroes, and it was said by some of the abolitionists that he feared that they would be freed, and that he did not want to give them up in his old age.

Edward R. Weir, sr., was a nephew of and a law student under Rumsey, who taught and impressed Weir so favorably with the principles of abolition that Weir still adhered to them even after Rumsey changed. Hence Weir and Rumsey stood on opposite sides in politics after the war broke out. After Rumsey had made known how his sympathies were he took no very active part in politics, but lived retired and devoted most of his time to his personal affairs.

Edward R. Weir, sr., became the leader and adviser of the Union element of the county, and Robert S. Russell headed the Secession element. Russell was selected by the Secession advocates to represent them in a Confederate legislature which met at Russellville, Kentucky, November 18 to 20, 1861. Russell, together with some two hundred others, adopted an ordinance of secession and declared Kentucky out of the Union. Three weeks later the Confederate Congress at Richmond, Virginia, went through the form of admitting the State into the Southern Confederacy. But the Russellville legislature was short-lived. It was routed by the Union army. Russell went south, and did not return until after the close of the war, when he came back and moved his effects to Clarksville, Tennessee, where he died in 1873.

The legislative race in 1861 took place between Judge Joseph Ricketts, representing the Union sentiment of the county, and R. D. Reynolds, representing the Secession element. Ricketts was elected by a very large majority.

The Home Guards met regularly. About the middle of September, while they were drilling in the western part of Greenville, a small company of young men who had been recruited for the Southern army in Daviess, McLean, and Ohio counties came through Greenville on their way south, and stopped in town for a few hours. Some of the Home Guards wanted to drive them out, but were told by Weir to let them alone unless they acted imprudently, in which event they could attack them. The southbound boys soon left without causing any trouble or raising any disturbance.

General Simon Bolivar Buckner, who was at the head of the State Guard, joined the Southern army in September, and took with him much of the State Guard equipment and nearly all of the men under him. He afterward had his headquarters at Bowling Green. In the meantime a number of the Home Guards began to disband, for many of them were divided in their sympathy. War was threatening on the southern border of the State; the guns of Weir's company of Home Guards were ordered in at Bethel Church, and were hauled from there in a two-horse wagon to Christian County, but they were soon returned to Muhlenberg. Some of these firearms were left in the Pisgah neighborhood, with the request that they be hidden away for safe-keeping. We boys, together with Uncle Richmond Pace (R. O. Pace's grandfather), hid about three dozen of the guns under the floor of Old Liberty Church, which had been abandoned as a place of worship before the war. The guns remained there for several months, when they were called for by the Federal authorities.

Excitement began to run high; the social relations of those who favored the Union were somewhat estranged from those who favored the South. They became like the Jews and the Samaritans, and had but little dealings with one another outside of business matters. "Birds of a feather flock together."

Some families and many old friends were divided upon the Union and Secession question, and consequently hard feelings and high words would often occur between the Secession and Union people of Muhlenberg. At that period a large majority of the citizens of Muhlenberg favored the Union. William G. Jones, who was reëlected county judge in 1858, was in sympathy with the South; so was Moses Wickliffe, who was elected sheriff in 1860 and who shortly after resigned and joined the Southern army. The remainder of the county officials were for the Union.

By the first of September, 1861, the war talk and feeling became general in Muhlenberg and throughout Kentucky, and preparations were made for recruiting the increasing number of volunteers.

Toward the last of September, 1861, General Buckner, with about fifteen hundred men, moved from Bowling Green to Hopkinsville. He marched by way of Rochester, where on September 26th he attempted to destroy the lock and dam on Green River. His soldiers created considerable excitement along the line of march. The rear guard of his army was very reckless, and treated the people along his route somewhat roughly.

On his way to Hopkinsville General Buckner passed through Greenville, where he viewed the remains of Charles Fox Wing, who had died the day before. He camped that same night at the Reuben Ellison spring, southwest of town. I well remember when, on the next morning a little after sun-up, he resumed his march. The day was clear and calm. We could distinctly hear the rattle of the war-drum as it sounded out on the morning

THE PROWSE OLD BRIDGE ACROSS POND RIVER

It stood near the site of the Old Reno Mill and was built in 1881 on piers that supported a former bridge, over which General Buckner and his men marched, September 27, 1861. This wooden bridge was replaced in September, 1911, by an iron bridge, a few days after this picture was taken

air, although we were five miles from the camp. This war tocsin sounded the alarm to the people of Muhlenberg that danger was ahead. Its music touched and fired the patriotism and nerve of the Union element in the county. This was the first army that had ever passed through Muhlenberg, and considerable excitement prevailed, especially along Buckner's line of march. A good many of the natives left their homes and took to the woods.

I had never seen a marching army, so I rode over to the upper Hopkinsville Road, believing that I could there see Buckner's entire command. But when I arrived there I found that part of the army had taken the lower Hopkinsville Road, which ran past our home, that I had left only an hour before. General Buckner was with that part of his army, and the General himself stopped at our house and talked with my father, who knew him when he was a boy at the old Buckner Furnace on Pond Creek.

I was informed that the divisions would be reunited at the Prowse Bridge, on the lower Hopkinsville Road. So I followed on to the bridge, where I saw General Buckner and his men, including the Muhlenberg boys with whom I was acquainted, who had joined the Southern army. They were all in good spirits, although marching to become targets for the missiles of death. Some of them never came back. Buckner's army continued its march and reached Hopkinsville on the 29th, after having had a little skirmish with some of the Home Guards in Christian County.

I do not think there were more than twenty-five or thirty men from Muhlenberg who joined the Southern army during 1861. Doctor John E. Pendleton, of Hartford, organized a company in Ohio County for the Southern army, and most of the Muhlenberg boys enlisted under him.

Buckner's passing through Butler, Muhlenberg, and Christian counties aroused the Union element, and gave impetus and acceleration to the organization of Colonel P. B. Hawkins' regiment of General Thomas L. Crittenden's division, which had commenced to form at Calhoun. I am under the impression that William James, jr., was the first man in the county to enlist in the Federal army. Five companies were recruited in Muhlenberg and became parts of the Eleventh Kentucky Infantry and Third Kentucky Cavalry. Company B of the Eleventh Infantry was the first formed, and was organized by Edward R. Weir, jr., and W. F. Ward; Company K by M. J. Roark and C. H. Martin; Company H by Isaac R. Sketo and J. K. Freeman. Company D, of the Third Kentucky Cavalry, commanded by Colonel J. S. Jackson, was organized by A. N. Davis. Captain Davis was taken prisoner at the battle of Sacramento, and was succeeded by T. J. Lovelace. Company F, of the same cavalry, was organized by Isaac Miller and Elisha Baker; Baker soon succeeded Captain Miller. These five companies were made up principally of Muhlenberg men.

General Buckner, during October, 1861, left a garrison at Hopkinsville under the command of Colonel James L. Alcorn, of Mississippi, who was later succeeded by Colonel Lloyd Tilghman. Colonel N. B. Forrest was also stationed at Hopkinsville until the first of February, 1862. During the stay of Forrest at Hopkinsville his men did a good deal of scouting, and often came into Muhlenberg. Their raids kept the people terrified, and were the means of driving some into the Federal army at Calhoun who might not otherwise have joined. A number were so frightened that they rushed to Calhoun for safety. Some of the strong Union people of Greenville also went to Calhoun for protection, and remained there until about the middle of February, 1862, when the Federal army left for the South.

To show that young people will have their fun and will play their pranks even during the terrors of war and in the face of battles, I will relate an occurrence that took place about three miles from Pisgah Church in November, 1861, shortly after one of Colonel Forrest's first raids into the county. There were some families living in that neighborhood at that time who were very easily scared, and who were good hands to frighten others with false reports.

For the sake of having a little fun, a dozen or fifteen boys, just grown up, led by some older ones, concluded that they would play "Forrest" and make a raid among the natives. So they met at a designated house on the upper Hopkinsville Road and in the vicinity of the place they had decided to "raid." The crowd met just about dark, and rigged themselves up in true cavalry style. They carried a number of pistols, which they loaded, but without balls; some of them fastened chains on their persons or horses, to rattle like sabers; many had sticks to represent guns. A little after the stars appeared this bogus cavalry started on its raid.

A few minutes before remounting their horses they sent a man ahead, named Wells, to call out at the fence of their first victim, to tell the family that there was a company of Southern cavalry at the house he had just passed who were tearing things up generally, and that he had come to warn them to be on the lookout. Wells was instructed to pretend to be in a great hurry and to change his voice as much as possible, so that no one would recognize him.

House in which the "Bogus Cavalry" was organized, as it appears to-day

He had the family pretty well aroused when the "cavalry" was heard approaching. "Here they come!" he said, and then started off on a gallop. There was a lane about two hundred yards long leading from the main road down to the house, and as Wells rushed up the lane the company dashed in and took after him, shooting rapidly and yelling "Halt! Halt!" As arranged in advance, they captured Wells within hearing distance of the house. Some of the boys called out, "Have you killed him?" and the answer came back, "No, but he is fearfully wounded." One man then asked in a very loud voice, "Captain, what must we do with him?" The captain, wanting every word to be heard, cried out, "Don't kill him—we want to find out what he was up to at this house. Surround the house and field at once!" Some were ordered to go around the field, but they did not go. In the meantime the frightened family threw chunks of fire out the front door, and made their escape. A few of the "raiders" then went down to the house, and found that everybody had fled. The family consisted of a father, three grown sons, two grown daughters, and a daughter-in-law. The crowd had reason to believe that the boys had run to the woods and that the old man and the women had hidden in the barn or stables. For the benefit of those who might be in these buildings some of the boys shouted, "Burn the stables!" Then the captain, in a voice that could be heard all over the place, said, "No! let the stables alone! I am confident that these people have all gone to the woods. Come, let's take our prisoner and move up the road to the next farm." The family little realized that this "cavalry" was composed of the same persons who, some two months before, had charivaried the married son at his father-in-law's home, located about three miles up the road. The noise on that occasion was kept up for many hours, and was discontinued only after the old lady had repeatedly requested the boys to "stop that there shiver-de-freezing."

Just before the "raiders" reached the next house they saw the family there run across the road and down to the woods. These people had heard the racket at their neighbors' and were doing the best they could to make their escape. When the crowd came up to the gate everything was still; no light was to be seen. The captain's loud voice now rang out "Nobody at home here!" The "cavalry" then turned and left the public highway and took a country road leading to a nearby neighbor's house.

When they entered the lane running by the house of their third victim they started one of their men in a fast run ahead of the crowd, and the others, shooting in every direction, charged after him, and as they passed the house shouted, "Halt! Halt!" They captured the man so noisily pursued, and then brought him back near to the farmer's front door. One of the leaders hallooed several times, and finally the old lady stuck her head out of the door. The captain asked her who lived there, and she told him. He then requested her to tell her husband to come out. She said that he was in bed sick, and not able to be up. As a matter of fact the crowd knew he had gone to Greenville that day. The captain then asked her whether he was a Lincolnite or a Southerner. She answered that he had never taken sides, but had always been neutral and stayed at home and attended to his own business. The captain then told her that he and his soldiers would camp up on the road and wanted her husband to come up early the next morning, and concluded by saying that if he did not come they would return and make him take the oath to support the South. Then the crowd rode off, feeling a little ashamed of themselves for having scared the old lady so badly. After a little talk on the subject they decided to disband. They agreed, however, that every one would deny any knowledge of the affair, and that all would meet at Pisgah Church the next day, Sunday, to hear the report of the raid.

All the parties were on hand before the church services began. The young men who were routed from their homes told a wonderful tale of how a company of Southern cavalry had raided the whole neighborhood, "torn up jack generally," and had wounded or killed a man near their house, and how all night long they had heard the raiders shooting. They said they believed that the man who was captured and perhaps killed was Wells. But while they were talking about the affair Wells came riding to the church, and after he had hitched and come up he was asked what he knew about the case. Wells said he had not noticed any signs of a disturbance and had not heard the shooting, and declared that this was the first he had heard about the excitement. He made many inquiries, and they told him that they took him to be the man who had notified them that the raiders were coming. He convinced them that they were mistaken in the man. The people were greatly puzzled for awhile, but it finally leaked out that this was a bogus raid.

It was learned that the three boys living in the first house "raided" ran about a mile to the home of some friends, and the whole family, with the refugees, slept in a straw-stack all night. It was a cold, frosty night. The people living in the second house stayed in the woods until just before sun-up, when they crept cautiously back home. The man who, the night before, was reported sick and not able to stir, got considerably better the next day; but he did not go to the camp to see about taking the oath.

This kind of procedure was, of course, a very dangerous one, and had it been carried on in some other neighborhood it probably would have terminated very seriously. In fact, after it was all over every one of the boys in this Saturday night "raid" began to realize what might have been the result of their wild frolic. As far as I know, there are but three now living who belonged to this "bogus cavalry" of 1861.

There were some youngsters who thought if the bogus cavalry could play "Forrest," they could play "Buckner." When General Buckner passed through the county he had several little brass cannons with him, that were greatly admired by all the young fellows who saw them. These boys concluded that they wanted a cannon to shoot and to scare the timid natives. Three or four of the youngsters got together and called on Edward O. Pace, then a blacksmith near the Pisgah neighborhood, and asked him if he could help get up a cannon. He said that he could. Pace was then a young man, and although he had been married a few years he nevertheless enjoyed the fun and pranks of boys. So he told the youngsters to go to the woods and cut out a black gum log eight or ten inches in diameter and about three feet long and bring it to his shop, and he would manufacture a cannon for them.

A log was procured, taken to Pace's shop at night, and the work on the cannon was commenced at once. The bark was shaved off nicely. Pace had a two-inch auger with a long shank, and with this he bored a hole in the end of the log down to a depth of fifteen or sixteen inches; he then bored a half-inch auger hole through the log to the bottom end of the two-inch auger hole. This smaller opening was for the fuse and served as a touch-hole. He had a lot of old wagon-tires in his shop, and out of these he made a number of bands and drove them on the wooden cannon as close as he could conveniently get them. He then loaded the big gun with some powder and made a trial shot to test its strength. It stood the test and was pronounced ready for "warfare."

The youngsters carried the cannon to a field near Pisgah Church. They procured all the powder they could get, and one night commenced a regular cannonading. They put in heavy charges of powder and the report fairly shook the earth; the noise rolled and reverberated in the distance like thunder. The whole neighborhood became alarmed. Some of the people were badly scared, for they thought Buckner or some other army was right in their midst. James Jones, of Long Creek, who happened to be visiting the nearby house of W. C. Martin, became so frightened at the first shot that he crawled under the bed and remained there for some time. The whole neighborhood was dumfounded at the loud shooting. The roaring of this cannon was heard in Greenville, over on Pond River, and near the Christian County line. The next day there was a considerable stir among the natives, for most of them inquired about the shooting. No one seemed to know who had kept up such a cannonading. In the meantime the boys were reaping the pleasure of having played "Buckner" so well.

After the cannon had rested a while it was taken over on the upper Hopkinsville Road, where some repairs were made on it at the James Rice blacksmith shop, then run by W. H. and E. Rice. E. Rice did the work for the boys, and a few nights later the cannonading was carried on in that neighborhood, where it caused considerable alarm.

The cannon was next carried near to a house in which Billy D. Rice then lived. There it was again put into service, but before discharging it E. Rice loaded it with a shop-hammer for a ball and aimed the barrel at a nearby tree. The cannon went off with a tremendous roar and sent the shop-hammer deep into the trunk of the tree, where I presume it has remained buried ever since.

During the last days of December, 1861, Colonel Forrest, with some three hundred men, made a raid down through Christian and Muhlenberg counties to near Sacramento in McLean County, where he came in contact with Major Eli H. Murray and about one hundred and eighty men of the Third Kentucky Cavalry. Colonel Forrest brought on the attack with part of his men, and Major Murray formed a line and repulsed the first charge. It is said that Murray might have stood his ground against Forrest's entire force had not some of Murray's recruits commenced a retreat to Sacramento, in consequence of which he was unable to check or rally his men. Colonel Forrest, seeing the disorder, charged them, and a running fight ensued which continued for a few miles, after which Forrest's cavalry returned. Murray's men never stopped on the road until they reached Calhoun, badly scattered and generally excited. Six of Murray's command were killed, including Captain A. G. Bacon, of Frankfort, and Isaac Mitchell, who lived near the old Buckner Furnace, and seven were wounded and captured, among whom was Captain A. N. Davis, then living near Friendship Church. Forrest's loss was two killed, one of whom was Captain Ned Merriwether, and three wounded. It was claimed that some of the citizens of Sacramento did damage by shooting at the Federals as they passed through the town. Some arrests were afterward made and the parties dealt with.

Colonel Forrest came back through Greenville, left some prisoners in town, and continued his march until he reached Pisgah Church, on the lower Hopkinsville Road, where he went into camp. Colonel Forrest and Major D. C. Kelly occupied a room in a residence near the church, where they ate supper and breakfast. In the meantime their men helped themselves to the corn and hay, and left a perfect wreck of feed from the crib and barn all the way to the church house. These things, however, were paid for in Confederate money.

While in this house Colonel Forrest related a good deal concerning the battle he had had with Major Murray. He told about the capture of Captain A. N. Davis and John L. Williams. He stated that in the running fight Davis rushed up behind him, and that he would have received a fatal thrust had not Davis' horse fallen, for in the fall of the animal Davis' arm was dislocated and he rose and surrendered. He also said that he saw John L. Williams, the Greenville carpenter, on the ground, rode up to him, and demanded that he surrender; but Williams looked him straight in the eye, and drew back his pistol and threw it with great force, striking him on the breast, and would have knocked him off his horse had he not been a large man; that immediately some of his (Forrest's) men rushed up and began using their sabers on Williams, but he (Forrest) stopped them at once. He remarked that Williams was too brave a man to be butchered when overpowered.

Williams was a Mason and so was Colonel Forrest. Forrest brought Williams to Greenville, the home of Williams, and left him with his family. He also brought a prisoner to Greenville whose name was, I think, Ed Baker, a lieutenant from Princeton, Kentucky. I saw this prisoner the next day at Reno's Hotel. He was badly wounded; shot in the legs, arms, and body, and was absolutely helpless. He remained in the hotel for two months, and then went home. This was the last raid made in Muhlenberg County by Colonel Forrest or his men.

I remember that when the battle of Fort Donelson was being fought on February 14 and 15, 1862, we could distinctly hear the cannon roar, although about fifty miles away. I also remember that on Wednesday, the 14th, it was cloudy in the forenoon and that in the afternoon it commenced to rain a little. The breeze was from the west, and about half-past two o'clock we heard some rumbling noise which we at first took to be thunder, but about three o'clock we were convinced that it was the roar of cannon, and that a battle was going on somewhere. A continuous rumble was heard until night. Snow commenced falling about sundown, and the next morning it was three or four inches deep. On the 15th the noise was more distinct, and from the information we could get we judged that the roaring came from Fort Donelson. Some Muhlenberg boys immediately started to Hopkinsville to learn what they could about the battle. Upon their return they told us how, after a two-days' battle, General Buckner had surrendered to General Grant.

After the Southern army left Hopkinsville, about the first of February, 1862, the people of the county felt some relief. They believed that the war was going from them; but the political sentiment of "Unionism" and what was called "Rebelism" was still being agitated. During the first part of 1862 "war talk" was the principal entertainment. During the first two years of the Civil War there were more lies told and more statements exaggerated about things connected with the war than during any other period of the country's history. One old gentleman, who made a trip to Greenville once or twice a week to get news about great battles, defeats, and surrenders, told me that when he went to Greenville and procured the truth, wrapped it up in a silk handkerchief, took it home and opened it, that it would then be a "durn lie."

Lying was a great feast for the people during the war, and did much good for a time. All preachers claim that lying is bad medicine and should be avoided, but I noticed that during the war it did many people good. I have seen whole crowds shake themselves, shout and halloo, on the presentation and reception of a lie, as if they had gotten religion. A well-woven and well-founded lie would last some time, and would be boosting and bracing to either the Union or Secession elements in the county. When the Union people received a favorable report, although unverified, they would get together, rejoice, and feel good. The Southern element sometimes got a favorable but unconfirmed report, and they too would have a rejoicing. Hence all the people were cheered and strengthened, at times, during their troubles. On the other hand, there was no time, from the commencement of the war until peace was declared, during which there was not a good deal of uneasiness and anxiety manifested by the people of the county.

Among the great events of the year 1862 was Morgan's march through Muhlenberg. His coming was a surprise to everybody. General John H. Morgan entered Greenville on Saturday, the 25th of October, 1862. Snow fell four inches deep that night and it was cold and chilly, although the trees were still green. It was an unfavorable day, nevertheless there was a large crowd in town, and Morgan's men did a good deal of trading and swapping of horses and saddles with the people who had come in from the country. They also contracted a large bill at Hancock & Reno's store for such things as they needed in military life. In making these trades and swaps Morgan's men always got the best of it. After they had finished trading with the natives they marched out the upper Hopkinsville Road about three miles from Greenville and camped near the residence of a Southern sympathizer, who was a large slave-owner and who had been a soldier in the War of 1812. He was as clever a man as ever lived in the county, always generous, kind, and accommodating. His home was open at all times to respectable people, rich or poor. No doubt he was glad to have an opportunity to extend his unreserved hospitality by entertaining so noted and distinguished a general and patriot of the South as General Morgan.

While General Morgan and the landlord were enjoying a nice repast, prepared especially for the occasion, and while being comfortably entertained before a nice wood fire, talking about the possibilities and probabilities of the Southern Confederacy, Morgan's men, who were left outside to brave the falling snow and bleak winds of the night, were helping themselves to the landlord's beehives. The next morning (Sunday) after breakfast, and after bidding General Morgan good-by and wishing him success, the old gentleman thought that he would look around and see if things were all in place. He soon discovered that his beehives were gone.

"Well, well, sirs!" he murmured. Then, returning to the house, he called his wife and said, "Well, well, sirs, Polly, those dirty rascals of Morgan's have actually taken our beehives!"

"You don't say so!" exclaimed his wife. "If I had known that, General Morgan would not have slept in our best bed or gotten anything to eat here!"

"Well, well, sirs," replied the old man, "they were hungry and cold, and we will just let it go at that, Polly."

The old man followed their tracks in the snow, found his empty beehives, a lot of frozen bees, and a little honey scattered over the abandoned camp. When he returned to the house he remarked to his wife, "That sure was a dirty act, Polly, but I was a soldier once myself and know something about such capers and shall not raise a fuss."

Some of Morgan's men, being of a religious turn of mind, went to church that same Sunday morning. General Morgan gave them leave to attend meeting at Friendship. Not many of the people were aware of Morgan's presence in the neighborhood. There was a large crowd present, including the religious part of Morgan's men. The sermon was a little too lengthy for Morgan's men, so they had to leave before services were over, for fear of getting too far behind their commander. But in their haste nearly all of them mistook somebody else's horse for their own, and rode off in such a hurry that they apparently never discovered their mistake. But when meeting broke, the people who owned the horses that were taken saw what had been done.

There was at least one horse-trade made that day in which the owners of the horses gave their consent to the exchange. I remember that H. N. Martin, then a young man living with his parents near Pisgah Church, owned a large, fine-looking black horse called "Rector," of which young Martin was very proud. Riding the horse out to Friendship Church on Sunday, he met up with Morgan's men and was induced to make an even swap with one of them. He exchanged "Rector" for an old broken-down stove-up, twist-tailed horse, which he rode home expecting to surprise his parents. Swapping horses on the Sabbath they thought was bad enough, but the trade made was even worse.

Morgan's march through Muhlenberg and Christian counties, as stated before, was unexpected. No one knew, at the time, for what purpose it was made. It was believed by some that General Morgan was induced to come into Muhlenberg and Christian counties to defeat Edward R. Weir, sr., for Congress. An election came off on the following Monday between Weir and George H. Yeaman. The presence of Morgan so terrified the people that not many went out to vote in Muhlenberg and Christian counties, Weir's stronghold, and consequently Weir was defeated. The Secessionists did not like Weir; he took an active part against them. For a long time Weir himself thought that some of the leading Secessionists had planned to have Morgan's raid in Muhlenberg and Christian counties take place at the time of the election.

During 1862 there was considerable excitement in Western Kentucky, caused by guerrilla warfare, recruiting, and bushwhacking. Companies of both Federal and Confederate armies were moving over different counties. Colonel Adam R. Johnson, of the Tenth Kentucky Cavalry, did some guerrilla work in various parts of the State. He lost his eyesight while fighting for the South. Detached companies from Johnson's command made raids, and plundered many of the towns and villages along their course. Al Fowler, Jack Porter, Jake Bennett, Ray, Sypert, and others belonging to some of his companies were troublesome and caused considerable uneasiness for a long time. These guerrillas were often chased, scattered, and driven out of the State by Federal troops, but most of them would slip back in again. As a general thing they were in squads of from twenty to fifty men.

Al Fowler and Jack Porter, both residents of Hopkins County, living between Pond River and Madisonville, did a good deal of scouting among the natives while recruiting men for the Southern army. Some of the Muhlenberg boys joined them. Fowler was active in the guerrilla service.

During the latter part of 1862 Fowler made a raid into Muhlenberg County, and was followed by a company of Federals commanded by Colonel James H. Holloway, of the Eighth Kentucky Cavalry. Colonel Holloway and some of his soldiers crossed Pond River near Hugh W. McNary's, and on reaching the McNary farm wanted to go into camp for the night. But McNary requested them to move farther up the road, explaining that some of his family were sick. McNary knew that Al Fowler and his men were in Muhlenberg, and suspecting that they were close by feared a fight would take place near his home. Colonel Holloway then marched up the road near the residence of Thomas C. Summers, where the town of Earles now stands, and went into camp at what was known as the Becky Summers house, a vacant house on the Greenville and Madisonville Road.

Fowler and his squad were south of the Summers place, and having located Holloway moved along a lane leading into the Greenville and Madisonville Road to where the Federals had gone into camp. It being night, Fowler and his men tried to slip up on the Federals, aiming to surprise and stampede them. But the Federals were ready for the attack, and when they were shot at returned the fire. Many said that the first volley fired by the Federals killed Fowler; others stated that the Federal picket killed Fowler. His own men believed he was accidentally shot by one of his own squad. After Fowler was killed his men were routed and scattered and left the county. Porter succeeded Fowler as captain of the company. Holloway passed through Greenville the next day, going east, carrying Fowler's hat on the end of a long stick. Captain Fowler was with Forrest in the Sacramento fight and also took part in the battle of Fort Donelson. It is said that Fowler was the man who used his saber on John L. Williams at Sacramento.

The brick residence erected by Thomas C. Summers at Earles in 1867 stands near the old store building and the abandoned log house, occupied by him during and before the Civil War.

After the death of Captain Fowler, Jack Porter made a raid into the county and through Greenville. Jack Porter was a son of Henry Porter, a strong Union man who lived on the Greenville and Madisonville Road near where Luzern is now located. Thomas C. Summers, who conducted a store and tobacco house at his home on the Madisonville Road near Pond River, was in Greenville one day during this raid, getting some cash for use in his business. When he heard that Porter intended capturing him and raiding his store, Summers, having no desire to be captured or raided, sprang into his saddle, left town, and rode home as fast as possible, hoping to reach his store before Porter could get there. Porter's men followed Summers for awhile, but he outdistanced them so much that they turned and moved in a body toward Pond River. Morris Moore and Dave Cain were with Porter. Both were Muhlenberg boys, and took great delight in bushwhacking around.

Moore, on one occasion, came to Greenville on a spying expedition and was run out of town by Buck Boone, a Federal soldier of the Third Kentucky Cavalry, who was at his home near town on a furlough. Boone determined to arrest Moore when apprised of his presence. Moore heard of this while in Sam Elliott's shoeshop on the Weir corner, and seeing Boone approach, snatched up a pair of boots and made for his horse, which was tied to a post on Cherry Street. Boone followed, and came within shooting distance of Moore just as Moore was getting on his horse. Boone blazed away, and Moore put spurs to his horse and left Greenville in double-quick time.

During the winter of '62-'63 Isaac Miller resigned as captain of Company F, of the Third Kentucky Cavalry, and returned to his home near Bremen. Moore, Cain, and a few others concluded that they would raid the Miller place and capture him and his horses, and they made a raid for that purpose. Captain Miller heard of the coming of the raiders just in time to mount his best horse and made his escape. After he had gotten out of their reach his horse fell and crippled him. Moore's raid proved a failure. Some Home Guards and Federal soldiers got together and followed his squad. Moore and his friends hastened back to their homes, located in the neighborhood that shortly after became McNary Station, on the Illinois Central Railroad. During this retreat Moore wanted his men to lay in ambush and fire on their pursuers as they passed, but he could not prevail on them to do so; each went his own way home. The Union squad, expecting to find Moore and his gang at Cain's home, on the Esquire John S. Eaves farm near Clark's Mill, moved on it during the night and commenced firing at the house. A ball passed through the wall and struck the headboard of the bed, about six inches above his wife's head. Cain rushed out of the room, and while running from the house was shot in the back; he ran a little farther, when he fell dead. Moore continued on the warpath, sometimes in the Southern army and sometimes out, and after the war closed was killed by his brother-in-law, who shot him in self-defense. Moore was a son of Bob Moore, who lived near McNary Station; he was a relative of Thomas C. Summers and a nephew of the Reverend Isaac Bard.

Through the winter and spring of 1863, squads of Federal and Confederate soldiers were occasionally seen in Muhlenberg County. A few Federal companies camped in Greenville some time during the spring and summer. Now and then a number of guerrilla companies would dash through the county, led by Jake Bennett and others. Six men belonging to the Thirty-fifth Kentucky Mounted Infantry came into Greenville one day during the month of November, 1863, and stopped at the Reno Hotel. They stacked their guns in the reception room and then took their horses to the livery stable. While they were gone Robert M. Martin, with fifteen or twenty men, rode up and seized the guns of the Federals, went to the livery stable, and there made prisoners of all the Federals except one, who tore out the back way and escaped.

The prisoners who were captured by Bob Martin informed him that about forty men of the Thirty-fifth Kentucky Mounted Infantry, commanded by Lieutenant Ed M. Randolph, were on their way to Greenville and would be in town in a short time. Martin at once sent the prisoners down to the bridge on Caney Creek and put out pickets on the different streets. Martin then made a visit to Hancock & Reno's store, and while there Lieutenant Randolph, with four or five men, came up but were halted by Martin's picket. When Martin heard what was going on he ran out, got on his horse, and, with his picket, rode down the street in a hurry. Lieutenant Randolph and his men came up, and after inquiry, pursued and came in collision with one of Martin's pickets, who fired on one of Randolph's men, named Brown, but to no effect. It being dark Lieutenant Randolph followed only a short distance. Martin went down to the bridge on Caney, paroled his five prisoners, and left the county.

One evening during the middle of December, 1863, Martin and some of his men dashed into Greenville after dark, and with a few shots came very near taking the town. At least the people kept shy of him. He and his squad robbed the post-office and helped themselves to such things as they could use. Bob called upon his brother, Lieutenant James H. Martin, who belonged to the Thirty-fifth Kentucky Mounted Infantry, and who was then at home visiting his family. While Bob's men were lining up near the blacksmith shop preparatory to leaving, by request of Charles and Alney McLean he dismounted and stepped into their store. The McLeans were strong Southern men, and while Martin was in the McLean brothers' store, Elisha Weir, a negro boy, came along and took Martin's saddle-packs off the horse, hid them near by, and then passed on down the street. When Bob came back to his horse he discovered that his saddle-packs were gone. He procured a lantern and made a search, but could not find them. The squad did not stay long in town and left without Bob's saddle-packs. After Martin and his men had gone, Elisha Weir hid the saddle-packs until the next morning, when he opened them and found they contained a number of handy tricks. The negro was highly pleased with his booty, and often remarked that he would like to see Bob Martin in town again.

The day following this raid there took place what we boys regarded as the greatest event of 1863. This was the battle at the Coal Bank, fought about two miles north of Greenville. This so-called battle took place between Colonel Robert M. Martin with a force of Southern troops, and Captain T. J. Lovelace in command of a force of Federals. Lovelace had been following Bob Martin for several days, and finally brought him to a stand near the Coal Bank. When these men faced each other, they hesitated. Captain Lovelace, doubting that he had a sufficient number of men to capture Martin, dispatched an orderly sergeant to

Greenville, where Captain M. J. Roark was teaching school, and asked for reinforcements, stating that a battle was going on at the Coal Bank.

Captain Roark had quite a number of scholars who were of the muster age, and they were requested to prepare to follow him as soon as possible to the field of blood. We were all glad of the chance to show our valor and chivalry on the battlefield. We got ready, and—together with other recruits obtained in the town—formed a considerable squad. We all galloped off down the Rumsey Road at breakneck speed. The rattling of our horses' hoofs resounded upon the still air of the evening as if a furious charge of a grand cavalcade of a thousand dragoons was taking place. On and on we sped until we reached the Coal Bank, where to our surprise everything was as still as death. Twilight had kissed the hilltops and day was fading into night. We looked in every direction, but could see no human being. We put our hands to our ears, but not a sound could we catch except the voice of a night-owl perched on a limb and crying out his uncouth interrogation, "Who—who are you all?"

Our leader, Captain Morgan, of an Indiana regiment, was outwitted. He said: "It is strange that a battle should be fought in so short a time, leaving no sign, and that everything should be so quiet. We surely have missed the place of engagement." But the orderly sergeant assured him that we were on the battlefield.

We then reconnoitered to the right to see if we could discover a camp. We swung around about two miles to the east and then turned toward Greenville, but were disappointed at the result of our chase. As we came into the road running from Greenville to South Carrollton we discovered a body of troops just ahead of us, so we followed on and when we reached the old Brank place near Greenville we found it was Lovelace's men going into camp.

We learned from the men that when the two squads had arrived near the Coal Bank they were within sight of each other. The two commanders, Bob Martin and Captain Lovelace, then rode forward and met between their forces to make terms, but they could not agree. However, Martin promised Lovelace that his men would not fire on Lovelace's men until Lovelace had gotten back to his place, for Lovelace had farther to go than Martin. But as soon as Martin got to his men, so we were told, they commenced firing on Lovelace's company, and Lovelace returned the fire and advanced on Martin. Martin then beat a retreat and Lovelace pursued. Martin was soon lost in the darkness of the night.

That same night we returned to Greenville, much disappointed in not having had an opportunity of immortalizing our names with heroic deeds achieved upon a battlefield in defense of our country. We went to bed meditating upon our misfortune in not having reached the Coal Bank sooner. But the war was not over, and we therefore looked forward to fighting on another day.

The next morning at daylight Colonel E. R. Weir, with a company of the Thirty-fifth Kentucky Mounted Infantry, appeared in the courthouse yard, where his men fed their horses and then had breakfast. A little while after sun-up Colonel Weir moved off with his command up the Mud River Road. In the meantime Captain Lovelace had left the Brank place and had moved down the Morton Ferry Road. Colonel Weir and Captain Lovelace joined forces about three miles east of Greenville and soon came up with the force under Bob Martin. After considerable skirmishing a regular encounter took place. Captain Sebastian C. Vick, who accompanied Colonel Weir, seeing Martin's forces beginning to waver, brandished his sword, ordered a charge, and succeeded in dividing Martin's command. Martin beat a rapid retreat, the right wing of his squad going north and the left wing south. Pursuit was made, but no one was captured, wounded, or killed.

Captain M. J. Roark was the Provost Marshal of Greenville. When the Bob Martin excitement began he declared martial law and put out pickets on every road leading into town. Captain Roark retained the schoolboys and some others to garrison the town in case there should be an attack.

News was received from the eastern part of the county that heavy firing could be heard in that section and that troops had been seen along the road. Rumors reached us that shooting was going on at various places in the county, but very little attention was paid to most of such statements. A dispatch came to Greenville ordering Captain Roark to send a squad of men to Lead Hill Church, on Long Creek, to intercept some of Martin's men. Captain Roark hated to disobey orders, but disliked very much to part with any of his reserve force, for in case of an attack he might not be able to hold possession of Greenville. However, he sent part of his reserve to Lead Hill Church. We, who remained in town, kept under arms and stood prepared.

Later in the evening another order came. It had been sent from the western part of the county and asked for help to be sent to Clark's Mill, on Pond River, to cut off the escape of some of Bob Martin's men. This was a "deadener" on Captain Roark, for to send off the remainder of his reserve would have left Greenville defenseless. But he saw that it had to be done, so he ordered the remainder of the reserve (which consisted principally of schoolboys) to go to Clark's Mill at once. We were very anxious for another chance, and hoped we would be more successful this time in getting into a real battle. Captain Morgan was our leader, and we moved off down the Madisonville Road.

There was an old gentleman with us who lived out on the road we traveled. He wanted to continue with our company, and had us stop at his home until he could see his wife and tell her where he was going, for he did not know but what he might be killed, and therefore wanted to kiss her goodbye. But it was some time before his wife came into the house. Captain Morgan did a little cussing while we were waiting. When the old lady returned, the gentleman informed his wife where he intended going and for what purpose. She told him that he could not go, but must stay at home. So he came out and said, "Well, boys, the jig is up with me— the old lady has done issued orders for me to stay at home!"

We rode on; as we neared Clark's Mill it began to get a little dusky. We noticed a woman on a horse, riding toward us. When she got within about one hundred yards of us, Captain Morgan cried out to her, "Halt!"

and she stopped. Some of the boys recognized her and told Captain Morgan that she was a well-known lady of the neighborhood, going home. Captain Morgan replied, "Sometimes men have on women's clothes." He said that he would investigate. When he came up to where she was Morgan took a good look at her. He let her pass, but she was nearly scared to death.

We arrived at Clark's Mill before it was entirely dark. As we came up, a gentleman, who seemed badly scared, told us that Bob Martin with part of his men had crossed the river not more than twenty minutes before. We were disappointed again. We felt that if we had not stopped to wait for the old man on the road, we would have had a chance for a glorious battle and could have had something to recommend us. In the meantime night came on and we went into camp, thinking there was still some chance for us with the remnant of Martin's "army." We put out pickets and relieved them every two hours. About eleven o'clock that night the pickets reported that some men had come down the hill toward the river near our camp, and had then gone back.

The next morning we started on our return to Greenville. A man living on the hill near by told us that a body of soldiers had come down close to the river, and seeing we were located there, went up the river above where we were encamped and crossed into Hopkins County. So that ended this campaign, and we returned, not as victors, but as would-be valiant sons of liberty. We reached Greenville and found everything quiet. We were told that Bob Martin's entire army had left the county and had gone into Hopkins.

However, Bob Martin was finally captured, and although that event took place nearly two years after the Battle at the Coal Bank, I shall here relate the incident and in that way try to give in a more connected form an account of Bob Martin's military career in Muhlenberg.

Martin's last romance in Muhlenberg took place during the fall of 1865. He had come to his father's, and while he was there a Federal officer, Major Nelson C. Lawrence, of the Seventeenth Kentucky Cavalry, of Russellville, was in Greenville for the purpose of capturing Martin. This Federal officer, with some of the citizens of Greenville, went to the residence of Hugh Martin, the father of Bob, arrested Bob, and brought him to town.

While Major Lawrence and a crowd of citizens were on the street in front of the Reno Hotel, Bob Martin stood near a raised parlor window of the hotel, where there chanced to be sitting a Miss Beard, of Hartford, a young lady who was visiting Mr. Reno's family. Martin, then under arrest, was near the window, and while conversing with Judge W. H. Yost, inquired who the lady was. Judge Yost told him, and Bob then asked for an introduction. After the introduction Bob asked Miss Beard if he could come in. She gave her consent. He then turned around and got permission from the officer, Major Lawrence, who had him in charge, to speak to a lady acquaintance in the hotel parlor. When the request was granted, Martin stepped into the house through the window. In the meantime, while the officer was busy talking and showing a silver pistol to the people who were standing around him, Martin went through the hotel and out the back way and had made some headway before any one knew of his escape. The alarm was given and a pursuit commenced. Martin headed toward the old brick college on Cherry Street, where Professor E. W. Hall was teaching school; but it happened that the scholars were then having recess and heard the racket. The boys saw Bob Martin running and the men after him. They joined the chase, but were ahead of the men and soon recaptured him and turned him over to the authorities. He was taken to Russellville and from there to Louisville and thence to New York, where a few months later he was pardoned.

Bob Martin was born in Muhlenberg in 1840 and lived in the county until a few months before the breaking out of the war. I knew him well. He frequently visited in the neighborhood where I was raised. Martin had spent four years in a great war, and had been in many dangerous and daring encounters. During the Civil War he faithfully spent all his time in active service for the South. His military experiences in Muhlenberg were trifles compared to his maneuvers in the South and in Canada and New York. He planned and executed with considerable military skill, but was at last captured by us schoolboys—at least we boys at that time felt confident that the men who were after him would not have recaptured him without our help.[1]

On one occasion during the year 1863, while a squad of Confederates skirmishing around Greenville had the town under pickets, two Federal soldiers—Captain C. H. Martin, of the Eleventh Kentucky Infantry, and Sergeant T. H. Martin, of the Third Kentucky Cavalry—were at home on a furlough. Both of them lived west of Greenville. They had called on some young ladies south of town, and were not aware of the presence of the Confederate soldiers. They expected to stop in Greenville a while on their return home. On arriving at the entrance to the Russellville Road they met a picket, who permitted them to pass, but seeing the Confederate soldiers on the streets they turned out on the Hopkinsville Road, desiring to get away as quickly as possible. They soon came to a picket on that road, who yelled "Halt!" to them as they were hurrying along. They, however, did not stop, but put spurs to their horses and were soon out of reach of the picket's fire. They made all possible speed for home, a distance of about six miles, and there kept watch for awhile. They happened to be wearing citizens' clothes, otherwise they would probably have been captured.

Several companies of Federal troops passed through Muhlenberg during 1864. Some of these camped for a while in Greenville; however, the people of the county were still more or less annoyed by guerrillas. Some of these bands were led by Jake Bennett and some by Bob Martin.

In the fall of 1864 Captain Quantrill, a noted guerrilla and a desperate man, came from Missouri to Kentucky with a company of men dressed in the Federal uniform. They passed through Hopkins County, where his men captured a horse from a man named Dick Davis. Davis, believing them to be Federals, followed them into Muhlenberg County and through Greenville. The people of Greenville were puzzled about the identity of

---

[1] See following chapter—"Robert M. Martin."

Quantrill and his men, but some of them were suspicious and advised Davis not to follow; however, Davis followed on. When they reached the Rhoads Settlement they killed Davis. When his body was found it was brought to Greenville and then conveyed to his home in Hopkins County. Some time afterward Quantrill was shot in an attempt to capture him in Meade County, and was taken to Louisville, where he died unrecognized in an hospital. It is said that Frank and Jesse James were with Quantrill when he passed through Muhlenberg.

Some time during the same year S. D. Chatham had a daring adventure. S. D. Chatham, or "Uncle Sam," as he was called, was for many years Muhlenberg's leading cabinet-maker.[2] He owned a fine mare, about four years old, which was grazing in a pasture where now stands the Greenville Light and Ice Plant. A band of guerrillas, after passing through Greenville, went into this field, took out the young mare, and rode her off. A few hours later, when Chatham went down to get his stock, he saw that the mare was gone. He immediately suspected the guerrilla company, and observed signs convincing him that they had taken her. He rushed back to town to get help. No one seemed disposed to follow, for it was getting late in the evening; so he determined to attempt the trip by himself. He mounted the dam of the stolen mare and started off, declaring he would get his highly prized four-year-old.

He traveled up the Russellville Road for some distance, and although it had grown quite dark continued his search. Finally his attention was attracted by a noise in a fence corner,

[2] S. D. CHATHAM, 1870

and upon investigation he discovered that it was the snoring of a sentinel, who had fallen asleep at his post. With ears alert and eyes now wider open than ever, he cautiously rode on. Before long he came to the guerrilla camp, where to his surprise he found all the men sound asleep, lying close to their horses. He paused, and while studying the situation heard a low nicker of recognition given by his stolen filly to her mother. By the dim light of the camp-fire he saw his four-year-old tied to a tree. He cautiously dismounted, slyly stepped over, untied her, and tiptoed back to the old mare, followed by the stolen animal. He remounted and slowly started away from the camp, the young mare walking behind her mother.

---

[2] S. D. Chatham was born in North Carolina February 14, 1810, came to Muhlenberg in 1836, and died in Greenville on April 25, 1882. Mr. Chatham and his wife, Madeline Gordon Chatham, were the parents of: L. Clark; Mrs. Martha (T. P.) Boggess; Joseph G.; Mrs. Lucy (T. J.) Tinsley; Mary A., who after the death of her first husband, W. H. Wilkinson, became the second wife of W. H. Dewitt; John E., and Mrs. Jennie (B. H.) Mann.

He again passed the sleeping sentinel, and with his two horses deliberately returned to Greenville. The next morning, when the guerrillas found that the stolen horse was gone, they believed it had worked loose by not being sufficiently well tied; the captain reprimanded the man who had had her in charge for not tying her better, and as a punishment made him walk to Russellville.

S. D. Chatham's feat was similar to those performed by Ethan Allen, Jasper, and Newton in the early history of the nation. It was a miracle he escaped with his life. Chatham was a brave and fearless man, as much so as any man who ever lived in the county, for in this incident he performed a feat that very few persons would have undertaken, and it is to be ranked as a remarkable act.

The next man who aroused the people in Muhlenberg was General H. B. Lyon. General Lyon was born and reared near Eddyville, in Lyon County, and was a member of a family of distinction. His grandfather, General Matthew Lyon, was a noted man. Lyon County was named after H. B. Lyon's uncle, Chittenden Lyon. General Lyon was graduated from West Point in 1856 and shortly afterward entered the United States army. He had some experience as an Indian fighter on the frontier before he joined the Southern forces. General Lyon started toward Greenville with the announced intention of burning the courthouse. When he entered the northern part of the county the people of Greenville were apprised of his plan, and prepared to fight him and defend the town. The schoolboys and citizens got together all the guns and ammunition that could be found. The crowd converted an old brick house on Main Street into a fort, had port-holes made in its walls, and prepared to hold Greenville at all hazards. We intended to give General Lyon the warmest reception of the war. The schoolboys and all the fighting men of the town fell into ranks. We were placed under the command of Captain Sebastian C. Vick, who was then in Greenville with his squad of scouts known as "The Bold Kentucky Zouaves."

There was a certain lawyer in town who was in sympathy with the South. He got his gun and joined our crowd to help defend the courthouse. In walking back to us he passed a lady who was also in sympathy with the South. She said to him, "What do you mean? Colonel Lyon is our friend." He replied, "Madam, I do not know who our friends are; nobody can be our friend who attempts to burn our property." The courthouse was this lawyer's den—the place where he made his living—and he felt, therefore, that his duty was to help defend it. All the Union lawyers stood with him, and like him would have died in the defense of the old courthouse.

After we had made our preparations for General Lyon we waited and waited, until the time he could have gotten to Greenville had long passed. But he did not appear, so Lieutenant Sid Lewis, one of Vick's most valiant scouts, was sent down the Rumsey Road—the road over which Lyon would be most likely to come—to see whether he could learn anything about the movements of the enemy. Sid started off and was gone some time. When he returned he stated that he had not seen nor heard anything of the expected enemy.

However, most of us still had hope that he would come. Later in the day a man from the northern part of the county came to town and reported that Lyon had gone west of Greenville. This news was a cloudburst on the fire. If anybody was ever disappointed it was the schoolboys and Captain Bass Vick's men. Upon receipt of this news Vick and his "Bold Zouaves" immediately mounted their chargers and galloped off toward Pond River, thinking that perhaps if they could not capture Lyon before he got out of the county they could, at least, scare him away from the courthouse. It turned out afterward that they were not only too late, but had gone in the wrong direction.

We schoolboys were also greatly disappointed the way matters turned out. We were expecting a glorious battle, in which we were to have immortalized ourselves upon the pages of our country's history as the most gallant and deserving heroes of the Civil War, for slaying the "Lyon of the Rebellion." But next morning, upon serious reflection, we came to the conclusion that a living man was worth more than a dead hero, and that several of us might have been killed in a battle with General Lyon. Such a loss, we boys thought, would have been a great blow to the county. We also knew that, after all, some of the greatest heroes in the world were those who had avoided many of the greatest difficulties in life. We had the consolation of having helped turn "the Lyon" from his prey and of preventing a great fright in Greenville, and of having saved the courthouse.

We later learned what might have been General Lyon's reason for not coming to Greenville. The Secessionists, at this stage of the game, had become bolder and more numerous in the town and in the county, and they had much better facilities for communication. The Secession leaders in town sent him word warning him not to enter Greenville, saying that if he did he would have one of the warmest receptions and hardest fights he had ever had during his military career, for the schoolboys and most of the citizens of Greenville, backed up by Captain Vick's "Bold Zouaves," were fortified and proposed to "do him up." He received the report, but to what extent it influenced him to change his route was never known. At any rate, General Lyon did not come to Greenville, and the great excitement was soon over.

What was probably the boldest prank that took place in Muhlenberg during war times occurred in Greenville a short time before the close of the rebellion. A dozen men, some of whom it is said lived in Christian County, east and south of Wildcat Hollow, had rigged themselves up on the order of guerrillas. They were led by Captain Sypert, and made a dash down through Muhlenberg and into Greenville, robbing a number of houses along the road they traveled. They rushed into Greenville, flourishing their old pistols as if there were a regiment of men just behind them. A good crowd was in town that day, and these boys made everybody stand in line, except a few who dodged back. They then commenced a general search through the pockets of about one hundred natives, and got some good-sized wads of greenbacks. After they had finished searching pockets they turned their attention to the stores, and procured a lot of calicoes, ribbons, shoes, gloves, and all kinds of wearing apparel. Then they mounted their horses, took their plunder, and returned the way they came. On reaching their homes they disposed of the booty, returning to their work as usual.

There was an incident that took place during this raid of the twelve men to Greenville which I shall here relate. It was on Saturday that the raid was made. On Friday evening Eugene Eaves and I went out from Greenville to my father's house near Pisgah Church, intending to go hunting the next day. So, early on Saturday morning, we took our guns and started to Pond River flats, where we hunted awhile and then turned back, reaching my father's about twelve o'clock. Upon our return we were told that twelve men had stopped there, ransacked the house and tore things up generally, and had then gone on toward Greenville.

I had bought a new suit, which I had worn home the day before and had left in the house, in the meantime wearing my old hunting-clothes. One of the men picked up this new suit and would have taken it had not my sister interfered. They also went into her trunk, and among other things got hold of an envelope in which, unknown to the robbers, she had her money. She snatched the envelope from the men, saying that it contained her sweetheart's letters, and she wanted to keep them. She followed them through all their search, and in a good-humored way stopped them from taking anything of value.

The twelve raiders did not stay long, but started for Greenville in a hurry. They had left our home about an hour and a half before Eaves and I got back. We put our guns away and all of us were talking about the daring men when James F. Shelton, who lived about a mile south, on the road along which the desperadoes had traveled, came dashing up at breakneck speed on his horse "Charlie," a large baldfaced sorrel with spraddled hind legs. He stopped and halloed out in an excited manner, "Boys, get your horses and let us go to Greenville and help fight the guerrillas!" We told him to get down, and that as soon as we could eat a bite we would go with him. He came in, and we continued our talk about the robbers. While Eugene Eaves and I were still eating, some one in the room suddenly cried out, "Here come the guerrillas back!" Everybody was thunderstruck, for this was something unexpected.

Shelton inquired if there were any guns about the house. My brother, Charles, told him that they were out in "the cabin." Our guns were always kept in order in what we called "the cabin," a one-room house in the back yard, about seventy-five feet from the main building. Shelton and Charles ran to this small house. Our available fighting force was Shelton, my two brothers (Charles and Tom), Eaves, and Lee. But before we could get together the desperadoes divided us and none but Shelton and Charles could get to the guns. The dash was so sudden that Eaves, Lee, my younger brother, and myself were cut off from the arsenal. Our force were all game men except myself, and I knew I would fight when hemmed.

About half of the robbers rushed into the house. Before they came into the room where Eaves and I were eating, I threw my pocket-book under the clothes-press. As soon as two of them entered the room, Eaves and Lee got up from the table. I kept my seat and continued to eat, but they seemed not to notice me. They searched Eaves and Lee, and got a plug of tobacco from one and a pocket-knife from the other.

One of them next stepped out on the porch fronting the cabin and in full view from where Shelton and Charles were located with the guns. He was getting a drink of water, and while standing and drinking, Charles leveled his gun and whispered to Shelton, "Jim, must I shoot?" Shelton said, "No, don't shoot." When the man left the porch Charles and Jim came out of the cabin with their guns, preferring to have an open field

PUBLIC ROAD NEAR OLD LIBERTY, TRAVELED BY THE TWELVE RAIDERS
As it appeared in 1900

fight. We do not know whether the marauders saw them or not. They probably did, for in the meantime one of them asked my sister what so many men were doing there, and she told them that they were neighbors. At any rate, the "Dirty Dozen" got away in a hurry.

As soon as the robbers had left the dining room Eaves, Lee, and myself made a break for the cabin, but Shelton and Charles were not there, and some of the guns were gone. We turned around and looked toward the road and saw the raiders leaving in a dash. We also saw Charles leveling his gun at one of the running men and heard him ask Shelton, "Jim, must I shoot?" And Jim answered, "No, don't shoot unless they take my horse." The robbers rushed up the road, but did not take his horse.

So they got off without any of them being killed. We were really glad of it, for we did not want to kill anybody, nor did we wish to be killed. It was Shelton's self-control and deliberate judgment that no doubt saved several lives. Shelton was game and would fight an elephant if necessary, but he was governed on this occasion by prudence and discretion. Several of us might have been shot if the fight had commenced, for we would all have taken part. Shelton said that it was folly for two men to attack a dozen. Shelton was then a young husband, and no doubt thought of his young wife and children who needed his assistance. If we had known that the raiders were coming back so soon we would have been properly prepared to give them a warm reception.

They did not remain long. On their return from Greenville my sister met them at the door as they came in, and in her good-natured way checked them from any molestation. She was shown the nice plunder they had gotten at Greenville and was offered some of it, but declined to accept any. After the robbers had been gone about half an hour, five neighbor men came riding up with guns. They had been hunting on Pond River. We told them of our experience. The crowd discussed the question of pursuit, but finally came to the conclusion that the "Twelve Raiders" could not be overtaken.

I remember that, on one occasion during 1864, Jake Bennett passed through the county and Greenville. He came in from the southern part of Muhlenberg, where he captured Jesse Taggart, who was a leader of the Home Guards and a very active Union man. Bennett shaved Taggart's head, then turned him loose, and came on to Greenville. He dashed into town one Sunday morning with about twenty men, greatly to the surprise of the people. Quite a crowd of negroes was on the streets at the time. Bennett's men began "shooting up" the town, and the negroes commenced running and scattered about like young partridges, some hallooing, "Oh, Lordy! Oh, Lordy!" After Bennett had cleared the street his men broke open the door of Hancock & Reno's store, went in and helped themselves, and then left town, going north. In about an hour a company of Federals came up in pursuit, but they did not overtake the Bennett band.

Jake Bennett made his last raid through Muhlenberg County in 1865. Bennett and Gentry, with parts of two companies, came down the Russellville Road the last Monday in March, 1865; it was county court day, and many people were in Greenville. It was Bennett's intention to pass through the town and raid the place, but when he heard that there was a company of Federal infantry then in Greenville he and his men turned out from the Russellville Road at a point about three miles south of town, and bore around east. All the people who had come to town and were returning home on the Russellville Road were stopped. Some were turned back, some captured; some were relieved of their money, and some were forced to swap or surrender horses. They kept picking up the natives, and soon had quite a crowd of prisoners on their hands.

They experienced some trouble with Alney Newman, who lived in that neighborhood near Pond Creek. A lieutenant under Gentry asked Newman what his politics were. Newman, being angry, answered in a stubborn manner that he was a Union man. He was then ordered to get off his horse; he refused, and they beat him over the head with their pistols. After he had been pretty badly bruised he got down. They next told him to take off his saddle, and when he refused to comply the lieutenant ordered the squad to cock their guns and level them at Newman. At this juncture

David Martin, one of the captives and a neighbor of Newman, rode up to Newman and advised him to take his saddle off. Newman then said, "If you say so, Dave, I will do it." Newman then removed his saddle, and in exchange for his young animal they gave him a poor old horse that died the next day.

Bennett in his march toward Greenville captured Joseph G. Chatham and his younger brother John, who were out after seed oats. Bennett told Joseph G. Chatham that if he would pilot them east of Greenville and toward South Carrollton he and his horse would not be molested. So

GREENVILLE HOTEL, GREENVILLE (BUILT IN 1855)
As it appears to-day

Chatham led them around until they struck the Greenville and South Carrollton Road below Powderly, where all their prisoners were turned loose. The captives, some twelve or fifteen in number, immediately started for Greenville. It was dark, but most of them were familiar with the old road. When they reached Caney Creek Bridge, just north of town, they were halted by a squad of Federals led by Captain Roark, who was on the lookout for Bennett. Roark's soldiers were as much frightened as surprised when they saw this squad of citizens coming up the public highway at that time of night. When Captain Roark learned that Bennett had taken the South Carrollton road he and his men started in pursuit, but soon returned. Bennett continued his march to South Carrollton, thence through the northern part of Muhlenberg and into Hopkins and Union counties, where they disbanded the first of April, a few days before the surrender of General Lee.

The Greenville Hotel, which still stands, on the east side of Main Street about fifty yards north of Main Cross Street, and the Reno House, which stood on the northwest corner of Main and Main Cross streets, were the war hotels.

The Greenville Hotel was the headquarters of the Secessionists and the hotbed of Southern sympathizers of the county. It was a general Confederate rendezvous, where the Confederate interests would be discussed, plans suggested, and secrets divulged by the lovers of Dixie living in the county. They would report at the Greenville Hotel to give and receive war news, and would sympathize with one another at the reception of unfavorable reports. The best drinks were always kept in this house, to help brace up those who might become despondent and disheartened as a consequence of the way in which matters went. The place was always kept lively and full of fun. It was a noted place for the relating of wonderful and windy narratives, conundrums, yarns, and sells. No melancholy disposition existed there. Its life and invigoration were kept up by the generous and affable disposition of the proprietors, together with the frequency of stimulating drinks. After the close of the war the Greenville Hotel became the Democratic headquarters of the county. Here all their councils took place and their methods and policies were adopted for the campaigns.

The Reno House was the Federal headquarters for the county during the war. Caucuses and consultations were held within its walls. Plans and methods were considered as to how to save the Union and put down the Rebellion. News was received and sent out from this hotel. In 1864 Major Hudson Brown, son of pioneer Nathaniel Brown, was shot and killed by Fred Harper in front of the Reno House, near the barroom. They were both Muhlenberg men and Federal soldiers. Brown was a young man, who had just been promoted to the rank of major in the Union army. After the war the Reno House was made the headquarters of the Republican party of the county, and remained so until the death of L. R. Reno.

Democratic leaders fought shy of the Reno House and the Republican leaders did likewise to the Greenville Hotel. The two houses were competitors in policies as well as in business.

The length and enormity of the Rebellion surpassed the expectations of everybody. To most of the people of the county the freeing of the negroes was an unexpected act. Lincoln's proclamation put a different phase on the situation and caused many Muhlenberg citizens to backslide and lose much of their love for the Union. Some of the people in the county came to the conclusion that they had been pulling too hard at the wrong end of the political rope. I shall here briefly refer to the development and changes in political affairs.

While the war was still going on some felt that the Rebellion with all its bullets was a failure. So in Muhlenberg County and in Kentucky a rebellion was raised and fought out with ballots. Many who had supported the Federal side in the Rebellion with bullets, joined the Secession forces to fight under their flag and colors in the battle with ballots. Those who joined the Secession ranks to fight with ballots called themselves Conservatives. They were opposed to the continuation of the war with bullets, saying that it was a failure and ought never to have been fought. So, by 1865, a general uprising against the Republican party took place.

The war with ballots began to flourish about the time the war with bullets ended. The Insurgents fused with the Secessionists to wage the war with ballots, which gave them a good majority in the county and State. This kind of warfare became national, and continued for a number of years.

Great was the change in some of the most determined and valiant Union men from positions they had occupied in 1861 and 1862. I recollect hearing a man say, in the fall of 1861, that he could hew the rebels down with a broadax, and in 1864 the same man declared that the war was all

THE RENO HOUSE, GREENVILLE
This hotel was managed by Lawson R. Reno from 1854 to 1890; destroyed by fire 1903.
A modern three story building now stands on this corner

wrong and that the negroes ought not to have been freed. He seemed to advocate the doctrine of Secession, but called himself a Conservative; yet he admitted his regeneration by Southern grace.

When the Secession element saw the stampede of the Union men coming from the support of the Federal government they rejoiced and were glad. They told the Insurgents and backslidden Unionists that the Radicals, as they called them, would certainly ruin the country by putting the negroes to rule over the white people of the South, and would make slaves of them. This kind of talk fired the simple-minded people to a high degree. The leading Secessionists of the county and State told the heart-broken people: "Vote with us, and we can save the country from an awful doom; it is the only way it can be done. Now we want the Insurgents to lead off in opposition to the Radicals, for opposition is all that we can recommend or propose, and we will follow you through evil as well as good report."

So, as stated before, in 1865, at the closing of the rebellion of bullets, a general uprising against the Republican party took place. The Republican party, that had put down the rebellion of bullets, had enacted and passed the thirteenth, fourteenth, and fifteenth amendments to the Constitution of the United States, in order to make our nation a great and progressive country, one that could be truly called "the land of the free and the home of the brave."

In order to defeat the Republicans for what they had already done and for what they might do, the Secessionists advised the selecting and nominating of candidates for office from among the Insurgent or deserting ranks, as a kind of feeler for the future. So in 1865 the Secessionists and Insurgents agreed on the nomination of a man for Congress in the Second Congressional District of Kentucky, of which Muhlenberg was then a part. This nominee, in 1861 and 1862, was a vehement uncompromising Union man, and at that time denounced the Secessionists and the rebellion of the South. But his feelings were hurt by the enactment of the amendments to the Constitution, which caused him to have different views. He was an example of where "circumstances alter cases." He made the race in 1865 and beat his Republican opponent by a considerable majority, opening up the way for better times. But in the next congressional election a thoroughbred, wool-dyed Secessionist got the nomination. The Insurgent then concluded that he would run on his Conservative strength, but in the race he received very few votes; the Secessionist won by a large majority over both the Insurgent and the Republican candidates. This was the retirement of the Insurgent, and he ever afterward remained passive in politics.

In 1866 the county election was held in Muhlenberg for county officers. The Union, or Republican, party had held the county offices during the war. The Secessionists thought best to bring out and nominate the Insurgents. So, for county judge, a man was nominated who had been a colonel in the Federal army but who had gotten his feelings hurt on account of the freeing of the negroes, which caused him to backslide. For county attorney they brought out an old man who had reached a point where he had conscientious scruples in regard to the emancipation of the negroes and the Republican management of the government, which caused him to apostatize. For county clerk they nominated a man who was at the beginning of the war an uncompromising Union man, but the changes resulting from the Rebellion did not altogether meet with his approval, for they stood between him and his Union patriotism, causing him to see as through a glass darkly. For sheriff they had a man who had always remained neutral, and stood for the Union and the Constitution as it was. For assessor they brought out a man who at the commencement of the Rebellion was a Union man, but became an Insurgent for the want of faith in the run of things. For jailer they nominated a man who never knew for certain what his political inclinations were. All of these men were elected over their Republican opponents. The Insurgents and the backslidden Unionists became stepping-stones for the regular Secessionists to get official control of the county and the State. They were then retired to the rear and became "hewers of wood and drawers of water," and were used as safeguards for the regular Secessionists, who held control of the county for a quarter of a century.

As remarked in the beginning of these reminiscences, my memory regarding these occurrences may not be correct in every detail. However, such are my recollections of some of the military, political, and other maneuvers that took place in Muhlenberg County during war times.

XXIV

ROBERT M. MARTIN

THE Civil War produced no higher type of the fearless and danger-loving soldier—no more perfect exemplar of the romantic and picturesque partisan ranger—than Robert Maxwell Martin of Muhlenberg, who came to be known, in war and in peace, as Colonel "Bob" Martin. His daring exploits, his narrow escapes, his coolness and good humor in the very face of death, his keen search ever for the post of danger, won the admiration of friend and foe alike, and have been noted generously in several books of Civil War history. These were written and published after his death, and were not the products of friends seeking to celebrate a living man. He was most modest, and always reticent of his own adventures. To the day of his death he possessed that natural quality of the buoyantly active man of living wholly in the present, and paying little regard to the glories of the past or to the prospects of the future.[1]

Robert Maxwell Martin was born in Muhlenberg a few miles northwest of Greenville, January 10, 1840, on what is now the County Poor Asylum farm. His father, Hugh Martin, reared four sons and three daughters, all of whom were born in the county, but who are no longer represented here. All of the family were followers of the Union cause except Robert. Two of the sons were in the Union army—Lieutenant Templeton B. Martin, of Company B, Eleventh Kentucky Infantry, and Lieutenant James H. Martin, of Company F, Thirty-fifth Kentucky Mounted Infantry. William, the eldest son, did not take up arms. The father was a strong Unionist, as were the McDonalds and Roarks, to whom the Martins were related. Robert was the only one who threw his fortunes in with the South, and he fought from the beginning of hostilities in Western Kentucky until the final surrender at Appomattox. He was twenty-one when the war began. He was an ideal free cavalry leader, unsurpassed as a scout, and the idol of his soldiers as the leader of a forlorn hope.

Martin was one of the first to enlist in Colonel N. B. Forrest's regiment of Confederate cavalry, where his qualities as a scout were quickly recognized and made use of. When Adam R. Johnson came up from Texas and enlisted with Forrest in 1861 it was on condition that he be made a

---

[1] Colonel Martin's military career is treated of at length in "The Partisan Rangers," by General Adam R. Johnson (1904); "Morgan's Cavalry," by General Basil W. Duke (1909); and "Confederate Operations in Canada and New York," by Captain John W. Headley (1906). Authority for many of the statements made in this sketch may be found in these books. General A. R. Johnson is now (1913) living at Burnet, Texas; General Duke and Captain Headley reside in Louisville.

scout, for which service long experience on the frontier well fitted him. "Very well," said Forrest. "If you can equal Bob Martin, I will have a fine team for scouting." Thus began a close association between the two daring and fast-moving riders.

When Colonel Forrest and his men were on their skirmish movement from Hopkinsville toward Rumsey, Martin and Johnson acted as chief scouts. On December 28, 1861, Forrest's cavalry arrived near Sacramento, McLean County, and Martin there fought his first battle.[2]

There were no limits to the audacity of Martin and Johnson, which they indulged at the outset with the delight of boys—as they were. On one occasion, getting information that Colonel James S. Jackson had collected a large number of cavalry horses for the Union army on the farm of Willis Field, near Owensboro, these two scouts, needing horses for their recruits, prepared an order for twelve horses in due form, to which they signed the name of General Thomas L. Crittenden, Jackson's superior officer. They then presented the order, got the horses—together with their breakfasts—

ROBERT M. MARTIN IN 1866

and departed in triumph. It was not until two days later that Field, Jackson, and Crittenden compared notes and discovered that they had been outwitted of a dozen fine mounts. The horses were delivered to Forrest.

On another occasion they, with one other companion, attacked under cover of night a garrison of Union troops at Henderson. From close range across the street on a summer night they fired into the garrison, causing excitement and confusion, alarming the town, and giving to the attack the appearance of an onset in force by a strong body. They made their escape, and Martin had the daring to return from the country three days later under a flag of truce, demanding the retraction of statements made in a town meeting and threatening an immediate attack on the town. The retractions were made, but the whole Confederate "force" amounted to three men, who greatly enjoyed the wild alarm they had created.

The thrilling experience of these daring scouts and spies of Forrest's at Donelson, and likewise during the Shiloh campaign, are told in detail by General Johnson. After the battle of Shiloh, Forrest loaned Johnson and Martin to General John C. Breckinridge, who sent them to Kentucky,

---

[2] A description of the fight at Sacramento, written by Adam R. Johnson, and another account by Richard T. Martin, are quoted elsewhere in this volume.

where they began recruiting in Webster and Henderson counties and inaugurated hostilities hundreds of miles in the rear of Grant's army, and here fought and dodged from county to county until November, 1862, by which time they had enlisted a regiment of cavalry.

During this expedition, with about twenty-five men, they crossed the Ohio from opposite Newburg, Indiana, and took the guns that had been stored there in the Union arsenal. Johnson says that, before crossing the river, "I ordered our horses to be placed where they would make as big a show as possible to the people on the other side, and from two pairs of

ROBERT M. MARTIN WAS BORN ON WHAT IS NOW THE COUNTY POOR ASYLUM
Up to about 1865 this was one of the best farms in Muhlenberg. Some of the brick houses built and occupied by his father, Hugh Martin, are still standing

old wagon wheels, with their axles, a stovepipe, and a charred log, I soon had manufactured two of the most formidable-looking pieces of artillery into whose gaping mouths a scared people ever looked." With these preparations Martin and Johnson alone crossed the river in a skiff, bearing a flag of truce. The Union garrison was a small one, guarding a hospital and supplies. The two scouts demanded possession of all the guns, and pointed to the frowning "cannon" on the opposite shore, discreetly masked behind bushes and just as discreetly revealed in part. Fearing a bombardment of the town, the guns were surrendered, with the ammunition, and Martin and Johnson transported them across the river.

The regiment they had raised was added to General John H. Morgan's command as the Tenth Kentucky Cavalry; C. S. A. Johnson, as the elder, was made Colonel, and Martin Lieutenant-Colonel. They went on Morgan's

December, 1862, raid into Kentucky. Later Johnson was detailed by the Secretary of War as the bearer of dispatches to General Magruder, in Texas. During his absence Martin commanded the regiment, and many daring feats are recorded of his adventures and of his conduct in battle by Johnson and also by General Duke in his history of Morgan's cavalry. Duke describes Martin as a man of extraordinary dash and resolution, very shrewd in partisan warfare. He was a very whirlwind to harry the enemy's supplies and interrupt their communication. He would charge his adversary on any good fighting chance, and would come out with a seemingly charmed life. At Snow's Hill, Tennessee, General Morgan sent him with his regiment to threaten the Union right, and he charged upon a battery with dauntless courage.

One incident at Milton, Tennessee, in March, 1863, was described to General Duke by an eyewitness. Martin's regiment had been ordered to charge a Union battery and capture it or keep it busy. They were repulsed at the first onset, but Martin rallied them from the rear and then, some distance in advance, again led them against the hill. "Just here," says the eyewitness quoted by Duke, "Martin performed one of those acts of heroic but useless courage, too common among our officers. When his regiment wavered and commenced to fall back, he halted until he was left alone; then at a slow walk rode to the pike, and with his hat off rode slowly out of fire. He was splendidly mounted, wore in his hat a long black plume, was himself a large and striking figure, and I have often thought that it was the handsomest picture of true and desperate courage I saw in the war."[3]

At McMinnville, Tennessee, in 1863, Martin received a bullet-wound in the lung, and was laid up for several months. He was at the head of his regiment on Morgan's disastrous raid into Ohio; he escaped into West Virginia with four hundred troops, and was soon clearing the country in East Tennessee of bushwhackers while Morgan's scattered troops were reassembling at Morristown.

This remnant of Morgan's command under Martin fought in Forrest's division at the battle of Chickamauga. Johnson says: "Colonel Martin, with one of the battalions, was chosen to open in advance of our infantry the great battle of Chickamauga, on the right. By their gallantry in charging and running out of their fortified position the Federal infantry, the Kentuckians attracted the attention of General Hill, who sought out General Forrest during the thickest of the fight and complimented him on their action. Subsequent to the battle it was again Martin who, with his battalion, drove the defeated Federals out of their advanced works at Chattanooga. . . . It was a memorable morning the next day after this brilliant feat of arms; Martin had formed our boys in the outskirts of Chattanooga, when General Forrest came riding down the line of the

---

[3] A Union soldier in the battery Martin charged, describing the circumstance after the Civil War, said: "He sat his walking horse with his hat in his hand, scratching his head as if to say, 'Well, I don't understand this running away.' It was so fine a display of supreme courage that our commander ordered the firing to cease, saying, 'It will be a d——d shame for so brave a man to be shot in the back.'"

Kentucky battalion, and taking off his hat in honor of the prowess they had shown, exclaimed, 'Any man who says that Morgan's men are not good soldiers and fine fighters tells a damn lie!' "

Duke says that this regiment of Morgan's men at Chickamauga, under Colonel Martin, "fired the first and last shots in that terrible struggle."

After Chickamauga, Colonel Martin chose a small detail and started for Western Kentucky to recruit a new regiment, most of his men being in Northern prisons or dead. He had many adventures in Christian, Trigg, and Hopkins counties. In December, 1863, at the head of his recruits, he entered Muhlenberg, and at eight o'clock at night charged unprotected Greenville, his men yelling like Indians. Captain Headley thus records the incident:

"There was a general stampede and great excitement among the population. This was a hotbed of Unionism, and the offensive Union men dreaded Martin. Others greeted us cordially. A detail went to the post-office and got the postage stamps and envelopes. We now had twenty dollars' worth of United States spoils. After Colonel Martin had spent an hour with his friends we rode out toward Hartford, soon turned, made a circuit around Greenville toward Hopkinsville, and camped with good fires until sunrise the next morning. After breakfast we went toward the Greenville and Madisonville Road to learn if we had been pursued. It was the purpose now to go back to Madisonville if any of its garrison had followed us to Greenville. We entered a long lane through a farm, and Colonel Martin inquired at the house, about midway. He heard of three different companies that were in pursuit, but got no information as to where they belonged. Just before we reached the end of the lane it was observed that dense woods were in front and extended around to the right over a hilly region. . . .

"The fence on the left extended about fifty yards farther than on the right side of the lane we were in. Cyrus Crabtree, wearing a Federal overcoat, was the advance guard, and at the end of the lane he observed a company of Federals about two hundred yards to the left across a little old unfenced field. There was a small ravine that ran through it, about midway between our ridge and the one where the Federals had halted. Crabtree stopped and motioned back to us. Martin halted the column and galloped up to Crabtree, then called out to the Federals and asked who was in command. 'Captain Jeff Roark,' was the response. 'Where from?' inquired Martin. 'Hopkinsville,' was the answer, followed with the inquiry, 'Who are you?' 'Captain Wilkes from Henderson. Send a man down half way,' answered Martin. 'All right,' said Roark. Martin directed Crabtree to go and get all that Roark knew about us. Crabtree and Roark met down in the little ravine, while both sides sat quietly and looked on. Colonel Martin called out to Crabtree, 'Is it all right?' 'Yes,' responded Crabtree; 'he wants to see you, Captain.' Martin trotted his horse down to meet his old friend. They had been boys together in the same neighborhood. Captain Roark was astonished when he recognized Colonel Bob Martin. I heard Martin laughing as he said, 'Well, Jeff, we ought to shake hands over a joke like this.' 'I think so too, Bob,' said

Roark, and they greeted each other cordially. They then talked for a few minutes, and separated, each galloping back to his command, and Martin announced that he was going to fight."

The small fight that ensued near the Coal Bank resulted in no serious casualties, although it continued as a running skirmish all next day. One incident illustrates Colonel Martin's marvelous resourcefulness and activity. In retreating across a "branch" with high banks, the overhanging boughs of a tree swept him over the rump of his horse. As he slid down he grasped the tail of the animal with both hands and held on until a soldier caught the bridle and he remounted coolly and pursued his way, laughing at the accident.[4]

Martin and his men found no welcome in Muhlenberg and he went South, where he joined General Morgan, who had by that time made his escape from prison. In Tennessee, Kentucky, and West Virginia he was ever busy and always in danger. At Mt. Sterling, June, 1864, he was badly wounded in the foot, and had his horse killed under him; but he was in the field next day in a buggy, keeping up with his column. Two days later he was in the saddle, his wounded foot on a pillow, his knee over the pommel of the saddle, woman-fashion, the other foot in the stirrup, leading a charge.

This wound disabled him for a time, and he was sent to Canada with letters from Judah P. Benjamin, Secretary of State for the Confederacy, where he was to aid in harrying the North from the frontier. At New York the plan of burning the city by setting fire to nineteen hotels at the same time was attempted; the fires were started, but were extinguished before much damage was done. He was at the head of a party of ten, including Captains J. Y. Beall, John W. Headley, and R. C. Kennedy, who were to attempt the rescue of seven Confederate generals while they were being transferred by rail from Johnson's Island to New York. They missed the prisoners, however, and the daring undertaking failed of accomplishment. Beall was arrested and hanged in February, 1865, as was also Kennedy soon afterward, but Martin and Headley managed to reach Cincinnati in safety and from there they went to Louisville.

Headley says there were about twenty thousand troops in camp in and around Louisville at this time, under Major-General John M. Palmer. Major Fossee, of his staff, kept three fine horses at headquarters. About ten o'clock one morning Martin and Headley cornered the orderly and hostler in the stable, who being unarmed readily surrendered. Martin and Headley led two of the horses out, handing the orderly a slip of paper on which Headley had written:

    Compliments of
        Col. Robert M. Martin
        Lieut. John W. Headley
            10th Kentucky Cavalry, C. S. A.

Feby. 28, 1864.

---

[4] The story of "Bob" Martin's military career as it appeared to Muhlenbergers is also told in Richard T. Martin's "Recollections of the Civil War," the preceding chapter.

On these horses they made their way to Virginia, only to hear of Lee's surrender a few days after their arrival. Martin, after spending a few months in Cuba and Tennessee, proceeded to Bowling Green, then down Green River to Paradise. He had been recognized at Bowling Green, and was followed. He was arrested in Greenville and taken in irons to Louisville and thence to New York, where he was thrown into Fort Lafayette on a charge of treason. He was one of those men who by their daring and activity, especially in the North, were relied upon to incense the Northern people and bring about the trial and conviction of Jefferson Davis and the other leaders of the Confederacy on this same charge of treason. Colonel Martin was examined and held for trial under indictment. An attempt was then made to induce him to give testimony against Davis, as the price of his life. But the prosecutors were dealing with a fearless man. "I not only have nothing to tell about Mr. Davis," he told his jailers, "but if I knew anything I would not tell it!" It is said that he was tried and convicted but that upon appeal his case was remanded for trial in another district. If this be true, he was the only man convicted of treason growing out of the Civil War. At any rate, he was not put on trial a second time. In the summer of 1866 he was pardoned unconditionally by President Johnson.

From war Colonel Martin returned to the paths of peace cheerfully, and plunged into business with all the energy he had displayed in war. He speculated in tobacco and made several fortunes, each of which he lost in turn. He traveled much abroad, and on one trip returning met on the steamer a Miss Wardlaw, of Murfreesboro, Tennessee. This chance meeting resulted in an early marriage. They had one daughter, named Oceania, after the steamship on which they had met. It was the death of this daughter, "Ocey" Martin Snead, that brought her mother and maternal relatives into such trying and pitiful prominence in New York in 1910, nearly ten years after Colonel Martin's death. There was no son.

Up to a few years before his death Colonel Martin occasionally visited friends in Muhlenberg. On one of his trips to Greenville, some fifteen years before the old and dilapidated courthouse was replaced by the present building, he jokingly remarked, "I have often regretted that I did not try to burn that old courthouse when I passed through here during the war, for if I had Muhlenberg would now have a better courthouse." Probably only those who remember the old brick courthouse during the last few years of its existence can fully appreciate the humor of this remark.

Martin was tall and slender, yet strongly built, walking with the erect, springy ease of an Indian until after he had received two severe wounds in war, one of which ultimately caused his death. He had a somewhat swarthy complexion, piercing blue eyes, a full nose with a hawk bridge, sandy hair that was inclined to curl, a winning smile, and a bearing in which courtesy and consideration united to render him attractive to all with whom he came in contact. He was devoid of all pretense, yet decisive, resourceful, and grim in the execution of his projects.

The life of Martin after the war is thus summarized by Captain Headley: "Colonel Robert M. Martin, after his release from prison, in

1866, settled at Evansville, Indiana, and engaged in the tobacco warehouse business. In 1874 he removed to New York City. For fourteen years he was manager of tobacco inspections for David Dowes & Co. in their Brooklyn warehouses. He located at Louisville in 1887, engaging in the tobacco brokerage business. In the fall of 1900, his old wound in the lung having produced frequent hemorrhages, his health gave way. He bade me good-by in October, 1900, upon his departure for New York, where he hoped some specialist might prolong his life, but he died on the 9th day of January, 1901. He was sixty-one years of age. . . . He is buried in Greenwood Cemetery, New York City.''

XXV

SOME OF MUHLENBERG'S CIVIL WAR SOLDIERS

MUHLENBERG was represented in the Civil War by about one thousand soldiers. About 85 per cent of these were in the Federal army, about 15 per cent in the Confederate army. The following are brief biographies of a few of Muhlenberg's soldiers who lived in the county during all or the greater part of their lives.

GENERAL DON CARLOS BUELL. For portrait see page 237.

JOHN COOMBS was born January 13, 1840. He is a son of Asa Coombs, who settled in Muhlenberg in 1848, near Rockport, Ohio County. He was a sergeant in Company H, Eleventh Kentucky Infantry (Federal), and served with that company during the greater part of the war. After its close he took up farming until he was elected jailer, when he moved to the county seat. He filled that office from 1882 to 1890. He continued to live in Greenville about ten years longer, filling in the meantime various town offices, after which he returned to his farm, where he remained until he retired from active life, when he again took up his residence in Greenville. He married Mary J., daughter of B. T. Casebier, who was an influential farmer in the eastern part of the county. Their only son is Joseph Edward Coombs, a merchant of Greenville.

JOHN COOMBS, WIFE AND SON, 1874

CAPTAIN ARTHUR N. DAVIS. For portrait see page 192.

JAPHA N. DURALL was born on a farm in the Bethel neighborhood, northwest of Greenville, March 19, 1844, and died on the same farm July 29, 1912. He was a corporal in Company H, Eleventh Kentucky Infantry (Federal). Some of the most largely attended soldiers' reunions held in the county have taken place on his farm. He was a farmer during the greater part of his life, and also operated a sawmill for a number of years. His wife was America Jane Woodburn, a sister of Doctor J. T. Woodburn. Most of their children still live in the Bethel neighborhood, where they occupy good farms.

FRANCIS M. FINLEY, a Federal soldier, and Thomas M. Finley, a Confederate soldier, were brothers, members of one of the dozen or more families in Muhlenberg that were represented in both armies. They were born in the Long Creek country on what is known as the Finley Farm, and were among the best-known farmers in that section of the county. They were sons of William H. Finley, who settled in the southern part of the county about 1830, where he died in 1852. His wife was Cynthia Wagner, daughter of a well-known local miller.

Francis Marion Finley was born April 15, 1833, enlisted in Company I, Forty-eighth Kentucky Infantry (Federal), in March, 1863, and remained with that company until it was mustered out of service in December, 1864. He married Susan S., daughter of John W. Shelton, who lived near Old Liberty and was of one of the oldest families in the county. Francis M. Finley died March

JAPHA N. DURALL, 1861

FRANCIS M. FINLEY, 1869

THOMAS M. FINLEY, 1869

14, 1908, on his farm near Greenbriar Church, eleven miles south of Greenville. Alexander Y. Finley, of the Pond Creek country, is his only son.

THOMAS MONROE FINLEY was born June 17, 1835. He enlisted in 1862 in Company D, Second Kentucky Cavalry (Confederate), at Allensville,

Todd County, and served with that regiment until the close of the war, when he returned to his Long Creek farm, afterward removing to Greenville, where he now lives. His wife was Nancy A., daughter of J. Jackson Robertson, who lived near the Buckner Stack. She died January 14, 1912. Mrs. Mollie C. (Charles M.) Shutt is their only child.

CAPTAIN JESSE KNOX FREEMAN, sr., was born February 26, 1837, in Hancock County, where he spent his youth. In 1858 he married Kittie Ann Mason, of Breckinridge County, and shortly after removed to Bremen. He enlisted in the Eleventh Kentucky Infantry (Federal) on September 28, 1861, and was elected first lieutenant of Company H. On April 8, 1862, after the death of Captain Isaac W. Sketo at Shiloh, he became captain of the company. For a time he acted as aide-de-camp to General William Soule Smith, and at one time served as commander of the convalescent camp of Union soldiers at Louisville; he also acted as provost marshal of Bowling Green. He was mustered out of service with his regiment on December 18, 1864. Captain Freeman moved to Central City shortly after the place was founded, and has since been identified with that town. He was postmaster of Central City from 1897 to 1905. His son J. K. Freeman, jr., is an attorney and at present the postmaster of Central City.

J. K. FREEMAN, 1864

WILLIAM S. GRUNDY. For portrait see page 230.

JUDGE S. P. LOVE, or, as he was more frequently called, Colonel S. P. Love, came to the county at the age of twenty-three, and after an active life here of more than half a century died in Greenville on March 26, 1903. No Muhlenberg man was more highly esteemed by his fellow-citizens than was Colonel Love. I quote in full from the Greenville Record:

"Colonel Smoloff Pallas Love died at his home at 7.15 o'clock last Thursday morning, after an illness that confined him to his bed for several weeks. He was born May 10, 1826, in Lincoln County, and was reared in Garrard County. In 1846 he enlisted as a private in Captain Donovan's command, being mustered into service at Mexico, Missouri, from which point he marched to Mexico, participating in numerous engagements during the Mexican War and being discharged from the service after the battle of Buena Vista. He had been appointed second lieutenant, but was never commissioned.

"In 1849 he came to this county, and on the 15th of July, 1850, was united in marriage by Rev. John N. Sharp to Miss Jane McConnell, daughter of John Henry McConnell, of this county. He was commissioned lieutenant-colonel in the Eleventh Kentucky Regiment of the Federal army, under Colonel P. B. Hawkins, in August, 1861, and in May, 1863, was made colonel of the regiment. He was constantly with his command, and his bravery, fidelity and consideration for his men endeared every member strongly to him. He was in the engagements at Shiloh and Perryville and in all the skirmishes in pursuit of Bragg's army when it retreated from Kentucky. He also participated in the siege of Knoxville, in the campaign under General Burnside in East Tennessee, and in all battles in which Sherman's army was engaged on the march from Ringgold to Atlanta. He was discharged at Bowling Green, December 16, 1864.

"In 1866 Colonel Love moved with his family from South Carrollton to Greenville, and in the same year was elected judge of the county, which position he held for two terms. After the expiration of his official term he engaged in the practice of law, and was an active and successful advocate. For some years he,had been a sufferer from a complication of diseases, and for the past few years had not been able to follow his profession.

"Burial was in Evergreen Cemetery Friday afternoon with full military honors, several hundred people being in attendance. Messrs. John A. Williams, W. C. Shannon, Nathan McClelland, D. E. Rhoads, John Coombs and Robert Casebier were pallbearers, and an escort of about forty men of his old command, and many other members of the G. A. R., aided in the ceremonies of last respect. Company F, Third Regiment Kentucky State Guard, under Captain R. C. McCracken, was in line and formed the firing squad, Bugler Clarence B. Hayes blowing taps that closed the service impressively.

S. P. LOVE, 1895

"The widow survives, and the following children: Mrs. Dan Mosely, Depoy; John G. Love, Central City; Mrs. Edward L. Yonts and Mrs. Annie R. White, of Greenville; Mrs. H. F. Young, Louisville; Mrs. George Gossett, Paducah; Mrs. J. W. Vomburg, Russellville; Mrs. Henry Nunan, Gurdon, Arkansas; Mrs. George A. Hillebert, Lehigh, Indian Territory. Their daughter Mrs. H. B. Barkis died in 1884, and their son Lucien T. Love in 1896. Colonel Love united with the Presbyterian Church at this place in 1882. Rev. G. F. Bell conducted a short service at the home, in which he was assisted by Rev. T. C. Peters, of the Methodist Church."

The few reunions of the veterans of the Mexican War that have taken place in Muhlenberg were proposed and conducted by Colonel Love, who probably took a more brotherly interest in the veterans of the Mexican and Civil wars than any other man in the county. He helped compile the history of the Eleventh Kentucky Infantry, published in "The Union Regiments of Kentucky" (1897).

R. T. VINCENT   J. L. WILKINS   WM. S. GRUNDY

These three pictures, made during the Civil War, represent three influential native sons and lifelong citizens of the Bremen country, who belonged to Colonel Love's regiment

Seven years after his death a poem written by Colonel Love was found among some of his personal papers. It was printed in the Greenville Record on July 14, 1910, by Orien L. Roark, who in his comment says: "His comrades in this county will recognize in this a personal appreciation of the soldier which was always manifest in their brave and true commander, who shared with the rank and file all the dangers and privations, and was first to give to the men the credit for the glories and fortunes of war."

Had Colonel Love published this poem during his life he probably would have dedicated it not only to the local veterans of the Civil War, but also to the Muhlenberg men in the Mexican War.

THE OLD SOLDIERS.

By S. P. Love.

Our ranks are growing thinner
    Every year,
And death is still a winner
    Every year,
Yet we still must stick together
Like the toughest kind of leather,
And in any kind of weather,
    Every year.

Our comrades have departed
    Every year,
And left us broken-hearted
    Every year,
But their spirits fondly greet us
And constantly entreat us
To come, that they may meet us,
    Every year.

Our steps are growing slower
    Every year,
Pale death is still a mower
    Every year,
Yet we faced him in the battle,
Amid the muskets' rattle,
And defied his final edict,
    Every year.

We are growing old and lonely
    Every year,
We have recollections only
    Every year,
That we bled for this great nation
On many a field and station
And with any kind of ration
    Every year.

Many people may forget us
    Every year,
And our enemies may fret us
    Every year,
But while onward we are drifting,
Our souls with hope are lifting
To heavenly scenes, still shifting,
    Every year.

In the May-time of the flowers
    Every year,
We shall live in golden hours
    Every year,
And our deeds be sung in story
Down the ages growing hoary—
With a blaze of living glory
    Every year.

COLONEL ROBERT M. MARTIN. For portrait see page 319.

HENRY C. MCCRACKEN was born May 28, 1838, in Pulaski County, Tennessee, and emigrated to Muhlenberg in 1856. He enlisted in Company K, Eleventh Kentucky Infantry (Federal), at Calhoun in 1861, and lost his right arm at the battle of Shiloh, April 7, 1862, shortly after which he was honorably discharged. In August, 1888, he was elected magistrate and served for two years. In 1896-97 he represented Muhlenberg in the Legislature. He was engaged in farming near Murphy's Lake until 1902, when he moved to Greenville. No man in the county has taken more interest in the local G. A. R. Post than Mr. McCracken. In 1866 he married Laura E. Green, daughter of William J. Green. Among their children are Captain Richard C. McCracken, contractor, and A. Elmer McCracken, jeweler, of Greenville.

HENRY C. McCRACKEN, 1861

CAPTAIN ISAAC MILLER was born in Tennessee in 1810 and came to Muhlenberg about 1832. He lived on a farm west of Bremen the greater part of his life, and died in South Carrollton in 1887. He was captain of Company F, Third Kentucky Cavalry (Federal), until he was wounded at Murfreesboro, when he resigned and was succeeded by Captain Elisha Baker, of Greenville. Captain Miller was for many years connected with the old militia musters. He married Bettie Crumbaker, daughter of Jacob Crumbaker. Among their children were: William T. (who was jailer from 1897 to 1905); James, who was a member of Company F; Alfred and Simon Miller; Mrs. Nancy (William) Short, Mrs. Malty (Anderson) Miller, Mrs. Mary (Wesley M. [son of N. B.]) Little, Mrs. Jennie (Jacob) Gish, and Mrs. Katie (Wm. G.) Whitmer—Mr. Whitmer also being a member of Company F. One of Captain Miller's brothers was James M., the father of John Simon Miller, who was jailer of the county from 1874 to 1882 and Greenville's postmaster from 1898 to 1912.

ISAAC MILLER, 1861

CAPTAIN JOSEPH MITCHELL was born in North Carolina, December 14, 1809, and came to Muhlenberg from Tennessee in 1846. He served as a colonel at many of the old militia musters. In the fall of 1863 he organized Company I, Forty-eighth Kentucky Mounted Infantry (Federal), of which he was made captain. He lived in the upper Pond Creek country and was one of the well-known farmers of the county. He died November 12, 1863. Among his children are Mrs. W. T. McWhirter and Mrs. Saluda A. Pace, who was the second wife of Edward O. Pace. Judge Richard O. Pace is a son of Edward O. and Saluda A. Pace. Isaac Mitchell, who was killed in the battle of Sacramento, was Captain Mitchell's brother.

JOSEPH F. RICHARDSON was born in Logan County in 1840 and died at his home in Central City on April 26, 1912. He was buried in his Con-

JOSEPH MITCHELL, 1861

federate uniform in Elmwood Cemetery, Owensboro. At the breaking out of the war he enlisted in Company A, Ninth Kentucky Infantry (Confederate), one of the regiments belonging to what was later known as the Orphan Brigade. He received a wound during the first day's battle at Shiloh which necessitated the immediate amputation of his left arm. He moved to Muhlenberg in 1864 and taught school for a number of years. In 1874 he was elected county superintendent of schools. In 1885 he moved to Daviess County, and seven years later returned to Central City. In 1900 he served as doorkeeper of the State Senate.

JOSEPH F. RICHARDSON, 1861

He represented Muhlenberg in the House of Representatives from January, 1910, to January, 1912. In January, 1912, he was chosen doorkeeper of the House of Representatives. In 1871 he married Jennie H. Morgan. Mrs. S. A. Burns, of Daviess County, and Miss Lulu Richardson, of Central City, are daughters of Mr. and Mrs. J. F. Richardson. "Uncle Joe," as he was called by his many friends, young and old, was a unique character, and one of the most highly respected men in the county.

J. L. ROARK, 1863   M. J. ROARK, 1863

LIEUTENANT JAMES LOUIS ROARK, son of John R. Roark and grandson of pioneer William Roark, was born in Muhlenberg County April 14, 1840, and died in Greenville on April 5, 1893. In 1861 he enlisted at Calhoun and was elected first lieutenant of Company K, Eleventh Kentucky Infantry (Federal), which office he held until his regiment was mustered out. On account of disabilities received in service he did not reënlist. He was in his day the best-known funeral director in the county. J. L. Roark married Jennie E. Morgan, daughter of Wm. K. Morgan. Their children are: Orien L., Cecil E., and Charles W. Roark of Greenville, and Doctor J. Louis Roark, now of Seattle, Washington.

CAPTAIN MARTIN JEFFERSON ROARK, son of pioneer William Roark, was born in Muhlenberg County June 26, 1833, and died in Greenville on October 22, 1908. He enlisted at Calhoun in 1861 and was elected captain of Company K, Eleventh Kentucky Infantry (Federal). He was severely wounded at Shiloh on April 7, 1862, and afterward was honorably discharged. Shortly after his return home he was made deputy provost marshal of Greenville. While a young man Captain Roark taught school in the county. In 1866-67 he represented Muhlenberg in the Legislature, after which he devoted his time to the practice of law and to the duties of the various county offices to which he was elected. Captain M. J. Roark and his wife Nannie W. (Davis) Roark were the parents of Professor R. N. Roark.

CAPTAIN WASHINGTON COLUMBUS SHANNON was born in Wilson County, Tennessee, October 4, 1838, and moved to Muhlenberg in 1854. On October 1, 1861, he enlisted at Calhoun as a private in Company K, Eleventh Kentucky Infantry (Federal), and after the battle of Shiloh became first sergeant of his company, which place he held until July, 1863, when he was commissioned first lieutenant and served in that capacity until December, when upon the death of Captain C. H. Martin he succeeded to the captaincy. On December 16, 1864, his term of enlistment having expired, he was mustered out at Bowling Green. He immediately reëntered the army and was commissioned captain of Company K, Seventeenth Kentucky Cavalry, and served until the close of the war, since which time he has lived in the Pond River country. Captain Shannon at various times has served the county as deputy assessor and deputy sheriff.

W. C. SHANNON, 1864

LIEUTENANT EUCLID E. C. SHULL was born at Paradise, October 29, 1842. He is a son of Peter Shull, jr., and a grandson of pioneer Peter Shull. On September 1, 1861, he enlisted in Company B, Twenty-sixth Kentucky U. S. V. I. He filled a number of regimental positions. On February 26, 1865, he became first lieutenant of Company G, U. S. Cavalry. He was mustered out of service September 28, 1865, since which time he has conducted the hotel in Paradise. During his more active years he was extensively engaged in farming. Few persons have visited Paradise within the past forty-five years without having had the pleasure of meeting Mr. and Mrs. Shull.

E. E. C. SHULL, 1862

WILLIAM H. SMITH was born near Paradise, September 30, 1841. He is a son of Leonard Smith and a grandson of pioneer Aaron Smith. He was a member of Company I, Eleventh Kentucky Infantry (Federal). His farm on Green River below Airdrie is one of the best preserved of the old farms in the county. Few men living along Green River are better known than "Billy" Smith, as he is called by his many friends. One of his nearest neighbors was General Buell, under whom he had fought during the first part of the Civil War and after whom his youngest son, Don Carlos R., is named. Mrs. Mary E. Humphrey, one of the most progressive women in the town of Paradise, is one of his daughters.

WILLIAM H. SMITH, 1862

JOHN L. G. THOMPSON was born in Clermont County, Ohio, August 15, 1836, and removed to Muhlenberg in 1858. While visiting in Illinois he enlisted in Company G, Second Illinois Cavalry (Federal). After the close of the Civil War he returned to his farm in Muhlenberg, and has ever since ranked among the best farmers in the county. His wife was Anna Woodburn, daughter of J. T. Woodburn, sr.

R. W. WALLACE was born near South Carrollton, October 5, 1829, and died at Paradise on July 13, 1876. He was a son of Jared and Polly (Dearing) Wallace. His grandfathers, Coulston Wallace and Bayless Dearing, came to Muhlenberg about 1808. He was a Confederate soldier—a member of Company C, Ninth Kentucky Infantry. Although a cripple, he took part in a number of battles. He had a store in Paradise, and at the time of his death was one of the leading merchants in the town. In 1866 he married Mary E. Kirtley, daughter of Elias V. Kirtley. R. W. Wallace and wife were the parents of Mrs. Gertrude W. (J. B.) Hocker of Owensboro, and R. E., J. E., and H. A. Wallace, well-known Muhlenberg merchants.

JOHN L. G. THOMPSON, 1861

R. T. VINCENT. For portrait see page 330.
COLONEL E. R. WEIR. For portrait see page 61.
JOHN K. WICKLIFFE. For portrait see page 256.
J. L. WILKINS. For portrait see page 330.

LIEUTENANT JOSEPH DAVIS YONTS was born near Paradise, October 25, 1841, and died in Greenville June 9, 1896. When the Eleventh Kentucky Infantry (Federal) was organizing he enlisted as a private in Company H, and after the battle of Shiloh became first lieutenant. Although he was wounded a number of times, he remained with his company until the close of the war. Immediately after the war he removed to Greenville, and for more than thirty years took an active interest in the business affairs of the town. In 1865 he became a clerk in the store of Edward R. Weir, sr., and continued in that work until the Greenville Grange Store was organized. He and Joseph G. Ellison managed this coöperative store during the few years of its existence. In the

R. W. WALLACE, 1865

JOSEPH D. YONTS, 1864

latter part of the seventies he and his brother, Edward L. Yonts, began rehandling tobacco in Greenville, and continued in that business until 1880, when they opened a drug store on the northeast corner of Main and Main Cross streets. A few years later he bought his brother's interest in this store, and remained in the drug business until the time of his death. Joseph D. Yonts was a son of Philip Yonts and his wife Adaline Davis Yonts. In 1872 he married Delia L. Kingsley, daughter of Edward Kingsley of Rochester and his wife Mary Susan Myers, daughter of David Myers of Myers' Chapel. Their only son is Morton K. Yonts, now of the Louisville bar.

XXVI

SLAVERY DAYS

A FEW slaves were probably brought by the first of the early settlers into what later became Muhlenberg County. Tradition has it that Colonel William Campbell, the founder of Caney Station and Greenville, brought slaves with him. A number of the other first-comers evidently brought slaves with them. There were very few, however, in what was called the "Dutch Settlement."

In 1800 there were 1,313 white inhabitants, five free negroes, and 125 slaves in Muhlenberg. By 1810 the white population had increased to 3,698 and there were 480 slaves. From that date to 1850 there was an increase in the proportion of slaves. In 1860 the population of the county was 9,101 white, 40 free colored, and 1,584 slaves. In 1910 the white population was 25,687 and the colored 2,911.[1]

In slavery days many persons who did not want to own negroes, or who did not approve of slavery, found themselves slaveholders. The slaves were acquired by inheritance or in the course of some business transaction as a necessity. It was not easy to dispose of a slave once owned, except by selling him as one would a horse or a cow.

Many stories might be told of the affectionate relations and personal devotion that sprang up between master and family and slave. It was not uncommon for masters who "hired out" slaves by the year, or were compelled to sell them, to consult the slave's choice of employer or new master. The "hiring out" and sale of slaves generally took place at New Year at Greenville, where there was a general assembling of those wanting to hire or buy, and a regular market opened. Administrators of estates would sometimes sell from one to a whole family of negroes to the highest bidder, at the courthouse door. Selling prices would range from $200 to $1,500. Hiring prices were from $50 to $200, according to the slave's worth. Richard T. Martin says: "In case of sale, as well as of hire, mothers would often be separated from their children. Most of the slaves seemed to be submissive to their fate and apparently enjoyed life as well as they do now with liberty. They were of course ignorant, without any training in self-reliance or self-protection. They did not then have much on their minds, only to do as they were told."

---

[1] The slave population in Muhlenberg was never proportionately large, ranging from one in five to one in seven of the whole population. The proportion in the State was about one slave to every five of population. The negro population of Muhlenberg and of Kentucky at present comprises about one eighth of the whole. In 1860 Muhlenberg's proportion was at the rate of one slave to every seven of population. See table of population of the county in chapter "Collins on Muhlenberg, Quoted and Extended," page 422.

The consideration that masters would show trusted slaves, and the affectionate feelings existing, have been verified from the recollections of a number of old former slaves still living in the county. All of them say they had a longing to remain in their first home or in the neighborhood where they had spent most of their lives. Local traditions contain many instances of the slave's love for his old home. An incident in the life of John Oates, one of the "old-time" negroes, will serve as an example.

"Uncle John," as he is called, still lives near the Wyatt Oates Old Place in the Pond River country, where he was born about 1845 and where, as he expressed it, he hopes to die "among his white folks." John's father belonged to pioneer Jesse Oates, and John in turn belonged to Wyatt Oates, one of the sons of Jesse. During the autumn of 1862 John, then a boy of about eighteen, while working near his master's blacksmith shop, was kidnaped by a band of guerrillas, who at the same time stole two horses belonging to Wyatt Oates. The young negro traveled with his captors through Hopkins, Christian, and Todd counties, and although not treated as a prisoner he was anxious to return home, and therefore took advantage of the first good chance that presented itself and made his escape. He left the guerrilla camp, then near Elkton, and although he avoided the public roads, succeeded in finding his way through the woods and over fields to what is now Cary's Bridge, where he entered Muhlenberg County. There he began traveling on the main road, for he was known in that neighborhood and felt safe from pursuers. He had not proceeded far when he arrived at the farm of a man who was well acquainted with his master. The owner of the place seemed glad to see him, and urged him to eat supper and stay all night. He accepted the invitation, and his friendly host informed him that Wyatt Oates was offering fifteen dollars reward for the return of his "lost, strayed or stolen John." The farmer proposed to lodge John that night and to return him to his master the next morning, receive the reward, and pay the slave five dollars of the proceeds. To this the slave replied that he thought his involuntary absence was in itself a loss to his master, and that

"UNCLE" JOHN OATES, 1912

under the circumstances no one was entitled to a reward. After he had been assigned a bed, and after all others had retired for the night, John quietly resumed his walk home, where upon his arrival he was received like a long-lost son by his master, who not only paid him the fifteen dollars reward but granted him two weeks' "lay-off" after hearing his story.

Notwithstanding the kindness shown, the slaves, after all, were held in ownership much as highly prized domestic animals are, and were treated in everything, except as regarded their work, as children requiring strict discipline and sometimes sharp punishment. They had no civil or educational rights or privileges. Slave-owners generally frowned upon the few who permitted slaves to be taught reading and writing, as the awakening of higher intelligence tended to arouse the slave's discontent with his condition and to give him longings for freedom. There was little or no attempt made to educate or Christianize the slave. He was left to his own devices, and even his morals—except as to personal honesty and conduct toward the whites—were disregarded. Slaves could not marry according to law. They cohabited by consent of their owners or according to their own choice, though many slave unions were as sacredly maintained as those of the white people.

Religion among them was a rude imitation of the worship of the whites. They were permitted to hold church meetings in schoolhouses and in white churches temporarily unoccupied. "Copper John," as he was called, who belonged to Edward R. Weir, Sam Elliott, owned by Edward Elliott, Peter McCormick, and Wilson Weir were the leading slave preachers for many years. They were men of some intelligence, and would preach in various parts of the county.

Slaves were housed usually in log cabins erected near the owner's residence. Edward R. Weir, sr., provided good brick, one-story houses for those he owned. The last of these brick slave cabins has disappeared, and only a few of the log huts are left standing in the county.

No slave could give testimony in court against a white man, and he was therefore without defense against brutal treatment of any kind unless it occurred in the presence of white witnesses. Any slave convicted of murder, attempt to murder, or of assault on a white woman was after trial in the circuit court sentenced to death, and a valuation placed on him by those before whom he was tried. The owner of the slave, upon presentation of the sheriff's certificate showing the date of execution and the appraised value, received from the State Treasurer the amount specified. The first legal hanging in the county was of a slave named Isaac, who was convicted of an attempt to murder Aylette H. Buckner, and, as related in the chapter on the "Story of the Stack," was valued at $1,000 and hanged July 6, 1838. The second legal execution was that of a slave known as Mitchell Martin, or Bogges, who was hanged April 26, 1850, and valued at $700. The third was a slave called Edmond Reno, or Edmond Elliott, who was hanged June 17, 1853, and his master, Jesse H. Reno, received $800 as compensation. All of these but Isaac were convicted of criminal assault.

Out of the slave's helplessness before the law there sprang up among many of them a unity of feeling almost Masonic, against cruel and harsh masters. Such masters were feared and hated, and among slave cabins, and even in the kitchen of the "big house," as the owner's residence was called, slave and white children alike were held in discipline and fear by stories of "ghost hauntings" of cruel slaveholders. The feeling extended to white men who were merely rigid disciplinarians, not sparing of the lash when they thought its use necessary. The ghost-stories were of course pure imaginings. One story that has long been heard of a haunted house near an old muster field evidently grew out of a substitution of identities, since the owner of the house was a liberal and kind-hearted man who, I found after careful investigation, always treated his slaves well. Nevertheless the story is told that he had caused two of his slaves to be buried

SLAVE CABINS BUILT ABOUT 1840 ON THE DOCTOR R. C. FRAZIER FARM
Near Powderly

near the milk-house in order to keep other slaves from entering and helping themselves to its contents. This tale is as improbable as the one that relates how, on a certain occasion, the same owner, wishing to punish a slave, took a barrel, drove two-inch nails from the outside through the one-inch staves, placed the negro in this barrel, and rolled it down the hill to the spring near the milk-house. The story is that the negro died from the effects of the treatment, and of course the place has been "ha'nted" ever since.

About twenty years before the beginning of the Civil War the mutterings of the movement for national emancipation of slaves began and rapidly grew louder. The idea had many followers in Muhlenberg and other parts of Kentucky. In 1845 Cassius M. Clay established an antislavery paper at Lexington, and by his fiery personality, eloquence, and fearlessness made many converts and induced many who already believed in emancipation by some gradual and businesslike method to take a bold stand publicly. By 1850 antislavery opinion had spread widely in the State and was openly discussed in Muhlenberg. In his diary, under date of June, 1849, the Reverend Isaac Bard records that at Colonel Wilson's home, near South Carrollton, "we debated emancipation. My great surprise is how any true Whig or true Democrat can oppose it. . . . They say if Kentucky should emancipate her slaves we would be ruined. Bob Wickliffe said, 'The darkies are the best shade I have ever seen.' . . . But I think some more sunshine would be better for health and a cure for empty corn-cribs and barns as well as a good cure for ignorant, idle and dissipated youth." Mr. Bard was traveling much of the time and was in close touch with public subjects.[2]

In Muhlenberg among prominent men who advocated emancipation were Edward R. Weir, sr., William L. Green, Edward Elliott, and Thomas Salsbury.[3] The latter died in 1848, and his will, dated May 30, 1844, provided for the immediate liberation, after the death of his wife, of all his slaves who had then reached the age of twenty-five, and for the later

---

[2] Robert Wickliffe, here referred to by Mr. Bard, was a son of pioneer Robert Wickliffe, and like his father was a slaveholder. He, like a number of slaveholders in the county, became an abolitionist about ten years before the Civil War.

Robert Wickliffe's will (that part dealing with his slaves) is here quoted as throwing light on the slavery question at the time. It was written in 1850 and recorded in 1855, in Will Book 3, page 153:

"Section Two: I will and direct, that after the death of my wife that all of my property (Negroes excepted) be sold, including my land, the proceeds to be applied as hereinafter directed.

"Section Three: I wish to provide for the comfort and happiness of my slaves, and wish the money arising from the sale of my other property as mentioned in section two applied for their benefit. I wish to colonize them, should the newly established Republic of Liberia continue to flourish. I desire that they may be removed to that country and the money raised from sale of property as before directed applied to their outfit and settlement in that country. I hereby will and direct that at the death of myself and wife all the slaves now owned by me and their increase shall be free and enjoy all the rights and privileges of free persons, but believing that they can do this but imperfectly in Kentucky I wish them removed to some country where they will be more advantageously situated, and for the purpose of providing for this and for their comfortable establishment do will and bequeath to them the proceeds of all my other property remaining after the death of myself and wife for the purposes aforesaid.

"Section Four: As it is likely that some important changes will be made in the organic law of our State by which negroes can not be emancipated and remain in the State, I hereby invest my executors with full and complete power to make such arrangements in regard to the future location of my slaves as may to them seem best, all circumstances considered, vesting them with power to send them to Liberia or colonize them in some other State as may be deemed most for their interest, retaining such control over said slaves as may be necessary to carry out the provisions of this section."

His wife, Aggy Wickliffe, in September, 1862, made her will bequeathing all her property "to and for the use of the slaves emancipated by the will of my deceased husband." Her will is recorded June 13, 1867, Book 3, page 230.

[3] Mrs. Salsbury (who was a daughter of John Dennis) died January 16, 1860, and the Salsbury tract of land, three miles southeast of Greenville, was divided among the freed negroes and the to-be-freed slaves. In 1910 only one family of Salsbury negroes lived in the "Salsbury Free Negro Settlement." The others, one after another, sold their farms to white men, and few, if any, ever owned a farm afterward. It may be well to add that Mr. and Mrs. Thomas Salsbury had no children, nor did Mr. and Mrs. Robert Wickliffe.

liberation of the others when they too had reached that age. Weir, Green, and Elliott were so convinced of their duty that they liberated all their slaves that were willing to accept freedom. They sent a few of them to the new Republic of Liberia in Africa, defraying their expenses, and then Green and Elliott removed to "free" States.

As early as about 1850 there began to arise fears of a "negro rising" or "slave insurrection" in many parts of the country, even in Muhlenberg. These rumors served to alarm many quiet persons and to frighten children, but there was never any "rising." Close watch was maintained and slaves were kept within rigid bounds. Runaway slaves would come into Muhlenberg from the South and from other counties in the State, but they were soon captured or driven from the county. In Greenville and all the towns in the county "patrollers" were paid to watch the conduct of slaves. Negroes were not allowed to stir out after nine o'clock at night. If caught abroad after that hour without passes from their owners they were severely whipped and driven in. The negroes living in the country did not go out much after nightfall except for "possum" and "coon" hunting, with the knowledge of their owners.

About this time a sort of temperance "order" had been established among the negroes. It had its start in Greenville. There were two bodies, apparently rival organizations. One was known as the "Washingtonians," headed by "Copper John" Weir; the other, known as the "Socodonians," was led by Sam Elliott. These orders appeared throughout the county. Members of both would meet at Greenville on Sundays and march, making considerable display. When the "abolition" movement had grown acute, however, the whites put a stop to the marchings, and the "orders" vanished. It was feared that they covered some secret understanding concerning freedom.

Suspicion and distrust between master and slave grew greater as a general proposition, although that fact did not disturb the confidence between some slaves and their masters. The Civil War put an end to all doubts and to the institution of slavery. There were many negroes in Muhlenberg who did not welcome freedom, and who were uneasy after it was conferred upon them. They had suffered like children, but they had had no sense of responsibility for their own maintenance. Some of the more intelligent had believed that some day they would be liberated, but they were not prepared when liberation came. A great many of the slaves never had to be punished while in slavery, but were obedient and kind-hearted and were treated well by their owners, some of whom often trusted particular slaves with important affairs.

It is paradoxical perhaps to say that many persons, former slaves as well as slave-owners, regretted the passing of the old days. As they got further and further away from slavery only its best and most sentimental sides were remembered. In the old days slaves were generally allowed a few holidays during Christmas week and at election days, which came on the first Monday in August in each year. Election days were always a feast for white boys and negroes. Slave-owners would allow their negroes, if they desired, to make cider and bake "ginger-cakes" on Saturday or

Sunday before the election on Monday, from the sale of which they would make a little pocket-money. Greenville would be full of boys and negroes, ginger-cakes and cider; fiddling and dancing on the streets would be an attraction of the occasion. Negroes were not allowed to drink or quarrel or to fight; if they did they were severely whipped. Negroes on election day kept more civil and sober than some of their masters. Sometimes a sober slave would have to care for his drunken master and take him home. These conditions and others connected with the intimate home relations between master and slave before the Civil War were of course entirely changed by the emancipation of the negroes.

XXVII

LOCAL WRITERS AND THE LOCAL PRESS

IT is likely that some of Muhlenberg's first-comers, and certainly some of the generation that followed them, occasionally wrote sketches; perhaps some expressed themselves in poetry—or, at least, in the form of verse. As far as I am aware, less than a half-dozen unpublished manuscripts and published pamphlets and sketches written by Muhlenberg men previous to 1850 have been preserved. Very little of what appeared in print between 1850 and 1870 can now be found. Up to 1870 no newspapers were printed in the county, and therefore comparatively few of the citizens who may have written prose or poetry previous to that time had opportunity to publish it. The files of the various local newspapers issued from 1870 to 1899 have been destroyed, and with them all the local literature they contained.

Pioneer James Weir was not only the first Muhlenberg man to write verses, but he also stands as the first and only local pioneer by whom sketches were written that are still preserved. His account of his trip, written shortly after his return from New Orleans in 1803, is given in full in Appendix B. His two sons—Edward R. Weir, sr., the author of a number of sketches published about the year 1840, and James Weir, who in 1850 published "Lonz Powers"—were men of literary ability. Their books and magazine stories are now out of circulation, and are reviewed or referred to elsewhere in this volume. Max Weir, a grandson of pioneer James Weir, was the author of "From the Father's Country," a pamphlet of a religious nature, published in 1904 and still preserved by many of his friends. Another grandson, Doctor James Weir, of Owensboro, has written several books of curious interest to medical and other professional students.

Stembridge's "The Western Speller" appeared in 1854. This book was compiled by John A. Stembridge, who was born in Muhlenberg in 1813 and died in Greenville in 1872. He was the only son of William Stembridge. His wife was a daughter of Larkin N. Akers. Their son, William junior, died in early manhood. Their two daughters removed to Evansville, Indiana, about 1875, and were connected with the public schools of that city for more than thirty years. John A. Stembridge, like his father, was a schoolteacher.

"The Western Speller" was written in Greenville in 1852 and published in 1854 by J. W. Boswell, of Hebardsville, Henderson County. The printing was done by Hull & Brothers and the binding by Hull Brothers & Caril, of Louisville. The "Preface" and "Recommendations" are here quoted in full:

PREFACE.

We live in an age of improvement, and as there have been improvements made on almost all theories, the author of this work thought that there could be an improvement made on the Spelling Books that are published by various authors. He had two reasons for writing this Book. The first reason, he saw some defects in all the various spellers. The most important reason was his ill health—not being able, for the last three years and a half, to labor. He came to the conclusion to write a Spelling Book on a new plan, which he has done, hoping that a generous public would examine it, and give his book the preference, as he knows of no other tribunal that would judge more correctly. With these remarks he submits it to the same.

GREENVILLE, KY., August, 1852.   THE AUTHOR.

RECOMMENDATIONS.

We have examined the spelling book compiled by Mr. John A. Stembridge, and consider it a valuable book. It contains a great variety of the most useful words, disposed in such order as will much facilitate the learner's progress in spelling and pronunciation. A large number of proper and Geographical names are appended. We think it an elementary book worthy of the attention of parents and Teachers.

GREENVILLE, KY., August, 1852.

Rev. John Donaldson, Principal Greenville Presbyterial Academy, Ky.
S. P. Love, Teacher Common Schools, Greenville, Ky.
B. E. Pittman, Common School Commissioner, Greenville, Ky.
Chas. F. Wing, Clerk Muhlenberg Circuit Court.
Wm. H. C. Wing, Clerk County Court.
A. C. DeWitt, Sec. Louisville Annual Con. M. E. C. South.
W. H. Yost.
Jonathan Short.
Joseph Ricketts.
Jesse H. Reno, P. J.
Edward Rumsey.
J. F. Kimbley, M. D.

All admit that Noah Webster has had to do with the foundation and elementary principles of the English Language, by his famed Spelling Book. And as improvements have been made on the theories of Newton, Galileo, Franklin, and Sir Humphry Davy, it is no disparagement to Dr. Webster, to say, we think an improvement has been made on his Book, by an humble but intelligent citizen of Muhlenberg County, Ky. The main important trait that distinguishes the work, as it appears to us, is its classification of words, Proper Names in Scripture, Geographical Names, and lastly a happy combination of words of our language, all so neatly and perspicuously arranged as to facilitate the young learner. Well done for Muhlenberg County, Kentucky.

ISAAC BARD, Pastor Mt. Pleasant Church and
Agent of Muhlenberg Presbytery.

I concur in the above recommendation of said book.

REV. C. C. BOSWELL, of the C. P. Church, Pastor
of Pleasant Hill Congregation.

This speller is a neatly bound book of 154 pages and contains about fifteen thousand words, classified in a convenient and original manner. Common words are arranged according to the number of syllables and the place of the accented syllable. Names of rivers, towns, mountains, etc., are given by continents or States, and are so placed that they, in a way, serve as lessons in geography. For example, under the three columns headed "States," "Capitals," and "People" are "Tennessee, Nashville, Tennesseeans," "Peru, Lima, Peruvians." Among the various other divisions appear many Biblical names, the names of the Presidents up to that date, and an "Alphabetical Vocabulary" in which he defines about one thousand words.

Although "The Western Speller" was regarded as "superior to any other now in use," as stated on the title-page, it was never widely known. It was used more or less extensively in Muhlenberg and adjoining counties from the time it was published up to about 1860, when its use was abandoned and Webster's American Spelling Book, better known as the "Old Blue-backed Speller," was again adopted in all the local schools. But two copies of Stembridge's book are now extant, so far as I have been able to ascertain.

It is probable that during the third quarter of the last century Buxton Harris wrote more for publication than any other one man in the county. He came to Muhlenberg in 1848. It is said that he was a good public speaker, that many of his poems and stories were printed in some of the then widely known newspapers and magazines, and that copies of his published works were preserved by him; all of them were destroyed thirteen years after his death, when his residence was burned to the ground. And now, after a lapse of less than fifty years, no one can recall the titles of more than two of his stories—"The Buried Trunk," and "Emma Legure, or the Lost Child."

Buxton Harris was born in Virginia in 1807, and at the age of forty-one he and his family moved from Tennessee to Muhlenberg County. He bought the Luckett farm (now the town of Powderly) and continued to live on it up to the time of his death, December 29, 1874. Before the emancipation of his slaves he was considered one of the wealthiest men in the county. Of his twelve children Bennett Harris, of Central City, and N. J. Harris, of Wichita, Kansas, are the only two now living.

In 1898 Professor William J. Johnson, then residing at Wells, published his "History of Hazel Creek Baptist Church," a pamphlet of 70 pages. It is the only history of a Muhlenberg church ever printed, and furthermore is the only pamphlet ever written that bears directly on the history of the county.

Professor Ruric Nevel Roark, son of Captain M. J. Roark, wrote three books on pedagogy—"Psychology in Education," "Method in Education," and "Economy in Education." These books were published in 1903, 1904, and 1905 by the American Book Company, and are considered standard works, not only in Kentucky but in other States and in some foreign countries.

No man in Kentucky was better known or more highly esteemed in educational circles than was Professor Roark. He contributed to many of the educational journals, and had a national reputation as a lecturer on educational subjects. He started the movement that resulted in the organizing of the Southern Educational Association. E. Polk Johnson, in his "History of Kentucky and Kentuckians," says: "Dr. Ruric N. Roark, the first president of the Eastern Kentucky State Normal School and a great educational leader, who took a pioneer interest in the establishment of State normal schools, . . . died while in the harness, and while fighting for the children of Kentucky."

RURIC N. ROARK, 1906

Professor Roark was born in Greenville, May 19, 1859, and after finishing a course of study in the Greenville Academy attended the National Normal University in Ohio, from which institution he was graduated in 1881. He was president of the Glasgow Normal School for three years, and from 1889 to 1904 served as dean of the department of pedagogy in the Kentucky State College. He was president of the Eastern Kentucky State Normal School at Richmond when, on April 14, 1909, he died after an illness of only a few weeks. He is buried at Richmond.

Among other pamphlets by Muhlenberg citizens are "Doctrines of the Cumberland Presbyterian Church," by Reverend J. E. Martin (son of David H. Martin) (1882); "A Treatise on Monometallism and Bimetallism," by Nicholas Royster (1898); "The World Lies Before Us," "The World Lies Behind Us," and "Down on Devil's Creek," by Theodore W. Whitmer (1899); "Sundry Sketches and Paragraphs," by J. R. Parker(1899); "The New Birth," by J. W. York (1902); "Outline of United States History," by Professor C. C. Hayden (1910); "Lost and Found, and Other Sketches," by Elsie J. James (1912). To this list may be added Edward Rumsey's speech on the invention of the steamboat, delivered before Congress in 1839 and published shortly afterward in pamphlet form, and also a number of booklets on medical subjects written during the past fifteen years by Doctor James Osborne DeCourcy, of St. Louis, who until a few years ago lived near Rosewood, where he was born.

In 1912 "Nisi Prius," an admirable collection of connected sketches, was published by J. Caldwell Browder, of Russellville. This book, although not by a Muhlenberg man, is here referred to because the scenes in the story are laid in Greenville and other parts of Muhlenberg County, or, as the author designates them, "Greenwood" and "Mecklenburg County." It is a story based on the happenings in a term of circuit court at Greenville in what the lawyers call "proceedings at nisi prius," hence the title.

All the poems by local writers that have been published and are still preserved were written within the past twenty-five years. Most of them were written since 1900. "Thou and I," by General Buell, appears in the chapter on the "Paradise Country and Old Airdrie"; "The Old Soldiers," by Judge Love, is given in the chapter on "Some of Muhlenberg's Civil War Soldiers," "God's Plow of Sorrow" appears in the chapter on Charles Eaves, and "The Cypress Trees" by Harry M. Dean is reprinted in "Collins Quoted and Extended." Mrs. Lou J. Mitchell and Clarence B. Hayes are each represented in Muhlenberg's published literature by a pamphlet of poems. These two writers were well known locally. Neither was born in the county, but both of them lived and died in Muhlenberg.

Mrs. Lou J. Mitchell was born in Logan County, June 24, 1852, and died near Friendship on April 24, 1910. Before her marriage to John W. Mitchell, of Muhlenberg, she taught school near Russellville. Shortly after she was married she became totally blind. About twenty years ago Mr. and Mrs. Mitchell moved to a farm in the Friendship neighborhood. After Mrs. Mitchell lost her eyesight she occupied much of her time writing verses. In 1892 twenty-four of these were published in a pamphlet entitled, "A Selection of Poems from the works of Mrs. Lou J. Mitchell, the Blind Poetess." Some of her verses describe the consolation she found in religion; others are optimistic reflections of one dwelling "in shadow-land."

Clarence B. Hayes—better known as "Peck" Hayes—was born in Hodgenville, Kentucky, July 23, 1878. In 1894 he moved to Muhlenberg with his father, J. H. Hayes. While serving as chief bugler under General F. D. Grant in the Spanish-American War he contracted tuberculosis, of which he died at his home in Greenville on February 10, 1908. He was a promising young man and a good musician. He wrote the words and music of a number of songs, among them "Mammy's Lullaby," which he dedicated to John G. Barkley, sr., and published in 1906. In March, 1908, Orien L. Roark, of the Greenville Record, issued "Some Verses by Clarence B. Hayes." This pamphlet contains fifteen of his poems. Had he lived longer he might have achieved wide fame as a dialect poet.

CLARENCE B. HAYES, 1905

Among Muhlenbergers who have in recent years contributed more or less to the local papers are Miss Amy M. Longest, of Powderly; Richard T. Martin and Harry M. Dean, of Greenville; John B. Kittinger, of Central City, and William H. Hoskinson, of Gus. Much of that which Mr. Martin has written is reprinted in this volume. Miss Longest is a student of good literature and local history, and is deeply interested in improving educational conditions in the county. She has published only a few poems and sketches in the local and metropolitan papers, but these few foretell a brilliant literary career. Harry M. Dean, although still a young man, is the most versatile writer Muhlenberg has ever produced. A number of his poems, stories, and sketches have appeared in some of the best-known papers in the country. Since the death of Clarence B. Hayes, Mr. Dean has been looked upon as the poet-laureate of Muhlenberg.

A "last week's paper," like a "last year's almanac," having served its purpose, is put to other uses or relegated to the waste-basket and soon disappears. Occasionally a copy is laid away with great care by a reader who for the sake of some specific article it contains, fully intends to pre-

PART OF FIRST PAGE OF MUHLENBERG'S FIRST NEWSPAPER
(Reduced Facsimile)

serve it. It is a well-known fact, however, that very few of such copies are preserved longer than a year or two. The same may also be said of clippings from papers. Although clippings are usually preserved longer than the entire copy of a paper, they are as a rule not marked to show when and where they were published, and as a consequence the information they contain does not fully serve its purpose. Unfortunately, like many of the old books and pamphlets that should have been preserved, many of the newspapers and clippings now being "preserved" seem destined to disappear sooner or later.

About twenty different newspapers have been printed in the county since 1870. Most of them lived only a few years. The Greenville Record, now in its fifteenth year, has existed longer by far than any other paper previously printed in Muhlenberg. Central City's Twice-a-Week Argus, formerly the Muhlenberg Argus, dates back seven years. Notwithstanding there were probably as many as several million copies of these various local papers printed and read, it is doubtful whether a hundred copies of the discontinued publications could now be found. Nevertheless each newspaper, in its day, had its influence on the people of the county. All of the Muhlenberg papers, regardless of their time or extent of circulation, are still remembered—some by one man, some by another.

The Kentucky Republican was the first paper published in the county. It was a weekly, established by W. L. Anthony and printed in Greenville. The first copy was issued March 16, 1870. Anthony was succeeded by

M. D. Hay, who printed a paper which, although styled "The Independent," was a Democratic sheet. The Independent was succeeded by the Gazette, a Democratic weekly conducted by John O'Flaherty. The Muhlenberg Echo was founded about 1876, and up to October, 1881, was edited by Urey Woodson, now editor of the Owensboro Messenger, and who is one of the best-known politicians in the country. Woodson was followed by C. W. Short, and he in turn by William H. Eaves, R. Y. Thomas, jr., Hayden C. Snoddy, and Orien L. Roark. The Muhlenberg Echo was succeeded by The Muhlenberger, a Democratic paper conducted first by T. J. Coates and later by Cardwell and Martin. The Muhlenberger was followed by another Democratic weekly, the Greenville Banner, under W. L. Phillips. In 1899 the Greenville Record, an independent paper, was started by Orien L. Roark, who is still at the head of the publication. Mr. Roark has served as an editor longer than any other man in the county. During the earlier days of the Greenville Record, William Sweeney published an independent paper called the Tribune, and D. J. Fleming another, also independent, known as the Muhlenberg Herald. The last paper founded in Greenville was the Muhlenberg Sentinel, a Republican organ, established by R. O. Pace in April, 1910, and now edited by E. E. Reno.

The first newspaper published in Central City was the Argus, founded by R. Y. Thomas, jr., in 1884. During the

Facsimile of editorial title, Muhlenberg's first newspaper

same year T. Coleman duPont bought this plant and established the Central City Republican, which continued until 1909. Its last three editors were John Lawton, Z. O. King, and E. E. Reno. In 1889 the Central City Herald was established by R. Y. Thomas, jr., and after changing hands a number of times was discontinued about 1894. During 1895 E. E. Reno and W. R. Barrett published the Central City Sun. In 1900 E. E. Reno and Doctor M. P. Creel began the Muhlenberg News, which paper was published until 1905, when the Central City Republican was reëstablished and bought their plant. The Muhlenberg Argus was launched September 20, 1906, with Leo Fentress as editor, who served in that capacity for a few years. In November, 1912, this weekly was changed to the Twice-a-Week Argus. This, the only paper now published in Central City, is owned and edited by C. E. Gregory.

The Farmers and Miners' Advocate, published in Central City by James D. Wood for several years, was discontinued in 1908, and the Muhlenberg Baptist, edited by Reverend F. M. Jones, also printed in Central City, appeared from 1906 to 1908. A paper called the Dunmor News was printed at Dunmor for a few months in 1888. During the year 1890 G. F. Swint published the South Carrollton Times, a local weekly.

It is probable that during the first third of this century as many books and pamphlets will be published by Muhlenberg writers as were produced during the first hundred years of the county's existence. And it is also probable that these publications by local writers will not only be preserved in the homes of a number of Muhlenbergers, but also in some of the public libraries throughout the country where books are not exposed to destruction by fire or ruin through improper exposure. If the county and circuit clerks were required by law to file copies of the local newspapers and to preserve them with the same care they do the official records of the county, much local history and interesting literature would be preserved for the present as well as for future generations.

Samuel E. Smith,[1] M. J. Roark, Mortimer D. Hay, J. W. McCall, B. E Pittman, S. P. Love, Finis M. Allison, Charles Eaves, Joseph Ricketts and W. H. Yost, all of whom have been called by the Supreme Judge except W. H. Yost, of Madisonville, who was considerably younger than his early contemporaries in law, and who stands to-day as the only living representative of the Greenville legal fraternity of 1870.

"On the medical board of Greenville and vicinity were Doctors W. H Yost, sr., Robert C. Frazier, R. M Crittenden, John W. Morehead, Alexander McCown,[2] J. W. Church (dentist), T. J. Slaton, and Samuel H Dempsey. Doctor T. J. Slaton is the only survivor. Peter H. Baker and David H. Myers were the druggists of Greenville.

"On the ecclesiastical board were R. Y. Thomas, sr., W. L. Casky, W. D Morton, J. F. Austin, and John D. Hanner, who have since gone to their eternal home.

"The principals of the mercantile board of Greenville were M. C. Hay & Co., J. C. Howard, M. Rowe, F. B. Hancock, jr., Lewis Reno, G. B. Eades & Co., T. J. Jones, William Irvin, J. H. Reno, and Julius Hesse. All have passed away, and the business houses they occupied have disappeared with them, except the one then occupied by M. C. Hay & Co., which remains a monument of 1870, having stood successfully two conflagrations.

DR. ALEXANDER McCOWN, 1870

"The hotels in that year were the Reno House, run by Lawson R. Reno, and the Greenville Hotel, run by John T. Reynolds, sr.

---

[1] At the election held in 1866 Samuel E. Smith was a candidate on the Republican ticket for Congress. The Democratic candidate was John Young Brown, then of Henderson and later Governor of the State. The election was contested, and after a wrangle extending over a period of more than a year was finally decided against Smith.

[2] Doctor Alexander McCown, one of the seven sons of pioneer Joseph McCown, was born in Muhlenberg County August 24, 1819. In 1840 he began preaching in the Methodist Church, and in 1860, after graduating from the Kentucky School of Medicine, Louisville, devoted his time to medicine, preaching, and farming. He died near Greenville January 24, 1894. In 1856 he married Mary Webster. Their only child, Archibald Webster McCown, is one of the most progressive farmers in Muhlenberg. Pioneer Joseph McCown, who settled a few miles east of Greenville about 1812, and pioneer Lewis McCown, who settled near what became South Carrollton, were brothers—sons of Alexander McCown, of Bardstown.

XXVIII

IN EIGHTEEN-SEVENTY

THE year 1870 marks the beginning of the end of the prolonged and trying times that followed the Civil War. The political manifestations of 1870 are typical of the period that extended from about 1865 to about 1875. It was in 1870 that the first railroad in the county was building. Shortly afterward began the long, costly, and troublesome wrangle on the validity of the railroad bonds. The building of the railroad was the beginning of the development of many of the county's resources. The local history of that year is summed up by Richard T. Martin, who in March, 1910, published in the Greenville Record a sketch entitled "Forty Years Ago." This article is so full of interest that I quote it almost entire, as revised. It must be borne in mind that under the good-humor with which the author describes the exciting political conditions of that year there is presented a graphic view of a condition of public alarm that was then of very serious moment.

"Many changes have taken place both in Greenville and Muhlenberg County since 1870. People have been born and have died, some have become rich and some poor, many have rejoiced and many have suffered, but the world has kept revolving in the same old way.

"In 1870 U. S. Grant was President of the United States; Thomas C. McCreary and Garrett Davis were the United States Senators from Kentucky; William N. Sweeny, of Owensboro, was our Congressman; John W. Stevenson was Governor of the State; Finis M. Allison, of Greenville, was our State Senator; Doctor John B. Hays was the representative of our county. In 1868 R. T. Petree, of Hopkinsville, the Civil War judge, was succeeded by George C. Rogers, of Bowling Green, who died during the summer of 1870 and whose unexpired term was filled by R. C. Bowling, of Russellville. Charles K. Milliken was Commonwealth's attorney; N. J. Harris was the circuit court clerk. All of these have since passed into the Great Beyond.

"The county officials in 1870 were S. P. Love, county judge; B. E. Pittman, county attorney; Thomas Bruce, county clerk; T. M. Morgan, sheriff; R. E. Humphrey, assessor; W. D. Shelton, jailer; James D. Craig, surveyor, and W. P. Hancock, coroner. These, too, have passed away, except T. M. Morgan, who is the only survivor of the county's official board of 1870.

"The magisterial board consisted of Joseph Adcock, J. H. Morton, A. J. Lyon, David Roll, J. P. Hendricks, and J. Hunt, all of whom are now dead. The Greenville bar was composed of J. H. Reno, J. C. Thompson,

"J. L. Roark and L. C. Chatham were the undertakers. Samuel Arnold and George Geibel were the millers. The tobacconists were H. N. Martin, J. C. Cary & Co., E. Rice, and R. T. & C. E. Martin. The saddlers were J. V. Ragon and John McIntire. F. B. Hancock was the broker and John Landrum the tailor. S. D. Chatham was the livery-stable man. Baker and Rhoads then conducted the Greenville Nursery. Green B. Steward was the leading barber. C. C. Jenkins ran 'The Railroad Saloon.'

"In 1870 Frank B. Hancock succeeded G. B. Eades as postmaster of Greenville. Most of the mail then came by way of Russellville and Owensboro. Each sent three mails a week to Greenville, and received the same number. Morganfield mail came and went only once every seven days.

"The railroad bonds had just been issued, and the Elizabethtown & Paducah Railroad was under construction. In March, 1870, W. L. Anthony printed the first copy of the Kentucky Republican, Muhlenberg's first newspaper. In May, 1870, Bob Gray, a negro, was lynched in Greenville for killing Mrs. Charles Newman.

The house occupied in 1870 by M. C. Hay & Co., Greenville, as it appears to-day

"New business houses, new church buildings, new law offices, new doctors' offices, new printing offices, and a new courthouse stand upon the sites of the old buildings that were used in 1870. The new houses are occupied by a new generation, and they, perhaps, will not be doing business here forty years hence.

"On a recent county court day I walked along the streets of Greenville. I looked at the new Y. M. C. A. building and the many other new houses facing the courthouse.[3] I surveyed the large crowd that was there gathered. I saw very few who, as middle-aged men, mingled together upon the streets in 1870. 1 noticed the commissioner standing high up on the large and beautiful steps of the new courthouse, and men standing around bidding at his sales; but they were not those who stood around and bid to the cry of the commissioner,

---

[3] The Greenville Young Men's Christian Association was organized June 26, 1886. Charles M. Howard was the first president and Max Weir the first secretary. In 1900 the Muhlenberg County Y. M. C. A. was formed at Greenville, and continued (with branches at Central City, Bremen, and Drakesboro) until 1904, or shortly after the death of Max Weir. On September 8, 1904, the Greenville Y. M. C. A. was incorporated. The local Association received $7,500 from the estate of Max Weir and with this erected the present building, which was formally opened May 17, 1910.

M. C. Hay, when he stood on the small stone steps in front of the old courthouse in 1870.

"In 1870 there occurred one of the greatest, most alarming, and perplexing political panics and epidemics that has ever been experienced in the history of our nation. It was known as the negro 'social equality panic.' This plague was prevalent south of the Mason and Dixon line, and symptons of it were felt in some of the Northern States. The 'negro equality' panic began in 1865, soon after the negroes were set free. It gradually grew and gained strength. In 1868, when the negroes were made citizens and clothed with the same civil rights as other citizens of the United States, fury was added to the flame already started, and it spread and became more fearful and distressing. People of a certain temperament and disposition, living in the State of Kentucky and the other Southern States, began to be most seriously affected by this epidemic. In 1870, shortly after the negroes were made voters, it reached its climax and highest degree of political force and alarm and became a monstrous and perplexing proposition.

"This panic was aggravated and agitated by speakers and office-seekers, who would present to the people dark forebodings of a fearful future by telling them that if the Republican party should be allowed to continue governing the country, negro equality would certainly follow. Uninformed and inconsiderate people began to shudder at the thought of having to come to negro equality. . . .

"This state of political affairs was very acute in Muhlenberg, as elsewhere. All who were subject to the epidemic in the county and State flocked that year into the Democratic or 'white man's party,' until it was swelled to an enormous majority. In 1871 Preston H. Leslie, Democratic candidate for Governor, defeated John M. Harlan, Republican candidate, by a majority of over forty thousand votes. Muhlenberg County gave a Democratic majority of between six and seven hundred.

"In 1870 the county election took place in Muhlenberg on the first Monday in August. There were full sets of Democratic and Republican candidates running for the various county offices, all good men. 'Negro equality' was the Democratic battle-cry used during the campaign. The general canvass commenced about the last of June. Lists were sent out showing where and when the various speakings would be held. The candidates on both sides met these appointments and addressed the large crowds that gathered. Most meetings were like picnics, and many ended in barn dances. There was plenty to eat; drink was always on hand.

"Usually S. P. Love, the Democratic candidate for county judge, and Wiley S. Hay, the Republican candidate, would furnish the oratory and eloquence. W. H. Yost, then about twenty-one years old, was the Democratic candidate for county attorney, and Clark Moore, some years older, was an independent candidate for the same office. They would occasionally take a tilt at each other. The remainder of the candidates, as a rule, would simply announce themselves for certain county offices and ask the people for support.

"When a Democratic candidate addressed the crowd that year he usually began by saying: 'Ladies and gentlemen, I am a Democratic candidate (which generally called for some applause). I have always been a Democrat. My father was a Democrat. (Applause.) I expect to live a Democrat and to die a Democrat and be buried in a Democratic coffin. (Great applause.) And if you elect me to serve you, I shall advo-

THE OLD CUMBERLAND PRESBYTERIAN CHURCH, CHERRY STREET, GREENVILLE
Built in 1848, is here shown as it appeared about 1870. It stood until 1902, when the congregation's present building was erected on the site of the old one

cate and practice Democratic principles. (Applause.) I want it distinctly understood that I am opposed to "negro equality" in any shape, form, or fashion whatever. (Great applause.) I am a candidate on the "White Man's Ticket," and I do not want any negro votes.' (Applause.)

"As already stated, Love and Hay did the principal speaking. Love had the advantage over Hay in several particulars. He could speak two words to Hay's one; he had a much louder voice, stronger lungs, and more wit, sarcasm, and ridicule than Hay. Having the public sentiment largely in his favor, he attempted to browbeat, and as the saying is 'to peck Hay's head,' all over the county.

"As a general thing when Love spoke he accused Hay and 'the Radical party,' as he called the Republican, of being in favor of negro equality. He would ask: 'Do you parents want to see young black, kinkyheaded negroes paying their respects to your daughters and marrying them? Do you want to see your sons making love to negro wenches and taking them for wives? Do you want negro daughters-in-law and negro sons-in-law?' A volley of 'No's!' would sound out from the crowd, and Love would continue: 'If you do, then vote for the "Piebald Buck"[4]; if you don't, then vote the Democratic ticket and you will save the country from negro equality, and if I am elected judge, I will not permit any of it in the county, nor will I allow any negro to testify in my court!'

"During this canvass Love, in closing his speeches, would sometimes say: 'I can't get Mr. Hay to answer my questions; he evades them.

> "'He wires in and he wires out,
> And he wires all round about;
> And like the snake that made the track,
> You can't tell if he's white or black."'

"In response to this, Hay would turn to Love and remark:

> "'Oh, do forsake such low pursuits
> And cultivate more generous fruits;
> Such acts will stigmatize your name,
> And bring reproach upon your fame."'

"One could see the animosity sparkling in the eyes of the parents, whose perturbed souls were deeply affected by the panic. They would cast a look of scorn at Hay, who sat quietly and calmly by, waiting his turn to speak. Generally when Love concluded his speech he would step off and all those who were enraged would follow, leaving Hay with only a small crowd of those conservative and immune to the panic.

"I remember on one occasion, after Love had finished speaking and the people commenced going away, a lady and two daughters, who had rosy cheeks and looked as sweet as angels, came running past where I stood, and a gentleman with whom I was talking asked the mother, 'Cousin Sally, why don't you stay and hear Mr. Hay speak?' She answered, 'I do not want to hear anybody speak that wants negro equality. I am going up to the dance with the girls!' And off she went.

"When Hay met his old associates and friends he would simply say to them, 'I am a candidate for the office of county judge, and if elected I will run the office for its fees. I shall ask no salary. I would like to have your support.' [It was customary for the fiscal court to allow the county judge five hundred dollars salary.]

"Many of the men who were under the influence of the panic would remark to him, 'Mr. Hay, we have known you for a long time and have always found you to be a perfect gentleman in all your dealings and have always known you to be a good citizen, but we can not support you and are sorry to tell you so. We would as soon vote against a father or

---

[4] Wiley S. Hay had a birthmark on his cheek.

brother.' Some would say, 'We have always believed in the principles of the Republican party, but since they have made the negro a voter and made it a negro party, we have joined the Democratic or "white man's party." We can not stand negro equality and expect to vote against it as long as we live.' Mr. Hay would repeatedly tell them that he was not for negro equality, but was as much opposed to it as any living mortal. Their usual reply was, 'But your party is, and you belong to the negro party, and a vote for you would be a vote for negro equality. We do not want to disgrace ourselves and our families by voting for negro equality.'

THE OLD BRICK BANK BUILING, GREENVILLE, ABOUT 1890, OR FOUR YEARS BEFORE ITS REMOVAL

This sort of consolation would throw a cloud of disappointment over the old sage, for he realized that he was the victim of political ignorance and prejudice and of deception carried on by persons who did not have aspirations as high as he had.

"Wiley S. Hay was one of the best men in the county. He was a pioneer of Muhlenberg, born in the first years of the Nineteenth Century, and was about sixty-eight years old during this campaign. His history was untainted. He was a man of broad mind and noble sentiment, an example of the highest type of American manhood. He represented the county in the Legislature in 1845-46 and was afterward a State Senator, but during this panic he was made a subject of ridicule and censure on account of his politics. No truer man ever lived in Muhlenberg County, and none who tried to do more for the betterment of his country. He had the nerve and the manhood to stand up and advocate his political principles and sentiments before an antagonistic majority of people who were greatly affected with the negro equality plague, and to defend that which he believed to be right.

"Hay was about six feet two inches tall. He was not an orator or trained speaker. He was well informed for his day; his speeches were logical and forcible, and when aroused he would straighten up and talk like a statesman. He was one of the leading Union men of the county during the war and a leading advisory Republican afterward. He was a slave-owner and well-to-do farmer. He rose from the vale of poverty; his parents were poor, his father, Kinnard Hay, having been a schoolteacher. W. S. Hay's oldest son, M. D. Hay, was a bright young lawyer

WILEY S. HAY, ABOUT 1850

of distinction. He was strong in sympathy with the South, and an ardent advocate of Secession. He became the mouthpiece and speaker for the Secession element of the county during the war. After the war he was a leader in the Democratic party. He died in 1875, about forty years of age. Mr. Hay's second son, M. C. Hay, joined the Southern army, was wounded at Shiloh, taken prisoner, and returned home at the close of the war. Hay's third son, David, died in the Southern army. Thus father and sons were at variance in politics.

"This negro equality panic or epidemic continued to vex and worry some of the people for twenty years. Most of those who were seriously affected died. Many of those who in the meantime grew up to manhood became immune to the epidemic, and the panic finally subsided.

"While the people of Muhlenberg were laboring under the fear of negro equality they were also under the pressure of another ordeal—the panic of railroad bonded indebtedness. This panic also ran twenty years, parallel, for a time, with the negro equality panic. Four judges and magistrates, all of whom were considered astute, worried with the two panics, but failed to bring about any relief. It was not until after the lapse of twenty years that both epidemics were subdued. Muhlenberg emerged from its former torpor and has since been traveling on the road of peace and prosperity, and the county is to-day worth at least threefold what it was during the years of the two great panics."

The careers of all the men referred to by Mr. Martin in his sketch are woven into Muhlenberg's history of their time. None of these citizens was better known and more highly esteemed, and none was more closely connected with the local history of their day, than Finis McLean Allison, of Greenville, who in 1870 was a member of the State Senate. He was a grandson of pioneer Samuel Allison, who was among the first to settle near where later Friendship Church was built. A few years before the death of Finis M. Allison the following sketch was published in "The Biographical Encyclopedia of Kentuckians":

"Finis McLean Allison, lawyer, was born March 4, 1829, in Muhlenberg County, Kentucky. His father, John Adair Allison, was a native of the same county; was of Scotch-Irish descent, and followed agricultural pursuits throughout his life. His mother's maiden name was Frances Watkins, and she was a native of Washington County, Kentucky. Mr. Allison was reared on a farm and received a common English education. At the age of fifteen he became deputy clerk in Muhlenberg county and circuit courts, holding the position until 1849. In the meantime, having studied law, he was admitted to the bar in the fall of 1850, and entered upon the practice of his profession. In 1852 he went to California and engaged for some time in gold-mining, but in 1854 returned and resumed the practice of his profession at Morgantown. In 1856 he was elected clerk of the county and circuit courts of Butler County, continuing in that position until 1865, when he again resumed the practice of law. In 1867 he was elected to the State Senate from the counties of Muhlenberg and Christian, serving until 1871.

FINIS McLEAN ALLISON, 1870

In that year he was appointed by Governor Leslie as inspector of tobacco at Louisville, but soon afterward resumed his professional business at Greenville, Kentucky. In politics he is a Democrat, and has taken an active interest in the affairs of his party. Mr. Allison was married August 1, 1849, to Julia A. Burks, and has six living children. His son Finis H. Allison is a physician in McLean County, and his son John Allison is a practicing lawyer at Greenville."

In 1874 Mr. Allison was appointed United States Commissioner for the District of Kentucky, and in 1882 was elected police judge of Greenville, which office he held until his death, April 12, 1886. The Muhlenberg Echo, published during the week of his death, after giving him his just praise as a citizen, lawyer, and judge, says: "Judge Allison's place in Greenville and the county will be hard to fill. His humble grave may never be marked by a lofty and costly monument, but his memory will live green and fresh in the hearts of this people long after many of us now living will have been forgotten."[5]

The lynching of the negro, referred to by Mr. Martin, was an act for which the county's entire population was censured, although not more than one hundred men took part in the affair. Those who attempt to give the

---

[5] Finis McLean Allison was the father of Mrs. Lucy (Joseph) Frazer, Mrs. Alice (Joseph) Stokes, Mrs. Naomi (Eugene) Lovell, Finis H., John, and James Allison.

details of this hanging usually wander far from the facts and invariably exaggerate the conduct of the lynching party. A clipping from a local newspaper, printed at the time, giving an account of this gruesome tragedy, has been preserved by Walter W. Langley. This I quote in full, in order to check the distorted tales now extant by giving the actual facts in the case. The Kentucky Republican of May 18, 1870, says:

Large logs were plentiful in 1870 and even as late as 1894, when this picture was made near Paradise

It becomes our painful duty as a public journalist to give to the readers of the Republican, this morning, the particulars of a most horrible tragedy enacted in Muhlenberg County. A most diabolical outrage and murder has been committed, the details of which will blanch the cheek and sicken the heart of every reader. Our blood curdles at the recital of the fiendish atrocity developed by the investigation. We shall endeavor to record the facts as we have gathered them from various sources, without coloring, and shall feel it our bounden duty as an humble exponent and defender of the principles of morality, law and good order, to deprecate and severely censure such riotous and violent proceedings as occurred on our streets last Saturday. These are the facts:

On Wednesday last, May 11th, Mrs. Elizabeth Newman, wife of Mr. Charles Newman, living about four miles south of Greenville, left her home, on foot in the morning, accompanied by her little boy aged four years, to spend the day with the family of Mr. John Gray, jr., but not finding them at home, she started to go toward the house of Mr. A. Newman, and here we lose trace of her. This was between seven and nine o'clock on Wednesday morning. At night, the husband and father, coming home from a log-rolling in the neighborhood, is surprised to find that his wife has not yet returned, and hastens to inquire after her of the neighbors, but fails to discover her whereabouts; and, thinking she must be safe at some one of her relatives' houses, he seeks his own couch for the night. The next morning the dead body of a woman, identified as that of Mrs. Newman, together with the child of Mrs. Newman, terribly mutilated, but still alive, are found in a little skirt of woods between Mr. A. Newman's and Mr. John Gray's. A coroner was summoned and an inquest held over the dead body, eliciting the following facts:

That Mrs. Elizabeth Newman came to her death from murderous blows, inflicted upon the head with rocks and sticks, and from a pistol-shot wound in the neck. In the opinion of several physicians, either wound would have caused instant death. Murderer unknown. Her skull was crushed in two places. The child was found about ten feet from the mother, with its skull broken and face much disfigured. It was still alive but in a stupor.

The woman was lying upon her face, her hair disheveled and matted with blood. The ground for seventy yards around bore marks of a desperate struggle. Drs. Yost, Crittenden and Frazier found unmistakable proof of violence to the person of the woman. At one place her breastpin was found, and the ground indicated a scuffle. At some distance farther on her sunbonnet and knitting work were found, and the disturbed condition of the dead leaves and ground, which bore evidence of a violent struggle, indicated that here the damning deed was committed. Here her cries for help were stopped by the hellish demon with a handful of leaves, fragments of which were on the spot. His fiendish purpose having been accomplished, the woman seems to have succeeded in escaping from the scoundrel and run on to about seventy yards from the point at which the first signs of a scuffle were seen. Here her body was found in the condition we have described. About a pint of seed corn was found scattered about upon the ground at the place where the woman seems to have been down the second time. The meeting, by Dr. A. McCown, and the suspicious conduct of a negro boy, Bob, living at John Gray's, in the woods, not a hundred yards from the scene of the outrage and murder at about the time Mrs. Newman must have passed that way, together with the fact that he was set to planting corn that morning in the field near John Gray's house, in full view of the road that Mrs. Newman took in going to and from the house, and the fact that the boy had no business in the wood at that time in the morning, seemed to point to him (the negro boy, Bob) as the author of the horrible murder, and on the evening of the same day he was arrested and placed in the county jail.

Great indignation was felt by the friends and relatives of the murdered woman, who was a daughter of Mr. Josiah Reid, living in this county, an estimable lady, a loving wife and fond mother. She was not yet thirty years of age; had been married to Mr. Newman about five years, and had but one child living, a bright, promising boy, who, as we have seen, escaped so narrowly with his life. Much excitement prevailed in the neighborhood of the murder, and a large number of persons visited the scene of the terrible tragedy. Strong additional proofs, fixing the negro boy's guilt beyond a doubt, having been found on Thursday, intimations were rife that a number of citizens of the county, together with the friends of the deceased, contemplated taking the prisoner by night from the custody of the jailer, and executing summary vengeance upon him. But an unwillingness to punish a prisoner in the hands of the law, until found guilty by an impartial trial, dictated moderation and the jail was not molested.

Saturday morning, May 14th, the time set for the investigating trial, the streets of our town were alive with an eager but quiet crowd of citizens of the county. Just before the hour of the trial, Mr. Josiah Reid spoke to the people from the courthouse steps, exhorting and cautioning them to use no violence upon the prisoner, as he was being brought from the jail to the court room; that he was interested far more than they were in the matter, as the murdered woman was his daughter, and if he could keep his hands off the prisoner, they certainly ought to. The court room was jammed to its fullest capacity, and the prisoner was brought before the court, Justices Adcock and Roll presiding. The prisoner, Bob Gray, had formerly belonged to Mr. John Gray, and was still living with his old master. He was about five feet five inches in height, of a dark copper color, and of strong muscular power. When asked in court if he had anything to say for himself, he stated that he was not guilty. Dr. Crittenden and Mr. Samuel E. Smith were sworn, and made in substance the following statement: They both visited the jail, in company, on the morning of the trial, and had a conversation with the prisoner, for the purpose of eliciting any confession he might choose to make. They stated that he at first denied the whole thing; then confessed that he killed the woman, but denied the rape, and stated that he attempted to take the life of the child and then murdered the mother; and then that he killed the mother and afterwards left the child for dead, so that it would not tell who did it. He equivocated and contradicted himself in every instance. When asked why he committed the murder, he said he had always wanted to kill some white woman.

Sufficient proof of the guilt of the prisoner having been adduced, by the investigation, to send him on for further trial, he was remanded back to jail. But before delivering him over to the jailer, the county attorney, B. E. Pittman, Esq., Judge Ricketts, and Hon. Samuel E. Smith addressed the crowd, in earnest language, in behalf of law and order, cautioning and entreating them to do nothing violent, but exhorting all to retire to their homes and leave the prisoner in the hands of the law; telling them that there was sufficient proof of his guilt to send him back to jail, and if convicted he would suffer the extreme penalty of the law. The muttering storm of a people's indignation at the enormity of the crime had been brewing all the morning, and rumors were afloat that five hundred determined men of the county, satisfied of the guilt of the prisoner, would never suffer him to go back to jail, but intended to take the law into their own hands and lynch the prisoner. Mr. Reid again made a noble appeal to the crowd, in which he said: "It was my daughter that was murdered. It is I that am interested more than any of you in this matter; and if I can bear it, surely you should. Harm him not. The law will deal with him as he deserves."

As the jailer and guard conducted the prisoner from the court room, the cry of "Hang him!" was heard on all sides, and as the prisoner, in charge of the officers of the law, issued from the courthouse, they were met by a crowd of from fifty to one hundred men, with pistols in hand, who demanded and dragged the prisoner from the officers and guard. The scene that followed beggars description. All was excitement and turmoil. It seemed to be the intention of the parties to hang the negro in the courthouse yard, and it is probably due to the earnestness and bold speaking of Judge Love, who mounted the fence and succeeded in arresting the attention of the leaders for a moment, that they desisted from this course. They, however, dragged him to the woods, distant half a mile from the courthouse, and there hanged him by the neck until he was dead.

After the body of the negro had hung suspended by a rope to the limb of a tree for an hour or more it was taken down, the head severed from the trunk, and the former, all gory and mangled, stuck on the end of a long pole, brought back to town and placed conspicuously in the courthouse yard, from whence it was removed soon after by Justice Adcock, placed with the body and decently buried.

Thus is mob-law satisfied. Thus is the death by violence of a noble, Christian woman avenged in the seditious, barbarous and disgraceful scenes we have hastily described. Thus has Muhlenberg County shown to the world her red-handed chivalry, in heroically cutting off the head of a dead negro, hanged by mob violence, and parading the bloody trophy before her halls of justice! Even if we sought to palliate (which we do not) the action of the mob in lynching the prisoner while in the hands of the law, this last flagrant offense against decency, civilization and Christianity merits denunciation in thunder tones by an indignant and outraged community. We blush to record the shame that now stains the hitherto fair fame of our county, but our imperative duty as a truthful journalist compels us to make the unwilling sacrifice. [6]

The year 1870 may be regarded as the beginning of banking in Muhlenberg. Shortly after the close of the Civil War most of the checks and drafts cashed in the county were handled in Greenville by F. B. Hancock, who about the year 1870 established "The Banking House of F. B. Hancock." Hancock conducted his banking business in connection with his other busi-

THE JONATHAN SHORT RESIDENCE, GREENVILLE
Built about 1850 and modernized in 1907 by Andrew W. Duncan, who now occupies it

ness until 1879. In the beginning he simply cashed checks. About 1870 he began to issue drafts, cash notes, and borrow and lend money and transact such other business as is done in a bank.

In the early days pioneer James Weir cashed practically all the drafts received by people in the county. In his Greenville store he kept a wooden chest heavily cleated with nails which, up to about 1840, served the purpose of a safe and vault. After his day his son Edward R. Weir, sr., and other leading merchants incidentally cashed checks for their customers. From 1865 to 1879, as already stated, F. B. Hancock made it a business to look after such matters. Hancock was succeeded by M. C. Hay, who

---

[6] Two men have been hanged by mobs in the county. The second was Dudley White, a negro, accused of killing Jonathan Gossett. He was taken from the jail on January 9, 1874, and hanged to a tree about three hundred yards east of the courthouse.

acted as financial agent for a few years. In 1882 M. C. Hay and Lewis Reno organized a bank in the "Old Brick Bank Building," which had been built in 1819 on the northwest corner of the courthouse square. This bank, started in 1882, was the first bank established in the county. In 1890 it became the First National Bank of Greenville, which is the oldest of the eight banks now in Muhlenberg.

More than sixty years before this, on February 9, 1819, the State Legislature, in an "Act authorizing the County Court of Muhlenberg to

YOUNG MEN'S CHRISTIAN ASSOCIATION BUILDING, GREENVILLE
Erected in 1910

dispose of part of their public ground," enabled the court, in accordance therewith, to sell the northwest corner of the courthouse lot to the "Bank of Greenville" for the purpose of erecting a bank building on it. Subscriptions for the sale of stock were "under the direction of James Weir, Alney McLean, William Campbell, sr., Charles F. Wing, Robert McLean and John S. Eaves." They erected a two-story brick house in 1819. Although their brick bank building was "condemned" immediately after it was finished, time showed that it was an exceptionally well-made house, for it was not torn down until seventy-five years later, and then only to make room for the more modern structure which now occupies that corner. In 1818 about fifty independent banks were incorporated throughout the State, among them the "Bank of Greenville." However, in 1820—shortly after the brick bank building was finished—the charters of these independent banks were repealed, and the organizers of the "Bank of Greenville" made no further attempt to establish a bank, but rented the various rooms in their bank building for office purposes.

Among those who in 1870 had an office in this old brick house was Doctor J. W. Church. In 1894 the famous "Old Brick Bank Building" was torn down and the building now standing on that corner was erected by the First National Bank of Greenville, by which corporation it was occupied until 1907, when the bank sold the house to the Greenville Coal Company and moved into the larger quarters across the street.

The building now occupied by the First National Bank stands on a corner which in 1870 was occupied by an old frame and log house that was torn down in the early seventies. It is said the old landmark that stood on that corner was removed by a wealthy widower, who erected in its place the present three-story (recently stuccoed) brick building—the second three-story brick house built in the county. When the widower began this new building—so runs the story, which although frequently told may nevertheless not be strictly true—he also began paying his attentions to a handsome young widow, who like himself then lived in the county. After he had finished the basement he proposed to his ladylove, but was coldly refused by her. He erected the first story, and in the meantime pressed his courtship. After the first story was finished he again proposed and was again refused, but not quite so emphatically as before. He then erected the second story, and carried on his courtship with more persistency. After the completion of the second story he again proposed and was once more refused, but this time with an hesitation that gave him hope. The widower then made up his mind to keep on building story after story until accepted by the widow. He added the third story, which made what was then considered a very tall and imposing building. After drawing his plans for the fourth story he again proposed to the widow. She now feared that if she continued to decline, the building would become too tall and unsafe, and she therefore accepted his offer. While the carpenters were finishing the roof the marriage ceremony took place, and the newly married couple lived happily ever after. Both have since died, but the story of their romantic courtship is still told, and will in all probability often be retold as one of the most interesting incidents connected with the houses built about the year 1870.

HUGH MARTIN HOUSE, GREENVILLE
Built in 1855 and a few years later sold to John McIntire; now the home of Doctors Louella and Emily Heltsley

XXIX

THE RAILROAD BONDS

FOR nearly forty years—to be exact, from 1868 to 1906—Muhlenberg staggered under a financial and political burden that greatly depreciated values, delayed industrial development, and harassed officials and taxpayers with most distressing legal uncertainties. The trouble arose out of the issuance by the county of $400,000 of 7 per cent twenty-year bonds in return for an equal amount of stock in the then projected Elizabethtown & Paducah Railroad, which was to be constructed through the counties intervening between Hardin and McCracken. Few questions of local importance have been more completely forgotten in detail than this of the railroad bonds, although it weighed more heavily on the generation that had to deal with it than perhaps any other episode in the county's history.

Muhlenberg was not alone in this matter. Other counties suffered in greater or less degree, but none suffered more severely than Muhlenberg; few suffered as much. It was the era of railroad building in Kentucky and in the entire West. The "flush days" after the war, that were hurrying on to the "blow-up" in the great panic of 1873, were in full swing in 1868-69. Counties all over the State were being persuaded to lend their credit by exchanging bonds for stock in order to help on these various railway projects. Many miles of what now are parts of the Louisville & Nashville Railroad system were financed in this way.[1]

The proposition to Muhlenberg asking for $400,000 of bond subscription was first advanced in 1867. That a railroad would be of great advantage to the county was not to be denied. Opponents of the measure were not wanting, but the railroad promoters made a vigorous house-to-house canvass and a county campaign. The question was formally submitted to the voters of the county at an election held May 30, 1868, resulting in 771 votes for the issue and 550 against it. There were times when memories of that campaign were often bitter, but with the passage of years even those who had suffered most began to see the humor of it. This situation is best described by Richard T. Martin, who was a close observer of the campaign for the bonds and who, writing of it forty-two years later, thus tells what went on in the public eye and mind in 1868:[2]

---

[1] The county was in nowise involved in the construction of any of the railroads that were built in Muhlenberg except the Elizabethtown & Paducah. This road has changed hands a number of times. For a while it was known as the Chesapeake, Ohio & Southwestern, and later as the Newport News & Mississippi Valley. Since 1897 it has been known as the Illinois Central.

[2] "Trying Times in Muhlenberg"; Muhlenberg Sentinel, September 23, 1910.

"One S. B. Thomas, of Elizabethtown, president of the railroad company, first presented such a proposition to the citizens of Muhlenberg County. He had an appointment to speak at Greenville about the necessity of the railroad, and an unusual crowd assembled there to hear him. Thomas was an orator of some distinction and ability. He made the promotion of the railroad his business. His speech was eloquent and persuasive. He was apparently very much interested in the welfare of Muhlenberg. He pictured a great future for the people of the county. He pointed to the advantages, facilities, and comfort that would be realized

ILLINOIS CENTRAL BRIDGE OVER GREEN RIVER, AT ROCKPORT

and enjoyed by the citizens from having a railroad running through the county, and showed that it would give strength and tone to all local industries and put the people on the way to success and wealth. According to Thomas' description and presentation of the scene, the hills and hollows of Muhlenberg County would be crowded with gilded homes of glittering wealth soon after the construction of the railroad.

"The thoughts and aspirations of his hearers were caught up and wafted on the wings of his magic eloquence to the highest realm of hope. The people gave Thomas their close and undivided attention, taking in his fast-flowing logic and eloquence as a sweet morsel.

"At that time all the products and goods were shipped and received by the way of Green River, and hauled to and from the various landings on the river to the different points in the county in wagons, which was a very slow, burdensome, inconvenient and undesirable system. Business men were eager for a better way. Thomas told them that if Muhlenberg would vote the bond issue they would get a paying road through the county, which would be made to run within a mile of the courthouse; that the road, when built, would enhance the value of the property of the county more than double the cost of the subscription. He explained that the stock taken would soon double in value, and that the receipts for the interest paid on the coupons of the bonds would be as certificates of the stock taken and could be sold above par after the railroad was completed. It would be a paying investment for the present generation, their children, and their children's posterity. He emphasized that the building of the road depended upon the people of the various counties along the line, and declared that all the other counties through which the road would run were to vote to take stock and issue bonds to cover the amount of stock taken. He also

TWIN TUNNEL, BETWEEN BELLTON AND PENROD
On Louisville & Nashville Railroad

promised that when the bonds were issued, the people would only have to pay the interest and lay up a sinking fund to liquidate the bonds when due; and that the whole amount could soon be paid off with the proceeds of poultry, potatoes, butter, eggs and blackberries.

"When Thomas mentioned blackberries, it did the people good, for they believed that they were solid on blackberries. It was then only a few years after the war. During the war the people did not know but what they would be killed, and were therefore careless about keeping up their farms. In all the fence corners and along the branches there had grown up an abundance of blackberry briars. Nearly every farmer had a large blackberry orchard, and was therefore confident that he could furnish a good many blackberries. So the outlook was very encouraging along that line. At that time there was also an abundance of greenbacks in circulation, and everybody had a pocketful of 'shin-plasters,' as they were called. Tobacco was selling at from twelve to fifteen dollars per hundred, and the people felt a good deal of independence and believed that they could buy or build a railroad, and could easily invest the sum of $400,000 and never miss it. Besides, they considered it the most convenient way to make a stock investment, for there were few banks, insurance or other stock companies handy, and as they preferred making an investment in their own county they could now venture $400,000 as a sort of feeler in speculation. At that time a great many of the citizens of Muhlenberg County had never seen a railroad, and knew about railroads only from hearsay.

"After Thomas had exhausted his fountain of prophecy on the people, he organized many of the prominent men of Greenville and other parts of the county as a company of agents to work up railroad interest. Among his Greenville boosters were J. Short, Joseph Ricketts, Jesse H. and J. Edmonds Reno, G. B. Eades, F. B. Hancock and Dr. W. H. Yost. The other speakers lived out in the county. Among these boosters there was an understanding that a general canvass of the county should be made and that an election should be called and a vote taken as soon as possible, for the road had already been chartered by the Legislature.

"Many of them started out at once and stumped the county. When some of those old orators were in high spirits they could make rattling speeches on railroad necessity. Their line of argument usually followed that of Thomas. They stirred up the people to a sense of their duty with respect to prosperity. There were some who opposed the measure of voting such a large bonded debt on the property of the county, and these were denounced as being 'contrary,' 'old fogies' and dogmatical drones opposed to the welfare of the community."

Many were the stories that grew out of the railroad campaign, some pathetic, many humorous, and all characteristic of the time and the people. One is told of a certain Greenville man who, while electioneering in the county, called on a country friend known to be one of the few "anti-levys" in the latter's neighborhood. The two men met at the farmer's pasture fence. After the usual salutations they climbed, each

THE BIG CUT, WEST OF MIDLAND
Kentucky Midland Railroad

from his own side, to the top of the rail fence, sat down, and began to argue the railroad question pro and con. Physically both were "on the fence," but not mentally, for each was firm in his own conviction regarding the railroad.

The town man deplored the neglect of the wonderful resources in the immediate vicinity—the forests, the coal, and the iron—none of which, he argued, could be developed until a railroad was built. Like nearly all other citizens of the county he felt convinced, and therefore argued, that the railroad debt could be met without a very noticeable increase in taxation. But the farmer insisted that as long as he could not see how or when the railroad tax could be paid, he was in favor of leaving the harvesting of the resources alone and thus rather "bear those ills we have than fly to others that we know not of."

The railroad enthusiast, after having presented all his arguments, noticed a white heifer and a spotted calf that chanced to be grazing in his friend's pasture. The idea suddenly occurred to him that he might offer to pay all the farmer's railroad tax in exchange for these two young cattle. So he made a proposition to that effect, and it was accepted. Both men were equally satisfied with the agreement, although both still held decidedly opposite views on the railroad question. The white heifer and spotted calf were brought to Greenville. The fatted calf was killed; the heifer, as years rolled on, grew old, and finally was sold and shipped away on the railroad to a city market. The town man, true to his word, not only paid the farmer's railroad tax in the beginning but kept on paying every assessment; and, it is said, he is doing so "even unto this day."

Another story is that a certain farmer, prompted by fear and pessimism, offered to give a thousand dollars to any one who would agree to pay all the railroad tax on his farm, which he then valued at a thousand dollars. Immediately after he had made this offer public a number of men showed their active anxiety to close such an agreement with him. The farmer then reconsidered the subject, and after a little more "figuring" and a little less "fearing" withdrew his proposition, for he came to the conclusion that he might gain more by holding his farm than by giving it away. He held on for a number of years, paid his taxes, and shortly after the bonds were compromised sold his place for $5,000.

The county's subscription to the railroad having been approved by the voters, the bonds were issued in March, 1869, delivered to the railroad company and sold. All of them read alike, differing only in denomination —$100, $500, and $1,000. As a souvenir of the exciting period that produced them and the gloomy times that followed, a verbatim copy of one of the bonds and a reduced facsimile of the same (from which ten coupons have been detached) is here presented:

United States of America. State of Kentucky. $500. County of Muhlenberg. No. 191. For the Elizabethtown & Paducah Railroad. Twenty years after date the County of Muhlenberg, in the State of Kentucky, promises to pay to Bearer the sum of Five Hundred Dollars, with interest thereon at the rate of Seven per Cent per annum, payable semi-annually upon presentation of the proper coupon hereto attached. The principal and interest being payable at the Bank of America in the City of New York, and to secure the payment of which the Property and Credit of the County are pledged.

IN TESTIMONY WHEREOF, the Judge of said County of Muhlenberg has here unto set his hand and affixed the Corporate Seal of the said County, this the first day of March, 1869, and caused the same to be attested by the signature hereto of the County Clerk, who has also signed the Coupons hereto attached.

  Thos. Bruce, County Clerk.   S. P. Love, County Judge.

Nobody could possibly have foreseen the long and troublesome complications that followed the sale of these bonds. The national panic of 1873 completed the disaster.

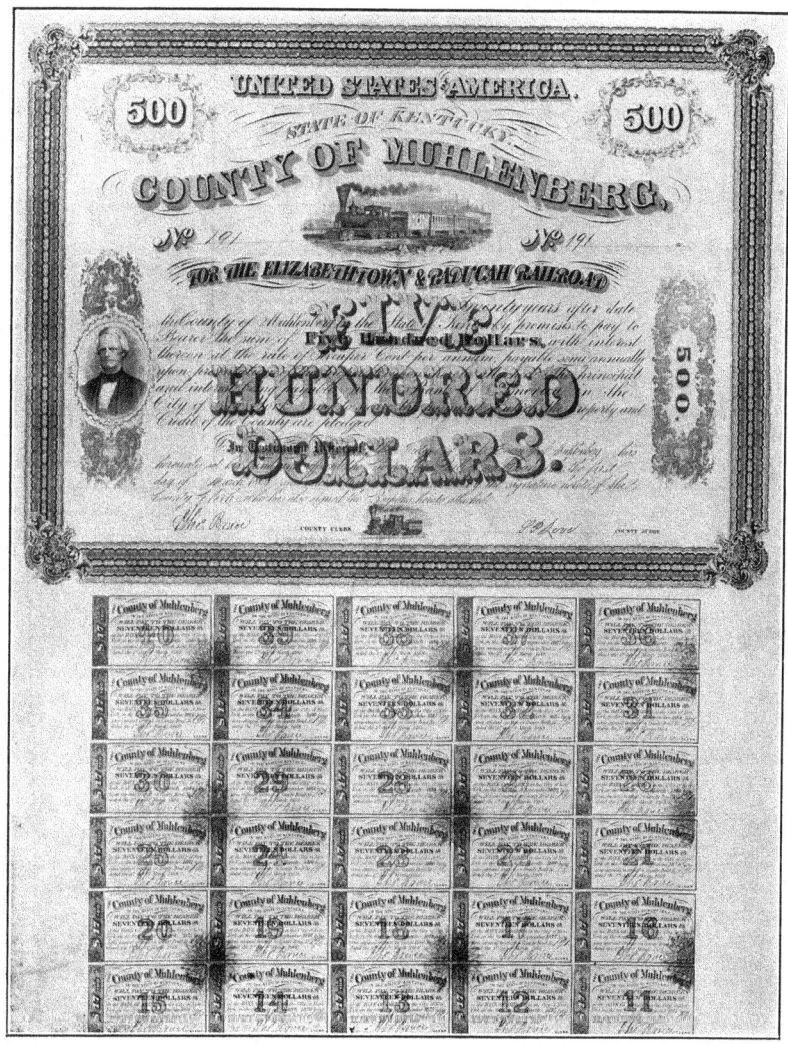

REDUCED FACSIMILE OF ONE OF THE ORIGINAL RAILROAD BONDS
Issued March, 1869; ten coupons detached, September, 1869—March, 1874

Construction of the railroad was begun at once, and the payment of interest on the bonds, amounting to $28,000 a year, was also begun. It was a heavy burden on the sparsely populated county. Interest was paid for several years, and the completed portion of the road was beginning to be used, when the company failed, the uncompleted road was sold, and the complications began. The portion completed, beginning nowhere and ending nowhere, was not taking in enough money to pay operating expenses, and the people of the county were thrown into a panic by the discovery that by the sale of the railroad under bankruptcy the $400,000 of stock to which the county was entitled in exchange for the bonds had been entirely wiped out, and even if completed the county would have no property interest whatever in the railroad it had paid so much to construct. A popular reaction at once set in, based on the belief that the county had been swindled. Talk of repudiating the bonds arose. This threw into a panic those in the county who had invested in the bonds, and alarmed outside holders also.

The original company had not gone through the form of issuing the county the $400,000 of stock due under the agreement, and thence grew an idea—encouraged by some lawyers—that the failure to turn over the printed certificates annulled the whole contract. Having nothing whatever to show for their bond subscription, property-owners began to refuse to pay their taxes, and the troubles broke in all their acuteness. Suits were brought to enforce the collection of the tax, the payment of the interest, and the formation of the sinking fund necessary to redeem the bonds at maturity. Litigation once begun was continued through all the courts; the county took the position that the bonds were illegal and invalid, but the courts necessarily held that they were legal, although the stock had never been issued.

Repudiation was actually if not legally accomplished. No interest was paid. An organization called the "Independent Order of Taxpayers" was formed in 1874, and many of the best citizens of the county joined it, for the purpose of resisting payment of the bonds and the collection of the tax by every means in their power. That year Judge S. P. Love was succeeded as county judge by Judge J. C. Thompson, and the people had the active sympathy of the court in fighting what was universally believed to be "the railroad swindle."

On March 18, 1878, the Legislature passed a special act known as the "Funding Act," giving to the county the power to compromise these bonds and to levy and collect a tax to pay the debt. Under this act a "Funding Board" was created. After the members had been duly elected the board met and proceeded to compromise, and did compromise, at the rate of fifty cents on the dollar, principal and interest. It had issued new bonds to the amount of about $93,000 when it was enjoined from further proceedings. The new bonds were then also resisted and litigated through all the courts; in the end they were held to be valid, as were the original bonds.

In 1886 Q. B. Coleman succeeded J. H. Morton as county judge. He was elected for the express purpose of defeating any attempt to enforce the collection of railroad taxes. Bondholders had court decisions and orders behind them, and were proceeding in form to compel Judge Coleman to act, when he cut the Gordian knot of the law by suddenly leaving the county for parts unknown. The higher courts held that "the county court shall have power to enforce the collection of said railroad tax." The county judge having left, and all the magistrates having resigned, there was no county court to make a levy and to "enforce the collection of said railroad tax." Legal proceedings had to wait until this complication could be cleared up. Mr. Martin says:[3]

"All business enterprise became more or less paralyzed and the energy of the people drooped and became languid; the coal mines that had been opened up along the railroad line were abandoned on account of no trade; the people of the county began to realize that to pay off the debt, as stipulated, would require almost a million dollars. So there was a very dark future presented for consideration. The property of the county decreased in valuation until the whole assessed value was only about two million dollars. A great many of the yeomanry wanted to sell out and save themselves by flight. The best farm land could be bought for six or seven dollars per acre. But no one wanted to buy. All immigration kept shy.

"When visitors came into the county they would remark: 'We understand that you people have an enormous railroad debt upon your shoulders. What a pity! We sympathize with you very much, but what on earth were you folks thinking about in Muhlenberg County—and not a very wealthy county at that—by voting such a debt upon your property? It is a shame that such a large debt should be saddled upon you good people. You who are now of middle age, perhaps, never shall see the end of the debt,' etc.

"Trials and investigations took place in all the courts, from the county court to the Supreme Court of the United States, and every court decided that the bonds were legal and should be paid, but that the levying of the

Ben and Bob Wickliffe (shown here as they appeared about 1890) were sons of pioneer Moses Wickliffe. They were born in Muhlenberg County in 1824, and died at their home, near Bevier, in 1893. They were twins, bachelors, well-known characters and inseparable companions. They went to California in 1849, but returned a few years later. To them every question had its humorous side. The railroad bond situation was a rich field for their wit.

---

[3] "Trying Times in Muhlenberg"; Muhlenberg Sentinel, September 23, 1910.

tax for the payment of the interest on the bonds belonged exclusively to the jurisdiction of the county court. Such decisions gave the county some advantage in the emergency. The county judge hid in the woods and could not be found to make the levy. The magistrates were then held to constitute the county court; in turn they were persuaded to resign their offices, which all of them did. The sheriff also resigned, and was appointed as State tax collector. This condition of affairs continued for a time, and blocked the bondholders to some extent. Attorneys on both sides and judges of ability handled the suits and kept them in the legal sieve. All those who favored high compromise were denounced as being enemies of the county.

"Some of the moneyed men of Muhlenberg purchased bonds sufficient to cover their property, and some few bought at low rate with a view to speculation, if possible. One man, especially, bought bonds at a very low rate and became very troublesome to the 'Non-Tax-Payers'; he was instrumental in having a number of suits brought against the county. He got a judgment against the county and succeeded in forcing a collection of ten thousand dollars by hiring a number of men and having the United States Marshal appoint them as deputies. He armed them with guns and regular camp equipment and brought them into the county. This terrified many, especially the women and children, and a general mass-meeting was held in Greenville. A number of legal lights were in attendance, and they advised the people to pay off the judgment of ten thousand dollars and by that procedure save a great deal of cost. This advice was taken; people poured into Greenville from all parts, paying their pro. rata in the case. The sheriff had to employ a number of deputies to take and receipt for the money. This ten thousand dollars was paid off and the deputy marshals left the county, the county paying their expenses and also buying the guns and camp equipment, which after being turned over to the county were sold at a discount.

"These proceedings were known as the Lance Capps Raid. Lance Capps was at that time a citizen of Muhlenberg, but he soon afterward left. The man who forced the collection also moved out of the county and died about the time a general settlement of the debt was effected."

In 1889 D. J. Fleming was elected county judge. In his campaign he declared that he could defeat the payment of the bonds. He made many strong efforts to do so. During his two terms of office lawsuits were pending in the State and Federal courts, every one of which was finally lost by the county.

In 1898 T. J. Sparks became county judge. He was elected on a platform declaring for the settlement of the entire bonded debt of the county, if it could be done at a reasonable figure. Immediately after his election steps were taken to bring about a settlement. The debt at that time amounted to about a million dollars. During Judge Sparks' administration the old bonds were settled at twenty cents on the dollar, principal and interest, and the new bonds, or the bonds issued by the "Funding Board," were paid dollar for dollar. [4]

---

[4] Judge Thomas Jefferson Sparks was born November 4, 1868, near Earles. He is the son of C. M. and Sallie (Miller) Sparks. Judge Sparks' father has

In settlement of this debt the county finally issued its bonds to the amount of $215,000; $25,000 payable in 1905, $25,000 in 1910, $80,000 in 1915, and $85,000 in 1920. This ended all of the railroad bond agitation in the county. The bonds due in 1905 and 1910 were met promptly at maturity. The interest of 5 per cent is now being paid and a sufficient sinking fund is being levied and accumulated for the redemption of the remaining bonds at maturity.

THOMAS JEFFERSON SPARKS, 1912

While all this mess and mass of litigation was in progress, property constantly depreciated in value and capital seeking investment drifted elsewhere. When the debt had increased to one million dollars the assessed property valuation of the county was two million dollars. The bondholders therefore had a lien on the property of the county for 50 per cent of its assessed value. When Judge Sparks' second term expired, January 1, 1906, the county's bonded indebtedness had decreased to $190,000, the assessed property valuation had increased to about four million dollars, and the bondholders' lien had been reduced to a little less than 5 per cent. As soon as the refunding compromise was effected, Muhlenberg and Greenville began to feel the good results of the railroad settlement.[5] Mr. Martin thus summarizes:

---

always been one of the leading citizens in his section of Muhlenberg. C. M. Sparks was a member of the Independent Order of Taxpayers, and took an active part in the fight of the people against the collection of the railroad debt. He was a member of the bond funding board, and served in that capacity as long as the board was in existence.

Judge Sparks went to the country school near his home, and later attended the Greenville schools and the State University. He taught in the public schools of Muhlenberg County for five years. In 1894 he married Miss Monte Oates, daughter of Edward and Nannie (Bridges) Oates, both of Muhlenberg County. In 1896 he was elected magistrate from the Fifth Magisterial District. Before his term expired he was made the nominee of his party for the office of county judge, to which position he was elected in 1897 and again in 1901. It was during his administration and principally through his efforts that a settlement of the railroad debt was made. Judge Sparks was Republican elector from the State-at-large in the presidential campaign of 1908, and in 1909 was appointed by Governor Willson as Commonwealth's attorney to fill out the unexpired term of Honorable R. Y. Thomas, who was that year elected to Congress. In 1900 he was admitted to the bar, and immediately after the expiration of his term as county judge formed a partnership with Mr. Newton Belcher for the practice of law. The firm of Belcher & Sparks is one of the strongest in Western Kentucky.

[5] Some of the fields that are now gully-washed and covered with scrub cedars were originally neglected and finally "thrown out" owing to the uncertainty of

"Peace was declared, and that mighty spectral monster disappeared. Although Muhlenberg had lost twenty-five years of its growth, yet the songs of industry were renewed and prosperity resumed its march; immigrants rushed in; the valuation of the property of the county rose at a rapid rate from two million dollars to about five millions. The railroad running through the county had been purchased, improved and extended by others; coal mines were opened up all along the line; potatoes, chickens, eggs and blackberries found a way to market. A large new courthouse was built; everybody was satisfied. However, only a few of those who voted the railroad bonds on the county lived to see the last act of this

ILLINOIS CENTRAL DEPOT, GREENVILLE

prolonged drama. Most of the men who had been vexed with and worried over the debt for years died in distress, not knowing that many of the promoters' promises and pictures would some day be realities.

"To-day the whole transaction appears as only a dream of the past, and those who have since come into active life and business can not realize the deep anxiety and perplexity that their fathers endured under the pressure of the 'Railroad Bonds.'

"It must be said in honor of the 'Non-Tax-Payers,' most all of the leaders of whom are to-day beneath the sod, that they stood in time of trouble as the eternal rocks against the lashing waves of a fearful storm and as an impenetrable wall in the dark hours of the panic, warding off and cutting down the enormous debt hanging over the county. Had it not been for their energies and devotion to the welfare of the county it might have had the entire debt to pay. It was undoubtedly their firmness that forced a satisfactory compromise of the debt, saving to the county $600,000. Although they were denounced by some, yet they were honest in their convictions of the right and felt that they had been betrayed and imposed on by designing persons."[6]

the outcome of the railroad bond question. The few that have not been redeemed are survivors of "old battlefields" in this "Forty Years' War."
[6] "Trying Times in Muhlenberg"; Muhlenberg Sentinel, September 23, 1910.

It will not be forgotten that one of the stipulations in the agreement with the railroad builders was that the track should be laid so as to come "within one mile of the courthouse." In order to comply with this agreement the surveyors were obliged to turn somewhat from a more direct course. The track was built "within a mile," with only some eighty feet to spare. An item published in the Greenville Record on October 6, 1910, illustrates the grim humor that grew out of this situation:

"Last week a traveling man made Greenville for the first time, and after some inquiries found the railroad was located almost a mile from the courthouse, and, of course, from the largest part of the business section. The traveler immediately sought Mr. W. G. Crawford, the courteous local agent of the Illinois Central Railroad, and asked, 'Why do you not have the station located up town?' Right off the reel the inquirer was given the response, 'Well, we find it more convenient to have the depot located near the railroad!'"

As has been said, Muhlenberg was not the only county that suffered from the era of railroad expansion. The State Auditor's report issued in 1871 shows that at that time thirty-five counties and fifteen cities in Kentucky were carrying similar railroad debts, amounting to $13,000,000. Along the Elizabethtown & Paducah Railroad were the counties of Grayson, $200,000; Muhlenberg, $400,000; Caldwell, $398,000; Lyon, $200,000; McCracken, $500,000, and the city of Louisville, $1,000,000, making a total of $2,698,000. The counties adjoining Muhlenberg that were then carrying railroad bonds were Logan, $736,000; Todd, $4,000; Christian, $200,000; city of Hopkinsville, $25,000; Hopkins, $165,000; city of Madisonville, $25,000, and two precincts in McLean County, $65,000.[7] Many of these bond issues became the subject of long litigation. Most of them were not paid until after a compromise had been effected. The railroad bonds of Green and Taylor counties date back to 1869, and are among the few that are still in litigation.

---

[7] Most of these figures are obtained from Collins, Vol. 1, page 211 (published in 1874).

XXX

TOBACCO

THE first tobacco cultivated in Muhlenberg, as far as is now known, was raised about the year 1802. Comparatively few large crops were produced in the county until about a quarter of a century after the plant had been introduced. Since the year 1830 tobacco has been one of the county's principal products. Muhlenberg's leaf and strips and its manufactured tobacco are now well known by the tobacco merchants and by the consumers of the weed. Over two and a half million pounds were raised annually as early as 1870, and since that time the county's yield has fluctuated between three million and five million pounds a year.

William Martin, who came to Muhlenberg in 1805, is the pioneer of the plug-tobacco business in the county. In the '30s of the last century he laid the foundations of an industry that after his time developed and gave to Greenville and Muhlenberg a wide reputation as a tobacco raising, rehandling, and manufacturing place. In the course of time William Martin was followed by three of his sons, and they in turn by some of their sons, and so on down through four generations. In fact most of the tobacco rehandling and manufacturing in Muhlenberg has been done by some of his descendants.

It was in 1835, in the Old Liberty neighborhood, that William Martin first manufactured plug tobacco. The tobacco raised in those days was about the same kind of Yellow Prior and shoestring still grown in some parts of the county. His son Dabney A. Martin later went to Virginia and there studied the culture of tobacco and introduced some other varieties equally well adapted to the soil in this section of the dark-tobacco district. William Martin selected the best leaf for his plug, using not only his own crop but also purchasing the crops of his neighbors. Most of the tobacco he handled was manufactured into plug each year during the course of a few months. His trash, lugs, and inferior leaf he prized into hogsheads and shipped to New Orleans via Kincheloe's Bluff. R. T. Martin, speaking of the poor transportation facilities the shippers of tobacco had during the early days, says: "They packed and prized the tobacco into hogsheads around a long pole which passed through the center. To the ends of the protruding pole they fastened two poles, to which horses were hitched, and in that way pulled and rolled the hogsheads to the Bluff. This 'carrying' was done when the roads were dry; nevertheless, mud holes were sometimes encountered and the tobacco would become more or less damaged."

William Martin had no wooden screws or any other contrivances that in any way approached modern appliances. He simply stemmed and re-dried the leaf and then packed it into crude forms or moulds, to which he applied pressure by pulling down on one end of a twenty-foot beam, the other end of which was tenoned in a mortise cut for that purpose in one of the heavy timbers of his barn. After the beam or lever had been pulled down by all the available human muscle it was held in position by means of a swordlike hickory peg stuck into one of a series of auger-holes in the wall. The pressure thus produced and held was so great that, according to local tradition, "it not only made the juice fly, but turned the tobacco into solid cakes as black as the niggers who done the squeezing." These plugs of "flat chewing" usually weighed about eight ounces, and were packed into boxes holding from one hundred to one hundred and fifty pounds. William Martin followed only a few years the manufacturing business he had started. However, before he quit, one of his sons, William Campbell Martin, took up the same work and continued in it until about 1840.

In 1840, Dabney A. and Ellington W. Martin, two of the younger sons of William Martin, established a plant on North Main Street in Greenville, and there began the making of the brand known as "Greenville Tobacco." This famous brand was manufactured in Greenville for more than half a century. From a good trade in the South it gradually spread to many other parts of the Union. Dabney A. and Ellington W. Martin were the first local men to use screws, and also the first to introduce flavoring and sweetening in plug tobacco. They loaded their manufactured product on six-mule wagons, each holding about four thousand pounds, and started them on long trips through the South. These large wagons were usually accompanied by one or two smaller ones, for the purpose of making side-trips from the main road and the moving source of supply. They delivered their goods on consignment; that is, to be paid for when sold, or to be returned when called for by the manufacturer. The quality of and the demand for their

DABNEY A. MARTIN, 1855

"Greenville Tobacco" was such that they seldom were obliged to relieve any one of unsold stock. There was no internal revenue tax on manufactured tobacco in those days, and their plug tobacco usually sold for "two bits," or twenty-five cents, a pound.

Dabney A. and Ellington W. Martin were the first men in Muhlenberg County to export strips or stemmed tobacco. As early as 1845 they added a stemmery to their factory. The plug and the strip business were both successful, and resulted in the accumulation of a large fortune. Most of their plug-tobacco trade, as already stated, was in the South. After the Civil War began they were unable to collect any bills. Furthermore, much of their tobacco was confiscated, and all their slaves were set free. The combined effect of these reverses was very disastrous. However, they continued in the business until shortly after the close of the war. In 1869 they sold their plant to Hugh N. Martin, who manufactured in the same building for a few years and then transferred the machinery to Chestnut Street, where in 1875 he added a stemmery and began putting up strips for the English market. In 1899 he removed to Louisville and there continued the leaf-and-strip business.

In the meantime other men went into the tobacco business in Greenville. Among those who began in the early days of this industry was George W. Short, who about 1843 began to manufacture plug tobacco. He operated until 1860. Shortly after his death his plant was converted into a rehandling house, and remained as such until its destruction by fire. A few years after the close of the war Hugh N. Martin, as already stated, began to make plug tobacco. About the year 1874 Ezekiel Rice, a grandnephew of the original William Martin, started the manufacturing of plug tobacco. He also handled leaf and put up a few strips. In 1899 Ezekiel Rice moved to Louisville and one year later sold out to the American Tobacco Company. Beginning about the year 1875 Charles E. Martin and William Irvin, and also D. A. Martin and T. M. Morgan, began manufacturing tobacco, but continued in that line only a short time. During the latter part of the '70s Richard T. Martin began the plug-tobacco business. In 1902 he sold his machinery and brands to a company in Hopkinsville, to which city the plant was then moved. Charles Y. Martin made plug and twist from 1880 to 1895; among his brands was the famous "XL Greenville." C. Y. Martin & Company now rehandle and export leaf tobacco and strips. In 1885 T. M. Green was among the manufacturers. A. J. Martin and Azel M. Terry made plug tobacco during the latter part of the '80s. In 1902 the S. E. Rice Tobacco Company began the manufacture of plug and pipe tobaccos, and in 1902 Buren Martin started in the plug business. The S. E. Rice Tobacco Company and Buren Martin & Company, of Greenville, are now the only tobacco manufacturers in the county.

The tobacco manufacturing business was at its height in Muhlenberg from about 1892 to 1898, when the four or five factories produced a total of about one million pounds a year.

Such, as I have given it, is a brief sketch of the first tobacco factory in the county and a glimpse of the more prominent establishments that followed. But all the men who handled tobacco in Muhlenberg did not drift into the plug-manufacturing business. Pioneer James Weir bought tobacco in Greenville during the earliest years of the county's history, shipping it in hogsheads to New Orleans. Edward R. Weir, sr., prized and shipped during 1840 and the years following. Thomas C. Summers, the father-in-law of Rufus Martin, bought leaf from 1850 up to the time of his death in March, 1886. Summers was one of the leading rehandlers of his day, and ran large houses at Earles and Bremen. John C. Carey, Charles W. Short, Joseph D. Yonts, and Charles B. Wickliffe were among the Greenville men who handled leaf in the '70s. Among the outsiders who put up leaf and strips about that time were Fattman & Company, of New York, who bought tobacco in Muhlenberg from 1865 to 1870, and Ackenberger & Company, who were represented by John Edmunds Reno about 1870 and after. Edward L. Yonts prized leaf from 1873 to 1890. Felix J. Martin handled tobacco from 1880 to 1885. George W. Eaves bought tobacco during the early '80s. Rufus Martin, a son of Felix J. Martin, began the leaf and strip business about the year 1880,

C. Y. MARTIN & COMPANY'S TOBACCO REHANDLING HOUSE, GREENVILLE

and was conducting a large establishment in Greenville when he died on November 3, 1902. As early as 1825 tobacco buyers were established at Paradise and a few other places in the county. H. D. Rothrock was one of the first buyers in South Carrollton. G. W. Briggs handled tobacco at Dunmor and Penrod for a number of years. William Shackleton was among the later buyers at Paradise.

For many years, up to about 1890, some of the farmers who raised tobacco occasionally bought the crops of their neighbors and prized them into hogsheads, which were shipped to Louisville and sold on the "breaks." Among such buyers and shippers were Thomas L. Martin,[1] William Y. Newman, Alney E. Newman, William Bell, Thomas B. Johnson, J. Lyles, Albert Miles, C. Cisney, and Daniel J. Gish.

The two manufacturers now in Greenville use much of the tobacco raised in the county. Most of Muhlenberg's crops, however, are "put on

---

[1] Thomas L. Martin was born in Woodford County May 4, 1801, came to Muhlenberg with his widowed mother in 1805, and died December 20, 1874. He lived near Old Liberty, where he raised many large crops of tobacco and was also engaged in rehandling tobacco. He was a successful farmer and did much toward the uplift of the county in general and the Old Liberty neighborhood in particular. He married Mahala Bell, daughter of pioneer William Bell. They were the parents of eight children: William, Dabney L., David H., Richard T., Charles Ellington, Thomas A., Mrs. Martha Jane (D. H.) Myers, and Mary Ann.

the open floor" or "pooled" and then sold to local or outside buyers, who ship the weed to Louisville and other tobacco-manufacturing cities. Since 1906 a control of the annual yield has been attempted by an organized body of men, who limit the size of their crops by following an agreement governing each farmer's acreage. During the past few years "pools" have been formed in which certain farmers coöperate to dispose of their combined crops to one buyer, to whom they sell at contract prices and who pays them their specified prices according to grades determined by the judges who grade it. The old way—the more independent way—of selling a crop is known as the "open floor." In this case the farmer raises as much tobacco as he cares to and sells it to any one who, in his judgment, makes the best offer.

THOMAS L. MARTIN, 1856

While the rehandlers and manufacturers are engaged in disposing of the tobacco that is raised year after year, and while the consumers of the weed are enjoying a smoke or a chew or a dip of snuff, many of the farmers of Muhlenberg are busy looking after another crop. The growing of good tobacco meant hard labor in the olden times, and it means hard labor now. No crop requires more care or greater patience than tobacco. From the sowing of the seed to the hauling of the product to market, every stage requires its own particular kind of weather. Should one of these ungovernable conditions fail to prevail at the right time, the quantity and quality of the tobacco are seriously affected. In fact, the uncertainty of the outcome has made it somewhat of a "gambling game." A crop of tobacco is the source of much worry, watching, and waiting. It usually represents a tenant's toil, for as a rule it is a "cropper's crop."

A tobacco crop now, as in the past, is worked along with other crops, and demands constant attention for "thirteen months of the year." The outdoor work begins with the clearing, burning, sowing, and canvasing of the plant bed, and continues down through the breaking of the ground, making of hills, setting and sometimes resetting of the plants; then follows the hoeing and plowing, the priming, topping, suckering, worming, cutting, and housing. After it is hung in the tobacco barn it is cured by either air-drying or by firing. After it has been cured and has "come in order" then the stripping, sorting, tying, and bulking take place. The next important event is to load the tobacco on a wagon and "carry" it to town and deliver it to the buyer.

At present many of the farmers in the northern part of the county cure their tobacco by air-drying it, while most of those living in the southern half fire it. The curing of tobacco by firing was probably introduced into Muhlenberg by the raisers of the first crops. However, it was not extensively practiced until about 1825, after which time until about 1850 all of the local product was fired. Since the Civil War the air-drying process has been resumed to some extent in the lower part of the county.

Although firing is the most disagreeable and hazardous part of the management of the crop, it, like all other barn work, nevertheless results usually in a pleasant time for those who participate.

One of the few surviving log cabins built for tobacco croppers when timber was plentiful.

On this occasion card-playing, potato-roasting, story-telling, and the playing of pranks take place around the slowly burning logs until long after the midnight hour. In fact, a jovial spirit generally prevails during all the indoor work, especially at the stripping. Old traditions are then recalled, the latest happenings discussed, new stories introduced, and many of the old jokes and tales retold. Among the latter are a number that have the reputation of being "as old as the hills." One is to the effect that Grandfather Somebody had a calf trained so that when he turned it into his tobacco patch it nipped off the tops of all the plants, thus sparing the farmer the trouble of topping. Another is that Uncle So-and-so had tobacco worms as large as the largest watermelons, and that he could not get rid of them in any other way than by shooting them. At one time,

An old-time log tobacco barn, near Long Creek, in which tobacco is cured by the firing process

so the tale is told, worms were so bad that the children could not go to school, not because they might be needed at home to pick the pests or kill the "green hail," but because the worms might attack and possibly devour the pupils on the road! The punster never fails to say that old man Somebody set out tobacco plants in his day until he became "stoop-ed."

The stripping is the first step toward the "winding up" of the crop, and every man who has worked on it is more or less interested in its weight and worth. Practically every one concerned either makes a guess or bets on the number of pounds, the proportion of leaf, lugs, and trash, and the price it will bring. Some not only guess or bet on the tobacco on which they have spent so many days of hard work, but often wager on other crops in the neighborhood.

The average crop raised in Muhlenberg consists of about three and one half acres, on each of which are planted about thirty-five hundred plants.

TOBACCO FIELD, A. B. CORNETT FARM, UPPER POND CREEK COUNTRY

Every acre produces from six hundred to a thousand pounds; in some instances the yield has reached eighteen hundred pounds. The average is about nine hundred pounds.[2] The weight is governed by the character of the season and the soil, and the worth by the quality and the supply and demand. Notwithstanding this complicated state of affairs, opinions regarding the pounds in the crop and the price it will bring vary only a little.

The history of every crop is a combination of tragedy, romance, and comedy. In spite of the constant work, unavoidable worry, and frequent disappointments, the raising and handling of tobacco now has and always has had many pleasant features, in the field as well as in the barn. Not the least among these features is watching the green leaves turn into greenbacks.

---

[2] Jacob Imbler, who lived west of Greenville, frequently raised over two thousand pounds of tobacco to the acre. It is said that about the year 1850 he offered to bet three thousand dollars that he could raise three thousand pounds of tobacco, regardless of the weather, on any acre of ground he might select on his farm or in his neighborhood. His plan was to do all the work by hand, spade the ground deep, and give each plant the very best of care. The people were so well convinced he could succeed that the wager was never accepted.

XXXI

COAL MINES AND IRON ORE

MUHLENBERG'S coal mines have a bearing on her past and present, and will undoubtedly form a prime factor in the county's future history. Iron ore has, so far, played a comparatively small part in Muhlenberg's bygone days; time alone can tell how great an effect the development of iron will have on the county's future history.

Much of the information gathered relative to the locating and developing of coal I found in geological reports. Local tradition has comparatively little to say on the subject. No written history of any of the local mines has ever been attempted. Incidents that have taken place around mines are soon forgotten, for current events usually form more interesting topics for discussion among miners than do matters pertaining to bygone days, and as a result much of the past is lost, as it were, in the dust and darkness of a deserted "entry" or an abandoned "room."

Fatalities occur in all coal-mining districts, and the cause and result of such accidents are among the things that are well remembered by sympathizing miners. In three of the disasters that have taken place in the county a distressingly large number of lives have been lost. Each of these three disasters was the result of an explosion. In the Moody Mine at South Carrollton two white men and eight negroes were killed on February 10, 1908; in the Browder Mine fifteen white men and nineteen negroes were killed on February 1, 1910; in the Central Coal and Iron Company Mine four white men and one negro were killed on January 17, 1912. A few accidents have occurred in each of which one man was killed; one or two resulted in the death of two men.

One of the few old stories occasionally told around the mines is of what is known as the "Dovey Robbery." One day during the summer of 1881 a stranger came to the Dovey mines at Mercer, then operated by John Dovey and his sons William and George B. Dovey. He asked for employment, and was told that he could go to work in a few days. In the conversation that followed he inquired in a casual way as to when the railroad pay-train would be due, and was informed that it had passed through the morning before. John Dovey incidentally remarked that the following day was pay-day for their miners, and that William Dovey had gone for the money and would return some time during the night. The next morning, after all the miners had gone to work, three strangers entered the Dovey store. Two of them immediately stepped in front of the building and guarded the place, while the third remained in the store and with cocked pistol in hand demanded the contents of the safe. George B. Dovey unhesitatingly opened the safe and proceeded to hand out all it contained —about thirteen dollars in cash and a gold watch with his father's name engraved on it. William Dovey, expected home the night before, had been delayed and had not yet arrived with the pay-roll money, which would have been in the safe had he come back at the time he originally intended to return. In the meantime two men and a woman, living near the mines, came to the store to make purchases. They entered the building, little suspecting that the two strangers in front were guarding the place. Immediately after they had stepped in, one of the strangers followed and with drawn pistol politely requested them to sit down and keep quiet while "young Mr. Dovey was transacting business with his friend." (George B. Dovey was then nineteen years of age.) After the robbers were satisfied that they had gotten all the cash and the only watch in the store, they quietly walked out of the building. By the time the three customers and George B. Dovey had recovered sufficiently from the shock to step to the front door the three strangers were nowhere to be seen. However, an investigation made shortly after showed that the robbers had gone toward Pond Creek, then to Rosewood, and across the cliffs into Logan County. It was not known until about a year later that Jesse James was the man who had robbed the store, and that he had come to Mercer for the purpose of robbing the pay-train. In April, 1882, when Jesse James was killed, the John Dovey watch was among the things found in his possession, and his administrator, seeing the name engraved on it, located the Doveys and returned the stolen property. [1]

In a sketch on "Powderly, Past and Present," published in the Greenville Record, March, 1911, Miss Amy M. Longest touches on the history of the mine in that town:

"The real birthday of Powderly was March 17, 1887. The place was so named in honor of T. V. Powderly, who was before the public at that time as a leader in the great labor movement. In the spring of 1887 a band of men bought some land near the railroad, two miles north of Greenville, and commenced the opening of a coal mine. This enterprise was a novel one: each shareholder in the Coöperative Coal Company put in twenty-five dollars or gave its equivalent in work. John D. Longest was the first president of the company.

---

[1] No Muhlenberger—native born or adopted son—was better known in professional athletics than George B. Dovey. After he became manager of the Boston National League Baseball Club he, in 1907 and in 1908, brought his "nine" to Central City and gave his "friends and fellow-citizens" an exhibition game of professional baseball.

From Sporting Life, Philadelphia, June 26, 1909, I quote: "The baseball world was shocked on Saturday, June 19, to learn of the sudden death of President George B. Dovey, of the Boston National League Club, on a Pennsylvania Railroad train while traveling in Ohio in search of players to strengthen his team. Mr. Dovey was forty-seven years old and a native of Philadelphia, whence he removed in early life to Central City, where his father owned coal property. Between times George played short field under the name of Colby on Barney Dreyfus' Paducah team, while a brother played second base under the name of Dayton. The Dovey boys, after giving up the mining business, turned their attention to other lines, and George B. became a railway man in Cleveland, Detroit, and St. Louis. . . . When, in the fall of 1906, he purchased the Boston Club, he resigned his position with the St. Louis Car Co. and removed

"Cottages were built by the miners, most of whom came from different localities and brought their families to live with them in the new town. All the members of this colony soon became acquainted and lived a quiet, congenial life. . . . But as a mine the enterprise, for lack of capital, was a failure. With the purchase of the Powderly Mine, in 1890, by the Greenville Coal Company, there began a change. All the stockholders sold their interest in the mine and many of them disposed of their houses and moved away. The vacated cottages were soon filled with other people and more new houses were built. The mine was better equipped . . . and now Powderly Mine is one of the best coal-producers in the county."

It is probable that some of the outcroppings of coal in Muhlenberg were observed by a number of the first-comers in the county, but the real nature and future value of the coal was not recognized by them. Timber was abundant, and the pioneers were more interested in the finding of good sandstone for chimneys and foundations than they were in the question of fuel.

Tradition has it that Alney McLean or his son, William D. McLean, accidentally discovered that the "black rock" found on the McLean farm, near Green River, would burn. About the year 1820 William D. McLean opened up what was known as the McLean drift bank below Paradise. He was one of the first men to report the existence of coal in Western Kentucky, and also one of the first to recognize Muhlenberg's coal as a desirable fuel. However, wood being plentiful and more convenient, his discovery was at that time regarded as a matter of little consequence.

About the year 1830 a few barges of coal were mined at the McLean bank and sent down Green River to Evansville and Owensboro. At about that time coal was also taken from near Ennis and the Mud River Mine and hauled to Russellville in ox wagons, a distance of about thirty miles. In the meantime a few men living near Pond River, among whom was William McNary, experimented on the coal that cropped out in that part of the county. In the central and southern sections a number of small drift banks were opened as early as about 1832, for the purpose of supplying the roadside blacksmiths. The early blacksmiths called this fuel "rock coal," thus distinguishing it from charcoal, which for many years was the only coal burned in their forges.

In 1838 and during a few years following Buckner and Churchill used charcoal in their furnace and also a little of the lower coal (probably No. 4), which they mined near The Stack. In 1854 Alexander reopened one of the McLean mines at Airdrie that had been worked more or less since about 1820, and also sank two shafts.

---

to Boston and assumed the duties of president and treasurer of the club. Mr. Dovey, albeit a shrewd business man, was thoroughly familiar with baseball and an ardent lover of the game. Personally he was most affable and companionable, a good talker and 'mixer,' and a man who made friends readily, and having made them held them; in short, he was just such a man as was needed to regain a National League following in Boston, and would have, without doubt, ultimately succeeded in giving Boston a winning National League team had his life been spared. He is survived by two brothers—John S., the secretary and treasurer of the Boston National League Club, and James, who lives at Latrobe, Pennsylvania, and by his mother, Mrs. Catherine J. Dovey, aged eighty-six, who lives in Brooklyn. Mr. Dovey was buried at Mount Moriah Cemetery, Philadelphia."

The coal along Green River received more attention in the early days than any found elsewhere in the county, because its location offered better transportation facilities. The McLean Bank, the Williams Shaft, the Vanlandingham Ledge, Pain's Mine, Kincheloe's Bluff Bank, the Rothrock Mine, and the Throckmorton Mine, all on or near Green River, and the Mud River Mine on Mud River, were among Muhlenberg's first commercial mines.

In 1847 Lewis Collins, in the short chapter on Muhlenberg County published in his first "History of Kentucky," says "the county abounds in coal and iron ore." But the great extent and probable value of the deposits of either the coal or the iron ore was given very little thought by local people before David Dale Owen, in 1854, published the First Report of the Geological Survey in Kentucky. In this report (pages 135 to 149) Doctor Owen calls attention to the existence of coal in about twenty-five different places in the county. Among other things he states (page 140) that the coal measures of Muhlenberg County are "rich in coal and iron ore." In the official publications that follow he and his successors report many other localities where thick veins of coal exist in the county. Doctor Owen observed that coals No. 12, No. 11, and No. 9, and all the lower numbers, are found throughout the northern half of Muhlenberg and in most of that part of the county that lies along Green River, and also that in the southern half of the county the lower numbers, down to the subcarboniferous, crop out in rotation, and beyond the limits of the county run out entirely. The many observations made since his day have merely verified his statements.

Regardless of the comparative value of these veins, the interesting fact in Muhlenberg's history is that these great deposits were studied and officially reported as early as 1854 by Doctor David Dale Owen, America's greatest geologist. Doctor Owen foresaw that the quality and abundance of this mineral was such that Muhlenberg would some day be a great coal-producer. Developments since his time, and especially in recent years, have undoubtedly gone far beyond any prophecy he then felt justified in making.

In the early '70s of the last century, after the completion of the Elizabethtown & Paducah Railroad through the county, and later after the construction of the Owensboro & Russellville Railroad from Owensboro to Owensboro Junction (now Central City), a number of mines were opened along these two lines. In 1875 no less than twelve mines were in operation on or near what is now the Illinois Central Railroad: Paine's Mine and the Collier and Woodcock Mine, near Green River; the Richmond Mine, near what is now Martwick; the Louisville and Stroud City Mine, the Galena, the Ross Mine, and the Finch Shaft, all four in the immediate vicinity of Central City; the Coppage Drift Mine; the Mercer Mine; the Muhlenberg Mine, and near Gordon Station (Depoy) the Gordon Mine, the Quinn Mine, and Arbuckle's Mine.

While these mines were being worked, land in the immediate vicinity of the railroad slowly advanced in price, but not until about 1880 did mine operators begin to appreciate the value of these deposits. In the meantime the county's railroad indebtedness became such that few capitalists cared to venture into the field. However, in the course of a few years more small mines were opened and also a few large ones. Mines are now operated along all four of the railroads in the county. Besides a number of "country banks," there are at present twenty-six commercial mines in Muhlenberg, whose total output has placed her at the head of the coal-producing counties in Kentucky.

Coal-mining methods have undergone many changes in recent years. All the commercial mines in Muhlenberg use modern machinery. Many of them are equipped with the latest electric appliances. The Midland Mine

MUD RIVER, NEAR MUD RIVER MINE

has a steel tipple. One modern improvement follows another so rapidly that the methods of a few years previous are soon regarded as out of date. During these rapid changes the early methods—the methods in vogue forty or more years ago—are almost lost sight of, for like the traditions bearing on the first mines in the county they are seldom or never referred to, and are as it were buried in the old dumps.

Among the very few men in the county who have made a study of early mining methods is William H. Hoskinson, who lives near Mud River Mine, and to whom I am indebted for data on the early history of this old mine.

Mud River Mine, although never a large one, was in the early days the largest in Muhlenberg, and is now considered "the oldest in the county." Its early history, vague as it is, is worth preserving, if for no other reason than the fact that it is the only one of the early mines regarding which any facts have been preserved by tradition.

The land known as the Mud River Mine property was originally a small tract. Adjoining surveys were purchased at various times, and the whole is now a body of about four thousand acres. During the past eighty years the place has been opened and closed a number of times, notwithstanding the fact that its coal has always been considered of a superior quality. It is said that every time the mine was shut down it was because the operator had failed to introduce modern methods.

In the early days the Mud River Mine was confined to the openings on the "river side"—the side of the hill that faces Mud River. The openings on the opposite side of the same long hill were made in comparatively recent times, and are on what is known as the "railroad side." It is so called because it is on the same side as the Louisville & Nashville Railroad and because a railroad track had been built from Penrod to the mine and used for a number of years.

Four entries, at different times, were driven into the hill at places on the river side. Regarding the oldest of these there is no reliable tradition as to when it was opened or abandoned. I infer, however, that it was opened as early as 1830. The second was probably opened shortly after, and was used until about 1858, when what is now called the old Hall & Payne entry was made and worked until about 1864. The Old Shop entry, the fourth and last on the river side, was opened in 1864, and for about twenty years produced all the coal mined at Mud River.

Although there were four mines on the river side, only two tipples had been built on the river bank. This verifies the tradition that all the coal produced from the two other entries was taken away in wagons. It was bought by a number of blacksmiths in Butler, Logan, and Muhlenberg counties, some of whom were obliged to haul it a great distance. The principal market, however, was at Russellville, about thirty miles away. What is still called the "Old Coal Road" began at the river side and ended in Russellville. It was at one time one of the best-known thoroughfares in the county.

Some of the people who burned this coal sent their own wagons after it, but generally it was hauled by men who lived near the mine and who made a business of delivering it. These wagoners, as a rule, drove a yoke of oxen, and often three or four yoke, to a load. It usually required about three days to make the trip to Russellville and return. The drivers always carried necessary supplies with them, and were prepared to camp any place where night might overtake them.

About the year 1850 Doctor Roberts appeared on the scene. He built a few substantial log cabins for his employes, and erected for his own use a house on the hill that divides the two sides. His residence is still standing. Doctor Roberts owned a number of slaves, among whom was one named Carter, who in all probability was as black as coal, for even to this day the expression "black as Carter" is used by many of the people living near Mud River Mine, few of whom know the origin of the phrase or give it any more thought than they do the whereabouts of that Carter who seems to have had an abundance of oats. Up to the arrival of Doctor Roberts all the coal that had been mined was taken away in wagons. He was the first to ship it in barges down Mud River. Shortly after 1850 the hauling of coal over the Old Coal Road began to fade into insignificance compared to the coal traffic on the river. The coal barges were taken up and down the river by men known as "river runners." Sometimes the boats were cordelled— that is, pulled by a rope that had been fastened to the bow and taken as far ahead as the length of the line or crookedness of the channel would allow. Most of them, however, were pushed along by means of set-poles manipulated by the crew. The men and boys seem to have enjoyed their work on the river as much as the drivers did theirs on the Old Coal Road.

THE DOCTOR ROBERTS HOUSE, MUD RIVER MINE

They were familiar with all the meanderings and landmarks along the stream, and although never measured, the distance from one point to another was well understood. It was considered two miles from the tipple to the mouth of Clifty or Rocky Creek, two more to Buzzards' Roost, and two more to the Old Mill Seat or the Half-Way. From there it was two miles farther to Conley's Lake, two more to Fleming's Landing, and two more down to the mouth—in all twelve miles to Rochester. Most of the barges, after they reached Green River, were sent farther on by means of tow-boats. Many of them were taken as far as Bowling Green.

Doctor B. W. Hall and William Payne operated the mine for a few years preceding the Civil War. They are now not as well remembered on account of their connection with the mine as they are because they introduced into the neighborhood a breed of hogs known as "mule-footed hogs." These hogs, in general appearance, were not unlike what their name implied. This breed gradually became mixed with other hogs around the mine and finally all trace of it disappeared. Up to a few years ago one could occasionally see a hog with some of its hoofs "mule-footed" and the others "split."

From 1860 to 1870 attempts to develop the mine were made at different times by men who had leased the property. Among these operators were Captain Phelps, Wesley Stevens, William Russell, and Colonel Taylor.

In 1870 Doctor B. W. Hall returned and brought with him Captain James B. Ryan, of Nashville, Tennessee. These two men did more toward developing the mine on the river side than any of their predecessors. After Doctor Hall withdrew, Captain Ryan opened the first mine on the railroad side of the hill and had a railroad track built to it from Penrod. Since his day the coal has been worked in a limited way. It is said that the present owners of the Mud River Mine are making a careful study of the mineral resources of their holdings, and that they contemplate equipping the mine with modern machinery and developing it on a scale larger than any before attempted.

Relative to early mining methods, William H. Hoskinson, in a letter written to me in November, 1912, says:

"Those who are familiar with none but the present methods of mining coal can not easily realize on how diminutive a scale the old Mud River Mine—or any other old coal mine—was worked. In 1871-72, when my father, Jackson Hoskinson, operated this mine under a contract with Hall & Ryan, he put out more coal than had ever before been produced at this place in the same length of time. But there are mines in Muhlenberg County now that produce more coal in one week than did old Mud River during the entire two years of my father's contract.

"Modern methods, as we know them to-day, were never in use at Mud River. In fact, the methods employed at any given time were never modern even at the time used. Much coal has been produced here by the light of candles and the old 'Dutch lamps,' but these were displaced long ago by the more convenient devices from which have evolved the present oil and carbide lamps. The drill, needle, and scraper were never seen here until about 1869. Before that time all coal was wedged down. A good steel sledge and five or six steel wedges were among the essentials of a collier's kit; he also had a heavy iron rake, with which he separated his coal, being careful to load nothing that would pass through the rake. His car was supposed to hold ten bushels. When it was filled a homemade wooden ticket was attached to it and a 'pusher' pushed it out of the room into the 'lie-way,' where it was coupled on to one or two other cars and pulled by a mule to the tipple. Only one mule was used in the mine, and he never went any farther than the 'lie-way.' In fact, small as he was, it was necessary in many places to remove some of the roof or bottom to make it possible for him to reach the 'lie-way.' The track throughout the mine was of wood. For a long time car wheels without flanges were used—the flange, or guard rail, being part of the wooden track. In the course of time these smooth-faced old wheels and the wooden tracks were superseded by flanged wheels and iron rails.

"Blasting powder, it is said, was first used here about 1869, by August Baker. This was the beginning of a new epoch at Mud River, for the churn-drill, needle, and scraper soon began to take the place of the sledge and wedges. All the coal was mined 'on the clear' and four or five inches of powder was considered a good shot. The little squib now so common was then unknown. In its stead the miners used a joint of wheat-straw filled with gunpowder, which was set off by means of an oiled paper placed under the straw and attached to the coal by a small lump of clay. When I was a boy I made many of these squibs, leaving the joint in one end of the straw and stopping the other end with soap to keep the powder from running out.

"The airing of the mine received very little consideration while the place was small, but as the entries increased in length this problem became greater. The general principle was the same then as now, except that fans

TIPPLE AND POWER HOUSE, CENTRAL MINE, CENTRAL CITY

were unknown. If any accident occurred around old Mud River in the early days worse than the scraping of a pusher's back on a bump in the roof, I never heard of it.

"There never were more than eight dwellings, a few barns and cribs, and a blacksmith shop in the town. As far as I am aware, the mine employes paid no rent, but they took good care of the houses assigned them. There was a small room in one end of the shop where a few groceries were kept for the accommodation of such families as might need them before they had an opportunity to have some brought up from Rochester. As a rule the miners sent to Rochester for enough supplies at one time to do them for a month or two. These purchases were brought to the mines by the 'river runners' on their return trips. Such small quantities as are now bought by many of the miners—a pound of coffee, a quarter's worth of sugar—were unheard of then. Nor were they guilty of such sinful and senseless extravagance as is now so often seen among miners. Milk, butter, eggs, and vegetables were seldom if ever bought, for each family produced its own. Many of the miners raised their own corn and meat; those who did not usually bought them from the farmers at the proper season and in sufficient quantities to run them for a year."

The oldest of the large mines in Muhlenberg now in operation is the Central Mine at Central City. Biederman duPont, the father of the present great mining industry in Muhlenberg, established the Central Coal & Iron Company, and in 1872, he being then a man of about thirty-five years, began developing (among that company's other holdings in Western Kentucky) two mines in the immediate vicinity of what later became Central City. The first of these was the Galena, west of town, and the other the Stroud Mine, both working the No. 11 vein. The shaft of what is now the Central Mine was sunk alongside the Stroud shaft in the fall of 1883. Coal

POWER HOUSE AND DOUBLE TIPPLE, GRAHAM-SKIBO MINE, GRAHAM

No. 9 was reached the day before Thanksgiving. This day is fixed in the minds of those who helped sink the shaft, for T. Coleman duPont, son of B. duPont, sent every one of them some of the coal from the new opening, and with it their Thanksgiving turkey was cooked. The Galena was in its day the largest mine in the county. The Central Mine, its successor, held the same position from the time it was opened down to twenty years after.[2]

The largest coal-producer in the county is the Graham-Skibo mine. This mine was opened in 1903 by the W. G. Duncan Coal Company of Greenville, who in 1900 opened the Luzerne Mine. No. 9 coal is worked at both of these mines. The Graham-Skibo tipple is a double one, serving the

---

[2] Among the well-known men who were identified with the Central Mine and with Central City were William D. McElhinny, who was vice-president and treasurer of the Central Coal & Iron Company from 1899 to 1911; Hywel Davies, now of Louisville, who was general manager from 1894 to 1900 and from 1909 to 1912, and who is serving as the first president of the Mine Owners Association of Kentucky; John S. Hobson, who until 1911 was sales agent, and the late Esquire F. Howey, who for many years was purchasing agent. The officers of the Central Coal & Iron Company are: T. Coleman duPont, president (who lived in Central City for a number of years, did much toward the upbuilding of the town, and who now lives in Wilmington, Delaware); John B. McElhinny, secretary (who has been identified with the mine since 1899); Samuel A. Yorks, vice-president, treasurer, and general manager (who although a newcomer is one of the best known and most influential young men in Central City).

Graham entry from one side and the Skibo from the other. Both divisions are equipped with the latest electric hauling and mining machinery. The tipple, like all other parts of this mine, is up to date in every respect and is kept always in neat condition. The town of Graham is one of the neatest and most orderly mining towns in the county.[3]

Muhlenberg County coal mines and their output for 1911 are given in the official report as follows:

Mine.	Tons.
W. G. Duncan Coal Co., Graham-Skibo, Graham	333,757
Crescent Coal Co., Bevier	252,945
Central Coal and Iron Co., Central City	190,716
W. G. Duncan Coal Co., Luzerne	190,395
Gibraltar Coal and Mining Co., Mercer	182,310
Greenville Coal Co., Powderly	103,050
Bevier Coal Co., Cleaton	94,830
Beech Creek Coal Co., Beech Creek	93,301
Lam Coal Co., Bevier	90,882
Black Diamond Mining Co., Drakesboro	89,670
Nelson Creek Coal Co., Nelson Station	81,629
Dovey Coal Co., Mercer	69,089
Elk Valley Coal Co., Diamond Block	66,845
Elk Valley Coal Co., Elk Valley	65,193
Hillside Coal Co., Oakland [1]	58,328
Elk Valley Coal Co., Browder Mine, Browder [2]	55,176
Kentucky-Midland Coal Co., Midland	50,154
Peerless Coal and Coke Co., Hillside [3]	48,658
Holt Coal Co., Central City	43,364
Hillside Coal Co., Hillside	15,425
Greenville Coal Co., Martwick	14,231
Elk Valley Coal Co., Radiant [2]	12,043
Rock Island Coal Co., South Carrollton	11,822
R. Morgan Coal, Coke and Mining Co., Mercer	9,691
Sunrise Coal Co., Drakesboro	1,682
Hendrie Coal Co., Drakesboro	476
	2,225,662

[1] And Oakland Coal Co.
[2] Succeeded by Muhlenberg Coal Co., December, 1911.
[3] And Advance Coal Co.

The output in Muhlenberg in 1911 was a little less than two and a quarter million tons, which at the rate of forty tons to the car made about 55,000 carloads of coal for that year.

The official report for 1911 shows that the average number of persons employed at and in these mines during the current year (excepting those in stores, offices, and similar positions) was 3,504, of whom 3,067 worked underground and 437 on the surface.

---

[3] The officers of the W. G. Duncan Coal Company are William G. Duncan, president, Charles W. Taylor, vice-president and manager, and Andrew W. Duncan, secretary and treasurer. William G. Duncan, jr., is the mining engineer. A. W. and W. G. Duncan, jr., are sons of William G. Duncan. The four men here referred to live in Greenville and in many ways have done much toward the advancement of the interests of both the county and the town.

The production of coal in Muhlenberg County for the years 1890 to 1911 inclusive, as shown by the records in the office of C. J. Norwood, Chief State Inspector of Mines, is as follows:

Year.	Output, Tons.	Year.	Output, Tons.
1890	231,080.16	1901	532,838
1891	265,065.84	1902	729,010
1892	299,541.00	1903	801,999
1893	315,724.16	1904	903,205
1894	269,579.84	1905	1,044,402
1895	267,353.02	1906	1,491,905
1896	256,268.19	1907	1,860,499
1897	261,783.32	1908	1,774,314
1898	268,507.40	1909	1,881,177
1899	414,846.34	1910	2,849,690
1900	409,581	1911	2,225,662

Muhlenberg County has an area of about four hundred square miles, all of which is underlaid with coal. However, only about two thirds of this area, or 270 square miles, is, it is said, underlaid with coal No. 9 and No. 11, which are the largest veins and practically the only ones now being worked. Each foot of thickness of a vein of this coal is estimated to produce 1,000 tons to the acre, and since No. 9 and No. 11 have a combined average thickness of from ten to eleven feet, these two veins will run, according to this estimate, about 10,000 tons to the acre, or 6,400,000 tons to the square mile, and 1,728,000,000 tons to the 270 square miles. Thus, assuming that the coal is uniform and estimating the output at three million tons per year, these two veins alone could be worked, according to these figures, for about six centuries, or until about the year 2500 A. D.

The mining of coal has passed the experimental stage and is now a well-established industry. The history of the two attempts to develop the iron ore is given in "The Story of The Stack" and "Paradise Country and Old Airdrie." As already stated, the Buckner Furnace was in operation about the year 1840 and the Airdrie furnace about the year 1855. Although the failure of both furnaces was due to causes other than the quality or quantity of the ore, no further attempt has been made to develop these extensive deposits.

In the case of iron ore, as in the case of coal, the first official record dates back to 1854, when Doctor Owen's report on these resources was published in the First Geological Survey of Kentucky. On page 59 he calls attention to the fact that "the lower coal measures in Muhlenberg and Hopkins counties include important beds of iron ore." In this same volume, pages 345 to 359, are published the results of chemical analyses made by Doctor Robert Peter of nine iron ores found near Green River and in the southern part of the county. They show that these ores contain from 31.17 per cent to 43.56 per cent of iron. The existence and character of these ores is not only discussed by Doctor Owen in the three succeeding reports compiled under his supervision, but the subject is also dwelt on by some of his successors. In Vol. I, New Series, Kentucky

Geological Survey, page 278, Doctor Robert Peter, having further investigated the iron ores of Muhlenberg, shows that they are composed of from 32.81 per cent to 48.82 per cent of iron. In Vol. II, New Series, pages 433 to 437, Professor N. S. Shaler, in 1876, writes:

"The most extensive and best developed ore region of Western Kentucky is called the Cumberland River iron region. . . . This region is capable of, and destined to, a much greater development than it has yet attained. . . . Already measures are in progress for the erection of extensive coke-works on the line of the Louisville, Paducah & Southwestern

TIPPLE AND POWER HOUSE, BLACK DIAMOND MINE, DRAKESBORO.

Railroad, which will doubtless prove but the first step in the successful development of a different form and more extensive iron industry than any yet established in Western Kentucky. . . . It is one of the most richly endowed undeveloped iron regions in the State. . . . In many other localities in the western coal-field iron ores have been found, but they have not been thoroughly prospected and little is known of their extent. One of the best-known localities of this sort is in Muhlenberg County. In this county are found, at Airdrie Furnace, on Green River, and at Buckner Furnace, near Greenville, deposits of so-called blackband iron ore, a ferruginous bituminous shale, yielding about thirty per cent of iron."

Such is in brief the history of the discovery of iron ore in Muhlenberg. Although two attempts to work this iron ore have been made, it has not yet been successfully accomplished. Many of the best mining experts and practical chemists of to-day declare that the local iron ore is not workable, and furthermore that the local coal can not be coked for the purpose of a flux. On the other hand a number of Muhlenberg men and some outsiders have prophesied that the development of this ore, like the coal, will some day be one of the leading industries of the county. At any rate, the Louisville Courier-Journal, in an editorial May 5, 1911, said:

"After the year 1800 the iron business in Kentucky made rapid progress, and from 1825 to 1860 it was a flourishing industry. The State is still dotted with the ruins of furnaces, for there is ore in various parts of Kentucky, but little of it being mined. There is ore both in the eastern and western coal fields and outside of them.

"The decline of the industry in Kentucky and Ohio may be attributed

POWER HOUSE AND STEEL TIPPLE, KENTUCKY-MIDLAND MINE, MIDLAND
Erected in 1908

to the discovery of the greater ore fields in the Northwest and elsewhere and also to the changed methods of mining, manufacturing, and distribution that have come about with the development of the country. Before the days of railroads Kentucky had many furnaces in successful operation. The ore was not exhausted and it is still here in great quantities. Will the industry ever 'come back?' Possibly not, and if it should it would be on a very different basis from what it was in the days of the old charcoal furnaces as they existed in Bath and Estill, in Nelson and Bullitt, in Lyon and Trigg and in other counties of Kentucky and in the counties of Southern Ohio. Nevertheless it is scarcely to be believed that these stores of iron will remain locked up forevermore. Next to coal Kentucky is more abundantly supplied with iron than with any other mineral. The country is using and exporting more iron every year. Whether or not there should be a resumption of furnace operations it is certain that some day this vast underground wealth will be in demand. While capital is so assiduously engaged in buying up Kentucky coal lands might it not be worth while to devote some attention to our latent iron deposits, which have been known to some extent to the outside world since the days of the Revolution? It is a queer phase of the mineral development of this country that a State which was the cradle of Bessemer steel and which once was dotted with furnaces from the Big Sandy to the Cumberland River should have ceased to figure seriously as a producer of iron.''

The mining of coal in Muhlenberg is an established industry, and since the supply is practically inexhaustible, its future record will undoubtedly form much of the county's local history. Capital, labor, and skill are the forces now successfully developing the wealth in the coal. But the development of the iron was for many years an unfortunate victim of operative blunders and bad transportation facilities, and is still a victim of doubt and neglect. King Coal will reign for many years, but I dare say the Iron Master will some day help rule. Then Doctor Owen's observation, made in 1854, that the coal measures of Muhlenberg are ''rich in coal and iron,'' and Collins' statement, published in 1847, that ''the county abounds in coal and iron ore'' will be more fully appreciated, and the records of science and history, long ignored, will receive the credit due them.

The three leading coal-mine operators residing in Muhlenberg to-day are William G. Duncan, James W. Lam, and William A. Wickliffe.

William G. Duncan, the Coal King of Muhlenberg County, was born in Scotland September 4, 1851. In 1855 his parents moved to Pennsylvania and the same year came to Airdrie, to which place his father, Andrew Duncan, a practical miner, had been invited by Alexander. After the Airdrie Furnace was abandoned Andrew Duncan operated coal mines near Paradise and Airdrie, where William G. Duncan spent his youth. After operating a number of mines in Ohio County and other places, William G. Duncan returned to Muhlenberg in 1900 and opened the Luzerne Mine. In 1903 he opened the Graham-Skibo Mine, which is the largest and best-equipped mine in Western Kentucky. These mines are owned by the W. G. Duncan Coal Company, of which corporation he is president. Mr. Duncan lives in Greenville in a house that is regarded as one of the most beautifully finished and furnished homes in the Green River country.

WILLIAM G. DUNCAN, 1912

No man has done more toward the development of Muhlenberg's coal industry, and no citizen is more liberal or has the interests of the county more at heart, than William G. Duncan.

James Wilson Lam was born in Muhlenberg County June 23, 1851. His father, Elijah Lam, was born in Tennessee in 1822, and his mother, Martha Cates, was born in North Carolina in 1818. His parents were married in Tennessee in 1842, removed to Muhlenberg in 1850, and settled on a farm near Hillside. J. W. Lam is one of their six children. In 1874 Mr. Lam married Nancy Eades, daughter of Nathaniel and Elizabeth Eades. Their two children are Mrs. Eula Margaret (Charles W.) Roark and Mrs. Mayme Elizabeth (Hubert) Meredith. Mr. Lam was in the mercantile business until 1891, when he entered the coal-mining business and opened Hillside Mine. In 1895 he opened Oakland Mine, within two hundred yards of the place of his birth. He has operated these two mines continuously from the time they were opened, and has mined coal from under the ground on which stood the house in which he was born. He has been identified with various coal-mining interests in the county, and is at present engaged in operating Hillside, Oakland, Morgan, and Dovey mines. He moved to Greenville in 1885. In 1901 he helped organize the Muhlenberg County Savings Bank, Greenville, and has served as its president since 1903. He has been for more than twenty-five years one of the most public-spirited citizens of the county. Unlike many self-made men, he is very liberal. Through his personal efforts and his financial contributions he has done much toward the material improvement and the moral uplift of Muhlenberg County in general and of Greenville in particular. He has erected more modern business houses there than any other citizen. He began his first term as mayor of the town in 1905, and is now serving his second term.

JAMES W. LAM, 1912

William A. Wickliffe is a son of William B. Wickliffe and a grandson of pioneer Arington Wickliffe. He was born in South Carrollton February 16, 1860. In 1879 he began reading law under Judge W. W. Sweeney, of Owensboro. In 1880 he graduated from the Law Department of the University of Louisville and the same year located in Greenville, where he began the practice of law, which he is still following. He served as county attorney from 1882 to 1886, was superintendent of county schools from 1888 to 1890, master commissioner of the Muhlenberg Circuit Court from 1889 to 1897, and mayor of the city of Greenville from 1893 to 1897. In 1901 he was elected president of the First

National Bank, Greenville, which office he still holds. In 1903 he organized the W. A. Wickliffe Coal Company, which operated at Browder. A few years later he sold his interests in that corporation, and having purchased a large interest in the Greenville Coal Company at Powderly, he with his associates, in 1910, bought large tracts of coal lands from the Central Coal & Iron Company and in the fall of 1911 opened the mine known as Martwick—a name derived from Martin and Wickliffe. Judge Wickliffe has made a success of mining, banking, and law, and is widely known in all three circles. In 1885 he married Mollie Reynolds, daughter of John T. Reynolds, sr., and a granddaughter of pioneer Joseph C. Reynolds. Their home in Greenville is one of the largest and handsomest residences in the county. Mr. and Mrs. Wickliffe are the parents of four sons and one daughter. Their two eldest sons, Paul R. and Matthew L., are connected with the Greenville Coal Company, and, like Judge Wickliffe, are interested in promoting the commercial welfare of Muhlenberg. Their other children are Miss Margaret Louise and Masters William B. and J. Edwin Wickliffe.

WILLIAM A. WICKLIFFE, 1912

XXXII

COLLINS ON MUHLENBERG, QUOTED AND EXTENDED

COLLINS' "History of Kentucky" is the only book in which an attempt has heretofore been made to record a history of Muhlenberg County. In 1784 John Filson published a history of "Kentucke," the first history of the Commonwealth ever printed. Among other early histories of the State are "The History of Kentucky" by Humphrey Marshall, in 1812 and 1824, and "The History of the Commonwealth of Kentucky" by Mann Butler, in 1834 and 1836. In 1847 Lewis Collins published the first edition of his "Historical Sketches of Kentucky," and in 1874 Richard H. Collins greatly enlarged and extended his father's work. Some of the other histories that followed are, "Kentucky, a Pioneer Commonwealth," by Nathaniel S. Shaler, in 1885; "The History of Kentucky," by Zachariah F. Smith, in 1886, 1892, and 1895, and "Kentucky in the Nation's History," by Robert McNutt McElroy, in 1909. All these histories are State histories. However, Lewis Collins includes in his work a brief history of each county, and the same plan is followed in the work of his son, Richard H. Collins. Kentuckians will owe an ever-increasing debt of gratitude to the two Collins for the patient labor and patriotic devotion that animated them in preparing their histories. These books are a mine of personal, political, and general facts concerning the early history of the counties of the State, much of which would have perished but for them. Lewis Collins is the Kentucky Herodotus, in point of material at least, and his collection and that of his son must ever remain the starting-point of the future histories of every county in the State.

The "Biographical Encyclopedia of Kentuckians," published in 1878, contains biographies of eight Muhlenberg men, and "Kentucky, a History of the State," by J. H. Battle, published in 1885 by the F. A. Battey Publishing Company, contains biographies of ninety-two local citizens. These sketches, with a few exceptions, contain merely short statements regarding the ancestry and life of the subject. Nevertheless, all serve the purpose for which they were intended and are well worth preserving. The one on Rumsey touches on the invention of the steamboat, and is quoted in full in the chapter on Edward Rumsey. The one of Charles Eaves is, from a literary standpoint, by far the best of these biographies, and a portion of it is quoted in the chapter devoted to the career of Judge Eaves.

The "Biographical Encyclopedia of Kentuckians" (1878) contains biographies of the following Muhlenberg men: Finis McLean Allison, Colonel S. P. Love, Judge Alney McLean, Honorable Edward Rumsey, James Weir, sr., James Weir, jr., Colonel E. R. Weir, and Charles Fox Wing.

The first half of Battle's "Kentucky, a History of the State" (1885), is devoted to a history of the Commonwealth; the last half of the edition prepared for the western part of the State contains biographies of a number of men living in the counties of Butler, Caldwell, Crittenden, Hancock, Hopkins, Livingston, Logan, Lyon, McLean, Muhlenberg, Ohio, Union, and Webster. The following appear under the head of Muhlenberg County:

Adams, R. W.
Adkins, William C.
Alexander, Wayland.
Allison, Finis McLean.
Baker, Elisha.
Bard, William H.
Barkley, J. G.
Bennett, William.
Blades, Thomas H.
Boggess, John H.
Bohannon, Dr. J. G.
Bourland, Dr. Charles A.
Brewer, Silas H.
Briggs, George I.
Briggs, George W.
Brown, Samuel.
Cates, J. G.
Clark, M. B.
Coleman, Quintus B.
Craig, Samuel S.
Creel, Dr. Milton P.
Crews, James B.
Drake, Albritton M.
Drake, Patrick H.
Eades, Charles E.
Eaves, Charles.
Eaves, George W., jr.
Fleming, David J.
Frazer, Dr. Robert C.
Gish, George W.
Gordon, George.
Haden, G. W.
Hay, Marcellus C.
Hemenway, Gilbert D.
Hendricks, Joseph P.
Hill, Jesse S.
Hope, Jeremiah M.
Howard, John C.
Humphrey, Rolley E.
Humphrey, Ivy W.
Irvin, Dr. William E.
James, Dr. A. D.
James, William Sevier.
Jones, William G.
Jones, Columbus W.
Kirkpatrick, Lucilius M.

Lile, T. J.
Long, Rufus E.
Lovell, William M.
McCown, Dr. Alexander.
McCracken, Henry C.
McDowell, Dr. W. R.
Martin, William H.
Martin, H. N.
Mendel, Charles.
Mills, Jonathan E.
Morgan, Thomas M.
Morman, James C.
Murphey, Samuel W.
Myers, James Gwinn.
Myers, David H.
Newman, Henry G.
Oates, William W.
Penrod, H. C.
Prowse, Mark L.
Prowse, Isaac S.
Putman, Jesse M.
Reno, J. H.
Reno, Lewis.
Reynolds, Thomas H.
Rhoads, David E.
Rice, Moses M.
Riley, Higerson.
Roark, M. J.
Robinson, William E.
Roll, David B.
Rust, Erastus P.
Ryan, James Buckner.
Sandusky, William H. H.
Scott, James H.
Stokes, Thomas R.
Sullivan, John K.
Sweatt, Dr. Edward.
Short, C. W.
Ward, William Flam.
Whitmer, Warren P.
Wickliffe, William B.
Williams, John A.
Williams, Daniel H.
Wood, John H.
Woodburn, Dr. Benjamin W.
Yost, Dr. W. H.

Collins' "History of Kentucky," as stated, is the only book in which is preserved a history of Muhlenberg County. Collins' first history was published in 1847, by Lewis Collins, and reprinted in 1850. In 1874 Richard H. Collins revised his father's work, enlarged it to a two-volume edition, and brought it down to date. A third edition appeared in 1877, a fourth in 1882, and a fifth in 1910. The last three editions are printed from the same plates, and do not include any history later than 1877. In all four of these editions by Richard H. Collins the first half of the work (Volume I) is devoted to a history of the State, while the second half (Volume II) deals with the histories of the counties, which are arranged in alphabetical order. The short sketch published of Muhlenberg in 1847 and the one published in 1874 are here reprinted. Although they are not much more than an outline of the county's history, and notwithstanding the fact that both contain a few errors, they will in all probability always be of great interest to readers of Muhlenberg's history.

In the preface to the 1847 edition Lewis Collins acknowledges his indebtedness to "Charles F. Wing, Esqr., of Muhlenburg," for information regarding the county. With the exception of a few lines giving a biography of General Muhlenberg, I here quote in full the first data ever published on the history of the county.

LEWIS COLLINS, IN 1847, ON MUHLENBERG COUNTY.[1]

MUHLENBURG county was formed in 1798, and named in honor of Gen. PETER MUHLENBURG, of the revolutionary army. It is situated in the south-western middle part of the State, and lies on the waters of Greene river: Bounded on the north and north-east by Greene river, which separates it from Daviess and Ohio; east by Butler; south by Todd and Logan; and west by Hopkins. In the southern portion of the county the surface is broken, and the lands comparatively poor; while the middle and northern divisions are undulating, and the soil productive. Corn, pork, and tobacco, are the staples. The county abounds in coal and iron ore. The "Henry Clay Iron Works," four miles from Greeneville is supplied with ore of a superior quality from the contiguous high grounds, which, as the quantity is inexhaustible, has obtained the name of the *Iron Mountain*. There are several mineral springs in Muhlenburg; and salt, in small quantities, was at one time manufactured in the county.

Number of acres of land in Muhlenburg, 274,809; average value of lands per acre, $1.93; valuation of taxable property in 1846, $1,298,019; number of white males over twenty-one years old, 1,366; number of children between five and sixteen years old, 1,744; population in 1840, 6,964.

There are five towns in the county, viz: Greeneville, Lewisburg, Rumsey, South Carrollton, and Skilesville.

---

[1] In this (the 1847 edition) Collins spells the name of the county, that of the county seat, and that of the river, "Muhlenburg," "Greeneville," and "Greene River." In the 1874 edition the spelling is "General Muhlenberg" and "Muhlenburg county." General Muhlenberg never spelled his name other than with the terminal "berg." It is frequently, but erroneously, printed "burg," not only on the early maps of the State but also in many other early publications. The name is rarely misspelled in the early county records, and never in those of a later date.

GREENEVILLE, the seat of justice, is one hundred and twenty miles from Frankfort. It contains, besides the usual public buildings, one Presbyterian and one Methodist church, six lawyers, three physicians, one seminary, six stores, one grocery, two taverns, one wool carding factory, two tobacco factories, and eight mechanics' shops. Population, 400. Established in 1812, and named after the distinguished revolutionary general, Greene.

Lewisburg is a small village, situated on Greene river, nine miles from Greeneville, containing two stores, one warehouse, and about 50 souls.

THE SHORT ROAD LEADING FROM THE BOAT-LANDING TO SOUTH CARROLLTON

Rumsey lies on Greene river, at lock and dam No. 2, about twenty-five miles north of Greeneville—contains one Union church, one lawyer, two physicians, two taverns, five stores, two groceries, one school, two saw-mills, two grist-mills, one carding factory, and six mechanics' shops. Population, 300. Named after James Rumsey, for whom the honor is claimed of having built the first steamboat in the United States.

South Carrollton, situated on Greene river, two miles below Lewisburg —has two stores, three warehouses, one Cumberland Presbyterian church, one physician, one tavern, and four mechanics' shops. Population, 75.

Skilesville is situated on Greene river, at lock and dam No. 3, fourteen miles east of Greeneville, and contains one physician, two stores, and about 15 souls. Named after James R. Skiles, who introduced the first steamboat upon Greene river, and who spent a fortune in promoting the navigation of the river.

Lewisburg, or Kincheloe's Bluff, on Green River (one of the five towns referred to by Lewis Collins), was a landing-place before 1798, and according to one tradition was declared "a port of entry" about 1800. James Weir, and practically all the other pioneer merchants in the county, received their merchandise from the East at the "Bluff," and also shipped their produce, hides, and pork south from there. It was from this point that pioneer James Weir embarked for New Orleans in 1803, his account of which trip is given in Appendix B. The place was so called in honor of pioneer Lewis Kincheloe. Although the town had been laid out and a plat of it had been recorded in January, 1817 (Order Book No. 4, p. 118), the place was not established by an act of the Legislature until January 12, 1825. There is a vague tradition to the effect that some time during the early part of last century Lewisburg made an effort to become the county seat. After South Carrollton was started, about 1838, Lewisburg gradually lost its business and finally became little more than a ferry crossing. An old brick residence, a frame house, and a small abandoned drift coal mine and tipple are all that is now standing on the site that in early days seemed destined to become one of the largest towns in the county. A short distance below the old "Bluff" landing, which is still used by a ferry-boat and some of the steamboats, is the pumping station of Central City's waterworks.

Rumsey, another of the towns referred to, is in that section of McLean County which up to 1854 was a part of Muhlenberg. Its population to-day is only about thirty per cent larger than it was in 1847, or at the time referred to by Collins. When, in 1834, work was begun on Lock and Dam No. 2, the small settlement that lay near by, on the left bank of Green River, began to develop into a village. Before 1837, when the gates of the lock were opened, the place had assumed the proportions of a town, and was called Rumsey. It was incorporated February 11, 1839. It lies opposite Calhoun—the Rhoadsville or Fort Vienna of the olden days. From 1840 to about 1855 Rumsey was larger than Calhoun, but to-day it has a population of only 413, while Calhoun has 742. One of the first steamboats ever built on Green River was built at Rumsey in 1846 by James and Philip Jones and named for a Greenville girl, "Lucy Wing."

A number of well-known Muhlenbergers were identified with the early history of Rumsey. Some of them lived and died in or near the town. Those who left the place and established themselves elsewhere always regarded Rumsey as their "old home." Many of the sons and daughters of its earliest citizens are still living, and point with pride to the fact that they at one time lived in "old Rumsey."

Doctor John M. Johnson, the father-in-law of Colonel Ed R. Weir, was a citizen of Rumsey. He represented Muhlenberg in the Legislature in 1837. About the year 1855 he moved to Paducah, and from 1859 to 1862 represented McCracken County in the Legislature, from which (according to Collins) he was expelled February 15, 1862, for "leaving his seat and taking position in the Rebel army." During the Civil War he settled in Atlanta, where he died in 1886. His second wife was a sister of General Howell Cobb, of the Confederate army. General Richard W. Johnson, the distinguished Federal soldier, was a brother of Doctor Johnson. General Johnson spent the greater part of his youth in Rumsey with Doctor Johnson, and was living in the town when, in 1845, he entered West Point as a cadet, from which military academy he was graduated in 1849. Another brother was James L. Johnson, who moved to Owensboro. There he studied law and was elected to Congress for the term 1849-1851. On the resignation of Honorable Martin H. Cofer, Mr. Johnson was appointed circuit judge by the Governor. He married Miss Harriet Triplett, daughter of Honorable Philip Triplett, a distinguished lawyer and former Congressman.

Doctor John M. Johnson's co-worker was Doctor Rufus Linthicum, the father of Doctors William A., Rufus, Edward, and Daniel A. Linthicum. Doctor Daniel A. Linthicum practiced medicine at Helena, Arkansas, and during the Civil War ranked among the best-known surgeons in the Southern army. Edward is now a prominent physician at Evansville, Indiana.

Dillis Dyer laid out the town of Rumsey, and continued to live there for a number of years; he frequently served as guide to pilots. He practiced law at Hartford for some years. He was secretary of the State Board of Commissioners under whose superintendence the locks and dams were built. He represented Ohio County in the Legislature from 1840 to 1846. His only son, Honorable Azro Dyer, of Evansville, is a distinguished member of the Indiana bar, and was elected and served as judge of the Superior Court in that city.

Alonzo Livermore, Russell McCreary, and Ezekiel Fleming were among the civil engineers who had charge of the lock and dam during their construction. Russell McCreary continued to live in Rumsey a few years after the work was finished. In 1843 and 1844 he represented the county in the Legislature, and a few years later returned to his former home in Frankfort. His son, Russell McCreary, is a well-known and prominent citizen of Frankfort.

Livermore, in McLean County, was so called in honor of Alonzo Livermore, who planned and superintended the construction of the lock and dam at Rumsey. In his day he was one of the best-known civil engineers in the country. He came from Pennsylvania in 1835, where he had served as chief engineer of the Pennsylvania canal. He left Rumsey in 1855, did engineering work in Arkansas and other States, and died in Mendota, Illinois, in 1888, aged eighty-seven. One of his sons, Alonzo Skiles Livermore, in 1880 established the Livermore Foundry & Machine Company, of Memphis, Tennessee. Another son was Doctor H. B. Livermore, who for many years lived at Macomb, Illinois. Robert S. Howard, one of Rumsey's most highly accomplished citizens, married Fidelia Livermore, a daughter of Alonzo Livermore. Robert S. Howard and William T. Short kept a general store in Rumsey for a number of years. Short remained in the county, but Howard moved to New Orleans, became a well-known wholesale merchant, and later engaged in business in Portland, Oregon.

Elisha Baker and Samuel M. Wing conducted a large store in Rumsey for some time; the former then returned to Greenville, and the latter was long in business in Owensboro, where he spent the remainder of his days.

Douglass Little made plows and built wagons in Rumsey from 1844 to 1851. His shop was in its day the largest in the county. His plows and wagons were hand-made, and had the reputation of being the best ever sold in Muhlenberg. He was a Whig as long as that party was in existence. The opposition to the Constitution of 1850 came mostly from the Whig party; nevertheless, he voted for the new constitution. He removed to Calhoun (then in Daviess County) in 1851, and was there elected justice of the peace. When McLean County was cut off from Daviess in 1854, he was again elected a justice. At the election in 1858 he was chosen county judge, and reëlected in 1862. In 1874, after an intermission of two terms, he was elected to the same office for the third time, and was serving at the time of his death, which occurred at Calhoun in April, 1877.

Douglass Little was the father of Judge Lucius P. Little, of Owensboro, who served as circuit judge from 1880 to 1893 in the Fourth District, and who has for many years been one of the prominent lawyers of Western Kentucky and who has long been regarded as one of the highest authorities on the State's history. He is the author of "Ben Hardin, His Times and Contemporaries," and has in preparation "Old Stories of Green River and Its People."

John G. Gooch was one of Rumsey's most interesting characters. He was a saddler by trade, and up to 1850, when he represented the county in the Legislature, spent much of his time in his shop, working at his trade and studying good books. He was one of the best-read men in the county, and was a devout and active churchman. When occasion arose where an orator was required to represent the citizens of this section of the Green River country, they invariably chose John G. Gooch. After he became a member of the State Legislature he began the study of law, and a few years later moved to Palestine, Texas, where he became a prominent lawyer.

John Vickers, who represented Muhlenberg in the Legislature in 1848, lived three miles south of Rumsey, near Sacramento, now in McLean County. Although Sacramento was not incorporated and officially named until March 1, 1860, a store, it is said, had been opened there before 1835. One version has it that John Vickers, a "Forty-niner," returned from California about 1850, and was the first to propose the name Sacramento for the settlement at the cross-roads. In 1870 Sacramento's population was about 200, and in 1912 about 450.

John Bender, a German by birth and also a "Forty-niner," lived at Sacramento in 1850 and later died there. He was a very intelligent and substantial citizen. He was a son-in-law of John Vickers. Honorable William B. Noe, the banker, who has as a lawyer long been at the head of the Calhoun bar, married the daughter of Mr. Bender.

Among the old citizens of Rumsey in the '40s were Charles M. Baber, hotel-keeper and magistrate; William A. Eaves and Leander Mitchell, superintendents of the lock and dam; Woodford Mitchell and Henry Williams, merchants; John Robbins, wool manufacturer; John A. Murray, grocer, and Ephraim Baker, a justice.

Richard H. Collins, in his "History of Kentucky" published in 1874, and in the reprints that follow, acknowledges his indebtedness for information regarding Muhlenberg County to "Joseph Ricketts and J. H. Pearson (who made a most beautiful map), of Muhlenburg county."

In 1874 Joseph Ricketts was fifty-six years of age and had lived in Greenville for more than a quarter of a century. He was one of the best-known lawyers in the Green River country. Collins' acknowledgment to "J. H. Pearson," and his reference to "a most beautiful map," is in all probability a mistake, and was intended to apply to some other county in Kentucky. At any rate, of the many persons I consulted in Muhlenberg —the Pearsons and others—none recall a man named J. H. Pearson, nor do any recall seeing a map that might have been made by either Pearson or Ricketts. Furthermore, in a search among the maps once owned by Collins, I failed to find one of Muhlenberg County. A map of the county, made years ago and showing some of the geographical details, even if somewhat inaccurate, would be worth preserving. As far as I have been able to ascertain, no such map, either in the form of a printed sheet or a pen-and-ink sketch, exists. [2]

During the course of what follows in this chapter I quote all that Collins published under the head of Muhlenberg County in the edition printed in 1874, except the brief sketches of Generals Muhlenberg and Buell. To his statements I add a number of my own, and thus, in a way, extend his history down to our times.

RICHARD H. COLLINS, IN 1874, ON MUHLENBERG COUNTY, QUOTED AND EXTENDED.

Muhlenburg county—the 34th in order of formation—was established in 1798, out of parts of Logan and Christian, and named in honor of General Peter Muhlenberg. Its original territory is still intact, except the small northern portion taken in 1854 to help form McLean county. It is situated in the southwestern middle portion of the state, and is bounded N. and N. E. by McLean and Ohio counties, from which it is separated by Green river; E. by Butler county, Big Muddy river being the dividing line; S. E. by Logan; S. by Todd and Christian; and W. by Hopkins county, the dividing line being Pond river. The surface of the county is generally rolling, part of it broken; the northern portion is good farming land, and all the county is fine grass land, and well timbered. The principal products are tobacco, corn, hay, and wool. Cattle and hogs are sold in large numbers to drovers. But the great wealth of the county is coal and iron.

What is here referred to as Big Muddy River has for many years been known as Mud River. Although Muhlenberg is no longer "well timbered,"

---

[2] Joseph Ricketts lived in Greenville for a period of about thirty years, and during that time was one of the most highly esteemed men in the county. He was a son of Thomas Ricketts, and was born in Warren County July 4, 1818. He attended Center College, Danville, and later taught school at Morgantown, where in 1845 he began the practice of law. In 1847 he moved to Greenville, and shortly after became one of the best-known lawyers in his section of the State. He represented Muhlenberg in the Legislature in 1855-57. In 1861 he was elected on the Union ticket and again represented the county for two years. In 1875 he and his family moved to Texas. At the time of his death (in Sherman, Texas, October 20, 1895) he was United States Commissioner. In 1846 he married Lucy James, daughter of Foster James, of Morgantown. Among their twelve children are Mrs. Charles T. Carlton, Mrs. R. E. Martin, Miss Julia Ricketts, and Eugene Ricketts.

much timber is still standing. Very large trees are now rare, and the few giants that still survive will in all probability soon be cut down and worked into lumber. However, much uncleared "cut-over" land, with its secondary timber and "second growth," is still to be found in the county. Reforestation and forest planting have not yet been attempted.

The table of statistics of Kentucky, compiled by Collins from official reports, shows that during the year 1870 Muhlenberg produced 2,594,930 pounds of tobacco, 2,095 tons of hay, 484,580 bushels of corn, and 32,676 bushels of wheat. In 1870 there were 8,254 hogs (over six months old), 3,162 horses, 1,041 mules, and 5,166 cattle in the county. The valuation of taxable property was then $2,462,757; in 1846 it was $1,298,019, and in 1912 it was $4,365,446. The number of acres of land in 1870 is given by Collins as 253,543.

Practically every farmer in the county raises tobacco. The annual yield since 1870 has always exceeded two and a half million pounds. Farmers now pay more attention to the raising of hay than heretofore. The corn crop is usually sufficient for the local demand. Muhlenberg has never produced enough wheat to supply the local demand for flour. Hogs and cattle are still extensively raised, but the number has not increased in proportion to the number of farms.

The Elizabethtown & Paducah Railroad, now known as the Illinois Central Railroad, was finished in 1871, and therefore had been in operation only a few years when Collins published his sketch. A time-table, published in 1873, shows the following stations along this line in the county: Green River, Nelson Creek, Owensboro Junction, Greenville, and Gordon Station (Depoy). The Owensboro & Russellville Railroad, now a branch of the Louisville & Nashville, was built from Owensboro to Central City in 1872, and ten years later was extended to Russellville. The Madisonville, Hartford & Eastern Railroad was finished in 1910. The Kentucky Midland was begun in 1910. It is built as far as the new town of Midland, and will, it is said, soon connect Central City with Madisonville.

Collins publishes data relative to seven of the towns that were in the county in 1874—Greenville, South Carrollton, Skilesville, Stroud City, Bremen, Paradise, and Airdrie:

Greenville, the county seat, on the Elizabethtown and Paducah railroad, 135 miles from Louisville, 120 from Frankfort, and 35 from Hopkinsville, contains, besides the usual public buildings, 5 churches (Baptist, Methodist, Presbyterian (Southern), Cumberland Presbyterian, and African), and 6 ministers, 12 lawyers, 4 physicians, 3 academies, 13 stores, 13 mechanics' shops, 3 hotels, 1 mill, 4 tobacco factories, 1 tannery; population in 1870, 557, and in 1873 estimated at 1,000; established in 1812, and named after Gen. Nathanael Greene.

Greenville, although started in the spring of 1799 and serving from its beginning as the county seat, was through an oversight not officially "established" by the Legislature until thirteen years later, when it and seven other towns in the State, that had existed for a number of years, were "established" by an act passed January 6, 1812. Collins gives 120 miles as the distance from Frankfort to Greenville. This is doubtless a typographical error, and was intended to read 210 miles.

Two opinions are now held regarding the origin of the name Greenville. On the one hand is the story that Mrs. Tabitha A. R. Campbell was so impressed with the expanse of green treetops, then extending in every direction from the hill selected for the location of the county seat, that she proposed the name Greenville, which was accepted. This version was supported by Mrs. Lucy Wing Yost, Judge Charles Eaves, and a few others who were well versed in the early traditions of the town. On the other hand there are oral and printed statements that the place was so called in honor of General Nathaniel Greene. After General Muhlenberg's name had been adopted for the county, the admirers of General Greene (so the story is told) endorsed the name of General Muhlenberg's friend and co-worker for the name of the county seat. At any rate, it is generally conceded that Greenville was so called in honor of General Greene. [3]

Greenville is the oldest town in Muhlenberg. It has always been regarded as the main meeting and trading place for the people "out in the county." After the adoption of the State Constitution of 1891, Greenville, in November, 1892, elected its first mayor. The following have served as mayors of Greenville: William A. Wickliffe, 1893-1896; Doctor J. G. Bohannon, two terms, 1897-1904; and J. W. Lam, who began his first term on January 1, 1905, and is now serving his second term.

South Carrollton, on W. bank of Green river, and on the Owensboro and Russellville railroad, 10 miles from Greenville; has 8 stores, 3 churches, 4 physicians, 2 mills, 3 tobacco factories, 3 taverns, 7 mechanics' shops; population in 1870, 240, and increasing steadily; incorporated in 1846.

South Carrollton was incorporated by an act approved February 23, 1849, and not in the year 1846, as stated by Collins. The town, however, was begun about the year 1838, and laid out by John Fentress on what

---

[3] General Nathaniel Greene, in the estimation of many critics, ranks next to Washington among the generals of the Revolution. He was born in Rhode Island on May 27, 1742. After taking part in many of the battles fought in the north he was, in 1780, placed in command of the army in the south, from which section he soon expelled the British. After the close of the Revolution the State of Georgia gave him a large plantation near Savannah, on which he lived from 1785 to the time of his death, June 19, 1786.

General Greene's popularity is attested by the many places throughout the Union now bearing his name. Rhode Island erected a monument to him in the national Statuary Hall. In Kentucky, Green County, formed in 1792, and its county seat, Greensburg, were so called in his honor.

Green River, however, in the opinion of most historians, was not named after General Greene. According to some of the local traditions the first German-American settlers of Muhlenberg frequently referred to this stream as The Grube—grube being a German word for a deep ditch or trench—although they knew it had already been designated as Green River by earlier pioneers. Some of the old deeds show that Green River was, in the early days, also called Muddy River. In two of them (Deed Book No. 10, page 79, and Deed Book No. 11, page 15) land referred to in the northeastern part of the county is described as lying "on the waters of Muddy River alias Green River." Either name is an appropriate one—its appropriateness, however, depending on the stage of the water. When the river is high or rising the water is muddy or yellow, while at other stages it is green.

was known as the "Randolph old farm," on which a tanyard had been operated for many years, near what is now known as the "Public Spring."

DOCTOR J. T. WOODBURN, 1912

Among the early citizens of South Carrollton were Bryant Bennett, Edmund M. Blacklock, James Carbon, Doctor Bryant Davis, John Fentress, Edmund Finch, N. B. Howard, S. Howell, Doctor A. M. Jackson, John Kittinger, Henderson Lovelace, Lewis McCown, Charles Morehead, sr., John Randolph, J. Edmunds Reno, and H. D. Rothrock. [4]

South Carrollton's first hotel was "White Hall" and its second "Our House" or "The Lovelace Tavern," both of which were in their day among the best-known places in the county. General Crittenden's army, as stated elsewhere in this history, was encamped in and near the town during the last half of January, 1862. It had a college for many years. Notwithstanding the fact that South Carrollton has the transportation facilities offered by a river and a railroad, the town has slowly decreased in business and population during the past twenty-five years.

Skilesville, on S. bank of Green river, at lock and dam No. 3, 16 miles E. of Greenville, has 2 stores and a mill; population about 100; named after Jas. R. Skiles, who introduced the first steamboat upon Green river, and spent a fortune in promoting the navigation of the river.

Skilesville was not incorporated until March 8, 1876, although the town had existed for more than forty years previous to that time.

Methodist Episcopal Church, Central City
Erected 1911

---

[4] Hugh Davis Rothrock was born in Greenville December 29, 1812, and died at his home in South Carrollton October 5, 1882. He was a son of John Rothrock, one of the influential pioneers of the county, who died in Greenville some time before 1820. About the year 1854 H. D. Rothrock moved to South Carrollton, where, with the exception of a few years, he spent the remainder of his life. He was one of South Carrollton's most progressive and cultured citizens. He conducted a large general store and handled leaf tobacco and strips. He also operated a coal mine near South Carrollton for a number of years. H. D. Rothrock married Susan Jones,

By an act approved December 21, 1837, an election precinct was "established at the house of Richard Simons in the town of Skilesville in Muhlenberg county." A map of the town drawn by Jacob Luce was recorded in 1844 (Record Book No. 11, page 650). The Skilesville post-office was established, abandoned, and reëstablished a number of times. Since 1907 the people of this neighborhood have received their mail at Rochester or Knightsburg. James Rumsey Skiles was a citizen of Warren County. Judge Lucius P. Little, in his forthcoming history of the Green River country, will publish a sketch of the career of this early promoter of Green River navigation. Lock and Dam No. 3, or the Rochester-Skilesville lock and dam, was opened in 1838.

St. Joseph's Roman Catholic Church, Central City, erected 1912

Stroud City, at the crossing of the O. & R. and E. & P. railroads,

Central City's first post-office (about 1871), as it appears to-day

35 miles from Owensboro, is growing fast.

Stroud City, or Owensboro Junction, later became Central City. Before the days of the railroad the well-known Morehead's Horse Mill stood on the site laid out for the new town. "An act to establish and incorporate the town of Stroud City" was approved April 19, 1873. Legislative acts regarding the regulation of the town were passed March 17, 1876, and April 24, 1880. By an act approved February 11, 1882, the name was changed to Central City. The building used as the town's first post-office is still standing. On August 7, 1871, George G. Shaver was appointed the

daughter of Peter Jones, who about the year 1798 came from Virginia and settled near South Carrollton. Mr. and Mrs. H. D. Rothrock were the parents of ten children, among them being Noah D. and Charles W. (two Confederate soldiers referred to elsewhere in this volume), John B., of Paducah, H. F. Given Rothrock, of Hanson, Kentucky, and Mrs. Bettie (Alfred H.) Edwards, Mrs. Annie (Ewing) Graham, and Mrs. Belle (James L.) Weir, of Lebanon, Tennessee.

first postmaster of what was then known as Owensboro Junction. He was succeeded on August 21, 1872, by Willis Kittinger, who served for a few years. In March, 1913, Congress appropriated $7,500 for the purchase of a site for a Federal building in Central City, which the Government contemplates erecting within a few years. The Sandusky House, opened about 1878 and run by Captain William H. H. Sandusky, was for more than twenty-five years one of the best-known hotels in Kentucky along the line of the Illinois Central Railroad. Among other churches in Central City is St. Joseph's Church, which was erected in 1912 and is the only Roman Catholic church in the county. This congregation's first building was built in 1886, when Reverend M. F. Melody, then stationed at Leitch-

BROAD STREET, CENTRAL CITY
Looking east from Louisville & Nashville Railroad track

field, was the priest-in-charge. Central City's first mayor was elected in November, 1892. The following have served as mayor of Central City: Doctor J. L. McDowell, 1893-1896; Doctor M. P. Creel, 1897-1900; Doctor W. R. McDowell, 1901-1904; W. D. McElhinny, 1905-1909; and Doctor J. T. Woodburn, who has served since January 1, 1910. [5]

---

[5] Doctor James Taylor Woodburn, mayor of Central City and one of the county's leading physicians, was born in Christian County December 28, 1848, and came to Muhlenberg at the age of four years. Doctor Woodburn was reared in the Bethel neighborhood. He worked on his mother's farm until 1873, when he began the study of medicine in the Louisville Medical College, from which school he was graduated in 1876. The following year he took a degree in the Kentucky School of Medicine. Doctor Woodburn practiced his profession in northern Muhlenberg and southern McLean until 1901, when he moved to Central City and bought the S. C. Gish drug store. Five years later he consolidated his business with that of Doctor W. R. McDowell, and together they formed the Woodburn & McDowell Drug Company. In the meantime he continued the practice of medicine, and in 1904 took a post-graduate course in the Chicago Clinical School. He has been on the county board of health for more than twenty years, and has been mayor of Central City since January 1, 1910.

In 1877 Doctor Woodburn married Betty Cosby. They are the parents of five children, their only son being Doctor B. Dudley Woodburn, of Central City.

Mrs. J. T. Woodburn, sr., the mother of Doctor J. T. Woodburn, came to Muhlenberg in 1852, a year after the death of her husband. She died near Bethel Church

Central City is the largest town in Muhlenberg. Since 1903 it has been the only place in the county where the sale of intoxicants is permitted. Relative to the early history of Central City the Muhlenberg Argus, on September 20, 1906, said:

Central City was begun about 1870, when what is now the Illinois Central Railroad was being built. Coal mining followed shortly after. The farm owned by John Stroud, including the one adjoining it which he bought from Charles S. Morehead and the farm owned by Joseph Settle, compose the principal part of the present (1906) site of Central City. Morehead ran a horse-mill for many years, and although it disappeared nearly forty years ago a few of the old citizens occasionally refer to the town as "Morehead's Horse Mill." In 1876 there were a few houses along the Greenville and South Carrollton dirt road, and in fact until about 1888 the principal business part of town was along that road, then and now known as Water Street. The old house where the first post-office was kept is still standing on the Greenville Road. Jonathan and Willis Kittinger kept a post-office and store in this building in the early '70s. One night, robbers broke in and hauled the entire stock away, but who they were has not been learned to this day.

Bremen, 14 miles from Greenville, has 2 stores and 2 tobacco factories; population about 75; incorporated in 1869.

Bremen post-office was originally established about 1825, in a residence on the Greenville and Rumsey Road near the McLean County line. About 1860 it was moved to Andrew Bennett's store and blacksmith shop, where the town of Bremen now stands; what was sometimes called Bennettsville became known as Bremen.

H. D. ROTHROCK, 1870

It was pioneer Peter Shaver who, in honor of his father's birthplace, Bremen, Germany, and in honor of the German-American pioneers of Muhlenberg, secured this appropriate name for a place in the county. As stated elsewhere, although the German-American pioneers of Muhlenberg are to-day represented by many descendants, all traces of the German language, manners, and customs disappeared a few generations ago, not only from the Bremen country—which was for many years called the "Dutch Settlement"—but also from other sections in which pioneers of German descent had settled.

---

in 1886. Her nine children are among the best-known citizens of the county: John A., Reverend William H., Mrs. Anna (John L. G.) Thompson, Doctor Benjamin W., Mrs. Terese A. (R. H.) Tolbert, Mrs. Charity (R. C.) Chandler, Mrs. Isabelle (B. F.) Reed, Mrs. America Jane (J. N.) Durall, and Doctor J. T. Woodburn, who is the youngest member of this family.

The Black Lake country lies east and northeast of Bremen. The soil of the so-called Black Lake swamps is regarded by many as the richest in the county, and its reclamation by drainage is now being considered by the citizens of Bremen and the Black Lake country. When this has been accomplished and the cypress and other swampland trees have been cleared away, then, as Harry M. Dean, of Greenville (who spent his boyhood in the Black Lake country), expresses it in his beautiful poem, "The Cypress Trees," this soil "that's black and deep" will be in condition "that men may sow and reap." The poem referred to was first printed in the Greenville Record on December 7, 1911, and has since been reprinted in many papers.

THE CYPRESS TREES.

We sentinel the lone waste places
  Of swamps that are low and dim;
Line on line for the conflict,
  Tall and silent and grim.
In the dawn of that far-off morning
  We stood in serried lines—
The trees all clustered together,
  And next to us stood the pines.
But great was the Master's cunning—
  A wisdom no man may know;
So He sends the pines to the uplands,
  While we to the swamps must go.

Mystic and brooding and silent,
  Huddled together we stand;
Pickets in reedy marshes,
  Guards of this lone, low land.
Dark are the aisles of our forests,
  Tangled with briars and vines;
Few there be who can know us,
  Few who can read our signs.
The lone owl broods in our branches,
  The brown snakes come and go,
And still we whisper a secret
  No man shall ever know.

Tall and mystic and brooding,
  Waiting the long years through;
Men drive us away from the swampland,
  But we come to the swampland anew.
For here we're master builders,
  Lifting the soil from the slime;
Holding the drifts in decaying,
  Bringing the earth to its prime.
Turning the low waste spaces
  To soil that's black and deep,
Until we are cleared from our places
  That men may sow and reap.

                HARRY M. DEAN.

Paradise, on Green river, 10 miles above (S. E. of) South Carrollton, in N. E. part of county; population about 300; has 4 stores and 2 tobacco factories; incorporated in 1856.

Paradise was not incorporated until March 10, 1856, which was more than half a century after the town had been settled. For a few years after the Mexican War it was sometimes referred to as Monterey. A deed recorded in 1854 incidentally states that Paradise then had an area of

BLACK LAKE AND CYPRESS TREES, NEAR BREMEN

thirteen acres. A plat drawn in 1871 shows an increase to twenty-six and one fourth acres. Although a few acres have been added to its limits, the population has slowly decreased since 1875. Its location and age make Paradise one of the most undisturbed and interesting villages along Green River.

Airdrie, on Green river, 17 miles from Greenville; population about 200, largely engaged in mining coal; incorporated in 1858.

Airdrie sprang into existence in 1854, and was on the point of being abandoned by many of the original citizens when, on February 17, 1858, the town was incorporated. Except during a few years, the people of Airdrie received their mail at Paradise. The old furnace, built in 1855, long ago became a picturesque ruin, and the house occupied for many years by General Buell was burned to the ground in 1907. A history of Airdrie is given in the chapter on "Paradise Country and Old Airdrie."

Drakesboro, now the third largest town in the county, was not in existence when, in 1874, Collins published the above-quoted data on the towns of Muhlenberg. About 1882, or about the time the Owensboro & Russellville Railroad was buit, Frank M. Rice began a store near what is now the depot, and there formed the nucleus of a village which for a few years was known as Ricedale. On February 21, 1888, the place was incorporated by an act of the Legislature and its name changed to Drakesboro, in honor of William Drake, who lived in that neighborhood for many years and died in 1868 in a house still standing near the town known as the Bill Drake Old Brick. Among other first-comers in this region was Bryant Cundiff.

In 1900 the town had a population of about two hundred. During the past twelve years it has increased to about twelve hundred. Much of Drakesboro's progress is due to the work and influence of such men as James T. Pierce, who in 1888 opened the Black Diamond Mine in the new town and has since been at the head of its affairs; William W. Bridges, who has been connected with the Black Diamond Mining Company since shortly after its organization; Doctor Jefferson D. Cundiff, who has lost no opportunity to contribute to the town's medical, educational, and commercial welfare, and B. Frank Green, who as cashier of the Citizens Bank looks after the financial interests of the citizens of the town and the Drakesboro country.

Of the seven towns commented on by Collins, all had post-offices in 1874 except Skilesville and Airdrie. There were eleven post-offices in the county at that time. The other six were: Earles, which was maintained in the S. W. Earle residence until about 1860, when the office was moved two miles south to the store of Thomas C. Summers, where it was continued under the old name of Earles until 1910, when, after rural free delivery Route No. 1 was established, the post-office was abandoned; Laurel Bluff, which was located on the Greenville Road about two miles from Dunmor (Laurel Bluff post-office was abolished when Home Valley was established, and Home Valley was later changed to Albritton and is now known as Penrod); Mercer and Nelson Station post-offices, which were then where they are now; Painstown, which was about two miles east of Nelson Station; Riverside, which was a small mining town on Green River about five miles above Paradise.

It may be well to add that about the middle of the last century there was a post-office in the Harpe's Hill country known as Unity, one at the Hugh W. McNary place called Ellwood or McNary's, one at Clark's Ferry called Pond River Mills, and one on Clifty Creek east of Cisney, near the Carver settlement, called Sulphur Springs. During 1884, and a few years before and after, a post-office was maintained in the Bethel Church neighborhood on the Greenville and Rumsey Road, called Bertram, and one near Old Liberty called Paceton.

Muhlenberg County now has thirty-four post-offices, eight star mail routes, and four rural free delivery routes. The star routes run: from Weir to Greenville, eight miles; from Haley's Mill, Christian County, via Bancroft to Greenville, eighteen miles; from Cisney to Yost, seven miles; from Rochester, Butler County, via Knightsburg and Ennis to Yost, nine and a half miles; from Wells to Yost, six and a fourth miles; from Penrod, via Gus, to Huntsville, Butler County, ten miles; from Beech Creek to Browder, two miles; and from Rochester, via boat to Paradise and Rockport, fifteen miles. There are three star routes from Dunmor into Butler and Todd counties. The rural free delivery routes run: No. 1, Greenville, Greenville to Earles, returning via Harpe's Hill, established in 1910, was the first in the county; No. 1, Central City, Central City to Gishton and Bethel Church, returning via Cherry Hill Church; No. 1, Bremen, extending from Bremen northeast into McLean County, returning via Millport; No. 2, Bremen, Bremen to Gishton and Earles, returning via Isaac's Creek and Briar Creek.

Most of the first-comers received their mail at Greenville, Worthington, or Lewisburg, or at "Hunt Settlement" or some of the other settlements.

POST-OFFICES IN MUHLENBERG COUNTY.

In 1830, 1840, 1850, 1860, 1874, 1884, and 1912.

1830.
Bremen.
Greenville.
Lewisburgh.
McNarys.
Mill Port.
Worthington.

1840.
Bremen.
Greenville.
Lewisburgh.
McNarys.
Rumsey.
Skilesville.
Worthington.

1850.
Bremen.
Ellwood.
Greenville.
Rumsey.
South Carrollton.
Unity.
Worthington.

1860.
Earles.
Ellwood.
Greenville.
Laurel Bluff.
Lead Hill.

Model Mills.
Pond River Mills.
South Carrollton.
Sulphur Springs.
Paradise.

1874.
Bremen.
Earles.
Greenville.
Laurel Bluff.
Mercer Station.
Nelson.
Owensboro Junction.
Painstown.
Paradise.
Riverside.
South Carrollton.

1884.
Albrittain.
Bertram.
Bevier.
Central City.
Dunmor.
Earles.
Greenville.
McNary.
Mercer Station.
Nelson.
Paceton.
Paradise.
Ricedale.
South Carrollton.
Yost.

1912.
Bancroft.
Beech Creek.
Bevier.
Bremen.
Browder.
Brucken.
Central City.
Cisney.
Cleaton.
Depoy.
Drakesboro.
Dunmor.
Ennis.
Gishton.
Graham.
Greenville.
Gus.
Hillside.
Knightsburg.
Luzerne.
McNary.
Martwick.
Mercer.
Midland.
Millport.
Moorman.
Nelson.
Paradise.
Penrod.
Powderly.
South Carrollton.
Weir.
Wells.
Yost.

POPULATION OF TOWNS IN MUHLENBERG COUNTY, AS GIVEN BY THE
CENSUS REPORTS FROM 1870 TO 1910.

TOWN	1910	1900	1890	1880	1870
Central City	2,545	1,348	1,144		
Greenville	1,604	1,051	968	866	557
Drakesboro	1,126	228			
South Carrollton	365	452	525	493	240
Bremen	254	180			
Dunmor	138	77	82		
Paradise	91	107		137	
Rosewood	89	82			
Penrod	68	80	72		
Skilesville	53	87		85	

MAIN STREET, DRAKESBORO
Looking west from Louisville & Nashville Railroad track

POPULATION OF MUHLENBERG COUNTY, AS GIVEN BY THE CENSUS
REPORTS FROM 1800 TO 1910.

YEAR	White	Free Colored	Slaves	Total
1800	1,313	5	125	1,443
1810	3,698	3	480	4,181
1820	4,302	2	675	4,979
1830	4,327	15	998	5,340
1840	5,755	13	1,196	6,964
1850	8,250	37	1,522	9,809
1860	9,101	40	1,584	10,725
1870	11,005	1,633		12,638
1880	13,020	2,078		15,098
1890	15,596	2,359		17,955
1900	18,584	2,157		20,741
1910	25,687	2,911		28,598

Muhlenberg Members of the House of Representatives.

In the following list the names and dates up to 1875 are copied verbatim from Collins:

Henry Rodes..........1800	John G. Gooch.....1850
Wm. Bradford..........1801, '03,'10,'11	David Dillman....1853–55
Christopher Tompkins.1805	Jos. Ricketts......1855–57, '61–63
John Morgan..........1806	Charles Eaves.....1857–59
John C. Russell.......1807, '09	Benj. J. Shaver....1859–61, '75–77
Alney McLean........1812, '13	M. Jeff. Roark.....1865–67
Wm. Bell ....1814, '15	Mortimer D. Hay..1867–69
Moses Wickliffe.......1816, '17,'18,'19	Dr. John B. Hays..1869–71
Edmund Watkins.....1820, '24,'25	James C. Moorman.1871–73
Edward Rumsey......1822	D. H. Baker.......1873–75
Micajah Wells........1826	Lewis Jones.......1877–85
John F. Coffman......1827, '33	R. Y. Thomas, jr...1885–87
David Short..........1828, '29,'32	C. W. Cisney......1887–89
Wm. C. McNary......1830,'31,'35,'36, '51–53	Chas. B. Wickliffe..1889–91
	Dr. A. D. James[6]...1891–93, '94–96
John S. Eaves 1834	W. J. Cox[7] 1893–93
John M. Johnson......1837	H. C. McCracken..1896–98
Jas. Taggart..........1838, '39	J. P. Jeffries.......1898–1900
B. E. Pittman........1840	W. W. Lewis 1900–04
Edward R. Weir......1841, '42,'63–65	T. G. Turner 1904–06
Russell McCreery.....1843, '44	Dr. T. J. Slaton[8] ...1906–08
Wiley S. Hay.........1845, '46	D. P. Taggart 1908–10
Wm. T. Short 1847	J. F. Richardson...1910–12
John Vickers.........1848	George Baker......1912–
George W. Short......1849	

Members of the State Senate from Muhlenberg County are given by Collins as follows: "Wm. Worthington, 1814-26; Wm. C. McNary, 1846-50; Wiley S. Hay, 1853-57; Finis M. Allison, 1867-71. From Muhlenburg, Butler, and Ohio counties—Robert S. Russell, 1850." Colonel William Campbell was a member of the State Senate in 1800, representing what was then "Livingston, Henderson, Muhlenburg, and Ohio counties."

---

[6] Doctor Addison D. James was born in Butler County, February 27, 1849, moved to Muhlenberg at the age of twenty, and died at his home near Penrod June 7, 1910. He received his degree of medicine from the University of Louisville in 1869 and the same year began the practice of his profession at Penrod, in which he continued until about 1890, when he entered politics. In 1891 he represented Muhlenberg in the State Constitutional Convention. He was twice elected to the lower house of the Legislature, and also served as State Senator. In 1893 he was a Commissioner at the World's Fair, Chicago. In 1897 he was appointed United States Marshal, which office he filled for eight years. In 1906 he was elected a member of Congress from the Third District. He was the third man who, while living in Muhlenberg, became a member of Congress. Doctor James was an energetic man, kind and accommodating to all, regardless of their politics.

[7] Doctor A. D. James resigned January 21, 1893, and W. J. Cox, who was elected to fill his unexpired term, took his seat February 8, 1893.

[8] D. P. Taggart took the oath of office and served until February 14, 1906, when the contest between him and Doctor T. J. Slaton was decided. The House of Representatives ordered and adjudged that Doctor T. J. Slaton was on November 7, 1905, duly elected Representative from Muhlenberg County and entitled to his seat, and on February 15, 1906, he took the oath of office and his seat in the Legislature.

The following Muhlenbergers have served as State Senators since the foregoing list was compiled: Louis Jones, December, 1887, to December, 1889; Doctor A. D. James, January, 1896, to March 11, 1896, when his seat was declared vacant by the Senate; Doctor T. G. Turner, January, 1898, to January, 1900; J. W. Wright, January, 1908, to January, 1912.

Relative to the county's coal and iron ore Collins, in 1874, says:

Coal.—At McNary's coal bank, on the E. side of Pond river, in the W. line of Muhlenburg county, is the singular phenomenon of two thick beds or veins of coal within 3½ feet of each other—the upper of 4¼ and the lower of 6¼ feet. The latter has a thin clay parting about the middle. They crop out at an elevation of 70 feet above high water in the river. Three miles S. E. of this, the Marcus coal occurs, 6 or 7 feet thick, a few feet above the bed of a branch. Three miles N. W. of Greenville, three beds of coal, 8 feet in all, occur in 110 feet of a section. A "general section" of Muhlenburg county (Kentucky Geol. Survey, iv, 399) shows some 26 feet of coal, in 9 different seams, within 440 feet—the seams varying from 10 inches to 5½ feet in thickness, except one thin seam; of these 5 seams are of workable thickness, 3 feet or over.

The completion of the railroads through this county is fast opening the way for large exports of coal to the Ohio river, Owensboro and Louisville. At Stroud City, the first bed of coal, 5½ feet thick, is reached at 14 feet from the surface, and the second bed, of superior quality, at only 20 feet. Many thousands of millions of bushels of coal can be taken from beneath the surface in Muhlenburg county, without injuring the surface in its farming value.

Black Band Iron Ore, a stratum 10 inches thick, ferruginous chocolate-colored, peculiar in its nature, color, composition, and paleontology, is found at Airdrie and elsewhere. It has been discovered, in one place at a depth of 25 feet, as thick as 19 inches, and yielding 36.8 per cent. of metallic iron.

Iron ore from the Jenkins ore bank, 2½ to 3 feet in thickness, yielded 43.56 per cent. of metallic iron; and that from the Hoskins ore bank, on Muddy river, 47.159 per cent. of iron.

The "Jenkins ore bank" referred to is about seven miles south of Greenville; the "Hoskins ore bank" is near the Mud River Mine, and was opened by Jackson Hoskinson. The history of the development of Muhlenberg's mineral resources is given in "The Story of The Stack," "Paradise Country and Old Airdrie," and "Coal Mines and Iron Ore."

Antiquities.—On a rock bank of Pond creek, four miles from Greenville, tracks of mules and horses are

DOCTOR ADDISON D. JAMES, 1905

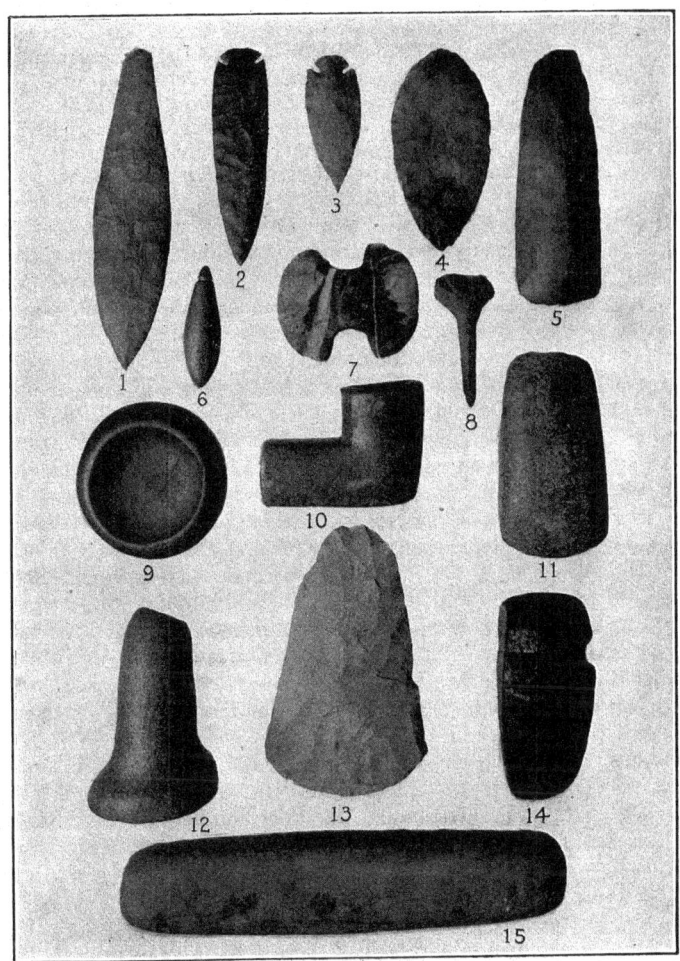

**INDIAN RELICS FROM THE AUTHOR'S COLLECTION
MADE IN MUHLENBERG COUNTY**

1. Flint knife or dagger, 8½ inches long, presented by Aaron B. McPherson.
2. Flint spear-head, presented by Lester W. Underwood.
3. Flint arrow-point, presented by Richard H. Pearson.
4. Leaf-shaped flint implement, presented by Amos M. Jenkins.
5. Polished flint celt, presented by Andrew Noffsinger.
6. Plummet of hematite, presented by Charles E. Whitmer.
7. Banner stone of variegated quartz, presented by A. Jackson Cornett.
8. Yellow chert perforator, presented by John K. Cundiff.
9. Discoidal of quartzite, presented by Glenn H. Stivers.
10. Pipe of steatite, presented by Bayless E. Oates.
11. Granite celt, presented by George W. Taylor.
12. Granite pestle, presented by James Wallace Oates.
13. Flint spade, presented by E. G. Conaster.
14. Grooved stone axe, presented by Andrew J. Taylor.
15. Rolling-pin pestle of stone, presented by Sidney J. Mohorn.

plainly to be seen in the solid sandstone. Some have been removed, and taken, it is said, to the St. Louis museum. On Muddy river is a sandstone rock with flat surface, 30 or 40 feet square, on which are carved hieroglyphics as yet undeciphered; the full form of an Indian, surrounded by different animals; the sun, moon, stars, and other symbolic signs.

Mounds.—One mile N. of Greenville, near the old Caney station—which was the first settlement in the county—are several mounds. From the largest, about 75 feet in diameter, have been dug portions of human skeletons. Trees of considerable size are now growing on the mounds.

Such "tracks" of mules and horses as are here referred to by Collins can be found in various parts of the county. They are, in my opinion, no more than evidence of the existence of a fossil shell that had been imbedded in a rock while the rock was being formed, and ages later, when the surface of the fossil-bearing strata was exposed, the fossil, being of softer material, was washed out, leaving a cavity the size and shape of the original fossil, which cavity resembles the track of a mule or horse.

The undeciphered hieroglyphics reported to have been seen on the rock on Mud River will probably always remain undeciphered. The place referred to by Collins is known as Indian Rock. It is one mile from Mud River Mine, near Cave Spring, on the Old Coal Road. If any Indian hieroglyphics were ever discovered there, the rocks on which they were carved have since eroded to such an extent that none of the marks are now visible. A number of "carvings," however, can still be seen on Indian Rock. One is a rough outline of the head and shoulders of a man, life size, above which is carved "H. H." Another is the crude outline of a man, about two feet high, wearing a "derby" hat. These and the few other carvings I saw on Indian Rock are such that I infer they have been made in comparatively recent years and were possibly cut with a hammer and nail by some men then connected with the old Mud River Mine.

In many parts of the county there can still be found mounds and other evidences of the Indians and Moundbuilders who lived in what is now Muhlenberg. But the old mounds, like the stone implements left by the aborigines, are rapidly disappearing. Stone implements, such as arrowpoints, spear-heads, and axes were picked up by the first settlers and are still occasionally found by plowmen and others. Practically none of these relics was preserved by the pioneers, and the same may be said of many of those that are found to-day. Even those that had been picked up and laid aside have, in most cases, disappeared—like old books, fire-arms, or farming tools. Many stone axes have served as nut-crackers, and in consequence are badly damaged, and thousands of large and perfect flints have been ruined by unappreciative people who broke them "just to see how hard they were." It is said that a woman who lived in the Pond River country picked up "wagon-loads of flints" during the course of her long life, pulverized them, and fed the "flint feed" to her chickens for grit. Although the stone relics of prehistoric men in Muhlenberg are far older than any of the wooden or iron implements made and left by the pioneers, many a stone axe and spear-point will be seen in the county long after the last old spinning-wheel or flintlock gun has disappeared.

Mounds, or traces of mounds, can still be found in many parts of the county, especially on hills near streams. Most of the mounds, having been plowed over during the course of years for the purpose of cultivating the fields in which they were located, are now almost leveled to the surrounding surface. A few years ago one in the upper Long Creek country was rooted up by hogs and the bones destroyed by them. The mounds near Caney Station, referred to by Collins, have worn away, and now nothing save a peculiarly rich soil marks their site.

PREHISTORIC MOUND NEAR BUCKNER'S STACK

Every one of the twenty-five mounds I have seen in Muhlenberg has apparently been opened one or more times. One in a wood near the Buckner Stack, although three partial excavations have been made therein, is the best preserved artificial earthwork of its kind in the county. It is now about five feet high and one hundred feet in circumference at the base. It was opened in 1870 and again in 1908 by boys who were looking for "gold," but not finding any, reinterred the bones they had exhumed. In 1910 I opened this mound and procured three somewhat mutilated skulls and a few other bones. These and other fragments of bones indicate that at least a dozen bodies of various sizes had been deposited in it. No stone or other Indian relics were found by me or by those who had "investigated" before me.

In this mound, as in most other mounds in Muhlenberg and in other parts of the Ohio Valley, all the bodies had apparently been deposited at one time, on the original surface of the hill, in a stone-walled sepulcher that was covered with flags of stone about four inches thick, and over all of which a circular mound of earth had been thrown. The fact that these mounds contain a number of skeletons apparently placed there at one time causes many to conclude that a battle must have been fought, and that all or some of the dead were buried in one place. From Professor F. W. Putnam, of the Peabody Museum of Archæology and Ethnology, I quote: "We know not if these burials indicate famine, pestilence, war, or unholy sacrifice. We can only conjecture that they were not the graves of persons who had died a natural death."

It is quite likely that many of the prehistoric men who lived in Muhlenberg were buried in individual graves. Many of their sepulchers, in all probability, were covered with small mounds that have since disappeared, leaving nothing to indicate or mark the place of such burials. A number of individual stone-lined graves have been discovered in the Long Creek country and a few other places in the southern part of the county by plowmen. Traces of three or four such stone graves, that were opened about 1870, can still be seen on Harpe's Hill, about one hundred feet from a mound that according to local tradition "has been dug into a dozen times or more."

All the mounds in the county, and probably all traces of them, will disappear long before the close of the present century, just as did the last of the earth rings, or house-site rings, about a quarter of a century ago. A few of these rings, it is said, were noticed on one of the hills overlooking the Murphy's Lake flats, and two were traced as late as about 1885 by W. S. Johnson, on his farm five miles south of Greenville, on the level surface of a hill overlooking Pond Creek. These circles were ridges of earth then a few inches high, a foot or two wide, and from fifteen to thirty feet in diameter. These more or less well-defined rings are, according to archæologists, the remains of circular huts, the ridges having been formed by the decay of the stick-and-pole walls and by the refuse that had accumulated against the walls when the huts were occupied. In the center of these circles charcoal and burnt clay were found, indicating that fires had been built therein.

A Sink, of the general appearance of similar sinks elsewhere in Kentucky, but comparatively bottomless, is in the barrens 6 miles E. of Munfordsville. It is funnel-shaped, tapering from about 70 feet diameter at top, to 10 feet, at the depth of 30 feet. Its depth has not been explored, but stones cast into it are not heard to strike bottom.

This description of a sink, although printed by Collins under the head of Muhlenberg County, was evidently intended to appear in his sketch of Hart County.

A Cave in the S. part of the county, 10 miles from Greenville, is worth attention. In Oct., 1872, an exploration for half a mile "reported" the discovery of two petrified figures, man and woman, dressed in the old Roman costume, and each holding in the arms a child—the man one of 10 years, and the woman a babe of 1 to 2 years. It was first discovered in the winter of 1852-3 by a person who tracked raccoons into it. In Aug.,

1853, G. P. McLean, of Mississippi, and others explored it for about 2 miles—to a pit beyond which they could not pass over for want of a ladder. Eight or ten branches led off in different directions, some of them apparently larger than the direct avenue. A petrified monkey, as perfect in shape as if alive, was found in the cave, a few weeks previous.

This cave is known as Lovell's Cave or Shutt's Cave, and is located south of Long Creek. Local tradition says it was first discovered in 1839 by Archibald Duvall, whose dog "treed" a "coon" in it. The opening

SITE OF A PREHISTORIC MOUND, JUDGE GODMAN FARM, NEAR MOORMAN, 1912
In 1895 this old mound was about six feet high in the center and had a diameter of about sixty feet. Like many of the other mounds, having been frequently plowed over, it is now almost leveled to the surrounding surface

was then a very small one, and "digging out the coon" resulted in the discovery of the cave. The "main hall" leads off from the entrance, and is about one hundred and twenty-five feet long and twenty-five feet wide. A much narrower hall, a passage three or four feet wide and about twenty-five feet high, leads to the left from the "main hall," winds in various directions, and finally comes back into the wider passage a short distance from where it started. A number of short branches turn off from the narrow hall, one of which goes to two "bottomless pits," that are about three feet wide and twelve feet deep. Recently a measurement was made with a string (but no compass) of the heretofore explored portions of the cave, which shows that the two halls have a combined length of about three hundred yards. It is probable that other halls exist, and that their discovery may show that this cave is (as is popularly reported) "a couple of miles long." Old citizens who are familiar with the history of the cave declare that no petrified figures were ever found in it, and that no signs indicating that the place was once occupied by prehistoric men have ever been observed.

Other small caves have been discovered in the Long Creek country within the past fifty years. The best known and most interesting of these is the John Jenkins Cave, three miles east of Lovell's Cave and near the Green F. Walker farm. The passages in this cave are walled with vertically fluted columns, while in Lovell's Cave the evidences of erosion are in the form of a series of small horizontal benches of rock projecting from the high walls. South of the John Jenkins Cave and within a mile of it are two caves, one on the farm of Charles Butler and the other on that of Riley Gates. These caves are in a rock which is more of a sandstone than a limestone. I found no stalactites, stalagmites, or gypsum in any of them. However, I noticed in places an incrustation resembling miniature stalactites.

There are a number of picturesque bluffs in the southern part of the county. Three miles south of Mud River Mine and near New Hebron Church is a small cavern, known by some as "Eternal Hole" and by others as "Internal Hole," which is said to have been occupied by Indians, although no evidences of such use are now visible. On Long Creek, on the Old Jones Peach Orchard Hill, two miles above Lead Hill Church, is a concave bluff known as "Saltpeter Cave." On one of the forks of Clifty Creek, between Dunmor and Cisney, is a high bluff and an old spring called "Sulphur Springs." Many of the bluffs in Muhlenberg along Clifty Creek and its branches are very picturesque, one of which is the Jesse McPherson "Cave Hut Cliff." The cliffs of Clifty increase in height and beauty as one goes up the creek into Todd County, and are there seen at their best as "Buzzards' Bald Yard," and "Wildcat Hollow."

There are many beautiful scenes and historic spots along the Muhlenberg bank of Green River. Pond River and Pond Creek are picturesque at all times, even during the driest seasons, when both streams become little more than broken chains of short and long ponds. Hence the names of the two streams.

Gen. Baron Steuben, the distinguished Prussian general of our Revolutionary war, located his Virginia military warrants, granted him for services in the war, in what is now Muhlenburg county. It was all lost (some 4,000 or more acres) to his estate, under the occupying claimant limitation law.

The land here referred to lies in the vicinity of South Carrollton.

In the War of 1812, the late Judge Alney McLean . . . commanded a company at the battle of New Orleans, Jan. 8, 1815. His lieutenant, E. M. Brank (still living, 1871), while the battle was raging hottest, mounted the breastworks to repel the British. The late L. N. Akers was taken prisoner at the battle of the River Raisin, and compelled to run the gauntlet; he drew a pension on account of wounds received.

Biographies of these three soldiers appear in the chapter on "Muhlenberg Men in the War of 1812."

During the War of the Rebellion, Greenville was for some time an outpost of both armies, or rather neutral ground between them. It was taken by Gen. Buckner in Feb., 1862, and some time after by John Morgan, and was once or twice partially sacked by guerrillas. Muhlenburg county sent 836 men to the Federal army.

This statement is quoted in the chapter on "Muhlenberg in the Civil War," where attention is called to the errors that occur in it, among them being the date on which Greenville was "taken" by General Buckner.

EDWARD RUMSEY was a prominent man of Muhlenburg county and of S. W. Kentucky, for more than forty-five years; represented the county in the state legislature, in 1822, and the district in congress, 1837-39; was an eloquent speaker, and a man of decided ability. Only his remarkable modesty and timidity prevented his taking a more leading part in the politics of the state and nation.

[9]R. Y. THOMAS, 1912

CHARLES F. WING was a captain at the battle of the Thames, and saw Tecumseh after he was slain. He was clerk of the Muhlenburg courts from the organization of the county in 1798 to 1856—58 years; a longer period than any other man ever held a clerkship in Kentucky.

Among the first chapters in this history is one on Edward Rumsey and another on Charles Fox Wing. Collins ends his notes on the history of Muhlenburg County with brief biographies of Generals Buell and Muhlenberg. Sketches of the lives of these two distinguished generals appear elsewhere in this volume.

---

[9] Robert Y. Thomas was born in Logan County in 1859; seven years later his parents, Reverend and Mrs. R. Y. Thomas, moved to Muhlenberg, since which time he has lived in the county. Reverend Thomas was a son of Jonathan Thomas, and his wife was a daughter of George Briggs, both of whom were pioneers in the Green River country. Reverend R. Y. Thomas was a Methodist minister. He began preaching in 1848, and continued that work in Muhlenberg and other parts of Western Kentucky until 1900. He died in January, 1905. R. Y. Thomas was educated at Bethel College, Russellville, from which institution he received the degree of A. B. in 1881 and of A. M. in 1884. He represented Muhlenberg in the State Legislature from 1885 to 1887. In 1903 he was elected Commonwealth's attorney, and held that office until March 1, 1909, when he resigned to take his seat in Congress. He is the fourth Muhlenberg man who while a citizen of the county became a member of Congress. He has been a member of Congress since he was first elected in 1908. R. Y. Thomas is one of the best-known men in the Green River country. His home is in Central City.

APPENDIX

APPENDIX

A

JUDGE HALL'S STORY OF THE HARPES

ABOUT a year after Muhlenberg County was formed, Big Harpe, one of the most brutal outlaws in the West, was killed. The following is a copy of the first written account of this affair. It was published in 1828 by Judge James Hall, of Cincinnati, in his "Letters from the West." At least four versions of the story of the Harpes have been printed since Judge Hall's was published. I reprint his account because it is the oldest, and as his books are rare it has become the least accessible version. Collins, in his "History of Kentucky," under the head of Hopkins County, gives two versions; Allen's "History of Kentucky" has one; T. Marshall Smith, in his "Legends of the War of Independence and of the Earlier Settlements in the West," published in 1855, gives another. Judge Hall's being the oldest, as already stated, is probably the truest. T. Marshall Smith's is by far the longest and most interesting. None of these, nor do any of the oral versions, agree on the details of any important point. Nevertheless all are, in a general way, the same.

Judge Hall's statement that the two wives of Big Harpe remained in Muhlenberg does not agree with local traditions nor with any of the other printed versions. T. Marshall Smith gives the names of the two Harpes as Bill and Joshua and shows that they came originally from North Carolina, were cousins, Tories and sons of Tories, and that neither had more than one wife. Writing about the unfortunate women who became the involuntary wives of the heartless Harpes, he says: "Susan Woods (wife of Bill Harpe) told them (deputy sheriff of Logan county and others) in the most humble and suppliant terms her own sad story and cruel sufferings. Maria Davidson (wife of Joshua Harpe) confirmed her statement, and related her own intolerable sufferings. . . . They both lived in the county of Logan many years after, where they were often seen, known and conversed with by the author of this narrative, and who received from the lips of Susan Woods herself most of the facts narrated in the foregoing pages, in reference to herself, Maria Davidson and the two Harpes, from the time they became so unhappily connected with them. . . ."

Edmund L. Starling, in his "History of Henderson County," published in 1887, says that on September 4, 1799, a court of quarter sessions was called for the examination of the three Harpe women, then committed in the Henderson jail as parties to the murder (on August 20, 1799) of Mrs. Moses Stigall, her infant son, and William Love, a school-teacher, and that the three prisoners were found guilty and remanded to jail, but were subsequently taken, under order of court, to Russellville, there to await the action of the grand jury, where they were tried and acquitted.

Joseph R. Underwood, in his account compiled in 1871, based on information supplied in 1838 by John B. Ruby, of Hopkins County, and published in Collins' history, writes: "The pursuers, armed with rifles, got on the trail of the Harpes and overtook them at their camp, upon the waters of Pond river; but whether in the present boundary of Hopkins or Muhlenburg county I have not satisfactorily ascertained."

Local tradition says Big Harpe crossed Pond River at Free Henry Ford and was killed in Muhlenberg County, near what has since been known as Harpe's Hill. An oak tree four feet in diameter, which until 1910 stood on the bank of Boat Yard Creek near the Slab Road leading from Harpe's Hill to Free Henry Ford, has always been pointed out as the tree under which John Leeper or Lieper, Moses Stigall or Stegal, and the other members of the pursuing party, killed Big Harpe, and under which the headless corpse of Big Harpe lay until it was devoured by wild animals. Clara Garris, who became the wife of James Stanley, and who during her long life lived near Harpe's Hill, frequently pointed out this spot, declaring that Big Harpe was killed near this tree and that when a child of about ten years she saw his headless body lying there.

THE HARPES.

Many years ago, two men, named Harpe, appeared in Kentucky, spreading death and terror wherever they went. Little else was known of them but that they passed for brothers, and came from the borders of Virginia. They had three women with them, who were treated as their wives, and several children, with whom they traversed the mountainous and thinly settled parts of Virginia into Kentucky, marking their course with blood. Their history is wonderful, as well from the number and variety, as the incredible atrocity of their adventures; and as it has never yet appeared in print, I shall compress within this letter a few of its most prominent facts.

In the autumn of the year 1799, a young gentleman, named Langford, of a respectable family in Mecklenburgh county, Virginia, set out from this state for Kentucky, with the intention of passing through the Wilderness, as it was then called, by the route generally known as Boon's Trace. On reaching the vicinity of the Wilderness, a mountainous and uninhabited tract which at that time separated the settled parts of Kentucky from those of Virginia, he stopped to breakfast at a public house near Big Rockcastle river. Travellers of this description—any other indeed than hardy woodsmen—were unwilling to pass singly through this lonely region; and they generally waited on its confines for others, and travelled through in parties. Mr. Langford, either not dreading danger, or not choosing to delay, determined to proceed alone. While breakfast was preparing, the Harpes and their women came up. Their appearance denoted poverty, with but little regard to cleanliness; two very indifferent horses, with some bags swung across them, and a rifle gun or two, composed nearly their whole equipage. Squalid and miserable, they seemed objects of pity, rather than of fear, and their ferocious glances were attributed more to hunger than to guilty passion. They were entire strangers in that neighborhood, and, like Mr. Langford, were about to cross the Wilderness. When breakfast was served up, the landlord, as was customary at such places, in those times, invited all the persons who were assembled in the commons, perhaps the only room of his little inn, to sit down; but the Harpes declined, alleging their want of money as the reason. Langford, who was of a lively, generous disposition, on hearing this, invited them to partake of the meal at his expense; they accepted the invitation, and ate voraciously. When they had thus refreshed themselves, and were about to renew their journey, Mr. Langford called for the bill, and in the act of discharging it imprudently displayed a handful of silver. They then set out together.

A few days after, some men who were conducting a drove of cattle to Virginia, by the same road which had been travelled by Mr. Langford and the Harpes, had arrived within a few miles of Big Rock-castle River, when their cattle took fright, and, quitting the road, rushed down a hill into the woods. In collecting them, the drovers discovered the dead body of a man concealed behind a log, and covered with brush and leaves. It was now evident that the cattle had been alarmed by the smell of blood in the road, and as the body exhibited marks of violence, it was at once suspected that a murder had been perpetrated but recently. The corpse was taken to the same house where the Harpes had breakfasted, and recognized to be that of Mr. Langford, whose name was marked upon several parts of his dress. Suspicion fell upon the Harpes, who were pursued and apprehended near the Crab Orchard. They were taken to Stanford, the seat of justice for Lincoln county, where they were examined and committed by an inquiring court, sent to Danville for safe keeping, and probably for trial, as the system of district courts was then in operation in Kentucky. Previous to the time of trial, they made their escape, and proceeded to Henderson county, which at that time was just beginning to be settled.

Here they soon acquired a dreadful celebrity. Neither avarice, want, nor any of the usual inducements to the commission of crime, seemed to govern their conduct. A savage thirst for blood—a deep-rooted malignity against human nature, could alone be discovered in their actions. They murdered every defenceless being who fell in their way, without distinction of age, sex, or colour. In the night they stole secretly to the cabin, slaughtered its inhabitants, and burned their dwelling—while the farmer who left his house by day, returned to witness the dying agonies of his wife and children, and the conflagration of his possessions. Plunder was not their object: travellers they robbed and murdered, but from the inhabitants they took only what would have been freely given to them; and no more than was immediately necessary to supply the wants of nature; they destroyed without having suffered injury, and without the prospect of gain. A negro boy, riding to a mill, with a bag of corn, was seized by them, and his brains dashed out against a tree; but the horse which he rode and the grain were left unmolested. Females, children, and servants, no longer dared to stir abroad; unarmed men feared to encounter a Harpe; and the solitary hunter, as he trod the forest, looked around him with a watchful eye, and when he saw a stranger, picked his flint and stood on the defensive.

It seems incredible that such atrocities could have been often repeated in a country famed for the hardihood and gallantry of its people; in Kentucky, the cradle of courage, and the nurse of warriors. But that part of Kentucky which was the scene of these barbarities was then almost a wilderness, and the vigilance of the Harpes for a time ensured impunity. The spoils of their dreadful warfare furnished them with the means of violence and of escape. Mounted on fine horses, they plunged into the forest, eluded pursuit by frequently changing their course, and appeared, unexpectedly, to perpetrate new enormities, at points distant from those where they were supposed to lurk. On these occasions, they often left their wives and children behind them; and it is a fact, honourable to the community, that vengeance for these bloody deeds was not wreaked on the helpless, but in some degree guilty, companions of the perpetrators. Justice, however, was not long delayed.

A frontier is often the retreat of loose individuals, who, if not familiar with crime, have very blunt perceptions of virtue. The genuine woodsmen, the real pioneers, are independent, brave, and upright; but as the jackal pursues the lion to devour his leavings, the footsteps of the sturdy hunter are closely pursued by miscreants destitute of his noble qualities. These are the poorest and the idlest of the human race—averse to labour, and impatient of the restraints of law and the courtesies of civilized society. Without the ardour, the activity, the love of sport, and patience of fatigue, which distinguish the bold backwoodsman, these are doomed to the forest by sheer laziness, and hunt for a bare subsistence; they are the "cankers of a calm world and a long peace," the helpless nobodies, who, in a country where none starve and few beg, sleep until hunger pinches, then stroll into the woods for a meal, and return to their slumber. Frequently they are as harmless as the wart upon a man's nose, and as unsightly; but they are sometimes mere wax in the hands of the designing, and become the accessories of that guilt which they have not the courage or the industry to perpetrate. With such men the Harpes are supposed to have sometimes lurked. None are known to have participated in their deeds of blood, nor suspected of sharing their counsels; but they sometimes crept to the miserable cabins of those who feared or were not inclined to betray them.

Two travelers came one night to the house of a man named Stegal, and, for want of better lodgings, claimed under his little roof that hospitality which in a new country is found at every habitation. Shortly after, the Harpes arrived. It was not, it seems, their first visit; for Mrs. Stegal had received instructions from them, which she dared not disobey, never to address them by their real names in the presence of third persons. On this occasion they contrived to inform her that they intended to personate Methodist preachers, and ordered her to arrange matters so that one of them should sleep with each of the strangers, whom they intended to murder. Stegal was absent, and the woman was obliged to obey. The strangers were completely deceived as to the character of the newly arrived guests; and when it was announced that the house contained but two beds, they cheerfully assented to the proposed arrangement: one crept into a bed on the lower floor with one ruffian, while the other retired to the loft with another. Both the strangers became their victims; but these bloody ruffians, who seemed neither to feel shame, nor dread punishment, determined to leave behind them no evidence of their crime, and consummated the foul tragedy by murdering their hostess and setting fire to the dwelling.

From this scene of arson, robbery, and murder, the perpetrators fled precipitately, favoured by a heavy fall of rain, which, as they believed, effaced their footsteps. They did not cease their flight until late the ensuing day, when they halted at a spot which they supposed to be far from any human habitation. Here they kindled a fire, and were drying their clothes, when an emigrant, who had pitched his tent hard by, strolled towards their camp. He was in search of his horses, which had strayed, and civilly asked if they had seen them. This unsuspecting woodsman they slew, and continued their retreat.

In the meanwhile, the outrages of these murderers had not escaped notice, nor were they tamely submitted to. The Governor of Kentucky had offered a reward for their heads, and parties of volunteers had pursued them; they had been so fortunate as to escape punishment by their cunning, but had not the prudence to desist, or to fly the country.

A man, named Leiper, in revenge for the murder of Mrs. Stegal, raised a party, pursued, and discovered the assassins, on the day succeeding that atrocious deed. They came so suddenly upon the Harpes that they had only time to fly in different directions. Accident aided the pursuers. One of the Harpes was a large, and the other a small man; the first usually rode a strong, powerful horse, the other a fleet, but much smaller animal, and in the hurry of flight they had exchanged horses. The chase was long and hot: the smaller Harpe escaped unnoticed, but the other, who was kept in view, spurred on the noble animal which he rode, and which, already jaded, began to fail at the end of five or six miles. Still the miscreant pressed forward; for, although none of his pursuers were near but Leiper, who had outridden his companions, he was not willing to risk a combat with a man as strong and perhaps bolder than himself, who was animated with a noble spirit of indignation against a shocking and unmanly outrage. Leiper was mounted on a horse of celebrated powers, which he had borrowed from a neighbor for this occasion. At the beginning of the chase, he had pressed his charger to the height of his speed, carefully keeping on the track of Harpe, of whom he sometimes caught a glimpse as he ascended the hills, and again lost sight in the valleys and the brush. But as he gained on the foe, and became sure of his victim, he slackened his pace, cocked his rifle, and deliberately pursued, sometimes calling upon the outlaw to surrender. At length, in leaping a ravine, Harpe's horse sprained a limb, and Leiper overtook him. Both were armed with rifles. Leiper fired, and wounded Harpe through the body; the latter turning in his seat, levelled his piece, which missed fire, and he dashed it to the ground, swearing it was the first time it had ever deceived him. He then drew a tomahawk, and waited the approach of Leiper, who, nothing daunted, unsheathed his long hunting-knife and rushed upon his desperate foe, grappled with him, hurled him to the ground, and wrested his only remaining weapon from his grasp. The prostrate wretch—exhausted with the loss of blood, conquered, but unsubdued in spirit—now lay passive at the feet of his adversary. Expecting every moment the arrival of the rest of his pursuers, he inquired if Stegal was of the party, and being answered in the affirmative, he exclaimed, "Then I am a dead man!"

"That would make no difference," replied Leiper, calmly. "You must die at any rate. I do not wish to kill you myself, but if nobody else will do it, I must." Leiper was a humane man, easy, slow-spoken, and not quickly excited, but a thorough soldier when roused. Without insulting the expiring criminal, he questioned him as to the motives of his late atrocities. The murderer attempted not to palliate or deny them, and confessed that he had been actuated by no inducement but a settled hatred of his species, whom he had sworn to destroy without distinction, in retaliation for some fancied injury. He expressed no regret for any of his bloody deeds, except that which he confessed he had perpetrated upon one of his own children. "It cried," said he, "and I killed it: I had always told the women, I would have no crying about me." He acknowledged that he had amassed large sums of money, and described the places of concealment; but as none was ever discovered, it is presumed he did not declare the truth. Leiper had fired several times at Harpe during the chase, and wounded him; and when the latter was asked why, when he found Leiper pursuing him alone, he did not dismount and take to a tree, from behind which he could inevitably have shot him as he approached, he replied that he had supposed there was not a horse in the country equal to the one which he rode, and that he was confident of making his escape. He thought also that the pursuit would be less eager, so long as he abstained from shedding the blood of any of his pursuers. On the arrival of the rest of the party, the wretch was dispatched, and he died as he had lived, in remorseless guilt. It is said, however, that he was about to make some disclosure, and had commenced in a tone of more sincerity than he had before evinced, when Stegal advanced and severed his head from his body. This bloody trophy they carried to the nearest magistrate, a Mr. Newman, before whom it was proved to be the head of Micajah Harpe; they then placed it in the fork of a tree, where it long remained a revolting object of horror. The spot, which is near the Highland Lick, in Union (then Henderson) County, is still called Harpe's Head, and a public road which passes it, is called the Harpe's Head Road.

The other Harpe made his way to the neighborhood of Natchez, where he joined a gang of robbers, headed by a man named Meason, whose villanies were so notorious that a reward was offered for his head. At that period, vast regions along the shores of the Ohio and Mississippi were still unsettled, through which boats navigating those rivers must necessarily pass; and the traders who, after selling their cargoes at New Orleans, attempted to return by land, had to cross immense wildernesses, totally destitute of inhabitants. Meason, who was a man rather above the ordinary stamp, infested these deserts, seldom committing murder, but robbing all who fell in his way. Sometimes he plundered the descending boats; but more frequently he allowed these to pass, preferring to rob their owners of their money as they returned, pleasantly observing, that "those people were taking their produce to market for him." Harpe took an opportunity, when the rest of his companions were absent, to slay Meason, and putting his head in a bag, carried it to Natchez, and claimed the reward. The claim was admitted; the head of Meason was recognized but so also was the face of Harpe, who was arrested, condemned, and executed.

In collecting oral testimony of events long past, a considerable variety will often be found in the statements of the persons conversant with the circumstances. In this case, I have found none, except as to the fact of the two Harpes having exchanged horses. A day or two before the fatal catastrophe which ended their career in Kentucky, they had murdered a gentleman named Love, and had taken his horse, a remarkably fine animal, which Big Harpe undoubtedly rode when he was overtaken. It is said that Little Harpe escaped on foot, and not on his brother's horse. Many of these facts were disclosed by the latter, while under sentence of death.

After Harpe's death the women came in and claimed protection. Two of them were the wives of the larger Harpe, the other one of his brother. The latter was a decent female, of delicate, prepossessing appearance, who stated that she had married her husband without any knowledge of his real character, shortly before they set out for the west; that she was so much shocked at the first murder which they committed, that she attempted to escape from them, but was prevented, and that she had since made similar attempts. She immediately wrote to her father in Virginia, who came for her, and took her home. The other women were in no way remarkable. They remained in Muhlenburgh county.

These horrid events will sound like fiction to your ears, when told as having happened in any part of the United States, so foreign are they from the generosity of the American character, the happy security of our institutions, and the moral habits of our people. But it is to be recollected that they happened twenty-seven years ago, in frontier settlements, far distant from the civilized parts of our country. The principal scene of Harpe's atrocities, and of his death, was in that part of Kentucky which lies south of Green river, a vast wilderness, then known by the general name of the Green river country, and containing a few small and thinly scattered settlements—the more dense population of that state being at that time confined to its northern and eastern parts. The Indians still possessed the country to the south and west. That enormities should sometimes have been practiced at these distant spots, cannot be matter of surprise; the only wonder is that they were so few. The first settlers were a hardy and an honest people; but they were too few in number, and too widely spread, to be able to create or enforce wholesale civil restraints. Desperadoes, flying from justice, or seeking a secure theatre for the perpetration of crime, might frequently escape discovery, and as often elude or openly defy the arm of justice.

B

WEIR'S TRIP TO NEW ORLEANS IN 1803

PIONEER James Weir, of Greenville, made a number of trips from Lewisburg, or Kincheloe's Bluff, to New Orleans in the early days. The date of the first was about six years after he settled in Muhlenberg, when he was about twenty-seven years old, and as far as known it is the only one of which he ever wrote a description. The original manuscript is still in existence, and for a copy of it I am indebted to Judge Lucius P. Little, of Owensboro, who will publish the story in his forthcoming book on "Old Stories of Green River and Its People."

JOURNAL, BY JAMES WEIR, 1803.

I arrived at Natchez on the 9th March. It is a beautiful little town situated on a high bluff rising from the river by a gradual ascent, & a fertile & level country seems to make off from the town. From the eligibility of this place I think it is found to be the center of trade for the Western Country. There are about 500 dwellings in this place. They are mostly Americans from South Carolina & Georgia. There is a number of large stores there. Goods are sold about the same price with Nashville. I suppose from what I have seen that Natchez is, or the inhabitants of the town are, as much given to luxury & dissipation as any place in America. There is great abundance of cotton in the vicinity of Natchez. That is their staple commodity. There were 5 sea-vessels (schooners or brigs) lying there waiting for loading. It is thought that in time shipping will come there in great numbers as it will not take them more than 5-6 days, if so long, to come up from Orleans if the wind is moderately in their favour. I left the Natchez on the 12th for the New Orleans and on the morning of the 13th I arrived at Loftier Heights just as the soldiers were firing the morning gun. Loftier Heights is a place of defense occupied by the troops of the United States under the command of Gen. Wilkinson. The garrison is in good order and the troops look well. This place is 45 miles below Natchez on the line between the Spaniards & Americans. The river is from there to the Orleans very good and we sailed night and day. From the Heights to the Atchafalaya is 15 miles. This is a place that boatmen dread as it has been said that boats were sucked out there and were not able to return but were taken into lakes that empty into the sea, though I found no difficulty in it, nor do I believe that it is so dangerous as has been represented. From this to Point Copee is 25 miles.

At Point Copee the French are settled on both sides in one continuous village which yields a beautiful prospect. From Point Copee to Baton

Rouge is 35 miles. Here is the principal Spanish garrison that is kept on the river & here did I experience some of their tyranical laws.

I arrived there in the evening and went to the Commandant & got my passport signed. He sent down to my boat & bought a ham of bacon. I thought from this example I might sell on without hesitation. I continued to sell till the next day at 12 o'clock when I was taken by a guard of Spanish Regulars who told me that I must go into confinement together with all my crew, save one to take care of the boat for selling without permission. I desired to see the Commandant for I hated the thought of going into a calaboose, but all in vain.

We were hurried into a nasty prison amongst a number of Spanish transgressors who were almost naked. I then began to think of Baron Trenk in the jail of Magdaburg & that it might perhaps be my lot to be there without cause, possibly for months or years as our liberation or confinement depended wholy on the will of a capricious tyrant. I walked through this nasty prison very uneasy still looking through the iron grates and ruminating on my sad misfortune. I sat down at length on the straw & began to console myself that I was not the first that had been in confinement unjustly & that I was not alone as I had one of my company with me, a Mr. Hobbs who was merely a passenger in my boat. After we had been there about half an hour the interpreter came & told us we must come out & go before the Commandant. We went out cheerfully expecting to be liberated knowing ourselves to be innocent.

We were brought before the Commandant who sat in his judgment hall. He demanded of me why I had sold bacon &c without permission from him. I told him that I did not know that it was necessary, and if I had transgressed against his laws it was through ignorance I being a stranger in their land & also that he was the first to purchase from me himself and that he did not tell me that it was necessary to have a permit & therefore I thought it ungenerous of him to put me into confinement. He took offense at this mode of expression and ordered us both back to confinement. The interpreter began to intercede for us but all in vain. Then Mr. Hobbs, who was with me, began to plead that he was only a passenger & that he ought to be set at liberty. The commandant agreed he should be liberated but I was sent back to confinement. I directed Hobbs to stay by my boat & not to leave the place till he saw the result. He said he would stay by me if it was for 6 months & use every exertion to get me out. He went to the boat & I to my prison with a heavy heart.

The poor dejected Spaniards that were my companions in this solitary place began to eye me with attention & one of them got up and made signs for me to sit down on his blankets. I sat down and mused to myself. I had no company for I could not understand them. While I sat thus in dejection & had no hopes of coming out shortly there came a messenger to the door & asked me what I had to advance in my behalf respecting the affair for which I was confined. I told him I had nothing more to say than what I had already told the Commandant, his master, & that he might tell him that if he did confine me here without a cause I would see the Governor at the New Orleans who would certainly see justice done &

perhaps by his removal from office. In about 10 minutes the messenger returned & told me I was to be set at liberty. The iron bolts were again turned & I was once more set at liberty.

When I returned to the boat the crew was overjoyed to see me once more. We then pushed off our boat & set out for the Orleans, resolving to stay at that unfortunate place no longer. From Baton Rouge to Orleans, 180 miles, nothing more particular occurred on our voyage. We sailed night & day as in this part of the river there are no sawyers. When we came within 100 miles of Orleans the river is levied on both sides to keep the water from over flowing the settlements. Here you are presented with beautiful prospects on the levy on both sides of which are houses, large & beautiful farms, orange groves, sugar cane & sugar houses all the way to the New Orleans. When we came in sight the masts of the vessels that lay in harbour appeared like a forest of old trees. We got in amongst them with some difficulty and landed just above the Gate.

I arrived at the New Orleans on the 23d of March 1803 a handsome city much larger & better situated than I did expect. There is a number of wealthy American merchants residing there & they carry on business largely; houses that may be relied upon either to deposit property with or to do business by consignment. Orleans is not a place of defence. Their garrisons and forts are out of repair. They have about 400 Spanish Regulars. They are a poor looking starved like crew. I am persuaded that 100 Kentucky men could take the place if it was the will of Government for I suppose that one third of the inhabitants of the Orleans are Americans in possession of the place.

New Orleans is situated low. The country falls off from it. About 3 miles back it is so swampy that no person can settle on it. It is a fine place for fish & oysters in the lake that lies about 3 miles back from the city. New Orleans is a very rich place and a great place for doing business & would be a great acquisition to the United States if they were in possession of it. The French & Spaniards living there are for the most part very much of gentlemen & more to be relied on than many of our American citizens that are settled there. Some of them that I became acquainted with treated me with the greatest civility & freindship.[1]

I set out from the Orleans for Philadelphia on the 6th of April on board the schooner Roby, Capt. Martain, Master (a very worthy and respectable

---

[1] The national and international complications involved in the question of keeping the Mississippi River open to American merchants were widely discussed by Kentuckians and others in 1803 and during a number of years preceding. Baton Rouge and New Orleans at the time referred to by Mr. Weir were, as he states, Spanish garrisons. Florida—then embracing the present State of Florida and the southern portions of Alabama and Mississippi and Louisiana, east of the Mississippi River—was ceded by Spain to Great Britain in 1763 and recovered by Spain in 1783. After the purchase of "Louisiana" in 1803 by the United States, much discussion arose regarding the boundary of the Spanish territory of Florida. The Perdido River was declared the western boundary of Florida, and is such to-day. What is now Florida remained Spanish territory until 1819, when it was ceded to the United States. It may be well to add that "Louisiana" was ceded by France to Spain in 1762 and re-ceded to France in 1800. In April, 1803, "Louisiana" was purchased from the French by the United States. What is now the State of Louisiana was admitted into the Union in 1812.

man, a Quaker). We had a fair wind down the river to the mouth viz 105 miles. Just before we came to the Balize or mouth of the river we struck a sander & stuck fast for 3 days. On the evening of the 4th we carried out our anchor & used every exertion by all hands & draw her off, yet nevertheless, I felt not satisfied, for I thought it was ominous of bad success. We had to wait till the next morning for a pilot to take us out the mouth of the river as the channel is very narrow and often changes so that it is impossible for any person to come out or in without a pilot who examines the channel every day & sets up stakes on each side next morning early.

The pilot came to us & the winds blew fair & we went out (together with seven other vessels) into the main ocean. Then it was that I began to feel sea sick in good earnest. The waves rolled high and the water looked green & loathsome as the hated Styx, (spoken of by the heathen poets.) We had 14 passengers on board. They were all sick save one. There was nothing to be heard but vomiting and cries of the sick. I bore it patiently knowing the sickness was not unto death & hoping that in a few days the worst would be over, but I continued sick almost throughout my whole journey. I had no appetite to eat & all kinds of victuals to me were loathsome till I arrived in the Delaware. We had a fair wind for 4 days after we left the Balize which blew us on rapidly. We sailed a south course till we came in sight of the Havannah. We then changed our course to E. N. E. The winds were contrary almost continually. We made no progress but were rather beaten back. Thus we were beat about in most horrid tempests, sometimes in sight of the Florida shore & sometimes in sight of the Land of Cuba & it was with difficulty that we could keep off the rocks & sands. The crew was in the utmost consternation & wished themselves on shore in any part. The Captain nevertheless preserved a calm and unshaken mind, bid us be of good cheer, that when adverse fortune had spent herself, we would have better winds & that he hoped to land us all safe at Philadelphia yet.

On the evening of the 4th of May one of the passengers a young man from Monongehala of the name of William Kelly jumped over board and drowned himself without any known cause (except the apparent danger of our voyage & seasickness of which he had greatly suffered.) He was noticed to sit pensive all that day till evening when he pulled off his shirt & immediately jumped overboard. We called to him and threw him a rope but he would not receive it, but swam immediately from the vessel. We turned the vessel about in order to take him up but it was impracticable as the wind blew very high. We could see him swimming for the space of 20 minutes, when he jumped up almost out of the water and cryed out twice very loud & sunk down & we saw him no more.

Great was the solemnity that pervaded through the whole crew. All seemed to regret the loss by so sudden death of so fine a young man who had so lately been our most jovial companion. We also seemed to conjecture that it did presage the destruction of all the crew & vessel. I went to bed but slept very little. I still fancied I could see poor Kelly jump out of the water & cry out for help.

The next morning there blew up a mighty storm with much thunder and dreadful flashes of lightning that rolled along the skies. The waves became most dreadful such as we had never seen before. They often ran over our vessel and came into the cabin windows till it was knee deep on the floor. Then it was that I began to think that we must certainly perish. However, through the skill of our captain & sailors & the mercy of God we were preserved to encounter a more eminent danger. Cruel & adverse fortune seemed never too weary to persecute us. The winds subsided & the clouds blew away & bright Phebus began to emerge from the deep & seemed to promise us a pleasant day. But how short was this interval of pleasant calm. It was like the prosperity of the wicked but of short duration.

We were calmly reclining ourselves on our beds talking over the dangers we had so recently escaped when it was cried out on deck "a waterspout! a waterspout! & it is coming towards us." We all ran up on deck when we perceived it not far distant from us & progressing on towards us. (Now a waterspout is a thing much feared by sea men. It is a body of water drawn up out of the sea into the clouds and then falls down with wonderful velocity and if it strikes a vessel it commonly sinks it.) I found our captain (who had hitherto appeared unmoved in all danger) began to appear much alarmed and the form of his visage was changed and all the sailors began to be in utmost confusion. The captain ordered all the passengers below. They mostly went down, but I resolved to stay on deck & see the event. The captain tried to make sail to get out of the way of it but it was all in vain. For then it seemed as though it would go before us. Then we struck sail thinking to fall back & let it pass on before us yet all our exertions seemed in vain. For though our vessel occupied but a small part of the wide extended ocean & this unhappy phenomenon was I suppose 2 miles off when we saw it first yet it came directly and immediately to us as though directed by a supernatural power for our certain destruction.

Now this horrid scene begins to approach, the air is darkened, it roars like one continual peal of thunder. The captain cried out, "It is done! we are all lost!" The stoniest hearted sailors began to cry out "death, certain death! Lord have mercy on us!" The passengers began to flock up from below. Horror & paleness overspread each countenance & all crying out for mercy. I stood near to the cabin door & held by a rope expecting every moment to launch into the unknown regions of eternity. It came up & struck the stern of our vessel with a dreadful shock. She wheeled round with a great force & sunk down into the sea till the water came up to our shoulders on the mail deck when I never expected to see her rise again. It tore away our main sail & our top sail & our flying jib & the greater part of our rigging & drew them up into the air as in a whirlwind so that we saw them no more. It took the hat off the mate's head together with a number of other articles off the deck. After having shattered us most intolerably it passed by our vessel which rose out of the water. We tried the pump & found that the hull of our vessel was yet sound to the inexpressable joy of the captain and all the crew. It was some time before we recovered from the shock we received. When it struck the vessel it was like the shock of thunder when near, or electrel fire. Indeed it was 3 days before some of the crew was well. Now all hands are employed in clearing away the shattered rigging & in trying to erect a small sail for we had no canvas on board & we had to sew together the ruins of the old in the evening. We raised two small sails tho of little consequence & tried to stand our course. Tho' the winds were yet contrary we kept in the Gulf Stream which beat us on to the North.

On the 26th & 27th the winds blew fair. On the 28th the wind shifted to the North & beat us back 2 degrees. We are now in the latitude of Charlestown & in sight of the Capes. The passengers prayed the captain to land them there for they began to despair of ever getting round to Philadelphia but he refused. So we beat on in great distress & confusion as our water was nearly exhausted & our ship in miserable repair, however the wind changed more favorably & on the 8th day of May we arrived in the Cape of Philadelphia & on the 9th we got a pilot & proceeded up the Delaware river (viz 120 miles to Philadelphia). We had a fair wind up the river & sailed up very pleasantly. A more beautiful prospect I never saw than in passing up the river. On either side is one continuous village with the most beautiful houses, meadows & orchards that yielded a most delightful prospect & a sweet & salutary perfume as the orchards & flowers were now in their bloom. I forgot all my difficulties, my seasickness left me and I felt uninterrupted felicity from the charming prospects. Vessels continually passing & repassing us with the same winds and towns arising on every side & ships coming in from all parts of the world. We spoke vessels in the river, some from the East & West Indies, from England, France & Spain & from all parts of the United States. On the 12th we arrived in Philadelphia, truly a large and elegant city most pleasantly situated. The people are remarkably plain & very civil. A great many of the inhabitants of this city are Quakers, mostly merchants and very attentive to business.

On the 23d I set out from Philadelphia for Pittsburg. On the 24th I arrived at Lancaster a beautiful inland town, I suppose superior to any in the United States. I stayed there 3 days, then set out for Pittsburg. On my way I passed through several handsome little towns. The country is well settled by industrious citizens. They have fine orchards meadows & barns, & houses tho they charge travelers very high. On the 13th of June I arrived at Pittsburg a handsome little town in the forks of the Monongahala & Allegheny rivers. It is the place where most of the Western merchants embark with their merchandise to come down the river which causes money to be very plenty there. I stayed there 4 days to wait till the wagons came in with my goods. I purchased a boat, put in my goods & set off down the river. We passed by some handsome little towns on the way. I think it will be one day a continuous village on the banks of the Ohio from Pittsburg to the New Orleans. The river was very low. I floated night & day yet I was 4 weeks & 4 days from Pittsburg to the Redbanks, where I arrived on the 4th day of July, being one day more than 5 months from the time I set out from Lewisburg to the New Orleans.

C

TWO LOCAL STORIES BY EDWARD R. WEIR, SR.

EDWARD R. WEIR, sr., of Greenville, son of pioneer James Weir, was the author of a number of short stories. Only two are still preserved, and they are here briefly outlined.

"A Visit to the Faith Doctor" was published in the November, 1836, issue of The Western Magazine of Cincinnati. When it first appeared in print it was the subject of much lively discussion in the Green River country, and especially in Muhlenberg County. Although the story caused Mr. Weir to lose a few votes, he nevertheless gained many others, when in 1841 he ran for the Legislature, to which he was elected by a large majority. The first half of the tale is a somewhat one-sided discussion of faith cures, in which the author quotes from the old Greek scribes and many of the writers of his own day. The last half is the account of an experience he had in visiting a "faith doctor" near "a little town on Green River," all of which is followed by a short argument on faith cures in general. The whole subject is treated ironically and by no means seriously. Nevertheless it was evidently written with a view of trying to prove what he considered "the absurdity of belief in faith doctors."

"A Deer Hunt" was published in the Knickerbocker Magazine of March, 1839, under the heading of "Random Sketches by a Kentuckian— E. R. W." In the same number of the magazine appears an article by Washington Irving and a poem by Oliver Wendell Holmes. Mr. Weir begins his story with a few remarks on the great forests around Greenville, which I have omitted.

A VISIT TO THE FAITH DOCTOR.

Many of the ancient writers held the belief of supernatural power being given to man, and that there were some who could cure as well as give diseases by prayer, exorcisms, laying on of hands, etc. . . .

Steele says in the Tatler, "It is not to be imagined how far the violence of our own desires will carry us toward our own deceit in the pursuit of what we wish for." Imagination is a powerful emotion, and it has been satisfactorily proven that it will not only effect cures of "incurable diseases," but will frequently produce death. Witness the case of the Jew in France, who on a very dark night passed safely over a bridge which consisted of a single log, whilst below him was an abyss of several hundred feet. On the next morning he was shown the fearful danger he had escaped, and so great was his emotion that he fell dead. Another is a case of a person whose fear of the plague was so great that when he entered a room where a plague-striken man was, he instantly expired. Again, where a criminal was bled to death without bleeding a drop of blood.

[Mr. Weir then proceeds to tell about a visit made by two ladies and himself to the Faith Doctor's farm. One of the ladies was afflicted with an inflamed eye, and had decided, as a last resort, to call on this wonderful man. Their party of three left Greenville "one warm day in August," and after an interesting ride, during which they paused long enough to partake of an excellent dinner, they arrived at the "Doctor's domicile." Tradition says this house was in Ohio County, near Livermore.]

It was a one-story log house with two rooms, and did not differ in any respect from those that we had passed during the day, save that a number of benches were ranged in front of the door. . . .

We dismounted and walked in. There was no person in the room, and we had time to look around the place into which we had thus introduced ourselves. But there was nothing to mark that we were in the dwelling-place of the wonderful man. I looked around for the books, the musty records of ancient knowledge, over which he might have pored and from which he might have gathered the power he was reputed to possess. But in vain we looked for these. No huge ironbound tome met our gaze. Everything was most provokingly plain, nothing mysterious, nothing which we might not find in any common farmer's cabin.

The neat little bed which stood in one corner of the room was like all other beds. The old-fashioned clock, enclosed in a still more antiquated case, ticked on like any other clock. From a furtive glance which I cast into a cupboard I found that the Doctor and his family did eat, for it was well stored with cold meats and cold pies.

Before I had time to extend my discoveries any farther his daughter came into the room. She was quite a pretty girl, but unfortunately for the poetry of the thing, she forgot to slip on her stockings. Shoes without stockings, you know, do not look well. We enquired for the Doctor. He was "in the meadow at work." We looked in that direction and beheld him astride of a haystack, which he appeared to be "topping off." A messenger was dispatched for him, and we prepared for the interesting interview.

From the house we had a full view of the meadow, and before it was possible for the little boy, whom we had sent, to reach him where he was, we saw him slide from the stack, snatch up his hat and start for the house at about half mast. Then thought I, "he has an intuitive sense that he is wanted," but the next moment "the woeful want of dignity" struck me more forcibly. The cause of his haste was soon explained: there was a rush among the green corn; then a bark, and a squeal, and forth rushed a gang of hogs, closely followed by Towser and Ponto, while just behind came the Doctor, encouraging his dogs by name, who soon succeeded in clearing the field from intruders.

His first salutation, when he saw me, was, "These nasty critters—people will leave the gate open, and they destroy all my truck!"

[The callers apologized for their negligence, after which the consultation began.]

Five minutes sufficed. He merely asked her name, which eye was affected, and how long it had been so. He took down her answers in writing and told her that the optic nerve, which we all knew before, was affected. I was very anxious to close the scene. So, hurrying the lady to her horse, I returned to bid the Doctor farewell. . . . We were told he accepts no compensation for his service—that he asks no pay; but he is not averse to his family receiving presents. Nevertheless I asked him if he would make any charge for what he had promised to try to do, to which he answered: "Yes, I charge you this: next time you come, shut the gate."

[Upon her return home the patient was confined to her room with a fever and headache. However, she rapidly recovered, and regained the full use of her eye, and the faith doctor had in her another enthusiastic convert.]

From the slight conversation I had with the Doctor, and from what he has said to others, I gather that his plan of operation is by prayer, and that his creed is founded upon that passage of Scripture, "Verily, if ye have faith as a grain of mustard seed," etc. By his neighbors he is said to be a truly pious and estimable man, and that he possesses some intelligence. From this I would humbly beg leave to differ: I think him a very ignorant man, who may probably have succeeded in forcing upon himself the belief that his prayers "avail much."

[The article concludes with the argument that if prayers and petitions can result in such wonders through this Faith Doctor, whom he declares "arrogant and impudent," how much more effective would be the result, and reverential the act, if the afflicted, instead of "laying his case before this pretender," would "pray to God and not to man."]

A DEER HUNT.

A bright, frosty morning in November, 1838, tempted me to visit this forest hunting-ground. . . . On this occasion I was followed by a fine-looking hound, which had been presented to me, a few days before, by a fellow-sportsman. I was anxious to test his qualities, and knowing that a mean dog will often hunt well with a good one, I tied up my eager and well-trained Bravo and was attended by the stranger dog alone.

[After a brisk canter of half an hour (which is very interestingly described) the sportsman sighted a deer, the object of his hunt. One version of the tradition has it that Mr. Weir first saw this stag on the hill three miles east of Greenville, which since the publication of this story has been called "Buck Knob."]

On the very summit of the ridge, full one hundred and fifty yards distant, every limb standing out in bold relief against the clear blue sky, the stag paused and looked proudly down upon us. After a moment of indecision I raised my rifle and sent the whizzing lead upon its errand. A single bound and the antlered monarch was hidden from my view.

[The chase continued for several hours, and led the hunter many miles from the starting-point, until finally he had a second shot at the animal.]

Again I poured forth the "leaden messenger of death," and meteorlike he flashed by us. One bound and the noble animal lay prostrate within fifty feet of where I stood. Leaping from my horse and placing one knee upon the stag's shoulder and a hand upon his antlers, I drew my hunting knife. But scarcely had the keen point touched his neck, when with a sudden bound he threw me from his body, and my knife was hurled from my hand. In hunter's parlance, I had "only creased him." I at once saw my danger; but it was too late. With one bound he was upon me, wounding and almost disabling me with his sharp feet and horns. I seized him by his widespread antlers and sought to regain possession of my knife, but in vain; each new struggle drew me farther from it. Cherokee (my horse), frightened at this unusual scene, had madly fled to the top of the ridge, where he stood looking down upon the combat, trembling and quivering in every limb.

The ridge road I had taken had placed us far in advance of the hound whose bay I could now hear. The struggles of the furious animal had become dreadful, and every moment I could feel his sharp hoofs cutting deep into my flesh; and yet I relinquished not my hold. The struggle had brought us near a deep ditch, washed by the heavy fall rains, and into this I endeavored to force my adversary; but my strength was unequal to the effort. When we approached the very brink he leaped over the drain; I relinquished my hold and rolled in, hoping thus to escape him. But he returned to the attack, and throwing himself upon me, inflicted numerous severe cuts upon my face and breast before I could again seize him. Locking my arms around his antlers, I drew his head close to my breast, and was thus, by a great effort, enabled to prevent his doing me any serious injury. But I felt that this could not last long; every muscle and fibre of my frame was called into action and human nature could not long bear up under such exertion. Faltering a silent prayer to Heaven, I prepared to meet my fate.

At the moment of despair I heard the faint bayings of the hound. The stag, too, heard the sound, and springing from the ditch, drew me with him. His efforts were now redoubled and I could scarcely cling to him. Yet that blessed sound came nearer and nearer! O how wildly beat my heart, as I saw the hound emerge from the ravine and spring forward, with short quick bark, as his eyes rested on his game. I released my hold of the stag, who turned upon this new enemy. Exhausted and unable to rise, I still cheered the dog, that dastard-like fled before the infuriated animal, who, seemingly despising such an enemy, again threw himself upon me. Again did I succeed in throwing my arms around his antlers, but not until he had inflicted several deep and dangerous wounds upon my head and face, cutting to the very bone.

Blinded by the flowing blood, exhausted and despairing, I cursed the coward dog, who stood near, baying furiously, yet refusing to seize his game. O how I prayed for Bravo! The thoughts of death were bitter. To die thus, in the wild forest, alone, with none to help! Thoughts of home and friends coursed like lightning through my brain. That moment of desperation, when hope itself had fled, deep and clear, over the neighboring hill, came the bay of my gallant Bravo! I should have known his voice among a thousand! I pealed forth, in one faint shout, "On, Bravo! on!" The next moment, with tigerlike bounds, the noble dog came leaping down the declivity, scattering the dried autumnal leaves like a whirlwind in its path. "No pause he knew," but fixing his fangs in the stag's throat, at once commenced the struggle.

I fell back completely exhausted. Blinded with blood, I only knew that a terrific struggle was going on. In a few moments all was still, and I felt the warm breath of my faithful dog as he licked my wounds. Clearing my eyes from gore, I saw my late adversary dead at my feet; and Bravo, "my own Bravo," as the heroine of a modern novel would say, standing over me. He yet bore around his neck a fragment of the rope with which I had tied him. He had gnawed it in two, and following his master through all his wanderings, arrived in time to rescue him from a horrible death.

D

DUVALL'S DISCOVERY OF "SILVER ORE"
BY RICHARD T. MARTIN.[1]

DURING the spring of 1851 an excitement was started in the western part of Muhlenberg County which continued for more than two years. Mark Duvall claimed he had found silver ore in the hills of his neighborhood. Mark Duvall was a son of Benjamin Duvall, an old settler who lived about six miles west of Greenville. Benjamin Duvall was the father of Howard, Mark, and Benjamin Duvall, jr., or "Darky," as he was commonly called.

Mark Duvall when a young man learned the tanner's trade under John Campbell of Greenville, who conducted a tannery near where the Greenville Milling Company's planing mill is now located. Mark had also devoted some time to the study of chemistry and mineralogy, and had become a good tanner. After remaining with Campbell for a few years he married and located near his father's farm, on which was a good running spring. There Mark established a tanyard of his own, which was well patronized. Mark was a quiet, sober, and well-liked man, and had the full confidence of all who knew him. In fact, the Duvall family stood high in the community.

There were about four hundred acres of hilly land lying east of Jarrell's Creek, all of which was owned by Benjamin Duvall and his neighbors. In the spring of 1851 Mark Duvall reported that he had discovered the existence of silver ore in this hilly section. He would not point out any particular spot where silver could be found, but declared that rich veins of it occurred throughout these hills. The proclamation of this news was very encouraging to those who owned the hills. Steps were at once taken and prospecting commenced, and soon the digging of holes and pits was carried on in earnest. As the news of the great silver discovery spread, prospecting extended until everybody in the western part of the county was on the lookout for ore, and in a short time the whole county was more or less interested.

This was only a few years after the excitement of the Buckner and Churchill Iron Works had subsided. Some people seemed to take a great interest in the matter, while others scouted the idea. Secret investigations were conducted in different parts of the county, but the investigations made among the hills were boldly carried on with greater assurance. Several of the moneyed men of Greenville became interested in the silver project, and made arrangements to become partners with those owning the hills and to furnish means for a thorough investigation of the matter.

When Mark Duvall had declared that there was silver in the hills, he backed up his statement by melting "silver" out of the rock that had

---
[1] Greenville Record, March 30, 1911.

been mined by the landowners. Different kinds of rock had been dug up; some limestone, some iron ore, and a blue sandstone which sparkled with particles of mica, and was considered the richest and most plentiful of the "silver" ore.

Duvall had a novel way of extracting silver from this blue sandstone. He used a deep iron bowl with a long handle attached. It was simply a large ladle. Nearly every family owned a similar small ladle, which they used in those days for melting lead to make bullets for hunting purposes.

During the first year of the silver excitement Duvall would have the different parties who were digging beat up some of their ore, and he would take his big ladle, go to their houses, and make a "run" for them. These "runs" were usually made at night. After a hot wood fire was started Duvall would fill his big ladle with the powdered ore and place it on the fire. He would then put a flux of soap and borax in the ladle to "increase the heat" and "help extract the metal." As a general thing there would be a gathering of neighbors to witness the "run." After the ore had become red-hot, Duvall would add some "nitric and sulphuric acid," which would soon disappear, and Duvall would say, "She has done her do!" He would next carry the ladle out doors, to cool off, and after it had cooled sufficiently a search would be made for silver. Small shots of metal would be found and selected out of the ore that had been heated, and much rejoicing would take place.

The next day digging would be resumed with more earnestness. After a while the natives tried to extract the silver from the ore themselves. They procured crucibles, small earthen melting pots, and would try to melt out the silver. But none was successful in getting out any metal unless Duvall happened to assist in making the "run." This was discouraging, and the experimenters would ask Duvall, "Why is it that we can not obtain the metal like you do?" He would answer that if they had good acids like his they could get metal.

Some one procured a mouth blow-pipe from Professor Donaldson, who was teaching school in the old brick college on Cherry Street in Greenville. With this instrument they attempted to test the richness of the ore. But with all their blowing they failed to "blow out" any silver.

On one occasion some Greenville men, who were interested in the project, went out to the Silver Hills to assist in trying to make a "run," but they failed to get any metal, although they made a thorough search after the ore had been put through a "run." The next morning Duvall, hearing of the unsuccessful "run," went over to the neighbor's house where it had been attempted. They told him that they had failed to get metal. They showed Duvall where they had poured the melted ore on the ground and had searched for the silver. Duvall began an examination, and found small shots of metal where they had failed to see any. A number of the others again investigated and they also found some shining shot, and every man present declared that after all it was a good "run." The parties from Greenville returned in good spirits.

After the news of the "silver discovery" had spread into other counties, quite a number of the citizens of the neighboring counties visited Silver

Hills. Among these visitors were expert "metal witches," who claimed they could locate any rich veins of metal. These "metal witches" would take a forked stick or small rod, like those used by "water witches," and "locate" veins of silver as easily as a "water witch" could locate a vein of water.

I recall a man named Culbertson, who wore trousers that did not reach his shoetops, and were therefore called "highwater pants." He carried a small, greasy bag, filled with various kinds of ores. He used a short hickory stick, split at one end. In order to find a vein of any particular metal he would place a piece of that kind of ore in the split end of the stick. With this loaded "metal-rod" he would walk over the hills and shake it around at arm's length and in every direction. If the ore that existed in the ground was the same as the ore in his split rod, then, he claimed, the attraction became so great that it jerked his arm like a fish.

John Vickers, who lived between Sacramento and Rumsey, was one of the great water and metal "witches" of his day. He was elected to the Legislature in 1848, went to California in 1849 when the gold fever broke out there, but returned to Muhlenberg in the fall of 1851 in time to assist Duvall in trying to convince the people that silver existed in the region of Jarrell's Creek. He claimed that he had found many silver veins with the assistance of his rod. He told the people that one day, while sitting in his house in Sacramento, he located, with his hickory rod, a rich gold vein in California, and that he had written to some of his relatives in that State to take possession of it until he could get there. He said that an abundance of silver undoubtedly existed in the Muhlenberg hills. His statements added luster and vigor to the project.

The various "water witches" became expert "silver witches," and "located" many rich veins throughout the neighborhood. There were several old women who followed telling fortunes with coffee-grounds. They also tried their skill on the silver question by "turning the cup," as they called it. They put some coffee-grounds into a cup with a little coffee and turned the cup around very rapidly, shook it, and then turned the cup upside down in the saucer. They would let the inverted cup remain in that position a few minutes, and then pick it up and examine the position of the grounds that still adhered to the sides. From the arrangement of the grounds they could tell whether the prospects were "clear" or "cloudy." If there was a clear space down the side of the cup it indicated "good luck" and "go ahead." If the side of the cup was clouded with grounds it foretold "bad luck" and "look out."

The rod was considered the most reliable way of determining the presence of silver ore. The "silver witch" in using the rod could answer questions with a "yes" or "no." The nodding up and down of the rod was for "yes" and the horizontal movement for "no." There was great confidence placed in these indications made by the rod.

As a general thing the people in the county had but little knowledge of mineralogy, metallurgy, or chemistry. Doctor W. H. Yost was considered the most competent man in Muhlenberg to make a test of the metal. After an examination he pronounced it tin. Howard Duvall, a brother of Mark, melted a silver dime and took it to Doctor Yost for analysis, who declared that it also was tin. The result was that the prospectors lost faith in Doctor Yost's knowledge of metals.

After Doctor Yost had made his tests it was thought best by the leaders of the silver enthusiasts to have the ore and metal analyzed by experienced chemists and mineralogists, for no one except Mark Duvall had succeeded in getting any metal from the blue sandstone which had been dug out of Silver Hills. A meeting was held by parties interested in the project. George W. Short, of Greenville, together with Duvall, was delegated to take some of the ore and metal that Duvall claimed to have extracted by the use of his iron ladle and a wood fire, and go to Cincinnati to an experienced assayer and have both rock and metal tested. This they did. The chemist stated that the so-called "silver" was a mixture of metals, and declared that it could not possibly have come out of the sand rock, for the rock contained no metal of any kind. Duvall argued that it did. So Short and Duvall left Cincinnati without any encouragement. Soon after this, Short lost all confidence in the silver business and withdrew his support and influence.

In spite of this set-back, much interest was still manifested by many of the owners of the so-called Silver Hills. Dabney A. Martin, a merchant and tobacconist of Greenville, wanted another test made. So when he went to Philadelphia after goods he took with him some of the blue sandstone and the metal that Duvall claimed to have "run" from the rock, and had them tested by chemists there. They also told him that the "silver" was a mixture of metals, and that it had not come out of the rock. In the fall of 1852, when Dabney A. Martin went to Europe on tobacco business, he took some of the ore and metal to England and had them analyzed in London. The chemists there likewise reported that the metal was a mixture and that it had not come out of the sand rock. This was another damper on the silver excitement. Martin, like Short, lost confidence in the silver situation.

However, Duvall kept "running" out the metal with his crucibles and iron ladle. On one occasion Duvall made a big "run" in an iron kettle over a wood fire. He extracted about five pounds of "silver." Nevertheless, doubt and distrust increased about Duvall's sincerity. He was accused of being a fakir and a fraud. After Duvall had made his five-pound "run," Vickers, who frequently prospected in Silver Hills, took Duvall's five-pound "run" and some of the blue sandstone silver ore, saying he would take them to New York and have them assayed there. Vickers left, but returned in about a month. He reported that the New York chemist, like all the other professional chemists, pronounced the "silver" a mixture of metals, and said that it had not come out of the sand rock. He explained that they rolled the metal into sheets for him. These he exhibited, and gave to all those who were interested in the silver question a small sheet of what looked very much like tinfoil, which it probably was. Vickers left Silver Hills and was never seen in that neighborhood again. It was afterward claimed that he did not take the metal and ore any farther than his home in McLean County.

Duvall proposed to the people that if they would construct a furnace he would show them that he was no fakir. So the neighbors joined in and built a small furnace near his tanyard. It was only nine feet high, and therefore a great deal smaller than Buckner's iron furnace on Pond Creek. When the silver furnace was finished and ready for action the neighbors gathered to see the silver "run." Duvall was watched very closely. After the smelter had been in operation two days and very little metal had been obtained, Duvall declared the furnace had not been properly constructed. Men who had lost confidence in his work did not hesitate to tell him so to his face. This resulted in a fight at the furnace, and the place was abandoned. The stone oven stood for several years, and was always known as Duvall's Silver Stack.

About the time the furnace was abandoned, Duvall claimed he had received letters telling him that unless he left the county he would be killed. Duvall decided it would not be safe for him to remain in the county, and therefore left. However, he always insisted that the hills he had explored were full of silver and would be opened up some day. Just before he moved to Ohio County, he requested three men of the neighborhood to meet him at a certain place in Silver Hills. After they met, he led them to the head of a deep hollow and there dug up several pieces of metal, which he carried back home with him. No questions were asked by any one of these men, but their eyes were opened; the tale was told, and the silver excitement was soon over.

The secret of all this silver excitement, which lasted for about two years, was well planned and manipulated by Mark Duvall, for what purpose no one can tell, unless it was to sell his father's land at a high price.

In the early history of the county, pewter utensils were used for domestic purposes. Pewter bowls, plates, pans, etc., of the early days had gone out of use at this period. The best quality of pewter—called also "white metal"—was made of tin hardened with copper. The cheap grade was made of lead, alloyed with antimony and bismuth. Duvall had secured some of these old pewter vessels, cut them up, and hidden them away for use in working the silver trick. Duvall was aware of the fact that his neighbors knew nothing about ores of any kind. He made his "silver runs" in his iron ladle on a wood fire, which in itself was absurd. He made these "silver runs" by dissolving a piece of pewter in acid. He would pour this solution on the hot crushed rock in the ladle. The acid would soon be consumed and the metal would remain in the ladle with the crushed rock, and when cooled off the metal would be formed into small shot and could be picked out. This would occur no matter what kind of rock might be used.

Mark Duvall moved to Ohio County, where he studied medicine and lived to a good old age, but as far as is known he never "discovered" any silver in that county.

E

"RIDING THE CIRCUIT"
By Lucius P. Little.

NO MAN in Western Kentucky stands higher as a citizen, lawyer, or student of literature and history than does Judge Lucius P. Little. In "Ben Hardin, His Times and Contemporaries," published in 1887, he wrote one of the best contributions ever printed bearing on the history of Kentucky from 1784 to 1852. He now has in course of preparation "Old Stories of Green River and Its People," which will appear during 1914. I have read the manuscript, and am confident that this book will take rank as one of the best written and most valuable histories of any of those concerning any section of the State. Judge Little was born in Calhoun February 15, 1838. He was graduated from the Law Department of Cumberland University, Lebanon, Tennessee, in 1857, and in 1868 moved to Owensboro, where he has since resided and where he has long stood at the head of his fellow lawyers. From 1880 to 1893 he served as circuit judge. He is a member of the Investigators' Club (Owensboro's literary and historical club) and the Kentucky State Historical Society. The following sketch was written by Judge Little in 1912, especially for this history.

"RIDING THE CIRCUIT."

The custom of the old-time lawyers in Kentucky of "riding the circuit" was almost coeval with the admission of the State into the Federal Union, and continued to the end of the fifties. After the Civil War ended, the increase of the local bar in numbers and in reputation as practitioners caused the custom gradually to decline.

While the custom was in vogue, on the Sunday before the beginning of a term of court the presiding judge, usually accompanied by the prosecuting attorney and a retinue of lawyers more or less numerous, mounted on horseback, might be seen entering the county town, destined for the principal tavern, not unlike an unarmed troop of cavalry. This might fitly be termed the "grand entry," and following it there quickly gathered about the inn a respectable number of the principal citizens, to greet the distinguished guests. After the first arrivals others followed, in parties of twos or threes or one by one. By nightfall the leading tavern was taxed to its utmost capacity.

The following morning, the first day of the term, the courthouse bell was rung vigorously at eight o'clock, and shortly thereafter the high sheriff proclaimed at the front door to the listening world the thrilling shibboleth, usual on such occasions: "O yez! O yez! The Circuit Court for Muhlenberg County is now in session! Let all persons having business therein draw near and be heard! God save the Commonwealth and this Honorable Court!" (This old preliminary formula has fallen into disuse, and unfortunately a neglected Deity has not always saved the Commonwealth from the enemies of law and order or protected the eminent judges who have presided over its courts.)

On entering the court room, all seats inside the bar are largely found already occupied by the unprivileged classes. The sheriff, however, gives the peremptory order that all persons not lawyers and officers of court are requested to retire from the bar, which mandate is quickly obeyed. Persons summoned as jurors and others (ready to be summoned) seek seats in easy earshot of any call of their names. Parties, witnesses, and mere lookers-on soon fill all remaining seats.

The judge has already taken what in legal parlance is "the bench," but which in reality is an easy chair behind a desk, which to the unsophisticated is strikingly like a pulpit. The clerk, sheriff, and jailer betake themselves to their respective posts and to the discharge of their several functions. At last the honorable court is opened in due form, and those having business therein draw near and (as opportunity offers) proceed to make themselves heard.

The particular term of court now to be mentioned occurred in the year 1859, when Honorable Thomas C. Dabney was judge of the district and Ed Campbell prosecuting attorney. The resident attorneys at that time were Charles Eaves, Jonathan Short, Joseph Ricketts, John Chapeze, B. E. Pittman, Edward R. Weir, sr., and Mortimer D. Hay. At the head of this roll, by extent of practice, long experience, and profound learning, easily stood Charles Eaves, then in the full vigor of manhood. The youngest member, familiarly called "Mort" Hay, was tall and slender, with a quick and bright mind, already giving assurance of the talents and ability for which he was subsequently distinguished in a career terminated by an untimely death. The visiting lawyers that term were Honorable B. L. D. Guffy, of Morgantown, who was later to occupy a seat on the Court of Appeals bench; Washington Ewing, of Russellville, sprung of a family distinguished for its talents; H. G. Petree, Samuel Kennedy, and Francis Bristow, from Elkton—and sometimes came also the latter's son Benjamin, physically strong and burly and of striking appearance, but not so widely distinguished then as to cause the subsequent inquiry, "Is there not good presidential timber produced in Elkton?" From the Daviess County bar answered John H. McHenry, sr., and William Anthony, both names very familiar in the region at that day. McLean County was also represented by two young lawyers who, having some business in court that term, were in attendance. One of these was the late William T. Owen, afterward for two terms circuit judge of his district. Each of these had secured two of Culver's best rigs for the trip—not, as it may be well to explain, that they necessarily required two separate conveyances for the thirty miles from Calhoun to Greenville, but because each had had the good fortune to secure as comrade for the journey two of the prettiest girls of that town. It is recalled that, on the bright day they fared forth, the two young gentlemen were arrayed in the height of the fashion of that time, but so clad that they would be a sight to the beholders in these later days. Picture them! Long hair, silk hats, swallow-tail coats, low-cut vests, close-fitting trousers, and low-quarter shoes, with white hose! Neither in that day nor at any time since, in Kentucky, has there ever been any discount on a pretty girl because of her raiment, but on this day these were charmingly gowned.

The weather was faultless, and the long, hot lanes were fewer than now. For the most part the road on either side was bordered by woodland, the scenery and fragrance of which would beggar the language that might attempt to describe it. It is better to forget the exquisite pleasure of such bright days in the dim light of the somberer and quieter ones that came later. The road, at one point, wound by a clearing where the timber had been cut away and the brush placed in piles for burning later. There an incident occurred worthy of note. A blacksnake, technically known as a "racer," six to seven feet in length, was discovered in the road by Owen, who was in advance. His fair companion expressed some girlish alarm, whereupon with becoming gallantry he leaped from the buggy and with whip in hand lashed the "racer" as he fled out through the clearing. After a chase of seventy-five yards the snake hid himself in a brush-pile, and Owen, exhilarated by the exercise, started to return. The snake, encouraged by the retreat of his pursuer, came forth, and with head erect nearly two feet made a good second on the return, although the young man did his best. Turning on the snake again and hitting him whenever in reach, the race out through the clearing was repeated, and the snake again sought refuge and again chased his pursuer. This performance was kept up without variation until four or five heats had been run. Meantime his traveling companion—secure from danger in the buggy—and the occupants of the other vehicle, had laughed and wept and laughed again. But Owen got excessively warm and was fairly outwinded, while the "racer" showed a discouraging degree of "bottom." By finally crawling into his buggy backwards, meanwhile demonstrating with his whip, he managed to terminate the unequal contest. *Docet hic fabula* if a beau wishes to show his mettle before the fair, he should beware of contests with "racers."

In the soft twilight of the day the journey ended. Having left their traveling companions with expectant friends, the attorneys found lodging at Captain Bob Russell's somewhat overcrowded hotel. The landlord was a large, portly man of fine presence, quite as dignified as any of his distinguished guests, with all of whom he maintained an easy familiarity. He carried a stout walking-cane as he mingled with his lodgers, discharging the duties of hospitality. His colloquial abilities were above the common, and he was not at loss whatever the topic. His stores of incident and anecdote were inexhaustible, and he gave his friends little opportunity for considering whether the accommodations of the house might not be amended in certain directions. He had honorably served his country in war and in peace in former years, and was still a valuable man in that quarter to the political party with which he affiliated.

The hotel building stood near the courthouse. It was a low, two-storied affair, with a few bed-chambers and these in the second story, but each large enough for three or four beds, and each bed was designed to accommodate two persons. The writer recalls that when he awoke at about four o'clock the first morning of his stay in Greenville, he beheld a large, fleshy, elderly man engaged in shaving a large area of fleshy face as with closed eyes he sat ponderously in a chair. (This was before the era of safety razors.)

"Mr. McHenry, how can you shave without a mirror?" inquired the freshly awakened young lawyer.

"I am not in the habit of using a mirror, and can shave just as readily without one," was the answer.

It was fortunate in his case, as our room in this respect was unfurnished, and the single candle in the bedroom shedding a radiance somewhat uncertain. It was also a provident arrangement of nature that morning that all the occupants of our chamber did not care to arise and dress at the same time; that operation was performed in detachments. The limited floor space forbade any other course. There was no ceiling or plaster beneath, and because of this the landlord was enabled with his cane to knock on our floor from time to time, as a warning that breakfast was about ready. All embarrassments were happily overcome, the morning meal dispatched, and the gentlemen of the bar were ready in due time for the opening of court.

One of the important cases to be tried was that of Arch Rutherford, charged with the murder of a man named Stark, in Todd County. After being indicted in Todd the defendant had procured a change of venue to Muhlenberg. The evidence in the case was circumstantial, and while the circumstances had been comparatively few they had been sufficient to lead to the conclusion on the part of the public generally that the accused was the guilty man, and that his motive had been robbery. A twenty-dollar bill which had been paid to Stark the day before the murder (which had occurred at night) was marked. It was found in possession of Rutherford and identified by the man who had paid it to Stark. The accused owned and was accustomed to ride a horse which, in motion, made a peculiar noise known as "rattling of the sheath." It was in proof at the trial that a horse making this peculiar noise was heard, on the night of the murder, to pass through the town of Elkton from Rutherford's residence, going in the direction of the place where Stark resided, and also that a short time afterward the horse was heard returning going toward defendant's residence. It was also made to appear that, in passing and repassing through town, the horse had been ridden in a gallop, and that next day he showed signs of having been recently hard ridden.

Honorable Francis Bristow was chief counsel for the accused. Mr. Campbell conducted the prosecution. The jury that tried the case returned a verdict of guilty, and sentence of death was pronounced. An appeal was prosecuted, and the judgment was reversed in the Court of Appeals and the case remanded for a new trial. While awaiting another trial the prisoner escaped from jail and was never afterward apprehended. Tradition has it that he fled to Texas, and during a long residence in that State accumulated considerable property and that he died there, but the date of his death is unknown.

At the same term there was also pending a case against S. P. Love, charged with killing Wesley M. Little at South Carrollton on August 16, 1857. The circumstances of the killing were that Love and Little, both residing in South Carrollton, became embroiled in a personal difficulty growing out of politics. Little kept a hotel in the town and was an active local politician. In a public speech he had denounced a statement made by Love as untrue. Early one Sunday morning, shortly afterward, Little, while standing alone in front of his hotel, was instantly killed by a shot in the back, fired by some one in concealment in the second story of a house across the street. Love was arrested and indicted for murder. At the autumn term of 1859 the case was tried, but the jury failed to agree. It was afterward continued from term to term until the outbreak of the Civil War. Love, meantime, joined the Federal army and during the war underwent final trial, which resulted in his acquittal.

Over half a century has gone by since the term of court herein referred to. More pages have been written in American history in that interval than in all the preceding years since Columbus first laid longing eyes on the palm trees of the West Indian island. In very truth old times have passed away, and behold all things are become new.

To one who saw Greenville and its people then, there are many things he would miss if he looked for them now. The portly and dignified landlord of Russell's Tavern has long slept in the silent grave. The small, old-fashioned courthouse has been supplanted by a stately edifice, the architectural graces of which entitle it to be called the Temple of Justice. The gentle Dabney has long since ceased to preside there, but has without fear answered the call of another Judge. Campbell, the prosecutor, is no longer a terror to evildoers, but has received the reward due a just man, and has claimed his right to be heard by that merciful Advocate who pleads for us all. Charles Eaves, when he left this world, took from it a store of legal knowledge possessed but rarely by any lawyer of his day and generation. The amiable, kind-hearted Guffy went through life doing his duty, dispensing good cheer among his friends, and finally meekly bowed his head to the fate that awaits us all. Owen, after marrying the pretty girl who had laughed so merrily at him in his contest with the "racer," rounded out an honorable career, and at its end he and she sleep well the last long sleep. Indeed, all the names here mentioned have long been numbered with the silent hosts who now rest in eternal peace.

INDEX

INDEX

A

Abbey, Edwin A., 7.
Abbott, Miss, 212.
Acrefield, Peter, 53.
Adams, John, 42.
Adams, Matthew, 32.
Adams, R. W., 405.
Adcock, Joseph, 353.
Adkins, William C., 405.
"Aftermath" (James Lane Allen), text, 242.
Agricultural products of county (in 1870), 412.
Airdrie, Old. See Paradise Country and Old Airdrie, 220-241.
  Abandoned houses at in 1895, 232.
  Alexander establishes town, 226.
  Coal mined at, 235.
  Collins on, 412, 419, 420.
  Entrance to the "McLean Old Bank," 236.
  Gen. Buell's private park, residence, and boathouse at, 1900, 238; residence, 1900, 239; ruins of, 1912, 240.
  McLean Old Spring, 236.
  Mill chimneys, 1900, 230.
  Old hotel building at in 1895, 235.
  Ruins at in 1900, 234.
  Stone House, 220, 221, 226, 229, 235.
  Stone steps, hillside, 221, 227.
Airdrie Furnace, 225, 398, 399, 401.
"Airdrie Furnace and Property, Report upon" (Kentucky State Geological Survey, text), 230-233.
Airdrie Hill, 220, 221, 239.
Airdrie mines, 190, 389, 401.
Airdrie Petroleum Co., 233.
Akers, Larkin N., 65, 66; family, 66; 289, 345, 430.
  Portrait of, 65.
Albritton P. O., 420.
Alcock, Duran, 105, 206.
Alcock, Richard Nelson, 50, 51.
Alexander, R. S. C. A., 188, 189, 190, 220, 224, 225, 226, 227, 228, 229, 233, 234, 235, 236, 237, 389, 401.
  Brought Scotch iron-workers to America, 226.
  Extensive investments, 226.
  Family of, 225.
  Furnace commercial failure, 227.
  "New Scotland," 226.
  Starts furnace at Airdrie, 226.
Alexander, Prof. Wayland, 215, 216, 405.
Alexander, William, 64.

Allen, G. W., 283.
Allen, James Lane ("Aftermath," text), 242.
Allen, Julian W., 13.
Allen, Linsey, 64.
Allen, William Booker, 122.
Allen's "History of Kentucky," 435.
Allison, B. Frank, 88.
Allison, Charles McLean, 64, 86.
Allison, Finis H., 361.
Allison, Finis M., 49, 87, 353, 354, 360, 404, 405, 423.
  Family of, 361.
  Political career, 361.
  Portrait of, 361.
  Sketch of in "Biographical Encyclopedia of Kentuckians" (text), 361.
Allison, James, 361.
Allison, John, 55, 361.
Allison, John Adair, 85, 86, 87, 108, 187, 361.
  Family of, 87.
  "Old Place," 87.
  Portrait of, 88.
Allison, Samuel, 85; family, 86; 127, 206, 360.
Allison, Samuel Henley, 86, 87.
Allison, William Dickson, 86, 87.
Allison, Young Ewing, 86, 87.
"Alvin's Avenue," 268.
Ambrose, C. C., 253.
Ambrose, John L. F., 253.
Anderson, John, 44, 64.
Anderson, John, jr., 64.
Anderson, Tom, 133, 139.
Andersons, the. See Story of Lonz Powers.
Andirons made at The Stack, 180, 181.
Anthony, Jacob, 53, 63.
Anthony, Miss Susan M., 212.
Anthony, William, 462.
Anthony, W. L., 350, 355.
Antiquities and Indian relics, 424-426.
Apling, Henry, 64.
Argus, Twice-a-Week, 350, 351, 352, 417.
Armstrong, William A., 15, 91, 105.
Arnold, Charles, sr., 116.
Arnold, Samuel, 355.
Ash, James, 63.
Atherton, A. J., 285.
Atkinson, John S., sr., 85.
Atkinson's Little Lake ("Fish Pond Hill"), 98.
Audubon ("Birds of America") on passenger pigeons, 116, 117.
Austin, J. F., 354.
Aycock, Richard, 98, 191.

B

Baber, Charles M., 410.
Bacon, Capt. Albert G., 261, 296.
Baker, D. H., 423.
Baker, Ed, 297.
Baker, Capt. Elisha, 253, 292, 332, 405, 409.
Baker, Ephraim, 410.
Baker, George, 423.
Baker, Peter H., 354.
Baldwin, Herbert W., 64.
Banking, beginning of in county, 365.
"Banking House of F. B. Hancock," 365.
Bank of Greenville, 366.
Baptists, 11, 46, 58.
Barbecue, Pond River country, 100.
Bard, H. C., 195, 197.
Bard, Rev. Isaac, 98, 126, 194-207, 301, 342, 346.
   Charges in county, 194.
   Death of, 194.
   Diary, extracts from, 198-205.
   Emancipation, debates on, 199, 200, 342.
   Family of, 195.
   Favored bond issue, 196.
   "Lecture on Muhlenberg County," 205-207.
   Letter to Henry Clay (text), 196-198.
   On railroad debt, 206, 207.
   Ordained in Greenville, 194.
   Portrait of, 195.
   Presbyterial Academy, laying cornerstone of, 203.
   Presbyterian Church of South Carrollton, laying cornerstone of, 198.
Bard, Dr. LaFayette, 195.
Bard, Luther, 195, 199.
Bard, William, 194.
Bard, William H., 405.
Bard's Ditch, 98.
Bard's Hill, 194.
Barker, Samuel, 64.
Barkley, J. G., 349, 405.
Barnett's Station, 8, 30, 31.
Barn, tobacco, old-time log; cropper's log cabin, 385.
Barrett, W. R., 352.
Battle at the Coal Bank, 302, 303, 323.
Battle, J. H. ("Kentucky, A History of the State"), 243, 404, 405.
Battle of New Orleans, 63, 64, 65, 67, 70, 72, 74.
Battle of the River Raisin, 65, 66.
Battle of the Thames, 21, 63, 64, 65, 66, 77.
"Battles and Leaders of the Civil War" (Century Co.), 240.
Baxter, John, 198, 199.
Beall, Capt. J. Y., 323.
Beasley, R. D. H., 11.
Beginning and Bounds of the County, 36-40.
   Act of General Assembly, establishing county, 36.
   Change made in southeastern boundary in 1890, 40.

Beginning and Bounds of the County—Continued.
   Line separating Logan and Christian counties before establishment of Muhlenberg, 39.
   Line separating McLean and Muhlenberg counties, 40.
Belcher, Newton, 377.
Belcher, W. O., 50, 55.
Belcher & Sparks, 377.
Bell, Thomas, 48, 50, 53, 167.
Bell, William, 32, 42, 45, 47; family, 48; 51, 52, 53, 165, 167, 383, 423.
Bell, William, 383.
Bender, John, 410.
"Ben Hardin, His Times and Contemporaries" (Little), 70, 132, 410, 461.
Bennett, Andrew, 417.
Bennett, Bryant, 414.
Bennett, Jake, 299, 301, 306, 312, 313.
Bennett, John, 63.
Bennett, William, 405.
Bennettsville, 417.
Benton's Ferry (Rockport), 12.
Berry's Lick, 8, 13, 19.
Bethel Church, 290, 416.
Bethel Church neighborhood, 326, 416, 420.
Bethlehem Baptist Church, 267.
Bevier, 23, 75.
Bibles in homes of pioneers, 127, 128, 222.
Big Bend (Fisherman's Bend), 97, 99.
Big Creek, 40.
Big Cut, the, west of Midland, 371.
"Big Harpe." See Harpe.
"Bill Drake Old Brick," 420.
"Biographical Encyclopedia of Kentuckians," 81, 361, 404.
"Birds of America" (Audubon), 116, 117.
Bishop, James, 64.
"Black as Carter," 392.
Black Band iron ore, 225, 226, 231, 424.
Black Diamond Mining Company, 420.
Black, Felix, Henry, and Judge Nathan, 105.
Black Lake, 19, 99, 110, 124.
Black Lake and Cypress Trees, near Bremen, 419.
Black Lake country, 418.
Blacklock, Edmund M., 24; family, 24; 414.
Blackwell, W. D., 55.
Blades, Thomas H., 405.
Bluffs, picturesque, in county, 430.
Boat Yard Creek (White Ash Pond), 98, 436.
Bodine, Isaac, 188.
Boggess, John H., 405.
Boggess, Peter, 44, 47, 48.
Boggess, Richard, 48; family, 48.
Boggess, William, 48, 51, 53.
Bohannon, Dr. J. G., 224, 405, 413.
"Bold Kentucky Zouaves," the, 308, 309
Bond, Cornelius, 63.
Bonds, Lott, 64.
Bonds. See Railroad Bonds, the.

INDEX

Bone, Cornelius, 64.
Bone, John, 9, 85; family, 86; 104, 127, 205, 206.
Bone, Thomas and Mark, 86, 104.
Boone, Buck, 301.
Boone, Daniel, 97.
Bourbon Furnace, 178.
Bourland, Dr. Charles A., 405.
Bowden, Rev. J. C., 212.
Bower, Jacob, 63.
Bowling Green, 257, 258, 290, 328, 329, 335, 393.
Bowling, John, 206.
Bowling, Judge Robert C., 54, 353.
Boyd, Rev. Adlai, 105, 108, 109; family, 109.
Bradford, William, 11, 15, 16, 43, 44, 46, 116, 166, 167, 423.
 "In Prison Bounds," 16.
Bradley, John, 42, 46.
Bragg, Gen. Braxton, 236, 271.
Brank, Ephraim M., 14, 48, 51, 64, 65, 67, 68, 69, 70, 74, 126, 203, 206, 289, 430.
 Family of, 70.
 Heroic conduct at battle of New Orleans described by McElroy (text), 67.
 House of, Greenville, 69.
 Portrait of, 68.
Brank, Rockwell S., 69, 70.
Branscome, Robert, 206.
Breastworks near South Carrollton, 262, 263.
Breathitt, John, 258.
Bremen, 27, 31, 219, 267, 332, 382, 417, 418.
 Post-office at, 27, 417.
 Public School Building, 218.
 Y. M. C. A., 355.
Bremen College and Perryman Male and Female Academy, 211, 216.
 Scholarships, 216.
Bremen country ("Dutch Settlement"), 25, 26, 27, 31, 126, 330, 338.
Brewer, Silas H., 405.
"Brick Bank Building," Old, Greenville, 126, 359, 366, 367.
Bridge Lake, 99.
Bridges, William W., 420.
Briggs, George I., 405.
Briggs, G. W., 383, 405.
Bristow, Benjamin, 462.
Bristow, Francis, 462, 464.
Broadnax, Judge Henry P., 53, 70, 203, 206.
Broad Street, Central City, 416.
Browder, 10, 30, 31, 387, 403.
Browder, J. Caldwell ("Nisi Prius"), 348.
Brown, George, 50.
Brown, Frederick, 64.
Brown, Maj. Hudson, 314.
Brown, James H., 252.
Brown, Milton T., 216.
Brown, pioneer Nathaniel, 314.
Brown, Samuel, 405.

Browning, Robert W., 33.
Bruce, Thomas, 55, 233, 353, 372.
Bryant, John, 206.
"Buck Knob," 451.
Buckner, Aylette H., 178, 179, 183, 184, 185, 187, 189, 340, 389.
 Portrait of, 184.
Buckner, Col. James F., 137.
Buckner, Philips, 187.
Buckner, Gen. Simon Bolivar, 78, 79, 176, 178, 185, 186, 187, 191, 252, 253, 257, 258, 291, 292, 297, 431.
 Portraits of, 185.
Buckner cradle, the, 187.
Buckner Furnace, 176, 178, 179, 180, 182, 183, 185, 187, 188, 190, 225, 229, 233, 291, 398, 399, 455.
 Owners of the land, 190.
Buckner house, occupants of, 189.
Buckner milk-house, ruins of, 179.
Buell, Gen. Don Carlos, 130, 190, 191, 192, 220, 221, 233, 234, 235, 238, 239, 240, 245, 262, 268, 326, 419.
 Biographical note, 233.
 Commissioner of State Agricultural College, 238.
 Death of, 236.
 Green River navigation, 234.
 "Kinship" between, and Gen. Braxton Bragg, 236.
 Marriage of, 236.
 Member Kentucky State Historical Society, 238.
 Member Shiloh Military Park Commission, 238.
 Park, residence, and boathouse, 1900, 238.
 Pension Agent for Kentucky, 238.
 Personal characteristics, 239.
 Portrait of, 237.
 "Prisoners" in Stone House, 235, 236.
 Residence of, 220, 224, 237, 239.
 Ruins of residence, 1912, 240.
 "Thou and I" (poem), 240, 241.
 Writings published in "Battles and Leaders of the Civil War" (Century Co.), 240.
Burney, W. D., 253.
Burying-grounds—
 Duke and Whitehouse, 75.
 Evergreen Cemetery, 329.
 Friendship Church, 183.
 Gish family, 26.
 Greenville Seminary, 126.
 New Hope Church, 279.
 Newman family, 131
 Old Caney Station, 12, 79, 200.
 Old Liberty, 85, 104, 108, 109.
 Private, 132.
 Rhoads family, 32.
Butler, Charles, 430.
Butler, Mann ("History of Commonwealth of Kentucky"), xv, 404.
Butler, Samuel, 64.
Butler County, 8, 13, 19, 40, 130, 423.
"Buzzard's Bald Yard," 430.

C

Cain, David, 252, 301.
Cain, John, 53.
Caldwell, Lieut.-Col. Samuel, 63.
Caldwell, Samuel, 52.
Caldwell & Martin, 351.
Calhoun (Rhoadsville, Vienna, Calhoon), 8, 10, 13, 30, 31, 54, 256, 258, 259, 261, 262, 267, 331, 334, 408, 410, 461.
Calhoun, Judge John, 53, 54, 71.
Campbell, Charles, 45, 63, 105.
Campbell, David, 45, 120.
Campbell, Ed, 462, 464, 465.
Campbell, John, 45, 107, 455.
Campbell, John, 206.
Campbell, Samuel, 14, 45.
Campbell, Mrs. Tabitha A. R., "the Mother of Greenville," 13, 14, 131, 413.
Campbell, Col. William, "the Father of Greenville," 11, 12, 13, 14, 15, 42, 45, 47, 50, 51, 69, 72, 129, 167, 338, 423.
  Family of, 14.
Campbell, William, jr., 63.
Campbell, William, sr., 63.
Campbell, William, sr., 127, 366.
Campbell, William, other men of same name, 45; families, 45.
Camp Ground, Old, 130.
Camp-meetings, early, 127, 130.
Caney Creek, 11, 124, 126, 302, 313.
Caney Station, 8, 9, 11, 12, 13, 15, 16, 426, 427.
Caney Station Graveyard, 12, 79, 200.
Cape, John A., 52.
Carbon, James, 414.
Carey, John C., 382.
Carey, J. C. & Co., 355.
Cargle, John, 53.
Carson, Thomas, 225.
Carter, Hugh, 127.
Carter, James, 64.
Carter, William, 63.
Carter's Creek Church, 188.
Cartwright, Peter, conducts meetings in county, 130.
  Describes "Great Revival" in his "Autobiography," 130.
Casebier, B. T., 326.
Casebier, David, 53.
Casebier, R. W., 283, 329.
Casky, Rev. W. L., 212, 354.
Cates, J. G., 405.
"Cave Hut Cliff," 16, 17, 430.
Caves, 428, 429, 430.
Central City (Stroud City, Owensboro Junction), 12, 124, 219, 328, 333, 351, 352, 388, 390, 395, 396, 412, 415, 416, 417.
  Broad Street, looking east, 416.
  Coal mines, 390, 395, 396.
  Early history of (Muhlenberg Argus), 417.
  Federal building at, appropriation for site of, 416.

Central City—Continued.
  First post-office (1871), 415, 417.
  G. A. R. post at, 283.
  Largest town in county, 417.
  Legislative acts regarding, 415.
  Mayors of, 416.
  Methodist Episcopal Church, 414.
  "Morehead's Horse Mill," 417.
  Only place in county where sale of intoxicants permitted, 417.
  Public School Building, 217.
  St. Joseph's Roman Catholic Church, 415, 416.
  Waterworks pumping station, 408.
  Y. M. C. A., 355.
Central Coal & Iron Company, 396, 403.
Chapeze, John, 462.
Charles Fox Wing. See Wing, Charles Fox.
Chatham, John E., 307, 313.
Chatham, Joseph G., 307, 313.
Chatham, L. Clark, 307, 355.
Chatham, S. D., 55, 307; family, 307; 308, 355.
  Portrait of, 307.
Chenoweth, Col. James Q., 280.
Chimneys, Some Old, 121.
Christian County, 39, 40, 129, 130, 133, 136, 137, 141, 142, 143, 147, 170, 271.
  Act for the division of (text), 40.
Church, Dr. J. W., 283, 354, 367.
Churches—
  Bethel, 290.
  Bethlehem Baptist, 267.
  "Brick Church," 202.
  Carter's Creek, 188.
  Cave Spring, 128.
  Central City, M. E., 414.
  Cumberland Presbyterian, Greenville, 109, 357.
  Ebenezer, 128.
  Friendship, 86, 183.
  Green's Chapel, 84.
  Greenville M. E., 212, 329.
  Greenville Seminary, 210.
  Hazel Creek Baptist, 128, 129.
  Lead Hill, 304.
  Macedonia, 128.
  Monticello (Midway), 128.
  Mt. Olivet, 128.
  Mt. Pisgah, 84, 104, 262, 280, 286, 288, 296.
  Mt. Pleasant, 194, 202.
  Mt. Zion, 128, 194, 202.
  Myers' Chapel, 254, 337.
  Nelson Creek Baptist, 22, 128.
  New Hebron, 128.
  New Hope, 279.
  Old Liberty, 84, 104-109, 127, 288.
  Old Presbyterian, Greenville, 126, 152.
  Olive Branch Chapel, 84.
  Olive Grove, 186.
  Pleasant Hill, 165.
  Pleasant Hill, 202.
  St. Joseph's Roman Catholic, 415.
  Sharon Baptist, 84.
  South Carrollton Presbyterian, 198.

INDEX 473

Churches—Continued.
  Station Church, Old, 11; New, 261.
  Sugar Grove, 128.
  Unity, 201, 202.
  Worthington's Chapel, 19, 21.
Churchill, Cadwalader, 178, 179, 183, 185, 189, 389, 455.
Circuit court, clerks of, 55.
Circuit court, judges of, 53, 54.
Circuit court, record of first meeting (text), 51, 52, 53.
  Grand jury, members of first, 53.
  Petit jury, members of first, 53.
Cisna, Robert, 42, 44.
Cisna, William, 50.
Cisney, 16, 192, 430.
Cisney, C., 383.
Cisney, C. W., 50, 423.
Citizens Bank, Drakesboro, 420.
Civil War. See Muhlenberg in the Civil War; Recollections of the Civil War (Martin).
Civil War soldiers, some of Muhlenberg's, 326-337.
Civil War veterans, some (1912), 283.
Clark, David, sugar camp, 90.
Clark, George Rogers, xv.
Clark, M. B., 405.
Clark's Ferry Bridge, 90, 93, 98.
Clark's Mill, 124, 272, 273, 301, 304, 305.
Claxton, Jeremiah, 64.
Clay, Cassius M., 341.
Clay, Henry, 23, 71.
  "Private Correspondence"; letter from Rev. Isaac Bard (text), 196-198.
Clemmons, Perry, 191.
Clifford, Harrison, 191.
Clifty Creek, 16, 110, 125, 430.
Clifty Creek country, 9, 115.
Coal Bank, battle at the, 302, 303, 323.
Coal Mines and Iron Ore, 387-403.
  Analyses of nine iron ores found in county (Peter), 398.
  Coal, estimated wealth of county in, 398.
  Coal-mine operators in county, biographical sketches of three leading, 401-403.
  Coal mines now in operation, 391, 396, 397.
  Coal mines operated in 1875, 390.
  Coal mines, output and statistics for 1911, 397.
  Coal traffic on river, 393.
  Collins on (1874, text), 424.
  Disasters, coal-mine, in county, 387.
  Early mining methods, 391, 394, 395.
  First commercial coal mines in county, 390.
  Iron industry in Kentucky and in Muhlenberg County, 400.
  McLean Drift Bank, opened in 1820, 389.
  Methods, coal-mining, 391.
  Mud River Mine, 389; oldest in county, history of, 391-394.

Coal Mines and Iron Ore—Continued.
  Number of persons employed in coal mines in 1911, 397.
  "Old Coal Road," 392, 393.
  Power house and double tipple, Graham-Skibo Mine, Graham, 396.
  Power house and steel tipple, Kentucky-Midland Mine, Midland, 400.
  Production of coal in county, 1890 to 1911, 398.
  "Rock coal," 389.
  Tipple and power house, Black Diamond Mine, Drakesboro, 399.
  Tipple and power house, Central Mine, Central City, 395.
Coates, T. J., 351.
Cob, Elijah, 64.
Cochran, Andrew, 202.
Cochran, Bryant, 63.
Cochran, John, 202.
Coffman, Benjamin, 25; family, 25; 120, 127.
Coffman, John F., 70, 423.
Coleman, Judge Q. B., 24, 55, 374, 405.
Coleman, Robert, 52.
Collins ("History of Kentucky"), 1, 8, 9, 10, 19, 30, 71, 176, 252, 379, 390, 401, 404-431, 435, 436.
  Five editions printed, 406.
  Spelling of county names, 1, 406.
Collins on Muhlenberg, Quoted and Extended, 404-431.
  Antiquities, 424-426.
  Cave, a (Lovell's or Shutt's Cave), 429.
  Coal and iron ore, 406, 424.
  Lewis, in 1847, on Muhlenberg County (text), 406, 407.
  Mounds and the Moundbuilders, 426-428.
  Richard H., in 1874, on Muhlenberg County, quoted and extended, 411-431.
  Sink, a (error), 428.
  Spelling of county name, changes in, 1, 406.
  Statistics (1870), 412.
Combs, Jesse, 64.
Commission of first justices of county, 43.
Commission of William Bradford as captain of militia, 166.
"Company land," 176.
Conaster, E. G., 425.
Conditt, Moses P., 63.
"Confederate Operations in Canada and New York" (Headley), 258, 318.
Convicts employed to quarry stone on Buell place, 235.
Cook, Judge George B., 54.
Cooksey's Mill, 124, 125.
Coombs, Asa, 326.
Coombs, John, 55, 283, 326, 329.
  Portrait of, 326.
Coombs, Joseph Edward, 326.
Coöperative Coal Company, 388.
Corder, James, 120.
Corley, Granville, 191, 192, 193.

Corley, James, 193.
Corley, Thaddeus E., 193.
Cornerstone of Presbyterian Church of South Carrollton, laying of, 198.
Cornett, A. B., farm, tobacco field on, Upper Pond Creek country, 386.
Cornett, A. Jackson, 42, 425.
Cornett, Rev. William Leftwich, 42; family, 42.
Cornstock Militia, 168.
Cornwall, John, 50, 51.
Cotton gin, 114, 122.
Cotton-growing, experiments in county, 114.
County, Beginning and Bounds of the. See Beginning and Bounds of.
County court days in olden times and at present, 127.
County court, first meetings of, 44-47.
First meeting of in present courthouse, 49.
County court records, first (text), 42.
First appearance of Greenville in, 45.
Second courthouse, 48.
County lines, 40.
County, naming the (1798), 7, 29, 31, 36.
County officers since 1850, tabulated, 55.
County offices, method of filling prior to adoption of Third Constitution, 55.
County Poor Asylum, 320.
Courthouse, first (1799), 11, 12, 13, 35, 45, 46, 47, 125.
Second (1834), 47, 48, 49, 279, 324.
Third (1907), 49, 52, 465.
Courthouses, burning of by Gen. Hylan B. Lyon, 280.
Courts and Courthouses, 41-55.
Cox, W. J., 423.
Crabtree, Cyrus, 322.
Cradle, Buckner, the, 187.
Craig, Garland D., 48, 178.
Craig, James, 42, 44, 45, 47; family, 47; 117.
Craig, James D., 353.
Craig, Joel, 253.
Craig, John, 64.
Craig, Robert, 64, 68.
Craig, Samuel S., 405.
Cravens, Jere S., 63.
Crawford, W. G., 379.
Creel, Dr. M. P., 352, 405, 416.
Crewdson, Judge Samuel R., 54.
Crews, James B., 405.
Crittenden, Dr. R. M., 354, 363.
Crittenden, Gen. Thomas L., 256, 258, 262, 267, 268, 292, 319, 413.
Breastworks near South Carrollton, 262, 263.
Forces under, movements of, 267, 268.
Headquarters at South Carrollton, 262.
Stay in Muhlenberg, history of, 262-267.
Crouch, Charles, 53.
Crouch, Isaac, 64.
Crumbaker, Jacob, 332.
Culbertson, John, 44, 46, 50, 51, 206.

Culbertson, Robert W., 64.
Culiver, Capt., 225.
Cumberland Presbyterian Church, the old, Greenville, 357.
Cumberland Presbyterians, 104 109, 212, 357.
Cummings, Moses, 63.
Cundiff, Bryant, 23, 420.
Cundiff, Dr. Jefferson D., 420.
Cundiff, John K., 425.
Curd, Clayton S., 55.
Cypress Creek, 19, 31, 99, 199.
"Cypress Trees, The" (poem, Harry M. Dean), 418.

D

Dabney, Judge Thomas C., 54, 462, 465.
"Daniel Boone Rock," 97.
Danner, Rev. Samuel, 25, 26; family, 25.
Davenport, Samuel, 18.
"David Short Old Brick," 95.
Davidge, Henry, 52.
Davidge, Reason, 52.
Davies, Hywel, 396.
Daviess County, 40, 410.
Davis, Arthur N., 191, 192, 253, 292, 296, 326.
Portrait of, 192.
Davis, Dr. Bryant, 414.
Davis, Dick, 306, 307.
Davis, George, 120.
Davis, Henry, 50, 53.
Davis, Isaac, 42, 45, 50, 64, 65, 72, 116.
Family of, 73.
House near Martwick, 73.
"Milk cellar," 73.
Davis, John, 52.
Davis, Randolph, 64.
Davis, Simon, 137.
Davis, W. Britton, 87, 187.
Davis, William, 63.
Davis Cave, 142.
Dean, Godman S., 25.
Dean, Harry M., 25, 349, 350, 418.
Dean, Summers, 25.
Dean, William Johnson, 24; family, 25.
Portrait of, 24.
Dearing, Bayless, 336.
DeCourcy, Dr. James Osborne, 348.
Deer and other game, 84, 110, 115, 181.
"Deer Hunt," a (Weir), 451-453.
Deer Lick, 182.
Dellium, Richard C., 19.
Dempsey, Sam H., 55, 354.
Dempsey, Westbrook, 51, 53.
Dennis, Abraham, 46, 63, 127.
Dennis, Alney McLean, 46.
Dennis, John, 9, 12, 13, 32, 41, 42, 44, 45, 46; family, 46; 50, 53, 342.
Dennis, Robert A., 46.
Dennis, Thomas, 53.
Dennis, Wm. Rufus, 46.
Dennis Tavern, 41.
DeWitt, Rev. A. C., 203, 346.
Dewitt, William, 64.

Diary of Rev. Isaac Bard, extracts from, 198-202.
Dillingham, Abner B. C., 64.
Dillman, David, 423.
Dobbs, R. J., 283.
Dobyns, John, 64.
Dog-irons made at The Stack, 180, 181, 185.
Donaldson, Prof. John, 199, 200, 202, 213, 346.
Donnald, James, 64.
Dovey, George B., 387, 388, 389.
Dovey, John, 387, 388.
Dovey, William, 387, 388.
"Dovey Robbery," the, 387.
Downing, Joel, 40.
Drake, Albritton, Revolutionary soldier, 67, 89, 130; family, 67, 130.
Drake, Albritton M., 67, 405.
Drake, Sir Francis, 67.
Drake, James, 254.
Drake, James, Revolutionary soldier, 67.
Drake, James P., 189.
Drake, John R., 67.
Drake, J. Perry, 130.
Drake, Mosley Collins, 64, 65, 66, 67, 89, 130, 165, 289.
    Family of, 67.
    House of, 173.
    Portrait of, 66.
Drake, Mosley Collins, jr., 67, 191.
Drake, Patrick H., 405.
Drake, Samuel, 127.
Drake, Rev. Silas, 67, 89, 130.
Drake, William, 67, 130, 420.
Drakesboro, 419, 420.
    Main Street, looking west, 422.
    Public School Building, 219.
    Tipple and power house, Black Diamond Mine, 399.
    Y. M. C. A., 355.
Driskell, Ferney, 189.
Driskell, Hutson, 189.
Driskell, J. F., 189.
Dudley, Robert, 63.
Duke and Whitehouse Burying-ground, 75.
Duke, Gen. Basil W. ("History of Morgan's Cavalry"), text, 271, 272; 318, 321, 322.
Dukes, pioneer family, 9.
Dukes, Samuel, 120.
Dukes, Starling, 121.
Duncan, Andrew, 228, 401.
Duncan, Andrew W., 397.
    Residence of, 365.
Duncan, David, 228.
Duncan, David John, 228.
Duncan, Robert, 228.
Duncan, W. G., 50, 228, 397, 401.
    Portrait of, 401.
    Residence of, 101.
Duncan, W. G., Coal Company, 396, 397, 401.
Duncan, William, 225.
Duncan, William G., jr., 397.
Dune, James, 189.
Dunkards, 25, 58.

Dunmor, 18, 219, 383, 420, 430.
duPont, Biederman, establishes Central Coal & Iron Company, 396.
duPont, T. Coleman, 352, 396.
Durall, Japha N., 283, 326, 417.
    Portrait of, 327.
"Dutch Farm," 90.
"Dutch Settlement" (Bremen country), 25, 26, 27, 31, 58, 126, 330, 338, 417.
Duvall, Archibald, 429.
Duvall, Benjamin, sr. and jr., 455.
Duvall, Howard, 455, 457.
Duvall, Mrs. James, 127.
Duvall, Mark, 455-459.
Duvall's Discovery of "Silver Ore" (Martin, Appendix D), 455-459.
"Duvall's Silver Stack," 459.
Dwyer, Louis, 269.
Dyer, Hon. Azro, 409.
Dyer, Dillis, 409.

E

Eades, Barnett, 99.
Eades, Charles E., 405.
Eades, Ellington, 99, 100.
Eades, G. B., 355, 371.
Eades, Nathaniel, 402.
Eades, R. W., 99.
Earle, Bayless, 92.
Earle, Rev. Ezias, 126, 156.
Earle, John, 63.
Earle, Richard Bayless, 92, 191.
Earles, 382, 420.
Early settlers, extraction of, 112.
Earth rings (house-site rings), disappearance of, 428.
Eaves, Judge Charles, 15, 16, 93, 238, 242-249, 251, 354, 404, 405, 413, 423, 462, 465.
    Biographical sketch (Battle, text), 243.
    Death of, 244.
    Family of, 244.
    "God's Plow of Sorrow" (poem), 249.
    Letter of, 245-248.
    Portrait of, 243.
    Residence, 247.
    Resolutions on death of, by members of local bar, 244.
    Sorrows of, 248.
    Student of law, history, literature, natural sciences, 242.
    Versed in local traditions, 244.
    Wing trial, appeal to jury in, 248.
Eaves, David W., 62; family, 62.
Eaves, Eugene, 55, 310, 311.
Eaves, George W., jr., 93, 95, 383, 405.
Eaves, John S., jr., 93, 242.
Eaves, John S., sr., 93; family, 93, 242; 99, 242, 301, 366, 423.
Eaves, Sanders, 62, 96, 242.
Eaves, William A., 410.
Eaves, William H., 351.
Eaves Creek, 242.
Edmonds, George, 63.

Education, higher, in Greenville, early history of (Martin, text), 211-213. In county, 208-219.
Edward Rumsey. See Rumsey, Edward.
Edwards, Ninian, 53.
"Egypt," 9.
Eighth Kentucky Cavalry, 300.
Election days (1860), slave privileges on, 343, 344.
Eleventh Kentucky Infantry, 193, 252, 253, 262, 268, 280, 282, 292, 318, 326, 328, 330, 331, 334, 335, 336, 337.
Elizabethtown & Paducah Railroad, 355, 368, 372, 379, 390, 412, 415, 416, 417.
Elkins, Joshua, 9.
Elkton, 8.
Elliott, Edward R., 60; family, 60; 340, 342, 343.
Elliott, Richard, 60, 88.
Elliott, Sam, 301, 340.
Ellison, Joe G., 55, 337.
Ellison Spring, 257, 258, 291.
Ellwood (McNary Place), 94.
Emancipation, beginning of movement in county, 341.
Emancipation, Rev. Isaac Bard on, 199, 200, 342.
English money in circulation in 1815, 118.
"Eternal Hole," 430.
Evans, James, 64.
Evans, John, 63.
Evergreen Cemetery, 329.
Everton, James, 63.
Everton, Thomas, 63.
Ewing, Robert, 43.
Ewing, Washington, 462.
Execution, legal, of slaves in county, 340.
Extraction of early settlers, 112.
Extracts from diary of Rev. Isaac Bard, 198-202.

F

Fair View Farm, 84.
"Faith Doctor, a Visit to the" (Weir), 449-451.
Faughender, James H., 253.
Fears of negro "risings" in county (1860), 343.
Fentress, John, 204, 413, 414.
Fentress, Leo, 352.
Ferguson, John, 63.
Ferguson, John K., 64.
Field, Willis, 319.
Fight at Sullivan's barn, 277-279.
Fight near Sacramento, 258-262, 296, 297.
Filson, John ("Kentucke"), xvi, 404.
Finch, Edmund, 414.
Finley, Alexander Y., 327.
Finley, Francis M., 327.
  Portrait of, 327.
Finley, Thomas Monroe, 188, 327.
  Portrait of, 327.
Finley, William H., 327.
First church organized in county (Hazel Creek Baptist), 128.

First-Comers, Some of the, 8-28.
First county court records (text), 42.
First justices, commission of, 43.
First Kentucky Cavalry (Confederate), 275.
First National Bank of Greenville, 366, 367, 402.
First Report of the Geological Survey in Kentucky, 176, 186 (text), 390, 398.
First settlements in county, 8.
First store opened in county, 59, 117.
Fisherman's Bend (Big Bend), 97, 99.
Five J. Coal Company, 236.
Flax, cultivation of in county, 114.
Fleming, Judge David J., 26, 55, 114, 351, 376, 405.
Fleming, David L., 115.
Fleming, Ezekiel, 409.
Fleming, Samuel C., 114.
Foley, Mason, 64.
Ford, Rev. G. W., 122; family, 122.
Ford, James R., 122.
Ford, John L., 122.
Ford, Laborn, 122; family, 122.
Ford, Napoleon M., 122.
Forgy, James, 19, 124.
Forrest, Gen. N. B., 252, 258-262, 271, 292, 296, 297, 318, 319, 321.
  "Life of" (Wyeth), 258.
Fort Meigs, siege of, 187.
Forty-eighth Kentucky Mounted Infantry, 253, 327, 333.
"Forty Years Ago" (Martin), 353-360.
Foster, Thomas, 63.
Fourth Regiment Kentucky Foot Volunteers, 191.
Fowler, Al, 299, 300.
Fowler, Jeremiah, 65.
Fox, Joseph, 253.
Fox, Nathan, 65.
Frazier, Joseph, 361.
Frazier, Dr. R. C., 341, 354, 363, 405.
Free Henry Ford, 12, 436.
Freeman, Rev. Azel, 212.
Freeman, Capt. Jesse Knox, sr., 253, 292, 328.
  Portrait of, 328.
Freeman, J. K., jr., 328.
Friendship Church, 86, 182, 183, 299, 360.
  Burying-ground, 183.
Friendship neighborhood, 86, 114, 122, 124, 181, 183, 349.
Furnace, Airdrie. See Airdrie Furnace.
Furnace, Bourbon, 178.
Furnace, Buckner. See Buckner Furnace.

G

Gamblin, John, 65.
Game in county, 33, 84, 110, 115, 181.
Gant, Thomas, 65.
Gany, Matthew, 65.
Garrard, Gov. James, 42, 43, 50.
Garrard, William, 51.
Garris, Benjamin, 50.
Garriz, Sihez, 9.

INDEX 477

Garst, Jacob, 25; family, 25.
Garst's Pond, 259, 261.
Gary, Mrs. Cynthia, 114.
Gasper River, 37.
Gates, Riley, 430.
Gatherings of the pioneers, 127.
Geibel, George, 355.
General elections for county and State officers, 55.
Geological Survey, Report of First Kentucky, 176, 186 (text), 390, 398.
German language, manners, and customs, disappearance of from former German-American settlements in county, 112, 417.
German Society of Pennsylvania, 6, 7.
"Ghost-hauntings," 341.
Ghost stories connected with old hotel building, Airdrie, 230, 236.
Gillingham, John B. C., 63.
Gilmour, James, 228, 229.
Gilmour, James G., 228.
Gilmour, Matthew, 228, 229.
Gish brothers, seven, 25, 26.
Gish, Christian, 26; family, 26.
Gish, Daniel J., 383.
Gish, George W., 405.
Gish, Shelby J., 236.
Gish, S. C., drugstore, 416.
Gish family burying-ground, 26.
Gleig, George Robert, on campaigns of British at Washington and New Orleans, 69.
Glenn, Andrew, 9, 205, 206.
Glenn, Moses F., 63.
Glenn, Thomas, 63, 120.
"Godfather of Muhlenberg County," grave of, 32.
Godman, Judge J. W. I., 22, 23, 24, 55, 429; family, 24.
"God's Plow of Sorrow" (poem, Judge Charles Eaves), 249.
Gooch, John G., 410, 423.
Good, John, 63.
Goodlove, Charles W., benchmark in courthouse yard, 50.
Goodnight, Judge I. Herschell, 54.
Goodnight, Stephen, 105.
Gordon, George, 405.
Gossett, John, 25; family, 26.
Grace, Divinity, 85.
Grace, Judge John R., 54.
Gragston, W. I., 41.
Graham, 396, 397.
Grand Army of the Republic, first post in county, 283.
Post at Central City, 283.
Post at Greenville, 283.
Grand juries, first in county, 50, 53.
Grave of the "Godfather of Muhlenberg County," 32.
Graves, John C., 64.
Graves marked with stone box-covers, 132.
Graveyard, Newman, 131.
Graveyards. See Burying-grounds.
Gray, Bob, negro, lynching of, 184, 355, 361-365.

Gray, John, jr., 362, 363.
Grayham, William, 65.
"Great Revival," the (1799), 129, 130.
Green, B. Frank, 420.
Green, N., 85; family, 86.
Green, Richard, 253.
Green, T. M., 86, 382.
Green, William J., 86, 332.
Green, Prof. William L., 60, 210, 211, 212, 213, 342, 343.
Portrait of, 212.
Greene, Gen. Nathaniel, 2, 407, 412, 413.
Green and Barren Rivers Navigation Company, 234.
Lease of purchased by Federal government, 234.
Green River, 9, 12, 19, 23, 39, 40, 44, 59, 98, 111, 112, 220, 234, 239, 271, 277, 280, 290, 369, 389, 390, 393, 407, 408, 413, 430, 449.
Green River country, 1, 7, 8, 21, 22, 29, 30, 72, 126, 441, 449.
Green's Bend, 98.
Green's Chapel, 84.
Greenup, Christopher, 53.
Greenville, 8, 11, 12, 13, 14, 15, 40, 41, 42, 45, 46, 47, 58, 59, 72, 78, 109, 111, 125, 126, 127, 143, 194, 219, 252, 253, 257, 258, 259, 262, 267, 271, 272, 279, 285, 290, 291, 296, 298, 300, 302, 304, 306, 308, 309, 310, 312, 313, 326, 328, 329, 332, 334, 335, 337, 339, 350, 353, 355, 361, 369, 379, 380, 381, 382, 402, 406, 407, 412, 413, 414, 431, 462, 465.
Academy building used as school and union church, 128.
Academy (Seminary), 126, 210.
As described in "Lonz Powers" (Weir, text), 150-164.
Bank of Greenville, 366.
Buckner, Gen., in, 257, 258, 290, 291.
County court days in, 127.
Courthouse, first (1799), 11, 12, 13, 35, 45, 46, 47, 125.
Second (1834), 47, 48, 49.
Third (1907), 49, 52.
Cumberland Presbyterian Church, old, 357.
"Established" by Legislature, 412.
"False alarm," a, 279, 309.
First National Bank, 366, 367, 402.
Forrest, Col., in, 258, 262, 296, 297.
Gatherings of the pioneers in, 127.
Hotel (1855), as it appears to-day, 313.
Illinois Central Depot, 378.
Jails, first county, 46.
Second, 49.
Third, and jailer's residence, 54.
Lynching of Bob Gray, negro, 355.
Mails in 1870, 355.
Main Street, 1912, 163.
Martin, Bob, in, 302-306.
Mass-meeting held at, to discuss railroad bonds, 376.
Mayors of, 413.

Greenville—Continued.
  Medical and ecclesiastical board in 1870, 354.
  Merchants of in 1870, 354, 355.
  Morgan, Gen., in, 272, 298.
  Muhlenberg County Savings Bank, 402.
  Nursery, the, 355.
  Occupied by Confederates under Martin (December, 1863), 322.
  "Old Brick Bank Building," 1890, 359, 366, 367.
  Oldest town in county, 413.
  Origin of name, 413.
  Population of in early years, 125.
  Presbyterian Church, 109, 126, 129, 152.
  Public School Building, 217.
  Raids on during the Civil War. See Muhlenberg in the Civil War; Recollections of the Civil War.
  Reno House, 315.
  Residences, business houses, and mechanic's shops about 1830, location of, 126.
  "Taken" by Gen. Buckner, 252, 431.
  Tobacco business, 380-386.
  Y. M. C. A., 355, 366.
Greenville Coal Company, 367, 389, 403.
Greenville College, 211, 214.
Greenville Cumberland Presbyterian Church, 109, 357.
  Memorial windows in, 109.
Greenville Female Academy, 203, 210, 211, 212, 213.
Greenville Grange Store, 337.
Greenville Hotel, Confederate rendezvous, 313, 314, 354.
Greenville in Fayette (later Franklin) County, xvi.
Greenville Ladies' College and Greenville College for Young Men, 214.
Greenville Record, 61, 104, 193, 285, 328, 330, 350, 351, 353, 388, 418, 455.
Greenville Seminary burying-ground, 126.
"Greenville Tobacco," 381.
Greenway, Louis, 182.
Greenwood, Henry, 191, 192.
Gregory, C. E., 352.
Gregory, Rev. Thomas, 21.
Griggs, Lorenzo D., 237, 280, 283.
Grist mills, old-time, 122-125.
Gross', James R., pocket memorandum book, 282.
Ground-sled or "landslide," 113, 114.
Grube, the (Green River), 413.
Grundy, William S., 328.
  Portrait of, 330.
Guerrilla raids and highway robberies during Civil War, 252.
Guffy, Hon. B. L. D., 462, 465.

H

Haden, Prof. C. C., 348.
Haden, George W., 124, 224; family, 224; 229, 257, 405.
  Portrait of, 224.
Haden, Joseph, 224.
Haden, Joseph C., 224.
Haden, Roy, 224.
Hall, Dr. B. W., 393, 394.
Hall, Prof. Elmer T., 214.
Hall, Prof. and Mrs. E. W., 211, 212, 213, 214, 215, 285, 306.
  Portrait of, 215.
Hall, Judge James ("Letters from the West"), 435.
Hall, Joseph, 253.
Hall, Prof. W. S., 214.
Ham, David, 64.
Hamm, J. Luther, 222.
Hamm, Matthew (Mattheis), 222.
  Bible, German, property of, 222.
Hancock, F. B., 355, 365, 371.
Hancock, Frank B., jr., 354.
Hancock, Isaiah, 206.
Hancock, William W., 48, 49.
Hancock, W. P., 353.
Hancock & Reno's store, 298, 302, 312.
Handley, Samuel, 53.
Hangings, legal, in county, 184.
Hanner, John D., 354.
Harbin, William, 55, 96.
Hardin, Benjamin, 39, 40.
Harpe, Big, 9, 93, 435-441.
Harper, Fred, 314.
Harpes, Judge Hall's Story of the (Appendix A), 435-441.
Harpe's Hill, 9, 12, 90, 91, 93, 94, 98, 242, 272, 428, 436.
"Harpe's House," so-called, 91.
Harris, Bennett, 347.
Harris, Buxton, 347.
Harris, Hume H., 253.
Harris, Nat J., 55, 347, 353.
Harris, Richard, 64.
Harris, Stephen, 206.
Harrison, Harvey, 286.
Harrison, Isaac, 63.
Harrison, William, 286-288.
Harrison, Gen. William Henry, 66.
Hartford, 8, 10, 12, 30, 32, 102, 253, 254, 257, 279, 280, 322, 409.
Hawkins, Col. Pierce B., 253, 292, 328.
Haws, John, 64.
Hay, Charles and Kincheon, 105.
Hay, David, 254, 360.
Hay, Kinnard, 105, 360.
Hay, M. C., 253, 269, 356, 360, 365, 366, 405, 462.
Hay, M. C. & Co., 354.
  House occupied in 1870, 355.
Hay, M. D., 351, 354, 360, 423.
Hay, Wiley S., 105, 356-360, 423.
  Portrait of, 360.
Hayes, Clarence B., 329, 349, 350.
  Portrait of, 349.
Hayes, J. H., 349.
Hayley's Mill, 142.
Hays, Andrew, 51.
Hays, Dr. John B., 353, 423.
Hazel Creek Baptist Church, 128, 129, 206.
  "History of" (Johnson), 128, 347.
  Twelve churches originating from, 128.

INDEX

Headley, John W. ("Confederate Operations in Canada and New York"), 258, 318, 322, 323.
Heck, Joseph, 222.
Helm, Gen. Ben Hardin, 275, 277.
Heltsley, Drs. Louella and Emily, 367.
Heltsley, Michael, 222.
Heltsley, William, 222.
Hemenway, Gilbert D., 405.
Hemman, George, 63.
Henderson, 258, 319.
Henderson, Richard, 112.
Hendricks, Harry, 253.
Hendricks, Joseph P., 353, 405.
Hendrie, Alexander ("Scotch Henry"), 188, 225, 226, 228, 229.
  Portrait of, 229.
Hendrie, Charles, 229.
Hendrie, Charles, sr., 225, 228.
Hendrie, John, 229, 237.
Henry Clay Furnace, the, 187.
"Henry Clay Iron Works," 176, 406.
Henry, Joseph G., 21.
Henry, Samuel, 256.
Hensley, Leftridge, 65.
Hesper Thomas, 120.
Hewlett, Alfred, 63.
Hewlett, Lemuel, 65.
Hewlett, Thomas, 65.
Hickory Withe Schoolhouse, 183.
Hieroglyphics, undeciphered, 426.
Higher education in Greenville, early history of (Martin, text), 211-213.
  In county, 208-219.
Hill, Asa, 64.
Hill, D. T., 55.
Hill, George, 64.
Hill, Jesse S., 405.
Hill, John, 64.
Hill, Samuel E., 63.
Hill, William, 63.
Hines, Isaac, 63.
Hines, John, 65.
"Hiring out" and sale of slaves, 338.
"History of Commonwealth of Kentucky," the (Butler), xv, 404.
"History of Hazel Creek Baptist Church" (Johnson), 128, 347.
"History of Henderson County" (Starling), 435.
History of Kentucky—
  Allen, William B., 435.
  Battle, J. H., 243, 404, 405.
  Butler, Mann, xv, 404.
  Collins, 1, 8, 9, 10, 19, 30, 71, 176, 252, 379, 390, 401, 404-431, 435, 436.
  Filson, John, xvi, 404.
  Hill, Samuel E., 63.
  Johnson, E. Polk, 348.
  McElroy (text), 67-69, 404.
  Marshall, 167, 404.
  Perrin (Battle), 29.
  Shaler, Nathaniel S., 404.
  Smith, Zachariah, xv, 404.
  Thompson, Ed Porter, 31, 253, 254.
"History of Morgan's Cavalry" (Duke), text, 271, 272; 318, 321, 322.

"History of the Orphan Brigade" (Thompson), 253, 254.
Hobson, John S., 396.
"Hoe-Cake Country," 84.
"Hog Eye" tippling house, 126.
"Hog Harvest" on the Alvin L. Taylor farm, 123.
Holidays, slave (1860), 343, 344.
Holloway, Col. James H., 300.
Holmes, Mrs. Anna Allison, 88, 109.
Home Valley P. O., 120.
Hope, Jeremiah M., 405.
Hopkins, Edmond, 120.
Hopkins, William, 10.
Hopkinsville, 8, 140, 142, 258, 259, 262, 271, 280, 290, 291, 292, 319, 322, 382.
Hoskinson, Jackson, 394, 424.
Hoskinson, William H., 349, 391, 394, 395.
"Hoskins ore bank," 424.
Hotel building at Airdrie, ghost stories connected with, 236.
  Remains of in 1895, 236.
Houser, Christopher, 63.
House-site rings (earth rings), disappearance of, 428.
Howard, Charles M., 355.
Howard, Isaac, 65.
Howard, J. C., 109, 405.
Howard, N. B., 414.
"Howards Settlements," 37.
Howell, S., 414.
Howey, Esquire F., 396.
Hubbard, Liner, 65.
Humphrey, Ivy W., 405.
Humphrey, John J., 216.
Humphrey, Mrs. Mary E., 336.
Humphrey, R. E., 353, 405.
Humphreys, D. C., letters of, 275-277.
Hunsacker, Isaac, 222.
Hunsinger, George, 63.
Hunt, Amos L., 18.
Hunt, John, 9, 18; family, 18.
Hunt, Jonathan, house, 18.
Hunt Settlement, 18, 421.
Hunting, local traditions regarding, 33, 34.
Hunting-shirt of the early pioneer, 102.
Hynes, William, 50, 53.

I

Illinois Central Bridge over Green River, 369.
Illinois Central Depot, Greenville, 378.
Illinois Central Railroad (Elizabethtown & Paducah), 355, 368, 372, 379, 390, 412, 415, 416, 417.
  Time table of 1873, 112.
Imbler, Jacob, 85, 386.
Imbler, William, 85.
Implements, stone, picked up by first settlers, 426.
"Independent Order of Taxpayers," 374, 376, 377.

Indian relics and antiquities, 424-426.
Indian Rock, "carvings" on, 426.
Indians, 10, 21, 90, 101, 102, 110, 430.
In Eighteen-Seventy, 353-367.
   Beginning of banking in county, 365.
   Campaign between Love and Hay, 356-360.
   County election, the, 356.
   County officials and magisterial board, 353.
   Courtship, story of a romantic, 367.
   "Forty Years Ago" (Martin, text), 353-360.
   Lynching of Bob Gray, negro, 355, 361-365.
   Mails, 355.
   Medical and ecclesiastical board, 354.
   Merchants and hotels, 354, 355.
   "Negro equality panic," 356-360.
   Panics, two great, 360.
   Railroad bonded indebtedness, panic of, 360.
Inman, James, 8, 10, 30.
"In Prison Bounds," 16.
Intermarriage of pioneers, 111, 112.
"Internal Hole," 430.
Intoxicants, Central City only place where sale is now permitted. 417
"Investigators' Club" (Owensboro), 461
Iron and iron ores. See Story of The Stack, Paradise Country and Old Airdrie, and Coal Mines and Iron Ores.
Iron industry in Kentucky and in Muhlenberg County, 400.
Iron ore, discovery of in county, 178, 179, 180, 225, 399.
Iron works and mines, ruins of at Airdrie, 220.
Irvin, Thomas, 9, 206.
Irvin, William, 55, 354, 382.
Irvin, Dr. William E., 405.
Isaac Bard. See Bard, Rev. Isaac.
Isaac's Creek, 124.
Isaac, negro, hanging of, 183, 184, 340.
Island Station, 19.
Island, town of, 19.

J

"Jack Ford" baptizing place, 99, 188.
Jackson, Dr. Alfred Metcalf, 204; family of, 204; 205, 414.
   Portrait of, 205.
Jackson, Gen. Andrew, 67, 70, 73.
Jackson, Col. James S., 253, 258, 292, 319.
Jackson, Jesse, 53.
Jackson, Leroy, 120.
Jackson, Samuel, 86.
Jackson, Dr. Shelby A., 233, 289.
Jagoe, Jacob, 96; family, 96.
Jail, first county, 46.
   Second, 49, 279.
   Third, and jailer's residence, 54.

James, Dr. A. D., 81, 405, 423, 424.
   Portrait of, 424.
James, Elsie J., 348.
James, Jesse, 307, 388.
James, W. H., 114.
James, William, jr., 292.
James, William Sevier, 405.
Janis, Edward, 65.
January, John, 63, 120, 126, 127, 206.
Jarrell's Creek, 124, 455, 457.
Jarroll, pioneer, 85.
Jarvis, Edward, 206.
Jarvis, Simon, 63.
Jeffries, J. P., 423.
Jenkins, pioneer Amos, 186; family, 186, 187.
Jenkins, Amos M., 116, 187, 425.
Jenkins, Bob, 169, 170.
Jenkins, C. C., 355.
Jenkins, Henry, 279.
Jenkins, Squire John, 55, 186, 430; family, 187.
   Portrait of, 186.
"Jenkins ore bank," 424.
Jernigan, Benjamin G., 253, 269.
Jernigan, John F., 253.
John Jenkins Cave, 430.
Johns, R. T., 50.
Johnson, Gen. Adam R. ("The Partisan Rangers," text), 258-262; 280, 299, 318, 319, 321.
Johnson, Alfred, 49, 90, 121, 178, 188, 189, 226, 279.
   Portrait of, 188.
Johnson, Benjamin, 120.
Johnson, E. Polk ("History of Kentucky and Kentuckians," text), 348.
Johnson (Johnston), Jacob, 189; family, 189.
Johnson, James L., 409.
Johnson, Dr. John M., 62, 408, 409, 423.
Johnson, Lonz, 226.
Johnson, Gen. Richard W., 408.
Johnson, Thomas B., 189, 383.
Johnson, Prof. William J. ("History of Hazel Creek Baptist Church"), 128, 347.
Johnson, W. S., 428.
Johnston, Rev. James, 104.
Jones, C. K., 254.
Jones, Columbus W., 405.
Jones, Fielding, 64.
Jones, Rev. F. M., 352.
Jones, James, 295.
Jones, James and Philip, 408.
Jones, James M., 90.
Jones, J. Ed, 254.
Jones, John M., 90, 254.
Jones, Lewis, 423, 424.
Jones, Peter, 415.
Jones, R. Wickliffe, 254.
Jones, Strother, 48, 89; family, 89, 90.
   Portrait of, 89.
Jones, Thomas J., 55, 89, 90, 354.
Jones, T. O., 55.
Jones, Judge William G., 55, 89, 290, 405.
Jonson, Judge Jeptha Crawford, 245.

INDEX 481

"Journal by James Weir" (Appendix B), 443-448.
Judge Hall's Story of the Harpes (Appendix A), 435-441.
Juries, first grand and petty in county, 50-53.

K

Keath, John, 51, 53.
Keith, Henry, 32, 50.
Keith, William, 199.
Kelley, Maj. D. C., 296.
Kelley, William, discovers so-called Bessemer process, 178.
Kennedy, George F., 65.
Kennedy, Capt. R. C., 323.
Kennedy, Samuel, 462.
"Kentucke" (John Filson), xvi, 404.
Kentucky—
  Early history of, xv-xvii.
  Histories of. See History of Kentucky.
  Map of (Munsell's), 38; Russell's, 37.
  Population of during closing years of Eighteenth Century, 8.
"Kentucky, a History of the State" (Battle), 243, 404, 405.
  Contains biographies of ninety-two local men, 405.
"Kentucky in the Nation's History" (McElroy, text), 67-69, 404.
Kentucky Midland R. R., 412.
Kern, George, 65.
Kimbley, J. F., 346.
Kincheloe, pioneer families of, 21.
Kincheloe, A. H., 254.
Kincheloe, Judge Jesse W., 21, 54.
Kincheloe, Lewis, 21, 44, 64, 66, 70, 77, 167, 408.
Kincheloe, R. M., 20.
Kincheloe, Thomas, 21.
Kincheloe, Lieut. William, 21.
Kincheloe, Rev. William, 20, 21, 50.
Kincheloe's Bluff (Lewisburg), 9, 21, 41, 44, 50, 59, 113, 165, 185, 199, 380, 406, 407, 408, 443.
Kincheloe's company, roll of in War of 1812, 64.
King, Z. O., 352.
Kingsley, Edward, 337.
Kipling, George S., 228.
Kipling, R. Henry, 228.
Kipling, Robert, 228; family, 228.
Kirby, Jesse, 85.
Kirkpatrick, H. L., 55; residence, 247.
Kirkpatrick, Lucilius M., 405.
Kirkpatrick, L. Z., residence of, 271.
Kirtley, A. J., 254.
Kirtley, Elias V., 336.
Kirtley, Elisha B., 254.
Kittinger, Jacob, family, 26.
Kittinger, John, 414.
Kittinger, John B., 349.
Kittinger, Jonathan, 417.
Kittinger, Joseph, 26.

Kittinger, O. T., 50.
Kittinger, Rudolph, 25, 26.
Kittinger, Willis, 416, 417.
Knight, Capt., 101, 102.
Knightsburg, 415.
Knoxville, 57.

L

Lam, Elijah, 402.
Lam, James Wilson, 50, 402; family, 402.
  Portrait of, 402.
"Lance Capps Raid," 376.
Lander, W. C., 254.
Landes, Samuel, 79.
Landrum, John, 355.
"Landslide" or ground-sled, 113.
Land warrants, location of, 112.
Langley, James, 64.
Langley, Jeremiah, 120, 127.
Langley, John W., 63.
Langley, Walter W., 362.
Larkins, Carrol, 195.
Laurel Bluff, 280, 420.
Lawrence, Maj. Nelson C., 305.
Lawton, Alexander, 21.
Lawton, John, 352.
Lead Hill Church, 133, 304, 430.
Lead Hill country, 89.
"Lecture on Muhlenberg County" (Bard), 205-207.
Ledger, old, of James Weir, sr., 117-121.
Lee, Stanford, 189.
Leece, Samuel, 65.
Leeper (Leiper), John, 436.
"Legends of the War of Independence" (Smith), 435.
Letner, N. R., 254.
"Letters from the West" (Hall), 435.
Lew Allen (Lewellyn) Hill, legend of, 101, 102.
  Origin of, 103.
Lewisburg (Kincheloe's Bluff), 9, 21, 41, 44, 50, 59, 113, 185, 380, 406, 407, 408, 443.
Lewis, Charles, 45, 50, 51, 116.
Lewis, F. L., 55.
Lewis, Henry C., residence of, 211, 214.
Lewis, Leonard, 286.
Lewis, Lieut. Sid, 308.
Lewis, W. W., 423.
Liberia, Republic of, 342, 343.
Liberty Church. See Old Liberty.
Liberty, political and religious, pioneers fought for, 127.
Life in the Olden Days (see also Pioneers), 110-132.
"Life of Ben Hardin" (Little), 70, 132, 410, 461.
"Life of Gen. Nathan Bedford Forrest" (Wyeth), 258.
Lile, T. J., 405.
Lincoln, Abraham, 275, 276, 286.
Linthicum, Dr. Daniel A., 409.
Linthicum, Dr. Edward, 409.
Linthicum, Dr. Rufus, 409.

Linthicum, Dr. Rufus, jr., 409.
Linthicum, Dr. William A., 409.
Little, Douglass, 409, 410.
Little, Judge Lucius P.—
    "Ben Hardin, His Times and Contemporaries," 70, 132, 410, 461.
    Green River country, letter on history of (text), 30.
    Life in the early days, 132.
    "Old Stories of Green River and its People," 410, 415, 443, 461.
    "Riding the Circuit" (Appendix E), 461-465.
Little, Wesley M., 332, 465.
"Little Lake at Fishpond Hill" (Atkinson's), 98.
Littlepage, Jesse, 51.
Littlepage, Thomas, 53.
Livermore, 409, 450.
Livermore, Alonzo, 409.
Livermore, Alonzo Skiles, 409.
Livermore, Dr. H. B., 409.
Local traditions regarding hunting, 33, 34.
Local Writers and the Local Press, 345-352.
    Newspapers, local, 350-352.
    Weirs, the, prominent local writers, 345.
    "Western Speller," the (Stembridge), 345, 346, 347.
    Writers, local, 347-350.
Lodge, Matthew, 52.
Logan County, 8, 30, 31, 36, 37, 39, 53, 129, 130, 333, 388.
Log Creek, 124, 304.
Logs, large, 362.
Long Creek, 124, 133.
Long Creek country, 9, 89, 125, 126, 187, 327, 328, 427, 428, 430.
Longest, Miss Amy M., 277, 349.
    "Powderly, Past and Present," 388.
Longest, John D., 388.
Long, Rufus E., 405.
"Lonz Powers," 60, 78, 87, 133-149, 150, 170.
Lott, James, 65.
Louisville, 23, 202, 323, 328.
Louisville & Nashville R. R., 31, 412.
Love, John G., 329.
Love, Col. S. P., 55, 191, 192, 233, 253, 258, 328, 329, 330, 346, 353, 354, 364, 372, 374, 404, 465.
    Biographical sketch, 328.
    Campaign between and Wiley S. Hay, 356-360.
    Family of, 329.
    Portrait of, 329.
    "The Old Soldiers" (poem), 330.
Lovelace, George, 167.
Lovelace, Henderson, 414.
Lovelace, Capt. Thomas J., 253, 292, 302, 303, 304.
Lovelace Tavern ("Our House"), 262, 265, 414.
Lovell, Charles W., 66, 86.
Lovell, Eugene, 361.

Lovell, Michael, "the Man from Maryland," 86, 120, 165.
    Family of, 86.
    "Old Place," 85.
    Portrait of, 86.
Lovell, William L., 405.
Lovell's Cave, 429.
Luce, David, 63.
Luce, Jacob, 415.
Luce, William, 50.
Luckett, Alfred, 100.
Luckett, John, 100.
"Lucy Wing," first steamboat built on Green River, 225, 408.
Lyles, J., 383.
Lynching of Bob Gray, negro, 355, 361-365.
    Dudley White, negro, 365.
Lynn, Gasham, 65.
Lynn, George, 63.
Lynn, Henry, 65.
Lyon, A. J., 353.
Lyon, Chittenden, 308.
Lyon, Gen. Hylan B., 279, 280, 308, 309.
Lyon, Gen. Matthew, 308.
Lyon, R. H., 55.

M

McBride, Charles, 269.
McBride, C. W., 281.
McBride, John, 282.
McCaleb, James, 206.
McClelland, Andrew, 286.
McClelland, Nathan, 329.
McClelland School, teacher and pupils, 209.
McClelland's Hill, 267, 268.
McCommons, William, 50, 120.
McConnell, John Henry, 328.
McCown, Dr. Alexander, 354, 363, 405.
    Portrait of, 354.
McCown, A. Webster, 86, 148, 354.
McCown, James, 121.
McCown, Joseph, 206, 289, 354.
McCown, Lewis, 354, 414.
McCown, W. Briggs, 55.
McCracken, A. Elmer, 332.
McCracken, H. C., 283, 331, 405, 423.
    Portrait of, 332.
McCracken, Capt. R. C., 329, 332.
McCreary, Russell, 409, 423.
McDonald, pioneer family, 318.
MacDougal, William, 229.
MacDougal, John, 229.
McDowell, Dr. J. L., 416.
McDowell, Dr. W. R., 405, 416.
McElhinny, John B., 396.
McElhinny, William D., 396, 416.
McElroy ("Kentucky in the Nation's History," text), 67-69, 404.
McFerson, James, 65.
McFerson, John, 18, 63.
McGee, John and William ("Great Revival"), 129.
McGill, James, 65.

INDEX 483

McHenry, Col. John H., 253.
McHenry, John H., sr., 71, 462, 463.
McIntire, John, 355.
McIntire, John, 367.
McIntire, J. P., 55.
McLarning, John, 137.
McLaughlen, James H., 52.
McLean, Judge Alney, 14, 42, 43, 46, 47, 53, 58, 63, 64, 65, 69-72, 74, 81, 86, 87, 120, 126, 167, 186, 206, 224, 302, 366, 389, 404, 423, 430.
  At battle of New Orleans, 70.
  Collins' biographical sketch of (text), 71.
  Family of, 72.
  First county surveyor, 72.
  Judge Little on, in "Life of Ben Hardin" (text), 70.
  Member of Congress, 71.
  Organized two companies during War of 1812, 70; rolls of, 63, 64.
  Portrait of, 71.
  Resolutions of respect by Muhlenberg Circuit Court, 1842 (text), 71.
McLean, Alney, jr., 72, 186.
McLean, Charles W., 72, 186, 302.
McLean, Ephraim, 72.
McLean, Ephraim, sr., 43.
McLean, Matthew, 51.
McLean, Dr. R. D., 14, 48, 69, 72, 126, 206, 366.
McLean, Mrs. Tabitha, 14, 72, 200.
McLean, Judge William C., 72.
McLean, William D., 72, 220, 224, 225, 389.
  First to mine coal at Airdrie, 224.
McLean's companies, rolls of, in War of 1812, 63, 64.
McLean County, 8, 10, 19, 30, 38, 71, 81, 258, 277, 408, 409, 410.
  Act to establish the county of, 40.
"McLean Old Bank," 220, 236.
McLean Old Spring, 236.
McNary, Hugh W., 94, 206; family, 95; 300.
  Portrait of, 96.
McNary, Miss Mattie, 95.
McNary, Dr. Thomas L., 94.
McNary, William, 94, 199, 206, 389; family, 94.
McNary, William C., 94, 204, 212, 423.
McNary house, 95.
McNary Station, 94, 301.
McPherson, Aaron B., 425.
McPherson, Alexander, 18, 124.
McPherson, Jesse, 9, 16, 17; family, 17, 18; 42.
McWhirter, W. T., 333.
Macons, Peter, 65.
Madisonville, 8, 61, 279.
Madisonville, Hartford & Eastern R. R., 412.
Mahan, John J., 254.
Maps of Muhlenberg and surrounding counties, 37-39.
Markers, grave, 132.
Marshall, Humphrey ("History of Kentucky"), 167, 404.

Martin, A. J., 109, 382.
Martin, Mrs. Anna L., 88.
Martin, Buren, 285, 382.
Martin, Charles E., 310, 311, 382, 383.
Martin, Capt. Columbus H., 253, 283, 292, 306, 335.
Martin, C. Y., 382.
Martin, D. A., 382.
Martin, Dabney A., 88, 380, 381, 458.
  Portrait of, 381.
Martin, David, 88, 313.
Martin, Ellington W., 88, 381.
Martin, Felix J., 88, 242, 383.
Martin, Hugh, 305, 318.
  Farm, now Poor Asylum, 320.
  House in Greenville, 367.
Martin, Hugh, sr., 205, 206.
Martin, Hugh N., 88, 299, 355, 382, 405.
Martin, Hutson, 88, 206; family, 88.
  "Old Place," 89.
Martin, James, 63.
Martin, Lieut. James H., 302, 318.
Martin, Rev. J. E., 348.
Martin, John, 65.
Martin, R. T., 88, 148, 214, 252, 258, 285-317, 338, 349, 380, 382, 383.
  Duvall's Discovery of "Silver Ore" (Appendix D), 455-459.
  Education, higher, early history of in Greenville, 211.
  "Forty Years Ago," 353-360.
  Old Liberty Church, 104-109.
  On the pioneers, 113.
  Portrait of, 287.
  Recollections of the Civil War, 252, 258, 285-317.
  "Trying Times in Muhlenberg," 368-371, 375, 378.
Martin, R. T. & C. E., 355.
Martin, Col. Robert M., 259, 262, 302, 303, 304, 318-325, 331.
  Birthplace of, 318, 320.
  Business career, 324.
  Family of, 324.
  Life of, after the war (Headley), 324, 325.
  Military career, 305, 306, 318-324.
  Occupies Greenville, 322.
  Opened the battle of Chickamauga, 321, 322.
  Operations in Canada and in the North, 323.
  Personal appearance, 324.
  Portrait of, 319.
  Qualities as a cavalry leader, 318, 321.
  Raid on Union arsenal at Newburg, Ind., 320.
  Recruiting, 320.
  Tried on charge of treason; pardoned, 324.
Martin, Rufus, 382, 383.
Martin, Samuel, 63.
Martin, Susannah Walker, widow of Thomas, 88; family, 88.
Martin, Templeton B., 318.
Martin, Thomas A., 310, 311, 383.
Martin, Sergt. T. H., 88, 306.

Martin, Thomas L., 88, 285, 383; family, 383.
Portrait of, 384.
Martin, W. C., 88, 295, 381.
Martin, William, 48, family, 88; 206, 380, 381, 382.
Martin, William H., 405.
Martin & Company, Buren, 382.
Martin & Company's, C. Y., tobacco re-handling house, 383.
Martin's Creek, 98.
Mason, Miss Nannie, 236, 240, 245.
Mason, Gen. Richard Barnes, 236.
Massacre after battle of River Raisin, 65, 66.
Matthews, Jacob, 65.
Matthews, Job, 127.
Matthews, Moses, 64.
Maxwell, Robert, 63.
Mayhan, John, 273, 274.
Melody, Rev. M. F., 416.
Mendel, Charles, 405.
Mercer P. O., 420.
Meredith, Hubert, 402.
Merriweather, Capt. Ned, 296.
Messic, James F., 105, 106, 107, 108.
"Metal witches," 457.
Metcalf, Enoch, 64.
Methodist Church, oldest in county (Mt. Olivet), 128.
Methodist Episcopal Church, Central City, 414.
Metzker, Charles, 154, 183.
House in 1895, 156.
Portrait of, 154.
Mexican War, Muhlenberg Men in the, 191-193.
Veterans, list of, 191.
Midland, 412.
Miles, Albert, 383.
Military grants, Virginia, 112.
"Military lines," 113.
Militia Muster, the old, 91, 165-175.
Commission, first militia officers', 166, 167.
Discontinuance of, 170.
Early history of, 166.
Features of, 168.
"Lonz Powers," described in, 170-175.
Places of meeting, 165, 166.
Milk-house, Buckner, ruins of, 179.
Mill Chimneys, Airdrie, 1900, 230.
Miller, Alfred, 332.
Miller, F. Marion, 26.
Miller, George, 64, 121.
Miller, Capt. Isaac, 96, 253, 292, 301, 332; family, 332.
Portrait of, 332.
Miller, James, 332.
Miller, James M., 332.
Miller, John S., 55, 332.
Miller, Simon, 332.
Miller, William, and the "Millerites," 177, 178.
Miller, William T., 55, 332.
Milligan, John C., 63.
Milliken, Charles K., 353.

Mills in the olden days, 122, 124.
Mills, Jonathan E., 405.
Mine Owners Association of Kentucky, 396.
Mitchell, Ben, 179, 189.
Mitchell, Isaac, 189, 296, 333.
Mitchell, Capt. Joseph, 189, 333; family, 333.
Portrait of, 333.
Mitchell, Leander, 410.
Mitchell, Mrs. Lou J., 349.
Mitchell, Mason, 283.
Mitchell, Woodford, 410.
Mitchusson, Lieut.-Col. William, 64.
Mohorn, Sidney J., 425.
Mohorn, W. A., 55.
Monterey (Paradise), 419.
Moore, Bob, 301.
Moore, Clark, 356.
Moore, Maurice, 195, 201, 206.
Moore, Morris, 252, 301.
Moore, Thomas, 65.
Moorman, James C., 423.
Moray, John, 83.
Morehead, Charles, sr., 414.
Morehead, Charles S., 165, 417.
Morehead, Dr. John W., 354.
"Morehead's Horse Mill," 124, 415, 417.
Morgan, Capt., 303, 304, 305.
Morgan, Charles, 50, 96.
Morgan, Dr. Daniel Boone, 97.
Morgan, George W., 251.
Morgan, John, 94, 96, 97; family, 97; 423.
Morgan, John B., 269.
Morgan, Gen. John H., 252, 271, 272, 298, 320, 323.
Morgan, Tom M., 55, 353, 382, 405.
Morgan, William K., 86, 97; family, 97; 334.
Morgan, Willis, 96.
Morgan's Cavalry. See History of.
"Morgan's Immortals," camping-ground of, 272, 298.
Morganfield Mail, 355.
Morgantown, 8.
Morman, James C., 405.
Morton, Rev. James, 212.
Morton, Judge John H., 55, 353, 374.
Morton, Richard, 26, 42, 44.
Morton, Thomas, 44.
Morton, W. D., 354.
Morton, William, 63.
Mothers and wives, moral and religious influence of pioneer, 130, 131.
Mounds and the Moundbuilders, 103, 182, 426-428.
Prehistoric Mound near Buckner's Stack, 427; on Judge Godman Farm, 429.
Mt. Olivet Church, 128.
Mt. Pisgah Church, 84, 104, 262, 280, 286, 288, 294, 295, 296.
Mt. Pleasant (Pleasant Hill) Church, 194, 202.
Mt. Zion Church, 128, 202.
"Muddy River" (Green River), 413.
"Muddy River" (Mud River), 37, 39, 411.

INDEX 485

Mud River, 13, 37, 39, 40, 99, 124, 178, 257, 271, 272, 390, 392, 393, 411, 426.
Mud River country, 9, 18, 19.
Mud River Mine, oldest in county, history of, 391-394; 424, 426.
Muhlenberg, Frederick Augustus, 2.
Muhlenberg, Henry A., 1.
Muhlenberg, Rev. Henry Melchoir, 1.
Muhlenberg, Gen. John Peter Gabriel, 1-7, 29, 31.
  Biographical sketch (text), 2, 3.
  Farewell sermon, scene at, 5; described by biographer (text), 4.
  In painting by Edwin A. Abbey, 7.
  "Life of," 1.
  Military career, 2, 4, 5.
  Ordination of, 2.
  Personal appearance, 7.
  Poems and dramas, subject of, 6.
  Political career, 2.
  Spelling of the name, 1, 406.
  Statue of in Statuary Hall, Washington, 6; in Philadelphia, 3, 5, 7.
  Two trips to Kentucky in 1784, 1, 2.
Muhlenberg County—
  Muhlenberg citizens in the Confederate Army, 253, 254.
  Agricultural products of (1870), 412.
  Beginnings and Bounds of the County, 36-40.
  Clark's trip, account of, earliest record of white people who visited the territory, xv.
  Coal mines in operation and output in 1911, 397.
  Courts and Courthouses, 41-55.
  Facsimile of commission of first justices, 43.
  Fair, 84.
  First settled by Revolutionary soldiers, 8.
  First settlements, 8, 9, 19.
  Jails, 46, 49, 54.
  Map of (1907-1912), 39.
  Members of House of Representatives (1800-1912), 423.
  Members of the State Senate, 423, 424.
  Naming of, xvii, 1, 7, 29, 31, 36.
  Population of, in 1800, 10; from 1800 to 1910, 422.
  Population of towns in county from 1870 to 1910, 422.
  Post-offices in county, 420, 421.
  Production of coal, 1890 to 1911, inclusive, 398.
  Revolutionary soldiers in (1800), 10.
  School Fair and Corn Show, first, 219.
  Some of the First-Comers, 8-28.
  Thirty-fourth, admitted 1798, xvii.
  Towns and post offices in county, 421.
  Vaterland customs and speech in, 112, 417.
Muhlenberg County Savings Bank, Greenville, 402.
"Muhlenberger's Recollections of 1862, A," (Randolph) text, 272-274.

Muhlenberg in the Civil War, 250-325.
  Alarms, true and false, 272-274, 279, 297.
  Buckner, Gen., in, 257, 258, 290-292.
  Citizens in the Confederate army, 253, 254.
  Civil War veterans, some (1912), 283.
  Crittenden, Gen., history of stay in, 262-267.
  Flags displayed, 257, 270.
  Forrest, Col., in, 258-262, 296, 297.
  G. A. R., first post in county, 283.
  Gross' (James R.) pocket memorandum book, 282.
  Guerrilla raids and highway robberies during, 252.
  Humphreys' (D. C.) letters as local history, 275-277.
  Letter on "Life with the Soldiers," 275.
  Lyon, Gen., in, 279, 280, 308, 309.
  Morgan, Gen., in, 271, 272, 298, 299.
  Names of officers and privates in Union regiments organized in State, 253.
  Reunions of Civil War soldiers, 283, 284.
  Sacramento, fight near, 258-262, 296, 297.
  Sullivan's barn, fight at, 277-279.
Muhlenberg Men in the Mexican War, 191-193.
Muhlenberg Men in the War of 1812, 63-75, 206.
  Daring deeds performed by Muhlenberg men, 65.
  List of officers and privates from Muhlenberg, 63-65.
  Local traditions of, 65.
  Three companies organized in Muhlenberg, 63.
Muhlenberg Sentinel, 285, 351, 368, 375, 378.
Muir, Gilbert, 229.
"Mule-footed hogs," 393.
Murphey, Samuel W., 97, 405.
Murphy, Jesse, 85, 97, 206; family, 97; 118.
Murphy, Samuel, 64.
Murphy, Thomas, 97, 100.
Murphy's Lake, 84, 90, 97, 98, 99, 100, 101, 127, 196, 332, 428.
  "Scatters," 98.
  Bard's Ditch, 98.
Murphy's Lake country, 12.
  First-comers, well-known, 85.
Murray, Maj. Eli H., 253, 258, 296.
Murray, John A., 410.
Muster, the old militia. See Militia Muster.
Myers, David, 337.
Myers, David H., 354, 383, 405.
Myers, Henry, 124.
Myers, James Gwinn, 405.
Myers' Old Chapel, 254, 337.

N

Naming the county (1798), 7, 29, 31, 36.
Nanny, Spencer, 65.
Nashville, 19, 41, 57, 267, 268.
Neal, Benjamin, 10.
Neff, Henry, 64.
"Negro equality panic," 356-360.
Nelson Creek Baptist Church, 22, 128.
Nelson Creek country, 9, 256.
Nelson Station P. O., 420.
Nevin, Blanche, 6.
New Hope Church burying-ground, 279.
Newman, Alney, 312, 313, 362, 383.
Newman, Charles, 362, 363, 364.
Newman, Henry G., 405.
Newman, William Y., 383.
Newman graveyard, 131.
New Orleans, 23, 73, 98, 99, 117, 380, 382, 408, 443.
New Orleans, battle of, 63, 64, 65, 70, 72, 74.
New Orleans, Weir's Trip to in 1803 (Appendix B), 443-448.
Newspaper, first printed in county, 355.
  Facsimile of editorial title, 351.
  Facsimile, reduced, of first page, 350.
Newspapers printed in county since 1870, 350-352.
New Station Church, 261.
Nexon, Rev. William, first licensed to solemnize rites of marriage, 46.
Nicholls, James, 24.
Ninth Kentucky Infantry (Confederate), 253, 254, 255, 256, 277, 333, 336.
"Nisi Prius" (Browder), 348.
Nixon, James, 65.
Noe, Hon. William B., 410.
Noffsinger, Andrew, 425.
Noffsinger, Daniel, Jacob, and Dr. John, 25, 26.
Noffsinger, Jacob, 25; family, 26.
Noffsinger, John and wife, 26.
  Portrait of, 25.
Norris, Thomas, 65.
Nott, George, 53.
Nunan, James, 191, 192.
Nunn, John, 64.
Nusell, Henry, 64.

O

Oates, Bayless E., 425.
Oates, Bayless Earle, 92, 93.
Oates, Charles R., 92.
Oates, Edward, 377.
Oates, Mrs. Elizabeth Earle, 92.
  Portrait of, 93.
Oates, George, 92.
Oates, James Wallace, 425.
Oates, Maj. Jesse, 91, 137. 206, 339.
  Duel between, and Coghill. 91, 92.
  Family of, 92.
Oates, "Uncle" John, 339.
  Incident in life of, 339.
  Portrait of, 339.
Oates, J. Wallace, 92.
Oates, Wallace W., 92.
Oates, William, 24, 63, 92; family, 93; 99.
Oates, William W., 405.
Oates, Wyatt, 92, 339.
Oberdorfer, Isaac and Samuel, 150.
O'Brien, Jordan, 64.
"Official Records of the War of the Rebellion" (text), 262-267.
O'Flaherty, John, 351.
Oglesby, Jacob, 85.
Ohio County, 8, 10, 40, 277, 279, 409.
"Old Brick Bank Building," Greenville, 126, 359, 366, 367.
Old Camp Ground, 130.
Old Caney Station graveyard, 12, 79, 200.
"Old Coal Road," 392, 393, 426.
"Old Ed's Rush to Rumsey," 270.
Oldest Baptist organization (Hazel Creek), 128.
Oldest Methodist Church (Mt. Olivet), 128.
Oldest Presbyterian organization (Mt. Zion), 128.
Old Jones Peach Orchard Hill, 430.
Old Lake, 98.
Old Liberty Church, 84, 85, 88, 100, 104-109, 127, 165, 285, 288, 290, 327, 380, 383, 420.
  Burying-ground, 85, 104, 108, 109.
  First-comers, well-known, 85.
  In 1900, 106.
  "Mother of preachers," 104.
  "Old Oaken Bucket" at, 105, 106.
  Political gatherings, barbecues, singing classes, 105, 108.
  Revivals at, 104.
  Ruins of in 1912, 107.
  School at, 105-108.
  Union church house, 104.
Old Millport, 96, 97, 124, 165, 421.
Old Prison, the (Stone House), 235.
Old Station Church (Station Church), 11.
"Old Stories of Green River and its People" (Little), 410, 415, 443, 461.
Old-time grist mills, 122-125.
Old trails, 12, 13.
Old White Plains, 170.
Olive Branch Chapel, 84.
O'Neal, Spencer, 64.
"Orders" negro, rival temperance, 343.
Ore, iron, discovery of in county, 178, 179, 180, 255, 399.
Orphan Brigade, the, 253, 254, 333.
"Our House" (Lovelace Tavern), 262, 265, 414.
Owen, David Dale, 186, 390, 398, 401.
Owen, Edmund and John, 53, 85.
Owen, William T., 462, 463, 465.
Owensboro (Yellow Banks), 13, 41, 258, 262, 267, 333, 355, 389, 390, 410, 412, 415, 461.
Owensboro Junction. See Central City.
Owensboro & Russellville Railroad, 19, 192, 390, 412, 413, 415, 420.

P

Pace, Daniel, 64.
Pace, Edward O., 295, 333.
Pace, Joel, 64.
Pace, Richmond, 290.
Pace, R. O., Judge, 50, 55, 290, 333, 351.
Painstown P. O., 420.
Pakenham, Gen., 74.
Panic, "negro equality," 356-360.
Pannell, Frank B., 183.
Pannell, James P., 183.
Pannell, Thomas B., 50, 55, 183.
Pannell, Rev. William Dodd, 183.
Panthers in county in pioneer times, 110, 115.
Paradise (Stum's Landing), 9, 117, 124, 205, 221, 383, 389, 401, 412, 419.
Paradise and the Highway Thereto, 221.
Paradise Country and Old Airdrie, 28, 220-241, 335, 336, 398.
   Coal discovered, 224.
   Coal mined at Airdrie, 235.
   Iron works and mines, ruins of, 220.
Parker, J. R., 348.
Parnham, Plunket, 189.
"Partisan Rangers, The" (Johnson, text), 258-262; 280, 318.
Patterson, Prof. James K., 80, 213.
   Portrait of, 213.
Patterson, Col. Robert, 13.
Patterson, Robert, 229.
Patterson, William, 213.
Paxton, Joseph, 154.
Payne, William, 393.
Pearson, J. H., 410, 411.
   "Map of county," 411.
Pearson, Richard H., 425.
Pearson, William H., 17.
Pendleton, Dr. John Ed, 253, 254, 257, 258, 292.
Pendleton, William C., 254.
Pennington, Lonz, execution of, 146, 147.
   Grave of, 148.
   House of, in 1912, 145.
Penningtons, the. See The Story of "Lonz Powers."
"Pennington's Farewell," 147.
"Pennsylvania Furnace," 176.
Penrod, 65, 383, 392, 394, 420, 423.
Penrod, George, 64, 65; family, 65; 289.
Penrod, H. C., 405.
Penrod, Tobias, 65.
Perrin (Battle's "History of Kentucky"), 29.
Perryman, Rev. John B., 216.
Peter, Dr. Robert, 398.
Peters, Christian, 27, 120.
Petit juries, members of first in county, 51, 53.
Potroo, H. G., 462.
Petree, Judge R. T., 54, 353.
Phelps, Capt., 394.
Philadelphia, 59, 117, 448.
Phillips, Henry, 120.
Phillips, W. L., 351.
Pierce, James T., 420.

Pigeons, passenger or wild, 84, 116, 117, 181.
Pilot Rock, 141, 143, 149.
Pioneers (see Life in the Olden Days, 110-132), 206.
   Gatherings of, 127.
   German Bibles in homes of, 128, 222.
   Graves of, 132.
   Hunting-shirt of the early, 102.
   Intermarriage of, 111, 112.
   Martin, R. T., on, 113.
   Political and religious liberty of—Flag and Bible symbolic of to, 127.
   Religion, interested in, 127.
   Religious exercises in homes of, 128.
   Revolutionary soldiers, 8, 10, 127.
   Settling and upbuilding of county, 28.
   Women, moral and religious influence of, 130, 131.
Pittman, B. E., 55, 346, 353, 354, 364, 423, 462.
Pleasant Hill (Mt. Pleasant) Church, 202.
Pleasant Hill Church, 165.
Poag, James W., 58.
Poag, Joseph, 58; family, 58.
Point Pleasant, 19, 277.
Pollard, Dr. Thomas, 120, 126, 206.
Pollock, Archie, 228.
Pond Creek, 9, 75, 99, 111, 178, 181, 188, 222, 291, 388, 428.
Pond Creek country, 327, 333.
Pond River, 9, 12, 39, 40, 90, 97, 98, 101, 102, 103, 111, 124, 140, 194, 196, 242, 258, 262, 272, 291, 389, 436.
Pond River and Pond Creek, origin of name, 430.
Pond River country, the, 28, 84-103, 126, 194, 335, 339.
   First-comers to, well-known, 89.
   Game, field for, 84.
Pond Station, 8, 10, 11, 13, 16, 30, 31.
   Site of, 11.
Pool, Raisin, 191, 192.
Poor Asylum, County, 320.
Population of county from 1800 to 1910, 422.
Population of towns in county from 1870 to 1910, 422.
Porter, Henry, 300.
Porter, Jack, 252, 299, 300, 301.
Portraits—
   Akers, Larkin N., 65.
   Allison, Finis McLean, 361.
   Allison, John Adair, 88.
   Bard, Isaac, 195.
   Brank, Ephraim M., 68.
   Buckner, Aylette Hartswell, 184.
   Buckner, Gen. Simon Bolivar, 185.
   Buell, Gen. Don Carlos, 237.
   Chatham, S. D., 307.
   Coombs, John, wife and son, 326.
   Davis, Arthur N., 192.
   Dean, Mr. and Mrs. William J., 24.
   Drake, Mosley Collins, 66.
   Duncan, William G., 401.
   Durall, Japha N., 327.
   Eaves, Charles, 243.

Portraits—Continued.
Finley, Francis M., 327.
Finley, Thomas M., 327.
Freeman, J. K., 328.
Green, William L., 212.
Grundy, William S., 330.
Haden, George W., 224.
Hall, Edwin W., 215.
Hay, Wiley S., 360.
Hayes, Clarence B., 349.
Hendrie, Alexander, 229.
Jackson, Dr. Alfred M., 205.
James, Dr. A. D., 424.
Jenkins, John, 186.
Johnson, Alfred, 188.
Jones, Strother, 89.
Lam, James W., 402.
Love, Col. S. P., 329.
Lovell, Michael, 86.
McCown, Dr. Alexander, 354.
McCracken, Henry C., 332.
McLean, Judge Alney, 71.
McNary, Hugh W., 96.
Martin, Dabney A., 381.
Martin, Richard T., 287.
Martin, Col. Robert M., 319.
Martin, Thomas L., 384.
Metzker, Charles, 154.
Miller, Isaac, 332.
Mitchell, Joseph, 333.
Noffsinger, Mr. and Mrs. John, 25.
Oates, Mrs. Elizabeth Earle, 93.
Oates, "Uncle" John, 339.
Patterson, Prof. James K., 213.
Reno, John Edmunds, 50.
Reynolds, Mr. and Mrs. Joseph C., 74.
Rhoads, Henry, wife and daughter, 33.
Rhoads, McHenry, 35.
Richardson, Joseph F., 333.
Roark, J. L., 334.
Roark, M. J., 334.
Roark, Prof. Ruric N., 348.
Rothrock, H. D., 417.
Rumsey, Edward, 82.
Russell, Robert S., 15.
Russell, Mrs. Samuel, 14.
Shannon, W. C., 335.
Shaver, Benjamin J., 251.
Shaver, Mr. and Mrs. Peter, 27.
Shull, E. E. C., 335.
Smith, William H., 336.
Sparks, Judge T. J., 377.
Stanley, Mrs. Clara G., 94.
Taylor, Alvin L., 189.
Thomas, R. Y., 431.
Thompson, John L. G., 336.
Vanlandingham, O. C., sr., 223.
Vincent, R. T., 330.
Wallace, R. W., 337.
Weir, Mrs. Anna C. R., 58.
Weir, Col. E. R., 61.
Weir, Edward R., sr., 59.
Weir, Mrs. Harriet R., 60.
Weir, pioneer James, 57.
Weir, James, 134.
Weir, Max, 62.
Wickliffe, Ben and Bob, 375.

Portraits—Continued.
Wickliffe, John K., 256.
Wickliffe, Col. Moses, 22.
Wickliffe, William A., 403.
Wilkins, J. L., 330.
Wing, Charles Fox, 77.
Wing, Mrs. Charles Fox, 78.
Wood, Zillman, 19.
Woodburn, Dr. J. T., 414.
Yonts, Joseph D., 337.
Yost, Judge William H., 51.
Yost, Mrs. William H., sr., 151.
Post-offices in county, 420, 421.
Post-primary Education in Muhlenberg, 208-219.
  Bremen College and Perryman Male and Female Academy, 211, 216.
    Scholarships, 216.
  Classes first taught by Prof. William Lewis Green, 210.
  Early history of higher education in Greenville (Martin, text), 211-213.
  Five colleges organized (1850-1900), 210, 218.
  "From shirt-sleeves to shirt-sleeves," 208.
  Greenville Academy (Seminary), 126, 210.
  Greenville College, 211, 214.
  Greenville Female Academy, 210, 211, 212, 213.
  Greenville Ladies' College and the Greenville College for Young Men, 214.
  Presbyterial Academy of Greenville, 203, 211, 212, 213.
  Present conditions and future progress, 219.
  South Carrollton Male and Female Institute, 211. 215.
    Scholarships, 215.
  West Kentucky Classical and Normal College (West Kentucky College), 211, 216.
Powderly Mine, 389, 403.
"Powderly, Past and Present" (Longest, text), 388, 389.
Power-house and Double Tipple, Graham-Skibo Mine, Graham, 396.
Power-house and Steel Tipple, Kentucky-Midland Mine, Midland, 400.
Prehistoric men in county, graves of, 428.
Prehistoric mound near Buckner's Stack, 427; on Judge Godman Farm, 429.
Presbyterial Academy of Greenville, 200, 202, 203, 211, 212, 213.
Presbyterian Church, Cumberland, of Greenville, 109, 357.
  Memorial windows in, 109.
Presbyterian Church of South Carrollton, laying corner-stone of, 198.
Presbyterian Church, old, in Greenville, 152.
Presbyterian, oldest organization (Mt. Zion), 128.
Presbyterians, Cumberland, in county, 104, 109.

Presentiments of death, 255.
Pritchett, Presley, 120.
Private burying-grounds, 132.
Proctor, Gen., 66.
Prowse, George O., 55, 85.
Prowse, Isaac S., 405.
Prowse, M. L., 55, 405.
Prowse or Reno Old Bridge, 101, 258, 291, 292.
Pruitt, Levi, 191, 192.
Public Road near Old Liberty (1900), 310.
Public School Building, Bremen, 218.
Public School Building, Central City, 217.
Public School Building, Drakesboro, 219.
Public School Building, Greenville, 217.
Public School Building, South Carrollton, 216.
"Public Spring," the (South Carrollton), 414.
Putman, Jesse M., 405.
Putnam, Prof. F. W., 428.
Putnam, Miles, 85.

Q

Quantrill, the guerrilla, 252, 306, 307.
Quarrying stone on Buell place, for penitentiary, 235.
Quarter sessions, court of, 41, 50, 51.
  First grand jury impaneled by members of, 50.
  First petit jury of, members, 51.

R

Raco, Henry, 64.
Ragan, J. V., 355.
Railroad Bonds, the, 207, 353, 355, 360, 368-379.
  Cities and counties in Kentucky carrying similar debts, 379.
  Complications, beginning of, 374.
  Copy and facsimile of, 372, 373.
  Election held, 368.
  Era of railroad building in Kentucky, 368.
  "Funding Act" — "Funding Board," new bonds issued by, 374, 376.
  "Independent Order of Taxpayers," 374, 376, 377, 378.
  Issuing of, 372.
  "Lance Capps Raid," 376.
  Legal proceedings, 375.
  Mass-meeting held in Greenville, 376.
  Proposition first advanced, 368, 369.
  Repudiation accomplished, 374.
  Settlement of, good results from, 377.
  Stories of the campaign, 371, 372.
  "Trying Times in Muhlenberg" (Martin, text), 368-371, 375, 378.
Randolph, Ashford D., 24, 93, 272.
Randolph, Lieut. Ed M., 24, 92, 302.
Randolph, Capt. John, 24; family, 24.
Randolph, John, jr., 24, 414.
Randolph, John R., 24 ("A Muhlenberger's Recollections of 1862," text), 272-274.
Randolph, Robert, 24; family, 24.
Randolph, Thomas, 53, 167.
Randolph, William Oates, 92.
"Randolph Old Farm" (South Carrollton), 414.
Raney, George, 254.
Rates, tavern, and ferry charges (1799), 44.
Recollections of the Civil War (R. T. Martin), 252, 258, 285-317.
  Antebellum times, customs of living in, 286.
  Bob Martin's military career in Muhlenberg, 305, 306.
  "Bogus cavalry" on a bogus raid, 293.
  Buckner's march through Muhlenberg, 290-292.
  Cannon, imitation, 292.
  Coal Bank, battle at the, 302, 303.
  Confederate legislature, meeting of at Russellville, 289.
  "Dirty Dozen," the, 310, 311, 312.
  Election agitation in 1860, 286.
  Enlistments, local, in 1861, 292.
  Forrest in Muhlenberg, 296, 297.
  Fort Donelson, conditions during battle of, 297.
  Guerrilla warfare, recruiting, and bushwhacking, 299, 301, 306, 307, 312.
  Home Guard companies organized, 289, 290.
  Lincoln, election of, a blessing, 286.
  Lyon in Muhlenberg, 308, 309.
  Morgan's march through Muhlenberg, 298, 299.
  Mt. Pisgah Church, disturbance at protracted meeting, 286-288.
  Neutrality sought by citizens of Kentucky, 288.
  Political affairs, developments and changes in, 314-316.
  Raids, 292, 296, 297, 300, 301, 302, 308, 309, 310, 311, 312.
  State admitted into Southern Confederacy, 289.
  State Guard and equipment, 290.
  War-time exaggerations, 297.
  War-time "prank," 309.
Record, Greenville, 61, 104, 193, 285, 328, 330, 350, 351, 353, 388, 418, 457.
Records, county court. See County Court records.
Redman, Parmenas, 64, 126.
Reeves, Judge Willis L., 54.
"Regulators," the. See Story of "Lonz Powers."
Reid, Josiah, 363, 364.
Reid, Lycurgus T., letter on death of Wickliffe, 255; 283.
Religion and slave preachers, 340.
Religion, pioneers interested in, 127.
Religious exercises in homes of pioneers, 128.

Reno, E. E., 351, 352.
Reno, Jesse H., 49, 50, 52, 55, 206, 268, 269, 340, 346, 353, 354, 371, 405.
Reno, John, 50.
Reno, John Edmunds, 50; family, 50; 55, 371, 383, 414.
  Portrait of, 50.
Reno, Mrs. John (Randolph), 24.
Reno, Lawson R., 50, 314, 315, 354.
Reno, Lewis, 50, 79, 354, 366, 405.
Reno, Lewis, sr., 50, 167.
Reno House, 50, 297, 301, 305, 313; Federal headquarters, 314; 315, 354.
"Report upon the Airdrie Furnace and Property" (Ky. State Geolog. Survey, text), 230.
Representatives, Muhlenberg members of House of (1800-1912), 423.
Reunions, soldiers', in county, 191, 283, 284, 289, 326, 330.
"Revival, Great" (1799), 129, 130.
Revolutionary soldiers, 9, 10, 126, 195, 205.
  Bone, John, 9, 86, 205.
  County first settled by, 8, 10, 127.
  Craig, James, 47.
  Drake, Albritton, 67, 130.
  Drake, James, 67.
  Earle, Bayless, 92.
  Elkins, Joshua, 9.
  Garriz, Sihez, 9.
  Glenn, Andrew, 9, 205.
  Hopkins, William, 10.
  Hunt, John, 18.
  Kincheloe, Lieut. William, 21.
  Martin, Hugh, sr., 205, 206.
  Martin, Thomas, 88.
  Neal, Benjamin, 10.
  Oates, Maj. Jesse, 91.
  Percentage of in county in 1800, 10.
  Reynolds, Richard D., sr., 74, 85, 104, 206.
  Rhoads, Henry, 29.
  Rice, William, 86.
  Russell, Gen. William, 13.
  Seven reported from county in 1840, 9, 10.
  Weir, William, 56.
  Wickliffe, Arrington, 22.
  Willis, Britain, 10.
  Wing, Barnabas, 76.
Reynolds, George and Thomas, 104.
Reynolds, John T., sr., 74, 104, 354, 403.
Reynolds, Joseph C., 65, 73, 74; family, 74; 85, 100, 272, 289, 403.
  Portrait of, 74.
Reynolds, R. D., 74, 290.
Reynolds, Richard D., sr., Revolutionary soldier, 74, 85, 104, 206.
Reynolds, Thomas H., 74, 405.
Rhoads, Absalom J., 29, 275.
Rhoads, Benjamin L., 254.
Rhoads, Bradford, 65.
Rhoads, Daniel, 33, 50, 51.
Rhoads, David, 30.
Rhoads, David, 33; family, 33; 51, 206.
Rhoads, D. E., 214, 237, 329, 405.
Rhoads, Gilbert Vaught, 275-277.

Rhoads, Henry, 8, 11, 29-35, 36, 42, 45, 46, 50, 128, 423.
  Biographical sketch (Perrin, text), 29, 30.
  Claim to land, trouble in establishing, 31, 32.
  Early settler, 10, 32.
  Family of, 33.
  "Godfather of Muhlenberg," 32, 35.
  Grave of, 32.
  Graveyard, old family, 32.
  House of, near Browder, 30.
  Influenced pioneers to settle in county, 35.
  "Last will and testament" of (text), 32, 33.
  Last years of, 35.
  Member of State Legislature, 31, 34.
  Naming the county, 7, 29, 31, 36.
  Plans for first courthouse, assisted in drawing, 35.
  Settled in Muhlenberg in 1793, 31.
Rhoads, Henry (grandson of pioneer Henry Rhoads), 33.
  Portrait of, 33.
Rhoads, Luther Bard, 33.
Rhoads, Prof. McHenry, 29, 32, 35.
  Portrait of, 35.
Rhoads, Solomon, 8, 30, 32, 33, 53.
Rhoads, Solomon (2d), 29, 33; family, 33; 127, 165, 167, 206.
Rhoads Settlement, 307.
Rhoadsville. See Calhoun.
Rice, Billy D., 296.
Rice, E., 296, 355, 382.
Rice, Ezekiel, 86, 120.
Rice, Frank M., 420.
Rice, James, 296.
Rice, Judge Jas. J., 55, 86.
Rice, Matthew, 86, 121.
Rice, Moses M., 67, 86, 405.
Rice, Samuel, 64.
Rice, T. J., 59, 86.
Rice Tobacco Company, S. E., 382.
Rice, W. H., 106, 296.
Rice, William, 85; family, 86.
Ricedale (Drakesboro), 420.
Richardson, John, 85.
Richardson, Joseph F., 333; family, 334, 423.
  Portrait of, 333.
Ricketts, Eugene, 411.
Ricketts, Joseph, 51, 55, 290, 346, 354, 364, 371, 410, 411, 423, 462.
Riddick, Newton B., 85.
"Riding the Circuit" (Little, Appendix E), 461-465.
Rights of slaves, civil or educational (1860), 340.
Riley, Higerson, 405.
Ripple, Jacob, 65.
Ripple, Michael, 65.
River Raisin, battle of the, 65, 66.
Riverside Mine, 229.
Riverside P. O., 420.
Roark, Cecil E., 334.
Roark, Charles W., 334, 402.
Roark, Dr. J. Louis, 334.

INDEX

Roark, J. Louis, 253, 334; family, 334; 355.
Portrait of, 334.
Roark, John R., 334.
Roark, Capt. M. J., 55, 210, 253, 269, 292, 303, 304, 313, 322, 334, 335, 354, 405, 423.
Portrait of, 334.
Roark, Orien L., 330, 334, 349, 351.
Roark, Prof. R. N., 335; portrait of, 348; works of, 347; 348.
Roark, William, 53, 64, 334.
Robbins, John, 410.
Roberts, Dr., 392; house, 393.
Robertson, David, 51, 53, 120.
Robertson, J. Jack, 188, 228, 328.
Door-props called, 228.
Family of, 188.
Robertson, John, 188; descendants of, 188.
Robertson, Robert, 53, 64, 188.
Robertson, Samuel, 283.
Robinson, William E., 405.
Rochester, 257, 393, 395, 415.
Rockport (Benton's Ferry), 12.
Rogers, Judge George C., 54, 353.
Rogers, J. L., 55, 80.
Rogers, John E. H., 120.
Roll, Abraham, 222; family, 223.
Roll, David B. ("Squire"), 223, 233, 353, 405.
Roll, James H., 254.
Roll, Michael F., 223.
Roll, Thomas J., 223.
Roll, T. L., 55.
Roll of Capt. Lewis Kincheloe's company in War of 1812, 64.
Rolls of Capt. Alney McLean's companies in War of 1812, 63, 64.
Rosewood, 16, 388.
Ross, Samuel M., 26.
"Roster of Volunteer Officers and Soldiers from Kentucky in War of 1812" (Hill), 63.
Rothrock, Charles W., 254, 269, 415.
Rothrock, H. D., 55, 383, 414.
Portrait of, 417.
Rothrock, H. F. Given, 415.
Rothrock, John, 206, 414.
Rothrock, John B., 415.
Rothrock, Noah D., 254, 255, 415.
Row, Adam, 65.
Row, Henry, 64.
Royster, Nicholas, 348.
Ruby, John B., 476.
Rumsey, 40, 81, 198, 271, 319, 406, 407, 408, 409, 410, 457.
Rumsey, Edward, 12, 48, 71, 81-83, 126, 134, 206, 257, 289, 346, 404, 423, 431.
Biographical sketch ("Biographical Encyclopedia," text), 81-83.
Family of, 81.
Famous speech, 83, 348.
Member of Congress, 81.
Portrait of, 82.
Rumsey, Dr. Edward, 60; family, 60; 83.

Rumsey, James, 81, 83, 134, 407.
Family of, 83.
Inventor of steamboat, 81-83.
Russell, Edward M., 14, 15.
Russell, John C., 11, 13, 14, 42, 170, 423.
Russell, Mrs. Lucy Roberts, 14.
Russell, Robert S., 14; family, 14; 257, 289, 423, 463, 465.
Portrait of, 15.
Russell, Samuel, 11, 13, 14, 46, 126, 206.
Russell, Mrs. Samuel, portrait of, 14.
Russell, William, 394.
Russell, Col. William, 13.
Russell, Gen. William, 11, 13, 45.
Russell County, 13.
Russell House, 14, 41, 46, 125, 126, 150, 463, 465.
Russell Old Field (race track), 14, 114, 165, 168, 169, 170.
Russellville, 8, 13, 41, 254, 355, 389, 392, 412, 436.
Rust, Erastus P., 405.
Rust, Isaac, 51.
Rutherford, Arch, 464.
Ryan, Capt. James B., 394, 405.

S

Sacramento, 31, 296, 319, 410, 457.
Fight near, 258-262, 292, 296, 319.
St. Joseph's Roman Catholic Church, Central City, 415.
"Salsbury Free Negro Settlement," 342.
Salsbury, Thomas, 64, 127, 342.
Salt and salt wells, 182, 406.
"Salting" a salt well, 182.
Salt Lick Creek, 178, 182.
"Saltpeter Cave," 430.
Sanders, George, 64.
Sandidge, Judge William P., 54.
Sandusky, Capt. William H. H., 405, 416.
Sandusky House, the, 416.
Saulsburg, David, 254.
School at Old Liberty Church, 105-108.
School Fair and Corn Show, first in county, 219.
"School History of Kentucky" (Thompson), 31, 253, 254.
Schools, county. See Post-Primary Education in Muhlenberg.
Schweizer, J. Otto, 3, 5, 7.
"Scotch fowl," a, 182.
"Scotch Henry" (Alexander Hendrie), 188.
Scott, James H., 405.
Second Kentucky Cavalry (Confederate), 327.
Segler, Jacob, 64.
Senate, State, members of from Muhlenberg County, 423, 424.
Sentinel, Muhlenberg, 285, 351, 368, 375, 378.
Settle, Joseph, 417.
"Settlements," Howards, 37.
Settlers, early, extraction of, 112.
Seventeenth Kentucky Cavalry, 305, 335.
Seventeenth Kentucky Infantry, 253.

Severs, Jacob, 46, 53.
Severs, Michael, 65, 67, 74, 75; family, 75; 206.
Shackelford, Judge Benjamin, 53, 54.
Shackleton, William, 237, 383.
Shaler, Prof. N. S., 399.
  "Kentucky, a Pioneer Commonwealth," 404.
Shannon, Capt. W. C., 253, 329, 335.
  Portrait of, 335.
Sharon Baptist Church, 84.
Sharp, William Mc., 73.
Shaver (Schaber), Andrew, sr., 25; family, 26.
Shaver, Andrew, jr., 25, 26, 27; family, 27.
Shaver, Judge Benjamin J., 27, 28, 55, 250, 251, 423.
  Portrait of, 251.
Shaver, George G., 415.
Shaver, J. A., 55, 216, 218.
Shaver, Peter, 25, 26, 27, 28, 417.
  Family of, 28.
  Letter of, 250, 251.
  Named town of Bremen in honor of his father's birthplace, 417.
  Portrait of, 27.
Shaver, Peter G., 216, 218.
Shaver, Robert A., 251.
Shaver Schoolhouse, 210.
Sheffield, Isom, 133, 169.
Shelton, C. Y., 107.
Shelton, James F., 106, 310, 311, 312.
Shelton, John, 64, 67, 206, 289, 327.
Shelton, W. D., 55, 353.
Shepherds, the. See Story of "Lonz Powers."
Shiloh, battle of, 268, 319.
  Weir, Col. E. R., letter of, on battlefield, 269, 270.
Short, C. W., 50, 351, 382, 405.
Short (Schartz), David, 95; family, 96; 423.
"Short, David, Old Brick," 95, 99.
Short, George W., 96, 382, 423, 458.
Short, Jacob, 96; family, 96.
Short, Jonathan, 50, 96, 151, 346, 371, 462.
  Residence of, 365.
Short, Samuel, 26, 96.
Short, William T., 96, 409, 423.
Shull, E. E. C., 222, 283, 335.
  Portrait of, 335.
Shull (Scholl), Peter, jr. and sr., 222, 335.
Shutt, Charles M., 328.
Shutt's Cave, 429.
Silver Hills, 456, 458.
"Silver Ore," Duvall's Discovery of (Martin, Appendix D), 455-459.
Simons, Richard, 415.
Simpson, James, 55.
Simrall, Col. James, 187
Site of Prehistoric Mound, Judge Goodman Farm, near Moorman, 1912, 429.
Sketo, Capt. Isaac R., 191, 192, 253, 269, 292, 328.
Skiles, James R., 407, 414, 415.
  Sketch of career (Little), 415.

Skilesville, 271, 406, 407, 412, 414, 415, 420.
  Incorporation of, 414.
  Post-office, 415.
Skillman, James, 64.
Skipworth, Eli, 189.
Slaton, Dr. Brank, 70.
Slaton, Dr. Henry Y., 70.
Slaton, Dr. T. J., 70, 213, 354, 423.
Slave cabins, 341.
Slave population of county (1800-1860), 338, 422.
Slavery Days, 338-344.
  Election days, slave privileges on, 343, 344.
  Emancipation, beginning of movement in county, 341.
  Execution, legal, of slaves, 340.
  Fears of negro "risings" in county, 343.
  "Ghost-hauntings," 341.
  "Hiring out" and sale of slaves, 338.
  Holidays, slave, 343, 344.
  "Orders," negro, rival temperance, 343.
  Religion and slave preachers, 340.
  Rights, civil or educational, of slaves, 340.
  "Salsbury Free Negro Settlement," 342.
  Selling prices of slaves, 118, 338.
  Slave cabins, 341.
  Slave population of county (1800-1860), 338.
Smith, Aaron and Leonard, 222, 236.
Smith, Aaron, Elias, and James, 222.
Smith, Don Carlos R., 336.
Smith, Eli, 124, 222.
Smith, Elias, 124.
Smith, Elias G., 254.
Smith, G. Marshall ("Legends of the War of Independence"), 435.
Smith, Hugh, 64.
Smith, Capt. John, 206.
Smith, Samuel E., 354, 363, 364.
Smith, William H., 222, 283, 284, 336.
  Portrait of, 336.
Smith, Zachariah F. ("History of Kentucky"), xv, 69, 404.
Smith's Landing, 44.
Snead, "Ocey" Martin, 324.
Snoddy, Hayden O., 351.
Some of the First-Comers, 8-28.
Some Old Chimneys, 121.
South Carrollton, 113, 185, 198, 219, 262, 263, 267, 277, 313, 329, 332, 383, 402, 406, 407, 408, 412, 413, 414, 430, 465.
  Breastworks at, 262.
  Early citizens of, some, 414.
  Hotels, old, 414.
  Incorporation of, 413.
  Road leading from Boat-landing to, 407.
South Carrollton Male and Female Institute, 211, 215.
  Scholarships, 215.
South Carrollton Public School, 215, 216.
Southerland, Henry, 229.

Southern Educational Association, 348.
Sparks, C. M., 376, 377.
Sparks, Judge T. J., 50, 55, 376, 377.
  Portrait of, 377.
Speed, Mrs. Fannie, 218.
Spurlin, J. Lindsey, 99, 100; family, 100.
Spurlin, Rev. James U., 100.
Spurlin, Theodore, 100.
"Stack House," the, 121, 181, 189.
Stack, Story of The, 41, 176-190, 220, 221, 229, 389, 398.
  Abandoned, 179, 187, 188.
  As it appeared in 1905, 177.
  Buckner Furnace, 176, 178, 179, 180, 182, 183, 185, 187, 188, 190, 225, 229, 233, 291, 398, 399.
  Buckner house, occupants of, 189.
  "Company land," 176.
  Dog-irons made at, 180, 181, 185.
  Erection of, 176.
  Geological Survey, First Kentucky, Report on, 186.
  "Henry Clay Iron Works," 176.
  Iron ore in county, 178, 179, 180.
  Owners of, 190.
  "Stack House," the, 121, 181, 189.
Stanley, Mrs. Clara Garris, 93, 436.
  Portrait of, 94.
Stanley, James, 93; family, 93; 436.
Stanley, Mark, 64.
Staples, John B., 114, 122.
Staples' Mill, 122, 124.
Starling, Edmund L. ("History of Henderson County"), 435.
State Constitutional Convention, 204, 423.
Station Church (Old Station Church), 11, 261.
Steamboat "Lucy Wing," 225, 408.
Stembridge, John A., 66.
  Family of, 345.
  "Western Speller," 345, 346.
Stephens, D. H., 127.
Steuben, Gen. Baron, 430.
Stevens, Wesley, 394.
Steward, Green B., 355.
Stigall (Stegal), Moses, 436.
Stiles, W. T., 55.
Stivers, Genn H., 425.
Stokes, John A., 74.
Stokes, Joseph, 361.
Stokes, Thomas R., 405.
Stom (Stum), John, 53.
Stom (Stum), Philip, 53.
Stone, Rev. Barton W., 14, 129.
  Describes "Great Revival" in Autobiography, 129.
Stone House, Airdrie, 220, 221, 226, 229, 235.
Stone implements picked up by first settlers, 426.
Stone Steps, Airdrie, 221, 227.
Stories, Two Local, by Edward R Weir, sr. (Appendix C), 449-453.
Story of "Lonz Powers," the, 133-149.
Story of The Stack. See Stack, Story of The.
Stroud City. See Central City.
Stroud, John, 64.
Stroud, John, 417.

Stroud, Lot, 25; family, 26.
Stroud, W. G., letter on Pond Station (text), 10.
Stuart, J. W., 50.
Studebaker, Jacob, 53.
Stull, John, 64.
Stum, George, 222.
Stum, Henry, 124, 221, 222.
Stum, Jacob, 221, 222.
Stum (Stom), pioneer Leonard, 124, 221, 222; family, 222.
Stum's Landing. See Paradise.
Sullivan, John K., 405.
Sullivan, Raleigh, 277.
Sullivan, Robert N., 278.
Sullivan's Barn, fight at, 277-279.
"Sulphur Springs," 430.
Summers, Charles, 206.
Summers, Rebecca, 203, 300.
Summers, Thomas C., 300, 301, 382, 420.
  Residence of, 300.
Sumner, Alney McLean, 226.
Sumner, Thomas, 65, 165, 226.
Sumner, Thomas E., 55.
Sumner, William, 32, 65.
Sunn, John F., 65.
Surveying, pioneer, 112, 113.
Sweatt, Dr. Edward, 405.
Sweeney, William, 351.
Swint, G. F., 352.
Sypert, Capt., 299, 309.

T

Taggart, D. P., 423.
Taggart, James, 48, 165, 277, 423.
  Ruins of the "Jim Taggart Old Place," 171.
Taggart, Jesse, 312.
"Tale of the Tails," 100.
Tarrants, Edward H., 64.
Tavern rates and ferry charges (1799), 44.
Taylor, Col., 394.
Taylor, Alvin L., xi, 123, 189, 190, 267.
  Portrait of, 189.
Taylor, Andrew J., 425.
Taylor, Charles W., 397.
Taylor, George W., 425.
Taylor, Jacob, 53.
Taylor, John L., 254, 262.
  Residence of, 264.
Tecumseh, Indian chief, 66, 77.
Temperance Hall, 213.
Tennell, George, 43.
Tenth Kentucky Cavalry (Confederate), 299, 320, 323.
Terry, Azel M., 88, 289, 382.
Terry, K. L., 100.
Terry, Thomas, 114, 289.
Thames, battle of the, 21, 63, 64, 65, 66, 77, 187.
"The Old Soldiers" (poem, Col. S. P. Love), 330.
Third Kentucky Cavalry, 192, 253, 261, 267, 292, 296, 301, 306, 332.
Thirty-fifth Kentucky Mounted Infantry, 252, 301, 302, 303, 318.
Thomas, Rev. R. Y., 354, 431.

INDEX

Thomas, R. Y., 81, 351, 352, 377, 423, 431.
  Portrait of, 431.
Thomas, S. B., 369, 370, 371.
Thompson, Ed Porter ("School History of Kentucky"), 31, 253, 254.
Thompson, Gus, 254.
Thompson, Judge J. C., 55, 353, 374.
Thompson, John L. G., 283, 336, 417.
  Portrait of, 336.
Thompson, Philip, 64.
Thompson, Richard, 85.
Thoroughfare, the, 19, 40.
"Thou and I" (poem, Gen. Don Carlos Buell), 240, 241.
Tinsley, Alex, 55.
Tippecanoe, 21.
Tipple and Power House, Black Diamond Mine, Drakesboro, 399.
Tipple and Power House, Central Mine, Central City, 395.
Tobacco, 73, 120, 380-386, 411, 412.
  Appliances used in early days, 380, 381.
  Average crop raised in county, 386.
  Barn, old-time log, and Cropper's Log Cabin, 385.
  Care and patience required in cultivating, 384.
  "Cropper's crop," a, 384.
  Curing, processes of, 384, 385.
  Field on A. B. Cornett Farm, upper Pond Creek country, 386.
  First cultivated in county, 380.
  "Flat chewing" plug, 381.
  "Greenville Tobacco," 381.
  Manufacturers of in Greenville, 382, 383.
  Open floor, 384.
  Plug-tobacco business in county, 380, 381, 382.
  Pools, 384.
  Price of in 1813-14, 120; in 1868, 370.
  Rehandling house (C. Y. Martin & Company), Greenville, 383.
  Social features of work in curing, 385, 386.
  Working of crop, 384.
  "XL Greenville," 382.
  Yield, county's annual, 380.
Todd, Alexander, 275.
Todd, Robert S., 275.
Todd, William, 64.
Todd County, 39, 133, 430.
Tolbert, Benjamin, 32, 206.
Toll, Frank, 228, 230.
Tompkins, Christopher, 52, 423.
Torrence, William, 230.
Townes, Dr. George W., 55.
Towns and post-offices in county, 420, 421.
"Tracks" (fossil), of mules and horses, 426.
Trails, old, in county, 12, 13.
Transportation facilities, poor, in early days, 380.
Transylvania Company, 112.
Triplett, Hon. Philip, 409.
Truck wagon, 113.
"Trying Times in Muhlenberg" (Martin), 368-371, 375, 378.

Turner, Joseph, 188.
Turner, Dr. T. G., 423, 424.
Twenty-sixth Kentucky Infantry, 253, 273, 277, 335.
Twice-a-Week Argus, 350, 351, 352.
Twin Tunnel, between Bellton and Penrod, 370.
Two Local Stories by Edward R. Weir, sr. (Appendix C), 449-453
Tyler, Charles, 64.
Tyler, Richard, 44.
Tyler Tavern, 41, 44.

U

Underwood, Joseph R., 436.
Underwood, Lester W., 425.
Union churches built by pioneers, 104, 128.
"Union Regiments of Kentucky" (1897), 253, 330.
Unity Church, 201, 202, 206.
Unsell, Henry, 53.
Uzzell, Thomas, 64.

V

Vanlandingham, Oliver C., sr., 59, 117, 165; house of, 169; 223.
  Portrait of, 223.
Vanlandingham, O. C., jr., 223, 224; family, 224.
Vanlandingham, Oliver C., 224.
Vanlandingham, Samuel P., 224.
Vaterland customs and speech in county, 112, 417.
Vaught, Abraham, 64.
Vaught, Gilbert, 50, 115.
Vaught, John, 115.
Veterans of the Mexican War (Muhlenberg), list of, 191.
Vick, Sebastian C. ("Capt. Bass"), 279, 280, 304, 308, 309.
Vickers, Capt. Henry L., 254, 277, 278, 279.
Vickers, John, 410, 423, 457, 458.
Vienna. See Calhoun.
Vincent brothers, three, 25, 26.
Vincent, Charles, 26, 121.
Vincent, R. T., 337.
  Portrait of, 330.
"Visit to the Faith Doctor," a (Weir), 449-451.
Voris, John, 65.

W

Wade, Hendley, 65.
Wagon, truck, 113.
Walcott, Walter, 69.
Walker, Green F., 430.
Walker, John, 126.
Walker, Jonas, 191.
Walker, massacre of family, 90.
Wallace, Coulston, 336.
Wallace, H. A., J. E., R. A., 336.

INDEX

Wallace, Jared, 336.
Wallace, Jesse H., 254.
Wallace, R. W., 254, 336; family, 336.
  Portrait of, 337.
Waller, Mrs. Lucy A., 190.
Ward, Thomas, 50.
Ward, William F., 253, 292, 405.
War of 1812. See Muhlenberg Men in.
Warrants, land, locating of, 112.
Warren, William, 189.
"Water witches," 457.
Watkins, Edmund, 206, 423.
Watkins, James, 86.
W. A. Wickliffe Coal Company, 403.
Webb, Lewis, 127.
Weeks, James W., 254.
Weir, Anna C., 62, 252, 270, 271.
Weir, Mrs. Anna C. R., 59.
  Portrait of, 58.
Weir, Edward R., sr., 60, 61, 124, 199,
  252, 257, 270, 271, 289, 299, 337,
  340, 342, 343, 345, 365, 382, 423,
  462.
  Author of stories and sketches, 61;
    two local stories by (Appendix C),
    449-453.
  Family of, 62.
  Portrait of, 59.
  Represented county in Legislature,
    60, 423.
  Residence of (1839), 271.
Weir, Col. E. R., 62, 252, 253, 268, 292,
  303, 304, 337, 404, 408.
  Family of, 62.
  Letter, 268-270.
  Portrait of, 61.
Weir, Emily, 60.
Weir, Harriet Rumsey ("Lady"), 61.
  Portrait of, 60.
Weir, Harry, 62, 117.
Weir, James, sr., 43, 44, 56-60, 69, 117,
  121, 126, 127, 133, 189, 194, 206, 223,
  345, 365, 366, 382, 404, 408, 449.
  Family of, 59, 60.
  First merchant and banker in Greenville, 59, 117.
  Horseback trips to Philadelphia, 59.
  Journal of (text), 56-58.
  Ledger of, 117-121.
  Portrait of, 57.
  Residence of, 137.
  Settled in county, 58.
  Trips down Mississippi to New Orleans, 59; trip to New Orleans in 1803 (text, Appendix B), 443-448.
Weir, James, 60, 78, 134-136, 345, 404.
  Author of "Lonz Powers" and other novels, 134.
  Describes Greenville in "Lonz Powers" (text), 150.
  Family of, 134.
  On the decline of the old militia muster (text), 170.
  Portrait of, 134.
  Sketch of in "Kentucky Biographies" (text), 134, 135.
Weir, Dr. James, 134, 345.
Weir, Max, 62, 345, 355.
  Portrait of, 62.

Weir, Miller, 62; family, 62.
Weir, Sallie Ann, 60.
Weir, Samuel, 53, 58; family, 58, 59; 167, 223.
Weir, Samuel M., 59, 223.
Weir, Susan, 58.
Weir, Susan M., 60, 211.
Weir, Virginia, 62.
Weir, William, 56.
Weirs, the, 28, 56-62, 117, 345.
"Weir Corner," the, 118, 126, 279.
Weir's Mill, 124, 126.
Weir's Trip to New Orleans in 1803
  (Appendix B), 443-448.
Welborn, pioneer family, 9.
Welborn, Thomas, 178.
Welborn, William, 133.
Wells, pioneer family, 9, 89.
Wells, Micajah, 67, 89; family, 89; 94, 423.
Wells, Wyatt, 89, 165.
Welsh, W. H., 55.
"Western Speller," the (Stembridge), 345, 346, 347.
West, J. W., 11.
West Kentucky Classical and Normal
  College (West Kentucky College), 35, 211, 216.
W. G. Duncan Coal Company, 396, 397, 401.
Wheat, old-time methods of shocking
  and threshing, 122, 123, 124.
White Ash Pond (Boat Yard Creek), 98.
"White Hall" hotel, South Carrollton, 414.
Whitmer, Charles E., 425.
Whitmer, David, 121.
Whitmer, David W., 97.
Whitmer, Jacob, 25, 26.
Whitmer, John, family, 26.
Whitmer, Joseph, 216.
Whitmer, Theodore W., 348.
Whitmer, Warren P., 405.
Whitmer, William G., 332.
Wickliffe, Aaron, 21.
Wickliffe, Arington, 22; family, 22; 402.
Wickliffe, Ben and Bob, 23, 375.
  Portrait of, 375.
Wickliffe, Charles B., 23, 55, 382, 423.
Wickliffe, John, 22.
Wickliffe, John K., 23, 254, 255, 256, 337.
  Portrait of, 256.
Wickliffe, Matthew L., 403.
Wickliffe, Col. Moses, 22, 23; family, 23;
  73, 191, 255, 375, 423.
  Portrait of, 22.
Wickliffe, Moses, 22, 55, 253, 254, 290.
Wickliffe, Paul R., 403.
Wickliffe, Robert, 22, 199, 342; will of, 342.
Wickliffe, W. A., Coal Company, 403.
Wickliffe, William A., 22, 50, 55, 156, 402, 403, 413.
  Family of, 403.
  Portrait of, 403.
  Residence, Greenville, 157.
Wickliffe, William B., 22, 402, 405.
Wilcox, Elias, 65.
Wilcox, Thomas, 64.

"Wildcat Hollow," 430.
Wilkins, Bryant, 64.
Wilkins, J. L., 337.
  Portrait of, 330.
Wilkins, Rev. Samuel M., 85, 88, 105.
Williams, Bryant, 50.
Williams, Daniel H., 405.
Williams, Ed, 283.
Williams, Henry, 410.
Williams, John A., 329, 405.
Williams, John L., 55, 296, 297, 300.
Williams, John M., 55.
Williams, Noah, 65.
Williams, Col. William, 64.
Williams, William, 65.
Willis, Britain, 10.
Wilson, John, 65.
Windows, memorial, in Greenville Presbyterian Church, 109.
Wing, Barnabas, 76.
Wing, Bert, 80, 248.
Wing, Charles Fox, 12, 14, 15, 32, 42, 44, 46, 48, 50, 52, 55, 64, 65, 74, 76-80, 87, 126, 127, 150, 167, 186, 201, 206, 213, 225, 257, 289, 291, 346, 366, 404, 406, 431.
  Appointed county clerk, 76.
  Biographical sketch (Louisville Daily Journal, 1861), 79.
  Clerk of court of quarter sessions and of circuit court, 76, 77.
  Family of, 79.
  Flag, devotion to his country's, 78.
  "Hero at Thames," 78.
  House of, center of hospitality, 80.
  "Old soldier of the second war" (in "Lonz Powers"), 156, 157.
  Organized company in War of 1812, 77.
  Portrait of, 77.
  Portrait of Mrs. Charles Fox Wing, 78.
  Residence, Greenville, 80.
Wing, E. Rumsey, 80.
Wing, John, 126.
Wing, Samuel M., 60, 80, 409.
Wing, William H. C., 55, 77, 79, 346.
Winlock, Joseph, 64.
Wise, James R., 253.
"Witches," water and metal, 457.
Wives and mothers, pioneer, moral and religious influence of, 130, 131.
Wolf Lick Fork, 36, 40.
"Wolf Sculp" certificates, 115, 116.
Wolves in county in early days, 115.
Wood, Ed S., 18, 55.
Wood, H. Y., 281, 282.
Wood, James, 9, 18; family, 18.
Wood, James D., 352.
Wood, James W., 18; letter of, 280, 281, 282.
Wood, John H., 280, 281, 405.
Wood, J. L., 281.
Wood, Zillman, 18.
  Portrait of, 19.
Woodburn, Dr. B. Dudley, 416.
Woodburn, Dr. Benjamin W., 405, 417.
Woodburn, John A., 417.
Woodburn, J. T., sr., 336, 416.
Woodburn, Dr. J. T., 326, 414, 416, 417.
  Portrait of, 414.

Woodburn, Rev. William H., 417.
Woodburn & McDowell Drug Company, 416.
Woods, Isaac, 276.
Woodson, Urey, 351.
Woodward, Ashby, 277, 279.
Woodward, Capt. Steven, 277, 278, 279.
Work, Samuel, 52.
Worthington, Isaac, 64.
Worthington, Thomas, 10, 19, 20, 21.
Worthington, T. M., 19.
Worthington, Judge William, 19, 20, 21, 42, 50, 51, 52, 53, 423.
  Family of, 20, 21.
  Graves of Judge and Mrs. William, 20.
Worthington's Chapel, 19, 21.
Worthington Post-office, 19, 421.
Wright, John, 121, 188.
Wright, J. W., 424.
Writers, local, 347-350.
Wyatt Oates Old Place, 339.
Wyeth, J. A. ("Life of Gen. Nathan Bedford Forrest"), 258.

X

"XL Greenville" tobacco, 382.

Y

Yeaman, George H., 299.
Yellow Banks. See Owensboro.
Yonts, Edward L., 337, 383.
Yonts, James W., 253.
Yonts, Joseph D., 253, 337, 382.
  Portrait of, 337.
Yonts, Lawrence, 65, 222.
Yonts, Morton K., 337.
Yonts, Philip, 222, 337.
Yonts, Rudolph, 222.
Yonts (Yontz) family, 222.
York, George M., 55.
York, J. W., 348.
Yorks, Samuel A., 396.
Yost, Dr. E. R., 70.
Yost, Mrs. Lucy Wing Short, 14, 79, 151, 225, 408, 413.
  Portrait of, 151.
Yost, "Old Doctor" William H., 50, 51, 70; family, 70; 206, 346, 354, 363, 371, 405, 457, 458.
Yost, Judge William H., 15, 50, 51, 55, 70, 305, 354, 356.
  Letter of (text), 15, 16.
  Portrait of, 51.
Yost, Mrs. William H., sr., portrait of, 151.
Yost & Laffoon, 51.
Young, Benjamin, 64.
Young, Henry and William, 256, 257.
Y. M. C. A., Greenville, 355, 366.

Z

Zimmerman, Jacob, 117, 127.
Zimmerman, Mathias, 120.
"Zouaves, the Bold Kentucky," 308, 309.

www.ingramcontent.com/pod-product-compliance
Lightning Source LLC
Chambersburg PA
CBHW060312230426
43663CB00009B/1677